CATALOGUE

OF

RECENTLY ADDED BOOKS,

LIBRARY OF CONGRESS,

1873–75.

WITH INDEX TO SUBJECTS AND TITLES.

WASHINGTON:
GOVERNMENT PRINTING OFFICE.
1876.

CONTENTS.

NOTE.

The publication of the annual supplements or catalogues of books added to the Library of Congress was discontinued with the issue for the year 1872. The great cost of these volumes, which were prepared on the plan of printing approximately full titles to each publication, old or new, was found to be quite out of proportion to their general utility. It has been determined to substitute for these annual volumes the publication of occasional brief finding-lists, or catalogues of the more important fresh additions to the Library.

The catalogue now issued embraces the principal accessions of the past three years, 1873–1875, and is arranged in three alphabets: 1st. Miscellaneous books, by names of authors; 2d. Law-books, by names of authors; 3d. Titles and subjects, in a single alphabet, at the end of the volume. In the latter arrangement, nearly every work appears twice, and in many cases several times.

There are omitted from this catalogue, as of minor importance, the titles of school-books, directories, almanacs, pamphlets, periodicals, and serials generally. The vast field covered by these classes of publications would involve much expenditure of type and paper, and the issue of a bulky volume, rendering it proper to reserve them for the general or complete catalogue of the Library.

LIBRARY OF CONGRESS,
Washington, May, 1876.

LIST OF ABBREVIATIONS EMPLOYED.

anon. Anonymous.
b. l. Black letter.
col. Colored.
ed. Edition.
eng. Engraved.
facs. Facsimile.
fol. Folio. 4°. Quarto. 8°. Octavo. 12°. Duodecimo, etc.
incl. Including.
l. Leaves.
n. d. No date.
n. p. No place of publication.
numb. Numbered.
obl. Oblong.
p. Page.
phot. Photograph.
pl. Plates.
p. l. Preliminary leaves.
pp. Pages.
pseud. Pseudonym.
sm. Small.
sq. Square.
t. Tome.
tab. Tables.
unp. Unpaged.
v. Volume or volumes.

The books are described as folio, quarto, octavo, duodecimo, etc., according to the apparent size of the volume, and not according to the printer's designations derived from the fold of the sheets.

In the alphabetical arrangement, the prefix *Mc*, *M'*, or *Mac*, is treated uniformly as a component part of the word, as if spelled *Mac*. Thus *McLeod* or *M'Leod* precedes *Maclure*. In like manner, the prefixes *New*, *La*, *Du*, etc., are treated as component parts of the words to which they belong. Thus, *New England* follows *Newell* instead of preceding it, as it would do if the prefix *New* were treated as a separate word.

It is one of the aims of the present catalogue to furnish with the titles a sufficiently full collation of each work. Thus it is made a part of the description to give the number of pages in the case of all works not exceeding two volumes, together with the number of maps and plates, if any, and the name of the publisher. The information thus conveyed will, it is believed, be found of practical value to readers, as conveying at a glance some idea of the extent of each work, while the addition of publishers' names is useful as supplying a guide to the identification of editions. In the case of books printed without date, the actual or approximate date is supplied in brackets.

Brackets in any part of a title indicate that the words included in them are not found in the title, but are inserted.

It is to be understood that long titles are uniformly abridged, the more significant words of the title only being inserted.

The letter s affixed to any title denotes that the work belongs to the Library of the Smithsonian Institution, now deposited in the Library of Congress.

CATALOGUE.

Abbott (John Stevens Cabot). American pioneers and patriots. 12°. *New York, Dodd & Mead,* [1874–75].

CONTENTS.

Life and adventures of rear-admiral John Paul Jones. 1 p. l. xi, 9–359 pp. 5 pl. [1874].
Adventures of the chevalier de la Salle and his companions. 384 pp. 5 pl. [1875].

——— History of christianity, from the earliest period to the present time. 504 pp. 6 pl. 2 maps. 8°. *Boston, B. B. Russell,* 1872.

——— History of Napoleon III. including a narrative of important events since the fall of Napoleon I. until the death of Napoleon III. 730 pp. 10 pl. 1 map. 8°. *Boston, B. B. Russell,* 1873.

Abbott (*Rev.* Lyman). New testament. v. 1, 12°. *New York, A. S. Barnes & co.* 1875.

CONTENTS.

Matthew and Mark. 399 pp. incl. 2 pl. and 1 map. 1875.

——— *and* **Conant** (Thomas Jefferson, *d. d.*) Dictionary of religious knowledge. xv, 1074 pp. 8°. *New York, Harper & brothers,* 1875.

Abdulla bin Abdulkadar, *mūnshi.* Translations from the hakayit Abdulla (bin Abdulkadar). With comments by J. T. Thompson. x pp. 1 l. 349 pp. 1 facs. 12°. *London, H. S. King & co.* 1874.

About (Edmond François Valentin). A B C du travailleur. 2e éd. 3 p. l. 317 pp. 16°. *Paris, L. Hachette & cie.* 1869.

——— Alsace, 1871–1872. 2e éd. 4 p. l. 348 pp. 1 l. 16°. *Paris, Hachette & cie.* 1873.

——— Causeries. 1e série. 2e éd. 2 p. l. 383 pp. 16°. *Paris, L. Hachette & cie.* 1867.

——— Same. 2e série. 2 p. l. 379 pp. 16°. *Paris, L. Hachette & cie.* 1866.

——— The fellah. Translated by sir Randal Roberts. iv, 340 pp. 12°. *London, Chapman & Hall,* 1870.

——— L'infâme. 2e éd. 2 p. l. 291 pp. 16°. *Paris, L. Hachette & cie.* 1873.

——— Maître Pierre. 4e éd. vi, 309 pp. 16°. *Paris, L. Hachette & cie.* 1862.

About (E. F. V.)—continued.

——— Notary's nose. From the french by Henry Holt. 3 p. l. 240 pp. 16°. *New York, H. Holt & co.* 1874.

[LEISURE hour series].

——— Rouge et noir. From the french by E. R. 1 p. l. 11–236 pp. 12°. *Philadelphia, Claxton, Remsen & Haffelfinger,* 1873.

——— Théâtre impossible. Guillery.—L'assassin.—L'éducation d'un prince.—Le chapeau de sainte Catherine. 2e éd. 2 p. l. 371 pp. 16°. *Paris, L. Hachette & cie.* 1864.

Acosta (Joaquin). Compendio del descubrimiento de la Nueva Granada. xvi, 400 pp. 4 pl. 8°. *Paris, imprenta de Beau,* 1848.

Acrelius (Israel). History of New Sweden. From the swedish, by W. M. Reynolds. 1, 17–468 pp. 2 pl. 1 map. 8°. *Philadelphia,* 1874.

[PENNSYLVANIA (Historical society of). Memoirs, v. 11].

Acrostics in prose and verse. 1st–3d series. 3 v. 18°. *London, T. Bosworth,* 1865–67.

CONTENTS.

1st series. Easy double acrostics. By A. H.
Scripture acrostics. Ed. by A. H.
Historical acrostics. By M. L. B.
Key to acrostics in prose and verse.
2d–3d series. Acrostics in prose and verse. Ed. by A. E. H.

Actes (Les) des apôtres modernes, voyages par les missionaires catholiques. Publiés sous la direction de l'abbé P.-A. Bosquet, de l'abbé Giraud, et de Gabriel Grimaud de Caux, [etc.] 12°. *Paris, au bureau,* 1852.

CONTENTS.

v. 1. Voyage aux lieux saints.—Voyage au mont Liban.—Voyage à Alep.—Voyage à Damas.
v. 2. Voyage à Bassora.—Voyage dans l'Asie mineure.—Voyage dans l'Archipel et au mont Athos.—Voyage en Crimée.

Acton (Roger). Abyssinian expedition and life of king Theodore. Reprinted from the illustrated London news. Eng. title, 3 p. l. 78 pp. 100 pl. on 72 l. 1 port. fol. [*London*], *office of the illustrated London news,* [1868].

Adams (Arthur, *f. l. s.*) Travels of a naturalist in Japan and Manchuria. x, 334 pp. front. 12°. *London, Hurst & Blackett,* 1870.

Adams (F. G. *compiler*). Homestead guide. 312 pp. incl. 11 pl. 1 map 8°. *Waterville, Kansas, F. G. Adams,* 1873.

Adams (Francis Ottiwell, *f. r. g. s.*) History of Japan from the earliest period. 2 v. xvi, 506 pp. 2 plans, 1 map; xiv, 356 pp. 2 maps. 8°. *London, H. S. King & co.* 1874–75.

Adams (John Quincy, *6th president of the United States*). Memoirs of John Quincy Adams, comprising portions of his diary from 1795 to 1848. Ed. by C. F. Adams. v. 1–7. 8°. *Philadelphia, J. B. Lippincott & co.* 1874–75.

Note.—Vols. 1 to 7 cover the years 1794 to 1828.

Adams (Louis). Décorations et meubles des époques Louis XIII & Louis XIV. 3 p. l. 100 pl. fol. *Paris, A. Morel,* 1865.

Adams (W. Davenport). Famous books, sketches in english literature. ix, 384 pp. incl. front. 12°. *London, Virtue, Spalding & co.* 1875.

Adams (William T.) Sunny shores; young America in Italy and Austria. Eng. title, 409 pp. 3 pl. 16°. *Boston, Lee & Shepard,* 1875.

[YOUNG America abroad, 2d series, v. 4].

——— Yacht club series. By Oliver Optic [*pseud.*] v. 2–6. 16°. *Boston, Lee & Shepard,* 1874–75.

CONTENTS.

v. 2. Yacht club, Eng. title, 340 pp. 12 pl. 1874.
v. 3. Money-maker. 361 pp. 13 pl. 1874.
v. 4. Coming wave; or, the hidden treasure. Eng. title, 353 pp. 12 pl. 1875.
v. 5. Dorcas club. Eng. title, 368 pp. 12 pl. 1875.
v. 6. Ocean-born. Eng. title, 368 pp. 12 pl. 1875.

Adeler (Max, *pseud.*) *See* **Clark** (Charles Heber).

Aermont (Paul, *pseud.*) Narrative of the travels of Paul Aermont among the planets. 192 pp. 12°. *Boston, Rand, Avery & co.* 1873.

Ahern (M. L.) Great revolution, history of the people's party in Chicago. 1 p. l. 7–265 pp. 8°. *Chicago, lakeside publishing co.* 1874.

Aikin (Lucy). Correspondence of W. E. Channing and Lucy Aikin, from 1826 to 1842. *See* **Channing** (W. E.) *and* **Aikin**.

Aikin (L. W.) Crystal gems for the sabbath-school. 192 pp. sq. 18°. *Philadelphia, Miller's bible & publishing house,* [1875].

Ainsworth (William Harrison). The good old times: story of the Manchester rebels of '45. 3 v. 12°. *London, Tinsley brothers,* 1873.

Album mexicano. Publicado por Ignacio Cumplido. v. 1. 8°. *Mexico, editor,* 1849. s.

Note.—Imperfect; pp. 565–572 duplicated and 581–589 wanting.

Alcott (Louisa May). Eight cousins. 2 p. l. 290 pp. incl. 6 pl. front. 1 facs. 16°. *Boston, Roberts brothers,* 1875.

——— Work. 3 p. l. 443 pp. 16°. *Boston, Roberts brothers,* 1873.

Alden (Ebenezer, *m. d.*) Memorial of the descendants of the hon. John Alden. 2 p. l. 164 pp. 8°. *Randolph, Mass. for the family,* 1867.

Alden (*Mrs.* Isabella M.) Household puzzles. By Pansy [*pseud.*] 370 pp. 2 pl. 16°. *Boston, D. Lothrop & co.* [1875].

——— Julia Reid. By Pansy [*pseud.*] 376 pp. 2 pl. 12°. *Cincinnati, western tract and book society,* 1872.

——— King's daughter. By Pansy [*pseud.*] 305 pp. 1 pl. 12°. *Cincinnati, western tract and book society,* 1873.

——— Wise and otherwise. By Pansy [*pseud.*] 388 pp. 3 pl. 12°. *Cincinnati, western tract and book society,* 1873.

——— *and* **Huntington** (Faye, *pseud.*) Modern prophets. By "Pansy" and "Faye Huntington". 354 pp. 3 pl. 16°. *Boston, D. Lothrop & co.* [1874].

Alderman (O. P.) Autobiography, up to 1874. 466 pp. 2 ports. 12°. *Buffalo, Baker, Jones & co.* 1874.

Aldrich (Thomas Bailey). Cloth of gold and other poems. 184 pp. 12°. *Boston, J. R. Osgood & co.* 1874.

——— Marjorie Daw and other people. 272, pp. 16°. *Boston, J. R. Osgood & co.* 1873.

——— Prudence Palfrey. 311 pp. incl. 1 pl. 12°. *Boston, J. R. Osgood & co.* 1874.

"**Alex.**" [*pseud.*] As it should be. 274 pp. 12°. *Philadelphia, J. B. Lippincott & co.* 1874.

Alexander (*Mrs.* —). Which shall it be? 1 p. l. 415 pp. 16°. *New York, H. Holt & co.* 1874.

[LEISURE hour series].

——— Wooing o't. 1 p. l. 483 pp. 16°. *New York, H. Holt & co.* 1873.

[LEISURE hour series].

Alexis-Alexandrovich (*Grand-duke of Russia*). His imperial highness Alexis in the United States, 1871–72. 2 p. l. 223 pp. 1

Alexis-Alexandrovich—continued. port. 8°. *Cambridge, [Ms.] the riverside press*, 1872. s.

Note.—The book consists of reprints of newspaper reports, anonymously compiled.

Alford (Henry, *d. d.*) Fireside homilies. xii, 196 pp. 16°. *London, Daldy, Isbister & co.* 1875.

——— Greek testament. 4 v. 8°. *London, [etc.] Rivingtons*, 1871-74.

——— Sons of God: sermons. vii, 200 pp. 16°. *London, Hodder & Stoughton*, 1872.

Alice Porter. [*anon.*] 338 pp. 3 pl. 16°. *New York, board of publication, reformed ch. in America*, [1873].

All round the world; a geographical and historical encyclopædia, [etc. *anon.*] 2 p. l. vii-512 pp. col. front. 4°. *New York, United States publishing co.* 1873.

Allan (*Prof.* W. *Washington & Lee university*). Notes on Rankine's applied mechanics and civil engineering. 1 p. l. 170 pp. 4°. [*Baltimore, A. Hunt & co.* 1873].

——— Theory of arches. 113 pp. 18°. *New York, D. Van Nostrand*, 1874.

[VAN NOSTRAND's science series, no. 11].

Allen (Asa W.) Genealogy of the Allen and Witter families. 1 p. l. 251 pp. 1 port. 12°. *Salem, O., L. W. Smith*, 1872.

Allen (Charles H.) Visit to Queensland, [Australia]. viii, 367 pp. 16°. *London, Chapman & Hall*, 1870.

Allen (Myron O. *m. d.*) History of Wenham [Mass.] 1639 to 1860. vii, 13-220 pp. 12°. *Boston, Bazin & Chandler*, 1860.

Allen (Stephen M.) Religion and science; the letters of "Alpha" on the influence of spirit upon imponderable actienic molecular substances, [etc.] By the author of Fibrilia, [etc. *anon.*] 1 p. l. 171 pp. 5 col. pl. 12°. *Boston, A. Mudge & son*, 1874.

Allen (Timothy F. *m. d. editor*). Encyclopædia of pure materia medica [homœopathic] v. 1-2 [A-Carduus]. 8°. *New York, [etc.] Boericke & Tafel*, [1874]-75.

Allen (W. F.) Gazetteer of railway stations in the United States and Canada. xxviii, 412 pp. 12°. *Philadelphia, national railway publication co.* 1874.

Allen (William H. *compiler*). Manual of devotion. 296 pp. 16°. *Philadelphia, J. B. Lippincott & co.* 1873.

Allibone (Samuel Austin). Poetical quotations, from Chaucer to Tennyson. 2 p. l. xiii-788 pp. 8°. *Philadelphia, J. B. Lippincott & co.* 1873.

Allibone (Samuel Austin)—continued.

——— Prose quotations from Socrates to Macaulay. 4 p. l. 13-764 pp. 8°. *Philadelphia, J. B. Lippincott & co.* 1876.

Allies (T. W.) The formation of christendom. pts. 1-2. xii, 389; xvi, 495 pp. 8°. *London, Longmans*, 1865-69.

Almanach du commerce et de l'industrie. [*anon.*] Année 1875. 8°. *New-York, H. de Mareil*, 1875.

Note.—Liste des résidents français de New York [et] des résidents français aux Etats-Unis, at end.

Alphand (A. *i. e.* J. Charles Adolphe). Promenades de Paris. Description des embellissements des bois de Boulogne et de Vincennes. 3 v. fol. *Paris, J. Rothschild*, 1867-73.

CONTENTS.

Texte: 9 p. l. lix, (1), 246 pp.
Atlas: Les bois de Boulogne, 6 p. l. 30 pl.

Alzog (*Dr.* Johannes). Manual of universal church history. From the 9th german ed. By F. J. Pabisch, and rev. Thomas S. Byrne v. 1. xiii, 779 pp. 1 map. 8°. *Cincinnati, R. Clarke & co.* 1874.

Amateur journalists' companion. For 1873. By Frank Cropper. Eng. title, 110 pp. 12 ports. 18°. *Louisville, Ky., F. Cropper*, 1873.

Ameilhon (Hubert Pascal). Histoire du Bas-empire. Par m. Le Beau. Continué par Ameilhon. [1255-1341].

[LEBEAU (Charles). Histoire du Bas-empire. 16°. *Paris, Desaint* [*etc.*] 1781-86. v. 22-24].

Amelia. From the french. [*anon.*] 246 pp. 16°. *Philadelphia, P. F. Cunningham & son*, 1874.

American annual cyclopædia and register of important events, for the years 1861-74. v. 1-14. 8°. *New York, D. Appleton & co.* 1862-75.

American cyclopædia. v. 1-13 [A-Printing]. 8°. *New York, D. Appleton & co.* 1873-75.

American firemen. [*anon.*] 256 pp. 16°. *Boston, H. L. Champlin*, 1875.

American fistiana, from 1816 to 1873. New ed. [*anon.*] 155 pp. 8°. *New York, R. M. De Witt*, [1873].

American guide to Europe. Ed. of 1874. [*anon.*] 1-368, 385-678 pp. 9 col. pl. 29 plans (2 in pockets), 12 maps (3 in pockets). 12°. *Philadelphia, [London printed], J. B. Lippincott & co.* [1874].

Note.—Contains also in pocket, "Vocabulary of travel talk", 15 pp. 18°.

American historical record. Edited by Benson J. Lossing, ll. d. [Monthly]. v. 3.

American—continued. sm. 4°. *Philadelphia, J. E. Potter & co.* [1874].

American household adviser. [*anon.*] 4 parts in 1 v. 12°. *New York, E. C. Bridgman,* 1875.

CONTENTS.

AMERICAN family receipt book, [etc.] By an american housekeeper. [*anon.*] 1 p. l. vii–100 pp.
REMINGTON (S. *m. d.*) The family doctor, [etc.] 1 p. l. vii–100 pp.
WHEELER (*Mrs.* E. A.) The frugal housekeeper's kitchen companion, [etc.] 96 pp.
WILLIAMS (T. B.) Farmer's guide in the management of domestic animals, [etc.] 1 p. l. 11–100 pp. front.

American iron and steel association. Ironworks of the United States. Directory of furnaces, rolling mills, [etc.] 106 pp. 8°. *Philadelphia,* [*J. B. Chandler*], 1874.

American Lloyd's register of american and foreign shipping. [1874]. obl. 8°. *New York, the society of american Lloyd's,* [1873].

——— Same. [1875]. obl. 8°. *New York, the society of american Lloyd's,* [1875]

American public health association. Public health reports and papers. [v. 1]. 1873. 1 p. l. xv, 563 pp. 19 charts, diagrams, etc. 8°. *New York, Hurd & Houghton,* 1875.

American railroad manual. By E. Vernon. [v. 1–2. 1873–74]. 8°. *New York, american railroad manual co.* 1873–74.

American railway and supply directory for 1873. [v. 1]. 8°. *Boston, Greenough, Jones & co.* 1873.

——— Same, 1874–75. List of officers and directors of the railroads in the United States and Canadas, [etc.] 8°. *Boston, Greenough, Jones & co.* 1874.

American rowing almanac. 1874. By Fred. J. Engelhardt. 18°. *New York, F. J. Engelhardt,* [1874].

American shipmasters' association. Record of american and foreign shipping. [1874]. 4°. *New York,* [*E. C. Root, Anthony & co.*] 1874.

——— Same. [1875]. 4°. *New York,* [*E. C. Root, Anthony & co.*] 1874.

American yacht list for 1874 and 1875. 2 v. 16°. *New York, L. H. Bigelow & co.* 1874–75.

Ames (Azel, *jr. m. d.*) Sex in industry. 158 pp. 16°. *Boston, J. R. Osgood & co.* 1875.

Ames (Mary Clemmer). His two wives. 585 pp. 12°. *New York, Hurd & Houghton,* 1875.

——— Outlines of men, women, and things. 3 p. l. 254 pp. 16°. *New York, Hurd & Houghton,* 1873.

Ames (Mary Clemmer)—continued.

——— Ten years in Washington. 587 pp. 17 pl. 8°. *Hartford, Conn., A. D. Worthington & co.* 1873.

Amos (Andrew). Four lectures on the advantages of a classical education. vii, 281 pp. 8°. *London, R. Bentley,* 1846.

Ampère (André Marie). Journal et correspondance. 3 p. l. vii, 277 pp. 8°. *Paris, J. Claye,* 1869.

——— Same. Story of his love: journal and correspondence during 1793–1804. From the french. viii, 328 pp. 8°. *London. R. Bentley & son,* 1873.

——— *and* **Ampère** (Jean Jacques Antoine). Correspondance et souvenirs (de 1805 à 1864). Recueillis par madame H. C. 3e éd. 2 v. 2 p. l. 508 pp; 2 p. l. 461 pp. 12°. *Paris, J. Hetzel & cie.* 1875.

Amunátegui (Miguel Luis). Precursores de la independencia de Chile. 3 v. 8°. *Santiago, imprenta de la "republica",* 1870–72. s.

Anderson (Rufus, *d. d., ll. d.*) History of the missions of the american board of commissioners in India. xvi, 443 pp. 3 maps. 12°. *Boston, congregational publishing soc.* 1875.

Anderson (R. B. *a. m.*) America not discovered by Columbus. 104 pp. 12°. *Chicago, S. C. Griggs & co.* 1874.

——— Norse mythology. 473 pp. front. 12°. *Chicago, S. C. Griggs & co.* 1875.

Andersson (Charles John). The lion and the elephant. xii, 386 pp. 4 pl. 12°. *London, Hurst & Blackett,* 1873.

Andrews (Israel Ward, *d.d.*) Manual of the constitution of the United States. 370, xxxviii pp. 8°. *Cincinnati, Wilson, Hinkle & co* [1874].

Angeberg (*Le comte* d', *pseud.*) Recueil des traités, conventions et actes diplomatiques concernant la Pologne, 1762–1862. 2 p. l. xvi, 1171 pp. 8°. *Paris, Amyot,* 1862.

Annales forestières. Collaborateurs: mm. Barral, de Buffévent, [etc.] Rédacteur en chef m. Ludovic Beaussire. 1842–65. 1st–3d ser. 24 v. 8°. *Paris, au bureau des Annales forestières,* [1842]–65.

1st ser. v. 1–5.
2d ser. v. 6–20.
Nouvelle période, v. 21–24.

Note.—From v. 14 in the 2d series, the title is: Annales forestières et métallurgiques.

——— Table alphabétique, années 1842 à 1846. 48 pp. 8°. *Paris, au bureau des Annales forestières,* 1848.

[*In* ANNALES forestières, v. 5, 1846, 8°, Paris].

Annals of Loch Cé. A chronicle of irish affairs, 1014–1590. [*anon.*] Edited, with a translation, by W. M. Hennessy. 2 v. lix, 653 pp. 1 fac; 4 p. l. 689 pp. 8°. *London, Longmans*, 1871.

[GREAT BRITAIN. *Treasury. (Public record office).* Rerum britannicarum medii aevi scriptores. 8°. *London*, 1871].

Annan (William). High church episcopacy. 283 pp. 12°. *Pittsburgh, R. S. Davis & co.* 1874.

Annuaire-almanach du commerce, de l'industrie, de la magistrature et de l'administration. (Didot–Bottin). 76e année, 1873. 8°. *Paris, F. Didot frères, fils & cie.* 1873.

Annuaire de l'économie politique et de la statistique; par mm. [Urbin Gilbert] Guillaumin, Joseph Garnier, Maurice Block, [etc.] 31e année. 2 p. l. 607 pp. 18°. *Paris, Guillaumin & cie.* 1874.

Annuaire de l'instruction publique pour les années 1867–1875, publié par J. Delalain. 9 v. 16°. *Paris, J. Delalain & fils*, [1867–75].

Annual record of homœopathic literature. 1874. Edited by C. G. Raue, [etc. v. 5]. 8°. *New York, Boericke & Tafel*, [1874].

Aoust (*L'abbé* Louis). Analyse infinitésimale des courbes planes. xxxvi, 418 pp. 8°. *Paris, Gauthier-Villars*, 1873. s.

Appleton's european guide book illustrated. [With] travel-talk in english, german, french and italian. 6th ed. 1873. Parts 1–2. 2 v. 16°. *New York, D. Appleton & co.* [*Chiswick press, London*, 1873].

Appletons' hand-book of american travel. Northern and eastern tour. Including New York, New Jersey, Pennsylvania, Connecticut, Rhode Island, Massachusetts, Maine, New Hampshire, Vermont, and the British dominions. Revised for 1873. 12°. *New York, D. Appleton & co.* 1873.

——— Same. Western tour. For 1872. 12°. *New York, D. Appleton & co.* 1872.

——— ——— Same. For 1873. x, 324 pp. incl. 2 maps, 7 maps. 12°. *New York, D. Appleton & co.* 1873.

Archaeologia cambrensis. 29 v. 8°. *London*, 1846–72.

CONTENTS.

1st series. 4 v. and supplement. 1846–51.
2d or new series. 5 v. 1850–54.
3d series. 15 v. and supplement. 1855–70.
4th series. v. 1–3. 1870–72.

Note.—The third and fourth series are entitled "Archaeologia cambrensis, the Journal of the Cambrian archæological association."

Architektonisches skizzen-buch. Jahrgang [1852–1873]. Parts 1–119. 10 v. fol. *Berlin, Ernst & Korn*, [1852–73].

Archiv für naturgeschichte. 78 v. 8°. *Berlin, Nicolaische buchhandlung*, 1835–73. s.

Archives de zoologie expérimentale et générale. v. 1–2. 8°. *Paris, G. Baillière*, [&] *C. Reinwald & cie.* 1872-73.

Armstrong (*Mrs.* M. F.) *and* **Ludlow** (Helen W.) Hampton and its students. With fifty songs, arranged by T. P. Fenner. 256 pp. incl. 5 pl. 1 pl. 8°. *New York, G. P. Putnam's sons*, 1874.

Arnold (I. F. K.) Bohömann, geheimer oberer und haupt der asiatischen brüder. [*anon.*] 8 p. l. 247 pp. 18°. *Hamburg & Mainz, G. Vollmer*, 1804.

Arnold (Matthew). Higher schools in Germany. lxxxvii, 270 pp. 12°. *London, Macmillan & co.* 1874.

——— Literature and dogma. xxxvi, 388 pp. 12°. *London, Smith, Elder, & co.* 1873.

——— On translating Homer, last words. 3 p. l. 70 pp. 12°. *London, Longmans*, 1862.

——— St. Paul and protestantism. 2d ed. xxxix, 182 pp. 12°. *London, Smith, Elder & co.* 1870.

Arnot (*Rev.* William). Laws from heaven for life on earth. [New ed.] 581 pp. 12°. *London, T. Nelson & sons*, 1873.

Arnould (*Sir* Joseph). Memoir of Thomas, first lord Denman. 2 v. xxviii, 436 pp. port; xx, 469 pp. port. 8°. *London, Longmans*, 1873.

Arrigoni (Ferdinando). Raccolta di vedute interne delle principali chiese di Milano. [*anon.*] Eng. title, 16 pl. fol. *Milano, R. Farfani*, 1826.

Arsac (Joanni d'). Brothers of the christian schools during the war of 1870-71. From the french. xvi, 415 pp. 32 pl. 8°. *West Chester, N. Y., New York catholic protectory*, 1873.

Art of dining. [*anon.*] 288 pp. sq. 18°. *New York, R. M. De Witt*, [1874].

Arthur (Timothy Shay). Woman to the rescue. A story of the new crusade. 226 pp. front. 12°. *Philadelphia, J. M. Stoddart & co.* [1875].

Art-Journal. New series. v. 12–13. 1873–74. 2 v. 4°. *London, Virtue & co.* [1873–74].

Arundell (Thomas). Historical reminiscences of the city of London. xii, 444 pp. 8°. *London, R. Bentley*, 1869.

Asbjörnsen (Peter Christian). Tales from the fjeld. From the norse. By G. W. Dasent. xv, 375 pp. front. 12°. *London, Chapman & Hall*, 1874.

Asher & Adams (*publishers*). American text-book for the million. 230, 193, 134 pp. 8°. *New York, Asher & Adams,* [1873].

——— New columbian rail road atlas. 2 p. l. 42 col. maps (interleaved with 42 l. of advertisements), 30 l. fol. *New York, Asher & Adams,* 1875.

——— New commercial and statistical gazetteer of the U. S. and Canada. 284 [+ 241ª–241ˢ] pp. 9 l. 41 maps paged 3–152. fol. *New York, Asher & Adams,* [1874].

——— Same. 241 pp. [+ 241ª – 241ˢ]. fol. *New York, Asher & Adams* [1875].

——— New statistical and topographical atlas of the United States 2 p. l. 29 col. maps on 58 l. paged 7–120, [36] pp. fol. *New York, Asher & Adams,* [1875].

Asheton (Francis). Modern Cressida; and On the church steps, by S. C. Hallowell. 94 pp. 1 pl. 8°. *Philadelphia, J. B. Lippincott & co.* 1875.

Assollant (Alfred, *i. e.* Jean Baptiste Alfred). Le puy de Montchal 2 p. l. 370 pp. 16°. *Paris, E. Dentu,* 1875.

——— Le seigneur de Lanterne. 2 p. l. 372 pp. 16°. *Paris, E. Dentu,* 1874.

Atkyns (*Sir* Robert, *jr. kt.* 1647–1711). Ancient and present state of Gloucestershire. 2d ed. 5 p. l. 452 pp. 3 l. 73 pl. fol. *London, T. Spilsbury, for W. Herbert,* 1768.

Atlantic coast guide. [*anon.*] 88, 136 pp. 2 maps. 16°. *New York, E. P. Dutton & co.* 1873.

Attfield (John, *ph. d.*) Chemistry. 5th ed. xv, 13–606 pp. 1 tab. fold. 12°. *Philadelphia, H. C. Lea,* 1873.

Attwell (Henry). Table of the aryan languages. iv, 27 pp. 4°. *London, Williams & Norgate,* 1874.

Atwater (Edward E.) History and significance of the sacred tabernacles of the Hebrews. xiv, 448 pp. 35 pl. 8°. *New York, Dodd & Mead,* 1875.

Auchincloss (William S. *c. e.*) Ninety days in the tropics. 60 pp. 9 photos. 12°. *Wilmington, Del.* 1874.

Auerbach (Berthold). Waldfried. Translated by S. A. Stern. 1 p. l. 514 pp. 12°. *New York. H. Holt & co.* 1874.

Aulagnier (Alexis François). Dictionnaire des alimens et des boissons. 3 p. l. 64, 731 pp. 8°. *Paris, Cousin,* 1839.

Aumale (Henri-Eugène-Philippe-Louis d'Orléans, *duc* d'). Histoire des princes de Condé pendant les XVIe et XVIIe siècles. 2 v. 1 p. l. 1 port. iii, 580 pp; 1 p. l. 1 port. 588 pp. map. 8°. *Paris, M. Lévy frères,* 1863–64.

——— Same. History of the princes de Condé in the XVIth and XVIIth centuries. From the french, by Robert Brown Borthwick. v. 1–2. xiv, 411 pp. port. 1 map; xiv, 448 pp. port. 8°. *London, R. Bentley & son,* 1872.

CONTENTS.

v. 1. Louis de Bourbon.
v. 2. Louis de Bourbon; Henry de Bourbon.

Austin (Alfred). Golden age. xi, 126 pp. 12°. *London, Chapman & Hall,* 1871.

——— Interludes. viii, 108 pp. 16°. *Edinburgh, W. Blackwood & sons,* 1872.

——— Madonna's child. 2d ed. vii, 80 pp. 2 pl. 8°. *Edinburgh, W. Blackwood & sons,* 1873.

——— Poetry of the period. 4 p. l. 294 pp. 12°. *London, R. Bentley,* 1870.

——— Rome or death! xi, 184 pp. sm. 4°. *Edinburgh, W. Blackwood & sons,* 1873.

Austin (Jane G.) Moonfolk. 205 pp. 12°. *New York, G. P. Putnam's sons,* 1874.

Autobiography (An). [*anon.*] vii, 307 pp. 12°. *Boston, A. Williams & co.* 1873.

Avellaneda (*Señora doña* Gertrudis Gomez de). *See* **Gomez de Avellaneda.**

Avery (M. A.) Rebel general's loyal bride. 417 pp. 4 pl. 12°. *Springfield, Mass. W. J. Holland & co.* 1873.

Avezac (Marie Pascal d'). Considérations géographiques sur l'histoire du Brésil. 2 p. l. 272 pp. 2 maps. 8°. *Paris, L. Martinet,* 1857.

——— Notice sur les anciens voyages de Tartarie en général, et sur celui de Jean du Plan Carpin en particulier.

[*In* PARIS. (*Société de géographie*). Recueil des voyages [etc.] 4°. *Paris,* 1830. v. 3, pp. 397–602].

Ayloffe (*Sir* Joseph, *bart.*) Calendars of the ancient charters, and of the welch and scottish rolls, in the tower of London. 1 p. l. lxxi, 462 pp. 16 l. 4 facs. 4°. *London, for B. White,* 1774.

Babbitt (E. D.) Health guide. 164 pp. 16°. *New York, E. D. Babbitt,* 1874.

Babcock (*Rev.* Rufus, *jr.*) Discourse occasioned by the death of the rev. George Leonard.

[*In* LEONARD (*Rev.* G.) Sermons on various subjects. 16°. *Portland,* [*Me.*] *Zion's advocate,* 1832. pp. v–xxxiii].

Babe (J. L.) South african diamond fields. 105 pp. 6 pl. 1 map fold. 12°. *New York, D. Wesley & co.* 1872.

Babington (Gervase). Very fruitfull exposition of the commandements. 24 p. l. 514 pp.

Babington (Gervase)—continued. 3 l. *b. l.* 16°. *London, H. Midleton for T. Charde*, 1586.

Baccalauréat (Le) ès sciences, résumé des connaissances exigées par le programme officiel. 3 v. 12°. *Paris, V. Masson & fils* [*et*] *G. Masson*, 1864–73.

CONTENTS.

BRISBARRE (J.) Philosophie. v. 1. 1864. pp. i–xliv, 111–209.
BURAT (E.) Précis de mécanique. 2e éd. 1869. v. 3, no. 6.
EDWARDS (A. M.) Précis d'histoire naturelle. 4e éd. 1873. v. 2, no. 4.
FERNET (É.) Précis de physique. 4e éd. 1873. v. 2, no. 2.

Bachelder (John B.) Gettysburg. iii–viii, 148 pp. 3 l. 9 pl. 1 map fold. 8°. *Boston, J. B. Bachelder*, 1873.

——— Illustrated tourist's guide of the United States. Including Gettysburg. 2 v. in 1. viii, 148, 82 pp. incl. 2 maps, 1 pl. 9 pl. 1 map fold. 8°. *Boston, J. B. Bachelder*, 1873.

——— Popular resorts in the United States. 192 pp. 8°. *Boston, J. B. Bachelder*, 1874.

——— Same. [3d ed.] 361 pp. front. 1 map. 8°. *Boston, J. B. Bachelder*, 1875.

Bacon (George Blagden). Siam. Eng. title, viii, 347 pp. 33 pl. 1 map. 12°. *New York, Scribner, Armstrong & co.* 1873.
[ILLUSTRATED library of travel and adventure].

Bacon (Leonard, *d.d.*) Genesis of the New England churches. 2 p. l. 7–485 pp. 8 pl. 2 maps, 2 ports. 12°. *New York, Harper & brothers*, 1874.

Bader (*Mlle.* Clarisse) La femme biblique. 2e éd. viii, 471 pp. 12°. *Paris, Didier & cie.* 1866.

Badgley (Jonathan). English grammar. 384 pp. 12°. *New York, author*, 1875.

Baer (*Mrs.* B. F.) Irene; or, beach-broken billows. 175 pp. 12°. *New York, authors' publishing co.* 1875.

Bagby (Geo. W.) For Virginians only. By Moses Adams [*pseud.*] 128 pp. 16°. *Philadelphia, J. B. Lippincott & co.* 1874.

Bagehot (Walter). Lombard street. viii, 359 pp. 12°. *New York, Scribner, Armstrong & co.* 1874.

Bailey (Henry D. B.) Local tales and historical sketches. 431 pp. port. 12°. *Fishkill Landing,* [*N. Y.*] *J. W. Spaight*, 1874.

Bailey (James M.) Life in Danbury. 6th thousand. 303 pp. 7 pl. 16°. *Boston, Shepard & Gill*, 1873.

Bailey (John Eglington). Life of Thomas Fuller. xxvi, 800 pp. 12 pl. 8 ports. (5 in facs.) 6 facs. pl. 1 plan, 1 tab. 8°. *London, B. M. Pickering*, 1874.

Bailey (Samuel W.) Náhbion. xvii, 698 pp. 8°. *Cambridge,* [*Ms*] *J. Wilson & son*, 1874

Bailey (W. T.) Richfield springs. 227 pp. incl. 2 pl. 2 pl. 12°. *New York, A. S. Barnes & co.* 1874.

Baillie (*Mrs.* —). Sail to Smyrna. iv, 253 pp. 6 pl. 12°. *London, Longmans, Green & co.* 1873.

Bain (Alexander, *ll.d.*) Mind and body. 2 p. l. 196 pp. 12°. *New York, D. Appleton & co.* 1873.
[INTERNATIONAL scientific series, no. 4].

Baird (Spencer Fullerton), **Brewer** (Thomas M.) *and* **Ridgway** (Robert). History of north american birds. 3 v. 4°. *Boston, Little, Brown, & co.* 1874.

Baker (D. W. C.) Brief history of Texas. 200 pp. incl. 1 port. 12°. *New York, A. S. Barnes & co.* 1873.

——— Texas scrap-book. 657 pp. 26 pl. 8°. *New York, A. S. Barnes & co.* [1875].

Baker (George). History and antiquities of Northampton. 2 v. 1 p. l. 780 pp; 2 p. l. 343 pp. 39 pl. fol. *London, J. B. Nichols & son, and J. Rodwell*, 1822–41.

Baker (George A. *jr.*) Point lace and diamonds. Poems. 132 pp. 10 pl. sq. 16°. *New York, F. B. Patterson*, 1875.

Baker (George M.) Amateur drama series. Eng. title, 248 pp. 3 pl. 16°. *Boston, Lee & Shepard*, 1875.

——— Maidenhood series. 16°. *Boston, Lee & Shepard*, 1875.

CONTENTS.

Running to waste. 245 pp. 6 pl. 1875.

——— Temperance drama. 230 pp. 16°. *Boston, Lee & Shepard*, 1874.

——— *editor.* Ballads of beauty. 167 pp. incl. 40 pl. sm. 4°. *Boston, Lee & Shepard*, 1875.

——— ——— Reading club and handy speaker. Selections in prose and poetry, [etc.] No. 1. iv, 92 pp. 16°. *Boston, Lee & Shepard*, 1874.

——— ——— Same. No. 2. 106 pp. 16°. *Boston, Lee & Shepard*, 1875.

Baker (*Mrs.* Harriet Newell Woods). Little princess. By "Aunt Hattie" [*pseud.*] 224 pp. 18°. *New York, Nelson & Phillips*, [1874].

Baker (Henry Barton). French society from the Fronde to the great revolution. 2 v. viii, 334 pp; iv, 340 pp. 12°. *London, R. Bentley & son*, 1874.

Baker (Osmon Clearder, *d. d.*) A guide-book in the administration of the discipline of the methodist episcopal church. Revised by bishop Harris. 253 pp. 16°. *New York, Nelson & Phillips*, 1873.

Baker (*Sir* Samuel W.) Ismailïa, narrative of the expedition to central Africa for the suppression of the slave trade. 2 v. viii, 447 pp. 1 map, 3 ports. on 2 pl. 20 pl; viii, 588 pp. 2 ports. 1 map, 28 pl. 8°. *London, Macmillan & co.* 1874.

Baker (William M.) Mose Evans. 3 p. l. 317 pp. 12°. *New York, Hurd & Houghton*, 1874.

Baker (William S.) Origin and antiquity of engraving. 10 pp. 1 l. 9-62 pp. 20 heliotype pl. 3 heliotype ports. sm. 4°. *Boston, J. R. Osgood & co.* 1875.

Ball (*Rev.* T. H.) Lake county, Indiana, from 1834 to 1872. 1 p. l. 364 pp. 1 map. 12°. *Chicago, J. W. Goodspeed*, 1873.

Ballads: scottish and english. [*anon.*] Ill. title, viii, 472 pp. 8 pl. 12°. *Edinburgh, W. P. Nimmo*, [1873].

Ballantyne (Robert Michael). Man on the ocean. 368 pp. 7 pl. 16°. *London, T. Nelson & sons*, 1874.

Balmes (*Rev.* Jaime Luciano). Criterion. Translated by a catholic priest. 321 pp. 12°. *New York, P. O'Shea*, 1875.

Balthassar de Medina. Chronica de la santa provincia de San Diego de Mexico. Vidas de illvstres, y venerables varones, que la han edificado [etc.] Eng. title, 22 p. l. 259 l. numb. 10 l. 1 map. sm. fol. *Mexico, J. de Ribero*, 1682.

Note.—The map at fol. 230 is the earliest specimen of copperplate engraving in Mexico.

——— Vida, martyrio, y beatificacion del martyr san Felipe de Jesus. 2da impression. 14 p. l. 176 pp. 1 port. 12°. *Madrid, herederos de la viuda de J. G. Infanzon*, 1751.

Balzac (Honoré de). Contes drolatiques. Droll stories. Translated into english. With designs by Doré. xxii, 651 pp. incl. 103 pl. 12°. *London, Chatto & Windus*, 1874.

Bancroft (Charles) Footprints of time. 671 pp. 11 pl. 8°. *Burlington, Iowa, R. T. Root*, 1874.

——— Same. [2d ed.] 734 pp. 4 pl. 1 port. 8°. *Burlington, R. T. Root*, 1875.

Bancroft (George). History of the United States. v. 10. 8°. *Boston, Little, Brown, & co.* 1874-75.

CONTENTS.

American revolution, v. 4, [and] General index to Bancroft's history of the United States. 741 pp.

Bancroft (Hubert Howe). Native races of the Pacific states of North America. v. 1-4. 8°. *San Francisco, author*, 1874-75.

CONTENTS.

v. 1. Wild tribes. xlix, 797 pp. 3 maps. 1874.
v. 2. Civilized nations. 1 p. l. x, 805 pp. 1 tab. 1875.
v. 3. Myths and languages. 1 p. l. x, 796 pp. 1875.
v. 4. Antiquities. 1 p. l. vii, 807 pp. 1875.
Note.—Author's copy.

Bangor [*Me.*] library association. Catalogue of books. 244 pp. 8°. [*Bangor*], *B. A. Burr*, 1873.

Banker's almanac for 1874. Edited by I. S. Homans. 23d annual volume. 8°. *New York, office of the Banker's magazine and statistical register*, [1874].

——— Same. 24th annual volume. 8°. *New York, Banker's magazine*, [1875].

——— Same. 2d ed. 8°. *New York, Banker's magazine*, [1875].

——— Same. 3d ed. 8°. *New York, Banker's magazine*, [1875].

Banvard (John, *artist*). Private life of a king. Suppressed memoirs of the prince of Wales, afterwards George IV, [etc.] 671 pp. 12°. *New York, literary and art publishing co.* 1875.

Banvard (Joseph, *d. d.*) Old Grips and little Tid. 146 pp. 1 pl. 18°. *New York, U. D. Ward*, 1873.

Barbier (Antoine Alexandre). Dictionnaire des ouvrages anonymes. 3e éd. Suite de la 2e éd. des Supercheries littéraires par J. M. Quérard. v. 1-2. A-L. 2 p. l. xlv, 1130 col; 2 p. l. 1160 col. 8°. *Paris, P. Daffis*, 1872-74.

Bard (*Dr.* Richard). Exegetical work on prophecy. 5 p. l. 5-185 pp. 12°. [*Denver, Col.*] 1873.

Bardsley (*Rev.* Charles Wareing). Our english surnames. x, 543 pp. 12°. *London, Chatto & Windus*, [1874].

Baret (John, *of Caius college, Cambridge*). Alvearie or triple dictionarie, in englishe, latin, and french. Eng. title, 5 p. l. 348 l. numb. c. i. [etc.] fol. [*London*, 1573].

Baring-Gould (*Rev.* Sabine). In exitu Israel. An historical novel. 2 v. xii, 292 pp; 1 p. l. 327 pp. 16°. *London, Macmillan & co.* 1870.

——— Legends of old testament characters. 2 v. xii, 237 pp; viii, 227 pp. 12°. *London, Macmillan & co.* 1871.

CONTENTS.

v. 1. Adam to Abraham.
v. 2. Melchizedek to Zechariah.

Baring-Gould (*Rev.* Sabine)—continued.
——— Lives of the saints. February–august. 8 v. 12°. *London, J. Hodges,* 1872–75.
Note.—Feb. march, april, and june are 2d ed. January wanting.
——— Lost and hostile gospels. xxxii, 305 pp. 12°. *London, Williams & Norgate,* 1874.
——— Yorkshire oddities, incidents, and strange events. 2 v. 3 p. l. 279 pp; 3 p. l. 271 pp. 12°. *London, J. Hodges,* 1874.
Barker (Fordyce, *m. d.*) Puerperal diseases. xiii, 526 pp. 8°. *New York, D. Appleton & co.* 1874.
Barley loaves. *See* **Hartley** (*Mrs.* Emily).
Barnard (Frederick Augustus Porter, *editor*). Johnson's new universal cyclopædia, v. 1, 1874. *See* **Johnson** (A. J. *& son*).
Barrett (*Rev.* Benjamin F.) Golden city. 253 pp. 12°. *Philadelphia, Claxton, Remsen & Haffelfinger,* 1874.
Barrett (*Rev.* Selah Hibbard, *editor*). Memoirs of eminent preachers in the freewill baptist denomination. 304 pp. 1 pl. 12°. *Rutland, Ohio, S. H. Barrett,* [1874].
Barrows (Albert Bradburn). Roland of Algernon and other poems. 207 pp. port. 18°. *Boston, A. B. Barrows,* 1875.
Barry (Herbert). Ivan at home. iii–xvi, 322 pp. 8 pl. 8°. *London, the publ. comp.* [*etc.*] 1872.
Barry (T. A.) *and* **Patten** (B. A.) Men and memories of San Francisco, in the "spring of '50". 296 pp. 12°. *San Francisco, A. L. Bancroft & co.* 1873.
Bartholomew (John). Zell's descriptive hand atlas of the world. Eng. title, xii, [174], 102 pp. 4 l. of pl. 35 double maps. fol. *Philadelphia, T. E. Zell,* 1873.
Bartlett (*Mrs.* C. A.) Lillie Ray. [Also, Eva, the prairie flower]. 267 pp. 1 port. 12°. *Hartford, Case, Lockwood & Brainard co.* 1874.
Bartlett (John). Familiar quotations. 7th ed. xvi, 864 pp. 12°. *Boston, Little, Brown & co.* 1875.
Bartlett (John Russell). Soldiers' national cemetery at Gettysburg. iv, 109 pp. 1 pl. 2 maps, 2 ports. 4°. *Providence,* [*R. I.*] *Providence press co. for the board of commissioners of the soldiers' national cemetery,* 1874.
Bartol (Cyrus Augustus, *d. d.*) The rising faith. 2 p. l. 386 pp. 16°. *Boston, Roberts brothers,* 1874.
Baschet (Armand). Le roi chez la reine, ou histoire secrète du mariage de Louis XIII et d'Anne d'Autriche. 2e éd. 2 p. l. 515 pp. 8°. *Paris, H. Plon,* 1866.
Bascom (John). Philosophy of english literature. xii, 318 pp. 12°. *New York, G. P. Putnam's sons,* 1874.
Bastian (Henry Charlton, *m. d.*) Beginnings of life. 2 v. xxxv, 475 pp; xi, 640, clv pp. 12°. *London, Macmillan & co.* 1872.
——— On paralysis from brain disease. xv, 340 pp. 12°. *London, Macmillan & co.* 1875.
Bastiat (Frédéric). Essays on political economy. [4th (people's) ed.] iv, 234 pp. 16°. *London, Provost & co.* [1874].
Bate (C. Spence, *f. r. s.*) *and* **Westwood** (John Obadiah, *m. a.*) History of the british sessile-eyed crustacea. 2 v. lvi, 507 pp; 1 p. l. 536 pp. 8°. *London, J. Van Voorst,* 1863–68.
Bates (Samuel P.) Battle of Gettysburg. 336 pp. 20 pl. incl. 13 ports. 8°. *Philadelphia, T. H. Davis & co.* 1875.
——— Martial deeds of Pennsylvania. Author's ed. 1116 pp. 4 maps, 2 pl. 74 ports. on 46 pl. 8°. *Philadelphia, T. H. Davis & co.* 1875.
Battey (Thomas C.) Life and adventures of a quaker among the Indians. xii, 9–339 pp. 7 ports. 1 pl. 12°. *Boston, Lee & Shepard,* 1875.
Baudelaire (Charles Pierre). Œuvres complètes. 7 v. 16°. *Paris, M. Lévy frères,* 1868–73.

CONTENTS.

v. 1. Les fleurs du mal. Précédées d'une notice par Théophile Gautier. 2 p. l. 411 pp. 1 port.
v. 2. Curiosités esthétiques. 2 p. l. 440 pp.
v. 3. L'art romantique. 2 p. l. 442 pp.
v. 4. Petits poëmes en prose.—Les paradis artificiels. 2e éd. 2 p. l. 471 pp.
v. 5. Histoires extraordinaires, par Edgar Poe. Traduction de C. Baudelaire. 2e éd. 2 p. l. 524 pp.
v. 6. Nouvelles histoires extraordinaires, par Edgar Poe. Traduction de C. Baudelaire. 2 p. l. 544 pp.
v. 7. Aventures d'Arthur Gordon Pym. Eureka. Par Edgar Poe. Traduction de C. Baudelaire. 2 p. l. 518 pp.

Baudrimont (Alexandre Édouard, *prof. à la faculté des sciences de Bordeaux*). Histoire des Basques. Nouv. éd. xii, v–x, 285 pp. 8°. *Paris, Maisonneuve & cie.* 1867.
Bauduy (Jerome K.) Lectures on diseases of the nervous system. 484 pp. 8°. *Philadelphia, J. B. Lippincott & co.* 1876.
Bauer (Clara). At Capri. From the german by Ms. 353 pp. 12°. *Philadelphia, Porter & Coates,* [1875].
[INTERNATIONAL series of new approved novels, v. 13].

Bauer (Clara)—continued.
——— Must it be? By Carl Detlef [*pseud.*] From the german by Ms. 134 pp. 8 pl. 8°. *Philadelphia, J. B. Lippincott & co.* 1873.
——— Valentine, the countess. By Carl Detlef [*pseud.*] From the german by M. S. 377 pp. 12°. *Philadelphia, Porter & Coates,* 1874.

Baur (*Dr.* Friedrich). Holzmesskunst. 2te aufl. xvi, 419 pp. 8°. *Wien, W. Braumüller,* 1875. s.

Baur (Wilhelm). Religious life in Germany. Translated. 2 v. xii, 362 pp; vi, 330 pp. 12°. *London, Strahan & co.* 1870.

Bausman (Benjamin, *d. d.*) Sinai und Zion. xvi, 448 pp. 6 pl. 12°. *Reading, Pa., D. Miller,* [1875].
——— Wayside gleanings in Europe. viii, 464 pp. 12°. *Reading, Pa. D. Miller,* [1875].

Baxter (William). Life of elder W. Scott. 450 pp. 1 port. 8°. *Cincinnati, Bosworth, Chase & Hall,* 1874.

Bayard (Samuel J.) Life of George Dashiel Bayard. 337 pp. 2 pl. 1 map. 12°. *New York, G. P. Putnam's sons,* 1874.

Bayles (Richard M.) Historical sketches of Suffolk county [N. Y.]; with outline of Long Island. 424, ix pp. 12°. *Port Jefferson, L. I., the author,* 1874.

Bayne (Peter). Life and letters of Hugh Miller. 2 v. viii, 432 pp. 2 pl. facs; vi, 504 pp. port. 8°. *London, Strahan & co.* 1871.

Bazar book of health. [*anon.*] 280 pp. 16°. *New York, Harper & brothers,* 1873.

Bazar book of the household. [*anon.*] 266 pp. 16°. *New York, Harper & brothers,* 1875.

Beach (Lewis). Cornwall, [Orange co. N. Y.] 200 pp. 8°. *Newburgh, N. Y., E. M. Ruttenber & son,* 1873.

Beadle (J. H.) Undeveloped west. 1 p. l. 15–823 pp. incl. 40 pl. 8 pl. 1 map. 8°. *Philadelphia, national publishing co.* [1873].
——— Women's war on whisky. 118 pp. 12°. *Cincinnati, Wilstach, Baldwin & co.* 1874.

Beale (Lionel S.) Bioplasm. xvi, 345 pp. 12°. *London, J. & A. Churchill,* 1872.
——— Protoplasm. 3d ed. xviii, 388 pp. 16 col. pl. 12°. *London, J. & A. Churchill,* 1874.

Bear (John W.) Life and travels. 2 p. l. 7–299 pp. port. 12°. *Baltimore, D. Binswanger & co.* 1873.

Beard (George M. *m. d.*) *and* **Rockwell** (Alphonso D. *m. d.*) Practical treatise on the

Beard *and* **Rockwell**—continued.
medical & surgical uses of electricity. 2d ed. xxviii pp. 1 l. 794 pp. 8°. *New York, W. Wood & co.* 1875.

Beardsley (E. Edwards, *d. d.*) Life and correspondence of Samuel Johnson, missionary in Connecticut. xii, 380 pp. port. 8°. *New York, Hurd & Houghton,* 1874.

Beaudry (Louis N.) Spiritual struggles of a roman catholic. iv, 275 pp. port. 16°. *New York, Nelson & Phillips,* 1875.

Beaufort (Emily A.) Egyptian sepulchres and syrian shrines. 2 v. 2 p. l. vii–xii, 411 pp. 2 col. pl; 4 p. l. 484 pp. 3 col. pl. 12°. *London, Longmans,* 1861.

Beauvoir (—, *marquis de*). Pekin, Jeddo, and San Francisco. From the french, by Agnes and Helen Stephenson. xi, 291 pp. 15 pl. 12°. *London, J. Murray,* 1872.

Becker (Bernard H.) Scientific London. viii, 340 pp. 12°. *London, H. S. King & co.* 1874.

Becker (Wilhelm Gottlieb). Augusteum ou description des monumens antiques à Dresde. 2 v. 3 p. l. viii, 148 pp. 1–34 pl. [2 col.]; iv, 121 pp. 35–94 pl. fol. *Leipzig, C. A. Hempel,* 1804–08.

Bedell (*Rev.* William, *rector of Rattlesden*). True relation of the life of rev. W. Bedell. xvii, 268 pp. sm. 4°. [*London*], *Camden society,* 1872.
[CAMDEN society publications, new series, no. 4].

Beebe (Carrie D.) Violets. 384 pp. 12°. *Middletown, N. Y., "Banner of liberty" publishing house,* 1873.

Beebe (Charles W.) Edmund Dawn. By Ravenswood [*pseud.*] 301 pp. 12°. *New York, G. W. Carleton & co.* 1873.

Beecher (Alvah C.) Recitations and readings. 180 pp. 16°. *New York, Dick & Fitzgerald,* [1874].

Beecher (*Miss* Catherine Esther). Housekeeper and healthkeeper. 482 pp. incl. 1 pl. 1 plan. 12°. *New York, Harper & brothers,* 1873.

Beecher (*Rev.* Henry Ward). Sermons. "Plymouth pulpit." 9th–10th series: sept. 1872–sept. 1873. 2 v. 482 pp; 503 pp. 8°. *New York, J. B. Ford & co.* 1874.
——— Summer parish: discourses, and morning services, at the "Twin mountain house". vi, 231 pp. photo. port. 12°. *New York, J. B. Ford & co.* 1875.
——— Yale lectures on preaching. xii, 263 pp. 12°. *New York, J. B. Ford & co.* 1872.

Beecher (*Rev.* Henry Ward)—continued.

——— Same. 2d series. viii, 330 pp. 12°. *New York, J. B. Ford & co.* 1873.

——— Same. 3d series. x, 326 pp. 12°. *New York, J. B. Ford & co.* 1874.

Beecher (*Rev.* Willis J.) Farmer Tompkins and his bibles. 320 pp. 3 pl. 3 facs. 12°. *Philadelphia, Presbyterian board of publication,* [1874].

Beers (D. G. *& co. publishers*). Atlas of Oneida county, N. Y. 139 pp. incl. 50 col. maps. fol. *Philadelphia, D. G. Beers & co.* 1874.

Beers (Frederick W.) County atlas of Litchfield, Connecticut. 76 pp. incl. 44 col. maps on 43 l. 4°. *New York, F. W. Beers & co.* 1874.

——— County atlas of Middlesex, Connecticut. 144 pp. incl. 45 col. maps on 66 l. 4°. *New York, F. W. Beers & co.* 1874.

——— Atlas of Douglas co. Kansas. 68 pp. incl. 20 maps. fol. *New York, F. W. Beers & co.* 1873.

——— Atlas of Shawnee co. Kansas. 1 p. l. 67 pp. incl. 17 maps. fol. *New York, F. W. Beers & co.* 1873.

——— County atlas of Hampshire, Massachusetts. 1 p. l. 105 pp. incl. 34 maps, 1 l. fol. *New York, F. W. Beers & co.* 1873.

——— Atlas of the city of Newton, Massachusetts. 119 pp. incl. 29 col. maps on 53 l. 4°. *New York, F. W. Beers & co.* 1874.

——— Atlas of Calhoun co. Michigan. 91 pp. incl. 39 maps, 1 l. fol. *New York, F. W. Beers & co.* 1873.

——— Atlas of Genesee co. Michigan. 119 pp. incl. 41 maps. 4°. *New York, F. W. Beers & co.* 1873.

——— County atlas of Ingham, Michigan. 104 pp. incl. 39 col. maps. 4°. *New York, F. W. Beers & co.* 1874.

——— Atlas of Ionia co. Michigan. 108 pp. incl. 37 col. maps. fol. *New York, F. W. Beers & co.* 1875.

——— Atlas of Kalamazoo co. Michigan. 95 pp. incl. 36 maps. fol. *New York, F. W. Beers & co.* 1873.

——— Atlas of Lapeer co. Michigan. 78 pp. incl. 38 col. maps. 4°. *New York, F. W. Beers & co.* 1874.

——— Atlas of Livingston co. Michigan. 86 pp. incl. 32 col. maps. fol. *New York, F. W. Beers & co.* 1875.

——— Atlas of Hunterdon co. New Jersey.

Beers (Frederick W.)—continued.

1 p. l. 77 pp. incl. 27 maps. 4°. *New York, Beers, Comstock & Cline,* 1873.

——— Atlas of Somerset co. New Jersey. Title, 62 pp. incl. 19 col. maps. fol. *New York, Beers, Comstock & Cline,* 1873.

——— County atlas of Warren, New Jersey. 96 pp. incl. 33 col. maps on 40 l. 4°. *New York, F. W. Beers & co.* 1874.

——— County atlas of Cayuga, New York. 147 pp. incl. 38 col. maps & 17 pl. fol. *New York, Walker & Jewett,* 1875.

——— Atlas of Livingston co. New York. 45 pp. incl. 30 maps, 1 l. fol. *New York, F. W. Beers & co.* 1872.

——— Atlas of Long Island, New York. 192 pp. incl. 98 col. maps fold. fol. *New York, Beers, Comstock & Cline,* 1873.

——— Atlas of Monroe co. New York. 115 pp. incl. 37 maps, 1 l. fol. *New York, F. W. Beers & co.* 1872.

——— Atlas of Staten Island, New York. Eng. title, 36 col. maps on 66 l. 4°. *New York, J. B. Beers & co.* 1874.

——— County atlas of Sullivan, New York. 96 pp. incl. 36 col. maps. fol. *New York, Walker & Jewett,* 1875.

——— County atlas of Ulster, New York. 140 pp. incl. 52 col. maps & 31 pl. fol. *New York, Walker & Jewett,* 1875.

——— County atlas of Carbon, Pennsylvania. 82 pp. incl. 26 col. maps, 3 pl. fol. *New York, F. W. Beers & co.* 1875.

——— Atlas of Cumberland co. Pennsylvania. 1 p. l. 48 pp. incl. 34 maps, 2 l. of pl. 1 l. fol. *New York, F. W. Beers & co.* 1872.

——— County atlas of Schuylkill, Pennsylvania 135+ pp. incl. 69 col. maps & 24 pl. fol. *New York, F. W. Beers & co.* 1875.

——— County atlas of Caledonia, Vermont. 99 pp. incl. 35 col. maps & 14 pl. fol. *New York, F. W. Beers & co.* 1875.

——— County atlas of Washington, Vermont. 1 p. l. 65 pp. incl. 32 maps, 1 l. fol. *New York, F. W. Beers & co.* 1873.

Beers (George A.) Vasquez; or, bandits of the San Joaquin. 141 pp. 8°. *New York, R. M. De Witt,* [1875].

Beever (Susanna). Book of reference to remarkable passages in Shakespeare. viii, 184 pp. 18°. *London, Bull, Simmons & co.* 1870.

Beever (*Rev.* W. Holt, *a. m.*) Daily life of our farm. xiii, 313 pp. incl. 1 pl. 12°. *London, Bradbury, Evans & co.* 1871.

Bégin (*Abbé* Louis Nazaire). Primauté et infaillibilité des souverains pontifes. 2 p. l. 430 pp. 12°. *Québec, l'imprimerie du "Canadien"*, 1873. s.

——— La sainte écriture et la règle de foi. xiii, 298 pp. 12°. *Québec, A. Coté & cie.* 1874. s.

Bell (Alexander Melville). Visible speech. 126 pp. 16 pl. 4°. *London, Simpkin, Marshall & co.* 1867.

Bell (Thomas, *f. r. s.*) History of british quadrupeds. 2d ed. xviii, 474 pp. 8°. *London, J. Van Voorst*, 1874.

Bell (*Major* William Morrison). Other countries. 2 v. xi, 392 pp. front; ix, 360 pp. front. 8°. *London, Chapman & Hall*, 1872.

Bellasis (Edward). Cherubini. xv, 429 pp. 12°. *London, Burns & Oates*, 1874.

Bellows (C. F. R. *c. e.*) Treatise on plane and spherical trigonometry. 166 pp. 8°. *New York, Sheldon & co.* 1874.

Bellows (John). Vrai dictionnaire de poche, français-anglais et anglais-français. Bonafide pocket dictionary of the french and english languages. 2 p. l. xvi, 548 pp. 1 l. 24°. *London, Trübner & co.* [1873].

Belot (Adolphe). Article 47. A romance. From the french. By James Furbish. 161 pp. 8°. *Philadelphia, J. B. Lippincott & co.* 1873.

——— Deux femmes, [etc.] 4e éd. 2 p. l. 304 pp. 16° *Paris, E. Dentu*, 1873.

——— La femme de feu. 9e éd. 2 p. l. 363 pp. 16°. *Paris, E. Dentu*, 1872.

——— *and* **Dautin** (Jules). Dacolard et Lubin. 4e éd. 2 p. l. 377 pp. 16°. *Paris, E. Dentu*, 1873.

——— ——— Le parricide. 4e éd. 2 p. l. 392 pp. 16°. *Paris, E. Dentu*, 1873.

Belt (Thomas). Naturalist in Nicaragua. xvi, 403 pp. 4 pl. 1 map. 12°. *London, J. Murray*, 1874.

Benedict (David). History of the donatists. With life of dr. Benedict, by H. C. Graves. Memorial ed. xxxii, 212 pp. port. 12°. *Providence, for M. M. Benedict*, 1875.

Benedict (Frank Lee). John Worthington's name. 197 pp. 8°. *New York, Harper & brothers*, 1874.

——— Miss Dorothy's charge. 7–195 pp. 8°. *New York, Harper & brothers*, 1873.

——— Mr. Vaughan's heir. 199 pp. 8°. *New York, Harper & brothers*, 1875.

——— St. Simon's niece. 189 pp. 8°. *New York, Harper & brothers*, 1875.

Benedict (Henry Marvin). Genealogy of the Benedicts in America. xix, 475 pp. 28 ports. 8°. *Albany, J. Munsell*, 1870.

Benedict (James L. *compiler*). Laws and regulations for the government of officers of customs. 218 pp. sq. 18°. *Washington, government printing office*, 1875.

Benjamin (E. Bedell). Brightside. 359 pp. 3 pl. 16°. *New York, R. Carter & brothers*, 1873.

Benndorf (Otto) *and* **Schöne** (Richard). Die antiken bildwerke des lateranensischen museums. x, 421 pp. 24 pl. 8°. *Leipzig, Breitkopf & Härtel*, 1867.

Bennett (Emerson). Orphan's trials. 1 p. l. 7–302 pp. 12°. *Philadelphia, T. B. Peterson & brothers*, [1874].

——— Outlaw's daughter. 4 p. l. 13–343 pp. port. 12°. *Philadelphia, Claxton, Remsen & Haffelfinger*, 1874.

——— Villeta Linden. 414 pp. 1 pl. 8°. *Philadelphia, Claxton, Remsen & Haffelfinger*, 1874.

Benning (Howe). Nix's offerings. 1 p. l. 400 pp. 3 pl. 16°. *New York, Warren & Wyman*, [1873].

[FIVE hundred dollar prize series of illustrated books].

Benn-Walsh (*Sir* John, *lord Ormathwaite*). Astronomy and geology compared. 4 p. l. 171 pp. 12°. *London, J. Murray*, 1872.

Benson (*Captain* L. *editor*). Book of remarkable trials and notorious characters. From 1700 to 1840. iv, 9–545 pp. 37 pl. 1 col. pl. 12°. *London, J. C. Hotten*, [1871].

Benson (Lawrence S.) My visit to the sun. v. 1. Physics. Electrotyped ed. 1 p. l. 164 pp. 8°. *New York, J. S. Burnton*, 1874.

Benson (Robert) *and* **Hatcher** (Henry). Old and new Sarum. xviii, 855 pp. 21 pl. fol. *London, J. B. Nichols & son*, 1843.

[HOARE (*Sir* R. C.) The history of modern Wiltshire, v. 6].

Bergius (Carl Julius). Grundsätze der finanzwissenschaft mit besonderer beziehung auf den preussischen staat. 2te aufl. vi, 749 pp. 8°. *Berlin, J. Guttentag*, 1871.

Beristain y Martin de Souza (*Dr.* José Mariano). Biblioteca hispano-americana septentrional. 3 v. fol. *México, A. Valdez*, 1816–21.

[Imperfect: some pages supplied in ms.]

Berjeau (Jean Philibert, *m. d.*) Early dutch, german, & english printers' marks. 1 p. l. 100 pl. on 60 l. 36 pp. 8°. *London, E. Rascol*, 1866[–69].

Berkeley (George, *d. d. bishop of Cloyne*). Writings of bishop Berkeley hitherto unpublished.

[*In* FRAZER (A. C.) Life and letters of George Berkeley, d. d. 8°. *Oxford*, 1871. pp. 417–658].

Berlin (E. A.) Earth angels and hidden oppression. 538 pp. incl. front. 12°. *Shelby, O.* [*Chicago printed*], *S. S. Bloom*, 1875.

Bernard (Charles Bernard Du Grail de la Villette, *known as* Charles de). Fatal passion; or, "Gerfaut". From the forty-first Paris ed. by O. Vibeur. 364 pp. 12°. *New York, G. W. Carleton & co.* 1874.

Bertrand (Louis Jacques Napoléon Aloisius). Gaspard de la nuit. 2 p. l. xxii, 324 pp. 8°. *Angers, V. Pavie*, 1842.

Beskow (Gustaf Emanuel). Reseminnen från Egypten, Sinai och Palestina, 1859–1860. 5e uppl. 3 p. l. 431 pp. 15 pl. 2 maps. 12°. *Stockholm, A. L. Norman*, 1866.

Besse (H. *m. d.*) Diploteratology. 202 pp. incl. 1 pl. 16°. *Delaware, Ohio, gazette office*, 1874.

Bicknell (Amos J.) Detail, cottage and constructive architecture. 2 p. l. 75 pl. front. fol. *New York, A. J. Bicknell & co.* [1873].

——— Wooden and brick buildings with details. 2 v. 4 p. l. pl. 1–80, 15 l. unp. front; 4 p. l. pl. 81–160, 12 l. unp. front. 4°. *New York, A. J. Bicknell & co.* 1875.

Bigelow (John). Life of B. Franklin, by himself, 3 v. 1874. *See* **Franklin** (Benjamin).

Bigland (Ralph). Historical, monumental and genealogical collections, relative to the county of Gloucester. 2 v. in 1. viii, 632 pp. 23 pl; 2 p. l. 312 pp. 11 pl. fol. *London, J. Nichols, for R. Bigland, of Frocester*, 1791–92.

Note.—This copy has pp. 253–312 in v. 2, not mentioned in Lowndes or Upcott. The work was never completed, the city of Gloucester being one of its principal deficiencies.

Billings (John S.) Report of the hygiene of the U. S. army. lix, 567 pp. 13 pl. 1 map. 4°. *Washington, government printing office*, 1875.

[UNITED STATES. *War department.* (*Surgeon general's office*). Circular no. 8].

Billingsly (*Rev.* A. S.) From the flag to the cross. 1 p. l. 429 pp. 21 pl. 8°. *Philadelphia, new-world publishing co.* 1872.

Biographical encyclopædia of Pennsylvania of the nineteenth century. 672 pp. 215 ports. 4°. *Philadelphia, Galaxy publishing co.* 1874.

Note.—Edited by Charles Robson.

Bird (*Rev.* Isaac). Bible work in bible lands. 432 pp. 12°. *Philadelphia, Presbyterian board of publication*, [1872].

Bird (Joseph). Protection against fire, and the best means of putting out fires. iv, 278 pp. 12°. *New York, Hurd & Houghton*, 1873.

Bird (Mary Atherstone). Winifred's jewels. 340 pp. front. 12°. *Philadelphia, H. N. McKinney & co.* [1875].

Biscoe (Ellen L.) Glimpses through. [*anon.*] Eng. title, 374 pp. 1 pl. 12°. *Boston, D. Lothrop & co.* 1873.

[THOUSAND dollar prize series].

Bissell (Edwin Cone). Historic origin of the bible. xxiii, 432 pp. 1 tab. 8°. *New York, A. D. F. Randolph & co.* [1873].

Bisset (Andrew). Essays on historical truth. 3 p. l. 468 pp. 8°. *London, Longmans*, 1871.

——— History of the commonwealth of England from the death of Charles I. to the expulsion of the long parliament by Cromwell: being omitted chapters of the history of England. 2 v. 1 p. l. xii, 392 pp; xvii, 505 pp. 8°. *London, J. Murray*, 1864–67.

Black (C. B.) Guide to France, Belgium, Holland, Germany, and north of Italy. 12 p. l. xxxiv, 715 pp. 14 pl. 51 maps. 16°. *London, S. Low, Marston, Low & Searle*, 1874.

——— Guide to Switzerland and the Italian lakes. 8 p. l. 170 pp. 10 maps. 16°. *London, S. Low, Marston, Low & Searle*, [1874].

Black (*Mrs.* S. S.) Rambling chats and chatty rambles. By J. O. Y. [*anon.*] 210 pp. 5 pl. 16°. *New York, E. P. Dutton & co.* 1873.

Black (William). Daughter of Heth. [*anon.*] 3 v. 12°. *London, S. Low son & Marston*, 1871.

——— Princess of Thule. 3d ed. 3 v. 12°. *London, Macmillan & co.* 1874.

——— Strange adventures of a phaeton. 3d ed. 2 v. viii, 328; viii, 312 pp. 12°. *London, Macmillan & co.* 1873.

Blackburn (Henry). Art in the mountains: the story of the passion play. 1 p. l. 167 pp. incl. 20 pl. 8°. *London, S. Low, son & Marston*, 1870.

——— Harz mountains. 184 pp. incl. 9 pl. 8°. *London, S. Low, Marston, Low & Searle*, 1873.

Blacklock (M. Strickland). City sounds and rural echoes. iv, 103 pp. 1 pl. 12°. *New York, J. M. Stevenson*, 1874.

Blackman (Emily C.) History of Susquehanna county, Pennsylvania. xi, 640 pp. incl. 1 pl. 22 pl. 6 maps. 8°. *Philadelphia, Claxton, Remsen & Haffelfinger*, 1873.

Blackmore (Richard D.) Maid of Sker. 3 v. 16°. *Edinburgh, W. Blackwood & sons*, 1872.

Blackwell (Antoinette Brown). The sexes throughout nature. 240 pp. 12°. *New York, G. P. Putnam's sons*, 1875.

Bladé (Jean François). Contes populaires. Traduction française et texte agenais suivis de notes par m. Reinhold Köhler. 2 p. l. iv, 164 pp. 8°. *Paris, J. Baer*, 1874.

Blake (E. Vale). Arctic experiences. 486 pp. incl. 10 pl. 1 map. 8°. *New York, Harper & brothers*, 1874.

Blake (Jonathan). History of the town of Warwick, Mass. to 1854. 240 pp. port. 12°. *Boston, Noyes, Holmes & co.* 1873.

Note.—Continued to the present time by rev. John Goldsbury and deacon Hervey Barber.

Blake (Lillie Devereux). Fettered for life. 379 pp. 12°. *New York, Sheldon & co.* 1874.

Blanc (Charles). L'art dans la parure et dans le vêtement. 2 p. l. 376 pp. 2 col. pl. 8°. *Paris, librairie Renouard*, 1875.

——— Grammar of painting and engraving. From the french by Kate Newell Doggett. xx, 330 pp. incl. 16 pl. 8°. *New York, Hurd & Houghton*, 1874.

——— Histoire des peintres de toutes les écoles. École bolonaise. 2 p. l. xix, [185] pp. 3 l. fol. *Paris, librairie Renouard*, 1874.

——— Same. École flamande. 2 p. l. 20, [488] pp. 4 l. fol. *Paris, veuve J. Renouard*, 1868.

——— Same. École française. 3 v. fol. *Paris, veuve J. Renouard*, 1863–65.

——— Same. École hollandaise. 2 v. 2 p. l. 20, [376] pp; 2 p. l. [380], 41 pp. 1 l. fol. *Paris, veuve J. Renouard*, 1861.

——— Same. École ombrienne et romaine. 2 p. l. 16, [363] pp. 4 l. fol. *Paris, veuve J. Renouard*, 1870.

[*With his* HISTOIRE des peintres de toutes les écoles. École bolonaise. fol. *Paris, librairie Renouard*, 1874].

——— Same. École vénitienne [et italienne]. 2 p. l. 16, [268], 60 pp. 1 l. fol. *Paris, veuve J. Renouard*, 1868.

——— L'œuvre de Rembrandt décrit et commenté. Catalogue raisonné de toutes les estampes du maître et de ses peintures. 2 v. 3 p. l. viii, 316 pp. incl. 21 pl. 1 l. 35 pl; 3 p. l. 308 pp. 1 l. 20 pl. 8 ports. 4°. *Paris, A. Lévy*, 1873.

——— *and others.* Histoire des peintres de toutes les écoles. École espagnole. 2 p. l. 19, [240] pp. 4 l. fol. *Paris, veuve J. Renouard*, 1869.

——— **Mantz** (Paul), *and* **Demmin** (Auguste). Histoire des peintres des toutes les écoles. École allemande. 2 p. l. xxiv, [472] pp. 1 l. fol. *Paris, librairie Renouard*, 1875.

Blasius (Wilhelm). Storms: their nature, classification and laws. 342 pp. 10 pl. 12°. *Philadelphia, Porter & Coates*, [1875].

Bleby (*Rev.* Henry). Romance without fiction. 582 pp. incl. 1 pl. 16°. *New York, Nelson & Phillips*, [1874].

Bleek (Friedrich). Introduction to the old testament. Translated from the 2d ed. (Berlin, 1865) by G. H. Venables. 2 v. xviii, 454 pp; xi, 484 pp. 12°. *London, Bell & Daldy*, 1869.

Bliss (Orville Justus). Three months in the orient; also, life in Rome, and the Vienna exposition. 198 pp. 12°. *Chicago, S. C. Griggs & co.* 1875.

Bliss (William R.) Paradise in the Pacific. 207 pp. 16°. *New York, Sheldon & co.* 1873.

Block (Maurice). Dictionnaire général de la politique. Nouv. éd. 2 v. 4 p. l. 1168 pp; 2 p. l. 1152 pp. 8°. *Paris, O. Lorenz*, 1873–74.

Blocqueville (Adélaide Louise d'Eckmühl, *marquise* de). Les soirées de la villa des jasmins. 4 v. 8°. *Paris, Didier & cie.* 1874.

Blomefield (*Rev.* Francis) *and* **Parkin** (*Rev.* Charles). Essay towards a topographical history of Norfolk. 5 v. fol. *Fersfield*, [*author*], *and Lynn, W. Whittingham*, 1739–75.

Boase (Clement Henry) *and* **Courtney** (William Prideaux). Bibliotheca cornubiensis. v. 1. A–O. 8°. *London, Longmans*, 1874.

Boaz: his tribulations. [*anon.*] 244 pp. 16°. *Nashville, Wheeler, Marshall & Bruce*, [1875].

Boddam-Whetham (J. W.) Western wanderings. xiii, 364 pp. 12 pl. 8°. *London, R. Bentley & son*, 1874.

Boigne (Éléonore Adèle d'Osmond, *comtesse* de). La maréchale d'Aubemer. 2 p. l. 329 pp. 1 l. 16°. *Paris, M. Lévy frères*, 1867.

Boissonade (Jean François). Critique littéraire sous le premier empire; précédée d'une notice sur m. Boissonade, par m. Naudet. 2 v. 2 p. l. ciii, 507 pp. port; 2 p. l. 648 pp. 8°. *Paris, Didier & cie.* 1863.

Boissonnas (*Mme.* B.) Un vaincu; souvenirs du général Robert Lee. 3e éd. 2 p. l. vii, 291 pp. port. 1 map. 16°. *Paris, J. Hetzel & cie.* 1875.

Bokum (Hermann). Tennessee hand-book and immigrant's guide. 2 p. l. 164 pp. 1 map. 12°. *Philadelphia, J. B. Lippincott & co.* 1868.

Bollaert (William). Wars of succession of Portugal and Spain, from 1826 to 1840. 2 v. viii, 485 pp. 1 l. 2 pl. 1 map, 2 ports; xi, 497, iii pp. 2 ports. 1 map. 8°. *London, E. Stanford,* 1870.

CONTENTS.

v. 1. Portugal.—Account of the siege of Oporto, 1832–33.
v. 2. Spain.—Flight of Isabella II. in September, 1868.

Bolles (Albert S.) Chapters in political economy. 4 p. l. 206 pp. 12°. *New York, D. Appleton & co.* 1874.

Bombaugh (Charles C. *a. m.*) Gleanings for the curious. [First series]. Eng. title, 864 pp. port. 8°. *Hartford, A. D. Worthington & co.* 1875.

Bonawitz (Johann Heinrich). Bride of Messina. Vocal score. 183 pp. 4°. *Philadelphia, Lee & Walker,* [1874].

Bond (John J.) Handy-book of rules and tables for verifying dates with the christian era; an account of the chief eras, and systems used by various nations, [etc.] xlii, 465 (+ 272^a-b^) pp. 12°. *London, G. Bell & sons,* 1875.

Bonneau (Alfred). Life of madame de Beauharnais de Miramion, 1629–1696. Translated by the baroness de Montaignac. xv, 349 pp. port. 12°. *London, R. Bentley,* 1870.

Bonnell (George W.) Topographical description of Texas. 150 pp. 18°. *Austin, Clark, Wing & Brown,* 1840.

Bonnet (Victor). Le crédit et les finances. 3 p. l. 396 pp. 8°. *Paris, A. R. Lainé,* 1865.

——— Le crédit et les banques d'émission. 2 p. l. xvi, 312 pp. 8°. *Paris, E. Plon & cie.* 1875.

Bonney (*Mrs.* Catharina V. R. *compiler*). Legacy of historical gleanings. 2 v. viii, 542 pp. 1 pl. 5 ports. 1 pl. containing 5 ports; viii, 544 pp. 3 pl. 2 ports. 8°. *Albany, J. Munsell,* 1875.

Bontier (Pierre) *and* **Verrier** (Jean C.) The Canarian; or, book of the conquest and conversion of the Canarians in 1402. Translated by R. H. Major. 7 p. l. lvi, 229 pp. 1 map, 1 port. 1 pl. 8°. *London, for the Hakluyt society,* 1872.

[HAKLUYT society publications, v. 46].

Bonwick (James, *f. r. g. s.*) Mormons and the silver mines. vii, 425 pp. 12°. *London, Hodder & Stoughton,* 1872.

Book of humorous poetry. [*anon.*] Illustrations by C. A. Doyle. Ill. title, xvi, 464 pp. 7 pl. 16°. *Edinburgh, W. P. Nimmo,* 1873.

Boone (T. B. *s. J.*) Manual of the blessed sacrament. From the french by mrs. Annie Blount Storrs. 506 pp. front. 18°. *New York, the catholic publication society,* 1875.

Boothby (Lætitia Lavinia). Memoirs by herself. Ed. by Clark Russell. viii, 322 pp. 12°. *London, H. S. King & co.* 1872.

Borbstædt (*Col.* A.) *and* **Dwyer** (*Maj.* F.) Franco-german war to the fall of Strassburg. viii, 701 pp. 15 maps and plans. 8°. *London, Asher & co.* 1873.

Borlase (*Rev.* William). Natural history of Cornwall. xix, 326 pp. 1 l. 29 pl. fol. *Oxford, for the author, by W. Jackson,* 1758.

Borlase (William Copeland). Nænia Cornubiæ. xvi, 288 pp. 8°. *London, Longmans,* 1872.

Bosgoed (D. Mulder). Bibliotheca ichthyologica et piscatoria. Catalogue de livres et d'écrits sur l'histoire naturelle des poissons et des cétacés, la pisciculture, les pêches, la législation des pêches, etc. 2 p. l. xxvi, 474 pp. 8°. *Haarlem, héritiers Loosjes,* 1874.

Boswell (James). Life of Samuel Johnson. With new notes, by Percy Fitzgerald. 3 v. 8°. *London, Bickers & son,* 1874.

Both (Carl, *m. d.*) Consumption and its treatment. 157 pp. incl. 1 pl. 8°. *Boston, A. Moore,* 1873.

Bouquet de la Grye (A.) Guide du forestier. 6e éd. 2 v. x, 302 pp; viii, 280 pp. 16°. *Paris, J. Rothschild,* 1870–72.

Bourgeois (L. X. *m. d.*) Passions in their relation to health and diseases. From the french, by Howard F. Damon. xi, 201 pp. 16°. *Boston, J. Campbell,* 1873.

Bourgoin (J.) Théorie de l'ornement. 2 p. l. xi, 366 pp. 24 pl. 8°. *Paris, A. Lévy,* 1873.

Bourne (H. R. Fox). English seamen under the Tudors. 2 v. xv, 304 pp. 5 maps on 4 pl; xi, 314 pp. 12°. *London, R. Bentley,* 1868.

——— Romance of trade. vi pp. 1 l. 379 pp. 12°. *London, Cassell, Petter & Galpin,* [1871].

Boutell (*Rev.* Charles). Heraldry. 3d ed. revised. xvi, 547 pp. 82 pl. 8°. *London, R. Bentley,* 1864.

Boutelle (John Alonzo) *and* **Burke** (William A.) Burke and Alvord memorial. 239 pp. 8°. *Boston, H. W. Dutton & son,* 1864.

Bowne (B. P.) Philosophy of Herbert Spencer. 283 pp. 12°. *New York, Nelson & Phillips,* 1874.

Boxer (*Rev.* James). Sacred dramas. 1. Naaman. 2. Finding of Moses. 3. Jephthah's

Boxer (*Rev.* James)—continued. daughter. 174 pp. 12°. *Boston, Lee & Shepard,* 1875.

Boyd (Andrew Kennedy Hutchison). Landscapes, churches and moralities. [*anon.*] vi, 320 pp. 12°. *London, Longmans,* 1874.

Boyd (*Mrs.* E. E.) Stones and diamonds 272 pp. 3 pl. 16°. *Boston, H. A. Young & co.* 1875.

Boyd (John). Annals and family records of Winchester, with centennial celebration, 1871. xi, 9–632 pp. 19 pl. 8°. *Hartford, Case, Lockwood & Brainard,* 1873.

Boyesen (Hjalmar Hjorth). Gunnar. 292 pp. 18°. *Boston, J. R. Osgood & co.* 1874.

——— A Norseman's pilgrimage. 301 pp. 16°. *New York, Sheldon & co.* 1875.

Boyle (Frederick). Camp notes. Stories of sport and adventure in Asia, Africa, and America. 4 p. l. 302 pp. 12°. *London, Chapman & Hall,* 1874.

Brachet (Auguste). Historical grammar of the french tongue. Translated by G. W. Kitchin. xvi, 221 pp. 16°. *Oxford, Clarendon press,* 1872.
[CLARENDON press series].

Brackel (Ferdinande, *freiin von*). Die tochter des kunstreiters. 2 p. l. 407 pp. 16°. *Köln, J. P. Bachem,* 1875.

Brackett (Anna C. *ed.*) Education of american girls. 401 pp. 12°. *New York, G. P. Putnam's sons,* 1874.

Braddon (Mary Elizabeth). Doctor's wife. [*anon.*] 4th ed. 3 v. 16°. *London, J. Maxwell & co.* 1864.

——— Lost for love. [*anon.*] 3 v. 12°. *London, Chatto & Windus,* 1874.

——— Lucius Davoren. [*anon.*] 3 v. 12°. *London, J. Maxwell & co.* 1873.

——— Strangers and pilgrims. [*anon.*] 3 v. 12°. *London, J. Maxwell & co.* 1873.

——— Taken at the flood. [*anon.*] 3 v. 12°. *London, J. Maxwell & co.* 1874.

Bradford (J. B. *& co. publishers*). Hotel guide to the United States and Canada. [1st ed. nov. 1874]. 16°. *Chicago, J. B. Bradford & co.* 1874.

Bradlaugh (Charles). Few words about the devil, and other biographical sketches and essays. 2 p. l. [246] pp. port. 12°. *New York, A. K. Butts & co.* 1874.

Bradley (Maria G. *compiler*). Golden gems. 114 pp. 12°. *Boston, D. Lothrop & co.* 1873.

Bradley (S. Messenger, *f. r. c. s.*) Manual of comparative anatomy and physiology. 3d ed. xi, 276 pp. 3 pl. 12°. *London, J. & A. Churchill,* 1875.

Bradshaw's general railway and steam navigation guide for Great Britain and Ireland, [etc.] No. 487 for feb. 1874. xlii, 374 pp. 1 map. sq. 16°. *London, W. J. Adams,* [1874].

Bradshaw's railway manual, shareholders' guide, for 1873. v. 25. 16°. *London, W. J. Adams,* 1873.

Brainard (Mary). Memorial pictures of war and peace. 208 pp. 12°. *Rockford, Ill. gazette steam printing house,* 1873.

Brandon (Raphael *and* J. Arthur). Analysis of gothick architecture. New ed. 2 v. vii, 118 pp. 51 pl; 1 p. l. 107 pl. 4°. *London, D. Bogue,* 1849.

——— Open timber roofs of the middle ages. viii, 87 pp. 43 pl. 4°. *London, D. Bogue,* 1849.

Brasseur de Bourbourg (*L'abbé* Charles Étienne). Bibliothèque mexico-guatémalienne [etc.] 2 p. l. xlvii, 183 pp. 8°. *Paris, Maisonneuve & cie.* 1871.

——— Quatre lettres sur le Mexique. xx, 463 pp. 8°. *Paris, Maisonneuve & cie.* 1868.
[COLLECTION de documents dans les langues indigènes pour servir à l'étude de l'histoire et de la philologie de l'Amérique ancienne, v. 4].

Brassey (Thomas, *m. p.*) On work and wages. 3d ed. xvi, 296 pp. 8°. *London, Bell & Daldy,* 1872.

Brayley (Edward Wedlake). History and antiquities of the abbey church of st. Peter, Westminster. Illustrated by John Preston Neale. 2 v. 2 eng. titles, 9 p. l. 228 pp. 9 l. 2 fronts. 72 pp. 5 l. 20 pl; 2 eng. titles, 1 p. l. 304 pp. 20 l. 94 pl. 2 fronts. 4°. *London, J. P. Neale,* [*&*] *Hurst, Robinson & co.* 1818–23.

Brehm (Alfred Edmund). Bird-life. From the german by H. M. Labouchere and W. Jesse. xxvii, 898 pp. 11 col. pl. 8°. *London, J. Van Voorst,* [1871–]74.

——— Vie des animaux illustrée. Éd. française, revue par Z. Gerbe. 4 v. 4°. *Paris, J. B. Baillière & fils,* [1869].

CONTENTS.

v. 1–2. Les mammifères. xxiv, 765 pp. 19 pl; 2 p. l. 870 pp. 21 pl.
v. 3–4. Les oiseaux. xxx, 791 pp. 19 pl; 2 p. l. 907 pp. 20 pl.

Brents (T. W.) Gospel plan of salvation. 667 pp. 8°. *Cincinnati, Bosworth, Chase & Hall,* 1874.

Brereton (*Sir* William, *bart.*) Travels in Holland, the United Provinces, England,

Brereton (*Sir* William, *bart.*)—continued. [etc.] 1634–35. 2 p. l. viii, 206 pp. sm. 4°. [*London*], 1844.

[CHETHAM society remains, v. 1].

Brevoort (James Carson). Verrazano the navigator. 159 pp. 1 l. 2 maps in facs. 8°. *New York*, [*Albany printed, Argus co.*] 1874.

Brewster (George). New philosophy of matter. New ed. 1 p. l. ix–361 pp. 8°. *Philadelphia, Claxton, Remsen & Haffelfinger, for the author*, 1874.

Bric-à-brac series. Edited by R. H. Stoddard. v. 1–9. 16°. *New York, Scribner, Armstrong & co.* 1874–75.

CONTENTS.

v. 1. Personal reminiscences by H. F. Chorley, J. R. Planché, and J. C. Young. xxiii, 297 pp. 1874.
v. 2. Anecdote biographies of Thackeray and Dickens. 2 p. l. vii–xxiv, 305 pp. 1874.
v. 3. Letters to an incognita by P. Merimée. With recollection by Lamartine and George Sand. [*pseud.*] 1 p. l. 350 pp. 1874.
v. 4. Personal reminiscences by Barham, Harness, and Hodder. 335 pp. 1875.
v. 5. The Greville memoirs, by C. C. F. Greville. xi, 346 pp. 1875.
v. 6. Personal reminiscences by Moore and Jerdan. 293 pp. 4 ports. 1 incl. in pag. 1875.
v. 7. Personal reminiscences by Cornelia Knight and Thomas Raikes. xvi, 339 pp. 4 ports. 1875.
v. 8. Personal reminiscences of O'Keefe, Kelly, and Taylor. xxi, 341 pp. 3 pl. 1 port. 1875.
v. 9. Personal recollections of Lamb, Hazlitt, and others. xxii, 322 pp. port. facs. 1875.

Bridges (John, *esq.*) *and* **Whalley** (*Rev.* Peter). History and antiquities of Northamptonshire. 2 v. 1 p. l. vi, 610 pp. 12 pl. 1 map inserted; 1 p. l. 672 pp. 1 l. 25 pl. fol. *Sold by T. Payne, London, D. Prince & J. Cooke, Oxford*, 1791.

Briggs (John Joseph). History of Melbourne. 2d ed. 8 p. l. 9–205 pp. 11 pl. 8°. *Derby, Bemrose & son*, [1852].

Briggs (Milton). Western farmer and stockgrower. 1 p. l. 291 pp. 12°. *Davenport*, [*Iowa*], *Day, Egbert & Fidlar*, 1873.

Brigham (William T.) Cast catalogue of antique sculpture. iv, 200 pp. 13 photos. 4°. *Boston, Lee & Shepard*, 1874.

Bright (Jonathan B.) The Brights of Suffolk, England; represented in America by the descendants of Henry Bright. xvii, 345 pp. [+ 4 l. numb. a–g], 2 ports. 12 pl. 2 plans, 1 map. 8°. *Boston, J. Wilson & son*, 1858.

Note.—Autograph letter of author inserted.

Brispot (*L'abbé* —). La vie de n. s. Jésus-Christ ou les saints évangiles coordonnés, expliqués, [etc.] 5ième éd. 3 v. 8°. *Paris, N. J. Philippart*, 1861.

British almanac for 1875, [etc. also] Companion to the almanac for 1875. 48th year. 2 v. in 1. 16°. *London, J. Greenhill*, [1874].

British association for the advancement of science. Notes and queries on anthropology. 1 p. l. xiv, 146 pp. 4 pl. 16°. *London, E. Stanford*, 1874.

Brittan (*Miss* Harriette G.) Shoshie. 222 pp. 7 pl. 16°. *New York, T. Whittaker*, [1873].

Brittlebank (William). Persia during the famine. x, 265 pp. front. 12°. *London, B. M. Pickering*, 1873.

Brock (Sallie A.) Kenneth. 417 pp. 12°. *New York, G. W. Carleton & co.* 1873.

Brockett (F. L.) Lodge of Washington. A history of the Alexandria Washington lodge, no. 22. 220 pp. 3 ports. 1 pl. 8°. *Alexandria, Va. G. E. French*, 1876.

Brockett (L. P. *m. d.*) Walter Powell, of Melbourne and London. Ed. and rewritten from B. Gregory's "Memoirs of Walter Powell". viii, 357 pp. 16°. *New York, G. Routledge & sons*, 1872.

Brome (Richard). Dramatic works. 3 v. 12°. *London, J. Pearson*, 1873.

Brookline (*City of, Mass.*) *Public library.* Catalogue. xii, 623 pp. 8°. *Cambridge, J. Wilson & son*, 1873.

Brooks (Elbridge Gerry, *d. d.*) Our new departure: or, the universalist church of America. 357 pp. 12°. *Boston, Universalist publishing house*, 1874.

Brotherhead (William). Centennial book of the signers. Title, viii, 297 pp. 2 l. 4°. *Philadelphia, J. M. Stoddart & co.* [1872].

Brothers-in-law. [*anon.*] 3 v. 12°. *London, Hurst & Blackett*, 1869.

Brotonne (F. *i. e* Frédéric Pascal de). Civilisation primitive. 2 p. l. 530 pp. 1 l. 2 tab. 8°. *Paris, C. Warée*, 1845.

Brougham (John) *and* **Elderkin** (John), *editors.* Lotos leaves, [etc.] xv pp. incl. eng. title & 1 facs. 1 l. 411 pp. 14 pl. 8°. *Boston, W. F. Gill & co.* 1875.

Broughton (*Miss* Rhoda). Nancy. 411 pp. 12°. *New York, D. Appleton & co.* 1874.

Brown (Alexander M.) Wintering at Menton. viii, 176 pp. 12°. *London, J. & A. Churchill*, 1872.

Brown (Charles R.) Brown's government of Indiana. 1 p. l. vi–210 pp. front. 16°. *Kalamazoo, Mich. governmental publishing co.* 1875.

——— Government of the state of Michigan. 160 pp. 1 pl. sq. 12°. *Kalamazoo, Mich. "Daily telegraph"*, 1874.

Brown (Charles R.)—continued.
——— Same. 2d ed. 195 pp. front. sq. 12°. *Kalamazoo, Mich. Moore & Quale*, 1874.

Brown (David Paul). Forensic speeches. 394 pp. 1 port. 8°. *Philadelphia, King & Baird*, 1873.

Brown (John Baldwin). Doctrine of annihilation in the light of the gospel of love. 2d ed. xi, 134 pp. 12°. *London, H. S. King & co.* 1875.

Brown (Robert, *m. a. president royal physical soc. Edinburgh*). Races of mankind. v. 1-2. viii, 320 pp. 10 pl; viii, 320 pp. 10 pl. 8°. *London, Cassell, Petter & Galpin*, [1873-74].

Brown (William H. *artist*). Portrait gallery of distinguished american citizens. 111 pp. 27 ports. 27 facs. fol. *Hartford, E. B. & E. C. Kellogg*, 1845.

Brown (William H. *of New York*). History of the first locomotives in America. Revised ed. 246 pp. 14 pl. 8°. *New York, D. Applèton & co.* 1874.

Brown (William Wells, *m. d.*) Rising son 552 pp. 1 port. 8°. *Boston, A. G. Brown & co.* 1874.

Browne (Charles Farrar). Artemus Ward [*pseud.*]: his works, complete. With a biographical sketch by Melville D. Landon. 347 pp. 23 pl. port. 12°. *New York, G. W. Carleton & co.* 1875.

Browne (Junius Henri). Sketches of travel and adventure in England, Ireland, France, Spain, [etc.] xxiv, 17-591 pp. 16 pl. 8°. *Hartford, Con. american publishing co.* 1871.

Browne (Thomas, *ll. d.*) Union dictionary, [etc.] 3d ed. xxii pp. 259 l. 12°. *London, for Wilkie & Robinson*, [*etc.*] 1810.

Brownell (Henry Howard). Lyrics of a day. 160 pp. 16°. *New York, Carleton*, 1864.

Browning (*Mrs.* Elizabeth Barrett). Poems of the intellect and the affections. Eng. title, 124 pp. 4 pl. 12°. *Philadelphia, Hubbard bros.* 1873.

[PARLOR treasury. Gems of poetry, v. 2, part 1].

Browning (Robert). Poetical works. 6 v. 16°. *London, Smith, Elder & co.* 1872-75.

CONTENTS.

v. 1. Pauline. Paracelsus. Strafford.
v. 2. Sordello. Pippa passes.
v. 3. King Victor and king Charles. Dramatic lyrics. The return of the Druses.
v. 4. A blot in the 'scutcheon. Colombe's birthday. Dramatic romances.
v. 5. A soul's tragedy. Luria. Christmas-eve and easter-day. Men and women.
v. 6. In a balcony. Dramatis personæ.

——— Red cotton night-cap country. 2 p. l. 282 pp. 12°. *London, Smith, Elder & co.* 1873.

Bruce (Sanders D.) American stud book. 2 v. 1 p. l. xi, 881 pp; v, 637 pp. 8°. *New York, S. D. Bruce*, 1873.

Bruce (Walter). Hudson river by daylight. [*anon.*] 135 pp. incl. 16 pl. 16°. *New York, J. Featherston*, 1873.

Brunson (Alfred, *d. d.*) Western pioneer. v. 1. 418 pp. 8°. *Cincinnati, Hitchcock & Walden*, 1872.

Brush (George J.) Manual of determinative mineralogy. iv pp. 1 l. 104 pp. 8°. *New York, J. Wiley & son*, 1875.

Note.—The tables consist of double leaves, and are numbered 63-98, forming 36 tables on 72 l.

Bryant (William Cullen). Among the trees. Illustrated. 39 pp. incl. eng. title & 1 pl. sq. 12°. *New York, G. P. Putnam's sons*, [1874].

——— Orations and addresses. 3 p. l. 393 pp. 1 port. 12°. *New York, G. P. Putnam's sons*, 1873.

Buchanan (Robert). Drama of kings. xvii, 471 pp. 12°. *London, Strahan & co.* 1871.

——— Land of Lorne. 2 v. xiii, 282 pp. 1 phot; vii, 277 pp. 1 phot. 12°. *London, Chapman & Hall*, 1871.

——— Napoleon fallen. xii, 142 pp. 12°. *London, Strahan & co.* 1871.

——— White rose and red. [*anon.*] xii, 243 pp. 16°. *Boston, J. R. Osgood & co.* 1873.

Buckingham (Catherinus P.) Elements of the differential and integral calculus. 343 pp. 12°. *Chicago, S. C. Griggs & co.* 1875.

Buckingham (Emma May). Self-made woman. 343 pp. 12°. *New York, S. R. Wells*, 1873.

Budge (*Dr.* Julius). Compendium der physiologie des menschen. 3te aufl. xxi, 433 pp. 12°. *Leipzig, A. Abel*, 1875. S.

Buel (Samuel, *d. d.*) Eucharistic presence, eucharistic sacrifice, and eucharistic adoration. 187 pp. 12°. *New York, T. Whittaker*, [1875].

Bulwer (Henry Lytton Earle, *lord Dalling and Bulwer*). Sir Robert Peel. viii, 147 pp. 8°. *London, R. Bentley & son*, 1874.

Bunnett (Fanny Elizabeth). Louise Juliane, electress palatine, and her times. xii, 263 pp. port. 1 pl. 1 facs. 12°. *London, J. Nisbet & co.* 1862.

Buonarotti (Michael Agnolo). Lawrence gallery. Series of fac-similes of drawings,

Buonarotti (Michael Agnolo)—continued. by M. Angelo Buonarotti. 4 pp. 31 pl. fol. *London, S. & A. Woodburn*, 1853.

Burckett (Florence). Wildmoor. 464 pp. 12°. *Philadelphia, J. B. Lippincott & co.* 1875.

Burckhardt (*Dr.* Jacob). Cicerone: or art guide to painting in Italy. Ed. by dr. A. von Zahn. Translated from the german by mrs. A. H. Clough. viii, 291 pp. 16°. *London, J. Murray*, 1873.

Burgh (N. P.) Modern marine engineering. 1 p. l. 403 pp. 35 pl. upon 34 sheets fold. 4°. *London, E. & F. N. Spon*, 1872.

Burke (*Sir* John Bernard, *ll. d.*) Genealogical and heraldic dictionary of the peerage and baronetage of the british empire. 36th ed. 1 p. l. lxxxvii, 1 l. 1348 pp. 8°. *London, Harrison*, 1874.

——— Same. 37th ed. 1 p. l. xcvii, 1367 pp. 8°. *London, Harrison*, 1875.

——— Rise of great families. iv, 371 pp. 8°. *London, Longmans*, 1873.

——— Royal descents and pedigrees of founders' kin. viii, [302] pp. 8°. *London, Harrison*, 1864.

Burke (*Rev.* Thomas N.) English misrule in Ireland. 299 pp. 1 port. 12°. *New York, Lynch, Cole & Meehan*, 1873.
[IRISH-AMERICAN library, v. 1].

——— Ireland and the Irish. 336 pp. 1 port. 12°. *New York, Lynch, Cole & Meehan*, 1873.
[IRISH-AMERICAN library, v. 2].

——— Lectures and sermons. 644 pp. 1 port. 8°. *New York, P. M. Haverty*, 1872.

——— Sermons, and lectures on moral and historical subjects. 335 pp. 1 port. 12°. *New York, Lynch, Cole & Meehan*, 1873.
[IRISH-AMERICAN library, v. 3].

Burke (Ulick Ralph). Handbook of sewage utilization. vii, 60 pp. 12°. *London, E. & F. N. Spon*, 1872.

Burmeister (Hermann Carl Conrad). Histoire de la création. Traduit de l'allemand d'après la 8e éd. par E. Maupas. 2 p. l. 689 pp. 8°. *Paris, F. Savy*, 1870

Burn (John Southerden). History of Henley-on-Thames. viii, 362 pp. 3 pl. 3 pedigrees. 8°. *London, Longmans*, 1861.

Burn (Robert Scott). Outlines of modern farming. 2d ed. 5 v. in 2. 12°. *London, Lockwood & co.* 1872.

Burnand (Francis Cowley). My time, and what I've done with it. An autobiography. Compiled from the diary of Cecil Colvin. 2d ed. xii, 447 pp. 12°. *London, Macmillan & co.* 1874.

Burnell (Henry L.) Arkansas. 2 p. l. 100, xxvi pp. 12°. *Fayetteville, Ark. H. L. Burnell*, 1873.

Burnham (Carrie S.) Woman suffrage. 112 pp. 8°. *Philadelphia, citizen's suffrage association*, 1873.

Burnouf (Émile Louis). Science des religions. 2e éd. 2 p. l. ix, 460 pp. 1 l. 12°. *Paris, Maisonneuve & cie.* 1872.

Burns (*Rev.* Dawson). Bases of the temperance reform. 224 pp. 12°. *New York, national temperance society*, 1873.

Burr (*Rev.* Enoch Fitch, *d. d.*) Pater mundi; or, doctrine of evolution. 2d series. xiv, 9–303 pp. 12°. *Boston, Noyes, Holmes & co.* 1873.

——— Sunday afternoons. 160 pp. 16°. *New York, Nelson & Phillips*, [1874].

——— Thy voyage, and other poems. 60 pp. incl. 16 pl. & port. 8°. *New York, Nelson & Phillips*, 1875.

——— Toward the strait gate. vi, 535 pp. 12°. *Boston, Lockwood, Brooks & co.* 1875.

Burris (*Rev.* F. H.) The trinity. xxvii, 216 pp. 12°. *Chicago, S. C. Griggs & co.* 1874.

Burritt (Elihu). Jacob and Joseph. viii, 162 pp. 12 pl. 12°. *London, S. Low, son & Marston*, 1870.

Burton (John, *m. d.*) Monasticon eboracense: and the ecclesiastical history of Yorkshire. xii, 448 pp. 18 l. 3 maps. fol. *York, for the author, by N. Nickson*, 1758.

Burton (Richard Francis). Zanzibar. 2 v. xiii, 503 pp. 3 pl. 4 maps; vii, 519 pp. 7 pl. 8°. *London, Tinsley brothers*, 1872.

——— *and* **Drake** (Charles F. Tyrwhitt). Unexplored Syria. 2 v. xx, 360 pp. incl. 1 pl; iii–vii, 400 pp. 9 pl. 7 pp. of facs. inscriptions. 8°. *London, Tinsley brothers*, 1872.

Bushnell (Horace, *d. d.*) Forgiveness and law. 256 pp. 12°. *New York, Scribner, Armstrong & co.* 1874.

——— Sermons on living subjects. 468 pp. 12°. *New York, Scribner, Armstrong & co.* 1872.

Business. By a merchant. [*anon.*] xi, 307 pp. 16°. *Edinburgh, Edmonston & Douglas*, 1873.

Busk (*Miss* R. H.) Folk-lore of Rome. xxiv, 439 pp. 8°. *London, Longmans*, 1874.

——— Valleys of Tirol. xxxi, 453 pp. front. 3 maps. 12°. *London, Longmans*, 1874.

Bussierre (Marie Théodore Renouard, *vicomte* de, 1802–1865). Histoire de la guerre des paysans. 2 v. 318 pp. 2 pl. 1 map; 2 p. l. 367 pp. 1 pl. 8°. *Plancy, société de saint Victor pour la propagation des bons livres,* 1852.

Butler (Clement Moore, *d. d.*) Addresses and lectures on public men and public affairs. 314 pp. 12°. *Cincinnati, H. W. Derby,* 1856.

Butler (Jessee H.) Home. 236 pp. port. 12°. *Boston, Colby & Rich,* 1875.

Butler (*Rev.* Thomas Ambrose). The Irish on the prairies, and other poems. 161 pp. 12°. *New York, D. & J. Sadlier & co.* 1874.

Butler (W. F.) Wild north land. x, 1, 358 pp. 1 map, 16 pl. 8°. *London, S. Low, Marston, son & Searle,* 1873.

Butterfield (C. W.) Historical account of the expedition against Sandusky in 1782. x, 403 pp. 1 port. 8°. *Cincinnati, R. Clarke & co.* 1873.

Butts (Isaac). Protection and free trade, [etc.] 190 pp. port. 12°. *New York, G. P. Putnam's sons,* 1875.

Byers (William N.) *and* **Kellom** (John H.) Hand book to the gold fields of Nebraska and Kansas. 113 pp. 12°. *Chicago, D. B. Cooke & co.* 1859.

Byrn (M. Lafayette, *m. d.*) Useful knowledge; or, repository of valuable information. 2 p. l. 339, v pp. 18°. *New York, M. L. Byrn,* 1872.

Byrne (*Rev.* Stephen). Irish emigration to the United States. 165 pp. 1 map. 12°. *New York, catholic publication society,* 1873.

Byrom (John). Private journal and literary remains. 4 v. sm. 4°. [*Manchester*], 1854–57.
[CHETHAM society remains, v. 32, 34 40, 44].

Cadwallader (Alonzo D.) Past, present and future. Poem. 158, ii pp. 12°. *Kalamazoo, Mich. Kalamazoo publishing co.* 1875.

Caillié (René). Journal d'un voyage à Temboctou et à Jenné, 1824–28. 3 v. 8°. & atlas 4°. *Paris, imprimerie royale,* 1830.
[Imperfect: atlas, pl. 1–3 to v. 2, and pl. 1, 4, 5, to v. 3 wanting].

Cairnes (John Elliott). Character and logical method of political economy. 2d ed. xix, 229 pp. 8°. *London, Macmillan & co.* 1875.

——— Essays in political economy. xi, 371 pp. 8°. *London, Macmillan & co.* 1873.

——— Political essays. ix, 350 pp. 8°. *London, Macmillan & co.* 1873.

Callet (Félix) *and* **Lesueur** (Jean Baptiste Cicéron). Architecture italienne septentrio nale. 2 p. l. 32 pl. fol. *Paris, Bance,* 1855.

Calliat (Victor). Parallèle des maisons de Paris, construites depuis 1830 jusqu'à nos jours. 2 v. Eng. title, 4 p. l. 128 pl; 3 p. l. 119 pl. fol. *Paris, Bance,* [*&*] *A. Morel & cie.* 1857–64.

Calthorpe. A novel. [*anon.*] 2 v. 246 pp; 242 pp. 12°. *Philadelphia, T. Desilver,* 1821.

Calvert (George Henry). Brief essays and brevities. 282 pp. 16°. *Boston, Lee & Shepard,* 1874.

——— Essays æsthetical. 264 pp. 16°. *Boston, Lee & Shepard,* 1875.

——— Goethe: his life and works. 276 pp. 16°. *Boston, Lee & Shepard,* 1872.

——— Maid of Orleans. 134 pp. 16°. *New York, G. P. Putnam's sons,* 1874.

——— Mirabeau: an historical drama. 103 pp. 16°. *Cambridge, Riverside press,* 1873.

——— Scenes and thoughts in Europe. 2d ser. 185 pp. 12°. *New York, G. P. Putnam,* 1852.

Cambrian journal. 1854–1864. 11 v. 8°. *London, Longmans, Tenby, R. Mason,* 1854–64.
Note.—Discontinued in 1864.

Cambry (Jacques). Voyage pittoresque en Suisse et en Italie. 2 v. 341 pp. 3 pl; 374 pp. 1 l. 1 pl. 8°. *Paris, H. J. Jansen,* 1801.

Cameron (Charles A.) Stock-feeder's manual. viii, 254 pp. 1 pl. 12°. *London, Cassell, Petter & Galpin,* 1868.

Campanella (Giuseppe Maria). My life and what I learnt in it. Autobiography. xix, 387 pp. port. 8°. *London, R. Bentley & son,* 1874.

Campbell (Alexander). History of Leith. 1 p. l. vi, 384 pp. 8°. *Leith, W. Reid & son,* 1827.

Campbell (Charles). Some materials to serve for a brief memoir of John Daly Burk. Ed. by Charles Campbell. 123 pp. 8°. *Albany, N. Y., J. Munsell,* 1868.

Campbell (Jesse H.) Georgia baptists. 288 pp. 1 l. 12°. *Richmond, H. K. Ellyson,* 1847.

——— Same. [New ed.] 502 pp. incl. front. 12°. *Macon, Ga. J. W. Burke & co.* 1874.

Campbell (Loomis J.) Pocket dictionary of the english language. 310 pp. 32°. *Boston, Brewer and Tileston,* 1872.

——— *and* **Root** (Oren, *jr.*) Columbian series. Columbian speaker. 240 pp. 16°. *Boston, Lee & Shepard,* 1874.

Campbell (Robert A.) Gazetteer of Missouri. [794] pp. 21 pl. 14 incl. in pag. 7 maps. 8°. *St. Louis, R. A. Campbell,* 1874.

——— New atlas of Missouri. [133 l. incl. 39 l. of maps]. 4°. *Saint Louis, R. A. Campbell,* 1873.

Campbell (Samuel M. *d. d.*) Across the desert. Life of Moses. 342 pp. incl. 4 maps & 7 pl. 12°. *Philadelphia, Presbyterian board of publication,* [1873].

Campbell (Thomas, *ll. d.*) Philosophical survey of the south of Ireland. [*anon.*] xvi, 478 pp. 6 pl. 8°. *Dublin, for W. Whitestone,* [*etc.*] 1778.

Campbell (*Rev.* William). Materials for a history of the reign of Henry VII. from original documents in the public record office. v. 1. xvi, 709 pp. 8°. *London, Longmans,* 1873.

[GREAT BRITAIN. *Treasury. (Public record office).* Rerum britannicarum medii aevi scriptores. 8°. *London,* 1873].

Canada (*Dominion of*). Census. 1870–71. Recensement. 3 v. 8°. *Ottawa, I. B. Taylor,* 1873–75.

[In english and french].

——— *Geological survey.* Alfred R. C. Selwyn, director. Report of progress for 1872–73 [&] 1873–74. 2 v. 8°. *Montreal, Dawson brothers,* 1873–74. s.

Canadien (Le). [Weekly]. 22 nov. 1806 to 4 march 1810. v. 1, no. 1 to v. 4, no. 16. 3 v. 4°. *Quebec,* 1806–10.

——— Same. [2d series, weekly]. 23 jan. 1822 to 16 feb. 1825. v. 3, no. 1 to v. 5, no. 5. 2 v. 4°. and fol. *Quebec,* 1822–25.

——— Same. [3d series, tri-weekly]. 7 may 1831 to 5 may 1862. v. 1–31. fol. *Quebec,* 1831–62.

Cannon (John). History of Grant's campaign for the capture of Richmond, (1864–1865). xi, 470 pp. 12°. *London, Longmans,* 1869.

Cantu (César). Histoire des Italiens. Traduite par m. Armand Lacombe, sur la 2e éd. italienne. 12 v. 8°. *Paris, F. Didot frères, fils & cie.* 1859–62.

Note.—Includes ancient as well as modern Italy.

Capefigue (Jean Baptiste Honoré Raymond). Philippe d'Orléans, regent de France. 1715–1723. 2 v. 2 p. l. 351 pp; 2 p. l. 342 pp. 18°. *Bruxelles, société belge de libraire,* 1839.

Caracci *or* **Carracci** (Annibale). Galeria nel palazzo farnese in Roma. Title, 30 pl. on 22 l. fol. *Roma, V. Monaldini,* 1657.

Carbajal Espinosa (Francisco). Historia de Mexico hasta mediados del siglo XIX. 2 v. 2 p. l. 688 pp. 4 l. 19 ports. 15 pl. 1 map; 704 pp. 4 l. 16 ports. 21 pl. 2 maps, 1 plan, 1 facs. 8°. *Mexico, J. Abadiano,* 1862.

Cardonne (Denis Dominic). Miscellany of eastern learning. From turkish, arabian, and persian manuscripts. 2 v. 2 p. l. xx, 275 pp; 6 p. l. 264 pp. 16°. *London, for J. Wilkie, & B. Law,* 1771.

Carey (Charles Stokes, *compiler*). Commonplace book of epigrams. 3 p. l. 247 pp. 16°. *London, W. Tegg,* 1872.

Carleton (Will.) Farm ballads. 108 pp. incl. 10 pl. 8°. *New York, Harper & brothers,* 1873.

Carlisle (Arthur Drummond). Round the world in 1870. xii, 408 pp. 4 maps. 8°. *London, H. S. King & co.* 1872.

Carmontel (—). Proverbes dramatiques. Nouv. éd. 4 v. 8°. *Paris, Delongchamps,* 1822.

——— Proverbes et comédies posthumes. 3 v. 8°. *Paris, Ladvocat,* 1825.

Carnegie (*Sir* James, *earl of Southesk*). Saskatchewan and the Rocky mountains. xxx, 448 pp. 7 pl. 1 facs. 4 tab. 2 maps. 8°. *Edinburgh, Edmonston & Douglas,* 1875.

Carnes (*Capt.* —, *pseud?*) Little Toss. 301 pp. 3 pl. 16°. *Boston, D. Lothrop & co.* 1873.

——— Uncle Anthony. 1 p. l. 7–333 pp. 3 pl. 16°. *Boston, D. Lothrop & co.* 1873.

Caro (Elme Marie). Études morales sur le temps présent. 2 p. l. xxxix, 377 pp. 1 l. 12°. *Paris, L. Hachette & cie.* 1855.

Carpenter (George T.) *and* **Hughes** (John). Debate on the destiny of the wicked. 469 pp. 12°. *Oskaloosa, Io. central book concern,* 1875.

Carpenter (Joseph Edwards, *editor*). Funny man's song book. 143 pp. 18°. *London, Routledge, Warne & Routledge,* 1863.

——— Humorous song book. viii, 280 pp. 18°. *London, G. Routledge & sons,* [1864].

Carpenter (Philip P. *b. a.*) Mollusks of western North America. xii, 325, 13–121 pp. 8°. *Washington, Smithsonian institution,* 1872.

[SMITHSONIAN miscellaneous collections, v. 10, art. 1].

Carpenter (William Benjamin, *m. d.*) Principles of human physiology. Ed. by Henry Power. 7th ed. xxiii, 1032 pp. 2 pl. 8°. *London, J. Churchill & sons,* 1869.

Carr (Ezra S.) Patrons of husbandry on the Pacific coast. 461 pp. 4 ports. 3 pl. 8°. *San Francisco, A. L. Bancroft & co.* 1875.

Carrara (Francesco). Antologia italiana. 5 v. 8°. *Vienna, nell'i. r. amministrazione per la vendita de' libri scolastici*, 1853–59.

CONTENTS.

v. 1. Il trecento e il quattrocento. 1853.
v. 2. Il cinquecento. 1858.
v. 3. Il seicento. 1858.
v. 4. Il settecento. 1858.
v. 5. L'ottocento. 1859.

Carroll (Lewis, *pseud.*) Alice's adventures in wonderland. 41st thousand. 5 p. l. 192 pp. 1 pl. 12°. *London, Macmillan & co.* 1874.

Note.—Attributed to Miss Dodgson and to Canon Lightfoot.

——— Same. Aventures d'Alice au pays des merveilles. Traduit de l'anglais par Henri Bué. 5 p. l. 196 pp. 1 pl. 12°. *Londres, Macmillan & co.* 1869.

——— Through the looking-glass. 5 p. l. 224 pp. 1 pl. 12°. *London, Macmillan & co.* 1872.

Carter (Edmund). History of the county of Cambridge, to the present time. First printed in 1753. iv, 376 pp. 8°. *London, [S. & R. Bentley]*, 1819.

Carter (John H.) Log of commodore Rollingpin. 258 pp. incl. 1 pl. 12°. *New York, G. W. Carleton & co.* 1874.

Cartoon portraits and biographical sketches of men of the day. [*anon.*] Drawings by Frederick Waddy. viii, 147 pp. 50 ports. 4°. *London, Tinsley brothers*, 1873.

Cary (Alice). Later poems.

[*In* AMES (Mary Clemmer). A memorial of Alice and Phœbe Cary. 12°. *New York, Hurd & Houghton*, 1873. pp. 237–312].

——— *and* **Carey** (Phœbe). Ballads for little folk. Edited by Mary Clemmer Ames. viii, 189 pp. 1 pl. 8°. *New York, Hurd & Houghton*, 1874.

——— ——— Last poems of Alice and Phœbe Cary. Edited by Mary Clemmer Ames. vii, 306 pp. 12°. *New York, Hurd & Houghton*, 1873.

Cary (Phœbe). Later poems.

[*In* AMES (Mary Clemmer). A memorial of Alice and Phœbe Cary. 12°. *New York, Hurd & Houghton*, 1873. pp. 313–351].

Cassani (Josef, *s. J.*) Historia de la provincia de Granada en la America. 14 p. l. 618 pp. 1 l. 1 map. sm. fol. *Madrid, M. Fernandez*, 1741.

Cassard (Andres). Cincuenta años de la vida de Andres Cassard. [*anon.*] 1 p. l. xvii, 3–269 pp. port. 8°. *Nueva York, G. R. Lockwood*, 1875.

Cassilda. [*anon.*] From the French by mrs. Mary C. Monroe. 181 pp. incl. front. 8°. *New-York, Benziger brothers*, 1875.

Castelar (Emilio). Life of lord Byron, and other sketches. Translated by mrs. Arthur Arnold. xix, 346 pp. 8°. *London, Tinsley brothers*, 1875.

——— Old Rome and new Italy. Translated by mrs. Arthur Arnold. vii, 352 pp. 1 port. 8°. *London, Tinsley brothers*, 1873.

Castellan (Antoine Louis). Lettres sur la Morée, l'Hellespont et Constantinople. 2e éd. 3 v. 8°. *Paris, A. Nepveu*, 1820.

Castellanos (José). Lira de Quisqueya. Poesias dominicanas escojidas por J. Castellanos. 1 p. l. 328 pp. 8°. *Santo Domingo, Garcia hermanos*, 1874.

Castleton (D. R.) Salem. 336 pp. 12°. *New York, Harper & brothers*, 1874.

Castro (Affonso de). As possessões portuguezas na Oceania. 3 p. l. xxiii, 461 pp. 2 maps. 8°. *Lisboa, imprensa nacional*, 1867.

Catel (L.) Prison de Dartmoor. 2 v. 230 pp. 1 l; 322 pp. 1 l. 8°. *Paris, chez les principaux libraires*, 1847.

[Imperfect: 2 l. (incl. title-page) of v. 1 wanting].

Catlin (George). Lifted and subsided rocks of America. xii, 228 pp. 1 map. 12°. *London, Trübner & co.* 1870. s.

Caverly (Robert B.) Heroism of Hannah Duston. 407 pp. 1 port. 12 pl. 12°. *Boston, B. B. Russell & co.* 1874.

Caylus (Anne-Claude-Philippe de Tubières, de Grimoard, de Pestels, de Levi, *comte* de). Recueil de trois cents têtes et sujets de composition, d'après les pierres gravées antiques du cabinet du roi. 2 p. l. 1 pl. 300 pl. on 150 l. 4°. [*Paris, Basan, about* 1775].

Cazelles (*Dr.* M. E.) Outline of the evolution-philosophy. From the french, by O. B. Frothingham. With appendix by E. L. Youmans. 167 pp. 12°. *New York, D. Appleton & co.* 1875.

Celebrated claimants ancient and modern. [*anon.*] 255 pp. 16°. *London, Chatto & Windus*, [1873].

Century of independence: documents and statistics; also, a chronological record. [*anon.*] 545 pp. front. 2 ports. 12°. *Indianapolis, [Cincinnati printed], J. R. Hussey & co.* 1876.

Cernuschi (Henri). Or et argent. 105 pp. 8°. *Paris, Guillaumin & cie.* 1874. s.

Cérutti (Joseph Antoine Joachim). Idées simples et précises sur le papier monnoie, [etc.] 2 p. l. 127 pp. 12°. *Paris, Desenne* 1790.

[MISCELLANEOUS pamphlets, v. 1025: 4].

Cesnola (*Gen.* Luigi Palma di). Antiquities of Cyprus discovered. Photographed by S.

Cesnola (*Gen.* L. P. di)—continued. Thompson, from a selection by C. T. Newton. 2 p. l. 5 pp. 36 pl. fol. *London, W. A. Mansell & co.* 1873.

Chaffers (William). Hall marks on gold and silver plate. 4th ed. 2 p. l. 112 pp. 2 pl. 8°. *London, J. Davy & sons,* 1872.

Chaffin (*Rev.* J. W.) Battle of Calvary. 236 pp. 16°. *Cincinnati, Hitchcock & Walden,* 1873.

Challice (*Mrs.* A. E.) Memories of french palaces. 3 p. l. 371 pp. 12°. *London, Bradbury, Evans & co.* 1871.

Chamberlain (Charles, *jr.*) Put to the test. 1 p. l. 7–362 pp. 16°. *New York, H. L. Hinton,* 1874.

Chamberlin (Edwin M.) Sovereigns of industry. 2 p. l. 165, xxi pp. 16°. *Boston, Lee & Shepard,* 1875.

Chamberlin (Everett). Chicago and its suburbs. 468 pp. incl. 11 pl. 1 map. 8°. *Chicago, T. A. Hungerford & co.* 1874.

Chambers (Robert). Index to heirs-at-law, next of kin, [etc.] 3d ed. revised and greatly enlarged. By E. Preston. 1 p. l. 411 pp. 8°. *London, Reeves & Turner,* 1872.

Chambliss (*Rev.* J. E.) New. Authentic. Complete. The life and labors of David Livingstone, [etc.] 805 pp. incl. 81 pl. 1 port. 3 facs. 1 map. 8°. *Philadelphia, Hubbard bros.* [1875].

Note.—Imperfect: 1 pl. wanting.

Chambrun (Adolphe, *marquis* de). Executive power in the United States. From the french by mrs. Madeleine Vinton Dahlgren. 288, 15 pp. 12°. *Lancaster, Pa. Inquirer co.* 1874.

Chamier (*Capt.* Frederick, *r. n.*) The saucy Arethusa. iv, 443 pp. 16°. *London, F. Warne & co.* 1867.

Champagny (François Joseph Marie Thérèse Nompère, *comte* de). Les Antonins—ans de J. C. 69–180. 3 v. 8°. *Paris, A. Bray,* 1863.

Chaney (George L.) F. Grant & co. or, partnerships. 281 pp. 3 pl. 16°. *Boston, Roberts brothers,* 1875.

Chaney (*Mrs.* George L.) William Henry. Dramatized from the works of mrs. A. M. Diaz. 73 pp. 16°. *Boston, J. R. Osgood & co.* 1875.

Channing (William Ellery, *d. d.*) *and* **Aikin** (Lucy). Correspondence, from 1826 to 1842. Ed. by Anna Letitia Le Breton. xx, 426 pp. 12°. *Boston, Roberts brothers,* 1874.

Channing (William Ellery, *nephew of William Ellery Channing, d. d.*) Thoreau. xii, 357 pp. 16°. *Boston, Roberts brothers,* 1873.

Chantreau (Pierre Nicolas). Philosophical, political, and literary travels in Russia, 1788 & 1789. From the french. 2 v. viii, 321 pp. 1 pl; vi, 316 pp. 2 pl. 1 map. 8°. *Perth, for R. Morison & son,* 1794.

Chaplin (Jeremiah *and* J. D.) Life of Charles Sumner. 504 pp. 4 pl. 3 facs. 2 ports. 12°. *Boston, D. Lothrop & co.* 1874.

Chapman (George). Comedies and tragedies. 3 v. 16°. *London, J. Pearson,* 1873.

Chapman (George Thomas, *d. d.*) Sketches of the alumni of Dartmouth college. 520 pp. 8°. *Cambridge,* [*Ms.*] *Riverside press,* 1867.

Chapman (Helen E.) Paul Brewster and son. 238 pp. front. 16°. *New York, national temperance soc. & publ. house,* 1875.

Chapman (Robert, *editor*). Picture of Glasgow. 3d ed. 6 p. l. 390 pp. 3 l. 3 pl. 2 maps. 16°. *Glasgow, R. Chapman,* 1818.

Charbonnier (J.) Organisation électorale et représentative de tous les pays civilisés. xi, 512 pp. 8°. *Paris, Guillaumin & cie.* 1874.

Charette. [*anon.*] 2 p. l. 7–327 pp. 12°. *New York, G. W. Carleton & co.* 1875.

Charles (Émile). Roger Bacon. xv, 416 pp. 8°. *Bordeaux, G. Gounouilhou,* 1861.

Charlton (*Rev.* William Henry). Burghley. Life of William Cecil, lord Burghley. xxi, 320 pp. 10 pl. 1 genealogy. 8°. *Stamford, W. Langley,* 1847.

"Charlton." [*pseud.*] Songs of the year, and other poems. 178 pp. 12°. *Cincinnati, R. Clarke & co.* 1875.

Charrière (Ernest). Politique de l'histoire. 2 v. 2 p. l. xv, 394 pp. 1 l; 2 p. l. xii, 574 pp. 1 l. 8°. *Paris, C. Gosselin,* 1841–42.

Chasles (Émile). Histoire nationale de la littérature française. Origines. 2 p. l. viii, 449 pp. front. 8°. *Paris, Ducrocq,* 1870.

Château Morville; or, life in Touraine. From the french. By E. R. [*anon.*] 2 p. l. 366 pp. 12°. *Philadelphia, Claxton, Remsen & Haffelfinger,* 1872.

[MORVILLE series].

Chatel (François). Histoire naturelle et philosophique de l'homme. 2 v. in 1. xxii, 308 pp; 2 p. l. 323 pp. 12°. *Paris, Duchesne,* 1816.

Chaussard (Jean Baptiste Publicola). Anténors modernes. [*anon.*] 3 v. 8°. *Paris, F. Buisson,* 1806.

Chellis (Mary Dwinell). Good work. 463 pp. 16°. *Boston, D. Lothrop & co.* 1873.

——— Mystery of the lodge. 388 pp. 12°. *Boston, D. Lothrop & co.* 1873.

——— Wealth and wine. 337 pp. 1 pl. 16°. *New York, national temperance society and publication house,* 1874.

Cheney (*Mrs.* Ednah D.) Child of the tide. 212 pp. 4 pl. 16°. *Boston, Lee & Shepard,* 1875.

——— Patience. 2d ed. 114 pp. incl. 4 pl. 18°. *Boston, Lee & Shepard,* 1875.

Cherbuliez (Victor). Comte Kostia. 4e éd. 2 p. l. 376 pp. 12°. *Paris, Hachette & cie.* 1872.

——— Le grand œuvre. 2 p. l. 299 pp. 16°. *Paris, L. Hachette & cie.* 1867.

——— Prosper. From the french. By Carl Benson. 1 p. l. 289 pp. 16°. *New York, H. Holt & co.* 1874.
[LEISURE hour series].

——— La revanche de Joseph Noirel. 3 p. l. 375 pp. 16°. *Paris, Hachette & cie.* 1872.

——— Roman d'une honnête femme. 4e éd. 2 p. l. 399 pp. 2 l. 12°. *Paris, Hachette & cie.* 1873.

Chesebro' (Caroline). Foe in the household. 114 pp. 8°. *Boston, J. R. Osgood & co.* 1871.

Chesebro (Frances M.) Smiles and tears. 146 pp. 1 pl. 16°. *Boston, Whittemore, Niles & Hall,* 1858.

Chesney (Charles Cornwallis). Essays in modern military biography. ix, 414 pp. 8°. *London, Longmans,* 1874.

Chesterman (Edwin). "You ask! — I'll tell!" [*anon.*] 3 p. l. 11–452 pp. 8°. *Philadelphia, Chesterman & Webster,* 1873.

Chetham society. Remains, historical and literary, connected with the palatine counties of Lancaster and Chester. v. 1–91, and index, 92 v. sm. 4°. [*Manchester*], *printed for the Chetham soc.* 1845–73.

Childe (Edward Lee). Life and campaigns of general [R. E.] Lee. From the french. xi, 336 pp. 1 port. 1 map. 12°. *London, Chatto & Windus,* 1875.

Chintreuil (Antoine). La vie et l'œuvre de Chintreuil par A. de La Fizelière, Champfleury, F. Henriet. xxxviii, 84 pp. 38 pl. 2 ports. fol. *Paris, Cadart,* 1874.

Chomet (Antoine Joseph, *called* Hector). Influence of music on health and life. From the french by mrs. Laura A. Flint. 1 p. l. 242 pp. 18°. *New York, G. P. Putnam's sons,* 1875.

Chompré (Pierre). Dictionnaire abrégé de la fable. Nouv. éd. 432 pp. 18°. *Paris, Billois, an* IX, [1801].

Chorley (Henry Fothergill). Recent art and society. Compiled by C. H. Jones. x, 317 pp. 12°. *New York, H. Holt & co.* 1874.

Chouppes (*Le marquis* Aimard de). Mémoires. 2 parts in 1 v. xii, 334 pp; 240 pp. 16°. *Paris, Duchesne,* 1753.

Christie (William D.) Life of Anthony Ashley Cooper, first earl of Shaftesbury. 1621–1683. 2 v. li, 317, lxxxi pp. port; xiii, 482, cxxix pp. port. 12°. *London, Macmillan & co.* 1871.

Christlieb (Theodor, *d. d.*) Best methods of counteracting modern infidelity. 89 pp. incl. 1 port. 12°. *New York, Harper & brothers,* 1874.

Chubb (George Hayter). Protection from fire and thieves. xii, 162 pp. 2 pl. 2 plans. 12°. *London, Longmans,* 1875.

Church (Florence Marryat, *mrs.* Ross). Her lord and master. 3 v. 16°. *London, R. Bentley & son,* 1871.
Note.—Wanting title and contents to v. 1.

——— Life and letters of captain Marryat. 2 v. xi, 260 pp; vii, 300 pp. 12°. *London, R. Bentley & son,* 1872.

——— Prey of the gods. 3 v. 16°. *London, R. Bentley & son,* 1871.

Churchill (Charles H.) Theory and practice of the electric telegraph. 2 p. l. ix–xvi, 144 pp. 12°. *Oberlin, O., Sherman & bros.* 1875.

Churton (Henry). Toinette. 510 pp. 12°. *New York, J. B. Ford & co.* 1874.

Cinelli Calvoli (Giovanni). Biblioteca vo lante. Continuata dal dottor Dionigi Andrea Sancassani. 4 v. 4°. *Venezia, G. Albrizzi, q. Girolamo,* 1734–47.

Clark (Alexander). Starting out. 1 p. l. vii–219 pp. 9 pl. 16°. *Philadelphia, J. B. Lippincott & co.* 1875.

Clark (Benjamin). On systematic botany and zoology. 1 p. l. v, 48, 55–56 pp. 8 tab. 1 pl. obl. fol. *London, author,* 1870.

Clark (Charles Hèber). Out of the hurly-burly. By Max Adeler, [*pseud.*] Eng. title, 398 pp. incl. 8 pl. 12°. *Philadelphia, "To-day" publishing co.* 1874.

Clark (Edward L.) Israel in Egypt. xvi, 9–352 pp. incl. 15 pl. 8°. *New York, Nelson & Phillips,* 1874.

Clark (Frank E.) Our vacations: where to go, how to go, and how to enjoy them. 208 pp. 18°. *Boston, Estes & Lauriat*, 1874.

Clark (*Mrs.* H. K. U.) Teachings of the ages. By A. C. Traveler [*pseud.*] 399 pp. 12°. *San Francisco, A. L. Bancroft & co.* 1874.

Clark (*Rev.* Peter, *a. m., pastor in Salem*). A defence of the divine rights of infant-baptism. 1 p. l. vi, 453 [+1] pp. 3 l. 12°. *Boston, S. Kneeland*, 1752.

Clark (Rufus W. *d. d.*) Work of God in Great Britain: under messrs. Moody and Sankey, 1873 to 1875. 371 pp. incl. 2 ports. & 1 pl. 12°. *New York, Harper & brothers*, 1875.

Clark (William M. *compiler*). Model dialogues. 371 pp. 12°. *Philadelphia, J. W. Daughaday & co.* [1874].

Clarke (Edward, *of Lincoln's Inn*). Treatise on the law of extradition. 2d ed. xvi, 194, clxxvi pp. 8°. *London, Stevens & Haynes*, 1874.

Clarke (Edward Hammond, *m. d.*) The building of a brain. 153 pp. 16°. *Boston, J. R. Osgood & co.* 1874.

——— Sex in education. 181 pp. 16°. *Boston, J. R. Osgood & co.* 1873.

Clarke (Frank Wigglesworth, *s. b.*) Constants of nature. Part 1. Specific gravities. vii, 263 pp. 8°. *Washington, Smithsonian institution*, 1873.

[SMITHSONIAN miscellaneous collections, v. 12, art. 2].

Clarke (*Mrs.* Henry Steele). Marble preacher. Eng. title, 476 pp. 1 pl. 16°. *Boston, D. Lothrop & co.* 1873.

[THOUSAND dollar prize series].

——— "Their children." 414 pp. 3 pl. 16°. *Boston, D. Lothrop & co.* [1875].

Clarke (James Freeman). Common sense in religion. 443 pp. 12°. *Boston, J. R. Osgood & co.* 1874.

——— *and* **Clarke** (Lilian). Exotics: attempts to domesticate them. By J. F. C. and L. C. [*anon.*] 141 pp. 18°. *Boston, J. R. Osgood & co.* 1875.

Clarke (John, *missionary*). Specimens of dialects: and notes of countries in Africa. 104 pp. 8°. *Berwick-upon-Tweed, D. Cameron*, 1848.

Clarke (James F. *m. r. c. s.*) Autobiographical recollections of the medical profession. xv, 537 pp. 12°. *London, J. & A. Churchill*, 1874.

Clarke (William Nelson). Parochial topography of the hundred of Wanting. 2 p. l. vii, 207 pp. 6 pedigrees. 4°. *Oxford, W. Baxter, for J. Parker*, [*etc.*] 1824.

Clavel (Adolphe, *m. d.*) Les races humaines. 2 p. l. 431 pp. 8°. *Paris, Poulet-Malassis & De Broise*, 1860.

Clavigero (Francisco Xavier). Historia de la antigua ó baja California. Traducida del italiano por don Nicolas Garcia de San Vincente. 4 p. l. v, 252 pp. 3 pl. 8°. *Méjico, J. R. Navarro*, 1852.

Note.—Contains also: Relacion historica de la vida del venerable padre fray Junipero Serra, por Francisco Palou, pp. 126–252.

Clemens (Samuel Langhorne) *and* **Warner** (Charles Dudley). Gilded age. 576 pp. 20 pl. 8°. *Hartford, american publishing co.* 1874.

Clement (*Mrs.* Clara Erskine). Painters, sculptors, architects, engravers, and their works. xii, 661 pp. incl. 9 pl. 12°. *New York, Hurd & Houghton*, 1874.

Clercq (Alexandre de). Recueil des traités de France. 10 v. 8°. *Paris, Amyot*, 1864–72.

CONTENTS.

v. 1. 1713–1802.	v. 6. 1850–1855.
2. 1803–1815.	7. 1856–1859.
3. 1816–1830.	8. 1860–1863.
4. 1831–1842.	9. 1864–1867.
5. 1843–1849.	10. 1867–1872.

Clergy directory of the clergy of the church of England. 1875. [5th ed.] 12°. *London, T. Bosworth*, 1875.

Cleveland (Cecilia). Story of a summer. 274 pp. 3 pl. 18°. *New York, G. W. Carleton & co.* 1874.

Cleveland (*Rev.* Edward). Bible sketches. Poem. 300 pp. 12°. *Boston, A. Mudge & son*, 1875.

Cleveland (Horace W. S.) Landscape architecture, as applied to the wants of the west. 3 p. l. 11–147 pp. 16°. *Chicago, Jansen, McClurg & co.* 1873.

Cleveland (Stafford C.) History and directory of Yates county, [N. Y.] v. 1. 2 p. l. xxiii, 766 pp. 7 l. 16 pl. 1 map. 8°. *Penn Yan, N. Y., S. C. Cleveland*, 1873.

Clevenger (Shobal V.) Treatise on the method of government surveying. 200 pp. 1 pl. 16°. *New York, D. Van Nostrand*, 1874.

Cliffe (John Henry). Notes and recollections of an angler: rambles among the mountains of Wales, [etc.] xii, 254 pp. 16°. *London, Hamilton, Adams & co.* 1870.

Cline & McHaffie. People's guide. A directory of Bartholomew co. Ind. 400 pp. 8°.

Cline & McHaffie—continued. *Indianapolis, Indianapolis printing & publishing house,* 1874.

——— Same. A directory of Hamilton co. Ind. 412 pp. 1 l. 8°. *Indianapolis, Indianapolis printing & publishing house,* 1874.

——— Same. A directory of Hendricks co. Ind. 400 pp. 8°. *Indianapolis, Indianapolis printing & publishing house,* 1874.

——— Same. A directory of Johnson co. Ind. 400 pp. 8°. *Indianapolis, Indianapolis printing & publishing house,* 1874.

——— Same. A directory of Marion co. Ind. 600 pp. 1 map. 8°. *Indianapolis, Indianapolis printing & publishing house,* 1874.

——— Same. A directory of Morgan co. Ind. 406 pp. 8°. *Indianapolis, Indianapolis printing & publishing house,* 1874.

——— Same. A directory of Vermillion co. Ind. 400 pp. 8°. *Indianapolis, Indianapolis printing & publishing house,* 1874.

Clodd (Edward). Childhood of the world. xi, 118 pp. front. 16°. *London, Macmillan & co.* 1873.

Cloud (D. C.) Monopolies and the people. 1 p. l. 462 pp. 8°. *Davenport, Iowa, Day, Egbert & Fidlar,* 1873.

——— Same. 3d ed. 2 p. l. 514, iii pp. 8°. *Davenport, Iowa, Day, Egbert & Fidlar,* 1873.

Clutterbuck (Robert, 1772–1831). History and antiquities of the county of Hertford. 3 v. (containing 54 pl.) fol. *London, Nichols, son & Bentley,* [*etc.*] 1815–27.

Cobb (Mary L.) Poetical dramas for home and school. 189 pp. 16°. *Boston, Lee & Shepard,* 1873.

Cobbe (Thomas). History of the norman kings of England. xciii, 387 pp. 12 tab. on 8 l. 8°. *London, Longmans,* 1869.

Cobden club essays. Local government and taxation. Edited by J. W. Probyn. vi, 454 pp. 8°. *London, Cassell, Petter & Galpin,* 1875.

Cochem (Martin von). Das leben unsers lieben herrn und heilandes Jesus Christus und seiner jungfräulichen mutter Maria. Col. front. col. title, 4 p. l. xvi, 1031 pp. incl. 1 pl. 7 pl. 8°. *Einsiedeln, gebr. C. & N. Benziger,* 1873.

Cochrane (Alexander Dundas Ross Wishart Baillie). Francis the first, and other historic studies. 2 v. ix, 280 pp; 2 p. l. 298 pp. 12°. *London, Hurst & Blackett,* 1870.

Cocker (B. F. *d. d., ll. d.*) Theistic conception of the world. 426 pp. 12°. *New York, Harper & brothers,* 1875.

Cockerell (Charles Robert), *and others.* Antiquities of Athens and other places in Greece, Sicily, etc. 61 pp. 55 pl. fol. *London, Priestley & Weale,* 1830.

Codman (John, *d. d.*) Narrative of a visit to England. iv, 9–248 pp. 16°. *Boston, Perkins & Marvin,* 1836.

Codman (*Capt.* John). The mormon country. 2 p. l. 225 pp. 10 pl. 1 map. 12°. *New York, United States publishing co.* 1874.

Coffin (Charles Carleton). Caleb Krinkle. vii, 500 pp. 12. *Boston, Lee & Shepard,* 1875.

——— Following the flag. By "Carleton" [*pseud.*] viii, 336 pp. 8 pl. 16°. *Boston, Ticknor & Fields,* 1865.

——— My days and nights on the battle field. By "Carleton" [*pseud.*] viii, 312 pp. 8 pl. 16°. *Boston, Ticknor & Fields,* 1864.

Coffin (Robert S.) Oriental harp. [*anon.*] Eng. title, 4 p. l. 13–254 pp. 8°. *Providence, Smith & Parmenter,* 1826.

Cohen (Henry). Guide de l'amateur de livres à vignettes du XVIIIe siècle. 2e éd. xvi, 273 pp. front. 8°. *Paris, P. Rouquette,* 1873.

Colange (L. *editor*). National encyclopedia. ix, 1002 pp. 8°. *New York & Philadelphia, national encyclopedia publishing co.* 1873.

Colbert (*Mrs.* Laura A.) Broken lines and southern soldiers. 269 pp. 12°. *Nashville, Tenn. southern methodist publishing house,* 1873.

Colby (Louis H.) Forty years' experience in veterinary practice. 474 pp. 7 pl. 12°. *Auburn, W. J. Moses,* 1875.

Cole (John). History of Filey, in the county of York. Eng. title, 1 p. l. vi, 160 pp. 4 pl. 8°. *Scarborough, J. Cole,* 1828.

Colebrooke (Henry Thomas). Miscellaneous essays. 3 v. 8°. *London, Trübner & co.* 1873.

CONTENTS.

v. 1. The life of H. T. Colebrooke, by his son, sir T. E. Colebrooke.
v. 2–3. Miscellaneous essays. A new edition, with notes, by E. B. Cowell.

Coleridge (Henry James, *s. J.*) Life and letters of st. Francis Xavier. 2 v. xxvii, 424 pp; xxiii, 579 pp. 12°. *London, Burns & Oates,* 1872.

Coleridge (Sara Henry). Memoir and letters. 2 p. l. ix–528 pp. 2 ports. 8°. *New York, Harper & brothers,* 1874.

Collé (Charles). Journal historique, ou mémoires critiques et littéraires, depuis 1748 jusqu'en 1772. 3 v. 12°. [*Paris*], *imprimerie bibliographique*, 1807.

Collin (Jacques Auguste Simon, *dit* de Plancy). Dictionnaire féodal. 2e éd. 2 v. in 1. 2 p. l. xxxv–l, 333 pp; 2 p. l. xxxv–l, 330 pp. 8°. *Paris, Brissot-Thivars*, 1820.

Collins (J. L.) Queen Krinaleen's plagues. By "Jonquil" [*pseud.*] 151 pp. 16°. *New York, american news co.* 1874.

Collins (Mortimer). Secret of long life. [*anon.*] 4 p. l. 145 pp. 8°. *London, H. S. King & co.* 1871.

——— Transmigration. 3 v. 12°. *London, Hurst & Blackett*, 1874.

Collins (William Wilkie). Basil. 1 p. l. 336 pp. 6 pl. 12°. *New York, Harper & brothers*, 1874.

——— Dead alive. 11th ed. 157 pp. 4 pl. 16°. *Boston, Shepard & Gill*, 1874.

——— Dead secret. 359 pp. 6 pl. 12°. *New York, Harper & brothers*, 1874.

——— Frozen deep. [Also, A terribly strange bed]. 237 pp. 4 pl. 12°. *Boston, W. F. Gill & co.* 1875.

——— Hide-and-seek. 412 pp. 5 pl. 8°. *New York, Harper & brothers*, 1874.

——— Miss or mrs.? viii, 325 pp. 12°. *London, R. Bentley & son*, 1873.

——— Moonstone. 491 pp. incl. 17 pl. 8°. *New York, Harper & brothers*, 1874.

——— My miscellanies. 2 v. vii, 291 pp; 2 p. l. 300 pp. 12°. *London, S. Low, son & co.* 1863.

——— New Magdalen. 3 p. l. 9–325 pp. 6 pl. 8°. *New York, Harper & brothers*, 1873.

——— No name. 609 pp. incl. 17 pl. 8°. *New York, Harper & brothers*, 1874.

——— Queen of hearts. 472 pp. 4 pl. 8°. *New York, Harper & brothers*, 1874.

——— Woman in white. 548 pp. incl. 16 pl. 8°. *New York, Harper & brothers*, 1873.

Collinson (*Rev.* John). History and antiquities of the county of Somerset. 3 v. (containing 41 pl. 1 map). 4°. *Bath, R. Cruttwell*, 1791.

Colombo (Fernando). Vie de Christofle Colomb. Composée par son fils, & traduite en françois [par C. Cotolendy]. 2 v. in 1. 12 p. l. 262 pp; 12 p. l. 260 pp. 12°. *Paris, Claude Barbin & Christophe Ballard*, 1681.

Colomera y Rodriguez (Venancio). Paleografía castellana: coleccion de documentos para comprender con perfeccion todas las formas de letras manuscritas que se usaron en los siglos XII, XIII, XIV, XV y XVI, alfabetos, [etc.] 1 p. l. eng. title, 188 pp. incl. 92 facs. sm. fol. *Valladolid, autor & R. L. Cruz*, 1862.

Comfort (George F.) *and* **Comfort** (*Mrs.* Anna Manning, *m. d.*) Woman's education. 155 pp. 16°. *Syracuse, T. W. Durston & co.* 1874.

Connelly (Emma M.) Under the surface. 332 pp. 12°. *Philadelphia, J. B. Lippincott & co.* 1873.

Connelly (William Montague). Four beasts: an identification of antichrist. 1 p. l. vi, 178 pp. 8°. *Baltimore*, [*J. Cox*], 1875.

Conscience (Hendrik). Ludovic and Gertrude. Translated for this edition. 161 pp. 12°. *Baltimore, J. Murphy & co.* 1875.

——— Merchant of Antwerp. From the flemish. By Revin Lyle. 1 p. l. 242 pp. 12°. *Baltimore, Kelly, Piet & co.* 1872.

——— Young doctor. Translated for this edition. 192 pp. 12°. *Baltimore, J. Murphy & co.* 1875.

Constable (Thomas). Archibald Constable and his literary correspondents. 3 v. 8°. *Edinburgh, Edmonston & Douglas*, 1873.

Conway (John D.) Complete poems. 200 pp. 12°. *Lawrence, Mass. J. D. Conway*, 1875.

Conway (Moncure Daniel). Rejected stone. [*anon.*] 132 pp. 12°. *Boston, Walker, Wise & co.* 1861.

——— Republican superstitions. xii, 130 pp. 12°. *London, H. S. King & co.* 1872.

——— *editor.* Sacred anthology. viii, 480 pp. 8°. *New York, H. Holt & co.* 1874.

Conyngham (David P. *ll. d.*) The O'Donnells of glen cottage. 498 pp. 12°. *New York, D. & J. Sadlier & co.* 1874.

Cook (Dutton). Art in England. 359 pp. 16°. *London, S. Low, son & Marston*, 1869.

Cooke (Augustus P. *U. S. n.*) Text-book of naval ordnance and gunnery. xiv, [842] pp. 8°. *New York, J. Wiley & son*, 1875.

Cooke (*Rev.* Henry A. *compiler*). Phineas Stowe, and bethel work. 1 p. l. 406 pp. incl. 2 pl. 12°. *Boston, J. H. Earle*, 1874.

Cooke (John, *m. d.*) Treatise on nervous diseases. 2 v. in 3. 8°. *London, Longmans*, 1820–21.

Cooke (John Esten). Pretty mrs. Gaston. 288 pp. incl. 1 pl. 12°. *New York, O. Judd co.* [1874].

Cooke (Josiah P. *jr.*) New chemistry. 326 pp. 12°. *New York, D. Appleton & co.* 1874. [INTERNATIONAL scientific series, v. 6].

Cooper (*Rev.* Thomas, "*the chartist*", *b.* 1805). Life of Thomas Cooper: by himself. viii, 400 pp. port. 12°. *London, Hodder & Stoughton,* 1872.

——— Verity of Christ's resurrection. xi, 176 pp. sq. 18°. *London, Hodder & Stoughton,* 1875.

Cooper (Thomas, *f. s. a.*) New biographical dictionary. 2 p. l. 1211 pp. 12°. *London, G. Bell & sons,* 1873.

Cooper (Thomas T.) Mishmee hills. viii, 270 pp. 4 col. pl. 1 map. 12°. *London, H. S. King & co.* 1873.

——— Travels of a pioneer of commerce in pigtail and petticoats. xv, 475 pp. front. 1 map. 8°. *London, J. Murray,* 1871.

Copp (Frank B.) Idle hour poems. 300 pp. 12°. *Easton, Pa. G. W. West,* 1874.

Coppée (Henry, *ll. d. editor*). Gallery of famous english and american poets. Front. illum. title, 488 pp. 4°. *Philadelphia, J. M. Stoddart & co.* 1873.

Coquand (Henri). Description du département de la Charente. 2 v. 2 p. l. 542 pp. 1 col. map; 420 pp. incl. 13 tab. 18°. *Besançon, Dodiviers & cie.* [&] *Marseille, Barlatier-Feissat & Demonchy,* 1858–62. s.

——— Monographie du genre ostrea. Terrain crétacé. 215 pp. 8°. *Marseille, H. Seren,* 1869. s.

——— Same. Atlas. 1 p. l. 75 pl. 4°. *Paris, J.-B. Baillière,* 1869.

Corbin (*Mrs.* Caroline Fairfield). His marriage vow. 1 p. l. 5–328 pp. 16°. *Boston, Lee & Shepard,* 1874.

Cordoba y Figueroa (Don Pedro de). Historia de Chile. 329 pp. 8°. [*Santiago de Chile, imprenta nacional,* 1873 ?] s.

Cordova *or* **Corduba** (Díego de). Vida, virtvdes, y milagros del apostol del Peru, fray Francisco Solano. Eng. title, 30 p. l. 686 pp. 6 l. 4°. *Madrid, emprenta real,* 1643.

Cornell (William Mason). How to enjoy life. 360 pp. incl. 2 pl. 12°. *Boston, B. B. Russell,* 1873.

——— Life and public career of hon. Horace Greeley. 312 pp. 2 ports. 12°. *Boston, Lee & Shepard,* 1872.

——— Sabbath made for man. 2d ed. 132 pp. 18°. *Boston, H. Hoyt,* 1873.

Cornell (William Mason)—continued.

——— *editor.* Charles Sumner: memoir and eulogies. 336 pp. 4 pl. port. 12°. *Boston, J. H. Earle,* 1874.

Corner (Sidney). Rural churches. 72 pp. 18 col. pl. 4°. *London, Groombridge & sons,* [1869].

Correa (Gaspar). Lendas da India. 4 v. 4°. *Lisboa, na typographia da academia real das sciencias,* 1858–66.

Corry (John). History of Lancashire. 2 v. 3 p. l. 616 pp. 9 pl; 2 p. l. 726, xliv pp. 2 l. 22 pl. 4°. *London, G. B. Whittaker,* 1825.

Corser (*Rev.* Thomas). Collectanea anglo-poetica. 5 v. sm. 4°. [*Manchester*], 1860–73. [CHETHAM society remains, v. 52, 55, 71, 77, 91].

Cortés *or* **Cortez** (Hernando *or* Fernando). Cartas y relaciones al emperador Carlos V. li, 575 pp. 8°. *Paris, A. Chaix & ca.* 1866. s.

Corvin-Wiersbitzki (Otto Julius Bernhard von). Life of adventure. Autobiography. 3 v. 8°. *London, R. Bentley & son,* 1871.

Cote (Wolfred Nelson). Baptism and baptisteries. 170 pp. 4 pl. 18°. *Philadelphia, bible & publication society,* [1874].

Cotgrave (Randle). Dictionarie of the french and english tongves. Eng. title, 2 p. l. 485 l. unp. fol. *London, A. Islip,* 1611.

——— Same. French and english dictionary; with another in english and french, [by Robert Sherwood]. With supplements. By James Howell. 2 parts in 1 v. 12 p. l. 396 l. unp; 2 p. l. 103 l. unp. fol. *London, for A. Dolle,* 1673.

Coues (Elliott). Birds of the northwest. xi, 791 pp. 8°. *Washington, government printing office,* 1874.
[UNITED STATES. *Department of the interior.* (*U. S. geological survey of the territories*). Miscellaneous publications, no. 3].

——— Field ornithology. 2 parts in 1 v. iv, 116 pp; 137 pp. 8°. *Salem,* [*Mass.*] *naturalists' agency,* 1874.

Coulson (George James Atkinson). Harwood. [*anon.*] 206 pp. 8°. *New York, E. J. Hale & son,* 1875.

——— Lacy diamonds. [*anon.*] 284 pp. 8°. *New York, E. J. Hale & son,* 1875.

——— Odd trump. [*anon.*] 326 pp. 8°. *New York, E. J. Hale & son,* 1875.

Courtet de L'Isle (Alexandre-Victor). Science politique fondée sur la science de l'homme. 2 p. l. xv, 400 pp. 8°. *Paris, A. Bertrand,* 1838.

Cousinéry (Esprit Marie). Voyage dans la Macédoine. 2 v. in 1. vii, 272 pp. 3 pl; vi,

Cousinéry (Esprit Marie)—continued. 204 pp. 4 pl. 4°. *Paris, imprimerie royale,* 1831.

Cowles (Henry, *d. d.*) Hebrew history. viii, 419 pp. 12°. *New York, D. Appleton & co.* 1875.

——— The minor prophets; with notes. x, 424 pp. 1 l. 12°. *New York, Appleton & co.* 1867.

——— The pentateuch, in its progressive revelations of God to men. x, 414 pp. 8°. *New York, D. Appleton & co.* 1874.

Cowley (Charlotte). Ladies history of England; to 1780. 704 pp. 6 l. 28 pl. 42 ports. on 14 pl. 2 maps. fol. *London, for the proprietors,* 1780.

Cox (George Valentine, *m. a*) Recollections of Oxford. 3 p. l. 437 pp. 12°. *London, Macmillan & co.* 1868.

Cox (*Rev.* George William). Mythology of the aryan nations. 2 v. xx, 460 pp; xv, 397 pp. 8°. *London, Longmans,* 1870.

——— *and* **Jones** (Eustace Hinton). Tales of the teutonic lands. xii, 394 pp. 12°. *London, Longmans,* 1872.

Coxe (*Rev.* Arthur Cleveland). Apollos. 277 pp. 12°. *Philadelphia, J. B. Lippincott & co.* 1873.

Cozzens (Samuel Woodworth). Marvellous country; or, three years in Arizona and New Mexico. Eng. title, 2 p. l. 7–532 pp. 26 pl. 1 map. 8°. *Boston, Shepard & Gill,* 1873.

Crafts (*Rev.* W. F.) Childhood: the textbook of the age. front. xii, 259 pp. 12°. *Boston, Lee & Shepard,* 1875.

——— Through the eye to the heart. Front. 224 pp. 12°. *New York, Nelson & Phillips,* [1873].

——— Trophies of song. 310 pp. 16°. *Boston, D. Lothrop & co.* [1875].

Craik (*Mrs.* Dinah Maria Muloch). Adventures of a brownie as told to my child. [*anon.*] 3 p. l. 116 pp. 6 pl. 12°. *London, S. Low, Marston, Low & Searle,* 1872.

——— My mother and I. [*anon.*] 3 p. l. 318 pp. 12°. *London, W. Isbister & co.* 1874.

Craik (Georgianna M.) Sylvia's choice. 2 v. 2 p. l. 306 pp; 2 p. l. 318 pp. 12°. *London, Hurst & Blackett,* 1874.

Cram atlas co. New commercial atlas of the U. S. 2 p. l. 35 col. maps on 22 l. fol. *New York & Chicago, Cram atlas co.* [1875].

Cranch (Christopher Pearse). The bird and the bell. xiii, 327 pp. 16°. *Boston, J. R. Osgood & co.* 1866.

Crawfurd (George). General description of the shire of Renfrew. 16, 9–523 pp. 6 pl. 4°. *Paisley, J. Neilson,* 1818.

Creuzé de Lesser (Auguste François, *baron*). La chevalerie. xii, 560 pp. 8°. *Paris, F. Ponce-Lebas & cie.* 1839.

Creuzer (Friedrich). Deutsche schriften. Erste abtheilung. Symbolik und mythologie der alten völker. 3te ausg. 4 v. 8°. *Leipzig, C. W. Leske,* 1836–43.

Croff (Gilbert B.) Progressive american architecture. 2 p. l. 97 pl. 4°. *New York, Orange Judd co.* [1875].

Crofton (Francis Blake). Bewildered querists and other nonsense. 127 pp. 12°. *New York, G. P. Putnam's sons,* 1875.

Croll (James). Climate and time in their geological relations. xvii, 577 pp. 8 pl. & charts. 8°. *London, Daldy, Isbister & co.* 1875.

Cromwell (Merritt). Flights and fancies. 215 pp. 12°. [*New York?* 1875].

Crosby (G. S.) The mystery, or platonic love. 564 pp. 6 pl. 12°. *Philadelphia, J. B. Lippincott & co.* 1875.

Crosby (*Rev.* Howard). Expository notes on Joshua. 236 pp. 12°. *New York, R. Carter & brothers,* 1875.

——— Thoughts on the decalogue. 164 pp. 16°. *Philadelphia, Presbyterian board of publication,* [1873].

Cross (Joseph, *d. d.*) American pastor in Europe. Edited by rev. J. Cumming. xxxv, 419 pp. 16°. *London, R. Bentley,* 1860.

Crossard (Louis, *baron* de). Mémoires militaires et historiques pour servir à l'histoire de la guerre depuis 1792 jusqu'en 1815 inclusivement. 5 v. 8°. *Paris, Migneret,* 1829.

Note.—Imperfect: v. 3, pp. 1–16 wanting.

Crotty (Daniel G.) Four years campaigning in the army of the Potomac. 207 pp. 8°. *Grand Rapids, Mich. Dygert bros. & co.* 1874.

Crowell (Eugene, *m. d.*) Identity of primitive christianity and modern spiritualism. v. 1. xiii, 523 pp. 8°. *New York, G. W. Carleton & co.* 1874.

Crowley (Robert). Select works. Edited with introduction, notes, and glossary by J. M. Cowper. xxxi, 185 pp. 1 l. 8°. *London, N. Trübner & co.* 1872.

[EARLY english text society, extra series, no. 15].

Cruden (Robert Peirce). History of the town of Gravesend and of the port of London. vii, 569 pp. 9 pl. 8°. *London, W. Pickering,* 1843.

Cruise in the Pacific. Edited by capt. Fenton Aylmer. [*anon.*] 2 v. 1 p. l. 319 pp. front; 1 p. l. 322 pp. front. 16°. *London, Hurst & Blackett*, 1860.

Cruse (*Miss* Mary Anne). Cameron Hall. By M. A. C. [*anon.*] 543 pp. 12°. *Philadelphia, J. B. Lippincott & co.* 1867.

Cudlip (Annie Thomas, *i. e. mrs.* Pender). "'He cometh not,' she said." 3 v. 12°. *London, Chapman & Hall*, 1873.

——— Only herself. 3 v. 12°. *London, Chapman & Hall*, 1869.

——— Passion in tatters. 3 v. 12°. *London, Chapman & Hall*, 1872.

Cudmore (P.) Civil government of the states, and constitutional history of the U. S. 254 pp. 8°. *New York, P. Cudmore*, 1875.

Cues from all quarters. [*anon.*] 3 p. l. 340 pp. 12°. *London, Hodder & Stoughton*, 1871.

Cumberland (Richard, 1732–1811). John de Lancaster. 2 v. 293 pp; 292 pp. 16°. *New-York, for E. Sargent & M. & W. Ward*, 1809.

Cumming (*Lt. col.* Gordon). Wild men & wild beasts. Eng. title, v–xv pp. 1 l. 351 pp. 18 pl. sq. 12°. *Edinburgh, Edmonston & Douglas*, 1871.

Cumming (*Rev.* Joseph George). The great Stanley. viii, 279 pp. 12°. *London, W. Macintosh*, 1867.

Cunningham (Allan). Paul Jones. 3 v. 12°. *Edinburgh, Oliver & Boyd*, 1826.

Curley (Edwin A.) Nebraska. viii, 433 pp. 8 maps, 12 pl. 8°. *New York, american and foreign publication co.* 1875.

Curtius (Ernst). History of Greece. Translated by A. W. Ward. 5 v. 8°. *London, R. Bentley & son*, 1868–73.

Custer (*Gen.* George A. *U. S. a.*) My life on the plains. 1 p. l. 5–256 pp. 5 ports. 3 pl. 8°. *New York, Sheldon & co.* 1874.

Cutts (Edward Lewes). Scenes and characters of the middle ages. xiii, 546 pp. 1 pl. sm. 4°. *London, Virtue & co.* 1872.

Cuvillier-Fleury (Alfred Auguste). Portraits politiques et révolutionnaires. 2e éd. 2 v. 2 p. l. 16, 310 pp; 2 p. l. 354 pp. 12°. *Paris, M. Lévy frères*, 1852.

D. (A. M.) John Dane, [1874]. *See* **Denison** (*Mrs.* Mary A.)

Dake (Orsamus Charles). Midland poems. vii, 284 pp. 16°. *Lincoln, [Neb.] state journal co.* 1873.

Dalgairns (John Bernard Dobrée). Holy communion. 3d ed. xiv, 440 pp. 12°. *Dublin, J. Duffy*, 1868.

Dall (*Mrs.* Caroline W. Healy). Romance of the association; or, one last glimpse of Charlotte Temple and Eliza Wharton. xii, 102 pp. 16°. *Cambridge, [Mass.] J. Wilson & son*, 1875.

Dallas (Robert Charles). Miscellaneous writings. 2 p. l. 5, viii, 300 pp. 1 pl. 4°. *London, for T. N. Longman*, 1797.

Dallaway (Harriet). Manual of heraldry for amateurs. viii, 169 pp. 12°. *London, W. Pickering*, 1828.

Dally (*Rev.* Joseph W.) Woodbridge and vicinity. The story of a New Jersey township. 391 pp. 8°. *New Brunswick, N. J., A. E. Gordon*, 1873.

D'Almeida (Anna). Lady's visit to Manilla and Japan. By Anna D'A. [*anon.*] xiii, 297 pp. col. front. 8°. *London, Hurst & Blackett*, 1873.

Dalrymple (Alexander). Collection of english songs. 16, 172, 33 pp. 12°. *London, W. Bennett*, 1796.

D'Alton (John, *barrister*). Illustrations, historical and genealogical, of king James's irish army list, 1689. 2d ed. enlarged. 2 v. xxiii, 462 pp; 1 p. l. 808 pp. 8°. *London, J. R. Smith*, 1861.

Dalton (William). Stories of the conquests of Mexico and Peru. viii, 499 pp. 7 pl. 16°. *London, J. Blackwood & co.* [1874].

Dana (James Dwight, *ll. d.*) Geological story briefly told. xii, 263 pp. 12°. *New York, Ivison, Blakeman, Taylor & co.* 1875.

——— Manual of geology. 2d ed. xvi, 828 pp. 1 pl. 1 map. 8°. *New York, Ivison, Blakeman, Taylor & co.* 1874.

——— Text-book of geology. 2d ed. vii, 358 pp. 12°. *New York & Chicago, Ivison, Blakeman, Taylor & co.* [1874].

Dana (*Rev.* J. Jay). Humpy Dumpy; or, the corner grocery. 314 pp. incl. 1 pl. 16°. *New York, national temperance society*, 1874.

Dancel (Jean-François, *m. d.*) De l'influence des voyages sur l'homme et sur ses maladies 3e éd. 504 pp. 8°. *Paris, E. Dentu*, 1858.

Daniell (W. H.) The voice and how to use it. 110 pp. 16°. *Boston, J. R. Osgood & co.* 1873.

Darwin (Charles Robert). Expression of the emotions. vi, 374 pp. 6 pl. 12°. *London, J. Murray*, 1872.

Darwin (Charles Robert)—continued.
——— Same. 4 p. l. 374 pp. 7 pl. 12°. *New York, D. Appleton & co.* 1873.
——— Insectivorous plants. 3d thousand. x, 462 pp. 12°. *London, J. Murray*, 1875.

Dasent (George Webbe). Jest and earnest. A collection of essays. 2 v. vii, 350 pp; 3 p. l. 388 pp. 12°. *London, Chapman & Hall*, 1873.

Dashiell (*Rev.* T. G.) Pastor's recollections. 208 pp. 12°. *New York, D. Appleton & co.* 1875.

Daudet (Alphonse). Lettres à un absent. Paris, 1870–1871. 2 p. l. 204 pp. 16°. *Paris, A. Lemerre*, 1871.
——— Lettres de mon moulin. 4e éd. 2 p. l. 302 pp. 16°. *Paris, J. Hetzel & cie.* [1874?]
——— Le petit Chose. Histoire d'un enfant. 6e éd. 3 p. l. 370 pp. 16°. *Paris, J. Hetzel & cie.* [1873].
——— Robert Helmont. 3e éd. 2 p. l. 304 pp. 1 l. 16°. *Paris, E. Dentu*, 1874.

Daumas (*Le général* Melchior Joseph Eugène). Mœurs et coutumes de l'Algérie. 4e éd. 2 p. l. vi, 442 pp. 16°. *Paris, L. Hachette & cie.* 1864.
——— La vie arabe. 1 p. l xv, 590 pp. 8°. *Paris, M. Lévy frères*, 1869.

Daussy (Jacques Mérault). Histoire des beaux-arts. xxxii, 319 pp. 8°. *Paris, Lorenzani*, 1849.

Davenport (Richard Alfred). Delusions, impostures, & deceptions. xvi, 368 pp. port. 18°. *London, W. Tegg*, 1869.

Davidson (Alexander) *and* **Stuvé** (Bernard). Complete history of Illinois from 1673 to 1873. x, 944 pp. 8°. *Springfield, Illinois journal co.* 1874.

Davies (Charles, *ll. d.*) Nature and utility of mathematics. 419 pp. 1 port. 8°. *New York, A. S. Barnes & co.* 1873.

Davies (Charles Maurice, *d. d.*) Heterodox London. 2 v. xvi, 386 pp; xix, 408 pp. 8°. *London, Tinsley brothers*, 1874.
——— Mystic London. vii, 406 pp. 8°. *London, Tinsley brothers*, 1875.
——— Orthodox London. [*anon.*] viii, 404 pp. 8°. *London, Tinsley brothers*, 1873.
——— Unorthodox London. 2d ed. viii, 448 pp. 8°. *London, Tinsley brothers*, 1874.

Davies (Clementina Drummond, *lady*). Recollections of society in France and England. 2 v. x, 304 pp; x, 308 pp. 12°. *London, Hurst & Blackett*, 1872.

Davies (*Rev.* David Peter). New historical and descriptive view of Derbyshire. 2 v. 1 p. l. ix, 358 pp. 2 pl. 1 map; 1 p. l. 359–717 pp. 7 l. 8°. *Belper, S. Mason*, 1811.

Davies (Theodore). Losing to win. 407 pp. 12°. *New York, Sheldon & co.* 1874.

Davies (Thomas A.) Genesis disclosed. 222 pp. 12°. *New York, G. W. Carleton & co.* 1874.

Davies (William). Pilgrimage of the Tiber. xii, 346 pp. 4 pl. 1 map. 8°. *London, S. Low, Marston, Low & Searle*, 1873.

Davies (William A.) Banks of Susquehanna. Translated into welsh by David Q. Davies. [English and welsh]. 189, iii pp. 12°. *East Nanticoke, Brannan & Ramsey*, 1872.

Davieson (*Dr.* —) *and* **Jordan** (*Dr.* —). Silent friend: a medical work on the organs of generation, [etc.] 192 pp. 11 pl. 18°. *New York, authors*, 1874.

Davila (Gil Gonzalez). Teatro eclesiastico de la primitiva iglesia de las Indias occidentales. 2 v. 7 p. l. 308 pp. 4 l; 8 p. l. 110 l. numb. fol. *Madrid, D. D. de la Carrera*, 1649–55.

Davis (Andrew Jackson). Free thoughts concerning religion. Revised. 215 pp. 12°. *Boston, W. White & co.* 1872.
——— Genesis and ethics of conjugal love. 142 pp. 16°. *New York, A. J. Davis & co.* 1874.
——— The harmonial man. Revised. 167 pp. 12°. *Boston, W. White & co.* 1872.

Davis (*Mrs.* Caroline E. Kelly). Miss Wealthy's hope. 410 pp. 1 pl. 16°. *Boston, D. Lothrop & co.* [1874].

Davis (James D.) History of Memphis. 320 pp. 1 l. 2 ports. 12°. *Memphis, Tenn. Hite, Crumpton & Kelly*, 1873.

Davis (Nathan S. *m. d.*) Clinical lectures. 1 p. l. 262 pp. 2 l. 12°. *Chicago, J. J. Spalding & co.* 1873.

Davis (*Mrs.* Rebecca Harding). John Andross. 324 pp. incl. 6 pl. 12°. *New York, O. Judd co.* [1874].

Davis (William M.) Nimrod of the sea. 1 p. l. 403 pp. incl. 15 pl. 1 pl. 12°. *New York, Harper & brothers*, 1874.

Davity (Pierre, *de Montmartin*). Les estats, empires, et principavtez du monde. Par le sr. D. T. V. Y. [*anon.*] 1 p. l. eng. title, 1396 pp. 4°. *Roven, A. Ovyn & I. Caillove*, 1625.

Dawkins (W. Boyd). Cave hunting. xxiv, 455 pp. col. front. 8°. *London, Macmillan & co.* 1874.

Dawson (Charles Carroll). Collection of records of families bearing the name Dawson. viii, 572 pp. 15 ports. 1 pl. 8°. *Albany, J. Munsell*, 1874.

——— Record of the descendants of Robert Dawson, of East Haven, Conn. 2 p. l. 115 pp. 3 ports. 8°. *Albany, J. Munsell*, 1874.
Note.—Forms part of his "Collection of records."

Dawson (John William, *ll. d.*) Nature and the bible. 257 pp. 10 pl. 12°. *New York, R. Carter & brothers*, 1875.

——— Story of the earth and man. xv, 403 pp. incl. 13 pl. 12°. *New York, Harper & brothers*, 1873.

Day (Henry). Lawyer abroad. 348 pp. 12 pl. 12°. *New York, R. Carter & brothers*, 1874.

Deane (John Bathurst). Life of Richard Deane. xii, 718 pp. 3 ports. 1 pl. 1 tab. 8°. *London, Longmans*, 1870.

De Costa (*Rev.* Benjamin Franklin). Northmen in Maine. 2 p. l. 146 pp. 8°. *Albany, J. Munsell*, 1870.

——— *editor.* Pre-columbian discovery of America by the Northmen. lx, 9–118 pp. 1 map. 8°. *Albany, J. Munsell*, 1868.

——— Sailing directions of Henry Hudson. With introduction and notes. 102 pp. 8°. *Albany, J. Munsell*, 1869.

De Foe (Daniel). Daniel De Foe: his life and recently discovered writings: extending from 1716 to 1729. By William Lee. 3 v. 8°. *London, J. C. Hotten*, 1869.

De Forest (John W.) Honest John Vane. 1 p. l. 259 pp. 16°. *New Haven, Richmond & Patten*, 1875.

——— Playing the mischief. 1 p. l. 185 pp. 8°. *New York, Harper & brothers*, 1875.
[HARPER'S library of select novels, v. 442].

——— Seacliff. 466 pp. 12°. *Boston, Phillips, Sampson & co.* 1859.

——— Wetherel affair. 222 pp. 8°. *New York, Sheldon & co.* 1873.

De Geer (*Mrs.* M. E.) Marian Lee. 216 pp. port. 12°. *Chicago, Chicago legal news co.* 1874.

Dekker (Thomas). Dramatic works: now first collected, with notes and a memoir of the author. 4 v. 12°. *London, J. Pearson*, 1873.

De Koninck (L. L.) *and* **Dietz** (E.) Practical manual of chemical analysis and assaying. Edited by R. Mallet. 1st am. ed. edited

DeKoninck (L. E.) *and* **Dietz** (E.)—contin'd. by A. A. Fesquet. xvi, 13–282 pp. 8°. *Philadelphia, H. C. Baird*, 1873.

Delandine de Saint-Esprit (Jérôme). Histoire de la révolution, 1747–1793. République. 544 pp. 12°. *Paris, Mallet & cie.* 1843.

De la Ramé (Louise). Dog of Flanders, and other stories. By "Ouida" [*pseud.*] 3 p. l. 293 pp. 4 pl. 12°. *London, Chapman & Hall*, 1872.

——— Pascarel. By "Ouida" [*pseud.*] 494 pp. 12°. *Philadelphia, J. B. Lippincott & co.* 1874.

——— Signa. By "Ouida" [*pseud.*] 501 pp. 12°. *Philadelphia, J. B. Lippincott & co.* 1875.

Delord (Taxile). Histoire du second empire, (1848–70). 6 v. 8°. *Paris, G. Baillière* 1869–74.

De Mille (James). Babes in the wood. 2 p. l. iv, 9–142 pp. 4 pl. 8°. *Boston, W. F. Gill & co.* 1875.
[GILL'S select novels].

——— A comedy of terrors. 2 p. l. 152 pp. 8°. *Boston, J. R. Osgood & co.* 1872.
[OSGOOD'S library of novels, no. 25].

——— Lily and the cross. 1 p. l. 5–264 pp. 6 pl. 12°. *Boston, Lee & Shepard*, 1875.

——— Living link. 1 p. l. 9–171 pp. 1 pl. 8°. *New York, Harper & brothers*, 1874.

——— An open question. 2 p. l. 233 pp. 20 pl. 8°. *New York, D. Appleton & co.* 1873.

——— Picked up adrift. 335 pp. 4 pl. 16°. *Boston, Lee & Shepard*, 1872.
["B. O. W. C." series, v. 5].

——— Seven hills. 331 pp. 4 pl. 16°. *New York, Lee & Shepard*, 1873.
[YOUNG dodge club, no. 2].

——— Treasure of the seas. 336 pp. 4 pl. 16°. *Boston, Lee & Shepard*, 1873.
["B. O. W. C." series, no. 6].

Demmin (Auguste Frédéric). Encyclopédie des beaux-arts plastiques; architecture et mosaïque, céramique, sculpture, peinture et gravure. 3 v. 8°. *Paris, Furne, Jouvet & cie.* [1873–74].

De Morgan (Augustus). A budget of paradoxes. vii, 511 pp. 8°. *London, Longmans*, 1872.

Demotier (Charles). Annales de Calais. 3 p. l. 402 pp. 2 pl. 2 maps. 8°. *Calais, Demotier*, 1856.

Dempsey (J. Maurice) *and* **Hughes** (William), *editors.* Our ocean highways. cciv, 482

Dempsey *and* **Hughes**—continued. pp. 1 l. 3 maps. 16°. *London, E. Stanford,* 1871.

Denis (Jean Baptiste). Recueil des mémoires et conférences qui ont esté présentées à monseigneur le dauphin pendant 1672[-83]. 4 p. l. 352 pp. incl. 5 pl. 4 pl. 4°. *Paris, F. Leonard,* 1672[-83].

Denison (*Rev.* Charles Wheeler). Antoine. By an ex-consul. [*anon.*] 316 pp. 3 pl. 16°. *Boston, H. Hoyt,* [1874].

Denison (*Rev.* F. *editor*). The evangelist; or, life and labors of rev. Jabez S. Swan. 466 pp. incl. 4 pl. 1 port. 8°. *Waterford, Conn. W. L. Peckham,* 1873.

Denison (*Mrs.* Mary Andrews). John Dane. By A. M. D. [*anon.*] 451 pp. 1 pl. 16°. *Boston, H. Hoyt,* [1874].

——— Little folks of Redbow. 362 pp. 3 pl. 16°. *Boston, H. A. Young & co.* [1875].

Dennis (John, *editor*). English sonnets. xii, 238 pp. 16°. *London, H. S. King & co.* 1873.

Densel (Mary). Lloyd Dalan. 284 pp. 4 pl. 16°. *New York, E. P. Dutton & co.* 1874.

Denton (William). Radical discourses on religious subjects. 4 p. l. 332 pp. 12°. *Boston, W. Denton,* 1872.

——— Servia and the Servians. xii, 294 pp. 5 pl. port. 12°. *London, Bell & Daldy,* 1862.

Denver (Mary Caroline) *and* **Denver** (Jane Campbell). Poems. 347 pp. 16°. *New York, for J. W. Denver,* 1875.

De Peyster (John Watts). History of the life of Leonard Torstenson. xviii, 284, viii pp. 8°. *Poughkeepsie, Platt & Schram,* 1855.

——— La royale. Parts i, ii, iii, iv, v, & vi in 1. By Anchor. [*pseud.*] vi, 70 pp. 1 port. 1 map. 4°. *New York, J. R. Huth,* 1872.

——— Same. Part vii. By Anchor [*pseud.*] 1 p. l. 10, xi, 150 pp. 3 ports. 2 maps. 4°. *New York, J. R. Huth,* 1874.

——— Same. Part viii. By Anchor. [*pseud.*] 1 p. l. iv, 48 pp. 1 port. 1 map. 4°. *New York, J. R. Huth,* 1872.

Dépret (Louis). Mémoires de n'importe qui. 2 p. l. 423 pp. 1 l. 16°. *Paris, Charpentier & cie.* 1875.

Derenbourg (Joseph). Essai sur l'histoire et la géographie de la Palestine. 2 p. l. iv, 486 pp. 8°. *Paris, l'imprimerie impériale,* 1867.

Des Barres (Joseph Frederick Wallet). Atlantic neptune. 3 v. narrow fol. [*London,* 1777-79].

Des Cars (*Le comte* Amédée Joseph). L'élagage des arbres. 7e éd. vi, 147 pp. 1 pl. 16°. *Paris, J. Rothschild,* 1870.

Deschamps (John). Scenery and reminiscences of Ceylon. Ill. title, 2 p. l. 48 pp. 12 col. pl. fol. *London, for the author,* 1845.

Deschiens (*M.* —). Collection de matériaux pour l'histoire de la révolution de France, depuis 1787 jusqu'à ce jour. Bibliographie des journaux. Par m. D. S . . . . s. [*anon.*] xxiv, 645 pp. 8°. *Paris, Barrois l'aîné,* 1829.

Desjardins (Gustave Adolphe). Recherches sur les drapeaux français. vii, 167 pp. 4 l. 42 pl. (40 col.) 1 col. facs. 8°. *Paris, veuve A. Morel & cie.* 1874.

Despard (*Mrs.* M. C.) Chaste as ice, pure as snow. 2d ed. 3 v. 12°. *London, S. Tinsley,* 1874.

Detlef (Carl, *pseud.*) *See* **Bauer** (Clara).

Deutsch (Emanuel Oscar Menahem). Literary remains. xx, 465 pp. 8°. *London, J. Murray,* 1874.

De Vere (Maximilian Schele, *ll. d.*) Modern magic. 466 pp. 12°. *New York, G. P. Putnam's sons,* 1873.

Devereaux (Francis, *compiler*). Missouri's manufacturers: her wealth, industry and commerce. 2 p. l. 21-186 pp. 1 l. 4°. *St. Louis, Comley brothers,* 1874.

Devey (J. *m. a.*) Comparative estimate of modern english poets. vii, 421 pp. 12°. *London, E. Moxon, son, & co.* 1873.

Deville (Achille). Histoire de l'art de la verrerie dans l'antiquité. 2 p. l. 108 pp. 113 col. pl. 4°. *Paris, veuve A. Morel & cie.* 1873.

De Vinné (Daniel). History of the irish primitive church. 228 pp. 12°. *New-York, F. Hart & co.* 1870.

Dewall (— Van). Great lady. From the german. By M. S. 125 pp. 8 pl. 8°. *Philadelphia, J. B. Lippincott & co.* 1874.

Dewees (Watson W.) Brief history of Westtown boarding school. 342 pp. 1 pl. 12°. *Philadelphia, Sherman & co.* 1872.

Dezallier d'Argenville (Antoine-Joseph). Abrégé de la vie des plus fameux peintres. Nouv. éd. [*anon.*] 4 v. 8°. *Paris, De Bure l'aîné,* 1762.

D'Heilly (Georges). Dictionnaire des pseudonymes. 4 p. l. 139 pp. 18°. *Paris,* [*D. Jouaust, pour l'auteur*], 1868.

Diard (*Mlle.* Louise). Great-grandmother's secret. From the french. By the lady Blanche Murphy. [*anon.*] 182 pp. incl. front. 8°. *New-York, Benziger brothers*, 1875.

Diaz (*Mrs.* Abby Morton). Domestic problem. 120 pp. 16°. *Boston, J. R. Osgood & co.* 1875.

——— Lucy Maria. 396 pp. 8 pl. 16°. *Boston, J. R. Osgood & co.* 1874.

——— Schoolmaster's trunk. 1 p. l. 118 pp. 16°. *Boston, J. R. Osgood & co.* 1874.

Dicey (Edward Stephen). Morning land. 2 v. in 1. viii, 258 pp; 1 p. l. 234 pp. 12°. *London, Macmillan & co.* 1870.

Dick (William B.) Encyclopedia of practical receipts and processes. 607 pp. 8°. *New York, Dick & Fitzgerald*, [1872].

——— Same. 2d ed. 607 pp. 8°. *New York, Dick & Fitzgerald*, [1874].

Dickinson (William). Antiquities in Nottinghamshire and the adjacent counties; comprising the histories of Southwell and of Newark. In four parts. [Parts 1–2, comprising v. 1. Southwell]. 1 p. l. xiv, 8, 344 pp. 23 pl. 17 l. of pedigrees. 4°. *Newark, Holt & Hage, for Cadell & Davies, London*, 1801.

Note—The rest of the work, intended originally for part 3-4, was published under the following title.

——— History and antiquities of the town of Newark, in Nottingham. 2 parts in 1 v. 3 p. l. xi, 401 pp. 13 pl. 9 l. of pedigrees. 4°. *Newark, M. Hage*, [1805–]1816.

Dickson (Alexander). All about Jesus. xii, 404 pp. 12°. *New York, R. Carter & brothers*, 1875.

Didier (Charles). Rome souterraine. 2 v. 3 p. l. 373 pp; 2 p. l. 396 pp. 4 l. 8°. *Paris, la revue encyclopédique*, 1833.

Diehl (*Mrs.* Anna T. Randall). Choice readings. New and rev. ed. 408 pp. 12°. *Philadelphia, Claxton, Remsen & Haffelfinger*, 1876.

Diemer (Joseph, *editor*). Deutsche gedichte des XI. und XII. jahrhunderts. Aufgefunden zu Vorau. 7 p. l. lxii, 384, 118 pp. 2 facs. 8°. *Wien, W. Braumüller*, 1849. S.

Dieterici (Friedrich). Reisebilder aus dem morgenlande. 2 v. xviii, 339 pp. 1 map; 3 p. l. 376 pp. 12°. *Berlin, Wiegandt & Grieben*, 1853.

Dieulafait (Louis). Diamonds and precious stones. From the french. By Fanchon Sanford. 2 p. l. xii, 292 pp. incl. 10 pl. 12°. *New York, Scribner, Armstrong & co.* 1874.

Diez (Friedrich Christian). Introduction to the grammar of the romance languages. Translated by C. B. Cayley. 2 p. l. 131 pp. 8°. *London, Williams & Norgate*, 1863.

Dillard (*Rev.* J. L.) Elements of medium theology. 498 pp. 12°. *Nashville, for the author*, 1874.

Dimsdale (*Prof.* Thomas J.) Vigilantes of Montana. 228 pp. 16°. *Virginia city, M. T. Montana post press*, 1866.

Disosway (E. T.) South Meadows. 2 p. l. 280 pp. 12°. *Philadelphia, Porter & Coates*, [1874].

Dixon (H. H.) Saddle and sirloin; or, english farm and sporting worthies. (Part north). [*anon.*] 2 p. l. 2, iv, 486 pp. port. 16°. *London, Rogerson & Tuxford*, 1870.

Dixon (William Hepworth). Free Russia. 2d ed. 2 v. viii, 352 pp. 1 pl; vi, 344 pp. 1 pl. 8°. *London, Hurst & Blackett*, 1870.

——— History of two queens. 1. Catharine of Aragon. 2. Anne Boleyn. 4 v. 8°. *London, Hurst & Blackett*, 1873–74.

Note.—v. 3 and 4 are 2d ed.

——— The Switzers. 2d ed. x, 364 pp. 8°. *London, Hurst & Blackett*, 1872.

——— White conquest. 2 v. viii, 356 pp; vi, 373 pp. 8°. *London, Chatto & Windus*, 1876.

Dodge (Mary Abigail). Nursery noonings. By Gail Hamilton. [*pseud.*] 310 pp. 16°. *New York, Harper & brothers*, 1875.

——— Twelve miles from a lemon. By Gail Hamilton. [*pseud.*] 320 pp. 12°. *New York, Harper & brothers*, 1874.

Dodge (*Mrs.* Mary Mapes). Rhymes and jingles. xii, 271 pp. 1 pl. 12°. *New York, Scribner, Armstrong & co.* 1875.

Doe (Charles H.) Buffets. 143 pp. 8°. *Boston, J. R. Osgood & co.* 1875.

Dollet (Victor), **Lacauchie** (A.) *and* **Lassalle** (Louis). Galérie dramatique. Costumes des théâtres de Paris. 10 v. 4°. *Paris, Hautecœur frères*, [18–].

Döllinger (*Dr.* Johann Joseph Ignatius von). Fables respecting the popes in the middle ages, translated by Alfred Plummer. xxiv, 463 pp. 12°. *New York, Dodd & Mead*, 1872.

Domenech (Emmanuel, *m. a.*) L'empire au Mexique. 2 p. l. 154 pp. 1 l. 8°. *Paris, Dentu*, 1862.

——— Histoire du Mexique. Juarez et Maximilien. 3 v. 8°. *Paris, librairie internationale*, 1868.

Dominguez (Ramon Joaquin). Diccionario nacional de la lengua española. 11ma ed. 2 v. 1019 pp; 2 p. l. 1021–1793, 302 pp. 4°. [*Madrid*], *Crespo, Martin & comp.* 1869.

Donald (James). Chambers's etymological dictionary of the english language. viii, 596 pp. 12°. *Edinburgh, W. & R. Chambers*, 1873.

Donné (Alphonse, *m. d.*) Change of air and scene. xi, 313 pp. 12°. *London, H. S. King & co.* 1872.

Donnelly (Eleanor C.) Domus Dei: religious and memorial poems. 106 pp. 8°. *Philadelphia, P. F. Cunningham*, 1875.

Doran (John, *ll. d.*) A lady of the last century (mrs. Elizabeth Montagu). xvi, 372 pp. 8°. *London, R. Bentley & son*, 1873.

Doré (Paul Gustave) *and* **Jerrold** (Blanchard). London. A pilgrimage. Eng. title, 6 p. l. xii, 191 pp. 54 pl. 4°. *London, Grant & co.* 1872.

Dorr (*Mrs.* Julia C. R.) Bride and bridegroom. 253 pp. 16°. *Cincinnati, Hitchcock & Walden*, 1873.

——— Expiation. 323 pp. 12°. *Philadelphia, J. B. Lippincott & co.* 1873.

——— Sibyl Huntington. 2 p. l. 7–359 pp. 12°. *New-York, Carleton*, 1870.

Dossi (Carlo). La colonia felice. 170 pp. 2 l. 8°. *Milano, Perelli*, 1874.

Doudouit (J. F. O.) Elegant biographical extracts. 2 v. viii, 230 pp; 210 pp. 18°. *Ludlow*, [*Eng.*] *H. Procter*, 1802.

Douglas (Amanda M.) Home nook. 384 pp. 12°. *Boston, Lee & Shepard*, 1874.

——— Old woman who lived in a shoe. 380 pp. 3 pl. 16°. *Boston, W. F. Gill & co.* 1875.

——— Seven daughters. 369 pp. 6 pl. 16°. *Boston, Lee & Shepard*, 1874.
[MAIDENHOOD series].

Douglas (Francis Wemyss Charteris, *lord Elcho*). Letters on military organization. xvi, 179 pp. 12°. *London, J. Murray*, 1871.

Douglas (Gawain, *bishop of Dunkeld*). Poetical works. 4 v. 12°. *Edinburgh, W. Paterson*, 1874.

Douglas (*Rev.* James). Nenia britannica: or, a sepulchral history of Great Britain. vi, 197 pp. 36 pl. fol. *London, J. Nichols, for G. Nicol*, 1793.

Douglas (*Mrs.* M.) Life of professor Gellert; with a course of moral lessons, delivered by him in the university of Leipsick; from a french translation. 3 v. 8°. *Kelso, A. Ballantyne*, 1805.

Note.—Appended to v. 3 is Instructions from a father to his son. 100 pp.

Douglas (Robert, *surgeon, r. n.*) Adventures of a medical student. 2 v. in 1. 168 pp; 168 pp. 12°. *New-York, Burgess, Stringer & co.* 1848.

Douglass (Elson). The social life. 464 pp. 10 pl. 12°. *Philadelphia, Belmont publishing co.* [1874].

Dowell (Stephen). History and explanation of the stamp duties. xxii, 380 pp. 8°. *London, Longmans*, 1873.

Dowley (M. Francis). History of the twelfth regiment, infantry, n. g. s. N. Y. xii, 216 pp. 12°. *New York, T. Farrell & son*, 1869.

Down east yarns. [*anon.*] 317 pp. 32°. [*n. p.*] *for the trade*, 1872.

Downs (Elizabeth). Nettie Loring: a tale. 353 pp. incl. 1 pl. 16°. *New York, national temperance society*, 1874.

Drake (Francis, *f. r. s. surgeon*, 1695–1770). Eboracum: or the history and antiquities of the city of York. 1 v. in 2. 14 p. l. 398 pp. 28 pl; 1 p. l. 399–627, cxi pp. incl. 12 pl. 17 l. 31 pl. fol. *London, W. Bowyer, for the author*, 1736.

Drake (Francis S.) Memorials of the society of the Cincinnati of Massachusetts. x, 565 pp. 1 l. 1 pl. 22 ports. 25 l. of facs. 8°. *Boston, for the society*, 1873.

Drake (Samuel Adams). Historic fields and mansions of Middlesex. xiv, 442 pp. incl. 1 pl. 21 pl. 1 map. 8°. *Boston, J. R. Osgood & co.* 1874.

——— Nooks and corners of the New England coast. 459 pp. incl. 3 pl. 1 map. 8°. *New York, Harper & brothers*, 1875.

——— Old landmarks and historic personages of Boston. xvii, 484 pp. 1 pl. 12°. *Boston, J. R. Osgood & co.* 1873.

Draper (James). History of Spencer, Mass. including a sketch of Leicester. 2d ed. 276 pp. 3 ports. 1 plan. 8°. *Worcester, H. J. Howland*, [1860].

Draper (John William, *m. d.*) History of the conflict between religion and science. xxii, 373 pp. 12°. *New York, D. Appleton & co.* 1875.
[INTERNATIONAL scientific series, v. 12].

Drinkwater (Jennie M.) Not bread alone. 386 pp. 4 pl. 16°. *New York, R. Carter & brothers*, 1873.

Drinkwater (Jennie M.)—continued.
——— Only Ned. 336 pp. 3 pl. 16°. *New York, R. Carter & brothers*, 1873.

Drummond (Robert Blackley, *b. a.*) Erasmus, his life and character. 2 v. 1 p. l. iv–xii, 413 pp. port; 1 p. l. v–vii, 380 pp. 12°. *London, Smith, Elder & co.* 1873.

Drysdale (John J. *m. d.*) *and* **Hayward** (John W. *m. d.*) Health and comfort in house building. vii, 114 pp. 2 tab. 6 pl. 8°. *London, E. & F. N. Spon*, 1872.

Dubois (Charles). Madame Agnes. Translated by M. P. T. 128 pp. 8°. *New York, catholic publication society*, 1874.

Du Boisgobey (Fortune). Golden tress. From the french. 422 pp. 12°. *Philadelphia, Claxton, Remsen & Haffelfinger*, 1876.

Du Camp (Maxime). Paris, ses organes, [etc.] dans la seconde moitié du XIX siècle. 6 v. 8°. *Paris, Hachette & cie.* 1873–75.

Du Deffand (Marie de Vichy-Chamrond, *marquise*). Correspondance inédite, précédée d'une notice par le marquis de Sainte-Aulaire. 2 v. 2 p. l. lxxxvii, 479 pp; 2 p. l. 441 pp. 8°. *Paris, M. Lévy frères*, 1859.

Dudevant (Amantine Lucile Aurore Dupin). Journal d'un voyageur pendant la guerre. Par George Sand. [*pseud.*] 2 p. l. 310 pp. 16°. *Paris, M. Lévy frères*, 1871.

——— My sister Jeannie. By George Sand. [*pseud.*] 2 p. l. 248 pp. 16°. *Boston, Roberts brothers*, 1874.

Du Fail (Noel, *sieur de la Hérissaye*). Les contes et discovrs d'Eutrapel. [1e éd.] 2 p. l. 223 l. numb. 16°. *Rennes, pour N. Glamet, de Quinpercorentin*, 1585.

——— Propos rustiques, baliverneries, contes et discours d'Eutrapel. Éd. annotée par J. M. Guichard. 2 p. l. 409 pp. 12°. *Paris, C. Gosselin*, 1842.

Dufau (Pierre Armand). Supplément aux constitutions chartes et lois fondamentales. 4 p. l. 220 pp.
[*In* LACROIX (J. V.) Constitutions des principaux états [etc.] 8°. *Paris, Pichon & Didier*, 1830. v. 7].

——— Traité de statistique. xii, 378 pp. 1 table. 8°. *Paris, H. L. Delloye*, 1840.

Duffey (*Mrs.* E. B.) No sex in education. A review of dr. E. H. Clarke's "Sex in education." 139 pp. 16°. *Philadelphia, J. M. Stoddart & co.* [1875].

——— What women should know. 320 pp. 12°. *Philadelphia, J. M. Stoddart & co.* [1873].

Dufour (Philippe, *m. d.*) Essai sur l'étude de l'homme. 2 v. in 1. 4 p. l. 405 pp; 2 p. l. 449 pp. 8°. *Paris, I. Pesron*, 1833.

Dufraisse (Marc Étienne Gustave). Histoire du droit de guerre et de paix de 1789 à 1815. 2e éd. 2 p. l. xvi, xxxii, 399 pp. 12°. *Paris, A. Le Chevalier*, 1868.

Dugdale (James, *ll. d.*) New british traveler. 4 v. in 2. 4°. *London, J. & J. Cundee*, 1814–19.

Dugdale (*Sir* William). Antiquities of Warwickshire illustrated. 2d ed. Revised by William Thomas, d. d. 2 v. 4 p. l. x pp. 2 l. 640 pp. incl. 23 pl. 10 pl; 641–1153 pp. incl. 26 pl. 15 l. 11 pl. fol. *London, for J. Osborn and T. Longman*, 1730.

——— Visitation of the county palatine of Lancaster in 1664–5. Edited by F. R. Raines. 3 v. sm. 4°. [*Manchester*], 1872–73.
[CHETHAM society remains, v. 84, 85, 88].

——— Visitation of the county of Yorke, begun in MDCLXV. and finished MDCLXVI. xxiii, 391 pp. 8°. *Durham*, 1859.
[SURTEES society. Publications, v. 36].

Duhring (Julia). Philosophers and fools. 357 pp. 8°. *Philadelphia, J. B. Lippincott & co.* 1874.

Dulaure (Jacques Antoine). Histoire de la révolution française, depuis 1814 jusqu'à 1830. Revue et continuée par m. [P. R.] Auguis. 8 v. 8°. *Paris, Poirée*, 1838.

Dulcken (Henry William). Picture history of England. 3 p. l. 328 pp. incl. 80 col. pl. sm. 4°. *London, G. Routledge & sons*, 1866.

Duller (Eduard). Die Donauländer. 2te aufl. 270 pp. 60 pl. 8°. *Leipzig, C. A. Haendel's verlag*, 1847.
[MALERISCHE (Das) und romantische Deutschland v. 9].

Dumas (Alexandre Davy). Œuvres complètes. Collection Michel Lévy. 257 v. 16°. *Paris, M. Lévy frères*, 1860–73.

CONTENTS.

v. 1. Acté. Nouv. éd. 2 p. l. 266 pp. 1871.
v. 2. Amaury. Nouv. éd. 2 p. l. 283 pp. 1871.
v. 3–4. Ange Pitou. Nouv. éd. 2 v. 2 p. l. 342 pp; 2 p. l. 338 pp. 1873.
v. 5–6. Ascanio. Nouv. éd. 2 v. 2 p. l. 300 pp; 2 p. l. 343 pp. 1872.
v. 7. Une aventure d'amour. Nouv. éd. 2 p. l. 275 pp. 1873.
v. 8–9. Aventures de John Davys. Nouv. éd. 2 v. 2 p. l. 322 pp; 2 p. l. 314 pp. 1872.
v. 10–11. Les baleiniers. Voyage aux terres antipodiques. Journal du docteur Maynard. 2 v. 2 p. l. 314 pp; 2 p. l. 311 pp. 1861.
v. 12–14. Le bâtard de Mauléon. Nouv. éd. 3 v. 1871.
v. 15. Black. Nouv. éd. 2 p. l. 319 pp. 1865.
v. 16–18. Les blancs et les bleus. 3 v. v. 1–2, nouv. éd. 1870–72; v. 3, 1868.

Dumas (Alexandre Davy)—continued.

v. 19. La bouillie de la comtesse Berthe. Nouv. éd. 2 p. l. 242 pp. 1871.
v. 20. La boule de neige. Nouv. éd. 2 p. l. 292 pp. 1866.
v. 21–22. Bric-à-brac. 2 v. 2 p. l. 304 pp; 2 p. l. 305 pp. 1861.
v. 23–25. Un cadet de famille. Traduit par Victor Perceval. 3 v. 1860.
v. 26. Le capitaine Pamphile. Nouv. éd. 3 p. l. 300 pp. 1873.
v. 27. Le capitaine Paul. Nouv. éd. 2 p. l. xlviii, 223 pp. 1869.
v. 28. Le capitaine Rhino. Nouv. éd. 2 p. l. 224 pp. 1873.
v. 29. Le capitaine Richard. Nouv. éd. 2 p. l. 307 pp. 1866.
v. 30. Catherine Blum. Nouv. éd. 2 p. l. 271 pp. 1867.
v. 31–32. Causeries. 1e–2e série. 2 v. 2 p. l. 280 pp; 2 p. l. 287 pp. 1860.
v. 33. Cécile. Nouv. éd. 2 p. l. 283 pp. 1871.
v. 34–35. Charles le téméraire. Nouv. éd. 2 v. 2 p. l. 324 pp; 2 p. l. 311 pp. 1871.
v. 36. Le chasseur de sauvagine. Nouv. éd. 2 p. l. 287 pp. 1872.
v. 37–38. Le château d'Eppstein. 2 v. 2 p. l. 261 pp; 2 p. l. 243 pp. 1860.
v. 39–40. Le chevalier d'Harmental. Nouv. éd. 2 v. 2 p. l. 296 pp; 2 p. l. 322 pp. 1873.
v. 41–42. Le chevalier de Maison-rouge. Nouv. éd. 2 v. 2 p. l. 312 pp; 2 p. l. 396 pp. 1872.
v. 43–45. Le collier de la reine. Nouv. éd. 3 v. 1873.
v. 46. La colombe. Maître Adam le Calabrais. Nouv. éd. 2 p. l. 305 pp. 1871.
v. 47–49. Les compagnons de Jéhu. Nouv. éd. 3 v. 1868.
v. 50–55. Le comte de Monte-Cristo. Nouv. éd. 6 v. 1871.
v. 56–61. La comtesse de Charny. Nouv. éd. 6 v. 1873.
v. 62–63. La comtesse de Salisbury. Nouv. éd. 2 v. 2 p. l. 290 pp; 2 p. l. 277 pp. 1861.
v. 64–65. Les confessions de la marquise.—Suite et fin des Mémoires d'une aveugle. Nouv. éd. 2 v. 2 p. l. 262 pp; 2 p. l. 267 pp. 1869.
v. 66–67. Conscience l'innocent. 2 v. 2 p. l. 256 pp; 2 p. l. 282 pp. 1861.
v. 68–69. Création et rédemption. Le docteur mystérieux. 2 v. 2 p. l. 320 pp; 2 p. l. 312 pp. 1872.
v. 70–71. Création et rédemption. La fille du marquis. 2 v. 2 p. l. 275 pp; 2 p. l. 283 pp. 1872.
v. 72–74. La dame de Monsoreau. Nouv. éd. 3 v. 1872.
v. 75–76. La dame de volupté. Mémoires de mlle. de Luynes. Nouv. éd. 2 v. v. 1, 2 p. l. 284 pp. 1872; v. 2, 2e éd. 2 p. l. 332 pp. 1865.
v. 77–79. Les deux Diane. [Par Paul Meurice]. Nouv. éd. 3 v. 1867.
v. 80–81. Les deux reines. Suite et fin des Mémoires de mlle. de Luynes. Nouv. éd. 2 v. 2 p. l. 333 pp; 2 p. l. 329 pp. 1870.
v. 82–83. Dieu dispose. Nouv. éd. 2 v. 2 p. l. 372 pp; 2 p. l. 368 pp. 1866.
v. 84–85. Les drames galants.—La marquise d'Escoman. 2 v. v. 1, nouv. éd. 1 p. l. 283 pp. [1872?]; v. 2, 2 p. l. 293 pp. 1860.
v. 86–88. Le drame de quatre-vingt-treize. 3 v. 1866–67.
v. 89. Les drames de la mer. Nouv. éd. 2 p. l. 304 pp. 1864.
v. 90. La femme au collier de velours. Nouv. éd. 2 p. l. 234 pp. 1873.
v. 91. Fernande. Nouv. éd. 2 p. l. 312 pp. 1873.
v. 92. Une fille du régent. Nouv. éd. 2 p. l. 356 pp. 1873.
v. 93. Filles, lorettes et courtisanes. Les serpents. Nouv. éd. 2 p. l. 283 pp. 1874.
v. 94. Le fils du forçat.—M. Coumbes. Nouv. éd. 2 p. l. 316 pp. 1873.
v. 95. Les frères corses. [Othon l'archer]. Nouv. éd. 2 p. l. 296 pp. 1867.
v. 96. Gabriel Lambert. [La pêche aux filets. Invraisemblance. Une âme à naître]. Nouv. éd. 2 p. l. 276 pp. 1868.
v. 97. Les Garibaldiens. Révolution de Sicile et de Naples. Nouv. éd. 2 p. l. 316 pp. 1 facs. 1868.

Dumas (Alexandre Davy)—continued.

v. 98. Gaule et France. Nouv. éd. 2 p. l. 295 pp. 1862.
v. 99. Georges. Nouv. éd. 2 p. l. 312 pp. 1873.
v. 100. Un Gil-Blas en Californie. 2 p. l. 324 pp. 1861.
v. 101–102. Les grands hommes en robe de chambre. César. 2 v. 2 p. l. 298 pp; 2 p. l. 304 pp. 1866.
v. 103–104. Les grands hommes en robe de chambre. Henri IV. Louis XIII et Richelieu. 2 v. 3 p. l. 307 pp; 2 p. l. 332 pp. 1866.
v. 105–106. La guerre des femmes. Nouv. éd. 2 v. 2 p. l. 337 pp; 2 p. l. 301 pp. 1868.
v. 107. Histoire d'un casse-noisette. Nouv. éd. 2 p. l. 284 pp. 1871.
v. 108. Les hommes de fer. 2 p. l. 307 pp. 1867.
v. 109. L'horoscope. 2 p. l. 284 pp. 1860.
v. 110–111. L'île de feu. 2 v. 2 p. l. 287 pp; 2 p. l. 255 pp. 1870.
v. 112. Impressions de voyage. Une année à Florence. Nouv. éd. 2 p. l. 279 pp. 1867.
v. 113–115. Impressions de voyage. L'Arabie heureuse. 3 v. 1860.
v. 116. Impressions de voyage. Le capitaine Aréna. Nouv. éd. 2 p. l. 291 pp. 1870.
v. 117–119. Impressions de voyage. Le Caucase. 3 v. 1865.
v. 120–121. Impressions de voyage. Le corricolo. Nouv. éd. 2 v. 2 p. l. 316 pp; 2 p. l. 311 pp. 1872.
v. 122–123. Impressions de voyage. Excursions sur les bords du Rhin. Nouv. éd. 2 v. 2 p. l. 287 pp; 2 p. l. 280 pp. 1869.
v. 124–125. Impressions de voyage. Midi de la France. Nouv. éd. 2 v. 2 p. l. 291 pp; 2 p. l. 324 pp. 1865.
v. 126–127. Impressions de voyage. De Paris à Cadix. Nouv. éd. 2 v. 2 p. l. 306 pp; 2 p. l. 305 pp. 1870.
v. 128. Impressions de voyage. Quinze jours au Sinai. Par A. Dumas et A. Dauzats. Nouv. éd. 2 p. l. 300 pp. 1868.
v. 129–132. Impressions de voyage. En Russie. [v. 1, nouv. éd.] 4 v. 1865–66.
v. 133–134. Impressions de voyage. Le spéronare. Nouv. éd. 2 v. 2 p. l. 320 pp; 2 p. l. 299 pp. 1873.
v. 135–137. Impressions de voyage. Suisse. Nouv. éd. 3 v. 1868–69.
v. 138–139. Impressions de voyage. Le véloce. Nouv. éd. 2 v. 2 p. l. 303 pp; 2 p. l. 296 pp. 1871.
v. 140. Impressions de voyage. La villa Palmieri. 2 p. l. 279 pp. 1865.
v. 141–142. Ingénue. 2 v. 2 p. l. 320 pp; 2 p. l. 331 pp. 1860.
v. 143–144. Isabel de Bavière. Nouv. éd. 2 v. 2 p. l. 288 pp; 2 p. l. 296 pp. 1872.
v. 145–146. Italiens et Flamands. 2 v. 2 p. l. 307 pp; 2 p. l. 301 pp. 1862.
v. 147–148. Ivanhoe. Par Walter Scott. Traduit par A. Dumas. 2 v. 2 p. l. 305 pp; 2 p. l. 287 pp. 1862.
v. 149. Jacques Ortis—les fous du docteur Miraglia. [Par Ugo Foscolo. Traduit] par A. Dumas. 2 p. l. 307 pp. 1867.
v. 150. Jacquot sans oreilles. 2e éd. 2 p. l. xxviii, 223 pp. 1873.
v. 151. Jane. Nouv. éd. 2 p. l. 324 pp. 1866.
v. 152. Jehanne la pucelle. Nouv. éd. 2 p. l. 296 pp. 1866.
v. 153–156. Louis XIV et son siècle. 4 v. 1866.
v. 157–158. Louis XV et sa cour. Nouv. éd. 2 v. 2 p. l. 296 pp; 2 p. l. 308 pp. 1873.
v. 159–160. Louis XVI et la révolution. 2 v. 2 p. l. 324 pp; 2 p. l. 336 pp. 1866.
v. 161–163. Les louves de Machecoul. 3 v. 1870.
v. 164–165. Madame de Chamblay. Nouv. éd. 2 v. 2 p. l. 268 pp; 2 p. l. 289 pp. 1866–73.
v. 166–167. La maison de glace. Nouv. éd. 2 v. 2 p. l. 326 pp; 2 p. l. 280 pp. 1867.
v. 168. Le maître d'armes. Nouv. éd. 2 p. l. 313 pp. 1873.
v. 169. Les mariages du père Olifus. Nouv. éd. 2 p. l. 264 pp. 1873.
v. 170. Les Médicis. Nouv. éd. 2 p. l. 271 pp. 1872.
v. 171–180. Mes mémoires. Nouv. éd. 10 v. 1865–70.
v. 181–182. Mémoires de Garibaldi. Traduits sur le manuscrit original. 3e éd. 2 v. 2 p. l. 312 pp; 2 p. l. 268 pp. 1866.
v. 183–184. Mémoires d'une aveugle. Nouv. éd. 2 v. 2 p. l. 303 pp; 2 p. l. 301 pp. 1867.
v. 185–189. Mémoires d'un médecin: Joseph Balsamo. Nouv. éd. 5 v. 1872.

Dumas (Alexandre Davy)—continued.

v. 190. Le meneur de loups. Nouv. éd. 2 p. l. 312 pp. 1868.
v. 191. Les mille et un fantômes. Nouv. éd. 2 p. l. 237 pp. 1873.
v. 192–195. Les Mohicans de Paris. 4 v. 1862.
v. 196–197. Les morts vont vite. 2 v. 2 p. l. 323 pp; 2 p. l. 295 pp. 1861.
v. 198. Napoléon. Nouv. éd. 2 p. l. 311 pp. 1873.
v. 199. Une nuit à Florence sous Alexandre de Médicis. Nouv. éd. 2 p. l. 251 pp. 1868.
v. 200–202. Olympe de Clèves. Nouv. éd. 3 v. 1872.
v. 203–204. Le page du duc de Savoie. Nouv. éd. 2 v. 2 p. l. 320 pp; 2 p. l. 292 pp. 1866.
v. 205–206. Parisiens et provinciaux. 2 v. 2 p. l. 326 pp; 2 p. l. 276 pp. 1868.
v. 207–208. Le pasteur d'Ashbourn. 2 v. 2 p. l. 320 pp; 2 p. l. 308 pp. 1860.
v. 209. Pauline et Pascal Bruno. Nouv. éd. 2 p. l. 311 pp. 1867.
v. 210. Un pays inconnu. Nouv. éd. 2 p. l. 320 pp. 1873.
v. 211–212. Le père gigogne. Contes pour les enfants. 2 v. 2 p. l. 312 pp; 2 p. l. 316 pp. 1860.
v. 213. Le père la ruine. 2 p. l. 320 pp. 1864.
v. 214–215. Le prince des voleurs. 2 v. 2 p. l. 293 pp; 2 p. l. 275 pp. 1872.
v. 216–217. La princesse de Monaco. 2 v. 2 p. l. 324 pp; 2 p. l. 320 pp. 1865.
v. 218. La princesse Flora. Nouv. éd. 2 p. l. 254 pp. 1871.
v. 219–221. Les quarante-cinq. Nouv. éd. 3 v. 1869.
v. 222. La régence. Nouv. éd. 2 p. l. 307 pp. 1872.
v. 223–224. La reine Margot. Nouv. éd. 2 v. 2 p. l. 319 pp; 2 p. l. 302 pp. 1868–73.
v. 225–226. Robin Hood le proscrit. 2 v. 2 p. l. 262 pp; 2 p. l. 273 pp. 1873.
v. 227. La route de Varennes. Nouv. éd. 2 p. l. 279 pp. 1869.
v. 228. Le salteador. Nouv. éd. 2 p. l. 320 pp. 1868.
v. 229–233. Salvator.—Suite et fin des Mohicans de Paris. 5 v. [v. 4–5, nouv. éd.] 1862–63.
v. 234. Souvenirs d'Antony. Nouv. éd. 2 p. l. 320 pp. 1868.
v. 235. Les Stuarts. Nouv. éd. 2 p. l. 307 pp. 1872.
v. 236. Sultanetta. 2 p. l. 320 pp. 1864.
v. 237. Sylvandire. Nouv. éd. 2 p. l. 319 pp. 1871.
v. 238–239. La terreur prussienne. 2 v. [v. 2, nouv. éd.] 2 p. l. 297 pp; 2 p. l. 294 pp. 1868–72.
v. 240. Le testament de m. Chauvelin. 2 p. l. 273 pp. 1861.
v. 241. Trois maîtres. Nouv. éd. 2 p. l. 264 pp. 1872.
v. 242–243. Les trois mousquetaires. Nouv. éd. 2 v. 2 p. l. 352 pp; 2 p. l. 340 pp. 1869.
v. 244. Le trou de l'enfer. Nouv. éd. 2 p. l. 364 pp. 1873.
v. 245. La tulipe noire. Nouv. éd. 2 p. l. 308 pp. 1872.
v. 246–251. Le vicomte de Bragelonne: ou, dix ans plus tard. Complément des Trois mousquetaires et de Vingt ans après. Nouv. éd. 6 v. 1872–74.
v. 252–253. La vie au désert. Cinq ans de chasse dans l'Afrique méridionale. Par Gordon Cumming. Nouv. éd. 2 v. 2 p. l. 288 pp; 2 p. l. 275 pp. 1869.
v. 254. Une vie d'artiste. Nouv. éd. 2 p. l. 312 pp. 1866.
v. 255–257. Vingt ans après. Suite de Trois mousquetaires. Nouv. éd. 3 v. 1873.

——— Théâtre complet. 1e–14e série. 14 v. 16°. *Paris, M. Lévy frères,* 1863–65.

——— Bragelonne. Conclusion of "The three guardsmen." 288 pp. 8°. *New York, W. E. Dean,* 1848,

——— The conscript. 400 pp. 12°. *Philadelphia, T. B. Peterson & brothers,* [1874].

——— The countess de Charny. Being the continuation of "The memoirs of a physician." 392 pp. 2 pl. 8°. *Philadelphia, T. B. Peterson,* [*about* 1850].

Dumas (Alexandre Davy)—continued.

——— The forty-five guardsmen. 233 pp. 8°. [*New York, Long & brothers,* 1850].
Note.—Title wanting.

——— Grand dictionnaire de cuisine. 1 p. l. vii, 1155 pp; (annexe) 24 pp. 2 pl. 8°. *Paris, A. Lemerre,* 1873.

——— Horrors of Paris. Sequel to "The Mohicans of Paris." 1 p. l. 190 pp. 8°. *Philadelphia, T. B. Peterson & brothers,* [1875].

——— The iron mask. Being the conclusion of "The three guardsmen." From the french by T. Williams. 420 pp. 2 pl. 8°. *Philadelphia, T. B. Peterson,* [*about* 1845].

——— Louise La Valliere; or, the second series and conclusion of the "Iron mask." From the french by T. Williams. 198 pp. 8°. *Philadelphia, T. B. Peterson,* [*about* 1846].

——— The Mohicans of Paris. 1 p. l. 189 pp. 8°. *Philadelphia, T. B. Peterson & brothers,* [1875].

——— The queen's necklace. Translated by T. Williams. 205 pp. 8°. *New York, W. F. Burgess,* 1850.

——— Six years later. Sequel to "The memoirs of a physician." From the french by T. Williams. 290 pp. 1 pl. 8°. *Philadelphia, T. B. Peterson,* [*about* 1850].

——— The three guardsmen. 239 pp. 8°. *New York, W. E. Dean,* 1848.

——— Twenty years after. A sequel to the "Three guardsmen." From the french by W. Barrow. 280 pp. 8°. *New York, W. F. Burgess,* 1850.

Dumas (Alexandre, *fils*). Théâtre complet. 1e–4e série. 3e éd. 4 v. 16°. *Paris, M. Lévy frères,* 1870–72.

CONTENTS.

v. 1. La dame aux camélias. Diane de Lys. Le bijou de la reine. 2 p. l. 424 pp.
v. 2. Le demi-monde. La question d'argent. 2 p. l. 385 pp.
v. 3. Le fils naturel. Le père prodigue. 2 p. l. 403 pp.
v. 4. L'ami des femmes. Les idées de madame Aubray. 2 p. l. 334 pp.

Dumesnil (Henri). La guerre. Avant-propos de m. Frédéric Passy. 1 p. l. 235 pp. 1 pl. 8°. *Paris, Pichon & cie.* 1872.

Dumesnil (Louis Alexis Lemaistre). Histoire de Philippe II, roi d'Espagne. 2e éd. vi, 367 pp. 8°. *Paris, A. Boucher,* 1824.

Dümling (*Dr.* Hermann). Illustrirtes thierleben. Die säugethiere. xvi, 349 pp. 10 col. pl. 4 pl. 8°. *Milwaukee, G. Brumder,* [1875].

Dumont (Léon). Des causes du rire. 2 p. l. iv, 133 pp. 8°. *Paris, A. Durand,* 1862.

Dumont (Léon A.) Haeckel et la théorie de l'évolution en Allemagne. 168 pp. 12°. *Paris, G. Baillière,* 1873.

Duncan (P. Martin, *f. r. s.*) Transformations of insects. An adaptation of m. Émile Blanchard's "Metamorphoses, mœurs et instincts des insectes"; [etc.] 2d ed. x pp. 1 l. 491 pp. 40 pl. 8°. *London, Cassell Petter & Galpin,* [1873].

Duncumb (John). Collections toward the history and antiquities of the county of Hereford. 2 v. xii, 604, [12] pp. 6 maps, 9 pl; 1 p l. 358, [10] pp. 3 pl. 4°. *Hereford, E. G. Wright,* 1804–12.

Dunn *or* **Dwnn** (Lewis). Heraldic visitations of Wales and part of the marches; between 1586 and 1613; edited by sir S. R. Meyrick. Published for the Welsh mss. society. 2 v. front. xxxii, 5–340 pp; front. 370 pp. 4°. *Llandovery, W. Rees,* 1846.

Dunn (*Rev.* Lewis R.) Holiness to the lord. 219 pp. 16°. *New York, Nelson & Phillips,* 1874.

Dunning (*Mrs.* A. K.) The minister's wife. 245 pp. 3 pl. 16°. *Philadelphia, am. s.-s. union,* [1874].
[SEMI-CENTENNIAL series].

Dupiney de Vorepierre (Jean François Marie Bertet-). Dictionnaire français illustré et encyclopédie universelle. 2 v. 2 p. l. 1328 pp; 2 p. l. 1376 pp. 4°. *Paris, bureau de la publication,* 1867–68.

Duplessi-Bertaux (J.) [Eaux forts. 125 etchings mounted on 56 l. obl. fol. *Paris,* 1797–1802].

Duplessis (Georges). Wonders of engraving. x, 338 pp. incl. 25 pl. 8 autotypes. 12°. *London, S. Low, son & Marston,* 1871.

Duplessis (Paul). Aventures mexicaines. 2 p. l. 324 pp. 12°. *Paris, A. Cadot,* [1860].

Du Pont (Alexandre). Roman de Mahomet, en vers du XIIIe siècle, par A. Du Pont, et livre de la loi au sarrazin, en prose du XIVe siècle, par Raymond Lulle, publiés par mm. Reinaud, et Francisque Michel. 2 p. l. xxiii, 140 pp. 2 l. 2 facs. 8°. *Paris, Silvestre,* 1831.

Duppa (Richard, *f. s. a.*) Heads from Michael Angelo: selection of twelve heads from the last judgment. 1 p. l. eng. title, ii, 9 pp. port. 14 pl. fol. *London, R. Duppa,* 1801.

——— Heads from the fresco pictures of Raffaello in the Vatican. 1 p. l. eng. title, ii, 39 pp. port. 5 sketches, 11 pl. fol. *London, R. Duppa,* 1802.

Duprat (Pierre-Pascal). Essai historique sur les races de l'Afrique septentrionale. 2 p. l. xv, 308 pp. 8°. *Paris, J. Labitte,* 1845.

Dupuis (Charles François). Origin of all religious worship. From the french. 1 p. l. 433 pp. 1 pl. 8°. *New Orleans,* 1872.

Dupuy (Eliza A.) All for love. 1 p. l. 19–415 pp. 12°. *Philadelphia, T. B. Peterson & brothers,* [1873].

——— The clandestine marriage. 1 p. l. 19–454 pp. 12°. *Philadelphia, T. B. Peterson & brothers,* [1875].

——— The dethroned heiress. 1 p. l. 19–471 pp. 12°. *Philadelphia, T. B. Peterson & brothers,* [1874].

——— The discarded wife. 1 p. l. 19–595 pp. 12°. *Philadelphia, T. B. Peterson & brothers,* [1875].

——— The gipsy's warning. 2 p. l. 21–450 pp. 12°. *Philadelphia, T. B. Peterson & brothers,* [1873].

——— The hidden sin. A sequel to "The dethroned heiress." 1 p. l. 19–357 pp. 12°. *Philadelphia, T. B. Peterson & brothers,* [1874].

——— How he did it. 456 pp. 12°. *Philadelphia, T. B. Peterson & brothers,* [1871].

——— The mysterious guest. 2 p. l. 21–406 pp. 12°. *Philadelphia, T. B. Peterson & brothers* [1873].

Durand-Brager (Jean Baptiste Henri). Sainte-Hélène. Histoire et vues pittoresques. 2 p. l. 54 pp. 1 l. 29 pl. fol. *Paris, Gide,* 1844.

Durau (Louis). Les curiosités de la ville de Milan, et de ses environs. [*anon.*] Eng. title, 71 pl. on india paper, 3 pl. inserted. sm. 4°. *Milano, Vallardi,* 1820.
Note.—The engravings are by L. Durau and published by Vallardi without descriptive text.

Durfee (*Rev.* Calvin). Sketch of the late rev. Ebenezer Fitch. 163 pp. 12°. *Boston, Mass. s. s. society,* 1865.

Durfee (Thomas). Village picnic and other poems. v, 214 pp. 12°. *Providence, R. I., G. H. Whitney,* 1872.

Dutcher (*Rev.* J. C.) The old home by the river. 230 pp. 3 pl. 16°. *New York, N. Tibbals & sons,* 1874.

Dutcher (Salem). Minority or proportional representation. 165 pp. 8°. *New York, United States publishing co.* 1872.

Dutertre (Jean Baptiste). Histoire des îsles de S. Christophe, de la Gvadelovpe, de la Martiniqve, et avtres dans l'Amériqve. 10 p. l. 482 pp. 3 l. 3 maps. *Paris, I. Langlois,* 1654.

Dutton (Amy). Streets and lanes of a city: reminiscences of Amy Dutton. viii, 159 pp. 16°. *London, Macmillan & co.* 1871.

——— *and* **Jones** (Agnes E.) Homes and hospitals: or two phases of woman's work. 336 pp. 12°. *Boston, am. tract society,* 1873.

Duval (Amaury Pineu). Les fontaines de Paris. Eng. title, 2 p. l. 144 pp. 60 pl. fol. *Paris, F. Didot,* [1813].

Duval (Ch.) **Kaufmann** (A.) **Renaud** (Ed.) *and others.* Petites maisons de ville et de campagne. 4 p. l. 60 pl. on 59 l. fol. *Paris, librairie centrale d'architecture,* [18—].

Duyckinck (Evert A.) *and* **Duyckinck** (George L.) Cyclopædia of american literature. Edited to date by M. Laird Simons. 2 v. Eng. title, xxii, 990 pp. 28 pl; eng. title, xiv, 1054 pp. 4°. *Philadelphia, T. E. Zell,* 1875.

Dwight (Benjamin W.) History of the descendants of elder John Strong, of Northampton, Mass. 2 v. lxii, 764 pp. 15 ports; 765–1586 pp. 1 l. 4 ports. 8°. *Albany, J. Munsell,* 1871.

Dwyer (Francis). Seats and saddles, bits and bitting. xiii, 265 pp. 7 pl. 12°. *Edinburgh, W. Blackwood & sons,* 1868.

Dyer (*Rev.* Sidney). Black diamonds. Ill. title, 320 pp. 8 pl. 16°. *Philadelphia, bible & publication society,* [1874].

——— Boys and birds. Ill. title, 414 pp. 3 col. pl. 12 pl. 16°. *Philadelphia, bible & publication society,* [1874].

——— Great wonders in little things. Eng. title, 333 pp. 8 col. pl. *Philadelphia, bible & publication society,* [1874].

——— Home and abroad. Col. title, 319 pp. 8 pl. 16°. *Philadelphia, bible & publication society,* [1872].

Earle (John Charles). English premiers. 2 v. in 1. xix, 334 pp; xiii, 312 pp. 12°. *London, Chapman & Hall,* 1871.

Eassie (William, *c. e.*) Cremation of the dead. xi, 132 pp. 6 pl. 8°. *London, Smith, Elder & co.* 1875.

Eastlake (*Sir* Charles Lock). Contributions to the literature of the fine arts. Second series. With memoir by lady Eastlake. v, 346 pp. 8°. *London, J. Murray,* 1870.

Eastlake (*Lady* Elizabeth Rigby). Life of John Gibson. ix, 255 pp. port. 8°. *London, Longmans,* 1870.

——— Memoir of sir Charles Lock Eastlake.
[*In* EASTLAKE (*Sir* Charles Lock). Contributions to the literature of the fine arts. Second series. 8°. *London,* 1870. pp. 1–192].

Eastman (Edwin). Seven and nine years among the Camanches and Apaches. 309 pp. 8 pl. 12°. *Jersey City, C. Johnson,* 1873.

Eastman (*Rev.* Hubbard). Noyesism unveiled. 432 pp. 12°. *Brattleboro, author,* 1849.

Eastwood (*Rev.* Jonathan). History of the parish of Ecclesfield, in the county of York. xvi, 558 pp. 2 pl. 1 pedigree. 8°. *London, Bell & Daldy,* 1862.

Eaton (*Rev.* John Richard Turner). Permanence of christianity. xix, 387 pp. 8°. *London, Rivingtons,* 1873.
[BAMPTON lectures, 1872].

Eaton (Lilley). Genealogical history of the town of Reading, Mass. xxviii, 815 pp. 14 pl. 8°. *Boston, A. Mudge & son,* 1874.

Ebeling (A.) Sketches of modern Paris. From the german by F. Locock. x, 324 pp. 12°. *London, R. Bentley,* 1870.

Eberhard (Johann August) *and* **Maasz** (Johann Gebhard Ehrenreich). Versuch einer allgemeinen teutschen synonymik in einem kritisch-philosophischen wörterbuche der sinnverwandten wörter der hochteutschen mundart. 3te ausg. fortgesetzt von J. G. Gruber. 6 v. in 3. 8°. *Leipzig, J. A. Barth,* 1826.

Eckel (Lizzie St. John). Maria Monk's daughter. xvi, 5–604 pp. 9 ports. 12 pl. 12°. *New York, for the author,* 1874.

Ecquevilly (Armand François Hennequin, *marquis* d'). Campagnes du corps sous les ordres de son altesse le prince de Condé. 3 v. 8°. *Paris, Le Normant,* 1818.

Edelfrida; a novel. [*anon.*] 4 v. 16°. *London, T. Hookham & J. Carpenter,* 1792.

Edgeworth (Mary L.) Southern gardener and receipt-book. 3d ed. 478 pp. 12°. *Philadelphia, J. B. Lippincott & co.* 1859.

Edwardes (Annie). Archie Lovell. 289 pp. 1 pl. 8°. *New York, W. P. & F. C. Church,* 1867.

——— Estelle. 432 pp. 12°. *New York, Sheldon & co.* 1874.

——— Ordeal for wives. [*anon.*] 448 pp. 12°. *New York, Sheldon & co.* [1873].

——— Ought we to visit her? 194 pp. 8°. *New York, Sheldon & co.* [1871].

——— Vagabond heroine. 1 p. l. 322 pp. 12°. *London, R. Bentley & son,* 1873.

Edwardes (*Sir* Herbert Benjamin) *and* **Merivale** (Herman). Life of sir Henry Lawrence. 2d ed. 2 v. xii, 492 pp; xii, 396 pp. 8°. *London, Smith, Elder & co.* 1872.

Edwards (Amelia Blandford). In the days of my youth. 454 pp. 8°. *Philadelphia, Porter & Coates*, 1874.

——— Outlines of english history. Am. ed. 106 pp. 16°. *Boston, Hickling, Swan & Brewer*, 1857.

——— Untrodden peaks and unfrequented valleys. xxvi, 385 pp. incl. 1 pl. 1 map, 7 pl. 8°. *London, Longmans*, 1873.

Edwards (Henry Sutherland). Life of Rossini. viii, 344 pp. port. 8°. *London, Hurst & Blackett*, 1869.

Edwards (Matilda Betham). Holiday letters from Athens, Cairo, and Weimar. 3 p. l. 247 pp. 12°. *London, Strahan & co.* 1873.

Effinger (*Rev.* Conrad Maria). Die betende seele. 432, 32 pp. incl. 4 pl. 3 pl. 18°. *Einsiedeln, C. & N. Benziger*, 1872.

——— Unser heil in Christo. 480 pp. 3 pl. 18°. *Einsiedeln, [etc.] C. & N. Benziger*, [1874].

Eggleston (Edward, *d. d.*) Christ in art. 295 pp. incl. 99 pl. front. 4°. *New York, J. B. Ford & co.* 1875.

——— Christ in literature. 421 pp. 1 l. 6 pl. 8°. *New York, J. B. Ford & co.* 1875.

——— Circuit rider. 2 p. l. 332 pp. 1 pl. 12°. *New York, J. B. Ford & co.* 1874.

——— End of the world. 299 pp. 15 pl. 12°. *New York, O. Judd & co.* [1872].

——— Schoolmaster's stories. 279 pp. incl. 4 pl. 12°. *Boston, H. L. Shepard & co.* 1874.

Eggleston (George Cary). How to make a living. 127 pp. 12°. *New York, G. P. Putnam's sons*, 1875.
[PUTNAM's handy book series].

——— Man of honor. 222 pp. incl. 10 pl. 12° *New York, O. Judd co.* [1873].

——— Rebel's recollections. vi pp. 1 l. 260 pp. 16°. *New York, Hurd & Houghton*, 1875.

Egleston (Thomas, *jr.*) Lectures on mineralogy. 1 p. l. xxix, 192 pp. 34 pl. on 17 l. 8°. *New York, D. Van Nostrand*, 1872.

Egmond van der Nyenburg (Johannes Ægidius van) *and* **Heyman** (John). Travels through part of Europe, Asia minor, the Archipelago, Syria, Palestine, Egypt, &c. From the low dutch. 2 v. xii, 395 pp. 4 pl; vi, 376 pp. 8 l. 2 pl. 8°. *London, for L. Davis & C. Rymers*, 1759.

Eguiara y Eguren (Juán José de). Bibliotheca mexicana. Tomus primus exhibens litteras A B C. 80 p. l. 544 pp. fol. *Mexici, ex nova typogr. in ædibus authoris*, 1755.
Note.—No more published.

Eiloart (C. J.) Out of her sphere. 3 v. 12°. *London, R. Bentley & son*, 1872.

Einhorn (*Rev.* David). Olath tamid. Book of prayers for israelitish congregations. vi, 394 pp. 8°. *New York, [Deutsch & Golderman, printers, Baltimore*, 1872].

Eisenmenger (Johann Andreas). Entdecktes judenthum. 2 v. in 1. 10 p. l. 1016 pp. 1 l; 2 p. l. 1111 pp. 4°. *Königsberg*, 1711.

Elder (Abraham). Tales and legends of the Isle of Wight. 2d ed. 1 p. l. v–viii, 336 pp. 14 pl. 16°. *London, Simpkin, Marshall & co.* 1843.

Elder (William). Questions of the day. 367 pp. 8°. *Philadelphia, H. C. Baird*, 1871.

Elderhorst (William). Manual of qualitative blow-pipe analysis. Edited by H. B. Nason, and C. F. Chandler. 4th ed. 310 pp. 12°. *Philadelphia, T. E. Zell*, 1874.

Eldridge (Abby, *pseud.*) Norman Brill's life-work. 218 pp. incl. front. 16°. *New York, national temperance publ. house*, 1875.

Eliot (*Sir* Edward Granville, 3*d earl of st. Germans*). Papers relating to lord Eliot's mission to Spain in 1835. ix, 148 pp. 8°. *London, [Bickers & son]*, 1871.

Eliot (Samuel). History of the United States. From 1492 to 1872. xvi, 507 pp. 4 maps. 12°. *Boston, Brewer & Tileston*, 1874.

Elliot (Frances). Diary of an idle woman in Italy. 2 v. in 1. x, 316 pp; vi, 329 pp. 16°. *London, Chapman & Hall*, 1871.

——— Pictures of old Rome. New ed. 4 p. l. 316 pp. 12°. *London, Chapman & Hall*, 1872.

——— Romance of old court-life in France. 3 p. l. 254 pp. 20 pl. 8°. *New York, D. Appleton & co.* 1873.

Elliot (Samuel H.) Look at home; or, life in the poorhouse of New England. New ed. 490 pp. 6 pl. 12°. *New-York, H. Dexter & co.* 1860.

Elliott (J. W.) National nursery rhymes and songs. Set to music by J. W. Elliott. With illustrations, by the brothers Dalziel. 4 p. l. 111 pp. front. 8°. *London, G. Routledge & sons*, [1870].

Ellis (*Sir* Henry). History of the parish of Saint Leonard Shoreditch, and liberty of Norton Folgate, in the suburbs of London. 2 p. l. 370 pp. 8 pl. 4°. *London, J. Nichols*, 1798.

Ellis (Sumner). At our best. 2 p. l. 307 pp. 16°. *Boston, Lee & Shepard*, 1873.

Elsner (Johann Gottfried). Ungarn durchreiset, beurtheilet und beschrieben. 2 v. in 1. v, 315, vi, 392 pp. 12°. *Leipzig, A. Frohberger,* 1840.

Elwes (Alfred). Through Spain by rail in 1872. xii, 340 pp. 12°. *London, E. Wilson,* 1873.

Emerson (Ralph Waldo, *editor*). Parnassus. 1 p. l. xlii, 534 pp. 12°. *Boston, J. R. Osgood & co.* 1875.

Emerson (William D.) Rhymes of culture, movement, and repose. 312 pp. 12°. *Cincinnati, G. E. Stevens & co.* 1874.

Emery (George Alexander). Ancient city of Gorgeana and modern town of York (Maine). 192 pp. incl. 1 pl. 18°. *Boston, G. A. Emery,* 1873.

Emigration: letters from Sussex emigrants, who sailed, in 1832, for Upper Canada. xii, 103, 4 pp. 1 map. 8°. *Petworth,* [*Eng.*] *J. Phillips,* 1833.

Emma; or the unfortunate attachment. New ed. [*anon.*] 2 v. xii, 250 pp. 1 pl; 292 pp. 1 pl. 16°. *London, for T. Hookham,* 1787.

Encyclopædia Britannica. 9th ed. [Edited by T. S. Baynes. A–Boissonade]. v. 1–3. 4°. *Edinburgh, A. & C. Black,* [*and*] *Boston, Little, Brown & co.* 1875.

——— Same. 9th ed. (Am. reprint). v. 1–2. 8°. *Philadelphia, J. M. Stoddart & co.* 1875.

Ensayo imparcial sobre el gobierno del rey d. Fernando VII. [*anon.*] 290 pp. 16°. *Paris, librería de Rosa,* 1824.

Ensayo sobre las libertades de la iglesia española en ambos mundos. [*anon.*] 1 p. l. 245 pp. 8°. *Londres, M. Calero,* 1826.

Épinay (Louise Florence Petronille Tardieu d'Esclavelles, *madame* de la Live d'). Mémoires. Éd. nouv. avec des additions des notes et des éclaircissements inédits par m. Paul Boiteau. 2 v. 2 p. l. viii, 460 pp; 2 p. l. 500 pp. 16°. *Paris, Charpentier,* 1865.

Episodes in an obscure life. [*anon.* New ed.] 2 v. 3 p. l. 221 pp; 3 p. l. 221 pp. 12°. *London, Strahan & co.* 1871.

Epps (John, *m. d.*) Life of John Walker, m. d. 2d ed. viii, 342 pp. 8°. *London, Whittaker, Treacher & co.* 1832.

Eppstein (*Rabbi* E.) Biblical history. 277 pp. 3 l. 8°. *Milwaukie, J. D. Razall & co.* 1873.

Equal to either fortune. [*anon.*] 3 v. 12°. *London, Tinsley brothers,* 1869.

Erckmann (Émile) *and* **Chatrian** (Alexandre). Histoire d'un sous-maître. [etc.]

Erckmann *and* **Chatrian**—continued.
8e éd. 284 pp. 16°. *Paris, J. Hetzel & cie.* 1873.

——— ——— La maison forestière. 5e éd. 3 p. l. 307 pp. 12°. *Paris, librairie internationale,* [1866].

——— ——— Same. Forest house and Catherine's lovers. Translated by J. Simms. 1 p. l. 272 pp. 1 pl. 16°. *London, S. Low, son & Marston,* 1871.

Erdeswicke (Sampson). Survey of Staffordshire. 3 p. l. 224 pp. 3 l. 8 pp. 5 l. 8°. *London, for W. Mears, and J. Hooke,* 1723.

——— Same. Collated with manuscript copies, and with additions by Wyrley and others, by Thomas Harwood, d. d. New ed. ci, 588 pp. 7 pl. 2 l. of pedigrees. 8°. *London, J. B. Nichols & son,* 1844.

——— Survey of Staffordshire. 1798–1801. *See* **Shaw** (S.) History and antiquities of Staffordshire.

Erhard (Heinrich August). Geschichte des wiederaufblühens wissenschaftlicher bildung. 3 v. 8°. *Magdeburg, Creutz'sche buchhandlung,* 1827–32.

Erizzo (Sebastiano). Le sei giornate. 406 pp. 1 l. port. 8°. *Milano, dalla società tipografica de' classici italiani,* 1805.

Ernst (Oswald H.) Manual of practical military engineering. 296 pp. 5 pl. 12°. *New York, D. Van Nostrand,* 1873.

Errázuriz (Crescente). Los oríjenes de la iglesia chilena, 1540–1603. 3 p. l. 9–562 pp. 8°. *Santiago, imprenta del Correo,* 1873. s.

Errázuriz (Federico). Chile bajo el imperio de la constitucion de 1828. 344 pp. 8°. *Santiago, imprenta chilena,* 1861. s.

Escosura y Hevia (Antonio de la). Juicio crítico del feudalismo en España. 2 p. l. 125 pp. 1 l. 8°. *Madrid, J. M. Alegria,* 1856. s.

Esquirol (Jean Étienne Dominique). Mental maladies. From the french, by E. K. Hunt, m. d. 496 pp. 8°. *Philadelphia, Lea & Blanchard,* 1845.

Essays in defence of women. [*anon.*] viii, 283 pp. 12°. *London, Tinsley brothers,* 1868.

Essex archæological society, *Colchester, Eng.* Transactions. v. 1–3. 8°. *Colchester, for the society,* 1858–65.

Étrennes de Polymnie; choix de chansons, avec de la musique nouvelle et des timbres d'airs connus. [*anon.*] 7 p. l. 308 pp. 18°. *Paris, Bélin,* 1788.

Eustace (Thomas). Adventures and providential deliverances. Eng. title, 1 p. l. 147 pp. 1 pl. 8°. *London, J. Hatchard & son,* 1820.

Evangelical alliance conference, 1873. History, essays, and other documents of the sixth conference, held in New York, oct. 2-12, 1873. Edited by rev. Philip Schaff, d. d. and rev. S. Irenæus Prime, d. d. iv, 773 pp. 8°. *New York, Harper & brothers,* 1874.

Evans (Albert S.) A la California. Life in the golden state. 379 pp. 24 pl. 8°. *San Francisco, A. L. Bancroft & co.* 1873.

Evans (David M.) Landmarks of truth. 1 p. l. 493 pp. 1 tab. 6 pl. 8°. *Philadelphia, Quaker city publishing co.* 1873.

Evans (Elizabeth Edson). Abuse of maternity. 129 pp. 12°. *Philadelphia, J. B. Lippincott & co.* 1875.

Evans (John). Ancient stone implements, weapons, and ornaments of Great Britain. xvi, 640 pp. 2 pl. 8°. *London, Longmans,* 1872.

Evans (Madison). Biographical sketches of the pioneer preachers of Indiana. 422 pp. 22 ports. 1 pl. 12°. *Philadelphia, J. Challen & sons,* 1862.

Evans (Marian). Wit and wisdom of George Eliot. [*pseud.*] 1 p. l. v, 260 pp. 18°. *Boston, Roberts brothers,* 1873.

Evans (Thomas William, *m. d. editor*). History of the american ambulance in Paris during the siege of 1870-71. xxxviii, 695 pp. incl. 1 pl. 10 pl. 8°. *London, for the autnor,* 1873.
[SANITARY associations during the franco-german war of 1870-1871, v. 1].

Everts (Hermann). Complete history of the ninth regiment New Jersey vols. infantry. 197 pp. 8°. *Newark, N. J., A. S. Holbrook,* 1865.

Evill (William). Winter journey to Rome and back. xi, 164 pp. 12°. *London, E. Stanford,* 1870.

Ewald (Alexander Charles). The crown and its advisers. vii, 222 pp. 12°. *Edinburgh, W. Blackwood & sons,* 1870.

——— Life and times of the hon. Algernon Sydney, 1622-1683. 2 v. xii, 405 pp. 1 tab; viii, 377 pp. 8°. *London, Tinsley brothers,* 1873.

——— Our public records. viii, 158 pp. 8°. *London, B. M. Pickering,* 1873.

Eyton (*Rev.* Robert Wynne). Antiquities of Shropshire. 12 v. in 11. 8°. *London, J. R. Smith,* 1854-60.

Faber (Johannes). Animalia mexicana, descriptionibus scholijsq. exposita. Thesavri rervm medicarvm Novae Hispaniae Francisci Hernandi et Nardi Antonii Recchi: scilicet primi tomi pars. 3 p. l. 459-840 pp. fol. *Romae, apud I. Mascardum,* 1628.

Fabre (Ferdinand). Abbé Tigrane. Translated by the rev. L. W. Bacon. 272 pp. 12°. *New York, J. B. Ford & co.* 1875.

Fabre-d'Olivet (Antoine). La langue hébraïque restitué. 2 v. in 1. xlviii, 197, 138 pp; 348 pp. 1 l. 4°. *Paris, l'auteur,* 1815-16.

——— *editor.* Le troubadour, poésies occitaniques du XIIIe. siècle; traduites par Fabre-d'Olivet. 2 v. Eng. title, 2 p. l. xi, lxviij, 222 pp. 1 l; eng. title. 1 p. l. 292 pp. 1 l. 8°. *Paris, Henrichs,* 1803.

Faden (William, *publisher*). North american atlas. 2 p. l. 27 maps. fol. *London, for W. Faden,* 1777.

Faehtz (Ernest F. M.) *and* **Pratt** (Frederick W.) Real estate directory of Washington, D. C. 1873-4. 3 v. fol. *Washington,* [*E. F. M. Faehtz & F. W. Pratt,* 1873-74].

——— ——— Washington in embryo; or, the national capital from 1791 to 1800, [etc.] iv, 78 pp. 3 plans. 4°. [*Washington, Gibson brothers*], 1874.

Fairfield (Francis Gerry). Clubs of New York. 349 pp. 8°. *New York, H. L. Hinton,* 1873.

——— Ten years with spiritual mediums. 182 pp. 12°. *New York, D. Appleton & co.* 1875.

——— *editor.* Poems by Henry Sylvester Cornwell, Francis Gerry Fairfield, Luther Granger Riggs, and Ruth G. D. Havens [etc.] 1 p. l. xxiv, 528 pp. 18°. *West Meriden, Conn. L. G. Riggs & co.* 1875.

Fairholt (Frederick William). Homes, haunts, and works of Rubens, Vandyke, Rembrandt, and Cuyp; [etc.] xiv, 266 pp. incl. 1 pl. 8°. *London, Virtue & co.* 1871.

——— Homes, works, and shrines of english artists. [Also] rambles in Rome. x, 182 pp. 23 pl. sq. 12°. *London, Virtue & co.* 1873.

——— *editor.* Dictionary of terms in art. vi, 474 pp. incl. front. 12°. *London, Strahan & co.* [1870].

Fairley (W.) Epitaphiana: or, the curiosities of churchyard literature. viii, 171 pp. 12°. *London, S. Tinsley,* 1873.

Faithfull (Emily). Reed shaken with the wind. vi, 11-286 pp. 12°. *New York, Adams, Victor & co.* [1873].

Falkner (W. C.) Spanish heroine. 136 pp. 12°. *Cincinnati, I. Hart & co.* 1851.

Falloux (Alfred Frédéric Pierre, *comte* de). Madame Swetchine: sa vie et ses œuvres. 6e éd. 2 v. 2 p. l. iv, 508 pp; 2 p. l. 432 pp. 16°. *Paris, Didier & cie.* 1863.

Fall-River (*Mass.*) Catalogue of the public library. xii, 383 pp. 8°. *Boston, Rand, Avery & co.* 1874.

Farjeon (B. L.) Joshua Marvel. 3 v. 12°. *London, Tinsley brothers,* 1871.

——— London's heart. 3 v. 12°. *London, Tinsley brothers,* 1873.

Farley (*Rev.* Stephen). Discourses and essays. vii, 400 pp. 12°. *Boston, H. Farley,* 1851.

Farman (Ella). Anna Maylie. 402 pp. 2 pl. 16°. *Boston, D. Lothrop & co.* 1873.

——— Girl's money. Eng. title, 272 pp. 2 pl. 16°. *Boston, D. Lothrop & co.* [1874].

——— Grandma Crosby's household. 1 p. l. 215 pp. 16°. *Boston, D. Lothrop & co.* 1873.

——— Little woman. 3 p. l. 11-195 pp. 1 pl. 16°. *Boston, D. Lothrop & co.* [1873].

——— White hand. 251 pp. front. 16°. *Boston, D. Lothrop & co.* 1875.

Farrar (Frederic William, *d. d.*) Life of Christ. 11th ed. 2 v. xxxii, 480 pp. 1 pl; xii, 516 pp. 1 pl. 8°. *London, Cassell, Petter & Galpin,* [1874].

——— Same. With an american appendix. 1 p. l. v-vi, 744 pp. 2 pl. 8°. *Albany, R. Wendell,* 1875.

Fastré (*Rev.* J. A. M.) Acts of the early martyrs. 3d series. 290 pp. 12°. *Philadelphia, P. F. Cunningham,* 1873.

Faulkner (Thomas, *m. d.*) Book of nature. 143 pp. 12°. *New York, Hurst & co.* [1875].

Faunce (*Rev.* D. W.) Fletcher prize essay.—Christian in the world. viii, 236 pp. 16°. *Boston, Roberts brothers,* 1875.

Fauriel (Claude Charles). Histoire de la poésie provençale. 3 v. 8°. *Paris, J. Labitte,* 1846.

Fawcett (Edgar). Purple and fine linen. 483 pp. 12°. *New York, G. W. Carleton & co.* 1873.

Fawcett (Henry) *and* **Fawcett** (*Mrs.* Millicent Garrett). Essays and lectures. vii, 368 pp. 8°. *London, Macmillan & co.* 1872.

Fawcett (J.) Dialogues on the other world. 5 p. l. 170 pp. 12°. *London, for the author,* 1759.

Fawcett (*Mrs.* Millicent Garrett). Tales in political economy. 4 p. l. 104 pp. 16°. *London, Macmillan & co.* 1874.

Faxon (Charles A. *publisher*). Illustrated hand-book of travel by the Fitchburg, Rutland and Saratoga railway line, to Saratoga, [etc.] 193 pp. 15 l. 3 maps. 16°. *Boston, C. A. Faxon,* 1873.

——— Same. Revised ed. 12, 210 pp. incl. 20 pl. 3 maps. 16°. *Boston, C. A. Faxon,* 1874.

Fay (Theodore S.) Views in New-York and its environs. From drawings, by Dakin, with illustrations by T. S. Fay. Eng. title, 1-58, 43-46 pp. 14 pl. 1 plan. 4°. *New York, Peabody & co.* 1831.

Fellöcker (*Padre* Sigmund). Geschichte der sternwarte der Benediktiner-abtei Kremsmünster. 2 p. l. 322 pp. 2 pl. 4°. *Linz, druck von J. Feichtinger's erben,* 1864. s.

Fellowes (*Rev.* Robert). Guide to immortality. 3 v. 8°. *London, J. White,* 1804.

Feltham (John). Tour through the Island of Man, in 1797-98. Edited by the rev. Robert Airey. xvi, 272 pp. 1 map, 1 pedigree, 2 pl. 8°. *Douglas,* [*Isle of Man*], 1861.

[MANX society. Publications, v. 6].

——— *and* **Wright** (Edward). Memorials of "God's acre", being monumental inscriptions in the Isle of Man, taken in 1797. Edited by William Harrison. xv, 132 pp. 8°. *Douglas,* [*Isle of Man*], 1868.

[MANX society. Publications, v. 14].

Feltman (William). Journal, 1781-82. Including the march into Virginia and siege of Yorktown. 48 pp. 8°. *Philadelphia, for the historical soc. of Pennsylvania,* 1853.

Fendler (Augustus). Mechanism of the universe. 158 pp. 1 l. 5 pl. 8°. *Wilmington, Del. "commercial printing co."* 1874.

Fenech (Johannes Lucas). Flores casvvm conscientiæ, [etc.] Quinta ed. 8 p. l. 576 pp. 4 l. 24°. *Coloniæ, apud J. W. Friessem,* 1692.

Fenn (George Manville, *editor*). Book of fair women. 166 pp. incl. 40 pl. 8°. *London, Cassell, Petter & Galpin,* [1873].

Fenner (C. S.) Vision. Embracing physical optics, physiological optics, errors of refraction. 3 p. l. xiii-299 pp. 8°. *Philadelphia, Lindsay & Blakiston,* 1875.

Ferber (Johann Jacob). Travels through Italy, in 1771 and 1772. From the german. By R. E. Raspe. xxxiv, 377 pp. 8°. *London, for L. Davis,* 1776.

Ferdinand IV. *king of Castile and Leon.* Memorias. Anotadas [etc.] por d. A. Bena-

Ferdinand IV.—continued. vides. 2 v. 2 p. l. cxvii, 696 pp. 2 l. 1 facs. 2 col. pl; 2 p. l. 912 pp. 1 l. 4°. *Madrid, J. Rodriguez,* 1860. s.

Ferguson (James). Life, in a brief autobiographical account, and further extended memoir. By Ebenezer Henderson. 2d ed. xxxvi, 503 pp. port. 1 map. 8°. *Edinburgh, A. Fullarton & co.* 1870.

Ferguson (Joseph). Life-struggles in rebel prisons. 206, xxiv pp. 4 pl. 1 port. 16°. *Philadelphia, J. M. Ferguson,* 1865

Ferland (*L'abbé* J. B. A.) Biographical notice of Joseph-Octave Plessis. Translated by T. B. French. xiv, 3–179 pp. 8°. *Quebec, G. & G. E. Desbrats,* 1864.

Fernald (Woodbury M.) True christian life and how to attain it. Essays. v, 309 pp. phot. port. 12°. *Boston, Noyes, Holmes & co.* 1874.

Fernandez (Juan Patricio). Historica relatio, de apostolicis missionibus patrum societatis Jesu apud Chiquitos. Hodie in linguam latinam translata. 20 p. l. 276 pp. 9 l. 4°. *Augustæ Vindelicorum, sumptibus M. Wolff,* 1733.

Fernandez de San Salvador (*Dr.* Augustin Pomposo). Los Jesuitas quitados y restituidos al mundo. Historia de la antigua California. 1–128, 179–214 pp. 5 l. 18°. *México, M. Ontiveros,* 1816.

Ferrand (*Comte* Antoine de). L'esprit de l'histoire. 5e éd. 4 v. 8°. *Paris, Déterville,* 1809.

Feugère (Léon). Essai sur la vie et les ouvrages de Henri Estienne. 2 p. l. 372 pp. 12°. *Paris, J. Delalain,* 1853.

Feuillée (Louis). Journal des observations physiques, mathématiques et botaniques, faites sur les côtes orientales de l'Amérique méridionale, & dans les Indes occidentales, depuis 1707 jusques en 1712. 2 v. [611] pp. 57 maps & pl; 4 p. l. 768 pp. 73 pl. 8°. *Paris, P. Giffart,* 1714.

Feuillet (Octave). Led astray. — The sphinx —"Bellah." From the latest Paris ed. by O. Vibeur. 412 pp. 12°. *New York, G. W. Carleton & co.* 1875.

Feuillet de Conches (Félix Sébastien, *baron*). Causeries d'un curieux. 4 v. 8°. *Paris, H. Plon,* 1862–68.

Féval (Paul Henri Corentin). Capitaine Simon. La fille de l'émigré. 2 p. l. 313 pp. 12°. *Paris, librairie nouvelle,* 1858.

[*With* ABOUT (E. F. V.) Trente et quarante. *Paris,* 1859].

Feydeau (Ernest Aimé). Histoire des usages funèbres et des sépultures des peuples anciens. 2 v. 2 p. l. 404 pp. 26 pl; 2 p. l. 164 pp. 21 pl. fol. *Paris, Gide & J. Baudry,* 1856–58.

[Wanting livraisons 20–22].

Feyjoo y Montenegro (Francisco Benito Geronimo). Essay on the learning, genius and abilities of the fair-sex. From the spanish. [*anon.*] 1 p. l. v–xx, 227 pp. 18°. *London, for D. Steel,* 1774.

——— Essays or discourses, from the works of Feyjoo, translated by J. Brett. 4 v. 8°. *London, for the translator,* 1780.

Field (*Mrs.* Henry Martyn). Home sketches in France, and other papers. 256 pp. port. 12°. *New York, G. P. Putnam's sons,* 1875.

Field (Kate). Hap-hazard. 253 pp. 18°. *Boston, J. R. Osgood & co.* 1873.

——— Ten days in Spain. 277 pp. 1 pl. 18°. *Boston, J. R. Osgood & co.* 1875.

Field (Margaret). Bertha Percy. 567 pp. 12°. *New York, D. Appleton & co.* 1860.

Field (Maunsell B.) Memories of many men and of some women. 2 p. l. 339 pp. 8°. *New York, Harper & brothers,* 1874.

Field (Thomas W.) Essay towards an indian bibliography. iv, 430 pp. 8°. *New York, Scribner, Armstrong & co.* 1873.

Figuier (Guillaume Louis). The human race. xvi, 548 pp. incl. 62 pl. 8 col. pl. 8°. *London, Chapman & Hall,* 1872.

Fillias (Achille). Géographie de l'Algérie. 3e éd. 2 p. l. 154 pp. 1 l. 1 col. map. 16°. *Paris, Hachette & cie.* 1874.

Finley (Martha). Elsie's womanhood. 1 p. l. 406 pp. 3 pl. 16°. *New York, Dodd & Mead,* [1875].

Fiorellio (Giuseppe). Pompeianarvm antiqvitatvm historia. Nvnc primvm collegit indicibvsqve instrvxit Ios. Fiorelli. 2 v. 4 p. l. 317, 189, 280 pp. 6 pl; 2 p. l. 688 pp. 8°. *Neapoli,* 1860–62.

Fish (E. J. *d. d.*) Ecclesiology. Constitution of the new testament church. With a supplement on ordination. 399 pp. 12°. *New York, authors' publishing co.* 1875.

Fish (Henry Clay, *d. d.*) Handbook of revivals. 428 pp. 12°. *Boston, J. H. Earle,* 1874.

——— Harry's conflicts. Ill. title, 224 pp. 4 pl. 16°. *Philadelphia, bible and publication society,* [1872].

——— Harry's conversion. Ill. title, 240 pp. 4 pl. 16°. *Philadelphia, bible and publication society,* [1872].

Fish (Henry Clay, *d. d.*)—continued.

——— Heaven in song. xxii, 742 pp. sm. 4°. *New York, Sheldon & co.* 1874.

——— Pulpit eloquence of the nineteenth century. With a supplement, to 1874, and introductory essay, by E. A. Park, d. d. 919 pp. 7 pl. 8°. *New York, Dodd & Mead,* [1874].

Fishbourne (E. Gardiner). Our ironclads and merchant ships. 108 pp. 11 pl. 8°. *London, E. & F. N. Spon,* 1874.

Fisher (Frances C.) Daughter of Bohemia. By Christian Reid [*pseud.*] 222 pp. 16 pl. 8°. *New York, D. Appleton & co.* 1874.

——— Hearts and hands. By Christian Reid [*pseud.*] 99 pp. 8°. *New York, D. Appleton & co.* 1875.

[APPLETON's library of american fiction].

——— Nina's atonement. By Christian Reid [*pseud.*] 2 p. l. 154 pp. 7 pl. 8°. *New York, D. Appleton & co.* 1873.

——— Question of honor. By Christian Reid [*pseud.*] iv, 501 pp. 12°. *New York, D. Appleton & co.* 1875.

Fisher (George Park, *d. d.*) The reformation. xxxiv, 620 pp. 8°. *New York, Scribner, Armstrong & co.* 1873.

Fiske (Albert A.) Fiske family. History of the family of William Fiske, sen. of Amherst, N. H. 2d ed. viii, [219] pp. 1 pl. 12°. *Ch ago,* 1867.

Fiske (John). Myths and myth-makers. 251 pp. 12°. *Boston, J. R. Osgood & co.* 1873.

——— Outlines of cosmic philosophy. 2 v. xv, 465 pp; vii, 523 pp. 12°. *Boston, J. R. Osgood & co.* 1875.

Fitzgerald (Percy). The Kembles. An account of the Kemble family. 2 v. xxiii, 353 pp. 7 ports. 1 facs; vi, 414 pp. 5 ports. 2 facs. 8°. *London, Tinsley brothers,* [1871].

——— Life of Alexander Dumas. 2 v. xiii, 302 pp. 1 port; viii, 314 pp. 8°. *London, Tinsley brothers,* 1873.

——— Principles of comedy and dramatic effect. 368 pp. 8°. *London, Tinsley brothers,* 1870.

——— Romance of the english stage. 2 v. xi, 334 pp; 3 p. l. 328 pp. 8°. *London, R. Bentley & son,* 1874.

——— Two fair daughters. 3 v. 12°. *London, Hurst & Blackett,* 1871.

Fitzmaurice (Edmond George, *lord*). Life of William, earl of Shelburne. v. 1. xiv, 413 pp. 8°. *London, Macmillan & co.* 1875.

Flagg (William). Good investment. 1 p. l. 9-116 pp. 1 pl. 8°. *New York, Harper & brothers,* 1872.

Flagg (Wilson). Birds and seasons of New England. vii, 457 pp. 12 heliot. pl. 12°. *Boston, J. R. Osgood & co.* 1875.

Flammarion (Camille). Stories of infinity. From the french by S. R. Crocker. 287 pp. 16°. *Boston, Roberts brothers,* 1873.

Flanders (Henry). Exposition of the constitution of the United States. 2d ed. rev. 295 pp. 12°. *Philadelphia, Claxton, Remsen & Haffelfinger,* 1874.

——— Lives and times of the chief justices of the supreme court of the United States. [2d ed.] 2 v. xxv, 647 pp. 1 port; xvi, 9-560 pp. 1 l. 1 port. 8°. *New York, J. Cockcroft & co.* 1875.

Fleming (George). Horse-shoes and horse-shoeing. xvi, 692 pp. col. front. 8°. *London, Chapman & Hall,* 1869.

——— Rabies and hydrophobia. xiii, 405 pp. 2 col. pl. 8°. *London, Chapman & Hall,* 1872.

Fleming (Howard). Narrow gauge railways in America. 79 pp. 1 pl. 8°. *Lancaster, Pa. inquirer print. co.* 1875.

Fleming (May Agnes). Guy Earlscourt's wife. 438 pp. 12°. *New York, G. W. Carleton & co.* 1873.

——— Mad marriage. 459 pp. 12°. *New York, G. W. Carleton & co.* 1875.

——— Terrible secret. 410 pp. 12°. *New York, G. W. Carleton & co.* 1874.

——— Wonderful woman. 544 pp. 12°. *New York, G. W. Carleton & co.* 1873.

Flemming (D. Lambden, *m. d.*) Life and death. vi, 500 pp. 5 pl. 8°. *Philadelphia, the author,* [1873].

Fletcher (Matilda). Practical ethics. viii, 154 pp. front. sq. 12°. *New York, A. S. Barnes & co.* 1875.

——— Same. viii, 154 pp. front. 12°. *Des Moines, Ia. Mills & co.* 1875.

Fleury (*L'abbé* Claude). Oeuvres de l'abbé Fleury, précédées d'un essai sur sa vie et ses ouvrages; par m. [L.] Aimé Martin. 2 v. 3 p. l. 714 pp; 2 p. l. 648 pp. 16°. *Paris, Lefèvre,* 1844.

——— Catéchisme historique. 2 p. l. 282 pp. 12°. *Paris, Lecoffre fils & cie.* 1868.

Flinn (Charles, *alias* Charles Mortimer). Life and career of Charles Mortimer. 111 pp. inc. 1 port. 8°. *Sacramento, record steam book printing house,* 1873.

Flint (Austin, *m. d.*) Essays on conservative medicine. 4 p. l. 13–214 pp. 12°. *Philadelphia, H. C. Lea*, 1874.

——— Phthisis. xi, 17–446 pp. 8°. *Philadelphia, H. C. Lea*, 1875.

Flint (Austin, *jr. m. d.*) Text-book of human physiology. xviii, 978 pp. 3 pl. 8°. *New York, D. Appleton & co.* 1876.

Flint (Charles Louis). Agricultural schools of Europe. 120 pp. 8°. *Boston*, 1864. s.

Flögel (Karl Friedrich). Geschichte der hofnarren. xx, 530 pp. 2 pl. 8°. *Liegnitz und Leipzig, D. Siegert*, 1789.

——— Geschichte des burlesken. x, 260 pp. 1 l. 8°. *Leipzig, im Schwickertschen verlage*, 1794.

Florencia (Francisco de, *s. J.*) Zodiaco Mariano, [etc.] Obra posthuma, reducida à compendio, [etc.] por el p. Jvan Antonio de Oviedo. 12 p. l. 328 pp. sm. 4°. *Mexico, real colegio de San Ildefonso*, 1755.

Florenzano (Giovanni). Della emigrazione italiana in America comparata alle altre emigrazioni europee. xv, 368 pp. 2 tab. 8°. *Napoli, F. Giannini*, 1874.

Flourens (Marie Jean Pierre). History of the discovery of the circulation of the blood. From the french, by J. C. Reeve, m. d. viii, 11–178 pp. 16°. *Cincinnati, Rickey, Mallory & co.* 1859.

Flower (William). Visitation of Lancaster, in 1567. Edited by the rev. F. R. Raines. 2 p. l. xvi, 141 pp. sm. 4°. [*Manchester*], 1870.

[CHETHAM society remains, v. 81].

Floy Lindsley and her friends. [*anon.*] 29 pp. 4 pl. 16°. *New York, am. tract society*, [1875].

Floyd (Cornelia). Mice at play. By Neil Forest [*pseud.*] 2 p. l. 271 pp. 16°. *Boston, Roberts brothers*, 1876.

Floyd (Mary Faith). The Nereid. 102 pp. 8°. *Macon, Ga. J. W. Burke & co.* 1871.

Fogg (Alonzo J.) Statistics and gazetteer of New-Hampshire. xiv, 674 pp. 11 pl. 1 map. 8°. *Concord, N. H., D. L. Guernsey*, 1874.

Folger (Isaac H.) Handbook of Nantucket, [Mass. *anon.*] 1 p. l. 91 pp. 1 map. 18°. *Nantucket*, [*Ms.*] *Island review office*, 1874.

——— Same. [New ed.] 1 p. l. 97 pp. 1 map. 18°. *Nantucket*, [*Ms.*] *Island review office*, 1875.

Follett (Eliza G.) Young housekeeper's assistant. 141 pp. 12°. *Sandusky, O. register steam print*, 1874.

Fonblanque (Albany). Life and labours. Edited by his nephew E. B. de Fonblanque. 2 p. l. 546 pp. 8°. *London, R. Bentley & son*, 1874.

Fontenelle (Bernard le Bovier de). Lives of philosophers. [Translated by John Chamberlayne]. 8 p. l. xxxv, 464 pp. 8°. *London, W. Innys*, 1717.

Foot (Samuel A.) Autobiography. 2 v. 436 pp. 5 ports; 1 p. l. 5–507 pp. 8°. *New York*, [*Smith & McDougal*], 1872.

Foote (Edward B. *m. d.*) Science in story. Sammy Tubbs, and "Spousie". 5 v. sq. 18°. *New York, Murray hill publishing co.* 1874.

Foote (Henry Stuart). Casket of reminiscences. 2 p. l. 498 pp. 8°. *Washington, chronicle publishing co.* 1874.

Foppens (Jean François). Bibliotheca belgica, ad annum M.D.C.LXXX. xliv, 600 pp. 77 ports; 1 p. l. 601–1233 pp. 67 ports. 4°. *Bruxellis, P. Foppens*, 1739.

Forbes (Archibald). My experiences of the war between France and Germany. 2 v. 5 p. l. 476 pp; 4 p. l. 503 pp. 8°. *London, Hurst & Blackett*, 1871.

Ford (Sally Rochester). Evangel Wiseman. 507 pp. 12°. *St. Louis, Barnes & Benyon*, 1874.

Ford (William F.) Industrial interests of Newark, N. J. 2 p. l. 271 pp. 1 col. map, 1 pl. 8°. *New York, Van Arsdale & co.* 1874.

Forman (H. Buxton). Our living poets. xii, 512 pp. 12°. *London, Tinsley brothers*, 1871.

Forney (John W.) Anecdotes of public men. 2 p. l. 9–444 pp. 12°. *New York, Harper & brothers*, 1873.

Forney (Matthias N.) Catechism of the locomotive. xvi, 609 pp. 1 pl. 12°. *New York, railroad gazette*, 1875.

Forrest (Neil). Honest and earnest. 257 pp. 3 pl. 16°. *New York, A. D. F. Randolph & co.* [1872].

Forrest (William S.) Great pestilence in Virginia; account of the yellow fever in Norfolk and Portsmouth in 1855. xiii, 326 pp. front. 12°. *New York, Derby & Jackson*, 1856.

Forsyth (William). Essays critical and narrative. 4 p. l. 462 pp. 8°. *London, Longmans*, 1874.

——— Novels and novelists of the eighteenth century. viii, 347 pp. 12°. *London, J. Murray*, 1871.

Fort (George F.) Early history and antiquities of freemasonry. front. 490 pp. 8°. *Philadelphia, S. P. Putnam*, 1875.

Forwood (W. Stump, *m. d.*) Historical and descriptive narrative of the Mammoth cave of Kentucky. 4th ed. 241 pp. 12 pl. 1 map. 16°. *Philadelphia, J. B. Lippincott & co.* 1875.

Fosbrooke (*Rev.* Thomas Dudley). Original history of the city of Gloucester. viii, 236 pp. 22 pl. fol. *London, J. Nichols & son*, 1819.

Foss (Edward). Biographia juridica. xv, 792 pp. 8°. *London, J. Murray*, 1870.

——— Memories of Westminster hall. v. 1. 3 p. l. 295 pp. 9 pl. 6 ports. 8°. *New York, J. Cockcroft & co.* 1874.

Foster (*Mrs.* J. H.) Mr. Mackenzie's answer. By Faye Huntington [*pseud.*] 351 pp. incl. front. 16°. *New York, national temperance pub. house*, 1875.

——— Those boys. By Faye Huntington [*pseud.*] 334 pp. 2 pl. 16°. *Boston, D. Lothrop & co.* [1875].

Foster (John William). Pre-historic races of the United States. 1 p. l. 415 pp. incl. 7 pl. 1 pl. 8°. *Chicago, S. C. Griggs & co.* 1873.

Foster (Joseph, *compiler*). Pedigrees of the county families of England. v. 1. Lancashire. 4°. *London, for the compiler*, 1873.

——— Pedigrees of the county families of Yorkshire. 3 v. 4°. *London, for the compiler*, 1874.

CONTENTS.

v. 1–2. West Riding.
v. 3. North and East Riding.

Fournier (Édouard). L'esprit dans l'histoire. 3e éd. 2 p. l. 468 pp. 18°. *Paris, E. Dentu*, 1867.

——— L'esprit des autres recueilli et raconté. 3e éd. 2 p. l. 288 pp. 18°. *Paris, E. Dentu*, 1867.

Fournier (Pierre, *s. J.*) Institutiones philosophicæ. viii, 647 pp. 8°. *Lutetiæ Parisiorum, Julien, Lanier, et soc.* 1854.

Fowle (Thomas Welbank). Reconciliation of religion and science. xix, 404 pp. 8°. *London, H. S. King & co.* 1873.

Fowler (William Worthington). Fighting fire. The great fires of history. [*anon.*] 716 pp. incl. 26 pl. 8°. *Hartford, Conn. Dustin, Gilman & co.* 1873.

Fox (Tilbury, *m. d.*) Skin diseases. 2d am. from 3d Lond. ed. xiv, 532 pp. 8°. *New York, W. Wood & co.* 1873.

Foy (Maximilien Sébastien). Discours, précédés d'une notice biographique par P. F. Tissot; d'une éloge par m. Étienne, et d'un essai sur l'éloquence politique en France, par m. Jay. 2 v. 1 p. l. cxxvii, 472 pp. port. 1 facs; 2 p. l. xxxix, 524 pp. 8°. *Paris, P. A. Moutardier*, 1826.

Fraas (Carl). Die schule des landbaues. 2te aufl. xii, 418, 12 pp. 8 pl. 8°. *München, literarisch-artistische anstalt*, 1852.

Fradesso da Silveira (Joaquim Henriques). Congresso meteorologico de Vienna de Austria em 1873. 2 p. l. 246 pp. 18°. *Lisboa, imprensa nacional*, 1874. S.

Francis (John). Annals, anecdotes and legends of life insurance. xii, 327 pp. 12°. *London, Longmans*, 1853.

Francis (Laura). Kate Parker. 464 pp. 2 pl. 16°. *Boston, congregational pub. soc.* [1874].

Francke (August Hermann). Guide to the holy scriptures. From the latin, by W. Jaques. 1st am. from the last Lond. ed. 249 pp. 16°. *Philadelphia, D. Hogan*, 1823.

Franco (Giovanni Giuseppe, *s. J.*) Tigranes. Abridged from the italian. 368 pp. 12°. *Philadelphia, P. F. Cunningham & son*, 1874.

Franco (Nicolo). Dialogi piacevoli. 8 p. l. 143 l. numb. 1 pl. 18°. *Vinegia, G. Giolito de Ferrari*, 1545.

François (Jean). Dictionnaire roman, walon, celtique et tudesque. [*anon.*] xii, 364 pp. 4°. *Bouillon, impr. de la soc. typog.* 1777.

Franklin (Benjamin). Life of Franklin. Now first edited from original manuscripts and from his correspondence, by John Bigelow. 3 v. 12°. *Philadelphia, J. B. Lippincott & co.* 1874.

Franklin (J.) History of Egypt. 3 v. 12°. *Newcastle on Tyne, J. Mitchell*, 1800–02.

Fraser (Alexander Campbell). Life and letters of George Berkeley; and an account of his philosophy. With many writings hitherto unpublished. xviii, 672 pp. port. 8°. *Oxford, Clarendon press*, 1871.

Fraser (Donald, *d. d.*) Life and diary of the rev. Ebenezer Erskine. xix, 543 pp. 1 port. 12°. *Edinburgh, W. Oliphant*, 1831.

——— Life and diary of the rev. John Henry Gardner. xvii, 252 pp. 1 port. 12°. *Edinburgh, M. Paterson*, 1836.

——— Life and diary of the rev. Ralph Erskine. 561 pp. 1 port. 12°. *Edinburgh, W. Oliphant & son*, 1834.

Fraser (John). Humorous chap-books of Scotland. Parts i–ii. xii, 156 pp; 2 p. l. 157–288 pp. 1 pl. 12°. *New York, H. L. Hinton*, 1873.

Freaks and follies of fabledom. [*anon.*] 2 p. l. 120 pp. 12°. *London, J. Ollivier*, 1852.

Free (John, *d. d.*) Essay towards an history of the English tongue. 4th ed. xxxiv, 29–148 pp. 8°. *London, for the author*, 1788.

Freeman (Edward Augustus). Comparative politics. ix, 522 pp. 8°. *London, Macmillan & co.* 1873.

——— Growth of the english constitution. xiv, 224 pp. 12°. *London, Macmillan & co.* 1872.

——— Outlines of history. ix, 366 pp. 16°. *New York, H. Holt & co.* 1873.

[FREEMAN (E. A.) Historical course for schools, v. 1].

——— *editor.* Historical course for schools. v. 1–5. 16°. *New York, H. Holt & co.* 1873–74.

CONTENTS.

1. FREEMAN (E. A.) Outlines of history. 1873.
2. THOMPSON (Edith). History of England. 1873.
3. MACARTHUR (M.) History of Scotland. 1874.
4. HUNT (W.) History of Italy. 1874.
5. SIME (James). History of Germany. 1874.

Freeman (*Rev.* James M.) Hand-book of bible manners and customs. 515 pp. incl. 11 pl. 12°. *New York, Nelson & Phillips*, 1874.

Frejes (Francisco). Memoria historica de la conquista particular de Jalisco por los Españoles. [*anon.*] 2 p. l. 212 pp. 18°. [1838?]

French home life. [*anon.*] 2 p. l. 349 pp. 12°. *Edinburgh, W. Blackwood & sons*, 1873.

Frere (Alice M.) The antipodes. 2 v. in 1. 4 p. l. 633 pp. 7 pl. 8°. *London, Hatchards*, 1870.

Frere (John Hookham). Works. In verse and prose. 2 v. ccxcv, 322 pp. 1 port; 496 pp. 1 port. 8°. *London, B. M. Pickering*, 1872.

Frescobaldi (Lionardo di Niccolo'). Viaggio in Egitto e in terra santa. 1 p. l. xiii, 196 pp. 1 l. 8°. *Roma, C. Mordacchini*, 1818.

Freshfield (Douglas W.) Travels in the central Caucasus and Bashan. 1 p. l. v–xv, 509 pp. 3 maps, 5 pl. incl. 1 col. 12°. *London, Longmans*, 1869.

Freytag (Georg Wilhelm Friedrich). Einleitung in das studium der arabischen sprache. xii, 511 pp. 8°. *Bonn, A. Marcus*, 1861.

Friedmann (Alexander). Rapport officiel sur la marine et les travaux maritimes à l'exposition universelle de Vienne en 1873. Traduction de l'allemand. 1 p. l. vii, 189 pp. 1 tab. on 2 l. 19 pl. 8°. *Vienne, imprimerie impériale et royale*, 1874. S.

Friswell (James Hain). A man's thoughts. xvi, 318 pp. 16°. *London, S. Low, Marston, Low & Searle*, 1872.

Fröhlich (E.) Der Rhein von Mannheim bis Düsseldorf. Eng. title, 24 pl. obl. 8°. *Mannheim, G. Zeiler*, [1840?]

Frost (Charles). Notices relative to the early history of Hull. xvi, 151, 58 pp. 7 pl. 2 pedigrees. 4°. *London, J. B. Nichols*, 1827.

Frost (Thomas). Old showmen, and the old London fairs. xii, 388 pp. 12°. *London, Tinsley brothers*, 1874.

Frothingham (*Rev.* Octavius Brooks). Religion of humanity. 338 pp. 16°. *New York, D. G. Francis*, 1873.

——— Theodore Parker: a biography. viii, 588 pp. 1 port. 8°. *Boston, J. R. Osgood & co.* 1874.

Frothingham (Richard). The centennial: battle of Bunker hill. 4 p. l. 136 pp. 1 plan, 1 facs. 16°. *Boston, Little, Brown & co.* 1875.

Fulford (Francis, *d. d.*) Sermons, addresses and statistics of the diocese of Montreal. xv, 308 pp. 1 pl. 8°. *Montreal, Dawson brothers*, 1865.

Fuller (Edwin W.) Sea-gift. A novel. 408 pp. 12°. *New York, E. J. Hale & son*, 1873.

Fuller (Harvey A.) Trimsharp's [*pseud.*] account of himself. 150 pp. incl. 2 pl. 12°. *Ann Arbor, Mich. Ann Arbor printing and publishing co.* 1873.

Fuller (Hiram). Grand transformation scenes in the United States. vii, 311 pp. 16°. *New York, G. W. Carleton & co.* 1875.

Fuller (John, *m. d.*) History of Berwick-upon-Tweed. xxi, 601, 50 pp. 8 pl. 8°. *Edinburgh, Bell & Bradfute*, 1799.

Fuller (Osgood E.) Candle of Latimer and daughter of Zion. [*anon.*] 224 pp. 16°. *Philadelphia, King & Baird*, 1875.

Fullerton (*Lt. col.* —). Views in the Himalaya and Neilgherry hills. 28 l. 24 col. pl. 1 map. obl. 8°. *London, Dickinson & co.* [1848].

Fullerton (Amy Fullerton). Lady's ride through Palestine & Syria. viii, 349 pp. 8 pl. 12°. *London, S. W. Partridge & co.* 1872.

Fulton (Charles Carroll). Europe viewed through american spectacles. 312 pp. 8°. *Philadelphia, J. B. Lippincott & co.* 1874.

Fulton (Justin D. *d. d.*) Show your colors. 209 pp. front. 16°. *New York, U. D. Ward,* [1875].

Furman (*Rev.* Charles E.) Home scenes, and other poems. 156 pp. 12°. *Rochester, E. Darrow,* 1874.

Furman (Gabriel). Antiquities of Long Island. [Also] bibliography by H. Onderdonk, jr. Edited by F. Moore. 478 pp. 12°. *New York, J. W. Bouton,* 1875.

——— Notes relating to the town of Brooklyn. *Brooklyn, A. Spooner,* 1824. Reprinted.

[*In* FURMAN (G.) Antiquities of Long Island. 12°. *New York,* 1875. pp. 273–434].

Furness (*Mrs.* Horace Howard). Concordance to Shakespeare's poems. iv, 422 pp. 8°. *Philadelphia, J. B. Lippincott,* 1874.

Furniss (William). Land of the Cæsar and doge. Eng. title, 384 pp. 12°. *New York, Cornish, Lamport & co.* [1852].

[Imperfect: wanting title].

——— Tetra-chordon: pot pourri of rhythms and prose. 144 pp. 12°. *New York, am. news co.* 1874.

——— Waraga, or the charms of the Nile. 456 pp. 8 col. pl. 12°. *New-York, Baker & Scribner,* 1850.

Fürst (Julius). Hebräisches und chaldäisches handwörterbuch über das alte testament. 2 v. in 1. vi, 806 pp. 2 l. 564 pp. 8°. *Leipzig, B. Tauchnitz,* 1857–61.

Fustel de Coulanges (Numa Denis). The ancient city: a study on the religion, laws, and institutions of Greece and Rome. From the latest french ed. by W. Small. 529 pp. 8°. *Boston, Lee & Shepard,* 1874.

G. (A. P. D.) Sketches of portuguese life. [*anon.*] xxvii, 364 pp. 1 l. 20 col. pl. 8°. *London, for G. B. Whittaker,* 1826.

Gabelentz (Hans Conon von der) *and* **Loebe** (J.) Glossarium der gothischen sprache. 1 p. l. xviii, 244 pp. 4°. *Leipzig, F. A. Brockhaus,* 1843.

[*In* BIBLE. (*Gothic*). Ulfilas. v. 2, part 1].

——— ——— Grammatik der gothischen sprache. viii, 298 pp. 1 pl. 4°. *Leipzig, F. A. Brockhaus,* 1846.

[*In* BIBLE. (*Gothic*). Ulfilas. v. 2, part 2].

Gabet (Gabriel). Traité élémentaire de la science de l'homme. 3 v. 8°. *Paris, J.-B. Baillière,* 1842.

Gaboriau (Émile). Clique of gold. From the french. 210 pp. 8°. *Boston, J. R. Osgood & co.* 1874.

——— La dégringolade. 5ème éd. 2 v. 2 p. l. 574 pp; 2 p. l. 545 pp. 16°. *Paris, E. Dentu,* 1874.

——— Other people's money. From the french. 188 pp. 8°. *Boston, J. R. Osgood & co.* 1875.

——— Widow Lerouge. From the french by F. Williams and G. A. O. Ernst. 156 pp. 8°. *Boston, J. R. Osgood & co.* 1873.

——— Within an inch of his life. From the french. 212 pp. 8°. *Boston, J. R. Osgood & co.* 1874.

[OSGOOD's library of novels, no. 41].

Gaddi (Giambattista). Roma nobilitata nelle sue fabbriche dalla santità di nostro signore Clemente XII. 4 p. l. 210 pp. 1 port. sm. fol. *Roma, A. de' Rossi,* 1736.

Gage (*Rev.* William Leonard). Home of God's people. 557 pp. incl. 16 pl. front. 8°. *Hartford, Dustin, Gilman & co.* 1874.

——— Light in darkness. [*anon.*] 123 pp. 16°. *Boston, Gould & Lincoln,* 1864.

——— Trinitarian sermons preached to a unitarian congregation. 3 p. l. 153 pp. 16°. *Boston, J. P. Jewett & co.* 1859.

——— *editor.* Favorite hymns. xii, 5–115 pp. 16°. *New York, A. S. Barnes & co.* 1874.

Gahan (*Rev.* William). Sermons for every sunday in the year. New ed. xix, 633 pp. 8°. *New York, D. & J. Sadlier & co.* 1875.

Gale (Ethel C.) Hints on dress. iv, 107 pp. 12°. *New York, G. P. Putnam & sons,* 1872.

[PUTNAM's handy-book series].

Galérie théâtrale. [*anon.*] 144 pl. in 3 v. fol. *Paris, Bance,* [1833–34].

[Imperfect; v. 1 wants pl. 11–12].

Gallenga (Antonio). Pearl of the Antilles. 2 p. l. 202 pp. 8°. *London, Chapman & Hall,* 1873.

Gallery of english and american women famous in song. [*anon.*] Ill. title, 576 pp. front. 4°. *Philadelphia, J. M. Stoddart & co.* [1875].

Galt (John). Last of the lairds. [*anon.*] 240 pp. 12°. *New York, J. & J. Harper,* 1827.

Galton (Francis). English men of science. xiv, 270 pp. 8°. *London, Macmillan & co.* 1874.

Gandillot (R.) Principes de la science des finances. 3 v. 8°. *Paris, Guillaumin & cie.* [1875].

Gannett (William C.) Ezra Stiles Gannett. A memoir. By his son. xv, 9–572 pp. port. 12°. *Boston, Roberts brothers,* 1875.

Gardiner (Samuel Rawson). History of England under the duke of Buckingham and Charles I. 1624–1628. 2 v. xxii, 366 pp. 1 map; xiv, 386 pp. 1 map. 8°. *London, Longmans,* 1875.

Gardner (Augustus Kinsley, *m. d.*) Old wine in new bottles: or, spare hours of a student in Paris. xii, 332 pp. 12°. *New-York, C. S. Francis & co.* 1848.

Gardner (Celia E.) Broken dreams. [Poems]. 252 pp. 6 pl. 12°. *New York, G. W. Carleton & co.* 1873.

——— Rich Medway's two loves. 463 pp. 12°. *New York, G. W. Carleton & co.* 1875.

——— Tested. 430 pp. 12°. *New York, G. W. Carleton & co.* 1874.

Gardner (E. C.) Homes, and how to make them. 314 pp. incl. 5 pl. 12°. *Boston, J. R. Osgood & co.* 1874.

——— Illustrated homes. 1 p. l. vii–287 pp. incl. 24 plans & 12 pl. 16°. *Boston, J. R. Osgood & co.* 1875.

Gardner (H. C.) Discontent, and other stories. 339 pp. 16°. *New York, Nelson & Phillips,* [1874].

——— Glimpses of our lake region in 1863. 420 pp. 16°. *New York, Nelson & Phillips,* [1874].

Gardner (Matthew). Autobiography. Edited by N. Summerbell, d. d. 286 pp. port. 2 facs. 8°. *Dayton, O. christian publishing association,* 1874.

Gardner (W. W. *d. d.*) Missiles of truth. x, 304 pp. 12°. *Cincinnati, G. E. Stevens & co.* 1874.

Garnier (Léon). Dictionnaire universel des contemporains. Par G. Vapereau. Supplément à la 4e éd. 2 p. l. iv, 181 pp. 8°. *Paris, Hachette & cie.* 1873.

[*With* VAPEREAU (G.) Dictionnaire universel des contemporains. 4e éd. 1870–73].

Garretson (*Dr.* James E.) Two thousand years after. By John Darby [*pseud.*] 166 pp. 16°. *Philadelphia, Claxton, Remsen & Haffelfinger,* 1876.

Garrett (Alexander Charles). Historical continuity: a series of sketches on the church. viii, 148 pp. 16°. *New-York, T. Whittaker,* [1875].

Gasc (Ferdinand E. A.) Dictionary of the english and french languages. [Eng. french part]. 2 p. l. 597–1182 pp. 1 l. 8°. *London, G. Bell & sons,* 1875.

Gascoyne (A. M.) Sunbeams from a western hemisphere. By A. M. G. [*anon.*] 117 pp. 16°. *Dublin, McGlashan & Gill,* 1874.

Gaskell (John). New elements from old subjects: presented as the basis for a science of the mind. xiii pp. 1 l. 196 pp. 8°. *Philadelphia, Claxton, Remsen & Haffelfinger,* 1874.

Gasparin (Valérie Boissier, *comtesse* Agenor de). Au bord de la mer. [*anon.*] 2 p. l. 353 pp. 12°. *Paris, M. Lévy frères,* 1866.

——— Vesper. Translated from the 3d french ed. by Mary L. Booth. 308 pp. 1 pl. 12°. *New York, R. Carter & brothers,* 1863.

Gattel (Claude Marie). Nuevo diccionario portatil, español é ingles. 8 p. l. 461 pp. sq. 16°. *Paris, Bossange, Masson y Besson,* 1803.

Gaulle (*Mme.* J. de, *née* Maillot). Adhemar de Belcastel. [*anon.*] From the french by P. S. A. 314 pp. 2 pl. 12°. *New York, catholic publication soc.* 1875.

Gaume (Jean Joseph). Christian cemetery in the nineteenth century. From the french by rev. Richard Brennan. 253 pp. 12°. *New York, Benziger brothers,* 1874.

——— Sign of the cross in the nineteenth century. From the last french ed. 330 pp. 12°. *Philadelphia, P. F. Cunningham,* 1873.

Gauthier (Jules). Histoire de Marie Stuart. 2e éd. 2 v. xvi, 593 pp. 3 l; 2 p. l. 575 pp. 8°. *Paris, E. Thorin,* 1875.

Gautier (Théophile). Constantinople. Nouv. éd. 364 pp. 16°. *Paris, M. Lévy frères,* 1873.

——— Same. Constantinople. From the french by R. H. Gould. Am. ed. 2 p. l. 363 pp. 12°. *New York, H. Holt & co.* 1875.

——— Les grotesques. Nouv. éd. xv, 400 pp. 16°. *Paris, M. Lévy frères,* 1873.

——— Les jeunes-France. Romans goguenards. Suivis de contes humoristiques. 2 p. l. xix, 371 pp. 16°. *Paris, Charpentier & cie.* 1873.

——— Mademoiselle de Maupin. Nouv. ed. 2 p. l. 384 pp. 16°. *Paris, Charpentier & cie.* 1873.

——— Militona. 5e éd. 1 p. l. 178 pp. 16°. *Paris, L. Hachette & cie.* 1869.

——— Nouvelles. 10e éd. 420 pp. 16°. *Paris, Charpentier & cie.* 1872.

——— Portraits contemporains. 3e éd. 2 p. l. 464 pp. port. 12°. *Paris, Charpentier & cie.* 1874.

Gautier (Théophile)—continued.
——— Portraits et souvenirs littéraires. 2 p. l. 320 pp. 16°. *Paris, M. Lévy frères,* 1875.
——— Quand on voyage. 2 p. l. 353 pp. 16°. *Paris, M. Lévy frères,* 1865.
——— Roman de la momie. Nouv. éd. 3 p. l. 306 pp. 16°. *Paris, Charpentier & cie.* 1873.
——— Romans et contes. 2 p. l. 459 pp. 16°. *Paris, Charpentier & cie.* 1872.
——— Les Vosges, par J. J. Bellel : vingt dessins d'après nature. Texte descriptif par Théophile Gautier. 2 p. l. 15 pp. 20 l. 20 pl. fol. *Paris, A. Morel & cie.* 1860.
——— Voyage en Espagne. Nouv. éd. vii, 375 pp. 16°. *Paris, Charpentier & cie.* 1873.
——— Voyage en Russie. 2 v. 2 p. l. 401 pp ; 2 p. l. 295 pp. 16°. *Paris, Charpentier & cie.* 1867.
——— Same. Winter in Russia. From the french by M. M. Ripley. 3 p. l. 348 pp. 12°. *New York, H. Holt & co.* 1874.
——— **Houssaye** (Arsène), *and* **Saint-Victor** (*Comte* Paul de). Les dieux et les demi-dieux de la peinture. Illustrations par m. Calamatta. 1 p. l. iii, 440 pp. 15 pl. 8°. *Paris, Morizot,* [1863].

Gay (Jean). Bibliographie des ouvrages relatifs à l'Afrique et à l'Arabie. xi, 312 pp. 8°. *San Remo, J. Gay & fils,* 1875.

Gay (Marie Françoise Sophie Nichault de Lavalette). Celebrated saloons, by madame Gay ; and Parisian letters, by madame Girardin. From the french, by L. Willard. vii, 260 pp. 18°. *Boston, W. Crosby & H. P. Nichols,* 1851.

Gay (Mary A. H.) Pastor's story and other pieces. 8th ed. iv, 265 pp. 12°. *Baltimore, Turnbull brothers,* 1873.

Gébé (Victor). Catalogue de journaux publiés ou paraissant à Paris en 1874. 2 p. l. 103 pp. 16°. *Paris, O. Lorenz,* 1875.

Gegenbaur (Carl). Grundzüge der vergleichenden anatomie. 2te aufl. xii, 892 pp. 8°. *Leipzig, W. Engelmann,* 1870.
——— Untersuchungen zur vergleichenden anatomie der wirbelthiere. 3 parts in 1 v. 4°. *Leipzig, W. Engelmann,* 1864–72.

Geiger (Abraham). Was hat Mohammed aus dem judenthume aufgenommen? 1 p. l. vi, 215 pp. 8°. *Bonn, gedruckt auf kosten des verfassers,* 1833.

Geiger (John Lewis). Peep at Mexico. xiv, 353 pp. 4 col. maps, 45 photos. 8°. *London, Trübner & co.* 1874.

Geikie (Cunningham, *d. d.*) Life in the woods. x, 405 pp. 4 pl. 16°. *London, Strahan & co.* 1873.

Genlis (Stéphanie Félicité Ducrest de Saint-Albin, *comtesse de, depuis marquise de Sillery*). The duchess de la Vallière and madame de Maintenon. Romances. 2 v. xix, 339 pp ; 1 p. l. xvi, 329 pp. 12°. *London, H. Colburn,* 1837.

Geoffroy Saint-Hilaire (Isidore). Vie, travaux et doctrine scientifique d'Étienne Geoffroy Saint-Hilaire. 3 p. l. 479 pp. port. 8°. *Paris, P. Bertrand,* 1847.

George (Augustus C. *d. d.*) Short sermons. 306 pp. 12°. *New York, Nelson & Phillips,* 1873.

George (*Rev.* Nathan D.) Universalism not of the bible. 2d ed. 458 pp. 12°. *New York, Nelson & Phillips,* 1873.

Gérard (François, *baron*). Oeuvre. 1789–1836. 3 v. fol. *Paris, Vignères* [*and*] *Rapilly,* 1852–57.

Gerbet (*L'abbé* Olympe Philippe). Lily of Israel; life of the virgin Mary. From the french. New ed. 1 p. l. 7–385 pp. 1 pl. 16°. *New York, D. & J. Sadlier & co.* 1873.

Gerstäcker (Friedrich). Streif- und jagdzüge durch die Vereinigten Staaten. 2 v. in 1. vii, 311 pp ; 2 p. l. 323 pp. 12°. *Leipzig, Arnoldische buchhandlung,* 1856.

Gervais (Paul). Éléments de zoologie. 2e éd. xii, 596 pp. 3 col. pl. 8°. *Paris, Hachette & cie.* 1871.
——— *and* **Van Beneden** (Pierre Joseph). Zoologie médicale. 2 v. xii, 504 pp ; viii, 455 pp. 8°. *Paris, J. B. Baillière & fils,* 1859.
——— **Marchand** (Léon), *and* **Raulin** (Félix Victor). Notions élémentaires d'histoire naturelle. [v. 1]. Année préparatoire. [v. 2]. Année première. 6 parts in 2 v. 16°. *Paris, Hachette & cie.* 1869–72.

Gesenius (Friederich Heinrich Wilhelm). Scripturae linguaeque Phoeniciae monumenta. 3 v. in 2. 4°. *Lipsiae, sumptibus F. C. G. Vogelii,* 1837.
——— Thesavrvs philologicvs criticvs lingvae hebraeae et chaldaeae veteris testamenti. Editio altera. 3 v. in 2. 4°. *Lipsiae, svmtibvs F. C. G. Vogelii,* 1829–58.

Gibbons (*Mrs.* P. E.) "Pennsylvania dutch." 2d ed. 318 pp. 16°. *Philadelphia, J. B. Lippincott & co.* 1874.

Gilchrist (J. G. *m. d.*) Homœopathic treatment of surgical diseases. 1 p. l. 9–421 pp. 8°. *Chicago, C. S. Halsey,* 1873.

Gilder (Richard Watson). The new day, a poem. 112 pp. sq. 16°. *New York, Scribner, Armstrong & co.* 1876.

Giles (Ella A.) Bachelor Ben. 308 pp. 12°. *Madison, Wis. Atwood & Culver,* 1875.

Gilfillan (Robert). Poems and songs. 4th ed. With memoir. xxx, 382 pp. 1 port. 16°. *Edinburgh, Sutherland & Knox,* 1851.

Gill (Thomas). Vallis Eboracensis: comprising the history of Easingwold and its neighbourhood. xiii, 17–456 pp. incl. 1 pl. 15 pl. 8°. *London, Simpkin, Marshall & co.* 1852.

Gill (*Rev.* William I.) Evolution and progress. 3 p. l. 295 pp. 12°. *New York, authors' publishing co.* 1874.

Gillet (Ransom H.) Life of Silas Wright. 2 v. xiv, 1008 pp. port. 1 pl; viii, 1009–2016 pp. 2 pl. 1 facs. 8°. *Albany, argus co.* 1874.

Gillett (E. H. *d. d.*) God in human thought. 2 v. 416 pp; 1 p. l. 417–834 pp. 8°. *New York, Scribner, Armstrong & co.* 1874.

——— Moral system. 231 pp. 12°. *New York, Scribner, Armstrong & co.* 1874.

Gillmore (Parker). Adventures afloat and ashore. 2 v. 1 p. l. v–x, 297 pp. front; 1 p. l. v–ix, 267 pp. front. 12°. *London, Hurst & Blackett,* 1873.

——— Prairie and forest. x, 383 pp. 13 pl. 12°. *London, Chapman & Hall,* 1874.

Gillray (James). Works; with the history of his life and times. Edited by T. Wright. 1 p. l. 376 pp. 82 pl. 4°. *London, Chatto & Windus,* [1873].

Gilman (Arthur). First steps in general history. x, 385 pp. 2 tab. 4 maps. 16°. *New York, Hurd & Houghton,* 1874.

——— Seven historic ages. iv, 144 pp. 8 pl. 16°. *New York, Hurd & Houghton,* 1874.

Gilmore (*Prof.* J. H.) Outlines of the art of expression. 103 pp. sq. 16°. *Rochester, [N. Y.] evening express printing co.* 1875.

Gilpin (William). Mission of the north american people. 217 pp. 6 col. maps. 8°. *Philadelphia, J. B. Lippincott & co.* 1873.

——— Same. 2d ed. 223 pp. 6 maps. 8°. *Philadelphia, J. B. Lippincott & co.* 1874.

Girard (C. F.) Lettre d'un citoyen des États-Unis sur la crise religieuse du canton de Vaud. viii, 272 pp. 12°. *Paris, [Basle printed], librairie protestante,* 1849.

Girard (C F.)—continued.

——— Scènes de la vie baloise pendant la semaine de la bataille de Saint-Jacques. viii, 148 pp. 12°. *Bâle, F. Schneider,* 1844.

Girard de Propiac (Cathérine Joseph Ferdinand, *chevalier*). Beautés de l'histoire du Pérou. xvi, 366 pp. 4 pl. 12°. *Paris, Vernarel & Tenon,* 1825.

Girardin (*Mme.* Émile de, *née* Delphine Gay). Parisian letters.

[*In* GAY (M. F. S. N. de L.) Celebrated saloons. 18°. *Boston, W. Crosby & H. P. Nichols,* 1851. pp. 191–260].

——— *and others.* Cross of Berny. 290 pp. 12°. *Philadelphia, Porter & Coates,* [1873].

Girtanner (Christoph). Historische nachrichten und politische betrachtungen über die französische revolution. 2te aufl. 13 v. 8°. *Berlin, [Schade],* 1794–98.

[Imperfect: title to v. 11 wanting].

——— Same. Fortgesetzt von Friedrich Buchholz. v. 15. 8°. *Berlin, [Schade],* 1802.

Gladstone (William Ewart). Rome and the newest fashions in religion. lxxxi, 190 pp. 8°. *London, J. Murray,* 1875.

——— Vatican decrees in their bearing on civil allegiance. [Also], a history of the Vatican council; with text of the papal syllabus. By Philip Schaff. 168 pp. 8°. *New York, Harper & brothers,* 1875.

Glapthorne (Henry). Plays and poems now first collected, with notes and a memoir of the author. 2 v. xxxvi pp. 1 l. 253 pp; vii, 271 pp. 12°. *London, J. Pearson,* 1874.

Glazier (Lewis). History of Gardner, Mass. to 1860. 163 pp. 12°. *Worcester, [Ms.] C. Hamilton,* 1860.

Glisan (R. *m. d.*) Journal of army life. [1849–58]. xi, 511 pp. 1 tab. 21 pl. 8°. *San Francisco, A. L. Bancroft & co.* 1874.

Glover (Mary Baker). Science and health. 456 pp. 12°. *Boston, christian scientist publishing co.* 1875.

Glover (Stephen). History and gazetteer of the county of Derby. Edited by T. Noble. v. 1–2, part 1 in 2 v. viii pp. 7 l. 365, 110 pp. 2 pl; viii, 623 pp. 8 pl. 4 pedigrees. 4°. *Derby, for the publishers by H. Mozley & sons,* 1831–33.

Glover (Townend). Manuscript notes from my journal. Diptera or two-winged flies. 2 p. l. 3, 120 l. pag. 13 pl. interleaved with 13 l. 4°. *Washington, J. F. Gedney,* 1874.

Goblet (H. F.) Theory of sight. 1 p. l. 310 pp. 8°. *London, Chapman & Hall,* 1869.

Godard d'Aucour de Saint-Just (Claude, *baron*). Essais littéraires de Saint-Just. 2 v. vii, 387 pp. 1 port; vii, 459 pp. 8°. *Paris, Le Normant père*, 1826.

Goddard (Abba A. *editor*). Trojan sketch book. 180 pp. 1 pl. 12°. *Troy, N. Y. Young & Hart*, 1846.

Goddard (Julia). Wonderful stories from northern lands. xxiv, 208 pp. 6 pl. 12°. *London, Longmans*, 1871.

Goddard (Martha L. B.) *and* **Preston** (Harriet W.) *compilers*. Sea and shore. Poems. [*anon.*] 2 p. l. 220 pp. 18°. *Boston, Roberts brothers*, 1874.

Godman (Frederick Du Cane). Natural history of the Azores. v pp. 1 l. 358 pp. 2 maps. 8°. *London, J. Van Voorst*, 1870.

Godwin (Francis, *d. d. bishop of Hereford*). Catalogve of the bishops of England. 6 p. l. 700 pp. 1 pl. 4°. *London, for T. Adams*, 1615.

Godwin (William). Essays. viii, 294 pp. 16°. *London, H. S. King & co.* 1873.

Goldsmid (*Sir* Frederic John). Telegraph and travel, [etc.] xv, 673 pp. 4 pl. 3 maps, 1 port. 8°. *London, Macmillan & co.* 1874.

Gomez de Avellaneda (*Señora doña* Gertrudis). Obras literarias. 5 v. 8°. *Madrid, M. Rivadeneyra*, 1869–71.

Gondrecourt (Henri Ange Aristide, *baron* de). La guerre des amoureux. 3 v. in 1. 18°. *Paris, G. Paetz*, 1866.

Gonzalès (Louis Jean Emmanuel) *and* **Demolière** (Hippolyte Jules). Les sept baisers de Buckingham. Par Emm. Gonzalès et Moléri [*pseud.*] 2 v. in 1. 160, 167 pp. 18°. *Paris, G. Paetz*, 1865.

Goodman (Walter). Pearl of the Antilles. xiv, 304 pp. 12°. *London, H. S. King & co.* 1873.

Goodrich (Aaron). History of the so-called Christopher Columbus. Front. viii, 403 pp. 8°. *New York, D. Appleton & co.* 1874.

Goodrich (De Witt C.) *and* **Tuttle** (Charles R.) Illustrated history of the state of Indiana. 736 pp. incl. 13 ports. & 30 ports. on 6 pl. 5 pl. 8°. *Indianapolis, R. S. Peale & co.* 1875.

Goodspeed (Edgar J. *d. d.*) *and* **Hicks** (*Rev.* E. W.) Life of Jesus: for young people. 551 pp. incl. 50 pl. 4°. *New York, H. S. Goodspeed & co.* [1874].

Goodwin (Daniel R. *d. d.*) Syllabus of lectures on systematic divinity. 3 v. in 1. 8°. *Philadelphia, Sherman & co.* 1874–75.

Goodwin (Henry M.) Christ and humanity. xxv pp. 1 l. 404 pp. 12°. *New York, Harper & brothers*, 1875.

Gordon (George Henry). History of the second Mass. regiment of infantry: third paper. viii, 3–231 pp. 8°. *Boston, A. Mudge & son*, 1875.

Gordon (*Lady* Lucie Duff). Last letters from Egypt. [Also] letters from the cape. With a memoir by her daughter mrs. Ross. 2 p. l. xl, 346 pp. port. 12°. *London, Macmillan & co.* 1875.

Görres (Jakob Joseph). Mythengeschichte der asiatischen welt. 2 v. 2 p. l. xxxvi, 324 pp; 3 p. l. 325–660 pp. 1 map. 8°. *Heidelberg, Mohr & Zimmer*, 1810.

Goschen (George Joachim). Reports and speeches on local taxation. viii, 218 pp. 8°. *London, Macmillan & co.* 1872.

Goss (Elbridge H.) Melrose memorial. xxix, 292 pp. 4°. [*Boston, A. Mudge & son*], *privately printed by subscription*, 1868.

Gossellin (Pascal François Joseph). Recherches sur la géographie systématique et positive des anciens. v. 1–3. 4°. *Paris, de l'imprimerie de la république, an* VI. [1798]–1813. [Imperfect: v. 4 wanting].

Gottschalk (Friedrich). Jahres-bericht über die leistungen der chemischen technologie. Von prof. R. Wagner. Generalregister über band i–x. 2 p. l. 307 pp. 8°. *Leipzig, O. Wigand*, 1866.

Götzinger (Max Wilhelm). Dichtersaal. Auserlesene deutsche gedichte für die jugend. 7te aufl. xvi, 685 pp. 8°. *Leipzig, J. F. Hartknoch*, 1870.

Goulburn (Edward Meyrick, *d. d.*) The principles of the cathedral system vindicated. xlvii, 151 pp. 12°. *London, Rivingtons*, 1870.

——— Thoughts on personal religion. 1st am. from the 5th Lond. ed. xxxvi, 400 pp. 16°. *New York, D. Appleton & co.* 1865.

Gould (Benjamin Apthorp). Ancestry and posterity of Zaccheus Gould of Topsfield 109 pp. 8°. *Salem,* [*Ms.*] *for the Essex institute*, 1872. s.

Gould (Jeanie T.) Marjorie's quest. 4 p. l. 356 pp. 8 pl. 12°. *Boston, J. R. Osgood & co.* 1872.

Gould (Lucius D.) American stair-builders' guide. 34 l. 32 pl. 8°. *New York, A. J. Bicknell & co.* 1875.

——— Carpenter's and builder's assistant. 70 pp. 23 pl. 8°. *New York, A. J. Bicknell & co.* 1874.

Gow (Alexander M.) Good morals and gentle manners. 252 pp. 12°. *Cincinnati, Wilson, Hinkle & co.* [1873].

Gower (*Lord* Ronald). Pocket guide to the public and private galleries of Holland and Belgium. viii, 276 pp. front. 24°. *London, S. Low, Marston, Low & Searle,* 1875.

Graham (F. Taverner). Reasonable elocution. 211 pp. 12°. *New York, A. S. Barnes & co.* 1875.

Graham (William A.) Addresses on the Mecklenburg declaration of independence of the 20th of may, 1775. 167 pp. incl. 1 facs. 16°. *New York, E. J. Hale & son,* 1875.

Grandclaude (Eugène). Principes du droit public. xxiii, 306 pp. 12°. *Paris, J. Lecoffre,* 1872.

Grandpierre (J. H.) Parisian pastor's glance at America. 132 pp. 16°. *Boston, Gould & Lincoln,* 1854.

Grant (James). Shall I win her? 3 v. 12°. *London, Tinsley brothers,* 1874.

Grant (Robert Edmund, *m. d.*) Outlines of comparative anatomy. 1 p. l. 656 pp. 8°. *London, H. Baillière,* 1841.

Granville (Augustus Bozzi). Autobiography. Edited by Paulina B. Granville. 2 v. xii, 452 pp. port; ix, 436 pp. 8°. *London, H. S. King & co.* 1874.

Graul (Karl). Reise nach Ostindien über Palästina und Egypten von 1849 bis 1853. 5 v. in 4. 8°. *Leipzig, Dorffling & Franke,* 1854–56.

Graves (J. R.) Bible doctrine of the middle life. 174 pp. 18°. *Memphis, Tenn. southern baptist publication society,* 1873.

Graves (Kersey). The world's sixteen crucified saviors, [etc.] 377 pp. 1 l. 12°. *Boston, Colby & Rich,* 1875.

Graves (*Rev.* Richard). Columella. [*anon.*] 2 v. front. iv, 240 pp; front. 1 p. l. 248 pp. 16°. *London, J. Dodsley,* 1779.

Gravier (Gabriel). Découverte de l'Amérique par les Normands au 10e siècle. xxxix, 250 pp. 1 l. 3 maps, 1 pl. sm. 4°. *Rouen, E. Cagniard,* 1874.

——— Découvertes et établissements de Cavalier de la Salle de Rouen dans l'Amérique du nord. xii, 412 pp. port. 1 col. pl. 2 maps. 8°. *Paris, Maisonneuve & cie.* 1870.

Gray (*Rev.* Horatio). Memoirs of rev. Benjamin C. Cutler, d. d. of Brooklyn, N. Y. Eng. title, viii, 439 pp. 1 pl. 1 port. 12°. *New York, A. D. F. Randolph,* 1865.

Gray (John Hamilton). Confederation; or, the history of Canada, 1864–71. In 2 v. v. 1. 432 pp. 8°. *Toronto, Copp, Clark & co.* 1872.

Gray (O. W.) Atlas of the United States. 175 (+12ª–14ª) pp. incl. 65 maps. fol. *Philadelphia, Stedman, Brown & Lyon,* 1873.

Gray (O. W.) *& son, publishers.* National atlas. 179 [+74ª] pp. incl. 57 maps, 16 plans, 3 l. fol. *Philadelphia, O. W. Gray & son,* 1875.

Note.—Edition for Allegany co. Md.

Grazebrook (H. Sydney.) Heraldry of Smith. Eng. title, xix, 120 pp. 32 pl. sm. 4°. *London, J. R. Smith,* 1870.

——— Heraldry of Worcestershire. 2 v. lvi, 363 pp; 1 p. l. 363–748 pp. sm. 4°. *London, J. R. Smith,* 1873.

Great bonanza. Illustrated narrative of adventure in gold mining, silver mining [etc.] By Oliver Optic [*pseud.* etc.] 263 pp. incl. 16 pl. 8°. *Boston, Lee & Shepard,* 1876.

Great Britain. *Parliament.* [Parliamentary reports and papers]. Session of 1872. 71 v. in 73. fol. [*London,* 1873].

——— Same. Session of 1873. 75 v. in 80. fol. [*London,* 1874].

——— Same. Session of 1874. 77 v. in 81. fol. [*London,* 1875].

[v. 31, 33, and 72 parts 1–2, wanting].

Great possessions. [*anon.*] 303 pp. incl. front. 16°. *Philadelphia, am. s.-s. union,* [1874].

Greaves (Arthur). Bubbles from the deep. vi, 194 pp. 12°. [*Philadelphia*], *for the author,* 1873.

Green (Henry). Shakespeare and the emblem writers. xvi, 571 pp. 16 facs. pl. front. 8°. *London, Trübner & co.* 1870.

Green (Jonathan H.) Secret band of brothers. 192 pp. 5 pl. 12°. *Philadelphia, G. B. Zieber & co.* 1847.

Green (Valentine). Account of the discovery of the body of king John, in the cathedral church of Worcester. 2 p. l. 8 pp. 1 pl. 4°. *London, V. & R. Green,* [*etc.*] 1797.

[*With* GREEN (V.) History and antiquities of Worcester, v. 2].

——— History and antiquities of the city and suburbs of Worcester. 2 v. Title, xviii, 300 pp. 2 l. 15 pl; title, iii, 114, clv [+i] pp. 2 l. 10 pl. 4°. *London, for the author by W. Bulmer & co.* 1796.

Green (William). Annals of George the third, to 1805. 2 v. 1 p. l. 334 pp; vii, 5–333 pp. 12°. *London, for S. Tipper,* 1808.

Green (William Henry, *d. d.*) Argument of the book of Job unfolded. 1 p. l. 369 pp. 12°. *New York, R. Carter & brothers*, 1874.

Greene (*Rev.* Joseph). Insect hunter's companion. 2d ed. With a chapter on coleoptera by Edward Newman. 2 p. l. 168 pp. 16°. *London, J. Van Voorst*, 1870.

Greene (William B.) Socialistic, communistic, mutualistic, and financial fragments. 271 pp. 16°. *Boston, Lee & Shepard*, 1875.

Greenleaf (Simon). Testimony of the evangelists examined by the rules of evidence. xxiii, 613 pp. 8°. *New York, J. Cockcroft & co.* 1874.

Greenough (A. J.) Boundbrook. 519 pp. 2 pl. 16°. *Boston, congregational pub. soc.* [1874].

Greg (William Rathbone). Enigmas of life. 4th ed. xxi, 308 pp. 12°. *London, Trübner & co.* 1873.

——— Rocks ahead. 4 p. l. 233 pp. 12°. *London, Trübner & co.* 1874.

Gregory (D. S. *d. d.*) Christian ethics. 346 pp. 12°. *Philadelphia, Eldredge & brother*, 1875.

Gregson (Matthew). Portfolio of fragments relative to Lancaster. 3d ed. Edited by John Harland. 1 p. l. xii, 426 pp. 21 pl. 1 map, 3 pedigrees. sm. fol. *London, G. Routledge & sons*, 1869.

Grellet (Stephen). Memoirs, edited by B. Seebohm. 2d ed. 2 v. xii, 369 pp. port; x, 385 pp. 12°. *London, A. W. Bennett*, 1861.

Grétry (André Ernest Modest). Mémoires. 3 v. 8°. *Paris, imprimerie de la république, an* 5, [1796].

Greville (Charles Cavendish Fulke). Greville memoirs. Edited by Henry Reeve. 2d ed. 3 v. 8°. *London, Longmans*, 1874.

——— Same. Edited by R. H. Stoddard. [Greatly condensed]. xi, 346 pp. 16°. *New York, Scribner, Armstrong & co.* 1875.
[BRIC-À-BRAC series, v. 5].

Grey (Charles, *editor*). Narrative of italian travels in Persia in the fifteenth and sixteenth centuries. Translated and edited. 2 p. l. xvii, 230 pp. 1 l. 8°. *London, Hakluyt society*, 1873.
[*In* HAKLUYT society publications, v. 47].

Gridley (*Rev.* A. D.) History of the town of Kirkland, [Oneida co.] New York. xv, 232 pp. 5 pl. 12°. *New York, Hurd & Houghton*, 1874.

Griffin (Richard Aldworth Neville, 3*d baron Braybrooke*). History of Audley end. xv, 331 pp. 26 pl. 4°. *London, S. Bentley*, 1836.

Grile (Dod, *pseud.*) Fiend's delight. 197 pp. 1 l. 16°. *London, J. C. Hotten*, [1874].

Grille (François Joseph). Introduction aux mémoires sur la révolution française. 2 v. 2 p. l. 496 pp; 2 p. l. 528 pp. 8°. *Paris, Pichard*, 1825.

Grindon (Leo Hartley). Little things of nature considered especially in relation to the divine benevolence. 2d ed. 105 pp. 16°. *London, F. Pitman*, 1865.

Griswold (Rufus Wilmot, *d. d.*) Female poets of America. With additions by R. H. Stoddard. 487 pp. 8 ports. 8°. *New York, J. Miller*, 1874.

——— Poets and poetry of England, in the nineteenth century. With additions by R. H. Stoddard. 582 pp. 1 l. 10 ports. 8°. *New York, J. Miller*, 1875.

Grote (Harriet). Personal life of George Grote. 2d ed. xv, 336 pp. 1 port. 1 facs. 8°. *London, J. Murray*, 1873.

Grotius (Hugo). De origine gentivm americanarum dissertatio. 15 pp. sm. 4°. [*n. p.*] 1642.

Gruner (Wilhelm Heinrich Ludwig). Specimens of ornamental art. With text by Emil Braun. 2 v. vii, 36 pp. 8 pl. 4°; 3 p. l. 80 pl. incl. 56 col. fol. *London, T. McLean*, 1850.

Guattani (Giuseppe Antonio). Memorie enciclopediche romane sulle belle arti, antichitá etc. [*anon.*] 7 v. 4°. *Roma, pel Salomoni, C. Mordacchini* [*&*] *de Romanis*, 1806–19.

Guenot (*L'abbé* C.) Village steeple. From the french by the lady Blanche Murphy. 193 pp. incl. front. 8°. *New-York, Benziger brothers*, 1875.

Guernsey (Clara F.) Elmira's ambitions. 1 p. l. 5–372 pp. 4 pl. 16°. *Philadelphia, am. s.-s. union*, [1875].

——— Mallory girls. 1 p. l. 5–446 pp. 5 pl. 16°. *Philadelphia, am. s.-s. union*, [1875].

——— A spirit in prison. 304 pp. 16°. *Boston, H. A. Young*, [1875].

Guernsey (Lucy Ellen). Grandmother Brown's school-days. 410 pp. 4 pl. 16°. *Philadelphia, am. s.-s. union*, [1875].

——— Lady Rosamond's book. 344 pp. 12°. *New York, T. Whittaker*, [1874].

Guerrazzi (Francesco Domenico). Manfred. From the italian by Luigi Monti. 447 pp. 12°. *New York, G. W. Carleton & co.* 1875.

Guersant (Paul Louis Benoît). Surgical diseases of infants and children. From the french by Richard J. Dunglison, m. d. viii, 17–354 pp. 8°. *Philadelphia, H. C. Lea,* 1873.

Guhl (Ernst) *and* **Koner** (Wilhelm). Life of the Greeks and Romans, described from antique monuments. From the 3d german ed. by F. Hueffer. xii, 620 pp. 8°. *London, Chapman & Hall,* 1875.

Guignes (Joseph de). Histoire générale des Huns, des Turcs, des Mogols, et des autres Tartares occidentaux, etc. Jusqu'à présent. 5 v. 4°. *Paris, Desaint & Saillant,* 1756.

Guild (C. S. *editor*). Hymns and rhymes for home and school. vii, 152 pp. 18°. *Boston, Nichols & Hall,* 1875.

Guillaume (*Le dr.* —). Le congrès pénitentiaire de Londres. Rapport présenté au conseil fédéral. 203 pp. 8°. *Berne, J. A. Weingart,* 1873. s.

Guillemain de Saint-Victor (Louis). Histoire critique des mystères de l'antiquité. [*anon.*] 1 p. l. 5–8, 234 pp. front. 18°. *Hispahan,* [*Paris*], 1788.

Guizot (François Pierre Guillaume). Collection des mémoires relatifs à l'histoire de France. Jusqu'au 13e siècle. 31 v. 8°. *Paris, dépôt central de la librairie,* 1823–34.

——— Le duc de Broglie. 2 p. l. 301 pp. 12°. *Paris, Hachette & cie.* 1872.

——— History of France to 1789. Translated by Robert Black. v. 1–4. 8°. *London, S. Low, Marston, Low & Searle,* 1872–75.

——— Un projet de mariage royal. 2 p. l. iii, 360 pp. 8°. *Paris, Hachette et cie.* 1863.

——— Washington. Translated by Henry Reeve. xvi, 230 pp. 12°. *London, J. Murray,* 1840.

Gustin (M. E.) Exposé of the grangers. 1 p. l. 130 pp. 12°. *Dayton, O. christian publishing association,* 1875.

Guthrie (James Cargill). Vale of Strathmore. xv, 524 pp. 12°. *Edinburgh, W. Paterson,* 1875.

Guthrie (*Mrs.* —). Through Russia. 2 v. 1 p. l. v–xi, 324 pp. front; 1 p. l. v–ix, 287 pp. front. 12°. *London, Hurst & Blackett,* 1874.

Guyse (Jacques de). Le premier [–] le tiers volume des illustrations de la Gaulle belgique [etc.] 3 v. in 1. fol. *b. l. Paris, G. du pre,* 1531–32.

Note.—From the latin of J. de Guise by Jean Lessabée.

H. (Hd.) My comrades; adventures in the Highlands. 3–327 pp. 6 pl. 12°. *New York, H. L. Hinton & co.* 1874.

Hadermann (Jeanette R.) Against the world. 334 pp. 12°. *Boston, Shepard & Gill,* 1873.

Hadley (James, *ll. d.*) Essays philological and critical. vii, 424 pp. 8°. *New York, Holt & Williams,* 1873.

Hagenbach (Karl Rudolph). Encyklopädie und methodologie der theologischen wissenschaften. 7te verb. aufl. xii, 444 pp. 8°. *Leipzig, S. Hirzel,* 1864.

Hailman (William N.) Kindergarten culture in the family and kindergarten. 119 pp. 12 pl. 12°. *Cincinnati, Wilson, Hinkle & co.* 1873.

——— Twelve lectures on the history of pedagogy. 130 pp. 12°. *Cincinnati, Wilson, Hinkle & co.* [1874].

Hale (*Rev.* Edward Everett). Our new crusade. 287 pp. 24°. *Boston, Roberts brothers,* 1874.

——— *and others.* Workingmen's homes. 2 p. l. 182 pp. 2 pl. 16°. *Boston, J. R. Osgood & co.* 1874.

Hale (Edwin M. *m. d.*) Materia medica and special therapeutics of the new remedies. [Homœopathic]. 4th ed. v. 1–2. 8°. *New York, Boericke & Tafel,* 1875.

CONTENTS.

v. 1. Special symptomatology. 672 pp. port.
2. Special therapeutics. 819 pp.

Hale (Thomas). Compleat body of husbandry. 2d ed. 4 v. 8°. *London, for T. Osborne,* [*etc.*] 1758–59.

Haley (John W.) Examination of the alleged discrepancies of the bible. xii, 473 pp. 12°. *Andover, W. F. Draper,* 1874.

Half-hours with freethinkers. Edited by John Watts and Iconoclast [*pseud.* 2d series, nos. 1–24, sept. 1, 1864–feb. 9, 1865]. 1 p. l. [212] pp. 12°. *London, Watts & co.* 1865.

Half hours with the poets. [*anon.*] 371 pp. 9 pl. 8°. *New York, J. Miller,* 1874.

Haliburton (Thomas Chandler). Rule and misrule of the English in America. [*anon.*] 1 p. l. xi–379 pp. 12°. *New York, Harper & brothers,* 1851.

Hall (Eugene J.) Poems of the farm and fireside. 114 pp. incl. 12 pl. 8°. *Chicago, Jansen, McClurg & co.* 1875.

Hall (Fitzedward). Modern english. xv, 394 pp. 12°. *New York, Scribner, Armstrong & co.* 1873.

Hall (Fitzedward)—continued.

——— Recent exemplifications of false philology. 1 p. l. 125 pp. 8°. *New York, Scribner, Armstrong & co.* 1872.

Hall (Henry) *and* **Hall** (James). Cayuga in the field. 2 v. in 1. 316 pp; 1 p. l. 9–269 pp. 8°. *Auburn, N. Y.* [*Truair, Smith & co. Syracuse*], 1873.

Hall (H. Byng). The bric-à-brac hunter; or chapters on chinamania. xi, 290 pp. front. 12°. *London, Chatto & Windus*, 1875.

Hall (John, *late principal of Ellington school*). How are the dead raised? 216 pp. 16° *Hartford, Brown & Gross*, 1875.

Hall (John, *d. d. New York*). God's word through preaching. The Lyman Beecher lectures before the theological department of Yale college. (4th series). 2 p. l. 274 pp. 12°. *New York, Dodd & Mead*, [1875].

——— Questions of the day. ix, 7–343 pp. 12°. *New York, Dodd & Mead*, 1873.

——— *and others.* Preparing to teach. For study by sabbath-school teachers. 408 pp. 5 pl. 1 map. 12°. *Philadelphia, presbyterian board of publication*, [1875].

——— *and* **Stuart** (George H.) The american evangelists, D. L. Moody and Ira D. Sankey, in Great Britain and Ireland. 455 pp. 2 ports. on 1 pl. 12°. *New York, Dodd & Mead*, [1875].

Hall (John Vine). Hope for the hopeless.—An autobiography. Abridged. 264 pp. port. 12°. *New York, am. tract society*, [*about* 1865].

Hall (*Mrs.* Matthew). Royal princesses of England, from the reign of George the first. iv, 540 pp. port. 16°. *London, G. Routledge & sons*, 1871.

Hall (Samuel Carter). Book of memories of great men and women of the age. xv, 488 pp. 8°. *London, Virtue & co.* 1871.

Hall (Theresa Oakey). Her mother's fancy. 201 pp. front. 12°. *Boston, H. L. Shepard & co.* 1875.

Hall (William Edward). Rights and duties of neutrals. x, 210 pp. 8°. *London, Longmans*, 1874.

Hall (William White, *m. d.*) How to live long. 316 pp. 12°. *New York, Hurd & Houghton*, 1875.

Hallock (Charles). Fishing tourist: angler's guide and reference book. 239 pp. incl. 1 pl. 12°. *New York, Harper & brothers*, 1873.

Hallock (William Allen, *d. d.*) The venerable Mayhews and the aboriginal Indians of Martha's Vineyard. 190 pp. 1 pl. 18°. *New York, am. tract society*, 1874.

Hallowell (*Mrs.* Joshua L.) Bec's bedtime. vii, 13–208 pp. incl. front. 12°. *Philadelphia, Porter & Coates*, 1873.

Hamerling (Robert). Ahasver in Rom. Eine dichtung. 10te aufl. 1 p. l. 276 pp. 1 l. 16°. *Hamburg, J. F. Richter*, 1874.

Hamerton (Philip Gilbert). Harry Blount. iv, 355 pp. front. 16°. *London, Seeley, Jackson, & Halliday*, 1875.

——— The intellectual life. xix, 455 pp. 1 port. 12°. *London, Macmillan & co.* 1873.

——— Same. xix, 455 pp. 1 port. 12°. *Boston, Roberts brothers*, 1873.

——— The unknown river. xv, 70 pp. 36 pl. 8°. *Boston, Roberts brothers*, 1872.

Hamilton (Alexander V.) Household cyclopædia of practical receipts. 423 pp. 9 pl. 12°. *Springfield,* [*Mass.*] *W. J. Holland & co.* 1873.

Hamilton (Allan McLane, *m. d.*) Clinical electro-therapeutics. 184 pp. 8°. *New York, D. Appleton & co.* 1873.

Hamilton (D. H. *d. d.*) Autology: an inductive system of mental science. xviii, 701 pp. 8°. *Boston, Lee & Shepard*, 1873.

Hamilton (*Mrs.* M. J. R.) Cachet. 3 p. l. 9–351 pp. 12°. *New York, G. W. Carleton & co.* 1873.

Hamlin (Augustus C. *m. d.*) The tourmaline. 107 pp. 4 col. pl. 12°. *Boston, J. R. Osgood & co.* 1873.

Hamlin (Benjamin). Bible explained. [In verse. v. 1]. 106 pp. 16°. *Santa Cruz, Cal. B. Hamlin & co.* 1874.

Hammer-Purgstall (Joseph, *baron* von). Geschichte der goldenen horde in Kiptschak. 2 p. l. li, 685 pp. 1 tab. 8°. *Pesth, C. A. Hartleben*, 1840.

——— Geschichte der osmanischen dichtkunst bis auf unsere zeit. 4 v. 8°. *Pesth, C. A. Hartleben*, 1836–38.

——— Geschichte des osmanischen reiches. 2te verb. aufl. 4. v. 8°. *Pesth, C. A. Hartleben*, 1834–36.

Hammond (William A. *m. d.*) Clinical lectures on diseases of the nervous system. Edited by T. M. B. Cross, m. d. viii, 291 pp. 8°. *New York, D. Appleton & co.* 1874.

Hand-book of Colorado. Third year of publication. 142 pp. 18°. *Denver, Col. J. A. Blake & F. C. Willett*, 1873.

Hand book to Monterey and vicinity. [*anon.*] 1 p. l. 152 pp. sq. 18°. *Monterey,* [*Cal. Walton & Curtis*], 1875.

Harbert (Lizzie Boynton). Out of her sphere 4 p. l. 184 pp. 12°. *Des Moines,* [*Iowa*] *Mills & co.* 1871.

Hardy (Campbell, *r. a.*) Forest life in Acadie. Sketches of sport in the Canadian dominion. ix, 371 pp. 10 pl. col. front. 8°. *London, Chapman & Hall,* 1869.

Hardy (Thomas). Far from the madding crowd. iv, 474 pp. 16°. *New York, H. Holt & co.* 1874.
[LEISURE hour series].

——— A pair of blue eyes. 1 p. l. 390 pp. 16°. *New York, H. Holt & co.* 1873.
[LEISURE hour series].

——— Under the greenwood tree. [*anon.*] 2 v. 3 p. l. 215 pp; 3 p. l. 216 pp. 12°. *London, Tinsley brothers,* 1872.

Hardy (*Sir* Thomas Duffus). Syllabus (in english) of the documents relating to England and other kingdoms contained in "Rymer's fœdera." 2 v. 2 p. l. [170], 479 pp; lxxi, 481–915 pp. 8°. *London, Longmans,* 1869–73.
[GREAT BRITAIN. *Public record office.* Publications].

Hare (Augustus John C) Days near Rome. 2 v. 333 pp; 363 pp. 12°. *London, Dalby, Isbister & co.* 1875.

——— Records of a quiet life. Revised for american readers by W. L. Gage. xv, 373 pp. 16°. *Boston, Roberts brothers,* 1873.

——— Wanderings in Spain. xxi pp. 2 l. 274 pp. 16 pl. 12°. *London, Strahan & co.* 1873.

Harford (John Scandrett). Recollections of William Wilberforce. xii, 326 pp. 12°. *London, Longman,* [*etc.*] 1864.

Harland (John). Collectanea relating to Manchester and its neighborhood. 2 v. 2 p. l. vii, 258 pp; 2 p. l. viii, 252 pp. sm. 4°. [*Manchester*], 1866–67.
[CHETHAM society remains, v. 68, 72].

——— *editor.* Lancashire lieutenancy under the Tudors and Stuarts. 2 v. 3 p. l. cxix, 96 pp; 3 p. l. 97–333 pp. 7 pl. sm. 4°. [*Manchester*], 1859.
[CHETHAM society remains, v. 49, 50.]

——— Mamecestre: chapters from the early recorded history of Manchester. 3 v. sm. 4°. [*Manchester*], 1861–62.
[CHETHAM society remains, v. 53, 56, 58].

——— Three Lancashire documents of the fourteenth and fifteenth centuries. 2 p. l. xv, 141 pp. sm. 4°. [*Manchester*], 1868.
[CHETHAM society remains, v. 74].

Harness (*Rev.* William). Personal reminiscences.
[*In* BRIC-À-BRAC series, v. 4, 1875. pp. 177–250].

Harris (James, 1*st earl of Malmesbury*). A series of letters, from 1745 to 1820. 2 v. xxvii, 511 pp; xx, 538 pp. 8° *London, R. Bentley,* 1870.

Harris (John, *d. d.*) History of Kent. v. 1. 1 p. l. [xiii], 592, xl pp. 39 pl. 4 maps. fol. *London, D. Midwinter,* 1719.
Note.—Imperfect: wants portrait of author. No more was published.

Harris (Samuel). Kingdom of Christ on earth. viii, 255 pp. 8°. *Andover, W. F. Draper,* 1874.

Harris (*Mrs.* Sidney S. *née* Miriam Cole). A perfect Adonis. [*anon.*] 1 p. l. 9–380 pp. 12°. *New York, G. W. Carleton & co.* 1875.

Harrison (James Albert). A group of poets and their haunts. vii, 319 pp. 16°. *New York, Hurd & Houghton,* 1875.

Harrison (Jennie). From four to fourteen. 294 pp. 4 pl. 16°. *New York, am. tract society,* [1874].

——— Little boots. 383 pp. 4 pl. 16°. *New York, Dodd & Mead,* [1874].

Harrison (Susan). Songs in the night. 2d am. ed. xiv, 196 pp. 24°. *Burlington, N. J., S. C. Ustick,* 1807.

Harrison (William). Bibliotheca monensis. viii, 208 pp. 8°. *Douglas,* [*Isle of Man*], 1861.
[MANX society. Publications, v. 8].

——— *editor.* Mona miscellany. 2 v. 2 p. l. xv pp. 1 l. 255 pp; xvi pp. 1 l. 294 pp. 2 pl. 8°. *Douglas,* [*Isle of Man*], 1869–73.
[MANX society. Publications, v. 16, 21].

——— Old historians of the Isle of Man. xii, 217 pp. 15 pl. 8°. *Douglas,* [*Isle of Man*], 1871.
[MANX society. Publications, v. 18].

Harrisse (Henry). Fernand Colomb; essai critique. [*anon.*] 3 p. l. 230 pp. 1 l. 8°. *Paris, Tross,* 1872.

Hart (James Morgan). German universities. 7 pp. 1 l. 398 pp. 12°. *New York, G. P. Putnam's sons,* 1874.

Hart (John Seely, *ll. d.*) Class book of poetry: selections from english and american poets, from Chaucer to Tennyson. New ed. 400 pp. 12°. *Philadelphia, Eldredge & brother,* 1875.

——— Short course in literature. 323 pp. 12°. *Philadelphia, Eldredge & brother,* 1873.

Harte (Francis Bret). Echoes of the foothills. 146 pp. 16°. *Boston, J. R. Osgood & co.* 1875.

Harte (Francis Bret)—continued.

——— Tales of the Argonauts, and other sketches. 2 p. l. 283 pp. 16°. *Boston, J. R. Osgood & co.* 1875.

Harting (James Edmund). Ornithology of Shakespeare. xxii pp. 1 l. 321 pp. incl. port. 8°. *London, J. Van Voorst,* 1871.

Hartley (*Mrs.* Emily). Barley loaves. [*anon.*] 339 pp. 3 pl. 16°. *Philadelphia, am. s.-s. union,* [1874].

Hartman (William D. *m. d.*) *and* **Michener** (Ezra, *m. d.*) Conchologia cestrica. Molluscous animals of Chester county, Pa. 114 pp. 12°. *Philadelphia, Claxton, Remsen & Haffelfinger,* 1874.

Hartmann (Eduard von). Philosophie des unbewussten. 6te aufl. iv, 846 pp. port. 8°. *Berlin, C. Duncker,* 1874.

Hartwell (Mary). Woman in armor. [Also Old Gargoyle & The man who "hadn't time"]. 2 p. l. 9–196 pp. 6 pl. 12°. *New York, G. W. Carleton & co.* 1875.

Hartwig (Georg, *m. d.*) Aerial world. xviii, 556 pp. 8 col. pl. 1 col. map. 8°. *London, Longmans,* 1874.

Harvey (William H. *m. d.*) *and* **Sonder** (Otto Wilhelm, *ph. d.*) Flora capensis: a systematic description of the plants of Cape Colony, Caffraria, & Port Natal. 3 v. 8°. *Dublin, Hodges, Smith & co.* 1859–65.

Harvey (*Mrs.* —). Turkish harems & circassian homes. x, 307 pp. 1 pl. 8°. *London, Hurst & Blackett,* 1871.

Haslewood (Joseph, *editor*). Ancient critical essays upon english poets and poësy. 2 v. 2 p. l. xxxviii pp. 5 l. 258 pp. 7 l. 1 pl; 4 p. l. xxiv, 316 pp. sm. 4°. *London, for R. Triphook,* 1811–15.

Hatin (L. Eugène). Histoire pittoresque de l'Algérie. 2 p. l. 256 pp. 2 ports. 1 map. 8°. *Paris, au bureau central de la publication,* [1840].

Hatton (Joseph). Clytie. 3 v. 12°. *London, Chapman & Hall,* 1874.

——— In the lap of fortune. 3 v. 12°. *London, Chapman & Hall,* 1873.

——— With a show in the north. Reminiscences of Mark Lemon. 2 p. l. 284 pp. front. 16°. *London, W. H. Allen & co.* 1871.

Haughton (*Rev.* Samuel). Principles of animal mechanics. 2d ed. xiv, 495 pp. 8°. *London, Longmans,* 1873.

Haven (*Rev.* Gilbert). Our next-door neighbor: bor: a winter in Mexico. 467 pp. incl. 11 pl. 3 pl. 2 maps. 12°. *New York, Harper & brothers,* 1875.

Haverty (Patrick M.) Legends and fairy tales of Ireland. [*anon.*] vi, 402 pp. 12°. *New York, P. M. Haverty,* 1872.

Haweis (Hugh Reginald). Ashes to ashes. Cremation prelude. 3 p. l. 260 pp. 12°. *London, Daldy, Isbister & co.* 1875.

——— Pet, or pastimes and penalties. 4 p. l. 314 pp. 1 l. front. 12°. *London, W. Isbister & co.* 1874.

Hawkins (Archibald). Life and times of Elijah Stansbury. 298 pp. 1 port. 12°. *Baltimore, J. Murphy & co.* 1874.

Hawkins (Thomas). Book of the great sea-dragons, ichthyosauri and plesiosauri, gedolim taninim, of Moses. 2 p. l. 27 pp. 30 pl. fol. *London, W. Pickering,* 1840.

Hawthorne (Julian). Bressant. 383 pp. 16°. *New York, D. Appleton & co.* 1873.

——— Idolatry. 372 pp. 12°. *Boston, J. R. Osgood & co.* 1874.

——— Saxon studies. 1 p. l. 452 pp. 12°. *Boston, J. R. Osgood & co.* 1876.

Hayden (A. S.) Early history of the disciples in the Western Reserve, Ohio. 476 pp. 12°. *Cincinnati, Chase & Hall,* 1875.

Hayne (Paul H.) Mountain of the lovers. 153 pp. 12°. *New York, E. J. Hale & son,* 1875.

Hayward (Abraham). Biographical and critical essays. New [2d] series. 2 v. 3 p. l. 434 pp; 3 p. l. 416 pp. 8°. *London, Longmans,* 1873.

——— Same. 3d series. 4 p. l. 411 pp. 8°. *London, Longmans,* 1874.

Hayward (W. Stephens). Ten years a rover. 1 p. l. 330 pp. 16°. *London, C. H. Clarke,* [187-].

Hazard (Elizabeth). Autumn musings. 128 pp. 12°. *Philadelphia, J. B. Lippincott & co.* 1874.

Hazard (Samuel). Santo Domingo, past and present. xxxi, 511 pp. 22 pl. 2 maps. 12°. *New York, Harper & brothers,* 1873.

Hazlitt (William Carew). Anecdotes and reminiscences of illustrious men and women of modern times. [*anon.*] viii, 357 pp. 16°. *London, Reeves & Turner,* 1872.

——— *editor.* New London jest book. xi, 374 pp. 16°. *London, Reeves & Turner,* 1871.

——— Shakespeare's library. The plays, romances, novels, poems and histories employed by Shakespeare in the composition of his works. With introduction and notes [by J. P. Collier]. 2d ed. 2 pts. in 6 v. 16°. *London, Reeves & Turner,* 1875.

Headley (Joel T.) The great riots of New York, 1712 to 1873. 2 p. l. 7–306, 331–359 pp. 12 pl. 12°. *New York, E. B. Treat*, 1873.

Headley (*Rev.* Phineas Camp). The island of fire; or, a thousand years of the old Northmen's home. 874–1874. 8, 5–339 pp. 8 pl. 12°. *Boston, Lee & Shepard*, 1875.

Healy (Mary). Lakeville. 238 pp. 4 pl. 8°. *New York, D. Appleton & co.* 1873.

Heath (John Benjamin). Some account of the company of grocers of London. 2d ed. xvi, 580 pp. 8 pl. 8°. *London, (privately printed), [C. Whittingham]*, 1854.

Hebberd (S. S.) Secret of christianity. 210 pp. 12°. *Boston, Lee & Shepard*, 1874.

Heber (Reginald, *bishop of Calcutta*). Poetical works. xii, 454 pp. 1 l. 1 pl. 16°. *London, J. Murray*, 1841.

Hecht (Emanuel). Biblical history for israelitish schools. Revised by S. Adler. From the german by M. Mayer. 7th ed. 144 pp. 16°. *New York, M. Thalmessinger & co.* 1874.

Hedges (Mary J.) White rose. 320 pp. 1 pl. 16°. *New York, national temperance society*, 1874.

Hefele (Carl Joseph von). Histoire des conciles. Traduite par m. l'abbé Goschler et m. l'abbé Delarc. [a. d. 52–1418]. 10 v. 8°. *Paris, A. Le Clere & cie.* 1869–74.

Heine (Heinrich). Prose miscellanies. Translated by S. L. Fleischman. 302 pp. 12°. *Philadelphia, J. B. Lippincott & co.* 1876.

Heine (Wilhelm). Reise um die erde nach Japan unter M. C. Perry in 1853, 1854 und 1855. Deutsche originalausg. 2 v. Eng. title, xvi, 321 pp. 5 col. pl; viii, 376 pp. 5 col. pl. 8°. *Leipzig, H. Costenoble*, 1856.

Helena's cloud with the silver lining. [*anon.*] 185 pp. incl. 2 pl. 16°. *New York, Nelson & Phillips*, [1874].

Heller (Karl Bartholomaeus). Reisen in Mexiko in 1845–48. xxiv, 432 pp. 1 pl. 2 maps. 8°. *Leipzig, W. Engelmann*, 1853.

Hellwald (Friedrich von). Russians in central Asia. From the german by T. Wirgman, ll. b. xx, 332 pp. 1 map. 8°. *London, H. S. King & co.* 1874.

Helmholtz (*Dr.* Hermann Louis Ferdinand). On the sensations of tone as a physiological basis for the theory of music. From the 3d german ed. By A. J. Ellis. xxiv, 824 pp. 8°. *London, Longmans, Green & co.* 1875.

——— Popular lectures on scientific subjects. Translated by E. Atkinson, ph. d. xvi, 397 pp. 8°. *London, Longmans*, 1873.

Helmuth (William Tod, *m. d.*) System of surgery. 1228 pp. 8°. *New York*, [1874].

——— Treatise on diphtheria. 125 pp. 8°. *St. Louis, H. C. G. Luyties*, 1862.

Helps (*Sir* Arthur). Ivan de Biron. [*anon.*] 3 v. 12°. *London, W. Isbister & co.* 1874.

——— Life and labours of mr. Brassey. xv, 386 pp. port. 3 pl. 4 maps. 8°. *London, Bell & Daldy*, 1872.

——— Social pressure. [*anon.*] vii, 412 pp. 12°. *London, Daldy, Isbister & co.* 1875.

——— Some talk about animals and their masters. [*anon.*] 4 p. l. 226 pp. 12°. *London, Strahan & co.* 1873.

Helvington. [*anon.*] 187 pp. 8°. *Memphis, bulletin publishing co.* 1867.

Hemans (Charles Isidore). Historic and monumental Rome. 2 p. l. iv, 734 pp. 12°. *London, Williams & Norgate*, 1874.

——— History of ancient christianity and sacred art in Italy. 1 p. l. 600 pp. 12°. *London, Williams & Norgate*, 1866.

——— History of mediaeval christianity and sacred art in Italy. v. 1–2. 2 p. l. 615 pp; vii, 664 pp. 12°. *London, Williams & Norgate*, 1869–72.

Hemenway (Abby Maria). Poets and poetry of Vermont. xii, 400 pp. 12°. *Rutland, G. A. Tuttle & co.* 1858.

Hemingway (Joseph). History of the city of Chester. 2 v. 2 p. l. v, 432 pp. 7 pl; 1 p. l. 444 pp. 2 l. 18 pl. 8°. *Chester, J. Fletcher*, 1831.

Hemlands-sånger, samlade och utgifne af swenska luth. tryckföreningen. 5e uppl. stereotyp-uppl. 400 pp. 24°. *Chicago, foreningens tryckeri*, 1874.

Hemmenway (John). Daily remembrancer on peace and war. 215 pp. 18°. *New Vienna, O. peace assoc. of friends in America*, 1875.

Hemsley (W. B. *compiler*). Handbook of hardy trees, shrubs, and herbaceous plants. Based on the french work of messrs. Decaisne and Naudin. With introduction by Edward S. Rand, jr. 1 p. l. xliii, 687 pp. 8°. *Boston, Estes & Lauriat*, 1873.

Hemstreet (William). Economical european tourist. A journalist three months abroad for $430. v, 230 pp. 1 l. 16°. *New York, S. W. Green*, 1875.

Henderson (Alfred). Latin proverbs and quotations. 2 p. l. vii, 505 pp. 8°. *London, S. Low, son & Marston*, 1869.

Henderson (John). Hand-book of the grasses of Great Britain and America. 238 pp. 12°. *Northport, L. I. journal publishing co.* 1875.

Henderson (Peter). Gardening for pleasure. 250 pp. 12°. *New York, O. Judd & co.* [1875].

——— Gardening for profit. New ed. 276 pp. 12°. *New York, O. Judd co.* [1874].

——— Practical floriculture. New ed. 288 pp. 12°. *New York, O. Judd co.* [1874].

Henne-AmRhyn (Otto). Kulturgeschichte der neuen zeit. 3 v. 8°. *Leipzig, O. Wigand*, 1870–72.

Henrich (*Rev.* A.) Afrikana oder Jordania? viii, 221 pp. incl. 3 pl. 1 l. 2 pl. 18°. [*Louisville*], *für den verfasser*, [1875].

——— Einer für alle and alle für einen in allen. Zwölf zeitpredigten. 2 p. l. 200 pp. 8°. *Cleveland, O. publikations-verein der deutschen baptisten*, [1875].

Henry (C. S. *d. d.*) About men and things. viii, 237 pp. 12°. *New York, T. Whi taker*, [1873].

——— Household liturgy. 82 pp. 16°. *New-York, T. Whittaker*, [1873].

Henry (Guy V.) Military record of army and civilian appointments in the U. S. army. v. 2. 391 pp. 8°. *New York, D. Van Nostrand*, 1873.

Henry (James). Sketches of moravian life and character. 316 pp. 1 l. front. 12°. *Philadelphia, J. B. Lippincott & co.* 1859.

Henry (James P.) Resources of Arkansas. 3d ed. 136 pp. 1 map. 8°. *Little Rock, Price & M'Clure*, 1873.

Henry (*Mrs.* Sarepta M. I.) After the truth. Finding. 286 pp. 16°. *Cincinnati, Hitchcock & Walden*, 1874.

——— Same. [Part 2]. Teaching. 286 pp. 16°. *Cincinnati, Hitchcock & Walden*, 1874.

——— Same. [Part 3]. Using. 339 pp. 16°. *Cincinnati, Hitchcock & Walden*, 1874.

Hepburn (J. C. *ll. d.*) Japanese-english and english-japanese dictionary. Abridged. vi, 330, 206 pp. sq. 16°. *New York, A. D. F. Randolph & co.* 1873.

Herbert (Henry John George, *3d earl of Carnarvon*). Reminiscences of Athens and the Morea, in 1839. xxxi, 230 pp. 1 map. 12°. *London, J. Murray*, 1869.

Herbert (Henry William). The fair puritan. 222 pp. 12°. *Philadelphia, J. B. Lippincott & co.* 1875.

Herbert (*Lady* —). Search after sunshine, or Algeria in 1871. 5 p. l. 265 pp. 8 pl. 8°. *London, R. Bentley & son*, 1872.

Herd (David, *compiler*). Ancient and modern scottish songs, heroic ballads, etc. Reprint of the edition of 1776. With memoir and notes by S. Gilpin. 2 v. xiv, xi, 327 pp; viii pp. 2 l. 304 pp. 12°. *Edinburgh, W. Paterson*, 1870.

Héricault (Charles d'). Maximilien et le Mexique. 2 p. l. 419 pp. front. 16°. *Paris, Garnier frères*, 1869.

Hermione. A novel. [*anon.*] 4 v. 16°. *London, for W. Lane*, 1791.

Hernandez (Jose Maria Perez). Compendio de la geografia de Michoacan de Ocampo. 145 pp. 1 l. *Mexico, N. Chavez*, 1872.

Herron (S. P.) Thoughts on life and character. 273 pp. 12°. *Philadelphia, J. B. Lippincott & co.* 1873.

Herschel (*Sir* John Frederick William, *bart.*) Familiar lectures on scientific subjects. [New ed.] 2 p. l. ix–xii, 507 pp. 12°. *London, A. Strahan & co.* 1871.

Hertford (Joseph). Personals; or, perils of the period. 339, viii pp. 1 pl. 12°. *New York, for the author*, 1870.

Hertslet (Edward). Map of Europe by treaty, showing changes since the general peace of 1814. 3 v. 8°. *London, Butterworths*, 1875.

Hervey (George Winfred). System of christian rhetoric. 5 p. l. 632 pp. 8°. *New York, Harper & brothers*, 1873.

Hewitt (Robert, *jr.*) Coffee: its history, cultivation, and uses. 102 pp. 1 col. pl. 1 map. 8°. *New York, D. Appleton & co.* 1872.

Heyl (Lewis). United States duties on imports. 1874. Revised to August 1st, 1874. viii, 238 pp. 1 l. 97, 110 pp. 1 l. 8°. *Washington, W. H. & O. H. Morrison*, 1874.

Heywood (Thomas). Dramatic works, now first collected, with notes and a memoir of the author. 6 v. 12°. *London, J. Pearson*, 1874.

Hézecques (Félix, *comte* de France d'). Recollections of a page at the court of Louis XVI. Edited, from the french, by Charlotte M. Yonge. 1 p. l. v–xi, 336 pp. 8°. *London, Hurst & Blackett*, 1873.

Hickling (William). Rector of Roxburgh. 272 pp. 16°. *New-York, E. P. Dutton & co.* 1873.

Hickman (William). Sketches on the Nipisaguit, New Brunswick, B. N. America. 2

Hickman (William)—continued.
p. l. ii, 2 pp. 8 col. pl. 8 l. fol. *Halifax, J. B. Strong*, 1860.

Hickok (Laurens P. *d. d.*) Humanity immortal. 362 pp. 8°. *Boston, Lee & Shepard*, 1872.

Hicks (J. M.) The north american bee-keepers' guide. 4 p. l. 103 pp. 4 l. 24°. *Lafayette, [Ind.] bee steam printing house*, 1875.

Higgins (S. B.) Ophidians, zoological arrangement of the different genera. 1st am. ed. 239 pp. 8°. *New York, Boericke & Tafel*, 1873.

Higginson (Thomas Wentworth). English statesmen. vii, 363 pp. 16°. *New York, G. P. Putnam's sons*, 1875.
[Brief biographies of eminent public men, v. 1].

——— Oldport days. 4 p. l. 11-268 pp. 10 pl. 12°. *Boston, J. R. Osgood & co.* 1873.

——— Young folks' history of the United States. vi, 370 pp. 1 map. 12°. *Boston, Lee & Shepard*, 1875.

Higham (*Mrs.* Mary R.) Athol. By M. R. H. [*anon.*] 2 p. l. 7-423 pp. 12°. *New York, Pott, Young & co.* 1873.

——— Rownie. By M. R. H. [*anon.*] 177 pp. incl. 1 pl. 16°. *New York, Pott, Young & co.* 1873.

Hill (Aaron). Full and just account of the present state of the ottoman empire. 4 p. l. xxvii pp. 4 l. 339 pp. 6 pl. 6 l. fol. *London, for the author*, 1709.

Hill (A. F.) Secrets of the sanctum. 312 pp. 12°. *Philadelphia, Claxton, Remsen & Haffelfinger*, 1875.

Hill (Britton A.) Liberty and law under federative government. 263 pp. 12°. *Philadelphia, J. B. Lippincott & co.* 1874.

Hill (Thomas E.) Manual of social & business forms. 305 pp. 4°. *Chicago, M. Warren & co.* 1874.

Hill (*Rev.* Walter H. *s. J.*) Elements of philosophy. 234 pp. 12°. *Baltimore, J. Murphy & co.* 1873.

Hillard (George Stillman). Memoir and correspondence of Jeremiah Mason. Privately printed. viii, 467 pp. 1 phot. 4°. *Cambridge, [Mass.] riverside press*, 1873.

Hiller (*Dr.* Ferdinand). Mendelssohn. Letters and recollections. Translated by M. E. von Glehn. xvii, 223 pp. port. 12°. *London, Macmillan & co.* 1874.

Hillern (Wilhelmine von). Twofold life. Translated by M. S. 343 pp. 1 port. 12°. *Philadelphia, J. B. Lippincott & co.* 1873.

Hills (Robert). Sketches in Flanders and Holland. viii, 215 pp. 36 pl. 4°. *London, J. Haines & J. Turner*, 1816.

Hincks (Thomas, *b. a.*) History of british hydroid zoophytes. 2 v. 5 p. l. lxviii, 338 pp. incl. 2 pl. 1 pl; 3 p. l. 67 pl. 67 l. unp. 8°. *London, J. Van Voorst*, 1868.

Hippeau (Célestin). L'instruction publique en Italie. 2 p. l. viii, 418 pp. 12°. *Paris, Didier & cie.* 1875. s.

Histoire générale des hommes vivants et des hommes morts dans le xixe siècle, [etc.] par des écrivains des diverses nations. Éd. où les articles se classent dans l'ordre alphabétique par tome. 5 v. fol. *Genève, à la direction de l'histoire générale*, 1860-74.

History and antiquities of the county of Norfolk. [*anon.*] 10 v. containing 62 pl. 8°. *Norwich, J. Crouse, for M. Booth*, 1781.

History of all the real and threatened invasions of England. [*anon.*] 4 p. l. iv, 196, 48 pp. 8°. *Windsor, [Eng-] for C. Knight*, 1794.

History of captain and miss Rivers. [*anon.*] 3 v. 16°. *London, for T. Hookham*, 1787.

History of Lincoln, [etc. *anon.*] ix, 224 pp. 5 l. 4 pl. 12°. *Lincoln, Drury & sons*, 1816.

History of man: in relation to virtues, vices and defects. [*anon.*] 3d ed. 258 pp. 18°. *Perth, R. Morison, jr.* 1796.

History of miss Sommervile. [*anon.*] 2 v. 2 p. l. 240 pp; 2 p. l. 259 pp. 16°. *London, for Newbery & Carnan*, 1769.

History of Stirling. [*anon.*] xi, 279 pp. 12°. *Stirling, [Scotland], M. Randall*, 1817.

History of the life and trials of Thomas McGehean. [*anon.*] 291 pp. 1 pl. 12°. *Cincinnati*, 1874.

Hittell (John S.) Brief history of culture. 329 pp. 12°. *New York, D. Appleton & co.* 1875.

Hoare (*Sir* Richard Colt, *bart.*) History of modern Wiltshire. 14 v. in 6. fol. *London, J. Nichols & son, and J. B. & J. G. Nichols*, 1822-43.

Hock (Carl, *freiherr* von). Die finanzen und die finanzgeschichte der Vereinigten Staaten von Amerika. xiv, 812 pp. 8°. *Stuttgart, J. G. Cotta*, 1867.

Hodder (Edwin). On "holy ground." 326 pp. 12°. *New York, Nelson & Phillips*, 1874.

Hodge (Charles). What is Darwinism? iv, 178 pp. 12°. *New York, Scribner, Armstrong & co.* 1874.

Hodges (William, *d. d.*) Baptism tested by scripture and history. 3d ed. x, 411 pp. 12°. *New York, E. P. Dutton & co.* 1874.

Hodgson (B. H.) Illustrations of the literature and religion of the buddhists. 4 p. l. 220 pp. 3 pl. 8°. *Serampore*, 1841.

Hodgson (William). The society of friends in the nineteenth century. v. 1. 349 pp. 12°. *Philadelphia, Smith, English & co.* 1875.

Hoffman (Charles Fenno). Poems. 238 pp. port. 16°. *Philadelphia, Porter & Coates*, 1873.

Hofmann (Carl). Practical treatise on the manufacture of paper. iv, 398 pp. incl. 4 pl. 5 pl. 4°. *Philadelphia, H. C. Baird*, 1873.

Hogg (*Rev.* David). Life of Allan Cunningham, with selections from his works. xii, 373 pp. 2 ports. 1 pl. 12°. *Dumfries*, [*Glasgow printed*], *J. Anderson & son*, 1875.

Holbrook (Martin L. *m. d.*) Eating for strength. 157 pp. 12°. *New York, Wood & Holbrook*, 1875.

Holcroft (Thomas). Travels from Hamburgh to Paris. Abridged by John Fulton. xvi, 392 pp. 8°. *Glasgow, for Gray, Maver & co.* 1804.

Holden (A. W. *m. d.*) History of the town of Queensbury, New York. viii pp. 1 l. 519 pp. 15 ports. 8°. *Albany, J. Munsell*, 1874.

Holden (Charles F.) Book on birds. 128 pp. 1 pl. port. 16°. *Boston, New-York bird-store*, 1875.

Holdsworth (Edmund W. H.) Deep-sea fishing and fishing boats. xvi, 429 pp. 15 pl. 8°. *London, E. Stanford*, 1874.

Hole (S. Reynolds). Book about roses. 4th ed. 3 p. l. 320 pp. col. front. sm. 4°. *Edinburgh, W. Blackwood & sons*, 1872.

——— Six of spades, a book about the garden and the gardener. viii, 236 pp. sq. 12°. *Edinburgh, W. Blackwood & sons*, 1872.

Holland (Josiah Gilbert). Arthur Bonnicastle. 401 pp. 12 pl. 12°. *New York, Scribner, Armstrong & co.* 1873.

——— Mistress of the manse. 245 pp. 12°. *New York, Scribner, Armstrong & co.* 1874.

——— Sevenoaks. 5 p. l. 441 pp. 12°. *New York, Scribner, Armstrong & co.* 1875.

Holliday (Fernandez C. *d. d.*) Indiana methodism. 360 pp. 8 ports. 8°. *Cincinnati, Hitchcock & Walden*, 1873.

Hollingshead (John). Miscellanies. Stories and essays. 3 v. 8°. *London, Tinsley brothers*, 1874.

Holloway (Laura Carter). In the home of the presidents. 2 p. l. 11–561 pp. 14 ports. 7 pl. 8°. *New York, United States publishing co.* 1875.

Holm (Saxe, *pseud.*) Saxe Holm's stories. 2 p. l. 350 pp. 12°. *New York, Scribner, Armstrong & co.* 1874.

Holmes (*Mrs.* Mary J.) West Lawn and the rector of St. Mark's. 413 pp. 12°. *New York, G. W. Carleton & co.* 1874.

Holmes (Oliver Wendell, *m. d.*) The poet at the breakfast table. [*anon.*] 1 p. l. 418 pp. 1 pl. 12°. *Boston, J. R. Osgood & co.* 1872.

——— Songs of many seasons. 1862–1874. xii, 216 pp. 16°. *Boston, J. R. Osgood & co.* 1875.

Holt (*Mrs.* M. A.) John Bentley's mistake. 177 pp. 1 pl. 18°. *New York, national temperance society*, 1873.

——— Work and reward. 183 pp. incl. 1 pl. 18°. *New York, national temperance society*, 1873.

Holwell (John Zephaniah). Interesting historical events, relative to Bengal, and the empire of Indostan. 2d ed. 2 parts in 1 v. 2 p. l. 233 pp. 4 pl; 3 p. l. 152 pp. 5 pl. 8°. *London, T. Becket & P. A. De Hondt*, 1766.

Holy-day stories. Translated by R. H. Schively. [*anon.*] 112 pp. 3 pl. 16°. *Philadelphia, reformed church publ. board*, [1869].

Holyoake (George Jacob). Christianity and secularism. Report of a public discussion, 1853. *See* **Grant** (*Rev.* Brewin) *and* **Holyoake.**

——— History of co-operation in England. v. 1. The pioneer period—1812–1844. xii, 419 pp. 12°. *London, Trübner & co.* 1875.

Holz (Ferdinand Wilhelm). Details griechischer haupt-gesimse. Eng. title, 1 l. 40 pl. 4°. *Berlin, T. Grieben*, [1854].

Homan (L. Beecher). Yaphank as it is, and was, and will be. Biographical sketches. 220 pp. incl. 10 ports. 1 pl. 8°. [*New York, J. Polhemus*, 1875].

Hooker (*Mrs.* Isabella Beecher). Womanhood. 108 pp. 16°. *Boston, Lee & Shepard*, 1874.

Hooker (Joseph Dalton) *and others.* Flora of British India. v. 1. Ranunculaceæ to sapindaceæ. 2 p. l. viii, xl, 740 pp. 8°. *London, L. Reeve & co.* [1872–]1875. s.

Hookham (Mary Ann). Life and times of Margaret of Anjou. 2 v. xii, 435 pp. 2 pl. 1 tab; xii, 446 pp. 3 pl. 8°. *London, Tinsley brothers*, 1872.

Hooper (*Col.* George W.) Down the river; or, practical lessons under the code duello. [*anon.*] 268 pp. 12 pl. 12°. *New York, E. J. Hale & son*, 1874.

Hooper (Henry). The lost model. 386 pp. 12°. *Philadelphia, J. B. Lippincott & co.* 1874.

Hope (Ascott R. *pseud.*) Book about dominies. 4th ed. vii, 248 pp. 12°. *Edinburgh, W. P. Nimmo*, 1871.

Hopkins (Caspar T.) Manual of american ideas. 2d rev. ed. 382 pp. incl. 1 chart. 12°. *San Francisco, A. L. Bancroft & co.* 1873.

Hopkins (G. Morgan) *& co.* Atlas of the city of Cambridge, Mass. 69 pp. incl. 19 maps. fol. *Philadelphia, G. M. Hopkins & co.* 1873.

——— City atlas of Lawrence, Mass. 2 p. l. 7–75 pp. cont. 18 maps. fol. *Philadelphia, G. M. Hopkins*, 1875.

——— Atlas of the city of Newton, Mass. 85 pp. incl. 23 maps. 4°. *Philadelphia, G. M. Hopkins & co.* 1874.

——— Atlas of the city of Salem, Mass. 2 p. l. 16 col. plans on 32 l. 1 l. 4°. *Philadelphia, G. M. Hopkins & co.* 1874.

——— Atlas of the city of Somerville, Mass. 53 pp. incl. 12 maps, 1 l. fol. *Philadelphia, G. M. Hopkins & co.* 1874.

——— Atlas of the county of Suffolk, Mass. 7 v. fol. *Philadelphia, G. M. Hopkins & co.* 1873–75.

CONTENTS.

v. 1. Boston proper. 1874.
2. Late city of Roxbury, now wards 13–14, and 15, city of Boston. 1873.
3. South Boston and Dorchester. 1874.
4. East Boston, city of Chelsea, Revere and Winthrop. 1874.
5. West Roxbury, now ward 17, Boston. 1874.
6. Late city of Charlestown, now wards 20, 21 and 22, city of Boston. 1875.
7. Late town of Brighton, now ward 19 of Boston. 1875.

——— Atlas of the town of Woburn, Mass. 67 pp. incl. 17 col. pl. 1 col. pl. fol. *Philadelphia, G. M. Hopkins & co.* 1875.

——— City atlas of Providence, Rhode-Island. v. 1. fol. *Philadelphia, G. M. Hopkins*, 1875.

——— City atlas of Rochester, New York. 1 p. l. 38 col. maps on 74 l. 1 l. fol. *Philadelphia, G. M. Hopkins*, 1875.

Hopkins (Mark, *d. d.*) Outline study of man. viii, 308 pp. 1 diagram. 12°. *New York, Scribner, Armstrong & co.* 1873.

——— Strength and beauty. 1 p. l. 7–361 pp. 12°. *New York, Dodd & Mead*, [1874].

Hopkins (Samuel, *d. d.*) System of doctrines, contained in divine revelation. 2d ed. 2 v. 518 pp; 538 pp. 8°. *Boston, Lincoln & Edmands*, 1811.

Hopley (Howard). Under egyptian palms. xv, 308 pp. 2 pl. 12°. *London, Chapman & Hall*, 1869.

Hoppin (James Mason). Life of Andrew Hull Foote. 411 pp. 8 pl. 2 maps. 8°. *New York, Harper & brothers*, 1874.

Horne (Richard Hengist). Cosmo de' Medici, and other poems. 4 p. l. 167 pp. port. 12°. *London, G. Rivers*, 1875.

——— Orion; an epic poem. 10th ed. xxvii, 158 pp. port. 12°. *London, Chatto & Windus*, 1874.

Horner (Susan) *and* **Horner** (Joanna). Walks in Florence. 2 v. xiii pp. 1 l. 476 pp. 10 pl. 1 plan, 1 table; vii pp. 1 l. 463 pp. 5 pl. 12°. *London, Strahan & co.* 1873.

Horstman (Ignatius F. *d. d. editor*). History of the holy catholic bible. 128 pp. 4°. *Philadelphia, J. E. Potter & co.* [1875].

Horton (Caroline W.) Architecture for general students. 2 p. l. 287 pp. 8 pl. 16°. *New York, Hurd & Houghton*, 1874.

Hosmer (*Mrs.* Margaret). John Hartman. 304 pp. 2 pl. 16°. *Philadelphia, J. P. Skelly & co.* 1872.

Hosmer (William Henry Cuyler). Later lays and lyrics. 2 p. l. 168 pp. 12°. *Rochester, N. Y., D. M. Dewey*, 1873.

——— Yonnondio, or warriors of the Genesee. 239 pp. 12°. *New-York, Wiley & Putnam*, 1844.

Hotten (John Camden, *editor*). Original lists of persons who went from Great Britain to the american plantations 1600–1700. 580 pp. (+ 159*–168*, and 315*–320*), 2 l. 4°. *London, Chatto & Windus*, 1874.

Hough (*Rev.* Alfred J.) Solomon's song resung. 1 p. l. 204 pp. 12°. *Boston, for the author*, 1874.

Housekeeping in the blue grass. A new cook book. Edited by the ladies of the presbyterian church, Paris, Ky. xv, 188 pp. 8°. *Cincinnati, G. E. Stevens & co.* 1875.

Houssaye (Arsène). Les courtisanes du monde. 4 v. 8°. *Paris, E. Dentu*, 1870.

——— Les grandes dames. Nouv. éd. 4 v. 8°. *Paris, E. Dentu*, 1869.

——— Notre-Dame de Thermidor. Histoire de madame Tallien. 2e éd. 2 p. l. 496 pp. 8 pl. 8°. *Paris, H. Plon*, 1867.

Houssaye (Arsène)—continued.

——— Les parisiennes. Nouv. ed. 4 v. 8°. *Paris, E. Dentu*, 1869.

——— Voyage à ma fenêtre. Voyage à Venise. Voyage au pays des tulipes. Voyage au paradis. 3 p. l. 405 pp. 2 pl. 8°. *Paris, H. Plon*, 1860.

Hovey (Alvah, *d. d.*) Religion and the state. Protection or alliance? Taxation or exemption? 175 pp. 16°. *Boston, Estes & Lauriat*, 1874.

How shall I woo thee? [*anon.*] 144 pp. 16°. *New York, happy hours co.* [1875].

How to become a clairvoyant. [*anon.*] 128 pp. 16°. *Newark, N. J. union publishing co.* 1874.

Howard (Alfred). Biographical illustrations: portraits and biography of the most eminent persons of all ages and nations. 1 p. l. 160 pp. 80 pl. cont. 720 ports. 4°. *London, for T. Tegg*, 1830.

Howard (Blanche). One summer. [*anon.*] 1 p. l. 7-254 pp. 18°. *Boston, J. R. Osgood & co.* 1875.

Howard (*Mrs.* B. C.) Fifty years in a Maryland kitchen. xvi, 378 pp. 12°. *Baltimore, Turnbull brothers*, 1873.

Howard (George W.) The monumental city. Front. 314 pp. 1 map. 8°. *Baltimore, J. D. Ehlers & co.* 1873.

Howard (John H.) Gymnasts and gymnastics. New ed. xix, 299 pp. incl. front. 12°. *London, Longmans*, 1873.

Howard (Marion). Fred's hard fight. 334 pp. 2 pl. 16°. *New York, national temperance publication house*, 1873.

——— Mr. Warner's household. 132 pp. 3 pl. 18°. *Philadelphia, presbyterian board of publication*, [1875].

Howe (A. Jackson, *m. d.*) Manual of eye surgery. 1 p. l. 5-204 pp. 8°. *Cincinnati, Wilstach, Baldwin & co.* 1874.

Howe (Joseph W. *m. d.*) The breath. 108 pp. 12°. *New York, D. Appleton & co.* 1874.

Howe (*Mrs.* Julia Ward, *editor*), *and others.* Sex and education. 203 pp. 16°. *Boston, Roberts brothers*, 1874.

Howells (William Dean). A chance acquaintance. 2 p. l. 279 pp. 18°. *Boston, J. R. Osgood & co.* 1873.

——— Same. 4 p. l. 13-271 pp. 7 pl. 12°. *Boston, J. R. Osgood & co.* 1874.

——— A foregone conclusion. 1 p. l. 265 pp. 12°. *Boston, J. R. Osgood & co.* 1875.

Howells (William Dean)—continued.

——— Poems. 1 p. l. 172 pp. 18°. *Boston, J. R. Osgood & co.* 1873.

Howitt (Mary). Vignettes of american history. 3 p. l. 138 pp. 19 pl. 12°. *London, S. W. Partridge & co.* [1868].

Howland (Marie). Papa's own girl. 547 pp. 12°. *New York, J. P. Jewett*, 1874.

Howson (John Saul, *d. d. editor*). Essays on cathedrals. By various writers. xi, 363 pp. 8°. *London, J. Murray*, 1872.

Huart (Louis). Muséum parisien. Histoire de toutes les bêtes curieuses de Paris et de la banlieue. 2 p. l. 395 pp. 8°. *Paris, Beauger et cie.* 1841.

——— Paris au bal. 110 pp. 12°. *Paris, Aubert & cie.* [1845].

Hübner (Joseph Alexander, *baron* von). Life and times of Sixtus the fifth. From the french by Hubert E. H. Jerningham. 2 v. viii, 444 pp; vi, 411 pp. 8°. *London, Longmans*, 1872.

——— Same. From the french by James F. Meline. 180 pp. 16°. *New York, catholic publication society*, 1873.

——— Promenade autour du monde. 2e éd. 2 v. 2 p. l. 478 pp; 2 p. l. 501 pp. 16°. *Paris, Hachette & cie.* 1873.

Hübner (Julius). The Dresden gallery in photographs, with comments by Julius Hübner. Translated by J. Pond. 1 p. l. 20 l. numb. & 20 phots. 1 l. 8°. *New York, Stroefer & Kirchner*, 1875.

Hudson (Elizabeth Harriot). Life and times of Louisa, queen of Prussia. 2 v. xvi, 362 pp; xi, 385 pp. 8°. *London, W. Isbister & co.* 1874.

Hudson (*Rev.* Henry Norman). Sermons. 423 pp. 16°. *Boston, Ginn brothers*, 1874.

——— Text-book of poetry. x, 694 pp. 12°. *Boston, Ginn brothers*, 1875.

Hudson (H. R.) Poems. iv, 214 pp. 12°. *Boston, J. R. Osgood & co.* 1874.

Hudson (William). Life of John Holland, of Sheffield park. viii, 567 pp. port. 5 pl. 1 facs. 8°. *London, Longmans*, 1874.

Huet (Pierre Daniel). Huetiana. xxiv, 436 pp. 8 l. 18°. *Paris, J. Estienne*, 1722.

Note.—Published by the abbé Joseph Thoulier d'Olivet.

——— Traité de la foiblesse de l'esprit humain. xl, 296 pp. 16°. *Londres, J. Nourse*, 1741.

——— Treatise of romances. Translated out of french. 7 p. l. 112 pp. 18°. *London, for S. Heyrick*, 1672.

Hugessen. *See* **Knatchbull-Hugessen.**

Hughes (John). Views in the south of France, chiefly on the Rhone; from drawings by P. Dewint. After original sketches by John Hughes, with descriptions. 2 p. l. 8 pp. 25 pl. sm. fol. *London, W. B. Cooke,* 1825.

Hughes (Thomas). Memoir of a brother. 2d ed. xvi, 178 pp. port. 12°. *London, Macmillan & co.* 1873.

Hughey (*Rev.* G. W.) Political romanism. 287 pp. 16°. *Cincinnati, Hitchcock & Walden,* 1872.

Hugo (Victor Marie, *vicomte*). Actes et paroles. Avant l'exil, 1841–1851. 2 p. l. xlviii, 516 pp. 8°. *Paris, M. Lévy frères,* 1875.

——— Quatrevingt-treize. Premier récit—la guerre civile. 3 v. 8°. *Paris, M. Lévy frères,* 1874.

——— Same. Ninety-three. Translated by F. L. Benedict. 356 pp. 8°. *New York, Harper & brothers,* 1874.

——— Same. "'93." Translated by E. B. d'Espinville Picot. 163 pp. 8°. *Philadelphia, "the evening telegraph,"* 1874.

Hulbert (Charles). Museum americanum. 346 pp. 3 pl. 18°. *Shrewsbury, C. Hulbert,* 1823.

[*With* HULBERT (C.) Museum europæum].

——— Museum europæum. 473 pp. 1 pl. port. 18°. *London, G. B. Whittaker,* 1825.

Hull (Daniel W.) The hereafter: a demonstration of a future life. 156 pp. 12°. *Boston, W. White & co.* 1873.

Hull (Moses). The contrast: evangelicalism and spiritualism compared. 236 pp. 12°. *Boston, W. White & co.* 1873.

——— *and* **Parker** (W. F.) Which: spiritualism or christianity? a friendly correspondence. 178 pp. 12°. *Boston, W. White & co.* 1873.

Humbert (Aimé). Japan and the japanese illustrated. Translated by mrs. Cashel Hoey. xix, 378 pp. incl. 6 pl. 4°. *London, R. Bentley & son,* 1874.

Humfrey (John). Veritas in semente. A moderate discourse concerning quakers. [*anon.*] 2d ed. xii, 3–15, 174 pp. 1 l. 16°. *London, J. Darby,* 1707.

Humphrey (*Mrs.* E. J.) Gems of India; sketches of distinguished hindoo and mahomedan women. 206 pp. incl. 1 pl. & 3 ports. 12°. *New York, Nelson & Phillips,* 1875.

Humphreys (David) *and others.* Anarchiad: a New England poem. viii, 120 pp. sq. 18°. *New Haven, T. H. Pease,* 1861.

Hunt (David). Essays on religious subjects. 152 pp. 12°. *New Vienna, O. author,* 1874.

Hunt (Helen Maria Fiske). Bits of talk about home matters. By H. H. [*anon.*] 1 p. l. vii–239 pp. 18°. *Boston, Roberts brothers,* 1873.

Hunt (James Henry Leigh). Wishing-cap papers. 455 pp. 16°. *Boston, Lee & Shepard,* 1873.

Hunt (Thomas Sterry, *ll. d.*) Chemical and geological essays. xxii, 489 pp. 12°. *Boston, J. R. Osgood & co.* 1875.

Hunt (William). History of Italy. xi, 273 pp. 16°. *New York, H. Holt & co.* 1874.

[FREEMAN (E. A.) Historical course for schools].

Hunter (W. W.) Comparative dictionary of the languages of India and high Asia. 6 p. l. 218 pp. 3 l. sm. fol. *London, Trübner & co.* 1868.

——— Orissa: [or the vicissitudes of an indian province]. 2 v. 3 p. l. 330 pp. 16 pl. 1 col. map in pocket; 2 p. l. 278 pp. 1 l. 219 pp. 1 pl. 8°. *London, Smith, Elder & co.* 1872.

Huntington (William S.) Road-master's assistant and section-master's guide. 2d ed. 144 pp. 18°. *New York, A. N. Kellogg & co.* 1872.

Hurst (Catherine E.) Queen Louisa of Prussia. 4 p. l. 228 pp. incl. 4 pl. port. 16°. *New York, Nelson & Phillips,* [1874].

Hurst (John F.) Life and literature in the fatherland. vi, 448 pp. 12°. *New York, Scribner, Armstrong & co.* 1875.

Hurtado (José) *and* **Hurtado** (Manuel Oliver). Munda Pompeiana. Memoria. 515 pp. 1 map, 1 pl. 8°. *Madrid, M. Galiano,* 1861. s.

Hussey (Elisha C.) National cottage architecture. 1 p. l. 24 pp. 63 pl. 4°. *New York, G. E. Woodward,* 1874.

Hutchings (*Rev.* Samuel). Mode of christian baptism. 344 pp. 4 pl. 16°. *New York, Warren & Wyman,* [1875].

Hutchins (John). History and antiquities of Sherbourne, Dorset. 1 p. l. 75–150 pp. 11 pl. 1 pedigree. fol. *London, Nichols, son, & Bentley,* 1815.

Hutchinson (Thomas J.) Two years in Peru. 2 v. xxiv, 343 pp. 1 col. map, 17 pl; xii, 334 pp. 15 pl. 8°. *London, S. Low, Marston, Low & Searle,* 1873.

Hutchison (Joseph C. *m. d.*) Treatise on physiology and hygiene. 1 p. l. 270 pp. 14 l. 2 col. pl. 12°. *New York, Clark & Maynard,* 1876.

Huth (Alfred Henry). Marriage of near kin. xii, 359, lxvii pp. 6 tables. 8°. *London, J. & A. Churchill*, 1875.

Hutton (Laurence). Plays and players. vii, 276 pp. 8°. *New York, Hurd & Houghton*, 1875.

Hutton (William). History of Derby to 1791. 2d ed. xii, 267 pp. 19 pl. 8°. *London, Nichols, son, & Bentley*, 1817.

Huyshe (G. L.) Red river expedition. xi, 275 pp. 1 tab. 1 port. 3 maps. 8°. *London, Macmillan & co.* 1871.

Hyde (Alexander). Agriculture. Twelve lectures. 372 pp. 7 pl. 12°. *Hartford, Conn. american publishing co.* 1871.

Hyde (Alexander), **Baldwin** (*Rev.* A. C.) *and* **Gage** (*Rev.* W. L.) Frozen zone and its explorers. xvi, 800 pp. incl. 36 pl. 3 maps, 32 pl. 8°. *Hartford, columbian book co.* 1874.

Hyde (Anna M.) Work, play, and profit; or, gardening for young folks. 162 pp. incl. 2 pl. 16°. *Philadelphia, J. B. Lippincott & co.* 1873.

Ignis fatuus: or, a voice from the clouds. [*anon.*] 136 pp. 12°. *Richmond, for the author*, 1827.

Ikhwánu-s safá; or, brothers of purity. From the hindustáni, by professor John Dowson. [*anon.*] viii, 156 pp. 16°. *London, Trübner & co.* 1869.

Illustrious lovers. Written originally in french. [*anon.*] 2 p. l. 244 pp. 4 l. 16°. *London, for W. Whitwood*, 1686.

Imbonati (Carlo Giuseppe). Bibliotheca latino-hebraica. 2 parts in 1 v. 8 p. l. 549 pp; 278 pp. 3 l. fol. *Romae*, 1694.

Note.—Forms continuation, or v. 5, to BARTOLOCCI (G.) Bibliotheca magna rabbinica.

Ingelow (Jean). Fated to be free. viii, 497 pp. 16°. *Boston, Roberts brothers*, 1875.

Ingersoll (Robert G.) The gods and other lectures. 4 p. l. 7-253 pp. 8°. *Peoria, Ill.* 1874.

Ingleby (Clement Mansfield). Shakespeare hermeneutics, or the still lion. 4 p. l. 168 pp. sm. 4°. *London, Trübner & co.* 1875.

——— Shakespeare's centurie of prayse. [*anon.*] xx, 362 pp. 1 facs. sm. 4°. *London, for the editor, Birmingham, printed by J. Allen*, 1874.

Inman (Thomas, *m. d.*) Ancient faiths embodied in ancient names. 2 v. viii, 789 pp. 6 pl; l, 1028 pp. 9 pl. 8°. *London, printed for the author*, 1868–69.

Inman (Thomas, *m. d.*)—continued.

——— Ancient faiths and modern. xx, 478, xlv pp. 8°. *New York, J. W. Bouton*, 1876.

International scientific series. v. 1–18. 12°. *London, H. S. King & co.* [&] *New York, D. Appleton & co.* 1872–75.

CONTENTS.

v. 1. TYNDALL (J.) The forms of water in clouds and rivers [etc.] 1872.
2. BAGEHOT (W.) Physics and politics. 1873.
3. SMITH (Edward). Foods. 3d ed. 1874.
4. BAIN (A.) Mind and body. 1873.
5. SPENCER (H.) The study of sociology. 1874.
6. STEWART (B.) The conservation of energy. 1874.
7. PETTIGREW (J. B.) Animal locomotion. 1873.
8. MAUDSLEY (H.) Responsibility in mental disease. 1874.
9. COOKE (J. P. *jr.*) The new chemistry. 1874.
10. AMOS (S.) The science of law. 2d ed. 1874.
11. MAREY (E. J.) Animal mechanism.
12. SCHMIDT (Oscar). The doctrine of descent and Darwinism. 2d ed. 1875.
13. DRAPER (J. W.) History of the conflict between religion and science. 1875.
14. COOKE (M. C.) Fungi.
15. VOGEL (H.) The chemical effects of light and photography.
16. WHITNEY (W. D.) The life and growth of language. 1875.
17. JEVONS (W. S.) Money and the mechanism of exchange. 1875.
18. LOMMEL (E.) The nature of light. 1875.

Irish (Phebe Matilda). Diary and letters. 219 pp. port. 16°. *Philadelphia, T. W. Stuckey*, 1876.

Irving (George Vere) *and* **Murray** (Alexander). Upper ward of Lanarkshire described and delineated. 3 v. 8°. *Glasgow, T. Murray & son*, 1864.

Irving (Joseph). Annals of our time: from june 20, 1837. New ed. to feb. 28, 1871. xiv, 1034 pp. 1 l. 8°. *London, Macmillan & co.* 1875.

——— Same. Supplement, from feb. 28, 1871, to march 19, 1874. 2 p. l. 170 pp. 8°. *London, Macmillan & co.* 1875.

——— History of Dumbartonshire; with genealogical notices. 2d ed. xii, 616+473*–500* pp. 7 pl. 4 facs. 4 pedigrees, 2 maps. 4°. *Dumbarton, for the author*, 1860.

J. (M. E.) Dayspring in the far west. Sketches of mission-work in north-west America. [*anon.*] xii, 215 pp. 21 pl. 3 ports. 1 col. map. sq. 12°. *London, Seeley, Jackson & Halliday*, 1875.

Jackson (Catherine Charlotte, *lady*). Fair Lusitania. xii, 406 pp. 20 pl. 8°. *London, R. Bentley & son*, 1874.

Jackson (Daniel, *jr.*) Alonzo and Melissa. 252 pp. 1 pl. 18°. *Philadelphia, J. B. Lippincott & co.* 1864.

Jackson (*Sir* George). Bath archives. A further selection from the diaries of sir George Jackson, from 1809 to 1816. 2 v. viii, 450

Jackson (*Sir* George)—continued. pp; x, 517 pp. 8°. *London, R. Bentley & co.* 1873.

Jackson (James, *sen. m. d.*) Memoir of James Jackson, jr. With abstracts from his letters. xiii, 228 pp. 16°. *Boston, Hilliard Gray & co.* 1836.

Jackson (*Rev.* John Edward). History and description of st. George's church at Doncaster. viii, 144, xci pp. 15 pl. fol. *London, for the author,* 1855.

Jackson (Mary Catherine). Word-sketches in the sweet south. 4 p. l. 301 pp. 8°. *London, R. Bentley & son,* 1873.

Note.—A tour to Gibraltar, Tangier, &c.

Jackson (Rowland). History of Barnsley, in Yorkshire. 2 p. l. 248 pp. 1 facs. 8 pedigrees. 8°. *London, Bell & Daldy,* 1858.

Jackson (T. G) Modern gothic architecture. viii, 206 pp. 12°. *London, H. S. King & co.* 1873.

Jacob (*Maj.-gen. sir* George Le Grand). Western India before and during the mutinies. viii, 262 pp. 12°. *London, H. S. King & co.* 1871.

Jacob (John J.) Biographical sketch of capt. Michael Cresap. [*anon.*] 124 pp. 16°. *Cumberland, Md. author,* 1826.

Jacox (Francis). At nightfall and midnight. xi, 466 pp. 12°. *London, Hodder & Stoughton,* 1873.

Jacquemart (Albert). History of the ceramic art. Translated by mrs. Bury Palliser. 4 p. l. 627 pp. 12 l. 12 pl. 8°. *London, S. Low, Marston, Low & Searle,* 1873.

Jacquemin (Raphaël). Iconographie générale et méthodique du costume du IVe au XIXe siècle (315–1815). 2 p. l. 199 col. pl. fol. *Paris, l'auteur,* [1863–69].

Jaillot (Charles Hubert Alexis). Atlas françois, contenant les cartes géographiques de l'Europe, de l'Asie, de l'Afrique et de l'Amérique. Eng. title, 1 p. l. 115 maps & tables. fol. *Paris, Iaillot,* 1695.

Note.—The p. l. or index leaf is an insertion which bears the imprint, "*Rotterdam, Reinier leers,* 1695." Of the 115 maps and tables which it enumerates, Nos. 44, 47, 59, 86, 103, and 105 are wanting.

Jal (Auguste). Dictionnaire critique de biographie et d'histoire. 2e éd. augmentée. 2 p. l. iv, 1357 pp. 8°. *Paris, H. Plon,* 1872.

James (Henry, *jr.*) Passionate pilgrim, and other tales. 496 pp. 12°. *Boston, J. R. Osgood & co.* 1875.

——— Transatlantic sketches. 401 pp. 12°. *Boston, J. R. Osgood & co.* 1875.

James (*Mrs.* Thomas Potts, *i. e.* Isabella). Memorial of Thomas Potts, junior; with an account of his descendants. xii, 416 pp. 1 l. 6 ports. 3 facs. 9 pl. sm. 4°. *Cambridge,* [*Ms.*] *privately printed,* 1874.

James (*Rev.* William). Grace for grace. 341 pp. 12°. *New York, Dodd & Mead,* [1874].

James (William, *of London*). Inquiry into the merits of the principal naval actions, between Great-Britain and the United States. vi, 102 pp. 3 tab. sq. 12°. *Halifax, for the author,* 1816.

Jameson (John Alexander). The constitutional convention. xix, 561 pp. 8°. *New York, C. Scribner & co.* 1867.

——— Same. 3d ed. xix, 561 pp. 8°. *Chicago, Callaghan & co.* 1873.

Jancigny (Adolphe Philibert Dubois de). Histoire de l'Inde ancienne et moderne. 371 pp. 5 tab. 16°. *Leipzig, A. Dürr,* 1858.

Janes (*Rev.* Frederic). Janes family. Genealogy. 419 pp. 4 pl. 8°. *New York, J. H. Dingman,* 1868.

Janin (Jules Gabriel). Histoire de la littérature dramatique. 6 v. 16°. *Paris, M. Lévy frères,* 1853–58.

——— Le livre. 2 p. l. xxxi, 404 pp. 8°. *Paris, H. Plon,* 1870.

Jātakatthavaṇṇanā. Jātaka with its commentary. Published in the original pāli by V. Fausbøll and translated by R. C. Childers. Text, v. 1, pt. 1. 4 p. l. 224 pp. 8°. *London,* [*Kopenhagen printed,*] *Trübner & co.* 1875.

Jaubert (Jean Baptiste) *and* **Barthélemy-Lapommeraye** (Christophe Jérôme). Richesses ornithologiques du midi de la France. 547 pp. 20 col. pl. 4°. *Marseille, Barlatier-Feissat & Demonchy,* 1859. s.

Jeaffreson (John Cordy). Book about the table. 2 v. 3 p. l. 324 pp; 3 p. l. 352 pp. 8°. *London, Hurst & Blackett,* 1875.

——— Brides and bridals. 2 v. vi, 362 pp; vi, 364 pp. 8°. *London, Hurst & Blackett,* 1872.

Jeannel (Julien François). De la prostitution dans les grandes villes au dix-neuvième siècle. 2e éd. x, 647 pp. 16°. *Paris, J.-B. Baillière & fils,* 1874.

Jefferson (Samuel). History and antiquities of Cumberland. 2 v. 1 p. l. xv, 515 pp. 14 pl; 1 p. l. xviii, 462 pp. 7 pl. 8°. *Carlisle, S. Jefferson,* 1840–42.

Jefferys (Thomas). The first part of the north american pilot: for Newfoundland, Labradore, and the gulf st. Lawrence [etc.]

Jefferys (Thomas)—continued.
New ed. 3 l. 25 charts. fol. *London, R. Laurie & J. Whittle,* 1806.
——— A new edition, enlarged, of the second part of the north american pilot, for New England, New York, Pennsylvania, New Jersey, Maryland, Virginia, North and South Carolina, Georgia, Florida, and the Havanna: [etc.] 1 l. 20 charts. fol. *London, R. Laurie & J. Whittle,* 1800.

Jeffrey (Alexander). History and antiquities of Roxburghshire. 4 v. 12°. *Edinburgh, Seton & Mackenzie,* 1864.

Jenkin (*Mrs.* Charles). Jupiter's daughters. v, 298 pp. 12°. *London, Smith, Elder & co.* 1874.

Jenness (John Scribner). Isles of Shoals. 182 pp. 2 maps, 1 port. 1 pl. 16°. *New York, Hurd & Houghton,* 1873.

Jennings (Hargrave) *and others.* Live lights or dead lights: (altar or table?) 16 p. l. 199 pp. 2 tab. 2 charts. 16°. *London, J. Hodges,* 1873.

Jerningham (Hubert E. H.) Life in a french chateau. 2d ed. xii, 278 pp. front. 12°. *London, Hurst & Blackett,* 1867.
——— To and from Constantinople. 1 p. l. v–xi, 365 pp. front. 8°. *London, Hurst & Blackett,* 1873.

Jerningham (*Mrs.* Matilda). Random rhymes, from january to december. viii, 192 pp. 12°. *Baltimore, the authoress,* 1873.

Jerningham; or, the inconsistent man. [*anon.*] 3 v. 12°. *London, Smith, Elder & co.* 1836.

Jerrold (Douglas William). Fireside saints, and other papers. 357 pp. 16°. *Boston, Lee & Shepard,* 1873.

Jerrold (William Blanchard). Life of Napoleon III. v. 1. x, 471 pp. 3 ports. 9 facs. 8°. *London, Longmans,* 1874.
——— London. A pilgrimage. 1872. *See* **Doré** (G.) *and* **Jerrold.**

Jervis (William Henley). Gallican church. From 1516 to the revolution. 2 v. xxiv, 476 pp. port; xii, 452 pp. port. 8°. *London, J. Murray,* 1872.

Jessup (Henry Harris, *d. d.*) Syrian home-life. Compiled by rev. Isaac Riley. From materials furnished by rev. H. H. Jessup. 366 pp. 2 pl. 12°. *New York, Dodd & Mead,* [1874].
——— Women of the Arabs. 1 p. l. x, 374 pp. 14 pl. 12°. *New York, Dodd & Mead,* [1873].

Jevons (William Stanley). Money and the mechanism of exchange. xviii, 349 pp. 12°. *London, H. S. King & co.* 1875.
[INTERNATIONAL scientific series, v. 17].
——— Same. 349 pp. 12°. *New York, D. Appleton & co.* 1875.
——— Principles of science. 2 v. xvi, 463 pp. 1 pl; vii, 480 pp. 8°. *London, Macmillan & co.* 1874.

Jewell (J. Grey, *m. d.*) Among our sailors. 311 pp. 12°. *New York, Harper & brothers,* 1874.

Jewitt (Llewellyn). Grave-mounds and their contents. xxiv, 306 pp. 1 pl. 12°. *London, Groombridge & sons,* 1870.
——— *and* **Hall** (Samuel Carter). Stately homes of England. 1 p. l. v–xi, 399 pp. sq. 12°. *London, Virtue & co.* 1874.

Joanne (Adolphe-Laurent). Dictionnaire géographique de la France. 2e éd. 2 v. 2 p. l. clxxxviii, 1288 pp; 1 p. l. 1289–2551 pp. 8°. *Paris, Hachette et cie.* 1872.
——— Paris illustré en 1870. 3e éd. 2 p. l. civ, 1087, 96 pp. incl. 114 pl. 14 maps. 16°. *Paris, Hachette & cie.* [1871].

Johns (Henry T.) Life with the forty-ninth Mass. volunteers. 391 pp. 14 pl. 12°. *Pittsfield, Mass. for the author,* 1864.

Johnson (George). Roll-call and other poems. 198 pp. 16°. *Philadelphia, J. B. Lippincott & co.* 1876.

Johnson (Helen Kendrick). Roddy's reality. 290 pp. front. 16°. *New York, G. P. Putnam's sons,* 1875.
——— Roddy's romance. 299 pp. 16°. *New York, G. P. Putnam's sons,* 1874.

Johnson (Laura Winthrop). Poems of twenty years. 148 pp. 12°. *New York, D. C. Lent,* 1874.

Johnson (Maria L.) In school and college. [*anon.*] 271 pp. 1 pl. 16°. *New York, Pott, Young & co.* [1873].

Johnson (Rossiter, *editor*). Little classics, 1874–75. *See* **Little** classics.

Johnson (Virginia W.) Calderwood secret. 1 p. l. 136 pp. 8°. *New York, Harper & brothers,* 1875.
[HARPER's library of select novels, no. 418].
——— Catskill fairies. Illustrated by A. Fredericks. 163 pp. incl. 7 pl. 8°. *New York, Harper & brothers,* 1876.
——— Joseph the Jew. [*anon.*] 131 pp. 8°. *New York, Harper & brothers,* 1874.
——— Sack of gold. 1 p. l. 121 pp. 8°. *New York, Harper & brothers,* 1874.
[HARPER's library of select novels, no. 419].

Johnson (Watson, *compiler*). Secret wealth; comprising over fifteen hundred receipts. Also, information on the horse, by dr. Hamilton, of England. 2 p. l. 9–360 pp. 7 l. 12°. *Syracuse,* [*Truair, Smith & co.*] 1875.

Johnston (Alexander Keith). Royal atlas of modern geography. New ed. ix pp. 74 l. of indexes, 49 maps on 98 l. fol. *Edinburgh, W. Blackwood & sons,* 1873.

Johnston (John, *ll. d.*) History of the towns of Bristol and Bremen, Maine. viii, 524 pp. 7 ports. 1 map. 8°. *Albany, J. Munsell,* 1873.

Johnston (Joseph E.) Narrative of military operations. 602 pp. 15 pl. 6 maps. 8°. *New York, D. Appleton & co.* 1874.

Jolowicz (Heinrich). Bibliotheca aegyptiaca. Repertorium über die bis 1857 in bezug auf Ägypten erschienenen schriften. viii, 244 pp. 8°. *Leipzig, W. Engelmann,* 1858.

Jonathan (*pseud.*) Brieven uit en over de Vereenigde Staaten. Door Jonathan [*pseud.*] Uitgegeven door dr. E. B. Swalue. xiv, 304 pp. 5 pl. 1 map. 8°. *Schoonhoven, S. E. Van Nooten,* 1853.

Jones (Charles C. *jr.*) Siege of Savannah, 1864, and confederate operations in Georgia during general Sherman's march to the sea. x, 184 pp. 12°. *Albany, for the author,* 1874.

Jones (Charles H.) Abridgement of the debates of congress. President's messages, treaties, [etc.] Forty-third congress—second session. vii pp. 1390 col. 8°. *New York, H. Holt & co.* 1875.

——— Africa, history of exploration and adventure from Herodotus to Livingstone. x, 496 pp. 28 pl. port. 1 map. 8°. *New York, H. Holt & co.* 1875.

——— *editor.* Vers de société. Eng. title, 401 pp. incl. 11 pl. 8°. *New York, H. Holt & co.* 1875.

——— *and* **Hamilton** (Theodore F. *compilers*). People's pictorial atlas. 88 pp. 54 l. of maps, 4 l. of pl. fol. *New York, J. D. Williams,* 1873.

Jones (Evan Rowland). Lincoln, Stanton and Grant. Historical sketches. xii, 342 pp. 3 ports. 8°. *London, F. Warne & co.* [1875].

Jones (G. H.) *& co.* Atlas of Philadelphia in fifteen volumes. v. 1–4. fol. *Philadelphia, G. H. Jones & co.* 1874–75.

Jones (John). History and antiquities of Harewood, York. 2 p. l. 312 pp. 11 pl. 8°. *London, Simpkin, Marshall & co.* 1859.

Jones (J. Hilton). Dominie's son. 264 pp. 12°. *New York,* [*G. P. Putnam's sons*], 1874.

Jones (J. William, *d. d.*) Personal reminiscences and letters of gen. Robert E. Lee. xvi, 509 pp. 6 ports. 13 pl. 8°. *New York, D. Appleton & co.* 1874.

Jones (*Rev.* William, *editor*). New testament illustrations: gathered from many sources. With articles from bishop Clark, rev. dr. Krummacher, [etc.] 959 pp. 12 pl. 8°. *Hartford, the J. B. Burr publishing co.* 1875.

Jouault (Alphonse). Abraham Lincoln, sa jeunesse et sa vie politique. 1 p. l. 256 pp. port. 16°. *Paris, Hachette & cie.* 1875.

Journal des débats politiques et littéraires. Mai 5, 1789–juin 30, 1875. 127 v. 8°. 176 v. fol. *Paris,* 1789–1875.

Joyce (P. W.) Origin and history of irish names of places. 1st–2d series. 2 v. xviii, 593 pp; viii, 509 pp. 16°. *Dublin, McGlashan & Gill,* 1875.
Note.—1st series is 4th ed.

Julienne (Eugène). L'orfévrerie française, les bronzes et la céramique. 2 p. l. 48 pl. fol. *Paris, A. Morel & cie.* 1864.

Junior (B.) Everybody's friend. 196 pp. 12°. *Saint Louis, book and news co.* 1873.

Kansas home for the friendless. (*Board of managers*). Kansas home cook-book. 264 pp. 16°. *Leavenworth, J. C. Ketcheson,* 1874.

Kardec (Allan, *pseud.*) 1874. *See* **Rivail** (Léon H. D.)

Karr (Jean Baptiste Alphonse). Alain family. From the french. By Robert B. Brough. Eng. title, 2 p. l. 311 pp. 7 pl. 12°. *London, Ingram, Cooke & co.* 1853.

Kastner (Jean Georges). Les danses des morts: dissertations et recherches. Accompagnées de la danse macabre, paroles d'Édouard Thierry, musique de G. Kastner. xvi, 310, 46 pp. 20 pl. 5 tab. 4°. *Paris, Brandus & cie.* 1852.

Kates (G. Whitfield). Lyceum stage, recitations, dialogues, etc. Part 1st. 119 pp. 18°. *Toledo, O., Bateson & Kates,* 1874.

Katsch (Adolph E.) Under the stork's nest. From the german, by Emily R. Steinestel. 233 pp. 12°. *Philadelphia, J. B. Lippincott & co.* 1875.

Keats (John). Endymion. Illustrated with engravings by F. Joubert. From paintings by E. J. Poynter. viii, 171 pp. fol. *London, E. Moxon, son & co.* 1873.

Keene (*Mrs.* Sarah F. Prince). "Led." 422 pp. 3 pl. 16°. *Boston, H. Hoyt*, [1873].

——— Viking heir. 330 pp. 3 pl. 16°. *Boston, H. Hoyt*, [1875].

Keim (De Benneville Randolph). Washington and its environs. Ed. for 1874. xx, 252 pp. 2 maps. 16°. *Washington, for the compiler*, 1874.

——— Same. Keim's illustrated hand-book. Washington and its environs. Ed. for 1874. 3d ed.—corrected to may, 1874. xx, 252 pp. 2 maps. 16°. *Washington city, for the compiler*, 1874.

——— Same. Ed. for 1874. 4th ed. Corrected to july, 1874. xx, 252 pp. 2 maps. 16°. *Washington, for the compiler*, 1874.

——— Same. 5th ed. Corrected to january, 1875. xx, 252 pp. 1 map, 1 plan. 16°. *Washington, for the compiler*, 1875.

——— Same. 6th ed. Corrected to january, 1875. xx, 252 pp. 1 map, 1 plan. 16°. *Washington, for the compiler*, 1875.

——— Same. 7th ed. Corrected to january, 1875. xx, 252 pp. 1 map, 1 plan. 16°. *Washington, for the compiler*, 1875.

Keller (Ferdinand). Lake dwellings of Switzerland and other parts of Europe. Translated by J. E. Lee. x, 424 pp. 99 pl. 8°. *London, Longmans*, 1866.

Keller (Franz). Amazon and Madeira rivers. xvi, 177 pp. 18 pl. fol. *London, Chapman & Hall*, 1874.

Kelley (O. H.) Origin and progress of the order of the patrons of husbandry; history from 1866 to 1873. 441 pp. 12°. *Philadelphia, J. A. Wagenseller*, 1875.

Kellogg (*Rev.* Elijah). Pleasant cove series. 16°. *Boston, Lee & Shepard*, 1873.

CONTENTS.

v. 5. John Godsoe's legacy. Eng. title, 304 pp. 3 pl.
v. 6. The fisher boys of Pleasant cove. Eng. title, 336 pp. 3 pl.

——— Whispering pine series. 16°. *Boston, Lee & Shepard*, 1873–74.

CONTENTS.

A stout heart. Eng. title, 224 pp. 6 pl.
The turning of the tide; or, Radcliffe Rich and his patients. Eng. title, 288 pp. 6 pl.

Kelly (Christopher). Solomon's temple spiritualized. Eng. title, ix, 477 pp. 8°. *Dublin, for the author*, 1803.

Kelly (E. R. *editor*). County topographies. 4 v. 12°. *London, Kelly & co.* 1875.

CONTENTS.

Dorsetshire. xv, 278 pp. 1 map.
Hampshire including the Isle of Wight. xvi, 455 pp. 1 map.
Somersetshire. xvii, 556 pp. 1 map.
Wiltshire. xv, 362 pp. 1 map.

Kelsall (Charles). Constantine and Eugene. By Junius Secundus [*pseud.*] 3 p. l. 252 pp. front. 18°. *Brussels, for the author*, 1818.

——— Remarks on scholastic and academic education, with an architectural detail. 2 p. l. 174 pp. 1 l. 19 pl. 2 maps. *London, for the author*, 1821.

Kemper (John). Treatise on the diseases of women. 212 pp. 12°. *Galesburg, Ill. Colville & bro.* 1875.

Kendall (Timothy). Flovvers of epigrammes. Reprinted from the original edition of 1577. xvi, 303 pp. 4°. [*Manchester*], *for the Spenser society*, 1874.

[SPENSER society publications, no. 15].

Kendall (William E.) Letters from Europe and the east. 137 pp. 12°. *New York, G. A. Whitehorne*, 1860.

Kenly (John R.) Memoirs of a Maryland volunteer. War with Mexico, in 1846–48. 521 pp. 8°. *Philadelphia, J. B. Lippincott & co.* 1873.

Kennedy (L.) *and* **Grainger** (T. B.) Present state of the tenancy of land in Great Britain. 2 v. xi, 384 pp. 1 pl; xix, 324 pp. 1 pl. 8°. *London, J. Ridgway*, 1828–29.

Kenney (Charles Lamb). Memoir of Michael William Balfe. x, 309 pp. incl. 1 pl. port. 1 facs. 8°. *London, Tinsley brothers*, 1875.

Kennicott (Benjamin, *d. d.*) State of the printed hebrew text of the old testament considered. 2 v. 572 pp. 4 l; x, 598 pp. 18 l. 8°. *Oxford, the theatre*, 1753–59.

——— Ten annual accounts of the collation of hebrew mss. of the old testament. 206 pp. 8°. *Oxford, Fletcher & Prince*, 1770.

Kenny (D. J.) Illustrated Cincinnati; a pictorial hand-book of the city. 368 pp. front. 1 map. 12°. *Cincinnati, R. Clarke & co.* 1875.

Kent (Charles). Charles Dickens as a reader. ix, 271 pp. 2 facs. 12°. *London, Chapman & Hall*, 1872.

Kenyon (George Thomas). Life of Lloyd, first lord Kenyon. xi, 403 pp. 2 ports. on 1 pl. 8°. *London, Longmans*, 1873.

Keon (Miles Gerald). Dion and the sibyls. 223 pp. 8°. *New York, catholic publication society*, 1875.

Kératry (Émile, *comte* de). La contre-guérilla française au Mexique. 2e éd. 2 p. l. 313 pp. 16°. *Paris, librairie internationale*, 1869.

Kermode (Tamar Anne). Poems. 1 p. l. 5–125 pp. sq. 18°. *Baltimore, G. Lycett*, 1874.

Kerr (Robert). Small country house, to cost from £2,000 to £5,000; with estimates up to £7,000. 100 pp. 12°. *London, J. Murray*, 1873.

Kersey (John). Dictionarium anglo-britannicum. 3d ed. 350 l. unnumb. 8°. *London, for J. Phillips*, [*etc.*] 1721.

Key (Thomas Hewitt). Language: its origin and development. xvii, 547 pp. 8°. *London, G. Bell & sons*, 1874.

Keyes (George L. *publisher*). Hand-book of travel: to the White and Franconia mountains, [etc.] 240 pp. 3 maps. 16°. *Boston, G. L. Keyes*, 1874.

——— Same. [2d ed.] 1 p. l. 284 pp. 3 l. 3 maps. 16°. *Boston, G. L. Keyes*, 1875.

Keyser (Charles S.) Fairmount park and the international exhibition at Philadelphia. 6th ed. 158 pp. 3 pl. 1 map. 12°. *Philadelphia, Claxton, Remsen & Haffelfinger*, 1875.

Kidder (Frederic). History of the Boston massacre, march 5, 1770. 2 p. l. 291 pp. 1 map, 1 pl. 8°. *Albany, J. Munsell*, 1870.

Kilbourne (Payne Kenyon). Sketches and chronicles of Litchfield, Conn. vii, 17–264 pp. 11 pl. 1 map. 8°. *Hartford, Case, Lockwood & co.* 1859.

Kimball (Harriet McEwen). Swallow-flights. [Poems]. v pp. 1 l. 131 pp. 18°. *New York, E. P. Dutton & co.* 1874.

Kimball (James William). Encouragements to faith. 3 p. l. 207 pp. 16°. *Boston, Willard tract repository*, [1873].

Kimball (Laura A. *compiler*). Manual of practical housekeeping. [*anon.*] 128 pp. 8°. *Fort Wayne, gazette book printing house*, 1873.

——— Same. [2d ed.] 132 pp. 8°. *For Wayne, Ind. gazette book printing house*, 1873.

King (Edmund Fillingham, *editor*). Ten thousand wonderful things. xvi, 684 pp. 16°. *London, G. Routledge & sons*, [1859] ?

Kingsbury (John H.) Kingsbury sketches. 296 pp. 6 pl. 12°. *New York, G. W. Carleton & co.* 1875.

Kingsley (Charles). Health and education. 2 p. l. 411 pp. 12°. *London, W. Isbister & co.* 1874.

——— King of the earth and other sermons. 2d ed. 1 p. l. v–viii, 319 pp. 18°. *London, Macmillan & co.* 1872.

——— Madam How and lady Why. xv, 350 pp. incl. 5 pl. 12°. *London, Bell & Daldy*, 1870.

Kingsley (Charles)—continued.

——— Plays and puritans, and other essays. 3 p. l. 271 pp. port. 12°. *London, Macmillan & co.* 1873.

CONTENTS.

Plays and puritans. pp. 1–80.
Sir Walter Raleigh and his time. pp. 81–208.
Froude's history of England. pp. 209–271.

——— Prose idylls, new and old. 2 p. l. 317 pp. 16°. *London, Macmillan & co.* 1873.

——— Town geology. 2d ed. lvi, 239 pp. 16°. *London, Strahan & co.* 1872.

Kingsley (Henry). Hornby mills; and other stories. 2 v. 4 p. l. 249 pp; 3 p. l. 234 pp. 12°. *London, Tinsley brothers*, 1872.

Kingsley (*Miss*). South by west or winter in the Rocky mountains and spring in Mexico. Edited by Charles Kingsley. [*anon.*] xix, 411 pp. incl. front. 1 map. 8°. *London, W. Isbister & co.* 1874.

Kingsman (A.) Over volcanoes, or through France and Spain in 1871. xi, 340 pp. 12°. *London, H. S. King*, 1872.

Kingston (William H. G.) Western world. 736 pp. 8°. *London, J. Nelson & sons*, 1874.

Kinney (Elizabeth C.) Bianca Capello. A tragedy. 146 pp. 16°. *New York, Hurd & Houghton*, 1873.

Kip (*Rev.* Francis M.) Memoirs of an old disciple and his descendants: Christian Miller [etc.] 309 pp. 12°. *New York, R. Carter*, 1848.

Kip (Leonard). Dead marquise. viii, 356 pp. 12°. *New York, G. P. Putnam's sons*, 1873.

Kip (William Ingraham). Historical scenes from the old jesuit missions. 375 pp. 12°. *New York, A. D. F. Randolph & co.* [1875].

Kirby (W. F.) Synonymic catalogue of diurnal lepidoptera. vii, 690 pp. 8°. *London, J. Van Voorst*, 1871. S.

Kirk (Eleanor). Up Broadway, and its sequel. 271 pp. 12°. *New York, Carleton*, 1870.

Kirkby (John de). Survey of the county of York. xxviii, 543 pp. 8°. *Durham*, 1867. [SURTEES society. Publications, v. 49].

Kite (Edward). Monumental brasses of Wiltshire. xv, 111 pp. 32 pl. 2 pedigrees. 8°. *London, for the author*, 1860.

Kitty Bourne. [*anon.*] 334 pp. incl. 53 pl. 12°. *New York, Dodd & Mead*, [1875].

Kleist (Heinrich von). Gesammelte schriften. Herausgegeben von Ludwig Tieck, mit einer biographischen einleitung von Julian Schmidt. 2te ausg. 3 v. 18°. *Berlin, G. Reimer*, 1863.

Klemm (Friedrich Gustav). Allgemeine cultur-geschichte der menschheit. 10 v. in 5. 8°. *Leipzig, B. G. Teubner*, 1843–52.

——— Allgemeine culturwissenschaft. v. 1. Werkzeuge und waffen. iv, 393 pp. 8°. *Leipzig, J. A. Romberg*, 1854.

——— Same. v. 2. Einleitung. Das feuer. Die nahrung. Getränke. Narkotica. 4 p. l. 399 pp. port. 8°. *Leipzig, J. A. Romberg*, 1855.

——— Freundschaftliche briefe. 2te aufl. xix, 429 pp. 1 pl. 16°. *Leipzig, B. G. Teubner*, 1850.

Klerk (Jean de, *d'Anvers*). Gestes des ducs de Brabant, publiés par J. F. Willems. 2 v. 6 p. l. lxxi, 904 pp. 20 pl; 6 p. l. xiii, 781 pp. 1 port. 1 facs. 4°. *Bruxelles, M. Hayez*, 1839–43. s.

[BELGIUM. *Académie royale des sciences, des lettres, et des beaux-arts.* Collection des chroniques belges inédites].

Klinkerfues (E. F. Wilhelm). Theoretische astronomie. xii, 474 pp. 8°. *Braunschweig, F. Vieweg & sohn*, 1874. s.

Knapp (*Rev.* W. C.) Funeral services. 168 pp. 16°. *Peoria*, [*Ill.*] *Franks & sons*, 1874.

Knatchbull - Hugessen (Edward-Hugessen). Whispers from fairyland. xi, 345 pp. 8 pl. 12°. *London, Longmans*, 1875.

——— Queer folk. Seven stories. ix, 357 pp. 6 pl. 16°. *London, Macmillan & co.* 1874.

Kneschke (Ernst Heinrich). Neues allgemeines deutsches adels-lexicon. 9 v. 8°. *Leipzig, F. Voigt*, 1859–70.

Knight (Edward H.) American mechanical dictionary. v. 1–2. [A–Pan]. 8°. *New York, J. B. Ford & co.* 1874–75.

Knoop (Johann Hermann). Dendrologia. 2 p. l. 87 pp. 2 l. sm. fol. *Leeuwarden, A. Ferwerda & G. Tresling*, [1763].

[*With* KNOOP (J. H.) Pomologia].

——— Fructologia. 2 p. l. 70 pp. 19 col. pl. sm. fol. *Leeuwarden, A. Ferwerda & G. Tresling*, [1763].

[*With* KNOOP (J. H.) Pomologia].

——— Pomologia. 1 p. l. 36 pp. 20 col. pl. sm. fol. *Leeuwarden, A. Ferwerda & G. Tresling*, [1758].

Knowles (Daniel Clark). A life that speaketh: a biography of rev. George P. Wilson. 229 pp. 16°. *New York, Nelson & Phillips*, [1874].

Knox (Thomas W.) Backsheesh! or life in the orient. With nearly two hundred and fifty illustrations. 694 pp. 1 port. 8°. *Hartford*, (*Conn.*) *A. D. Worthington & co.* 1875.

Knox (Thomas W.)—continued.

——— Underground or life below the surface. 942 pp. incl. 80 pl. 8°. *Hartford, J. B. Burr & Hyde*, 1873.

Koeppen (Karl Friedrich). Die religion des Buddha. viii, 616 pp. 8°. *Berlin, F. Schneider*, 1857.

Kohlrausch (*Dr.* F.) Introduction to physical measurements, etc. From the second german ed. by T. H. Waller and H. R. Procter. xii, 249 pp. 8°. *London, J. & A. Churchill*, 1873. s.

Kohn (Ignaz). Eisenbahn-jahrbuch der Österreichisch-ungarischen monarchie. 3ter jahrg. xi, 444 pp. 2 tab. 1 map. 8°. *Wien, Lehmann & Wentzel*, 1870.

Koldewey (Karl). German arctic expedition of 1869–70. Translated and abridged by the rev. L. Mercier. viii, 590 pp. 2 ports. 29 pl. 4 col. pl. 2 col. maps. 8°. *London, S. Low, Marston, Low & Searle*, 1874.

Koltz (J. P. J.) Traité de pisciculture pratique. 3e éd. vi, 160 pp. 16°. *Paris, V. Masson & fils*, 1866.

Koran (The): translated from the arabic. By J. M. Rodwell. xxviii, 659 pp. 12°. *London, Williams & Norgate*, 1861.

Körber (Philipp). The herdsman of Dambach. From the German. By Sarah A. Flory. 156 pp. 2 pl. 16°. *Philadelphia, lutheran board of publication*, 1875.

[FATHERLAND series].

Krabbe (*Dr.* Otto). Die universität Rostock im fünfzehnten und sechzehnten jahrhundert. 2 v. in 1. xiv pp. 1 l. 304 pp; 1 p. l. 305–764 pp. 8°. *Rostock, Adler's erben*, 1854. s.

Krasinski (*Count* Zygmund Napoleon). The undivine comedy. Polish poetry in the nineteenth century, by Julian Klaczko. Translated by Martha Walker Cook. 513 pp. 12°. *Philadelphia, J. B. Lippincott & co.* 1875.

Krilof (Ivan Andrievitch). Krilof and his fables. By W. R. S. Ralston. xliii, 180 pp. 12°. *London, Strahan & co.* 1869.

Kroeger (A. E.) The minnesinger of Germany. 4 p. l. 284 pp. 12°. *New York, Hurd & Houghton*, 1873.

Kruse (Theodor). Indiens alte geschichte. 1 p. l. 438 pp. 8°. *Leipzig, Dyk'sche buchhandlung*, 1856.

Krüsi (Hermann). Pestalozzi: his life, work, and influence. 248 pp. incl. port. 8°. *Cincinnati, Wilson, Hinkle & co.* [1875].

Laborde (Alexandre). Description d'un pavé en mosaïque découvert dans l'ancienne ville

Laborde (Alexandre)—continued. d'Italica, aujourd'hui le village de Santiponce près de Séville. Eng. title, 2 p. l. 103 pp. 22 pl. 8 vignettes. fol. *Paris, P. Didot l'aîné,* 1802.

Lacombe (Albert). Dictionnaire de la langue des Cris. 4 p. l. xx, 708 pp. 2 l. 1 map. 8°. *Montréal, C. O. Beauchemin & Valois,* 1874. s.

——— Grammaire de la langue des Cris. 1 p. l. iii, 190 pp. 1 tab. 8°. *Montréal, C. O. Beauchemin & Valois,* 1874. s.

[*With* LACOMBE (A.) Dictionnaire de la langue des Cris].

Lacombe (P.) Arms and armour in antiquity and the middle ages. From the French, by Charles Boutell. xvi, 296 pp. incl. 24 pl. 12°. *London, Reeves & Turner,* 1874.

Lacon (*pseud.*) The devil in America: a dramatic satire. By Lacon [*pseud.*] 225 pp. 12°. *Mobile, J. K. Randall,* 1867.

Lacroix (Henry). Canadian guide and book of reference. 1st ed. Title, xii, 116 pp. 1 map. 12°. *Montreal, "witness" printing house,* 1873.

Lacroix (John P.) Life of Rudolf Stier. xiii, 332 pp. 12°. *New York, Nelson & Phillips,* 1874.

Lacroix (Paul). Bibliographie et iconographie de tous les ouvrages de Restif de la Brétonne. Par P. L. Jacob [*pseud.*] 2 p. l. xv, 510 pp. port. 8°. *Paris, A. Fontaine,* 1875.

——— Curiosités de l'histoire des arts. Par P. L. Jacob, bibliophile, [*pseud.*] 2 p. l. 411 pp. 16°. *Paris, A. Delahays,* 1858.

——— Manners, customs, and dress during the middle ages, and the renaissance. xix, 554 pp. 15 col. pl. 4°. *London, Chapman & Hall,* 1874.

——— Military and religious life in the middle ages and the renaissance. xx, 504 pp. 14 col. pl. 4°. *London, Chapman & Hall,* 1874.

Lady of Lawford and other stories. [*anon.*] 346 pp. 15 pl. 12°. *Troy, N. Y., H. B. Nims & co.* [1875].

Laferrière (Édouard Louis Julien, *compiler*). Les constitutions d'Europe et d'Amérique. Revues par M. A. Batbie. vii, cxliv, 654 pp. 8°. *Paris, Cotillon,* 1869.

Lafever (Minard). Young builder's general instructor. 175 pp. 66 pl. 4°. *Newark, N. J., W. Tuttle & co.* 1829.

La Fontaine (Jean de). Fables. Now first translated from the french; by Robert Thomson. 4 v. in 2. 12°. *Paris, Chenu,* 1806.

Lake (D. J.) Atlas of Athens co. Ohio. 88 pp. incl. 24 col. maps & plans, & 31 pl. 2 col. maps. fol. *Philadelphia, Titus, Simmons & Titus,* 1875.

——— Atlas of Jackson county, Ohio. 51 pp. incl. 18 col. maps and 6 pl. fol. *Philadelphia, Titus, Simmons & Titus,* 1875.

Lamartine (Alphonse Marie Louis Prat de). Mémoires inédits, 1790–1815. ix, 369 pp. 8°. *Paris, Hachette & cie.* 1870.

——— Graziella: a story of italian love. From the french, by James B. Runnion. 235 pp. sq. 16°. *Chicago, Jansen, McClurg & co.* 1876.

Lamb (Charles). Complete works in prose and verse. From original editions, with the cancelled passages restored. Edited by R. H. Shepherd. xv, 776 pp. 2 ports. 1 facs. 12°. *London, Chatto & Windus,* 1875.

Lamb (*Mrs.* Martha J.) Spicy. A novel. 178 pp. 3 pl. 8°. *New York, D. Appleton & co.* 1873.

Lamb (Mary) *and* **Lamb** (Charles). Poems, letters, and remains: now first collected, with notes. By W. Carew Hazlitt. 307, 31[+88$^{1-4}$] pp. 9 pl. 1 port. 8 facs. 12°. *London, Chatto & Windus,* 1874.

Lambing (*Rev.* A. A.) The orphan's friend. 306 pp. 16°. *New York, D. & J. Sadlier & co.* 1875.

Lameth (*Baron* Alex.) Histoire de l'assemblée constituante. 2 v. 2 p. l. ciii, 434 pp; 2 p. l. 499 pp. 8°. *Paris, Moutardier,* 1828–29.

La Métherie (Jean Claude de). De l'homme considéré moralement. 2 v. xcvj, 415 pp; 1 p. l. 498 pp. 8°. *Paris, Maradan,* 1802.

Lance (Adolphe). Excursion en Italie. Eaux-fortes par L. Gaucherel. [2e éd.] viii, 317 pp. 1 l. 15 pl. 8°. *Paris, vve. A. Morel & cie.* 1873.

Landon (Melville D.) The franco-prussian war in a nutshell. 486 pp. 15 maps. 12°. *New York, G. W. Carleton & co.* 1871.

Landor (Walter Savage). Cameos, selected by E. C. Stedman and T. B. Aldrich. With an introduction. 128 pp. sq. 16°. *Boston, J. R. Osgood & co.* 1874.

Landriot (Jean François Anne Thomas). Conférences aux dames du monde pour faire suite à La femme forte et à La femme pieuse.

Landriot (J. F. A. T.)—continued. 5e éd. 2 v. 2 p. l. xii, 312 pp; 2 p. l. 316 pp. 16°. *Paris, V. Palmé*, 1866.

Landseer (Thomas, *editor*). Life and letters of William Bewick. 2 v. xii, 300 pp. port; viii, 262 pp. 12°. *London, Hurst & Blackett*, 1871.

Lange (Johann Peter, *d. d. editor*). A commentary on the holy scriptures: critical, doctrinal, and homiletical. Translated from the german, and edited, by **P.** Schaff, d. d. Old testament. v. 1, 4, 6, 7, 9, 10, 13, 16. 8 v. 8°. *New York, C. Scribner & co.* 1868–74.

CONTENTS.

v. 1. General introduction. Genesis, by J. P. Lange.
v. 4. Joshua, by F. R. Fay; Judges and Ruth, by P. Cassel.
v. 6. Kings, by C. W. F. Bähr.
v. 7. Job, a rhythmical version by T. Lewis, and a commentary by O. Zöckler.
v. 9. Psalms, by C. B. Moll, with a new version by T. J. Conant.
v. 10. Proverbs, Ecclesiastes, and song of Solomon, by O. Zöckler.
v. 13. Jeremiah, and Lamentations, by C. W. E. Naegelsbach.
v. 16. Minor prophets, by P. Kleinert, O. Schmoller, T. W. Chambers, J. F. McCurdy, and J. Packard.

——— Same. New testament. 10 v. 8°. *New York, C. Scribner & co.* 1868–74.

CONTENTS.

v. 1. General introduction. Matthew, by J. P. Lange.
v. 2. Mark, by J. P. Lange; Luke, by J. J. van Oosterzee.
v. 3. John, by J. P. Lange.
v. 4. Acts of the Apostles, by G. V. Lechler, and C. Gerok.
v. 5. Romans, by J. P. Lange, and F. R. Fay.
v. 6. Corinthians, by C. F. Kling.
v. 7. Galatians, by O. Schmoller; Ephesians, Philippians, and Colossians, by K. Braune.
v. 8. Thessalonians, by C. A. Auberlen, and C. J. Riggenbach; Timothy, Titus, and Philemon, by J. J. van Oosterzee; Hebrews, by C. B. Moll.
v. 9. James, by J. P. Lange, and J. J. van Oosterzee; Peter, and Jude, by G. F. C. Fronmüller; John, by K. Braune.
v. 10. Revelation of John, by J. P. Lange.

Lange (*Dr.* Ludwig). Original-ansichten der vornehmsten städte in Deutschland. Mit text von Georg Lange. 6 v. in 2. 4°. *Darmstadt, G. G. Lange*, 1832–46.

[Imperfect: v. 5, pl. 16 and 20 wanting; v. 6, pl. 16 wanting].

Langevin (Edmond). 1674–1874. Deuxième-centenaire. Notice biographique sur François de Laval de Montmorency. 1 p. l. xvi, 322 pp. port. 8°. *Montréal, la compagnie d'impression* [*etc.*] *de Lovell*, 1874. s.

Lanier (Sidney). Florida: its scenery, climate, and history. 336 pp. incl. 6 pl. 12°. *Philadelphia, J. B. Lippincott & co.* 1876.

La Place (P. Ant. de), **La Croix** (J. Fr. de) *and* **Hornot** (Ant.) Anecdotes du nord. [*anon.*] 4 pts. in 1 v. 16°. *Paris, Vincent*, 1770.

Larcom (Lucy). Childhood songs. 202 pp. incl. 9 pl. 12°. *Boston, J. R. Osgood & co.* 1875.

——— An idyl of work. 183 pp. 16°. *Boston, J. R. Osgood & co.* 1875.

Larkins (William George). Handbook of english literature. 2 v. in 1. 4 p. l. 184 pp; 2 p. l. vii–ix, 174 pp. 16°. *London, G. Routledge & sons*, 1867.

Larned (Ellen D.) History of Windham county, Connecticut. v. 1. 1600–1760. 582 pp. 1 l. 1 map. 1 facs. 8°. *Worcester, Mass. author*, 1874.

Larrabee (*Prof.* W. H.) *and* **Buttz** (*Prof.* H. A.) Helps to speak and write correctly. 216 pp. 12°. *New York, N. Tibbals & son*, [1873].

Larwood (Jacob). Story of the London parks. 2 v. 3 p. l. 331 pp. 2 pl; 3 p. l. 272 pp. 2 pl. 12°. *London, J. C. Hotten*, [1871].

Lassen (Christian). Indische alterthumskunde. 4 v. 8°. v. 1–2, *Bonn, H. B. Koenig*, 1847–52; v. 3–4, *Leipzig, L. A. Kittler*, 1857–62.

——— *and* **Westergaard** (Niels Ludwig). Ueber die keilinschriften der ersten und zweiten gattung. 2 p. l. 130, ii pp. 8 pl. 8°. *Bonn, H. B. König*, 1845.

Latham (Robert Gordon, *m. d.*) Dictionary of the english language. Founded on that of Johnson. 2 v. in 4. 4°. *London, Longmans*, 1870–72.

Lauder (*Sir* Thomas Dick). Legendary tales of the highlands. 3 v. 12°. *London, H. Colburn*, 1841.

Laugel (Auguste). England political and social. Translated by J. M. Hart. 325 pp. 12°. *New York, G. P. Putnam's sons*, 1874.

Lawlor (Denys Shyne). Pilgrimages in the Pyrenees and Landes. xxiii, 634 pp. 1 pl. 8°. *London, Longmans*, 1870.

Lawrence (John). Genealogy of the family of John Lawrence. 4 p. l. 191 pp. 8°. *Boston, for the author*, 1857.

Lawrence (William Beach, *ll. d.*) Belligerent and sovereign rights as regards neutrals during the war of secession. xiv, 89, 40 pp. 8°. *Boston, A. Mudge & son*, 1873.

Lawrence (William V.) Ellina. [A poem]. viii, 264 pp. 12°. *Cambridge*, [*Mass.*] *riverside press*, 1873.

Lawrence (*City of, Mass.*) *Free public library.* Catalogue. 1873. viii, 341 pp. 8°. *Lawrence, G. S. Merrill & Crocker*, 1873.

Lawson (*Mrs.* J. W.) Brockley moor. By J. W. L. [*anon.*] 307 pp. 8°. *New York, D. Appleton & co.* 1874.

Lawson (William), **Hunter** (Charles D.) *and others.* Ten years of gentleman farming at Blennerhasset. viii, 408 pp. 2 pl. 12°. *London, Longmans,* 1874.

Lazarus (Emma). Alide: an episode of Goethe's life. 214 pp. 12°. *Philadelphia, J. B. Lippincott & co.* 1874.

Lea (William). Tables of the strength and deflection of timber. xl, 152 pp. 12°. *London, Simpkin, Marshall & co.* 1850.

Leanti (Arcangiolo). Lo stato presente della Sicilia. 2 v. 1 p. l. xxi, 222 pp. 36 pl; 1 p. l. 223–407, 45 pp. 8 pl. 12°. *Palermo, F. Valenza,* 1761.

Leavenworth (Elias Warner, *ll. d.*) Genealogy of the Leavenworth family in the United States. 376 pp. 17 ports. 2 pl. ill. front. 8°. *Syracuse, N. Y., S. G. Hitchcock & co.* 1873.

Le Bouvier-Desmortiers (Urbain René Thomas). Vie du général Charette. 3 v. 8°. *Paris, chez les marchands de nouveautés* [*&*] *P. Didot l'aîné,* 1809–14.

Lecomte (*L'abbé* A.) Le Darwinisme et l'origine de l'homme. 2e éd. xiii, 411 pp. 12°. *Bruxelles, A. Vromant,* 1873.

Le Conte (Joseph). Religion and science. 324 pp. 12°. *New York, D. Appleton & co.* 1874.

Lee (*Rev.* Alfred Theophilus). History of Tetbury, in Gloucester. xxiii, 320 pp. 11 pl. 8°. *London, J. H. & J. Parker,* 1857.

Lee (Charles Carter). Virginia georgics. 122 pp. 2 l. 8°. *Richmond, J. Woodhouse & co.* 1858.

Lee (Samuel). Bible regained, and the God of the bible ours. 1 p. l. 285 pp. 16°. *Boston, Lee & Shepard,* 1874.

Lee (William, *m. d. of Washington*). Currency of the confederate states of America. 27 pp. 10 photog. pl. 4°. *Washington,* 1875.

Lee (William, *of London*). Life of Daniel De Foe.

[DE FOE (D.) Daniel De Foe: his life and recently discovered writings. 8°. *London, J. C. Hotten,* 1869. v. 1].

Lees (*Lady* Maria Charlotte Sullivan). A few days in Belgium and Holland. iv, 148 pp. 12°. *London, E. Stanford,* 1872.

Lefevre (*Sir* George, *m. d.*) The life of a travelling physician. [*anon.*] 3 v. 12°. *London, Longmans,* 1843.

Legends and fairy tales of Ireland. 1872. *See* **Haverty** (P. M.)

Legrand D'Aussy (Pierre Jean Baptiste) *and* **Roquefort** (Jean Baptiste Bonaventure de). Des sépultures nationales, et particulièrement de celles des rois de France. 528 pp. 8°. *Paris, J. Esneaux,* 1824.

Leguével de Lacombe (B. F.) Voyage à Madagascar et aux îles Comores (1823 à 1830). Précédé d'une notice historique par m. Eugène de Froberville. 2 v. 2 p. l. iv, 101 pp. 1 l. 294, 4 pp. 4 pl. 1 map; 2 p. l. iv, 375 pp. 1 pl. 1 map. 8°. *Paris, L. Desessart,* 1840.

Leishman (William). System of midwifery. 2d american from the 2d english ed. xxiv, 17–766 pp. 8°. *Philadelphia, H. C. Lea,* 1875.

Leitch (Richard Pettigrew). Course of painting in neutral tint. 32 pp. 24 col. pl. obl. 4°. *London, Cassell, Petter & Galpin,* [1875].

——— Course of sepia painting. 32 pp. 24 pl. obl. 4°. *London, Cassell, Petter & Galpin,* [1875].

Leland (Charles Godfrey). Egyptian sketch book. ix, 331 pp. 12°. *New York, Hurd & Houghton,* 1874.

——— English gipsies and their language. xv, 259 pp. 12°. *New York, Hurd & Houghton,* 1873.

——— **Palmer** (*Prof.* E. H.) *and* **Tuckey** (Janet). English-gipsy songs. In rommany with metrical translations. xii, 276 pp. 12°. *Philadelphia, J. B. Lippincott & co.* 1875.

Lemaire (Nicolas Éloi). Bibliotheca classica latina, cum notis et indicibus. 141 v. 8°. *Parisiis, colligebat N. E. Lemaire,* 1819–32.

CONTENTS.

v. 1–4. CAESAR (Caius Julius) ad codices parisinos recensitus. 4 v. 1819–22.
v. 5. CATULLUS (C. Valerius) ex editione F. G. Doeringii. 1826.
v. 6–24. CICERONIS (M. T.) quae exstant omnia opera. 19 v. 1827–32.
v. 25–26. CLAUDIANI (Claudii) opera omnia. 2 v. 1824.
v. 27. NEPOS (Cornelius) recensitus, curante J. B. F. Descuret. 1820.
v. 28. FLORII (Lucii) epitome rerum romanarum. Item Lucii Ampelii liber memorialis. 1827.
v. 29–31. HORATIUS FLACCUS (Quintus) curante et emendante N. E. Lemaire. 3 v. 1829–31.
v. 32. JUSTINI historiarum philippicarum ex Trogo Pompeio libri 44. 1823.
v. 33–34. JUVENALIS (D. Junii) sexdecim satyræ ad codices parisinos recensitæ. 2 v. 1823–25.
v. 35. PERSIUS FLACCUS (A.): item Lucilii fragmenta, satyra sulpiciæ; curante A. Perreau. 1830.
v. 36–38. LUCANUS (M. Annæi) Pharsalia, cum Thomae Maii supplemento. 3 v. 1830–32.
v. 39–41. MARTIALIS (M. V.) epigrammata ad codices parisinos recensita. 3 v. 1825.
v. 42–51. OVIDII NASONIS (Publii) quae exstant omnia opera. 9 v. in 10. 1820–24.
v. 52–53. PHÆDRI fabularum Æsopiarum libri quinque. 2 v. 1826.
v. 54–57. PLAUTI (M. Accii) comœdiæ, curante J. Naudet. 4 v. 1830–32.

Lemaire (Nicolas Éloi)—continued.

v. 58-68. PLINII SECUNDI (Caii) historiæ naturalis libri xxxvii. 10 v. in 11. 1827-32.
v. 69-70. PLINII CÆCILII SECUNDI (C.) epistolarum libri decem et panegyricus. 2 v. 1822-23.
v. 71. PROPERTII (Sextii Aurelii) elegiarum libri quatuor; quibus accedunt imitationes. 1832.
v. 72-74. CURTIUS RUFUS (Q.) ad codices parisinos recensitus. 3 v. 1822-25.
v. 75-81. QUINTILIANUS (Marcus Fabius). Opera. 7 v. 1821-25.
v. 82. SALLUSTIUS (Caius Crispus) ad codices parisinos recensitus. Item Julius Exsuperantius emendatus. 1821.
v. 83-91. SENECA (L. A.) Omnia opera quae exstant, philosophica, declamatoria, et tragica. 9 v. 1827-32.
v. 92-93. SILIUS ITALICUS (Caius). Punicorum libri septemdecim. 2 v. 1823.
v. 94-97. STATII (Papinii) quæ exstant omnia opera. 4 v. 1825-30.
v. 98-99. SUETONII TRANQUILLI (C.) duodecim Cæsares, et minora opera. 2 v. 1828.
v. 100-104. TACITUS (Caius Cornelius) qualem publicavit J. J. Oberlin. 6 v. in 5. 1819-20.
v. 105-106. TERENTIUS AFER (P.) Comœdiæ. 3 v. in 2. 1827-28.
v. 107. TIBULLI (Albii) quæ supersunt omnia opera. 1826.
v. 108-119. LIVIUS PATAVINUS (Titus) ad codices parisinos recensitus. 13 v. in 12. 1822-25.
v. 120-121. VALERII FLACCI (C.) argonauticon libros octo edidit N. E. Lemaire. 2 v. 1824-25.
v. 122-124. VALERIUS MAXIMUS de dictis factisque memorabilibus, et Jul. Obsequens de prodigiis. 2 v. in 3. 1822-23.
v. 125. VELLEIUS PATERCULUS (Caius) qualem publicavit D. Ruhnkenius. 1822.
v. 126-133. VIRGILIUS MARO (P.) qualem publicavit C. G. Heyne, etc. 8 v. 1819-22.
v. 134. Poetæ latini minores. v. 1. Gratii et Nemesiani cynegetica, T. Calpurnii siculi eclogæ, Q. Ennii, Severi Sancti, Bedae, Septimii Sereni Ausonii, Cassii Parmensis, Optatiani Porphyrii, et aliorum carmina, quae notis illustravit N. E. Lemaire. xii, 722 pp. 1824.
v. 135. ——— v. 2. Satirica, elegiaca, lyrica, et alia quædam carmina, quæ notis illustravit N. E. Lemaire. 4 p. l. 554 pp. 1824.
v. 136. ——— v. 3. Lucilii Junioris, Saleii Bassi, et aliorum carmina heroica, epithalamia, et homeristarum latinorum opera, quæ notis illustravit N. E. Lemaire. 4 p. l. 662 pp. 1824.
v. 137. ——— v. 4. Rutilii Numatiani itinerarium, Prisciani periegesis et alia opera, Ausonii et variorum auctorum carmina geographica, Varronis Atacini fragmenta, quæ notis illustravit N. E. Lemaire. 4 p. l. 592 pp. 1825.
v. 138. ——— v. 5. Rufi Festi Avieni descriptio orbis terræ, ora maritima, et carmina minora; ejusdem Aratea phænomena et prognostica, quæ notis illustravit N. E. Lemaire. 4 p. l. 643 pp. 1825.
v. 139. ——— v. 6. De re astronomica Ciceronis et Germanici carmina ex Arato translata; item M. Manilii astronomicon libri quinque ex recensione Jos. Scaligeri, quæ notis illustravit N. E. Lemaire. 3 p. l. 666 pp. 1826.
v. 140. ——— v. 7. De re hortensi et villatica carmina Columellæ, Palladii, Vomani, et aliorum; item amatoria et ludicra Maximiani Etrusci, Ofilii, Juventini, Sperati, Symposii, Hosidii Getæ, et Ausonii. [Item, indices varios in septem voluminum carminibus, etc. disposuit et emendavit N. E. Lemaire]. 2 v. in 1. viii, 563 pp. 3 p. l. 441 pp. 1826.
v. 141. Appendix. [Notice sur N. E. Lemaire. Ejusdem carmina, etc. Indices in bibliothecam classicam latinam]. 120 pp. 10 l. 1 port. 1832.

——— Same. Complementum. 2 v. xv, 600 pp; 4 p. l. 591 pp. 8°. *Parisiis, colligebat olim N. E. Lemaire*, 1838.

CONTENTS.

v. 1-2. LUCRETII CARI (Titi) de rerum natura libri sex. 2 v. 1838.

Lemercier (Adrien). Augustine. From the french. 145 pp. 1 pl. 18°. *New York, D. & J. Sadlier & co.* 1873.

——— The two brothers. From the french. 135 pp. 1 pl. 18°. *New York, D. & J. Sadlier & co.* 1873.

Lena Landon. [*anon.*] 1 p. l. 347 pp. 4 pl. 16°. *Philadelphia, am. baptist publication society*, [1874].

Lening (Gustav). Dark side of New York life. [*anon.*] 832 pp. 8°. *New York, F. Gerhard*, 1873.

Lennox (*Lord* William Pitt). Sport at home and abroad. 2 v. viii, 330 pp; viii, 309 pp. 12°. *London, Hurst & Blackett*, 1872.

Lenormant (François). Student's manual of oriental history. Ancient history to the commencement of the median wars. 2 v. xx, 538 pp. 1 l; xii, 394 pp. 1 l. 12°. *London, Asher & co.* 1869-70.

Leo (Heinrich). Lehrbuch der universalgeschichte. v. 1-2. 3te aufl. v. 3-6. 2te aufl. 6 v. 8°. *Halle, E. Anton*, 1840-51.

——— Vorlesungen über die geschichte des jüdischen staates. 266 pp. 8°. *Reutlingen, J. J. Mäcken'sche buchhandlung*, 1829.

Leonard (Charles C.) History of Pithole: by "Crocus" [*pseud.*] 106 pp. 16°. *Pithole city, Pa. Morton, Longwell & co.* 1867.

Leonard (Henry C.) Pigeon cove [Mass.] and vicinity. viii, 193 pp. incl. 1 pl. 16°. *Boston, F. A. Searle*, 1873.

Leonard (*Rev.* William). Via sacra: or, footprints of Christ. With introduction by C. H. Hall. 209 pp. front. 18°. *Brooklyn, orphans' press*, 1875.

Leonhardt (Josephus, *d. d. pseud.*) Confessions of a minister. Being leaves from the diary of the rev. Josephus Leonhardt. 136 pp. 16°. *Philadelphia, H. Peterson & co.* 1874.

Lepautre (Jean). Collection des plus belles compositions de Lepautre gravé par Decloux et Doury. 2 p. l. 100 pl. fol. *Paris, E. Noblet* [*etc.* 187-].

L'Épinois (Henri de). Galilée: son procès, sa condamnation. 108 pp. 8°. *Paris, V. Palmé*, 1867.

Lepsius (Karl Richard). Briefe aus Aegypten, in 1842-1845. vi, 456 pp. 2 pl. 8°. *Berlin, W. Hertz*, 1852.

——— Über die xxii. ägyptische königsdynastie. 1 p. l. 259-320 pp. 2 tab. 4°. *Berlin, k. akademie der wissenschaften*, 1856.

Lequien de la Neufville (Jacques). Origine des postes. 11 p. l. 446 (+*63–*76) pp. 16 l. 16°. *Paris, P. Giffart,* 1708.

Leroy-Beaulieu (Paul). De la colonization chez les peuples modernes. 2 p. l. vii, 616 pp. 8°. *Paris, Guillaumin & cie.* 1874.

Le Saint (L.) Guerre du Mexique 1861–67. 2e éd. 223 pp. front. 8°. *Lille, J. Lefort,* [1871].

Leslie (Eliza). Miss Leslie's new receipts for cooking. 520 pp. 12°. *Philadelphia, T. B. Peterson & brothers,* [1874].

Leslie (Emma). Flavia. 311 pp. incl. 4 pl. 12°. *New York, Nelson & Phillips,* [1875].

——— Glaucia. 308 pp. incl. 2 pl. front. 16°. *New York, Nelson & Phillips,* [1874].

——— Leofwine the saxon. 301 pp. incl. 3 pl. 12°. *New York, Nelson & Phillips,* [1875].

——— Quadratus. 308 pp. incl. 3 pl. 12°. *New York, Nelson & Phillips,* [1875].

——— Sunshine of Blackpool. 239 pp. 18°. *New York, Nelson & Phillips,* [1875].

Lessing (Gotthold Ephraim). Laocoon. Translated by Ellen Frothingham. xi, 245 pp. 16°. *Boston, Roberts brothers,* 1874.

Lester (A. Hoyle). The pre-adamite, or who tempted Eve? 164 pp. 1 pl. 2 maps. 12°. *Philadelphia, for the author,* 1875.

Lester (Charles Edwards). Life and public services of Charles Sumner. 3 p. l. 596 pp. 12 pl. 8°. *New York, United States publishing co.* 1874.

——— Life and voyages of Americus Vespucius. 10th ed. 470, vii pp. 12 pl. port. 8°. *New Haven, H. Mansfield,* 1867.

——— Our first hundred years. 2 v. 5 p. l. 7, 482+8 pp. 4 l. port; 4 p. l. 480 pp. 4 l. 8°. *New York, United States publishing co.* 1875.

Lester (John Erastus). The Atlantic to the Pacific. 365 pp. 1 map. 16°. *Boston, Shepard & Gill,* 1873.

L'Estrange (*Rev.* Alfred Guy Kingham). From the Thames to the Tamar. viii, 341 pp. front. 8°. *London, Hurst & Blackett,* 1873.

L'Estrange (*Sir* George B.) Recollections. The peninsular war. viii, 280 pp. 7 pl. port. 8°. *London, S. Low, Marston, Low & Searle,* [1874].

Letchworth (William P.) Sketch of the life of Samuel F. Pratt. 1 p. l. 7–211 pp. 3 pl. 8°. *Buffalo, Warren, Johnson & co.* 1874.

Letheby (Henry). The sewage question; with additions, from "Medical press and circular." viii, 204 pp. 12°. *London, Baillière, Tindall & Cox,* 1872.

Lettres édifiantes et curieuses. Cartas edificantes, y curiosas, escritas de las missiones estrangeras, por missioneros de la compañia de Jesus. Traducidas del frances por Diego Davin. 16 v. sm. 4°. *Madrid, viuda de M. Fernandez & el supremo consejo de la inquisicion,* 1753–57.
[Imperfect: v. 16, pl. 4 wanting].

Leuret (François) *and* **Gratiolet** (Louis Pierre). Anatomie comparée du système nerveux. 2 v. xxxii, 592 pp; xii, 692 pp. 8°. Atlas, 2 p. l. 60 pp. 32 col. pl. fol. *Paris, J.-B. Baillière et fils,* 1839–57.

Leverett (*Rev.* Charles Edward). Memoir of sir John Leverett, governor of Mass. 1673–79. [*anon.*] 203 pp. 4 pl. 1 chart. 8°. *Boston, Crosby, Nichols & co.* 1856.

Levi (Moses Raffael, *m. d.*) Die cellular-pathologie in ihren grundlagen und anwendungen betrachtet. xiv, 334 pp. 8°. *Braunschweig, F. Vieweg & sohn,* 1865. S.

Lévy (Edmond, *de Rouen*). Histoire de la peinture sur verre en Europe. 4 p. l. 272, 206 pp. 36 col. pl. 4°. *Bruxelles, Tircher,* 1860.
[Imperfect: pl. 7 wanting].

Lewald (Fanny). Hulda; or, the deliverer. After the german, by mrs. A. L. Wister. 394 pp. 12°. *Philadelphia, J. B. Lippincott & co.* 1874.

Lewes (George Henry). Problems of life and mind. First series, the foundations of a creed. 2 v. xv, 472 pp; viii, 542 pp. 8°. *London, Trübner & co.* 1874–75.

Lewis (Charles B.) Goaks and tears. By M. Quad [*pseud.*] 1 p. l. 72 pp. 12°. *Boston, H. L. Shepard & co.* 1875.

——— "Quad's odds;" by M. Quad [*pseud.*] 480 pp. 15 pl. port. 8°. *Detroit, R. D. S. Tyler & co.* 1875.

Lewis (Charlton T.) History of Germany. Founded on Müller's history. 1 p. l. v–viii pp. 1 l. 799 pp. 2 ports. 1 map. 12°. *New York, Harper & brothers,* 1874.

Lewis (Dio, *m. d.*) Chastity. 320 pp. 12°. *Philadelphia,* [*etc.*] *G. Maclean & co.* 1875.

——— Five-minutes chats with young women. 2 p. l. 9–426 pp. 12°. *New York, Harper & brothers,* 1874.

——— Prohibition a failure. 266 pp. 12°. *Boston, J. R. Osgood & co.* 1875.

Lewis (E.) *and* **Sturtevant** (Joseph N.) North american Ayrshire register. 1 p l.

Lewis *and* **Sturtevant**—continued. 5-174 pp. 2 pl. 8°. *South Framingham, Mass.* [*Boston printed, A. Mudge & sons*], 1875.

Lewis (*Rev.* George). Impressions of America and the american churches. viii, 432 pp. 8°. *Edinburgh, W. P. Kennedy*, 1845.
[Imperfect: pp. 301-338 wanting].

Lewis (Tayler). Vedder lectures, 1875. "The light by which we see light." 246 pp. 12°. *New York, board of publication of the r. c. a.* 1875.

Liais (Emmanuel). Climats, géologie, faune, et géographie botanique du Brésil. viii, 640 pp. 1 map. 8°. *Paris, Garnier frères*, 1872.

Lichtenberg (Georg Christoph). Vermischte schriften. 8 v. in 7. 16°. *Göttingen, Dieterich*, 1800-1804.

Lieber (Francis, *ll. d.*) Manual of political ethics. Edited by T. D. Woolsey. 2d ed. 2 v. 472 pp; 459 pp. 8°. *Philadelphia, J. B. Lippincott & co.* 1875.

——— On civil liberty. 3d ed. Edited by T. D. Woolsey. 622 pp. 8°. *Philadelphia, J. B. Lippincott & co.* 1874.

Liechtenstein (*Princess* Marie Henriette Norberte). Holland house. 2 v. xvi, 289 pp. 11 pl. 1 facs; xi, 255 pp. incl 7 pl. 1 pl. 7 facs. 8°. *London, Macmillan & co.* 1874.

Life and doctrine of Saint Catherine of Genoa. From the italian. [*anon.*] xiv, 7-386 pp. 12°. *New York, catholic publication society*, 1874.

Likins (*Mrs.* J. W.) Six years experience as a book agent in California. 168 pp. 8 pl. 8°. *San Francisco, women's union printing office*, 1874.

Lincoln (David F. *m. d.*) Electro-therapeutics. 186 pp. 8°. *Philadelphia, H. C. Lea*, 1874.

Lindsay (Robert, *of Pitscottie*). History of Scotland. 3d ed. 1 p. l. xvi, 367, 55 pp. 12°. *Edinburgh, for C. Elliot*, 1778.

Lindsley (David Philip). Elements of tachygraphy. 128 pp. 3 l. 12°. *Boston, O. Clapp & son*, 1873.

——— Same. 4th ed. 116 pp. 1 l. 113-128 pp. 12°. *Boston, O. Clapp & son*, 1874.

Linton (*Mrs.* Eliza Lynn). True history of Joshua Davidson, communist. [*anon.*] viii, 279 pp. 12°. *Philadelphia, J. B. Lippincott & co.* 1873.

Lippincott (*Mrs.* Sara Jane Clarke). Heads and tails. By Grace Greenwood [*pseud.*]

Lippincott (*Mrs.* S. J. C.)—continued. 1 p. l. 185 pp. 12°. *New York, J. B. Ford & co.* 1875.

Little (George). American cruiser. 390 pp. incl. 12 pl. 12°. *Boston, W. J. Reynolds & co.* 1847.

Little classics. Edited by Rossiter Johnson. 16 v. 18°. *Boston, J. R. Osgood & co.* 1874-75.

CONTENTS.

v. 1. Exile.	v. 11. Heroism.
v. 2. Intellect.	v. 12. Fortune.
v. 3. Tragedy.	v. 13. Poems narrative.
v. 4. Life.	v. 14. Poems lyrical.
v. 5. Laughter.	v. 15. Minor poems.
v. 6. Love.	v. 16. Authors. Biographical sketches of the authors represented in the series. With a general index.
v. 7. Romance.	
v. 8. Mystery.	
v. 9. Comedy.	
v. 10. Childhood.	

Littlejohn (F. J.) Legends of Michigan. 614 pp. incl. 13 pl. & 16 ports. 8°. *Allegan, Mich. northwestern bible and publishing co.* 1875.

Liverseege (Henry). Engravings from the works of Henry Liverseege. 1 p. l. port. eng. title, 35 pl. fol. *London, Hodgson, Boys & Graves*, [1833-35].

Livingstone (David). Last journals, in central Africa, from 1865 to his death. Continued by Horace Waller. 2 v. xvi, 360 pp. 6 pl. port. 1 map; viii, 346 pp. 12 pl. 3 facs. 1 map. 8°. *London, J. Murray*, 1874.

——— Same. (Abridged from the London edition). 448 pp. incl. port. 24 pl. 1 facs. 1 map. 8°. *Hartford, R. W. Bliss & co.* 1875.

Livre (Le) noir de la commune de Paris. [*anon.*] 3e éd. 396 pp. 12°. *Bruxelles, office de publicité*, 1871.

Lloyd (Humphrey). Treatise on magnetism, general and terrestrial. xvii, 239 pp. 3 pl. 8°. *London, Longmans*, 1874.

Lloyd (William Watkiss). Age of Pericles, a history of the politics and arts of Greece. 2 v. xix, 390 pp; xv, 416 pp. 8°. *London, Macmillan & co.* 1875.

——— History of Sicily to the athenian war. xi, 396 pp. 1 map. 8°. *London, J. Murray*, 1872.

Lobé (Guillaume). Guide aux droits civils et commerciaux des étrangers en Espagne. 2e éd. viii, 499 pp. 8°. *Paris, Guilbert*, 1837.

Locke (David Ross). Eastern fruit on western dishes. The morals of Abou Ben Adhem. 231 pp. 12°. *Boston, Lee & Shepard*, 1875.

Locker (Frederick). London lyrics. 7th ed. x, 203 pp. 16°. *London, W. Isbister & co.* 1874.

Lockhart (C. S. M.) Centenary memorial of sir Walter Scott. xxiii, 171 pp. 12 pl. 3 facs. 12°. *London, Virtue & co.* 1871.

Lockyer (Joseph Norman). Contributions to solar physics. xxiii, 676 pp. 3 col. pl. 4 pl. 8°. *London, Macmillan & co.* 1874.

Lodge (Thomas). Margarite of America. Edited by J. O. Halliwell. viii, 139 pp. 8°. *London, T. Richards*, 1859.

Note.—26 copies printed.

Loew (Hermann). Monographs of the diptera of North America. Edited by R. Osten Sacken. 2 parts. xxiv, 221 pp. 2 pl; xi, 360 pp. 5 pl. 8°. *Washington, Smithsonian institution*, 1862–64.

[*In* SMITHSONIAN miscellaneous collections, v. 6].

——— Same. Part 3. vii, 351, 13 pp. 8–11 pl. 8°. *Washington, Smithsonian institution*, 1873.

[*In* SMITHSONIAN miscellaneous collections, v. 11, art. 3].

Löffelholz-Colberg (Friedrich *freiherr* von). Forstliche chrestomathie. 4 v. in 3. 8°. *Berlin, J. Springer*, 1866–71.

Logan (Algernon Sydney). Mirror of a mind 116 pp. sq. 16°. *New York, for the author*, 1875.

Logan (Thomas A.) Breech-loaders. By "Gloan" [*pseud.*] 192 pp. incl. 8 pl. 1 pl. 8°. *New York, G. E. Woodward*, 1873.

Logan (W. H. *editor*). A pedlar's pack of ballads and songs. xv, 479 pp. 12°. *Edinburgh, W. Paterson*, 1869.

Lommel (Eugen). The nature of light. xiv, 356 pp. col. front. 12°. *London, H. S. King & co.* 1875.

[INTERNATIONAL scientific series, v. 18].

London (*City of, Eng.*) Post office London directory, 1873. 8°. *London, for F. Kelly*, [1872].

London guide. How to get from or to any part of London. [*anon.*] viii, 120 pp. 1 map. 12°. *London, E. Stanford*, 1875.

London (*Company of stationers of*). Transcript of the registers; 1554–1640. Edited by Edward Arber. v. 1–2. 4°. *London, privately printed*, 1875.

CONTENTS.

v. 1. Text. Detailed cash accounts to 22 july 1571. Summary cash abstracts onward to 2 august 1596.

v. 2. Text. Entries of books to 25 june 1595. Entries of apprentices and freemen, calls on the livery, and fines to 2 july 1605.

London (*New library and museum of the corporation of*). Catalogue of engraved portraits, topographical drawings and prints, coins, gems, autographs, [etc.] exhibited at the opening of the new library and museum, 1872. Edited by W. H. Overall. 322 l. unp. 4°. *London*, 1872. s.

Long (*Rev.* Edwin M.) Illustrated history of hymns and their authors. [v. 1]. 560 pp. incl. 38 ports. & 19 pl. 12°. *Philadelphia, J. F. Jaggers*, [1875].

Long (Joseph W.) American wild-fowl shooting. 2 p. l. ix–285 pp. 4 pl. 12°. *New York, J. B. Ford & co.* 1874.

Longfellow (Henry Wadsworth). Aftermath. vi, 144 pp. 1 pl. 16°. *Boston, J. R. Osgood & co.* 1873.

——— The hanging of the crane. With illustrations. 1 p. l. 7–64 pp. front. 12°. *Boston, J. R. Osgood & co.* 1875.

——— Masque of Pandora and other poems. iv, 146 pp. 16°. *Boston, J. R. Osgood & co.* 1875.

——— Poetical works. Household ed. ix, 363 pp. 12°. *Boston, J. R. Osgood & co.* 1874.

——— *editor.* Poets and poetry of Europe. xviii, 1, 779 pp. 8°. *Philadelphia, Carey & Hart*, 1845.

——— Same. New ed. Eng. title, xxvii, 916 pp. port. 8°. *Philadelphia, Porter & Coates*, 1871.

Loomis (Alfred L. *m. d.*) Lectures on diseases of the respiratory organs, heart and kidneys. xii pp. 1 l. 549 pp. 8°. *New York, W. Wood & co.* 1875.

Loomis (*Rev.* Harmon). The great conflict, Christ and antichrist. 249 pp. 16°. *New York, Nelson & Phillips*, 1874.

——— The land of shadowing wings: or, the empire of the sea. 279 pp. 16°. *New York, Nelson & Phillips*, 1873.

Lord (Eleazar). On credit, currency and banking. 2d ed. 130 pp. 8°. *New-York, G. & C. & H. Carvill*, 1834.

Lord (John, *ll. d*) Life of Emma Willard. 351 pp. 2 ports. 12°. *New York, D. Appleton & co.* 1873.

Lord (Willis, *d. d.*) Christian theology. 623 pp. 8°. *New York, R. Carter & brothers*, 1875.

Lorentz (Bernard), **Parade** (A.) *and others.* Cours élémentaire de culture des bois. 5e éd. xxviii, 698, xxix pp. 1 pl. 8°. *Paris, ve. Bouchard-Huzard*, 1867.

Lorimer (*Rev.* Peter). Patrick Hamilton, first preacher and martyr of the scottish ref-

Lorimer (*Rev.* Peter)—continued. ormation. xvi, 267 pp. 12°. *Edinburgh, T. Constable & co.* 1857.

Lorra Baquio (Francisco). Manval mexicano de la administracion de los santos sacramentos. 7 p. l. 1–80, 89–96, 89–132 l. [+111bis] numb. 18°. *Mexico, D. Gutierrez*, 1634.

Lossing (Benson John, *ll. d.*) Outline history of the United States. 399 pp. incl. front. 4 maps. 12°. *New York, Sheldon & co.* 1875.

Loth (Moritz). "The forgiving kiss." 364 pp. 12°. *New York, G. W. Carleton & co.* 1874.

Lottin de Laval (René Victorien). Voyage dans la péninsule arabique du Sinaï et l'Égypte moyenne. [Texte] 2 p. l. 356 pp. 4° ; [atlas] 2 p. l. 1 map, 15 pl. 17 photolith. facs. 80 pl. of facs. inscriptions on 40 l. fol. *Paris, vve. A. Morel & cie.* 1873.

Louage (*Rev.* A.) Course of philosophy. 237 pp. 12°. *Baltimore, Kelly, Piet & co.* 1873.

——— History of greek and roman classical literature. 220 pp. 12°. *New York, D. Appleton & co.* 1873.

Loubat (J. F.) Narrative of the mission to Russia, in 1866. 444 pp. 13 pl. 1 tab. 8°. *New York, D. Appleton & co.* 1873.

Lover (Samuel). Songs and ballads. 3d ed. xvi, 224 pp. 12°. *New York, Wiley & Putnam*, 1847.

Low (Charles Rathbone). Land of the sun; sketches of travel in the east. xii, 356 pp. 12°. *London, Hodder & Stoughton*, 1870.

Lowe (Edward Joseph). Our native ferns. 2 v. vii, 348 pp. 37 col. pl ; vii, 492 pp. 42 col. pl. 8°. *London, Groombridge & sons*, 1867–69.

Lowe (Richard Thomas). History of the fishes of Madeira. Pts. 1–5. 4 p. l. v–xvi, 196 pp. (+4* & 43*) 1 pl. 16 col. pl. 8°. *London, J. Van Voorst*, 1843–[60].
[No more published].

Lowell (James Russell). The courtin'. Illustrated by Winslow Homer. 18 l. 7 pl. 4°. *Boston, J. R. Osgood & co.* 1874.

Lowell (Robert). Antony Brade. viii, 416 pp. 16°. *Boston, Roberts brothers*, 1874.

Lowne (Benjamin Thompson). Anatomy & physiology of the blow-fly. viii, 121 pp. 10 pl. 8°. *London, J. Van Voorst*, 1870.

Lowrie (John C.) Manual of the foreign missions of the presbyterian church in the United States. [3d ed.] 359 pp. 1 pl. 4 maps. 12°. *New York, W. Rankin*, 1868.

Lubbock (*Sir* John, *bart.*) On british wild flowers considered in relation to insects. 2d ed. 1 p. l. vii–xvi, 186 pp. front. 12°. *London, Macmillan & co.* 1875.
[NATURE series].

——— On the origin and metamorphoses of insects. 1 p. l. vii–xvi, 108 pp. incl. 7 pl. front. 12°. *London, Macmillan & co.* 1874.
[NATURE series].

Lübke (*Dr.* Wilhelm). Ecclesiastical art in Germany during the middle ages. From the fifth german edition. 1 p. l. x pp. 1 l. 299 pp. 19 pl. 8°. *London, Cassell, Petter & Galpin*, 1870.

——— Same. 2d ed. xi, 299 pp. 19 pl. 8°. *Edinburgh, T. C. Jack*, 1873.

Lucas (Hippolyte). Histoire naturelle des crustacés, des arachnides, et des myriapodes. 1° partie. 2 p. l. 600 pp. [46] pl. 8°. *Paris, société bibliophile*, 1851.

——— Histoire naturelle des lépidoptères d'Europe. 2e éd. 2 p. l. 288, iv pp. 82 pl. 8°. *Paris, F. Savy*, 1864.

Lucas (Paul). Voyage fait par ordre du roi dans la Grèce, l'Asie Mineure, la Macédoine et l'Afrique. 2 v. in 1. 15 p. l. 323 pp, 10 pl. 1 tab ; 5 p. l. 328 pp. 9 pl. 1 tab. 18°. *Amsterdam, aux dépens de la compagnie*, 1714.

Lucy (—). Men and manner in parliament, by the member for the Chiltern hundreds. [*anon.*] 3 p. l. 286 pp. 12°. *London, Tinsley brothers*, 1874.

Lum (Dyer D.) The spiritual delusion. 252 pp. 12°. *Philadelphia, J. B. Lippincott & co.* 1873.

Lunt (George, *editor*). Old New England traits. v, 244 pp. 16°. *New York, Hurd & Houghton*, 1873.

Lurine (Louis) *and* **Brot** (Alphonse). Les couvents. 2 p. l. vii, 516 pp. 18 pl. 8°. *Paris, J. Mallet & cie.* 1846.

Lyell (*Sir* Charles). Geological evidences of the antiquity of man. 4th ed. xix, 572 pp. 2 pl. 8°. *London, J. Murray*, 1873.

——— Principles of geology. 11th ed. 2 v. xx, 671 pp. 5 pl ; xviii, 652 pp. 3 pl. 8°. *London, J. Murray*, 1872.

——— Student's elements of geology. 2d ed. 1 pl. vii–xix, 672 pp. front. 12°. *London, J. Murray*, 1874.

Lyell (K. M.) Geographical handbook of all the known ferns. xi, 225 pp. 12°. *London, J. Murray*, 1870.

Lyman (Willis). Collection of tactical studies. Translated by W. Lyman. 138 pp. 18°. *New York, D. Appleton & co.* 1874.

Lytton (Edward George Earle Lytton Bulwer, *baron Lytton*). The Caxtons. New ed. iv, 380 pp. 1 pl. 16°. *London, G. Routledge & sons,* [1873].

——— Kenelm Chillingly. Globe ed. 2 v. in 1. 363, 352 pp. 1 pl. 16°. *Philadelphia, J. B. Lippincott & co.* 1873.

——— "My novel." The lord Lytton ed. 4 v. in 2. 12°. *Philadelphia, J. B. Lippincott & co.* 1874.

——— The Parisians. Globe ed. 3 v. in 1. 16°. *Philadelphia, J. B. Lippincott & co.* 1874.

——— Same. 2 v. in 1. 350, 337 pp. incl. 4 pl. 12 pl. 12°. *New York, Harper & brothers,* 1874.
[HARPER's library edition]

——— What will he do with it? The lord Lytton ed. 3 v. in 2. 12°. *Philadelphia, J. B. Lippincott & co.* 1874.

Lytton (*Sir* Edward Robert Bulwer, *baron Lytton*). Fables in song. 2 v. vi, 203 pp; vi, 218 pp. 12°. *Edinburgh, W. Blackwood & sons,* 1874.

M . . . . Madame de Lavalle's bequest: counsels to young ladies. From the fourth french ed. [By M . . . . *anon.*] 355 pp. 12°. *Philadelphia, P. F. Cunningham & son,* 1875.

M'Allister (*Mrs.* M. E.) Sunshine among the clouds. 213 pp. 16°. *Cincinnati, Hitchcock & Walden,* 1873.

Macarthur (Margaret). History of Scotland. Ed. for american students. xiv, 199 pp. 16°. *New York, H. Holt & co.* 1874.
[FREEMAN's historical course for schools, no. 3].

Macaulay (Angus). Rudiments of political science. Part the first. xxiv, 390 pp. 1 l. 8°. *London, for the author,* 1796.

Macaulay (James). Ireland in 1872. xii, 419 pp. 12°. *London, H. S. King & co.* 1873.

Macbeth (John Walker Vilant). Might and mirth of literature. 2 p. l. 542 pp. 8°. *New York, Harper & brothers,* 1875.

McBride (H. Elliott). All kinds of dialogues. 180 pp. 16°. *New York, Dick & Fitzgerald,* [1874].

——— Comic dialogues. 179 pp. 16°. *New York, Dick & Fitzgerald,* [1873].

McCabe (James D. *jr.*) Centennial history of the United States. 925 pp. 7 pl. 2 ports. 1 facs. 8°. *Philadelphia, the national publishing co.* [1875].

——— Cross and crown. 619 pp. 11 pl. 8°. *Cincinnati, national publishing co.* 1874.

Maccall (William). Foreign biographies. 2 v. vii, 320 pp; 3 p. l. 283 pp. 8°. *London, Tinsley brothers,* 1873.

McCarthy (Justin). "Con amore;" or, critical chapters. viii, 360 pp. 12°. *London, Tinsley brothers,* 1868.

——— A fair saxon. 3 v. 12°. *London, Tinsley brothers,* 1873.

McCaul (Alexander, *d. d.*) Old paths; a comparison of modern judaism with the religion of Moses. xii, 660 pp. 8°. *London, London society's house,* 1846.

McCaul (*Rev.* John). Britanno-roman inscriptions, with critical notes. xlvii, 290 pp. front. 8°. *Toronto, H. Rowsell,* 1863.

M'Conkey (*Miss* Rebecca). True stories of the american fathers. 329 pp. 3 pl. 16°. *New York, Nelson & Phillips,* [1874].

McCosh (James, *d. d.*) Scottish philosophy. vii, 481 pp. 8°. *New York, R. Carter & brothers,* 1875.

McCrary (George W.) Treatise on the american law of elections. 487 pp. 8°. *Keokuk, Io. R. B. Ogden,* 1875.

M'Donald (Alexander). Narrative of some passages in the history of Eenoolovapik. 2 p. l. iii, 149 pp. 1 map, 1 facs. port. 12°. *Edinburgh, Fraser & co. & J. Hogg,* 1841.

Macdonald (Frederika). Nathaniel Vaughan. 3 v. 12°. *London, Hurst & Blackett,* 1874.

Macedo (Joaquim Manoel de). Notions on the chorography of Brazil. Translated by H. Le Sage. vi, 576 pp. 6 l. 8°. *Leipzig, F. A. Brockhaus,* 1873.

McElgun (John). Annie Reilly. 245 pp. 2 l. port. 16°. *New York, J. A. McGee,* 1873.

Maceuen (Malcolm). Celebrities of the past and present. Chiefly adapted from Sainte-Beuve. vii, 5–240 pp. 12°. *Philadelphia, Porter & Coates,* 1874.

Macfarlane (James). Coal-regions of America. xvi, 680 pp. incl. 30 maps and pl. 2 pl. 5 maps, 1 tab. 8°. *New York, D. Appleton & co.* 1873.

——— Same. 3d ed. With supplement for 1874. xvi, 695 pp. incl. 8 pl. and 11 maps, 2 tab. 2 pl. 11 maps. 8°. *New York, D. Appleton & co.* 1875.

M'Ferrin (John B. *d. d.*) History of methodism in Tennessee. v. 3. 1818 to 1840 538 pp. 1 pl. 12°. *Nashville, Tenn. southern methodist publishing house,* 1873.

Mac Gahan (J. A.) Campaigning on the Oxus, and the fall of Khiva. x, 438 pp.

Mac Gahan (J. A.)—continued. 21 pl. 2 ports. 12°. *New York, Harper & brothers*, 1874.

McGee (James E.) Lives of Irishmen's sons and their descendants. 292 pp. 1 pl. 16°. *New York, J. A. McGee*, 1874.

——— Sketches of irish soldiers in every land. xii, 329 pp. 1 pl. 16°. *New York, J. A. McGee*, 1873.

McGuire (*Mrs.* Judith White). General Robert E. Lee, the christian soldier. [*anon.*] 1 p. l. ix–198 pp. 16°. *Philadelphia, Claxton, Remsen & Haffelfinger*, 1873.

McIlvain (Charlotte L.) Ebon and gold. [*anon.*] 2 p. l. 7–335 pp. 12°. *New York, G. W. Carleton & co.* 1874.

Mackay (Charles). Lost beauties of the english language. xxiv, 288 pp. 12°. *New York, J. W. Bouton*, 1874.

——— Under the blue sky. viii, 344 pp. 12°. *London, S. Low, Marston, Low & Searle*, 1871.

McKeen (Phebe F.) Theodora. vi, 480 pp. 12°. *New York, A. D. F. Randolph & co.* [1875].

Mackenzie (G. Muir), *and* **Irby** (A. P.) Turks, Greeks, & Slavons. xxxii, 688 pp. 19 pl. 4 maps. 8°. *London, Bell & Daldy*, 1867.

Mackenzie (*Rev.* William). History of Galloway. 2 v. 4 p. l. viii, 544, 48 pp. map; 2 p. l. vii, 498, 75 pp. map. 12°. *Kirkcudbright, J. Nicholson*, 1841.

Mackey (Albert Gallatin, *m. d.*) Encylopædia of freemasonry. vii, 947 pp. 1 pl. 8°. *Philadelphia, Moss & co.* 1874.

——— Masonic parliamentary law. 240 pp. 12°. *Philadelphia, Moss & co.* 1875.

——— The mystic tie: or, facts illustrative of freemasonry. viii, 220 pp. 12°. *Charleston, S. C., Miller & Browne*, 1849.

McKnight (Charles). Old fort Duquesne. 501 pp. 8 pl. 12°. *Pittsburgh, people's monthly publishing co.* 1873.

——— Our western border one hundred years ago. xi, 756 pp. 15 pl. 8°. *Philadelphia, J. C. McCurdy & co.* 1875.

McLain (*Miss* Mary Webster.) Keeping open house. 104 pp. 8°. *Hartford, Conn. M. H. Mallory & co.* 1872.

——— Wedding garments. 1 p. l. 265 pp. 16°. *New York, Scribner, Armstrong & co.* 1875.

Maclean (J. P.) Manual of the antiquity of man. 159 pp. incl. 2 pl. 1 port. 12°. *New York, author*, 1875.

Macleod (Henry Dunning). Principles of economical philosophy. 2d ed. v. 1, v. 2, part 1. xliv, 676 pp; xiv, 522 pp. 8°. *London, Longmans*, 1872–75.

Maclise (Daniel). Gallery of illustrious literary characters (1830–38), accompanied by notices chiefly by W. Maginn, ll. d. Edited by W. Bates. xii, 10–239 pp. 84 pl. 4°. *London, Chatto and Windus*, [1873].

Macmillan (Hugh). Holidays on high lands. vii, 300 pp. 16°. *London, Macmillan & co.* 1869.

McPherson (Edward). Hand-book of politics for 1874. vii, 246 pp. 8°. *Washington, Solomons & Chapman*, 1874.

——— Political history of the United States during reconstruction, (april 15, 1865, to july 15, 1870). 2d ed. 9, 648 pp. 8°. *Washington, Solomons & Chapman*, 1875.

Macquart (Pierre Justin Marie). Les arbres et arbrisseaux d'Europe et leurs insectes. 366 pp. 8°. *Lille, L. Danel*, 1852. s.

Macquoid (Katharine S.) Miriam's marriage. 3 v. 12°. *London, Smith, Elder & co.* 1872.

——— My story. 1 p. l. 189 pp. 8 pl. 8°. *New York, D. Appleton & co.* 1875.
[Library of choice novels, no. 47].

——— Too soon. [*anon.*] 3 v. 12°. *London, R. Bentley & son*, 1873.

Macready (William Charles). Reminiscences, and selections from his diaries and letters. 2 v. xii, 476 pp. port; x, 486 pp. port. 8°. *London, Macmillan & co.* 1875.

Mactaggart (John). Scottish gallovidian encyclopedia, or, the curiosities of the south of Scotland. xii, 504 pp. 8°. *London, for the author*, 1824.

Macvicar (John G. *ll. d.*) Sketch of a philosophy. Parts i–iv. 4 v. 8°. *London, Williams & Norgate*, 1868–74. s.

CONTENTS.

Part i. Mind: its powers and capacities, and its relation to matter. xvi, 160 pp. 1868.
Part ii. Matter and molecular morphology. [*anon.*] xx, 96 pp. 1868.
Part iii. The chemistry of natural substances. xx, 163 pp. 2 pl. 1870.
Part iv. Biology and theodicy: a prelude to the biology of the future. 1 p. l. xx, 180 pp. 1 pl. 1874.

"**Made** in heaven." A novel. [*anon.*] 2 v. 2 p. l. 298 pp; 2 p. l. 310 pp. 12°. *London, R. Bentley & son*, 1873.

Maffei (Paolo Alessandro). Raccôlta di státve antiche e moderne. Illvstrata di P. A. Maffei. 2 p. l. eng. dedication, xii pp. 1 l. 43 l. containing 170 numb. columns, 7 l. clxiii pl.

Maffei (Paolo Alessandro)—continued. numb. fol. *Roma, D. de Rossi e G. Zenobj,* 1704.

Maffitt (*Rev.* John Newland). Pulpit sketches. First series. 178 pp. 12°. *Louisville, Ky. W. H. Johnston,* 1839.

——— Tears of contrition; or sketches of the life of John N. Maffitt. 260, 40 pp. 16°. *New-London, S. Green,* 1821.

Magee (*Rev.* James H.) Night of affliction and morning of recovery. An autobiography. 173 pp. 1 port. 12°. *Cincinnati, author,* 1873.

Maguire (T. H.) The art of figure drawing. x, 59 pp. 30 pl. 4°. *London, G. Routledge & sons,* [1869].

Mahabharata. Nalopâkhyânam, or, the tale of Nala; sanskrit text in roman characters, followed by a vocabulary and a sanskrit grammar. By the rev. Thomas Jarrett. [*anon.*] 4 p. l. 160 pp. 5 tab. on 7 l. 8°. *Cambridge* [*Eng.*] *university press,* 1875.

Mahaffy (*Rev.* John P.) Social life in Greece from Homer to Menander. xii, 390 pp. 12°. *London, Macmillan & co.* 1874.

Maid of Kent. [*anon.*] 3 v. 16°. *London, for T. Hookham,* 1790.

Maidment (James, *editor*). Book of scottish pasquils. 1568–1715. xxviii, 438 pp. 12°. *Edinburgh, W. Paterson,* 1868.

——— Scottish ballads and songs. 2 v. xv, 364 pp; vi, 344 pp. 8°. *Edinburgh, W. Paterson,* 1868.

Maillard (Firmin). Histoire des journaux publiés à Paris pendant le siége et sous la commune. 267 pp. 16°. *Paris, E. Dentu,* 1871.

——— Les publications de la rue pendant le siége et la commune. 1 p. l. xii, 198 pp. front. 16°. *Paris, A. Aubry,* 1874.

Maillard (L.) Note sur l'Ile de la Réunion (Bourbon). 344 pp. 111 l. 25 pl. (10 col.) 3 col. maps. 8°. *Paris, Dentu,* 1862.

Maillet (Benoît de). Description de l'Égypte. Composée sur les mémoires de M. de Maillet, par l'abbé Le Mascrier. xxiv, 328, 242 pp. 5 l. 8 pl. 1 map. 4°. *Paris, L. Genneau & J. Rollin, fils,* 1735.

Maimbourg (Claude). Life of st. Thomas of Villanova, archbishop of Valentia. 1st am. ed. 352 pp. 1 pl. 12°. *Philadelphia, P. F. Cunningham & son,* 1874.

Maine (*Sir* Henry Sumner). Lectures on the early history of institutions. viii pp. 1 l. 412 pp. 8°. *London, J. Murray,* 1875.

Mainyô-i-khard. Book of the Mainyô i-khard. Pazand and sanskrit texts, (in roman characters) as arranged by Neriosengh Dhaval, in the fifteenth century. With an english translation, a glossary of the pazand text, containing the sanskrit, persian and pahlavi equivalents, a sketch of pazand grammar, and an introduction by E. W. West. viii, xxiv, 188, 264 pp. 8°. *Stuttgart, C. Grüninger,* 1871.

Mair (James Allan). Handbook of proverbs and family mottoes. 192 pp. 16°. *London, G. Routledge & sons,* [1873].

Maison rustique du XIXe siècle. Encyclopédie d'agriculture pratique; sous la direction de mm. E. Bailly, A. Bixio, Malepeyre aîné, et Ysabeau. 5 v. 8°. *Paris, bureau du journal d'agriculture pratique,* 1842–44. S.

Maitland (Edward). Higher law. A romance. [*anon.*] 3 v. 12°. *London, Chapman & Hall,* 1870.

Maitland (William). History and antiquities of Scotland. [*anon.*] v. 1. 1 p. l. xxiv, 615 pp. fol. *London, for A. Millar,* 1757.

Malcolm (James Peller). Excursions in the counties of Kent, Gloucester, Hereford, Monmouth, and Somerset, in 1802, 1803, and 1805. 2d ed. Eng. title, 3 p. l. 245 pp. 21 pl. 8°. *London, Nichols, son, & Bentley,* 1814.

Malerische (Das) und romantische Deutschland. 2te aufl. 10 v. 8°. *Leipzig, C. A. Haendel's verlag,* 1847.

CONTENTS.

v. 1. SCHWAB (G.) Schwaben. 200 pp. 30 pl.
2. HEERINGEN (G. von). Franken. 128 pp. 30 pl.
3. BECHSTEIN (L.) Thüringen. 205 pp. 30 pl.
4. BLUMENHAGEN (W.) Der Harz. 192 pp. 30 pl.
5. SPORSCHIL (J.) Sachsen. 168 pp. 30 pl.
6. HERLOSSSOHN (C.) Das riesengebirge und die grafschaft Glatz. Nebst einem ausfluge nach Prag und Karlstein. 182 pp. 30 pl.
7. CORNELIUS (W.) *and* KOBBE (T. von). Ost- und Nordsee. 191 pp. 30 pl.
8. SIMROCK (K.) Der Rhein. 376 pp. 60 pl.
9. DULLER (E.) Die Donauländer. 270 pp. 60 pl.
10. SEIDL (J. G.) Tyrol und Steyermark. 392 pp. 60 pl.

Malijay (Paul de). Méditations sociales. Saint Jean-Baptiste, l'évangile et le Canada. 3 p. l. 210 pp. 1 l. 8°. *Montréal, des presses à vapeur de "La Minerve",* 1874.

Malmesbury (*Earl of*). *See* **Harris** (James Howard).

Malot (Hector). Romain Kalbris. From the french by mrs. J. McNair Wright. 386 pp. incl. 18 pl. 12°. *Philadelphia, Porter & Coates,* [1873].

Malzine (Omer de). Flore mexicaine aux environs de Cordova. (1869–1870). 102 pp. 8°. *Gand, C. Annoot-Braeckman,* 1873. S.

Mandet (Francisque). Histoire de la langue romane. xi, 388 pp. 8°. *Paris, Dauvin & Fontaine,* 1840.

Mangin (Arthur). Mysteries of the ocean. Translated and enlarged. 470 pp. 8°. *London, T. Nelson & sons*, 1868.

Mann (Jonathan B.) Life of Henry Wilson, vice-president. vi, 120 pp. 1 port. 8°. *Boston, J. R. Osgood & co.* 1872.

Mann (*Mrs.* Mary Peabody, *wife of Horace Mann*). Flower people. New ed. 176 pp. 7 pl. sq. 12°. *Boston, J. R. Osgood & co.* 1875.

Manners (R. Rutland). Pasco, and other poems. 1 p. l. 107 pp. 1 l. 16°. [*New York*]? *for the author*, [1875].

Mannert (Konrad). Geographie der Griechen und Römer. 10 v. in 14. 8°. *Nürnberg*, [*etc.*] *Grattenauer*, [*etc.*] 1788–1825.

Manning (Jacob M. *d. d.*) Helps to a life of prayer. 159 pp. 16°. *Boston, Lee & Shepard*, 1875.

Manning (Samuel, *ll. d.*) Italian pictures drawn with pen and pencil. [*anon.*] 214 pp. incl. 36 pl. roy. 8°. *London, the religious tract society*, [1872].

——— The land of the Pharaohs. Egypt and Sinai: illustrated by pen and pencil. 224 pp. incl. 33 pl. roy. 8°. *London, the religious tract society*, [1875].

——— Spanish pictures drawn with pen and pencil. With illustrations by Gustave Doré and other artists. [*anon.*] 200 pp. incl. 29 pl. roy. 8°. *London, the religious tract society*, [1870].

——— "Those holy fields." Palestine, illustrated by pen and pencil. 223 pp. incl. 24 pl. & 3 maps. 8°. *London, the religious tract society*, [1874].

Manning (Thomas, *compiler*). Commodore's signal book and vade mecum. 98 pp. 5 col. pl. fold. 12°. *New York, J. Filmer*, [1874].

——— Yachting annual. 124 pp. 36 l. numb. containing col. ensigns, 2 pl. 12°. *New York, J. Filmer*, [1875].

Manningham (John). Diary. 1602, 1603. Edited by J. Bruce. xx, 188 pp. sm. 4°. *Westminster, J. B. Nichols & sons*, 1868.

[CAMDEN society publications, no. 99].

Manœuvres of artillery. [*anon.*] 4 v. 16°. *Metz, lithography of Dupuy and Tavernier*, 1828.

CONTENTS.

1. School of the cannonier, and service of field artillery.
2. Service of siege, garrison and coast artillery.
3. Manœuvres of field batteries.
4. Plates.

Man's age in the world according to holy scripture and science. By an Essex rector. [*anon.*] vii, 264 pp. 8°. *London, L. Reeve & co.* 1865.

Mansel (Henry Longueville, *d. d.*) Gnostic heresies of the first and second centuries. Edited by J. B. Lightfoot. xxxii, 288 pp. 8°. *London, J. Murray*, 1875.

——— Letters, lectures, and reviews, including the phrontisterion, or, Oxford in the 19th century. vii, 408 pp. 8°. *London, J. Murray*, 1873.

Mantell (Gideon Algernon, *ll. d.*) A day's ramble in and about the ancient town of Lewes. 157 pp. front. 16°. *London, H. G. Bohn*, 1846.

Manteuffel (Hans Ernst, *baron* von). Art de planter. Traduit sur la 3e éd. allemande par J. P. Stumper. 2e éd. xxxii, 224 pp. 16°. *Paris, J. Rothschild*, 1874.

Mantz (Paul). Chefs d'œuvre de la peinture italienne. viii, 268 pp. 1 l. 50 pl. fol. *Paris, F. Didot frères, fils & cie.* 1870.

Manufactories and manufacturers of Pennsylvania in the nineteenth century. [*anon.*] 533 pp. 90 ports. 83 pl. sm. 4°. *Philadelphia, galaxy publishing co.* 1875.

Note.—Edited by C. Robson.

Manville (Helen A.) Heart echoes. By Nellie A. Mann [*pseud.*] xii, 169 pp. 12°. *New York, S. R. Wells & co.* 1875.

Manx society. [Publications]. v. 1–19 & 21. 8°. *Douglas, Isle of Man*, 1859–73.

CONTENTS.

BROWN (Thomas). The mona of Cæsar and Tacitus. (v. 1).
CHALONER (James). Treatise on the Isle of Man, 1656. (v. 10).
CLAY (Charles, *m. d.*) Currency of the Isle of Man, 1869. (v. 17).
CRELLIN (J. Frissell). Paper money of the Isle of Man. (v. 17).
CUMMING (*Rev.* James George, *editor*). Antiquitates Manniæ, 1868. (v. 15).
FELTHAM (John). Tour through the Isle of Man, 1797–98. (v. 6).
——— *and* WRIGHT (Edward). Memorials of "God's acre," 1797. (v. 14).
GILL (*Rev.* William) *and* CLARKE (*Rev.* John Thomas, *editors*). English and Manx dictionary, 1866. (v. 13).
HARRISON (William). Bibliotheca Monensis, 1861. (v. 8).
——— *editor.* Mona miscellany. 2 v. (v. 16, 21).
——— Records of Tyrwald & st. John's chapel. (v. 19).
——— The old historians of the Isle of Man, 1871. (v. 18).
KELLY (John, *d. d.*) The Manx dictionary, 1866. (v. 13).
——— Grammar of the antient gaelic language of the Isle of Man, 1859. (v. 2).
MACKENZIE (*Rev.* William, *editor*). Legislation of the thirteen Stanleys, kings of Man. (v. 3).
OLIVER (John Robert, *m. d. editor*). Monumenta de insula Manniæ. 3 v. 1860–62. (v. 4, 7, 9).
OSWALD (H. R.) Vestigia insulæ Manniæ antiquiora, 1860. (v. 5).
PARR (John). Abstract of the laws [etc.] of the Isle of Man, 1867. (v. 12).

Manx society—continued.

SACHEVERELL (William). Account of the Isle of Man. (v. 1).
STANLEY (James, *7th earl of Derby*). History and antiquities of the Isle of Man. (v. 3).
WALDRON (George). A description of the Isle of Man. (v. 11).

Many lands and many people. [*anon.*] 256 pp. incl. front. 8°. *Philadelphia, J. B. Lippincott & co.* 1875.

March (Francis A. *ll. d.*) Latin hymns, with english notes. xii, 333 pp. 12°. *New York, Harper & brothers*, 1874.

[DOUGLASS series of christian greek and latin writers, v. 1].

Marckes (Theodore von). Franco-german war. 1 p. l. 19-126 pp. incl. 17 pl. 1 pl. 1 map. 8°. *Philadelphia, Barclay & co.* [1871].

Marcoy (Paul). Travels in South America. [Translated by Elihu Rich]. 2 v. xii, 524 pp. 1 pl. 4 maps; viii, 496 pp. 1 pl. 6 maps. 4°. *London, Blackie & son*, 1875.

Marcus (Louis). Histoire des Wandales. 2 p. l. viii, 96, 423 pp. 8°. *Paris, A. Bertrand*, 1836.

Marguerite d'Angoulême *or* **de Valois**, *queen of Navarre.* Les marguerites de la marguerite des princesses. Texte de l'édition de 1547 avec introduction, notes et glossaire par Félix Frank. 4 v. 16°. *Paris, librairie des bibliophiles*, 1873.

[CABINET du bibliophile, no. 16].

Marguerite's journal. With introduction by the author of "Rutledge." [*anon.*] 328 pp. 12°. *New York, G. W. Carleton & co.* 1875.

Marin (François). Les dons de Comus. Nouv. éd. [*anon.*] 3 v. 16°. *Paris, L. Cellot*, 1775.

Markham (Albert Hastings). Cruise of the "Rosario" amongst the New Hebrides and Santa Cruz islands. xvi, 304 pp. 8 pl. 1 map. 8°. *London, S. Low, Marston, Low & Searle*, 1873.

Markham (Clements Robert). General sketch of the history of Persia. xxxviii, 565 pp. map. 8°. *London, Longmans*, 1874.

——— Memoir of lady Ana de Osorio, vice-queen of Peru (a. d. 1629-39). xii, 99 pp. 2 col. pl. 1 col. map. sm. 4°. *London, Trübner & co.* 1874.

——— Narratives of the rites and laws of the Yncas. Translated and edited with notes and introduction. 1 p. l. xx, 220 pp. 8°. *London, Hakluyt society*, 1873.

[HAKLUYT society publications, v. 48].

Markham (Clements Robert)—continued.

——— Threshold of the unknown region. 2d ed. xviii, 358 pp. 9 maps. 8°. *London, S. Low, Marston, Low & Searle*, 1873.

Marlay (*Rev.* John F.) Life of rev. Thomas A. Morris. iv, 407 pp. port. 12°. *Cincinnati, Hitchcock & Walden*, 1875.

Marlès (J. Lacroix de). Paris ancien et moderne. 3 v. 4°. *Paris, Parent-Desbarres*, 1837-38.

[Imperfect: wanting the vol. of plates].

Marr (Fannie H.) Heart-life in song. 165 pp. 16°. *Baltimore, Turnbull brothers*, 1874.

Marriott (Wharton Booth). Testimony of the catacombs and of other monuments of christian art, concerning doctrine. viii, 223 pp. 10 pl. 8°. *London, Hatchards*, 1870.

Marsh (George Perkins, *ll. d.*) The earth as modified by human action. A new edition of Man and nature. xxi, 656 pp. 8°. *New York, Scribner, Armstrong & co.* 1874.

Marsh (J. C. Lory, *m. d.*) A book about shams. vii, 240 pp. 5 pl. 12°. *London, Ward, Lock & Tyler*, 1870.

Marshall (Frederic). International vanities. 4 p. l. 360 pp. 8°. *Edinburgh, W. Blackwood & sons*, 1875.

Marshall (T. W. M.) Christian missions. 2d ed. 2 v. 2 p. l. 644 pp; 2 p. l. 479, xxxvi pp. 8°. *London, Longman*, 1863.

——— My clerical friends and their relations to modern thought. [*anon.*] 3 p. l. 388 pp. 8°. *London, Burns, Oates & co.* 1873.

Marston (Philip Bourke). Song-tide and other poems. 2d ed. xi, 210 pp. 12°. *London, Chatto & Windus*, 1874.

Martenet (S. J.) **Walling** (H. F.) *and* **Gray** (O. W.) New topographical atlas of Maryland and the district of Columbia. 108 pp. incl. 29 maps, 7 l. fol. *Baltimore, Stedman, Brown & Lyon*, 1873.

Martensen (Hans Lassen). Christliche dogmatik. xi, 460 pp. 8°. *Berlin, G. Schlawitz*, 1856.

Martin (Benjamin N. *d. d.*) Choice specimens of american literature. 2d ed. xviii, 518 pp. 12°. *New York, Sheldon & co.* [1875].

Martin (Charles). Précis des événements de la campagne du Mexique en 1862. Précédé d'une notice sur le Mexique par Léon Deluzy. 2 p. l. 372 pp. 1 map, 1 plan. 8°. *Paris, C. Tanera*, 1863.

Martin (Edward Winslow). History of the grange movement. 539 pp. incl. 11 pl. 7 pl.

Martin (Edward Winslow)—continued. 8°. *Philadelphia, national publishing co.* [1873].

Martin (Frederick). Statesman's year-book, 1874, 1875. 11th and 12th annual publication. 2 v. 12°. *London, Macmillan & co.* 1874–75.

Martin (George H.) Text book of civil government in the United States. 330 pp. 12°. *New York, A. S. Barnes & co.* 1875.

Martin (Louis Aimé, *editor*). Lettres édifiantes et curieuses concernant l'Asie, l'Afrique et l'Amérique. 4 v. 8°. *Paris, A. Desrez*, 1838–43.

[PANTHÉON littéraire].

Martin (Theodore). Life of the prince consort [Albert]. 3d ed. v. 1. xv, 516 pp. 3 ports. 2 pl. 8°. *London, Smith, Elder & co.* 1875.

Martin (Thomas Henri). Galilée; les droits de la science et la méthode des sciences physiques. 2 p. l. xi, 428 pp. 16°. *Paris, Didier & cie.* 1868.

Martin (William T.) History of Franklin county [Ohio]. v, 450 pp. 7 pl. 8°. *Columbus, Follett, Foster & co.* 1858.

Martin de Moussy (V.) Description de la Confédération argentine. 3 v. 8°. & atlas. 2d ed. fol. *Paris, Didot frères, fils & cie.* 1860–73. s

Martineau (Harriet). Life in the sick-room. 2d ed. [*anon*]. xv, 221 pp. 8°. *London, E. Moxon*, 1844.

Martinet (Antoine, *abbé*). Ark of the people, by Plato Punchinello [*pseud.*] Translated from the french. 458 pp. 12°. *Philadelphia, P. F. Cunningham*, 1873.

Martinez (Victor José). Sinopsis historica, filosofica y politica de las revoluciones mexicanas. v. 1. 2 p. l. 24, xxxii, 286 pp. 1 l. 8°. *Mexico, D. de Leon y White*, 1874.

Marvin (Frederic Rowland). Dream music. 107 pp. 12°. *New York, Carleton*, 1870.

Mary-Lafon (Jean Bernard Lafon, *dit*). Histoire politique, religieuse et littéraire du midi de la France. 4 v. 8°. *Paris, P. Mellier*, 1845.

Mason (C. Welsh). Rape of the gamp. A novel. 1 p. l. 9–152 pp. front. 8°. *New York, Harper & brothers*, 1875.

Mason (J. A. *m. d.*) Treatise on the climate and meteorology of Madeira; edited by J. S. Knowles. xv, 388 pp. 3 pl. 8°. *London, J. Churchill*, 1850.

Mason (Mary Murdoch). Mae Madden. 192 pp. 18°. *Chicago, Jansen, McClurg & co.* 1876.

Mason (Richard S. *d. d.*) Baptizing of infants defended. 127 pp. 12°. *New York, E. J. Hale & son*, 1874.

Masson (David). Chatterton. viii, 284 pp. 12°. *London, Macmillan & co.* 1874.

Massy (Richard Tuthill). Analytical ethnology. v, 245 pp. 6 pl. 16°. *London, H. Bailliere*, 1855.

Mathews (Joanna H.) Miss Ashton's girls. 6 v. 16°. *New York, R. Carter & brothers*, 1874–76.

CONTENTS.

i. Fanny's birthday gift. 368 pp. 3 pl. 1874.
ii. The new scholars. 376 pp. 3 pl. 1874.
iii. Rosalie's pet. 373 pp. 3 pl. 1875.
iv. Eleanor's visit. 352 pp. 3 pl. 1875.
v. Mabel Walton's experiment. 347 pp. 3 pl. 1875.
vi. Elsie's Santa Claus. 1 p. l. 346 pp. 3 pl. 1876.

Mathews (William, *ll. d.*) Great conversers, and other essays. 304 pp. incl. 1 map. 8°. *Chicago, S. C. Griggs & co.* 1874.

Matson (N.) French and Indians of Illinois river. 260 pp. 1 pl. 16°. *Princeton, Ill. republican printing establishment*, 1874.

Maudsley (Henry, *m. d.*) Responsibility in mental disease. x, 313 pp. 12°. *London, H. S. King & co.* 1874.

[INTERNATIONAL scientific series, v. 8].

Maunder (Samuel). Little lexicon of the english language. 5th ed. Eng. title, viii, 856 pp. 1 pl. 32°. *London, F. J. Mason*, [18—].

Mauny de Mornay (Marie Joseph de). Pratique et législation des irrigations dans l'Italie supérieure et dans quelques états d'Allemagne. 2me ptie. Législation. 2 p. l. lii, 166 pp. 8°. *Paris, imprimerie royale*, 1844.

Maurault (J. A. *abbé*). Histoire des Abenakis, depuis 1605 jusqu'à nos jours. 1 p. l. iii, xi, 631 pp. 4 l. 8°. *Sorel, [C. E.] "Gazette de Sorel,"* 1866.

Maurice (C. Edmund). Lives of English popular leaders. i. 12°. *London, H. S. King & co.* 1872.

CONTENTS.

i. Stephen Langton. xv, 276 pp. 1872.

Maurice (*Rev.* John Frederick Denison). Friendship of books; and other lectures. With a preface, by T. Hughes. xxxvi, 389 pp. 12°. *London, Macmillan & co.* 1874.

Maurice (Thomas). Dissertation on the oriental trinities. 2 p. l. 17–460 pp. 6 pl. 8°. *London, for the author*, 1801.

Maurin (Albert). Galérie historique de la révolution française. 5 v. 8°. *Paris, la société des travailleurs réunis,* [1849-50].

Maury (Louis Ferdinand Alfred). Forêts de la Gaule et de l'ancienne France. vii, 501 pp. 8°. *Paris, Ladrange,* 1867.

Mawe (Thomas), **Abercrombie** (John), *and others.* Every man his own gardener. 2 p. l. 616 pp. 10 l. front. 16°. *London, for T. Longman,* [*etc.*] 1794.

Maxwell (James Clerk). Treatise on electricity and magnetism. 2 v. xxxi, 2, 425 pp. 1 l. 14 pl; xxiii, 2, 444 pp. 1 l. 6 pl. 8°. *Oxford,* [*Eng.*] *Clarendon press,* 1873.
[CLARENDON press series].

May (Frederick L.) *& co. publishers.* British and irish press guide. (Second year). 1875. 8°. *London, F. L. May & co.* [1875].

May (*Col.* John). Journal and letters relative to two journeys to the Ohio country in 1788 and '89. 160 pp. 8°. *Cincinnati, R. Clarke & co.* 1873.
[OHIO (Historical and philosophical society of). Publications. New series. v. 1].

Mayerne (Louis Turquet de). Histoire générale d'Espagne, comprise en xxx livres. 10 p. l. 1536 [1524] pp. fol. *Paris, A. l'Angelier,* 1608.

Mayne (J. T.) Short notes of tours in America and India. 1 p. l. v, 193 pp. 5 pl. 8°. *Madras, Gantz brothers,* 1869.

Mayne (Leger D. *pseud.*) What shall we do to-night? or social amusements. 366 pp. incl. 1 pl. 12°. *New York, Dick & Fitzgerald,* [1873].

Maynwaring (Arthur). Life and posthumous works. xviii, 356 pp. 12 l. 8°. *London, for A. Bell,* 1715.

Mayo (*Mrs.* Isabella). By still waters; by Edward Garrett [*pseud.*] 2 p. l. 362 pp. 12 pl. 12°. *New York, Dodd & Mead,* 1874.

——— Premiums paid to experience. By Edward Garrett [*pseud.*] 2 v. 3 p. l. 269 pp; 3 p. l. 286 pp. 12°. *London, Strahan & co.* 1872.

Mayo (William Starbuck, *m. d.*) Flood and field. 2 p. l. 9-284 pp. 7 pl. 12°. *Philadelphia, W. P. Hazard,* 1855.

Mead (Whitman). Travels in North America. Parts 1 & 2 in 1 v. 160 pp. 8°. *New-York, C. S. Van Winkle,* 1820.

Meade (Herbert). Ride through the disturbed districts of New Zealand. xi, 375 pp. 4 col. pl. 2 maps. 8°. *London, J. Murray,* 1870.

Mears (John W. *d. d.*) Story of Madagascar. 313 pp. 11 pl. 16°. *Philadelphia, presbyterian board of publication,* [1873].

Medley (J. G.) The Roorkee treatise on civil engineering in India. v. 1. 3d ed. xii, xii, 592, 1, xiii pp. 70 pl. 3 tab. 8°. *Roorkee, Thomason college press,* 1873 s.
[Imperfect: pl. 46 wanting].

Melek-Hanum, *wife of* Kibrizli-Mehemet-Pasha. Six years in Europe. Edited by L. A. Chamerovzow. viii, 334 pp. 8°. *London, Chapman & Hall,* 1873.

Meline (Mary Miller). Charteris. A romance. 260 pp. 12°. *Philadelphia, J. B Lippincott & co.* 1874.

——— In six months. 3 p. l. 299 pp. 16°. *Baltimore, Kelly, Piet & co.* 1874.

Mellen (Grenville). Sad tales and glad tales; by Reginald Reverie [*pseud.*] vi, 185 pp. 16°. *Boston, S. G. Goodrich,* 1828.

——— *editor.* Book of the United States. vi, 13-804 pp. front. 1 pl. with 7 ports. 8°. *Hartford, H. F. Sumner & co.* 1838.
[Imperfect: pp. 795-802 wanting].

Memorial of lt. Daniel Perkins Dewey. [*anon.*] 126 pp. port. 16°. *Hartford, Case, Lockwood & co.* 1864.

Memories: a story of german love. From the german, by George P. Upton. [*anon.*] 173 pp. sq. 16°. *Chicago, Jansen, McClurg & co.* 1875.

Men of the second empire. [*anon.*] 2 p. l. xvi, 281 pp. 12°. *London, Smith, Elder & co.* 1872.

Ménant (Joachim). Exposé des éléments de la grammaire assyrienne. 2 p. l. iv, 392 pp. 8°. *Paris, l'imprimerie impériale,* 1868.

Mendelssohn-Bartholdy (*Dr.* Karl). Goethe and Mendelssohn. (1821-1831). From the german, by M. E. von Glehn. xxi, 159 pp. 2 ports. 12°. *London, Macmillan & co.* 1872.

Mendez (Francisco). Noticias sobre la vida, escritos y viajes del rmo. p. Enrique Florez. 2da ed. xx, 444 pp. 1 l. port. 1 pl. 8°. *Madrid, J. Rodriguez,* 1860. s.

Mendieta (Gerónimo de). Historia eclesiástica indiana. La publica J. G. Icazbalceta. xlv, 790 pp. 8°. *México, antigua libreria,* 1870.

Mendoza (Eufemio) *and* **Rosa** (Manuel A.) Nociones de cronologia universal. 7 p. l. 11-398 pp. 2 l. 4 pl. 1 tab. 8°. *Mexico,* [*imprenta del gobierno*], 1874. s.

Mercier (*Doctor* Alfred). Le fou de Palerme. Par M.* * *, louisianais [*pseud.*] 140 pp. 1 l.

Mercier (*Doctor* Alfred)—continued. 8°. *Nouvelle-Orléans, imprimerie du "Carillon,"* 1873.

Meredith (Isabella Grant). The old house on Briar hill. 352 pp. 4 pl. 16°. *New York, Dodd & Mead,* [1875].

Merewether (Henry Alworth). By sea and by land: a trip all round the world. xvi, 343 pp. incl. 1 pl. 8°. *London, Macmillan & co.* 1874.

Mérimée (Prosper). Lettres à une inconnue. Précédées d'une étude sur Mérimée par H. Taine. 6e éd. 2 v. 2 p. l. xxxii, 368 pp; 2 p. l. 373 pp. 16°. *Paris, M. Lévy frères,* 1874.

——— Same. Letters to an incognita; with recollections by Lamartine and George Sand [*pseud.*] Edited by R. H. Stoddard. 1 p. l. 350 pp. 16°. *New York, Scribner, Armstrong & co.* 1874.

[BRIC-À-BRAC series, no. 3].

Merivale (Charles, *d. d.*) General history of Rome. 2d ed. xxxvi, 708 pp. 5 col. maps. 12°. *London, Longmans,* 1875.

Merle (Gibbons) *and* **Reitch** (John, *m. d.*) Domestic dictionary and housekeepers manual. 2 p. l. xii, 457 pp. 8°. *London, W. Strange,* 1845.

Merli (A.) *and* **Belgrana** (L. T.) Il palazzo del principe D'Oria. 1 p. l. 11 pl. 1 l. fol. *Genova, tipografía del r. istituto sordo-muti,* 1874. s.

Méry (Joseph). Through thick and thin: or, "La guerre du Nizam." From the 35th Paris ed. by O. Vibeur. 425 pp. 12°. *New York, G. W. Carleton & co.* 1874.

Merz (Karl). Musical hints for the million. 1 p. l. 216 pp. sq. 16°. *Cleveland, S. Brainard's sons,* 1875.

Messler (Abraham, *d. d.*) Forty years at Raritan.—Eight memorial sermons. viii, 5–327 pp. 8°. *New-York, A. Lloyd,* 1873.

Metz (Conrad Mart). Studies of the human figure. 1 p. l. 27 pl. fol. *London, J. & J. Boydell,* [1809].

[Imperfect: wanting pl. no. 17].

Meunier (Victor). Les ancêtres d'Adam, histoire de l'homme fossile. xix, 282 pp. 1 l. 18°. *Paris, J. Rothschild,* 1875.

Meurice (Paul). Les deux Diane [publié] par A. Dumas. Nouv. ed. 3 v. 16°. *Paris, M. Lévy frères,* 1867.

[DUMAS (A. D.) Oeuvres complètes. 16°. *Paris.* v. 77–79].

Mexia (J. Carlos). Manual de la constitucion de los Estados Unidos. 7, ix, 258 pp. 1 l. 8°. *Washington, R. Beresford,* 1874.

Mexico (*Republic of*). Révélations sur l'occupation française au Mexique. Documents officiels, publiés par ordre du gouvernement constitutionnel de la république. 107 pp. 8°. *Bruxelles,* [*D. Brismée*], 1869.

Mézières (Alfred). Prédécesseurs et contemporains de Shakspeare. xv, 403 pp. 8°. *Paris, Charpentier,* 1863.

Mézières (Louis). Histoire critique de la littérature anglaise. Morale, roman, genre épistolaire. 3 v. 8°. *Paris, Baudry,* 1834.

Micali (Giuseppe). Monuments antiques, pour l'intelligence de l'ouvrage: L'Italie avant la domination des Romains. 2 p. l. 24 pp. 52 pl. 1 map. fol. *Paris, Treuttel & Würtz,* 1824.

Michaelis (Adolf). Der parthenon. Text, xvi, 370 pp. 1 pl. 8°; & atlas, 3 p. l. 15 pl. fol. *Leipzig, Breitkopf & Härtel,* 1870–71.

Michelet (Jules). Histoire du XIXe siècle. [v. 1]. Directoire. Origine des Bonaparte. 2 p. l. xxiv, 443 pp. 8°. *Paris, G. Baillière,* 1872.

——— The mountain. From the french. 323 pp. 8°. *London, T. Nelson & sons,* 1872.

Michelet (*Madame* Jules). Nature; or, the poetry of earth and sea. xxxi, 431 pp. 8°. *London, T. Nelson & sons,* 1872.

Midland counties historical collector. [Monthly]. Aug. 1854–dec. 1856. v. 1–2. 8°. *Leicester, T. C. Browne,* 1854–56.

Military monitor and american register. A record of the war between the United States and Great Britain, 1812. v. 1. Aug. 17, 1812–aug. 23, 1813. 4°. *New York, J. Desnoues,* 1813.

Mill (John Stuart). Autobiography. vi, 313 pp. 8°. *London, Longmans,* 1873.

——— Same. 3 p. l. 313 pp. 8°. *New York, H. Holt & co.* 1873.

——— Chapters and speeches on the irish land question. 2 p. l. 125 pp. 12°. *London, Longmans,* 1870.

Millard (David Edmund). Memoir; with selections from his writings. By his son. 456 pp. 8°. *Dayton, O. christian publishing assoc.* 1874.

Miller (Elizabeth S.) In the kitchen. 568 pp. sm. 4°. *Boston, Lee & Shepard,* 1875.

Miller (Joaquin, *i. e.* Cincinnatus Hiner). The ship in the desert. 205 pp. 16°. *Boston, Roberts brothers,* 1875.

Miller (Joaquin)—continued.

——— Songs of the sun-lands. vii, 243 pp. 8°. [*London, Longmans & co.* 1873].

——— Unwritten history: life amongst the Modocs. 445 pp. 23 pl. port. 8°. *Hartford, american publishing co.* 1874.

Miller (*Rev.* John). Fetich in theology. 261 pp. 12°. *New York, Dodd & Mead,* 1874.

——— Metaphysics. xxiv, 17–402 pp. 8°. *New York, Dodd & Mead,* [1875].

Miller (*Rev.* J. R.) Woman's ministry. 160 pp. port. 16°. *Philadelphia, J. B. Lippincott & co.* 1875.

Miller (*Rev.* M. R.) The luminous unity. Is unitarianism a principle of heathenism rather than of judaism? 263 pp. 12°. *Philadelphia, J. B. Lippincott & co.* 1874.

Milligan (Robert). Analysis of the new testament. v. 1. The gospels and acts. 1 p. l. 5–413 pp. 3 col. maps. 8°. *Cincinnati, Bosworth, Chase & Hall,* 1874.

——— The great commission of Jesus Christ to his apostles. New ed. 257 pp. 12°. *Lexington, Ky. J. B. Morton & co.* 1873.

Milligan (William, *d. d.*) *and* **Roberts** (Alexander, *d. d.*) The words of the new testament. x, 262 pp. 12°. *Edinburgh, T. & T. Clark,* 1873.

Millingen (James). Ancient unedited monuments. Painted greek vases. 1 p. l. viii, 106 pp. 60 col. pl. fol. *London,* 1822.

——— Ancient unedited monuments. Statues, busts, bas-reliefs, and other remains of grecian art. 1 p. l. ii, 40 pp. 22 pl. fol. *London,* 1826.

[*With* MILLINGEN (J.) Ancient unedited monuments. Painted greek vases].

Mills (Lucy A.) Peter's strange story. 421 pp. 2 pl. 16°. *Boston, D. Lothrop & co.* 1873.

Milner (Vincent L.) Religious denominations of the world. A new and improved ed. with appendix up to the present time, by J. N. Brown. 629 pp. 7 ports. *Philadelphia, Bradley, Garretson & co.* 1874.

Milnes (Richard-Monckton, *lord Houghton*). Monographs, personal and social. xi, 339 pp. 4 ports. 12°. *London, J. Murray,* 1873.

Milton (J. L.) The stream of life on our globe. xxiv, 620 pp. 12°. *London, R. Hardwicke,* 1864.

Minnesota (*State of*). *Commissioner of statistics.* Statistics for 1871[–74]. 4 v. 8°. *St. Paul, St. Paul press co.* 1872–75.

Miscellanea scotica. A collection of tracts relating to Scotland. 4 v. 16°. *Glasgow, J. Wylie & co.* 1818–20.

Mischna, oder der text des talmuds. Aus dem hebräischen von J. J. Rabe. 6 v. in 3. 4°. *Onolzbach, J. C. Posch,* 1760–63.

Mishaps of mr. Ezekiel Pelter. [*anon.*] 2 p. l. 11–302 pp. incl. 12 pl. 12°. *Chicago, S. C. Griggs & co.* 1875.

Missirini (Melchiorre). Pericolo di seppellire gli uomini vivi creduti morti. xl, 431 pp. 8°. *Milano, C. Branca,* 1837.

Mitchel (John). The crusade of the period: and last conquest of Ireland (perhaps.) 332 pp. 1 port. 12°. *New York, Lynch, Cole & Meehan,* 1873.

[IRISH-AMERICAN library, no. 4].

Mitchell (C.) *& co. publishers.* Newspaper press directory and advertisers' guide. 30th annual issue. 1875. 8°. *London, C. Mitchell & co.* 1875.

Mitchell (Thomas). Rudimentary manual of architecture. xiv, 304 pp. 3 pl. 12°. *London, Longmans,* 1870.

Mixer (A. H.) Manual of french poetry. xxxiv, 501 pp. 12°. *New York, Ivison, Blakeman, Taylor & co.* 1874.

Modern thinker: an organ for the most advanced speculations in philosophy, science, sociology and religion. No. 1. 3d ed. 3 p. l. 248 pp. 8°. *New York, am. news co.* 1870.

——— Same. No. 2. 2d ed. 2 p. l. 160 pp. 8°. *New York, D. Wesley & co.* 1873.

Moe (Adelaide T.) The old fountain inn, and other poems. 123 pp. 16°. *Philadelphia, J. B. Lippincott & co.* 1875.

Moehler (Johann Adam). De l'unité de l'église, ou du principe du catholicisme. Traduit de l'allemand, par Ph. Bernard. vi, 300 pp. 8°. *Bruxelles, H. Rémy,* 1839.

Moffat (James C. *d. d.*) Comparative history of religions. Part ii. v, 316 pp. 12°. *New York, Dodd & Mead,* [1874].

——— Song and scenery; a summer ramble in Scotland. 2 p. l. 288 pp. 16°. *New York, L. D. Robertson,* 1874.

Moggridge (J. Traherne). Harvesting ants and trap-door spiders. xi, 156 pp. 12 pl. 8°. *London, L. Reeve & co.* 1873.

Molesworth (William Nassau). History of England, 1830–1874. New ed. 3 v. 12°. *London, Chapman & Hall,* 1874.

Molière (Jean Baptiste Poquelin). Dramatic works, rendered into english by H. Van

Molière (J. B. P.)—continued. Laun. v. 1–2. 8°. *Edinburgh, W. Paterson*, 1875.

Molloy (James L.) Our autumn holiday on french rivers. xviii, 391 pp. incl. eng. title, 16 pl. 8°. *London, Bradbury, Agnew & co.* 1874.

Monckton (James H.) National builder. Eng. title, 22 pp. 87 l. 86, 6 pl. 4°. *New York, G. E. Woodward*, [1872].

——— National carpenter and joiner. 1 p. l. 8 pp. 46 l. 48 pl. 4°. *New York, G. E. Woodward*, [1873].

——— National stair-builder. 14 pp. 46 l. 47 pl. 4°. *New York, G. E. Woodward*, [1873].

Monnier (Antoine). Eaux-forts et rêves creux. 2 p. l. 84 pp. 2 l. 20 pl. 8°. *Paris, L. Willem*, 1873.

Monod (Adolphe). Parting words. October, 1855, to march, 1856. From the fifth Paris ed. 205 pp. port. 12°. *New York, D. Appleton & co.* 1873.

Monroe (*Dr.* J. R.) Dramas and miscellaneous poems. 190 pp. 8°. *Chicago, Knight & Leonard*, 1875.

Montagu (George). Dictionary of british birds. Edited by E. Newman. xxiv, 400 pp. 8°. *London, J. Van Voorst*, 1866.

Montbarey (Alexandre Marie Léonor de Saint Maurice, *prince* de). Mémoires autographes. v. 1–3. 8°. *Paris, A. Eymery*, 1826–27.
[Imperfect: v. 4 wanting].

Montgomery (Florence). Thrown together. [*anon.*] 2 v. 12°. *London, R. Bentley & son*, 1872.

——— Thwarted, or ducks' eggs in a hen's nest. [*anon.*] viii, 255 pp. 12°. *London, R. Bentley & son*, 1874.

Month (A) at Gastein. [*anon.*] ix, 317 pp. incl. 21 pl. 12°. *London, R. Bentley & son*, [1873].

Montjoie (Christophe Félix Louis Ventre de Latouloubre, *better known as* Galart de.) Éloge historique et funèbre de Louis XVI. Nouv. éd. 2 p. l. 316 pp. 8°. *Paris, Lebéque*, 1814.

Moody (F. W.) Lectures and lessons on art. vii, 139 pp. 25 pl. 21 l. 8°. *London, Bell & Daldy*, 1873.

Moon (George Washington). Bad english exposed: criticisms on L. Murray and other grammarians. 4th ed. xvi, 227 pp. 16°. *London, Hatchards*, 1871.

Moor (Henry). Visit to Russia in 1862. vi, 234 pp. 8 pl. 12°. *London, Chapman & Hall*, 1863.

Moore (*Rev.* Thomas). History of Devonshire. 2 v. Eng. title, 574 pp. 94 pl. 1 map; eng. title, 908 pp. 2 l. 1 map. 8°. *London, R. Jennings*, 1829.

Moosmüller (Oswald). St. Vincenz in Pennsylvanien. Von O. M. [*anon.*] 2 p. l. 385 pp. 19 pl. 8°. *New York, F. Pustet & co.* [1873].

Morabin (Jacques). Histoire de Cicéron. 2 v. 3 p. l. 325, ccxlv pp; 1 p. l. 481, ccxlvi–ccccxxxii pp. 4°. *Paris, P. N. Lottin*, 1745.

Morando (Bernardo). Rosalinda, a novel. [*anon.*] From the french. 8 p. l. 347 pp. 8°. *London, for C. Davis*, 1733.

Morant (*Rev.* Philip). History and antiquities of the county of Essex. 2 v. [790] pp. 20 pl. 53 ins. pl; 3 p. l. 646 pp. 13 pl. 64 l. of pl. 9 l. ms. and 3 l. ins. fol. *London, for T. Osborne*, [*etc.*] 1768.
[Imperfect: v. 2 wants the preface, 2 pp.]

Moreau (Célestin). Bibliographie des mazarinades. 3 v. 8°. *Paris, J. Renouard & cie.* 1850–51.

Moreau de Jonnès (Alexandre). Recherches statistiques sur esclavage colonial. 2 p. l. 272 pp. 8°. *Paris, Bourgogne & Martinet*, 1842.
[Imperfect: wanting all after p. 272].

Morell (*Dr.* J. M. D.) Dr. Morell's english series. Biographical history of english literature. 564 pp. 12°. *London, Longmans*, [1873].

Morford (Henry). Rhymes of an editor. viii, 303 pp. 4 pl. 12°. *London, E. Moxon, son & co.* 1873.

Morgan (*Rev.* Henry). Shadowy hand; or, life-struggles. Eng. title, 448 pp. 5 pl. port. 16°. *Boston, author*, 1874.

Morgan (Henry J.) Bibliotheca canadensis: a manual of canadian literature. xiv, 411 pp. 8°. *Ottawa, G. E. Desbarats*, 1867.

Morgan (John Ed.) University oars; enquiry into the after health of the men who rowed in the Oxford and Cambridge boat-race, from 1829 to 1869. xvi, 397 pp. 12°. *London, Macmillan & co.* 1873.

Morgan (Sydney Owenson, *lady*). The missionary. 3 v. in 1. 279 pp. 16°. *New-York, the Franklin co. and Butler & White*, 1811.

——— Woman; or, Ida of Athens. 4 v. in 2. 1 p. l. xi, 186 pp; 1 p. l. 193–379 pp. 12°. *Philadelphia, Bradford & Inskeep*, 1809.

Morley (Henry). First sketch of english literature. viii, 912 pp. 16°. *London, Cassell, Petter & Galpin,* [1873].

Morley (John). Critical miscellanies. xii, 375 pp. 8°. *London, Chapman & Hall,* 1871.

——— On compromise. x, 214 pp. 8°. *London, Chapman & Hall,* 1874.

Morphis (J. M.) History of Texas. 591 pp. 5 pl. 5 ports. 1 plan, 1 col. map. 8°. *New York, United States publishing co.* 1874.

Morren (Charles). Palmes et couronnes de l'horticulture de Belgique. 1 p. l. 547 pp. 16°. *Liège,* 1851. s.

Morren (Édouard) *and* **De Vos** (André). Mémorial du naturaliste et du cultivateur. x, 146 pp. 8°. *Liège, aux bureau de la belge horticole,* 1872. s.

Morris (Herbert W.) Present conflict of science with christian religion. 686 pp. incl. 7 pl. 2 maps, 13 pl. 8°. *Philadelphia, P. W. Ziegler & co.* 1875.

Morris (John Williams). Memoirs of rev. Andrew Fuller. 1st am. from last Lond. ed. 320 pp. 1 port. 8°. *Boston, Lincoln & Edmands,* 1830.

Morris (Rob. *ll. d.*) Masonic martyr. Biography of Eli Bruce. xvi, 316 pp. incl. 3 pl. & 1 map. 12°. *Louisville, Ky. Morris & Monsarrat,* 1861.

Morris (William). Letters sent home. Canada and the United States. xv, 477 pp. 12°. *London, F. Warne & co.* [1875].

Morrison (*Rev.* A. B.) Spiritualism and necromancy. iii, 203 pp. 16°. *Cincinnati, Hitchcock & Walden,* 1873.

Morrison (W. H. & O. H. *publishers*). Stranger's guide for Washington. 116 pp. map. 18°. *Washington, W. H. & O. H. Morrison,* 1875.

Morse (*Rev.* Abner). Genealogical register of the descendants of several ancient puritans. v. 2. The Brigham family. 2 p. l. 96 pp. 1 l. 11 ports. 1 pl. 8°. *Boston, H. W. Dutton & son,* 1859.

——— Genealogy of the descendants of several ancient puritans, Adams, Bullard, Holbrook, Rockwood, Sanger, Wood, Grout, Goulding, and Twitchell. 2 p. l. [250] pp. 19 ports. 2 pl. 8°. *Boston, for the author,* 1857.

Morstadt (V.) Prag im neunzehnten jahrhunderte. Nach der natur gezeichnet, von V. Morstadt, gestochen von F. Geissler.

Morstadt (V.)—continued.
15 p. l. 42 pp. 10 pl. sm. fo'. *Prag, Borrosch & André,* 1835.

Note.—Text in german and french in parallel columns.

Morton (John S.) History of the origin of the appellation keystone state, as applied to Pennsylvania. [*anon.*] 190 pp. 1 pl. 8°. *Philadelphia, Claxton, Remsen & Haffelfinger,* 1874.

Mosaico (El) mexicano. 7 v. 8°. *México, I. Cumplido,* 1837–42.

Mosblech (*L'abbé* Boniface). Vocabulaire océanien-français et français-océanien des dialectes parlés aux îles Marquises, Sandwich, Gambier, etc. xv, 318 pp. 12°. *Paris, J. Renouard & cie.* 1843.

Mossman (Samuel). New Japan. vii, 484 pp. map. 8°. *London, J. Murray,* 1873.

——— Origin of the seasons from a geological point of view. xvi, 472 pp. 1 map. 12°. *Edinburgh, W. Blackwood & sons,* 1869.

Mossman (Thomas Wimberley). History of the catholic church of Jesus Christ from the death of saint John to the middle of the second century [etc.] xx, 514 pp. 8°. *London, Longmans,* 1873.

Motley (John Lothrop, *ll. d.*) Life and death of John of Barneveld. 2 v. xvi, 389 pp. 2 pl; vii, 475 pp. 2 pl. 8°. *London, J. Murray,* 1874.

——— Same. 2 v. xvi, 389 pp. 2 pl; vii, 475 pp. 2 p'. 8°. *New York, Harper & brothers,* 1874.

Moulart (Ferdinand Joseph). De sepultura et coemeteriis. 4 p. l. 422 pp. 8°. *Lovanii, Valinthout et socii,* [1862]. s.

Moulton (*Mrs.* Louise Chandler). Bed-time stories. 239 pp. 6 pl. 16°. *Boston, Roberts brothers,* 1874.

——— More bed-time stories. 238 pp. 4 pl. 16°. *Boston, Roberts brothers,* 1874.

——— Some women's hearts. 3 p. l. 364 pp. 16°. *Boston, Roberts brothers,* 1874.

Mounsey (Augustus H.) Journey through the Caucasus and the interior of Persia. xi, 336 pp. 1 map. 12°. *London, Smith, Elder & co.* 1872.

Movers (Franz Karl). Die Phönizier. Band I–II, theil 3, abth. 1, in 4 v. 8°. *Bonn,* 1841–56.

Mrs. Limber's raffle. [*anon.*] 162 pp. 16°. *New York, D. Appleton & co.* 1876.

Mudge (*Rev.* Z. A.) Arctic heroes. 304 pp. incl. 4 pl. 16°. *New York, Nelson & Phillips,* [1875].

Mudge (*Rev.* Z. A.)—continued.
——— Luck of Alden farm. Eng. title, 396 pp. 1 pl. 16°. *Boston, D. Lothrop & co.* 1873. [THOUSAND dollar prize series].

Muir (John). Religious and moral sentiments from sanskrit writers, with exact translations in prose. [New ed.] 128, 4 pp. 12°. *London, Williams & Norgate,* 1875.

Mulhall (M. G.) *and* **Mulhall** (E. T.) Handbook of the river Plate republics. viii, 432 pp. 1 map, 2 plans. 12°. *London, E. Stanford,* 1875.

Müller (Frederic Max). Chips from a german workshop. v. 4. Essays chiefly on the science of language. 8°. *London, Longmans,* 1875.

Müller (*Rev.* Michael). Charity to the souls in purgatory. 351 pp. 1 pl. 24°. *Boston, P. Donahoe,* [1873].

Müller (W. I. L.) Ueber London und Paris nach Rom. Von W I L M [*pseud.*] 2 v. xvi, 419 pp; iv, 454 pp. 8°. *Berlin, G. W. F. Müller,* 1853.

Münch (Ernst von). Erinnerungen, reisebilder, phantasiegemälde und fastenpredigten aus den jahren 1828 bis 1840. 2 v. vii, 421 pp; v, 208 pp. 8°. *Stuttgart, verlag der I. F. Cast'schen buchhandlung,* 1841–42.

Munger (Charles Alanson). Poems. vi, 9–144 pp. 16°. *New York, G. P. Putnam's sons,* 1874.

Munson (James E.) Munson's system of phonography.—Dictionary of practical phonography. xxxv, 328 pp. 12°. *New York Hurd & Houghton,* 1875.

Murphy (John Mortimer). Oregon handbook and emigrant's guide. 136 pp. 5 pl. 8°. *Portland, O., S. J. McCormick,* 1873.

Murphy (John R.) Mineral resources of Utah. 104 pp. 11 maps & tables. 8°. *London, Trübner & co.* 1872.

Murray (John, *publisher*). Handbook for Shropshire, Cheshire, and Lancashire. [*anon.*] xc, 328, 80 pp. 1 map. 12°. *London, J. Murray,* 1870.
——— Handbook for Wiltshire, Dorsetshire, and Somersetshire. New ed. [*anon.*] lv, 440, 88 pp. 1 map. 12°. *London, J. Murray,* 1869.
——— Handbook for Algeria. [*anon.*] viii, 115, 80 pp. 1 plan, 1 map. 12°. *London, J. Murray,* 1873.
——— Handbook for Corsica and Sardinia. [*anon.*] 94, 80 pp. 2 maps. 12°. *London, J. Murray,* 1868.

Murray (John)—continued.
——— Handbook for Egypt. 4th ed. [*anon.*] xx, 2, 505, 80 pp. 3 maps. 12°. *London, J. Murray,* 1873.
——— Handbook for central Italy. 8th ed. [*anon.*] 438, 88 pp. 1 plan, 1 map. 12°. *London, J. Murray,* 1874.
——— Handbook for northern Italy. 13th ed. [*anon.*] xlviii pp. 1 l. 564, 88 pp. incl 9 plans, 4 plans, 1 map. 12°. *London, J. Murray,* 1874.
——— Handbook for southern Italy. 7th ed. [*anon.*] xlv, 449, 80 pp. 2 plans, 2 maps. 12°. *London, J. Murray,* 1873.

Murray (J. Clark, *ll. d.*) Ballads and songs of Scotland. xvi, 205 pp. 12°. *London, Macmillan & co.* 1874.

Murray (*Rev.* William Henry Harrison). Music-hall sermons. Second series. 207 pp. 12°. *Boston, J. R. Osgood & co.* 1873.
——— The perfect horse. 8 p. l. 480 pp. 14 pl. 8°. *Boston, J. R. Osgood & co.* 1873.

Musical recollections of the last half-century. [*anon.*] 2 v. xv, 345 pp; vi, 370 pp. 8°. *London, Tinsley brothers,* 1872.

Musikalisches conversations-lexikon. Bearbeitet von Hermann Mendel. [A–Harmonielehre]. v. 1–4. 8°. *Berlin, L. Heimann & R. Oppenheim,* 1870–74.

Musset (Paul Edme de). Mr. Wind and madam Rain. Translated by Emily Makepeace. 126 pp. incl. 4 pl. sq. 18°. *New York, Harper & brothers,* 1864.

Musset-Pathay (Victor Donatien de). Anecdotes inédites pour faire suite aux mémoires de madame D'Épinai. [*anon.*] 115 pp. 8°. *Paris, Baudouin frères,* 1818.

Myers (Edward H. *d. d.*) The disruption of the methodist episcopal church, 1844–46. 216 pp. 12°. *Nashville, A. H. Redford,* 1875.

Myers (P. Hamilton). Ensenore, and other poems. 196 pp. 16°. *New York, Dodd & Mead,* [1875].

Myers (P. V. N.) Remains of lost empires: the ruins of Palmyra, Nineveh, Babylon, and Persepolis. 2 p. l. 531 pp. 11 pl. *New York, Harper & brothers,* 1875.

Nadal (Bernard H. *d. d.*) The new life dawning, and other discourses. Edited, with a memoir, by rev. Henry A. Buttz, and an introduction by bishop R. S. Foster. 421 pp. port. 12°. *New York, Nelson & Phillips,* 1873.

Nadal (E. S.) Impressions of London social life, with other papers. x, 223 pp. *New York, Scribner, Armstrong & co.* 1875.

Naglee (Henry Morris). The love life of brig. gen. H. M. Naglee, consisting of a correspondence on love, war and politics. 182 pp. incl. 1 port. 12°. [*New York, Hilton & co.*] 1867.

Nanquette (Henri). Exploitation, débit et estimation des bois. 2e éd. xvi, 368, 48 pp. 8 pl. 12 col. pl. 8°. *Nancy, ve. Raybois,* 1868.

Narragansett club. Publications. (First series). v. 6. 4°. *Providence, R. I.* [*Providence press co.*] 1874.

CONTENTS.

v. 6. Letters of Roger Williams, 1632-1682. Now first collected. Edited by John Russell Bartlett. 1874.

Nason (*Rev.* Elias). A gazetteer of the state of Massachusetts. 576 pp. 3 pl. 1 map. 8°. *Boston, B. B. Russell,* 1874.

——— The life and times of Charles Sumner. His boyhood, education, and public career. 356 pp. port. 3 pl. 12°. *Boston, B. B. Russell,* 1874.

Nassau (*Rev.* Robert H.) Crowned in palmland. A story of african mission life. 390 pp. 10 pl. 1 map. port. 12°. *Philadelphia, J. B. Lippincott & co.* 1874.

Note.—A memoir of mrs. Mary Cloyd Nassau.

Nasser-ed-Din Shah Qajar (*shah of Persia*). Diary of his tour through Europe in 1873. By J. W. Redhouse. A verbatim translation. 3d thousand. Ill. title, xx, 427 pp. port. 12°. *London, J. Murray,* 1874.

National portrait gallery of distinguished americans; with biographical sketches. [*anon.*] 3 v. 8°. *Philadelphia, Rice, Rutter & co.* [1868].

Nauclerus (Johann Verge *or* Vergehans, *known as*). Memorabilivm omnis aetatis et omnivm gentivm chronici commentarii. Adiecta Germanorum rebus historia de Svevorum ortu, institutis ac imperio. Compleuit opus F. N. Basellivs annis XIIII. ad M.D. additis. 2 v. in 1. 8 p. l. clxxxxi l. numb. 14 l. cccxvii l. numb. fol. *Impressum Tubingæ opera T. Anshelmi,* 1516.

Naxera (Manuel Crisostomo). Disertacion sobre la lengua othomi; traducida al castellano. 1 p. l. xiii, 145 pp. 8°. *Mexico, imprenta del aguila,* 1845.

Neal (John). Portland illustrated. 160 pp. port. 8°. *Portland,* [*Me.*] *W. S. Jones,* 1874.

Neale (W. Johnson). The lost ship. [*anon.*] 3 v. 8°. *London, H. Colburn,* 1843.

[Imperfect: v. 2 wanting pp. 265-266].

Neaves (*Lord* Charles). Greek anthology. 3 p. l. 210 pp. 1 l. 16°. *Edinburgh, W. Blackwood & sons,* 1874.

Neff (Félix). Lettres, avec quelques additions. Par A. Bost. 2 v. 536 pp. port. 3 pl; 1 p. l. 564 pp. 8°. *Genève, chez l'auteur,* 1842.

Neill (Edward Duffield). History of Minnesota. 2d ed. lii, 50-758 pp. 3 ports. 4 maps. 8°. *Philadelphia, J. B. Lippincott & co.* 1873.

Nellie West. From ten to twenty. [*anon.*] 284 pp. 3 pl. 16°. *Philadelphia, am. s.-s. union,* [1875].

Nelme (L. D.) Essay towards an investigation of the origin and elements of language and letters. 1 p. l. xiv, 134 pp. 1 l. 1 tab. 4°. *London, for S. Leacroft,* 1772.

Nelson (John). History and antiquities of Islington, in Middlesex. 2d ed. 2 p. l. 357 pp. 9 l. 22 pl. 1 map. 8°. *London, the author,* 1823.

Nelson (Richard). Suburban homes on the line of the Marietta railroad. 1 p. l. 164 pp. 1 l. 4 pl. 1 map, 1 plan. 8°. *Cincinnati, Nelson & Bolles,* [1875].

Nesfield (William Eden). Specimens of mediæval architecture. Eng. title, 6 l. 100 pl. fol. *London, Day & son,* 1862.

Nevada state library. Catalogue, 1874. 132 pp. 8°. *Carson city, C. A. V. Putnam,* 1874.

Neve y Molina (Luis de). Reglas de ortografía, diccionario y arte del idioma othomi. 254 pp. 1 l. 24°. *Mexico, M. Villanueva,* 1863.

Newcome (*Rev.* Henry). Autobiography. Edited by R. Parkinson, d. d. 2 v. 3 p. l. xxv, 184 pp; 3 p. l. 185-390 pp. sm. 4°. [*Manchester*], 1852.

[CHETHAM society remains, v. 26, 27].

——— Diary, from sep. 30, 1661 to sep. 29, 1663. Edited by Thomas Heywood. 3 p. l. xl, 242 pp. sm. 4°. [*Manchester*], 1849.

[CHETHAM society remains, v. 18].

Newell (Robert H.) The cloven foot: an adaptation of "The mystery of Edwin Drood" to american scenes. By Orpheus C. Kerr [*pseud.*] 279 pp. 12°. *New York, Carleton,* 1870.

New Hampshire (*Province of*). Provincial papers. Documents and records relating to New Hampshire: 1623-1776. Edited by N. Bouton. 7 v. 8°. *Concord, Manchester & Nashua,* 1867-73.

——— (*State of*). *Geological survey.* Geology of New Hampshire. Report comprising the results of explorations ordered by the legislature. C. H. Hitchcock, state geolo-

New Hampshire (*State of*)—continued. gist. Pt. 1. Physical geography. xi, 668 pp. 29 pl. 20 maps. 8°. *Concord, E. A. Jenks*, 1874.

New Jersey. *Historical society.* Proceedings, v. 10; 2d series, v. 1-3. 4 v. 8°. *Newark, N. J. daily advertiser*, 1867-74.

Newman (John Henry, *d. d.*) Essay in aid of a grammar of assent. 3 p. l. 485 pp. 12°. *London, Burns, Oates & co.* 1870.

Newman (John P. *d. d.*) Thrones and palaces of Babylon and Nineveh. 2 p. l. 11-455 pp. incl. 22 pl. 1 map. 8°. *New York, Harper & brothers*, 1876.

Newman (*Rev.* M. W.) Alice Harmon. [*anon.*] 2 p. l. 263 pp. 16°. *New York, D. & J. Sadlier & co.* 1874.

Newton (A. V.) Saloon keeper's companion. Containing jokes and stories, laws and business forms, Hoyle's games, [etc. *anon.*] 2 v. in 1. 336 pp; 120 pp. 12°. *Worcester*, [*Ms.*] *West & Lee game & printing co.* 1875.

Newton (Charles Thomas, *editor*). Collection of ancient greek inscriptions in the British museum. Pt. 1. Attika. Edited by E. L. Hicks. 4 p. l. 160 pp. 1 l. 7 facs. 3 pl. fol. *Oxford*, [*Eng.*] *trustees*, 1874.

Newton (Richard, *d. d.*) The giants, and how to fight them. Eng. title, 325 pp. 5 pl. 16°. *New York, R. Carter & brothers*, 1875.

——— Illustrated rambles in bible lands. 1 p. l. 254 pp. 60 pl. 12°. *Philadelphia, am. s.-s. union*, [1875].

——— Leaves from the tree of life. 320 pp. 6 pl. 16°. *New York, R. Carter & brothers*, 1874.

Niboyet (Paulin Fortunio). L'américaine. P. N. Fortunio [*pseud.*] 2 p. l. xi, 438 pp. 16°. *Paris, C. Pont*, 1875.

Niccols (Iohn). Iohn Niccols pilgrimage, wherein is displaied the liues of the proude popes, ambitious cardinals, [etc.] *b.l.* 9 p. l. 137 l. unp. 16°. *London, T. Dawson, for T. Butter & G. Isaac*, 1581.

Nichols (Catherine). Wild flowers of the west. [*anon.*] 3 p. l. 170 pp. 16°. *Chicago, H. H. Frary*, 1874.

Nichols (John). Memoirs of George Hardinge, esq. viii, 560 pp. 1 l. 2 pl. 8°. *London, author*, 1818.

Nichols (John Gough). Ancient paintings, in fresco, discovered in 1804, at Stratford-upon-Avon, from drawings, by Thomas Fisher. [etc.] Described by John Gough

Nichols (John Gough)—continued. Nichols. Eng. title, 2 p. l. 14 pp. 56 pl. fol. *London, H. G. Bohn*, 1838.

Nicolaysen (N.) Norske fornlevninger. xi, 859 pp. 8°. *Kristiania, C. C. Werner & co.* 1862-66. s.
[FORENINGEN til norske fortidsminnesmerkers bevaring. Publications].

Nicole (Pierre). Pensées. Éd. stéréotype. 140 pp. 24°. *Paris, Fortin, Masson & cie.* 1840.

Nicolson (A.) Sketch of the german constitution and of events in Germany from 1815 to 1871. viii, 126 pp. 8°. *London, Longmans*, 1875.

Niebuhr (Marcus von). Geschichte Assur's und Babel's seit Phul. Nebst versuchen über die vorgeschichtliche zeit. vi, 529 pp. 1 map. 8°. *Berlin, W. Hertz*, 1857.

Niemann (A.) French campaign 1870-1871. Military description. From the german by E. Newdigate. 420 pp. 22 maps & plans. 12°. *London, W. Mitchell & co.* 1872.

Nieritz (Carl Gustav). The dumb boy of Fribourg. From the german by J. B. J. Champagnac. Revised english translation by A. T. S. 166 pp. 1 pl. 18°. *New York, D. & J. Sadlier & co.* 1873.

——— The rich man and the poor man. From the german. By rev. Wm. H. Gotwald. 120 pp. 1 pl. 16°. *Philadelphia, lutheran board of publication*, 1875.
[FATHERLAND series].

Nieuhoff (Jan). Die gesandtschaft der ostindischen gesellschaft in den vereinigten Niederländern, an den tartarischen cham, durch Peter de Gojern, und Jacob Keisern. Eng. title, 3 p. l. 444 pp. 6 l. port. 1 map, 34 pl. 4°. *Amsterdam, J. Mörs*, 1666.

Nimmo (*Rev.* William). History of Stirlingshire. 2d ed. brought down to the present time, by rev. W. M. Stirling. 2 v. vii, 384 pp; 1 p. l. 385-772 pp. 3 pl. 2 l. 8°. *Stirling, for A. Bean*, 1817.

Nimrod (Harry, *pseud.*) Fudge family in Washington. 8, 109 pp. 16°. *Baltimore, J. Robinson*, 1820.

Ninety-second Illinois reunion association. Ninety-second Illinois volunteers. 390 pp. 12°. *Freeport, Ill. journal*, 1875.

Nitzsch (Christian Ludwig). Osteographische beiträge zur naturgeschichte der vögel. x, 122 pp. 2 pl. 8°. *Leipzig, C. H. Reclam*, 1811.

Noack (Ludwig). Die biblische theologie. viii, 392 pp. 8°. *Halle, C. E. M. Pfeffer,* 1853.

——— Die christliche mystik nach ihrem geschichtlichen entwickelungsgange dargestellt. 2 v. in 1. viii, 352 pp; iv, 332 pp. 8°. *Königsberg, gebrüder Bornträger,* 1853.

Noble (John). National finance: a review of the policy of the last two parliaments, and of the results of modern fiscal legislation. 4 p. l. 368 pp. 8°. *London, Longmans,* 1875.

Noble (*Rev.* W. F. P.) Prophets of the bible and the seven churches. 552 pp. 16 pl. 8°. *Philadelphia, new world publishing co.* [1873].

Nodier (Charles). Promenade from Dieppe to the mountains of Scotland. From the french. xii, 211 pp. 18°. *Edinburgh, W. Blackwood,* 1822.

Nolan (Frederick). Egyptian chronology analysed. xxxi, 483 pp. 8°. *London, Seeleys,* 1848.

Noon (Alfred, *compiler*). Ludlow: a century and a centennial; sketch of Ludlow, Mass. with celebration of its centennial anniversary, june 17th 1874. xix, 208 pp. 8 ports. on 5 pl. 8°. *Springfield, Mass. C. W. Bryan & co.* 1875.

Nordhoff (Charles). Communistic societies of the United States. 2 p. l. vii–439 pp. 14 pl. 1 map, 2 ports. 8°. *New York, Harper & brothers,* 1875.

——— Northern California, Oregon, and the Sandwich islands. 256 pp. incl. 1 port. & 1 map, 1 map. 8°. *New York, Harper & brothers,* 1874.

——— Politics for young Americans. 259 pp. 12°. *New York, Harper & brothers,* 1875.

Norfolk and Norwich archæological society. Norfolk archæology. v. 1–7. 8°. *Norwich, C. Muskett, Cundall, Miller & Leavins, and Miller & Leavins,* 1847–72.

Noriac (Charles Antoine Jules Cayron, *dit*). La bêtise humaine. 3e éd. 2 p. l. 284 pp. 16°. *Paris, A. Bourdilliat & cie.* 1860.

——— Le grain de sable. Nouv. série de la bêtise humaine. 6e éd. 2 p. l. 283 pp. 16°. *Paris, A. Bourdilliat & cie.* 1861.

Nork (F.) Etymologisch-symbolisch-mythologisches real-wörterbuch. 4 v. in 2. 8°. *Stuttgart, J. F. Cast,* 1843–45.

Norman (William). The american pilot. 3 p. l. 9 maps. fol. *Boston, W. Norman,* 1798.

Normand (Louis Marie). Arc de triomphe des tuileries, érigé en 1806, d'après les dessins et sous la direction de mm. C. Percier et P. F. L. Fontaine, architects, avec un texte explicatif par m. [Jean Pierre] Brès. 5 p. l. 27 pl. fol. *Paris, Normand fils,* 1828.

Norris (George W. *m. d.*) Contributions to practical surgery. 318 pp. 8°. *Philadelphia, Lindsay & Blakiston,* 1873.

Norris (Mary H.) Fräulein Mina. 253 pp. incl. 1 pl. 16°. *New York, Nelson & Phillips,* [1873].

Norton (Harry J.) Wonder-land illustrated; or, horseback rides through the Yellowstone national park. 111 pp. 16 pl. 1 map. 12°. *Virginia city, Montana, H. J. Norton,* [1874].

Norton (John N.) Every sunday: a course of sermons for the year. 501 pp. 8°. *Hartford, Conn. M. H. Mallory & co.* 1873.

Notredame (Michel de). Die erstaunlichen bücher des grossen Nostradamus in's deutsche übertragen von Eduard Roesch. 2 v. 267 pp; 263 pp. 18°. *Stuttgart, J. Scheible,* 1850.

[BIBLIOTHEK der zauber-, geheimniss- und offenbarungs-bücher und der wunder-hausschatz-literatur aller nationen [etc.] 9te–10te abth.]

Nougarède de Fayet (Auguste). Des anciens peuples de l'Europe, et de leurs premières migrations. 2 p. l. 236 pp. 7 maps. 8°. *Paris, F. Didot frères,* 1842.

Nouveau dictionnaire d'histoire naturelle. Par une société de naturalistes et d'agriculteurs. Nouv. éd. 36 v. 8°. *Paris, Deterville,* 1816–19. S.

Nouveau recüeil d'apophthegmes. [*anon.*] 3 p. l. 250 pp. front. 16°. *Toulouse, J. Boude,* 1695.

Noyes (C. P.) Recollections of India. 120 pp. 1 l. 18°. *Providence, [R. I.] G. H. Whitney,* 1852.

Noyes (John Humphrey). Home-talks. Edited by A. Barron and G. Noyes Miller. v. 1. 1 p. l. 358 pp. port. 12°. *Oneida, [N. Y.] published by the community,* 1875.

Nunez (H. Helen). Leisure moments. [Poems]. 374 pp. 12°. *Philadelphia, J. B. Lippincott & co.* 1873.

Nuñez de Haro y Peralta (Alonso, *archbishop of Mexico*). Al rector, vice-rector, catedráticos, y directores del real colegio seminario de instruccion, de retiro voluntario, y correccion de Tepozatlan, [etc.] 266 pp. 1 l. sm. 4°. [*México,* 1776]. S.

Nürnberg's merkwürdigkeiten und kunstschätze. 1stes–2tes heft in 1 v. *Nürnberg, F. Campe,* 1831.

CONTENTS.

1stes heft. Die kirche des heiligen Sebaldus beschrieben von Moritz Maximilian Mayer. 40 pp. 4 pl.
2tes heft. Die kirche des heiligen Laurentius beschrieben von Johann Wolfgang Hilpert. 48 pp. 4 pl.

Nuttall (P. Austin). Dictionary of scientific terms. xviii, 325 pp. 12°. *London, Strahan & co.* 1869.

——— Standard pronouncing dictionary of the english language. New ed. xxii, 896 pp. 16°. *London, F. Warne & co.* [1873].

Nützliche (Eine) anweisung, oder beyhülffe vor die Teutschen um englisch zu lernen. [*anon.*] 2 p. l. 287 pp. 2 l. 16°. *Germanton,* [*Pa.*] *C. Saur,* 1762.

Nye (Gideon, *jr.*) Peking the goal,—the sole hope of peace. 1 p. l. 104 pp. 8°. *Canton,* 1873.

Oberholtzer (Sara Louisa). Violet Lee, and other poems. 143 pp. 12°. *Philadelphia, J. B. Lippincott & co.* 1873.

Oberleitner (Andreas). Chrestomathia syriaca una cum glossario syriaco-latino, huic chrestomathiae adcommodato. 2 v. xii, 292 pp; 246 pp. 8°. *Viennae, typis A. de Schmid,* 1826–27.

——— Fundamenta linguae arabicae. xvi, 390, vi pp. 8°. *Viennae, typis A. Schmid,* 1822.

Obookiah (Henry). Memoirs. 129, 32 pp. port. 18°. *New Haven, N. Whiting,* 1819.

O'Brien (Dillon). Dead broke, a western tale. 193 pp. 12°. *St. Paul, pioneer co. print,* 1873.

O'Brien (*Rev.* James H.) The franciscan way to the heavenly Jerusalem. 508 pp. 1 l. 4 pl. 24°. *New York, T. W. Strong,* [1875].

Occioni (Onorato). Cajo Silio Italico e il suo poema. 2 p. l. 270 pp. 12°. *Padova, P. Prosperini,* 1869. s.

O'Curry (Eugene). On the manners and customs of the ancient Irish. Edited by W. K. Sullivan. 3 v. 8°. *London, Williams & Norgate,* 1873.

Odd fellows (Independent order of). *Grand lodge of the United States.* Digest of the laws, decisions and enactments of the r. w. grand lodge, from its organization to 1870. [Also] constitution, by-laws, [etc.] By John H. White. [3d ed.] 547 pp. 62 l. in the pag. 8°. [*Albany, N. Y.*] *for the grand lodge of the United States,* 1871.

——— ——— Journal of proceedings, including the annual reports of its officers from its formation in feb. 1821, to the close of 1874. [Also] the constitution, by-laws [etc.] v. 1–7. 8°. *Baltimore, J. L. Ridgeley,* 1874.

Odolant-Desnos (Joseph). Mythologie pittoresque. 4e éd. 2 p. l. 550 pp. 30 pl. 8°. *Paris, E. Picard,* 1849.

Oekonomische neuigkeiten und verhandlungen. Zeitschrift. Herausgegeben von C. C. André. 19ter–29ster band in 8 v. 4°. *Prag, J. G. Calve,* 1820–25. s.

——— Same. Begründet von C. C. André, fortgesetzt von prof. dr. F. X. Hlubek. 1847–1850. 73ster–80ster band. 4°. *Prag, J. G. Calve,* [1847–50]. s.

O'Gallagher (S. F.) Brief reply to a short answer to a true exposition of the doctrine of the catholic church, touching penance, &c. 176 pp. 8°. *New-York, for the author,* 1815.

O'Gorman (Daniel). Intuitive calculations. 24th ed. by J. R. Young. xvi, 241 pp. 16°. *London, Lockwood & co.* 1871.

O'Kane (T. C.) Every sabbath: a collection of music. 160 pp. obl. 16°. *Cincinnati, J. Church & co.* 1874.

O'Keefe (*Rev.* Matthew). Key to true christianity. 151, 42 pp. 8°. *Philadelphia, W. P. Kildare,* 1874.

O'Kelly (James J.) The Mambi-land, or adventures in Cuba. 359 pp. 1 pl. 12°. *Philadelphia, J. B. Lippincott & co.* 1874.

Olcott (Henry S.) People from the other world. 492 pp. incl. 49 pl. & 7 ports. 12°. *Hartford, american publishing co.* 1875.

Old sights with new eyes. [*anon.*] 372 pp. 12°. *New York, M. W. Dodd,* 1854.

Oldfield (Edmund). Topographical and historical account of Wainfleet and the wapentake of Candleshoe, in the county of Lincoln. 4 p. l. 370, 39 pp. 8 pl. 4°. *London, Longmans,* 1829.

Oldfield (Joshua, *d. d.*) Essay towards the improvement of reason. 3 parts in 1 v. 24 p. l. viii, 424 pp. 8 l. 8°. *London, T. Parkhurst,* 1707.

O'Leary (James, *d. d.*) Bible history. xii pp. 1 l. xiii–480 pp. incl. 60 pl. front. 12 maps. 12°. *New York, D. & J. Sadlier & co.* 1873.

——— Ireland among the nations. xiv, 11–208 pp. 16°. *New York, J. A. McGee,* 1874.

Oliphant (Margaret O. Wilson). For love and life. 3 v. 12°. *London, Hurst & Blackett,* 1874.

——— Innocent. 3 v. 12°. *London, S. Low, Marston, Low & Searle,* 1873.

Oliphant (M. O. W.)—continued.

——— May. 209 pp. 8°. *New York, Scribner, Armstrong & co.* 1873.

——— A rose in june. 2 v. 2 p. l. 303 pp; 2 p. l. 264 pp. 12°. *London, Hurst & Blackett,* 1874.

——— Three brothers. 3 v. 12°. *London, Hurst & Blackett,* 1870.

Oliphant (Thomas Lawrence Kington). Sources of standard english. xxiii, 408 pp. 16°. *London, Macmillan & co.* 1873.

Oliver (Henry K.) Original hymn tunes, chants, sentences, and motets. 117 pp. obl. 8°. *Boston, O. Ditson & co.* 1875.

Oliver (John Robert, *m. d. editor*). Monumenta de insula Manniæ, or a collection of national documents relating to the Isle of Man. 3 v. 8°. *Douglas,* [*Isle of Man*], 1860–62.

[MANX society. Publications, v. 4, 7, 9].

Oliver (William). Scenery of the Pyrenees. Eng. title, 1 l. 25 pl. fol. *London, Colnaghi & Puckle,* 1842.

Oordt (A. M. van). Schetsen uit de muzikale wereld. 3 p. l. 268 pp. 8°. *Leiden, A. W. Sijthoff,* 1874.

Opal (*pseud.*) The cloud of witnesses. By Opal [*pseud.*] 522 pp. 12°. *New York, J. Miller,* 1874.

Opfer der andacht. Gebet- und erbauungsbuch für katholische christen. [*anon.*] 432 pp. 2 col. pl. 24°. *Einsiedeln, gebr. K. & N. Benziger,* 1873.

Opium eating. An autobiographical sketch. [*anon.*] 150 pp. 12°. *Philadelphia, Claxton, Remsen & Haffelfinger,* 1876.

Oppel (Karl). Das alte wunderland der pyramiden. Eng. title, xii, 316 pp. incl. 7 pl. 11 pl. 12°. *Leipzig, O. Spamer,* 1863.

[ILLUSTRIRTE jugend- und haus-bibliothek. 3te serie: 6ter band. Erzählungen aus dem alterthum. I].

Oran, the outcast. [*anon.*] 2 v. in 1. 199 pp; 3–180 pp. 12°. *New York, Peabody & co.* 1833.

[Imperfect v. 2 wanting title and pp. 77–80].

Orchard (Robert). New select collection of epitaphs and monumental inscriptions. 2d ed. 1 p. l. 106 pp. 1 port. 12°. *London, J. Taylor & son,* 1827.

Orcutt (Franklin B.) Light of the age: or miracles explained. 109 pp. 12°. *Chicago, for the author,* 1866.

Orcutt (Hiram). Parents' manual. 290 pp. 1 pl. 16°. *Boston, Thompson, Brown & co.* [1874].

O'Reilly (A. J. *d. d.*) Victims of the Mamertine. 2d series. 1 p. l. 13–573 pp. front. 12°. *New York, D. & J. Sadlier & co.* 1875.

O'Reilly (John Boyle). Songs from the southern seas. 227 pp. 16°. *Boston, Roberts brothers,* 1873.

Orendorff (Charles, *m. d.*) The pantheist. 109 pp. 8°. *Springfield, Ill. Baker & Phillips,* 1865.

Oribasius. XXI veterum et clarorum medicorum græcorum varia opuscula. Interpretationem latinam Io. B. Rasarii. [Gr. and lat.] xvi, 416 pp. 4°. *Mosquæ, litteris caesareae universitatis,* 1808.

Orléans (Élisabeth Charlotte, de Bavière, *duchesse* d'). Fragments of original letters, written 1715 to 1720. From the french. 2 v. in 1. xii, 228 pp. 2 l. 238 pp. 16°. *London, for T. Hookham,* 1790.

——— Secret memoirs of the court of Louis XIV. and of the regency. Extracted from the german correspondence of the duchess of Orleans. viii, 472 pp. port. 8°. *London, G. & W. B. Whittaker,* 1824.

Ormathwaite (*Lord*). *See* **Benn-Walsh** (*Sir* J.)

Ormerod (George, *editor*). Tracts relating to military proceedings in Lancashire during the great civil war. 2 p. l. xxxii, 372 pp. sm. 4°. [*London*], 1844.

[CHETHAM society remains, v. 2].

Orozco y Berra (Manuel). Geografía de las lenguas y carta etnográfica de México. xiv, 302 pp. 1 col. map. 8°. *México, J. M. Andrade & F. Escalante,* 1864.

——— Materiales para una cartografia mexicana. xii, 340 pp. 8°. *Mexico, imprenta del gobierno,* 1871.

[SOCIEDAD mexicana de geografía y estadística. Publications].

Ortega (C. F.) Poesias. 1 p. l. xi, 346 pp. 24°. *Mejico, Ojedo,* 1839.

Orton (James). Underground treasures. 1 p. l. 137 pp. incl. 5 pl. 16°. *Hartford, Worthington, Dustin & co.* 1872.

——— *editor.* The liberal education of women. x, 9–328 pp. 12°. *New York, A. S. Barnes & co.* 1873.

Osborn (Laughton). Mariamne. Being the third of the tragedies of jewish and biblical history. 2 p. l. 167–269 pp. 12°. *New York, H. L. Hinton,* 1873.

Osburn (William, *jr.*) Antiquities of Egypt. 236 pp. 7 pl. 8°. *London, religious tract society,* 1847.

O'Shaughnessy (Arthur). Music and moonlight, poems and songs. vii, 208, 7 pp. 18°. *London, Chatto & Windus,* 1874.

Oswald (F.) Manual of good manners. 2 p. l. vii–x pp. 1 l. 178 pp. 32°. *Baltimore, Kreuzer brothers,* 1874.

Oswald (H. R.) Vestigia insulæ Manniæ antiquiora, or a dissertation on the armorial bearings of the Isle of Man, (etc.) 4 p. l. ix, 218 pp. 1 l. 2 col. pl. 8 pl. 8°. *Douglas,* 1860.

[Manx society. Publications, v. 5].

Otis (George Edmund). The river of dreams and other poems. 97 pp. 16°. *Boston, Lee & Shepard,* 1875.

——— Thurid and other poems. By G. E. O. [*anon.*] 2 p. l. 123 pp. 8°. *Boston, Lee & Shepard,* 1874.

Our national obligation! [*anon.*] 182 pp. 18°. *Cincinnati, western tract & book soc.* 1873.

Our own family doctor, and medical adviser. [*anon.*] 607 pp. 8°. *New York, T. D. Hurst,* [1873].

Ouvry (Henry Aimé). Stein and his reforms in Prussia, with reference to the land question in England. 2d ed. xii, 195 pp. 12°. *London, Kerby & Endean,* 1875.

Overbeke *or* **Overbeck** (Bonaventura van). Les restes de l'ancienne Rome. 3 v. fol. *La Haye, P. Gosse jun. & D. Pinet,* 1763.

Ovidius Naso (Publius). P. Ovidii metamorphosis, oder: wunderbarliche beschreibung, von der menschen, thiern vnd anderer creaturen veränderung. Jetzt widerum̃ auff ein newes, dem gemeinen vatterlande teutscher sprach, renouiert, corrigiert, vnd an tag geben, durch S. Feyerabendt. Eng. title, 7 p. l. 198 pp. fol. *Franckfort am Mayn, S. Feyerabendt,* 1581.

——— Same. Metamorphoses. Translated into english blank verse by Henry King. xi, 548 pp. 12°. *Edinburgh, W. Blackwood & sons,* 1871.

——— Three books, de arte amandi. Translated, with annotations. By Francis Wolferston. 3 p. l. 112 pp. 12°. *London, for J. Cranford,* 1661.

——— Traduction des fastes d'Ovide, avec des notes: par m. Bayeux. 4 v. 4°. *Rouen & Paris, Boucher le jeune,* [*etc.*] 1783–88.

Ovilo y Otero (Manuel). Manual de biografía y de bibliografía de los escritores españoles del siglo xix. 2 v. vii, 288 pp; 252 pp. 16°. *Paris, Rosa y Bouret,* 1859.

[Enciclopedia popular mejicana].

Owen (Francis Browning). Poems. By Francis Browning [*pseud.*] 90 pp. sq. 12°. *Detroit, free press printing house,* 1874.

Owen (George W.) The leech club. 298 pp. 12°. *Boston, Lee & Shepard,* 1874.

Owen (John). Travels into different parts of Europe, in 1791 and 1792. 2 v. 2 p. l. lxxvi, 400 pp; 2 p. l. 579 pp. 8°. *London, for T. Cadell, jr. & W. Davies,* 1796.

Owen (Robert Dale). Twenty-seven years of autobiography. Threading my way. 360 pp. 12°. *New York, G. W. Carleton & co.* 1874.

Oxford (William). Oxford's senior speaker. 432 pp. 12°. *Philadelphia, J. H. Butler & co.* [1873].

Ozanam (Alphonse Frédéric). Pilgrimage to the land of the Cid. From the french, by P. S. 192 pp. 2 pl. 16°. *New York, catholic publication soc.* 1875.

P. (I. M. B.) History of the city of Chester. [*anon.*] 2 p. l. iii, 334, ii pp. 4 pl. 8°. *Chester, for T. Poole,* 1815.

P. (S. D.) Ugly-girl papers. [*anon.*] 3 p. l. 283 pp. 16°. *New York, Harper & brothers,* 1875.

Paciaudi (Paolo Maria). Descrizione delle feste celebrate in Parma l'anno 1769. Per le auguste nozze di don Ferdinando colla reale arciduchessa Maria Amalia. [*anon.*] Eng. title, 3 p. l. 76 pp. 36 pl. fol. *Parma, nella stamperia reale,* [1769]?

Note.—The plates are by E. A. Petitot. Text in italian and french in parallel columns; the italian by Paciaudi, the french by abbé Millot.

Packard (Alpheus Spring, *jr. m. d.*) Our common insects. viii, iii–225 pp. incl. 4 pl. 1 pl. 12°. *Salem, naturalist's agency,* 1873.

Paddock (Wilbur F. *d. d. editor*). Half-century of church life. 498 pp. 12°. *Philadelphia, M'Calla & Stavely,* 1873.

Paddock (Zachariah, *d. d.*) Memoir of rev. Benjamin G. Paddock, with notices of early ministerial associates. Also, sketches of rev. George Gary, Abner Chase, William Case, [etc.] 377 pp. 2 ports. 12°. *New York, Nelson & Phillips,* 1875.

Padilla (Juan de, *el cartuxano*). Los doze triumphos de los doze apostoles, fechos por el cartuxano. Poema heroico cristiano. Trasladado de un exemplar que hoy existe en la libreria del Museo británico. Editor don Miguel del Riego. 6, 136 pp. 2 facs. 4°. *Londres, C. Wood,* 1841.

[*In* Riego (M. del). Coleccion de obras poeticas españolas. 1843].

Paetel (Fr.) Molluscorum systema et catalogus. System und aufzählung sämmtlicher conchylien der sammlung von Fr. Paetel. 3 p. l. xiv, 119 pp. 8°. *Dresden, O. Weiske,* 1869. s.

Paez (Ramon). Travels and adventures in South and Central America. 523 pp. 12 pl. 1 map. 12°. *Hartford, T. Belknap,* 1873.

Paganel (*L'abbé* Camille). Mémoires secrets sur m. l'archevêque de Paris. 1 p. l. ii, 426 pp. 8°. *Paris, Tenon,* 1831.
[MISCELLANEOUS pamphlets, v. 1008 : 2].

Page (H. A.) Memoir of Nathaniel Hawthorne with stories now first published in this country. xiii, 301 pp. 12°. *London, H. S. King & co.* 1872.

Pagès (François Xavier). Vies, amours et aventures de plusieurs illustres solitaires des Alpes. 4 v. in 2. 12°. *Paris, Laurens,* 1800.

Paget (Francis E.) The living and the dead: sermons on the burial service. xvii, 358 pp. 12°. *Cambridge,* [*Eng.*] *J. T. Walters,* 1845.

Paget (John). Paradoxes and puzzles, historical, judicial, and literary. xii, 472 pp. 8°. *Edinburgh, W. Blackwood & sons,* 1874.

Paine (William, *m. d.*) New school remedies. 633 pp. 1 col. pl. 12°. *Philadelphia, Claxton, Remsen & Haffelfinger,* 1874.

Paixhans (Henri Joseph). Expériences faites par la marine française, sur une arme nouvelle. 106 pp. 2 l. 8°. *Paris, Bachelier,* 1825.

Palafox y Mendoza (Juan, *bishop of Osma*). El pastor de noche buena. Duodecima impression. 8 p. l. 224 pp. 4 l. 18°. *Madrid, viuda de J. Muñoz,* 1761.

Palermo (Polycarpo). De vera C. Plini Secundi superioris patria. 4 p. l. 181 pp. 1 l. sm. 4°. *Veronæ, ex officina Tamiana,* 1608.

Palfrey (John Gorham). History of New England, to the revolution of the seventeenth century. 2 v. xx, 408 pp ; xii, 426 pp. 12°. *New York, Hurd & Houghton,* 1866.

Palgrave (William Gifford). Hermann Agha. vi, 281 pp. 16°. *New York, Holt & Williams,* 1872.
[LEISURE hour series].

Palliser (F.) *and* **Palliser** (M. A.) Mottoes for monuments or epitaphs. 4 p. l. 156 pp. 9 pl. 12°. *London, J. Murray,* 1872.

Palma (Luigi). Del principio di nazionalità nella moderna società europea. viii, 326 pp. 1 l. 12°. *Milano, editori della biblioteca utile,* 1867. s.
[BIBLIOTECA utile, 44 & 45].

Palmer (B. M. *d. d.*) Life and letters of James Henley Thornwell. xiii, 614 pp. port. 8°. *Richmond, Whittet & Shepperson,* 1875.

Palmer (Charles John). History and illustrations of a house in the elizabethan style of architecture. Property of J. D. Palmer. 29 pp. 3 l. 43 pl. port. fol. *London, printed for private distribution* [*by C. Whittingham*], 1838.

Palmer (Edward Henry). History of the jewish nation. Revised by rev. F. S. Smith. 119 pp. 5 l. 21 pl. 3 maps, 1 plan. 8°. *Boston, D. Lothrop & co.* [1875].

Palmer (Phœbe). The useful disciple; a narrative of mrs. Mary Gardner. 175 pp. 18°. *Cincinnati, for the methodist episcopal church,* 1851. s.

Palmer (Ray). Earnest words on true success in life. 1 p. l. 295 pp. 12°. *New York, A. S. Barnes & co.* 1873.

——— Poetical works. Complete ed. 372 pp. 1 port. 12°. *New York, A. S. Barnes & co.* 1876.

Palmieri de Micciché (Michel). Pensées et souvenirs historiques et contemporains. 2 v. in 1. 1 p. l. 362 pp ; 1 p. l. v–vii, 334 pp. 8°. *Paris, auteur,* 1830.

Papillon (Fernand). Nature and life. From the second french ed. by A. R. Macdonough. vii, 363 pp. 12°. *New York, D. Appleton & co.* 1875.

Papon (*L'abbé* Jean Pierre). Histoire de la révolution de France, depuis 1789. 2e éd. 6 v. 8°. *Paris, Poulet,* 1817.

——— Relation de la peste de Marseille, en 1720, et de celle de Montpellier, en 1629. 2 p. l. 93 pp. 2 l. 8°. *Montpellier, A. Seguin,* 1820.

Papworth (John W.) Alphabetical dictionary of coats of arms belonging to families in Great Britain and Ireland. xxii, 1125 pp. 8°. *London, T. Richards,* 1858–74.

Paquet (*L'abbé* Benjamin). Le libéralisme. 103 pp. 8°. *Québec, l'imprimerie du "Canadien",* 1872. s.

Paradise of God; or, the virtues of the sacred heart of Jesus. [*anon.*] 2 p. l. xiii–365 pp. 16°. *Baltimore, J. Murphy & co.* 1874.

Parchappe (Jean Baptiste Maximien). Galilée, sa vie, ses découvertes et ses travaux. 404 pp. 16°. *Paris, L. Hachette & cie.* 1866.

Pardon (George Frederick). Book of manly games for boys. By captain Crawley [*pseud.*] xi, 532 pp. 8 pl. 12°. *London, W. Tegg,* [1873].

Pareus (David Wœngler de). Davidis Parei in s. Matthæi evangelivm commentarivs. 6 p. l. 800, 120 pp. 4°. *Oxoniæ, excudebat J. Lichfield, impensis H. Corteyne,* 1631.

Paris (Louis Philippe d'Orléans, *comte* de). Histoire de la guerre civile en Amérique. v. 1-4. 8°, & atlas. 1e-2e livr. fol. *Paris, M. Lévy frères,* 1874-75.

——— Same. History of the civil war in America. Translated by Louis F. Tasistro. v. 1. xvi, 640 pp. 6 maps. 8°. *Philadelphia, J. H. Coates & co.* 1875.

Note.—Containing v. 1 and 2 of the Paris ed.

Paris at night. [*anon.*] Ill. title, 150 pp. 1 col. pl. 12°. *Boston, Boston and Paris publ. co.* [1875].

Parizel (Prosper). De vita et scriptis s. Aviti. 4 p. l. 328 pp. 8°. *Lovanii, Valinthout et socii,* [1859]. s.

[LOUVAIN. *Universitas catholica in oppido Lovaniensi.* Facultas philosophiæ et literarum. 1857-58. no. 11].

Parker (Caroline E. R.) Twenty stories and twenty poems. 154 pp. 10 pl. 18°. *New York, am. tract soc.* [1874].

——— Wilsons' kindling-dépôt. 144 pp. 1 pl. 18°. *New York, am. tract soc.* [1873].

Parker (Charles). Villa rustica: scenes in the vicinity of Rome and Florence. 2d ed. iv pp. 28 l. 72 pl. 4°. *London, J. Weale,* 1848.

Parker (*Rev.* Daniel). Proscription delineated. 290 pp. 8°. *Hudson,* [*N. Y.*] *author,* 1819.

Parker (Granville). Formation of the state of West Virginia. x, 482 pp. 8°. *Wellsburg, W. Va. Glass & son,* 1875.

Parker (John A.) Quadrature of the circle. 3 p. l. [301] pp. 1 map. 8°. *New York, J. Wiley & son,* 1874.

Parker (John Henry). Archæology of Rome. v. 1 in 2 v. [413] pp; 2 p. l. 9 l. 85 pl. 8°. *Oxford, J. Parker & co.* 1874.

Parker (Langston, *m. d.*) Treatment of syphilitic diseases by the mercurial vapour bath. From the 5th London ed. by J. W. Foye. 17, [156] pp. 1 pl. 12°. [*Boston*], *A. Williams & co.* 1874.

Parker (Lizzie G.) Miscellaneous selections. 194 pp. 16°. *Wellsburg, W. Va. A. Glass,* 1873.

Parkhurst (Clint). Poems. 2 p. l. 9-154 pp. 12°. *Chicago, western news co.* 1874.

Parkman (Francis). France and England in North America. Part 4. The old régime in Canada. xvi, 448 pp. 1 map. 8°. *Boston, Little, Brown & co.* 1874.

Parks (Isaac, *d. d.*) Lectures on punishment. 298 pp. 12°. *Troy, N. Y. Brainerd & Brown,* 1873.

Parks (Sam. Frank). Edena. A verse romance. 100 pp. 8°. *Knoxville, Tenn. press and herald book and job printing office,* 1872.

Parlor treasury. Gems of poetry. 6 v. 12°. *Philadelphia, Hubbard bros.* 1873.

Parr (John). Abstract of the laws, customs, and ordinances of the Isle of Man. v. 1. Edited by J. Gell. xvi, 241 pp. 8°. *Douglas,* [*Isle of Man*], 1867.

[MANX society. Publications, v. 12].

Parry (John S.) Extra-uterine pregnancy. xii, 17-276 pp. 8°. *Philadelphia, H. C. Lea,* 1876.

Parsonage in the Hartz. Adapted from the german by Cornelia McFadden. [*anon.*] 288 pp. 4 pl. 16°. *Philadelphia, presbyterian board of publication,* [1873].

Parsons (Eliza). Woman as she should be. 4 v. 16°. *London, for W. Lane,* 1793.

[Imperfect: title-page of v. 2 wanting].

Parsons (Reuben, *d. d.*) Biographical dictionary. New ed. 398 pp. incl. 9 ports. 1 pl. 12°. *New York, D. & J. Sadlier & co.* 1874.

Parson's (The) wife. [*anon.*] 2 v. 2 p. l. 283 pp; 2 p. l. 287 pp. 16°. *London, logographic press,* 1789.

Parton (James). Life of Thomas Jefferson. vi, 764 pp. 1 pl. 12°. *Boston, J. R. Osgood & co.* 1874.

Parton (*Mrs.* Sara Parker Willis). Fanny Fern. A memorial volume. Containing her select writings and a memoir. By J. Parton 502 pp. 1 l. ins. 6 pl. 12°. *New York, G W. Carleton & co.* 1873.

——— Fern leaves from Fanny's portfolio. [By Fanny Fern, *pseud.*] Eng. title, 400 pp. 7 pl. 12°. *Auburn, Derby & Miller,* 1853.

——— Same. Second series. [By Fanny Fern, *pseud.*] Eng. title, 400 pp. 6 pl. 12°. *Auburn, Miller, Orton & Mulligan,* 1854.

——— Ginger-snaps. By Fanny Fern [*pseud.*] 312 pp. 12°. *New York, Carleton,* 1870.

Pascoe (Charles Eyre). London directory for american travellers for 1874. 12°. *Boston, Lee & Shepard,* 1874.

——— Same. London guide and directory for american travellers. [etc.] 1875. 3d ed. 12°. *Boston,* [*London printed*], *Lee & Shepard,* [1875].

Pashley (Robert). Travels in Crete. 2 v. xl, 321 pp. 7 pl. 1 facs; xi, 327 pp. 8 pl. 8°. *Cambridge, J. W. Parker,* 1837.

Passidius (*Saint*). Vita di s. Aurelio Agostino vescovo d'Ippona, tradotta in italiano. 8 p. l. 103 pp. 1 port. 8°. *Milano, A. Agnelli,* 1764.

Pastoral sketches. From the "American pastor's journal." [*anon.*] 124 pp. 18°. *Springfield, G. & C. Merriam,* 1834.

Pastoret (Emm. Claude Joseph Pierre, *marquis* de). Zoroastre, Confucius et Mahomet, comparés comme sectaires, legislateurs & moralistes. 4 parts in 1 v. 2 p. l. 402 pp. 12°. *Paris, chez Buisson,* 1787.

Pater (Walter H.) Studies in the history of the renaissance. xv, 213 pp. 12°. *London, Macmillan & co.* 1873.

Paterson (James). History of the counties of Ayr and Wigton, [Scotland]. 3 v. in 5. 8°. *Edinburgh, J. Stillie,* 1863–66.

Patin (Charles). Relations historiqves et cvrievses de voyages en Allemagne, Angleterre, Hollande, Bohème, Suisse, &c. Eng. title, 6 p. l. 274 pp. 5 pl. 1 map, 1 port. 18°. *Lyon, C. Mvgvet,* 1674.

Paton (Chalmers I.) Freemasonry. xxvi, 484 pp. 8°. *London, Reeves & Turner,* 1873.

Patterson (Robert M.) Paradise. 220 pp. 16°. *Philadelphia, presbyterian board of publication,* [1874].

Patterson (*Rev.* W. M.) Manual of architecture: for churches, parsonages, and school houses. 133 pp. 15 pl. 4°. *Nashville, publishing house of the methodist episcopal church, south,* 1875.

Patton (Charles U.) Common-sense horse book. 1 p. l. 128 pp. 16°. *Cincinnati, Mecklenborg & Rosenthal,* 1875.

Patton (William W. *d. d.*) Prayer and its remarkable answers. 408 pp. front. 12°. *Chicago, J. S. Goodman,* 1876.

Pauke (Florian). Reise in die missionen nach Paraguay. Herausgegeben von P. Johann Frast. 164 pp. 12°. *Wien, bey A. Edlam von Schmid,* 1829.

Paul (Sara T.) Cookery from experience. 338 pp. 12°. *Philadelphia, Porter & Coates,* [1875].

Paulmier (J. P. D. C. J.) Mémoires tovchant l'établissement d'vne mission chrestienne dans le troisième monde. [*anon.*] 12 p. l. 216 pp. 16°. *Paris, C. Cramoisy,* 1663.

Paulus (Heinrich Eberhard Gottlob). Compendivm grammaticae arabicae. 4 p. l. 114 pp. 1 l. 5 tab. 8°. *Ienæ, apvd C. H. Cvnonis hæredes,* 1790.
[Imperfect: wanting, except one leaf, all after p. 114].

Pauly (Alphonse). Bibliographie des sciences médicales. xx pp. 1758 col. 36 l. unp. 8°. *Paris, Tross,* 1874.

Pavels (Claus, *bishop of Bergen*). Biografi og dagbøger, udgivne af C. P. Riis. xii, 516 pp. port. 12°. *Bergen, C. Floor,* 1864. s.

Payne (A. M. Mitchell). The odd one. 350 pp. 3 pl. 16°. *New York, R. Carter & brothers,* 1876.

——— Rhoda's corner. 361 pp. 3 pl. 16°. *New York, R. Carter & brothers,* 1873.

Payne (John). Dictionary of the Grebo language. 153 pp. 16°. *Philadelphia, King & Baird,* 1867.

Payne (Seth Wilbur). Behind the bars. 3 p. l. 242 pp. 16°. *New York, Vincent & co.* 1873.

Payne (William H.) Chapters on school supervision. 215 pp. 4 l. 12°. *Cincinnati, Wilson, Hinkle & co.* [1875].

Payson (Edward, *d. d.*) Mementos of rev. E. Payson, d. d. Sketch of his life, and selections from his works. By rev. Edwin L. Janes. 351 pp. 12°. *New York, Nelson & Phillips,* 1873.

——— Memoir, select thoughts and sermons. Compiled by rev. A. Cummings. 3 v. 8°. *Portland, Hyde, Lord & Duren,* 1846.

Paz-Soldan (José Gregorio, *editor*). Anales universitarios del Perú. 2 v. xvi, 392 pp. photo. port; 1 p. l. 344 pp. 2 l. 8°. *Lima, imprenta del gobierno & de la "Epoca,"* 1862.

Peabody (Andrew Preston, *d. d.*) Christian belief and life. 326 pp. 12°. *Boston, Roberts brothers,* 1875.

——— Manual of moral philosophy. vii, 225 pp. 12°. *New York, A. S. Barnes & co.* 1873.

Peabody (Andrew W. *d. d.*) Christianity and science. viii, 287 pp. 12°. *New York, R. Carter & brothers,* 1874.

Peabody (Elizabeth Palmer). Record of mr. Alcott's school. 3d ed. 297 pp. 16°. *Boston, Roberts brothers,* 1874.

Peacock (Thomas Brower). Poems. 119 pp. 12°. *Independence, Kansas, democrat publishing house,* 1872.

Peacock (Thomas Love). Melincourt. [*anon.*] 2 v. in 1. 253 pp. 1 l; 232 pp. 18°. *Philadelphia, M. Thomas,* 1817.

Peak (*Rev.* John). Memoir of elder John Peak, by himself. 203 pp. port. 12°. *Boston, J. Howe,* 1832.

Peake (Elizabeth). History of the german emperors and their contemporaries. From

Peake (Elizabeth)—continued. the german. 589 pp. 8°. *Philadelphia, J. B. Lippincott & co.* 1874.

——— Pen pictures of Europe. 591 pp. 66 pl. 8°. *Philadelphia, J. B. Lippincott & co.* 1874.

Peale (Rembrandt). Graphics; a popular system of drawing and writing. 4th ed. 129 pp. 12°. *Philadelphia, C. Sherman & co.* 1841.

Pearson (*Rev.* F. C.) Sparks among the ashes. 327 pp. 12°. *Philadelphia, J. B. Lippincott & co.* 1873.

Pearson (Jonathan). Contributions for the genealogies of the descendants of the first settlers of the patent and city of Schenectady, 1662 to 1800. iv, 324 pp. 1 pl. sm. 4°. *Albany, J. Munsell,* 1873.

Pease (*Rev.* A. G.) Philosophy of trinitarian doctrine. xii, 183 pp. 12°. *New York, G. P. Putnam's sons,* 1875.

Peck (George, *d. d.*) Life and times of rev. George Peck, d. d. By himself. 409 pp. port. *New York, Nelson & Phillips,* 1874.

Peck (Ira B.) Genealogical history of the descendants of Joseph Peck. 442 pp. 2 pl. incl. 1 col. 1 chart, 13 ports. 8°. *Boston, A. Mudge & son,* 1868.

Peckham (P. Annetta). Welded links. 1st ed. 116 pp. photog. port. sq. 12°. *Chicago, P. A. Peckham,* 1875.

Pedder (Henry C.) Issues of the age. v, 175 pp. 12°. *New York, A. K. Butts & co.* 1874.

Peddie (James, *d. d.*) Practical exposition of Jonah. 180 pp. 16°. *Edinburgh, W. Oliphant & son,* 1842.

Peebles (J. M.) Around the world; or, travels in Polynesia, China, India, Arabia, Egypt, Syria, and other "heathen" countries. iv, 414 pp. 8°. *Boston, Colby & Rich,* 1875.

Peet (Harvey Prindle, *ll. d.*) Elementary lessons, being a course of instruction for the deaf and dumb; part 1. 12th ed. xii, viii, 13–308 pp. 18°. *New York, Baker, Pratt & co.* 1875.

——— Same, part 3. 10th ed. 252 pp. 12°. *New York, Baker, Pratt & co.* 1875.

Peet (Isaac Lewis). Language lessons. 232 pp. 12°. *New York, Baker, Pratt & co.* 1875.

Pégot-Ogier (Eugène). The Fortunate Isles. From the french by Frances Locock. 2 v. iv, 318 pp; vi, 298 pp. 8°. *London, R. Bentley & son,* 1871.

Peigné (J. Marie-Étienne). Lamennais: sa vie intime à la Chênaie. Nouv. éd. 102 pp. 1 port. 18°. *Paris, mme. Bachelin-Deflorenne,* 1864.

Peirce (Bradford K. *d. d.*) The chaplain with the children. By B. K. P. [*anon.*] 317 pp. 8 pl. 16°. *New York, W. C. Palmer, jr.* 1870.

——— The recovery of Jerusalem. 144 pp. 18°. *Boston, Mass. s. s. society,* 1851.

Pember (Arthur). Mysteries and miseries of the great metropolis. By "A. P." [*anon.*] viii, 462 pp. 12 pl. 8°. *New York, D. Appleton & co.* 1874.

Penhallow (Samuel). History of the wars of New-England, with the eastern Indians. 1 p. l. iv pp. 1 l. 134 pp. 1 l. 16°. *Boston, for S. Gerrish, & D. Henchman,* 1726.

Pennell (R. F.) Ancient Greece. 2 p. l. 126 pp. 1 map. 16°. *Boston, J. Allyn,* 1874.

Penney (*Miss L. editor*). National temperance orator. 288 pp. 12°. *New York, national temperance publication house,* 1874.

Pennsylvania (*State of*). *2d geological survey:* 1874–5. [Publications]. 8°. *Harrisburg, board of commissioners for the second geological survey,* 1875.

CONTENTS.

D. PRIME (F. *jr.*) Report of progress on the brown hematite ore ranges of Lehigh county. 1875.
I. CARLL (J. F.) Report of progress in the Venango county district. Observations on the geology around Warren. By F. A. Randall. Note on the comparative geology of north-eastern Ohio and north-western Pennsylvania [etc.] By J. P. Lesley. 1875.
J. WRIGLEY (H. E.) Special report on the petroleum of Pennsylvania [etc.] 1875.
M. M'CREATH (A. S.) Report of progress in the laboratory. 1875.

Pennsylvania archives. 2d series. Edited by J. B. Linn & Wm. H. Egle, m. d. v. 1. 8°. *Harrisburg, B. Singerly,* 1874.

Pennsylvania railroad company. Report of the investigating committee. Appointed march 10th, 1874. 240 pp. 2 maps. 8°. *Philadelphia, Allen, Lane & Scott's printing house,* 1874.

Penzance (*Eng.*) public library. Catalogue. Compiled by J. Kinsman. viii, 421 (+320^{a-d}) pp. 8°. *Penzance,* [*London printed*], 1874.

People's history of America. Containing: Belknap's biographies of the early discoverers; Robertson's history of South America; Ramsay's history of the United States, the whole brought down to the present time. [*anon.*] Eng. title, xi, 720 pp. 20 pl. 2 ports. 1 facs. 4°. *New York, H. S. Allen,* 1874.

Pepys (*Lady* Charlotte Maria). Diary and houres of the ladye Adolie, 1552. viii, 360 pp. 4°. *London, Addey & co.* 1853.

Percier (Charles) *and* **Fontaine** (Pierre François Léonard). Choix des plus célèbres maisons de plaisance de Rome. 2e éd. 2 p. l. 72 pp. 77 pl. fol. *Paris, J. Didot aîné,* 1824.

——— ——— Plans de plusieurs châteaux, palais et résidences de souverains, de France, [etc.] 14 pl. ou 15 l. incl. eng. title. folio. *Paris,* [1835?]

——— ——— Résidences de souverains. Parallèle entre plusieurs résidences de souverains de France, d'Allemagne, de Suède, de Russie, d'Espagne, et d'Italie. 1 p. l. vii, 354 pp. 4°. *Paris, chez les auteurs,* 1833.

Percival (James Gates). Annual report of the geological survey of Wisconsin. 111 pp. 8°. *Madison, Calkins & Proudfit,* 1856.

——— Clio. 203 pp. 12°. *New-York, G. & C. Carvill,* 1827.

Percival (*Rev.* P.) Tamil proverbs with their english translation. 3d ed. xi, 573 pp. 12°. *London, H. S. King & co.* 1875.

Perez (Jerónimo). Memorias para la historia de la revolucion de Nicaragua, 1854 á 1857. 1a parte. 1 p. l. ii, 173 pp. 2 l. sm. 4°. *Managua, imprenta del gobierno,* 1865.

——— Same. Memorias para la historia de la campaña nacional. Contra el filibusterismo. 1856 y 57. 2da parte. 3 p. l. 215 pp. 2 l. sm. 4°. *Masayo, imprenta del órden,* 1873.

[*With* PEREZ (J.) Memorias para la historia de la revolucion, 1865].

Perez de Montoro (Joseph). Obras posthumas, lyricas humanas. v. 1. 12 p. l. 468 pp. 9 l. 8°. *Madrid, A. Marin,* 1736. s.

Perez de Moya (Juan). Tratado de cosas de astronomia, y cosmographia, y philosophia natural. 249 l. numb. 7 l. sm. fol. *Alcala, I. Gracian,* 1573.

——— Tratado de geometria practica, y speculatiua. 255 l. numb. 5 l. sm. fol. *Alcala, I. Gracian,* 1573.

Perier (J. A. N. *m. d.*) Fragments ethnologiques. 2 p. l. 124 pp. 8°. *Paris, V. Masson,* 1857.

Perkins (Samuel). The world as it is. 2d ed. 457 pp. incl. 1 map. 12°. [*New Haven*], *T. Belknap,* 1837.

[Imperfect: pp. 219-226, 231-238, 243-250, 255-262, are wanting].

Perreyve (*L'abbé* Henri). La journée des malades. Daily life of the sick. From the french. 288 pp. 12°. *Philadelphia, P. F. Cunningham & son,* 1875.

Perrier (Amelia). A winter in Morocco. viii 365 pp. 4 pl. 12°. *London, H. S. King & co.* 1873.

Perry (Arthur Latham). Elements of political economy. 11th ed. xxiv, 543 pp. 8°. *New York, Scribner, Armstrong & co.* 1874.

Perry (*Rev.* J.) Full course of instruction in explanation of the catechism. 435 pp. 16°. *St. Louis, P. Fox,* 1875.

Perry (Nora). After the ball, and other poems. 192 pp. 16°. *Boston, J. R. Osgood & co.* 1875.

Perry (William). General dictionary of the english language. 184 l. unp. port. 16°. *London, for J. Stockdale,* 1795.

Perry (William Stevens, *d. d.*) Handbook of the general convention of the protestant episcopal church, 1785-1874. xiv, 277 pp. 12°. *New York, T. Whittaker,* [1874].

——— Historical collections relating to the american colonial church. v. 3. Massachusetts. xxv, 720 pp. 4°. [*Hartford, Conn.*] *for the subscribers,* 1873.

Perryman (E. G.) Our new minister. 157 pp. 16°. *New-York, T. Whittaker,* [1875].

Peters (Dewitt C.) Kit Carson's life and adventures. 604 pp. incl. 30 pl. 2 ports. 8°. *Hartford, Conn. Dustin, Gilman & co.* 1874.

Peters (Jeremy, *pseud.*) Chronicles of Turkeytown; or, the works of Jeremy Peters [*pseud.*] 1st series. 238 pp. 12°. *Philadelphia, R. H. Small,* 1829.

Peters (John C.) *and* **McClellan** (Ely). History of the travels of asiatic cholera. In Asia and Europe: by John C. Peters. In North America: by Ely McClellan.

[*In* UNITED STATES. *War department.* (*Surgeon-general's office*). Cholera epidemic of 1873. 8°. *Washington, government printing office,* 1875. pp. 515-705, 7 maps].

Petronius Arbiter (Titus). Pétrone latin et françois, traduction entière. Nouv. éd. 2 v. 1 p. l. xlix pp. 1 l. 383 pp. 4 pl; 1 p. l. 293 pp. 1 l. 126 pp. 7 pl. 16°. [*Paris,* 1713].

Pettenkofer (Max von, *m. d.*) Relations of the air to the clothes we wear, the house we live in, and the soil we dwell on. Translated by Aug. Hess. viii, 94 pp. 1 l. 12°. *London, N. Trübner & co.* 1873.

Pettigrew (James Bell, *m. d.*) Animal locomotion, with a dissertation on aëronautics. xiv pp. 1 l. 264 pp. 3 pl. 12°. *London, H. S. King & co.* 1873.

[INTERNATIONAL scientific series, v. 7].

Pettigrew (J. B. *m. d.*)—*continued.*
——— Physiology of the circulation in plants, in the lower animals, and in man. viii, 329 pp. 8°. *London, Macmillan & co.* 1874.

Pettus (*Sir* John). Volatiles from the history of Adam and Eve. 4 p. l. 188 pp. 1 l. 16°. *London, T. Bassett,* 1674.
[Imperfect: 2 pp. wanting at p. 152, and the pagination of pp. 153–168 incorrect].

Peugnet (Eugène, *m. d.*) Nature of gun-shot wounds of the abdomen. 4 p. l. 96 pp. 8°. *New York, W. Wood & co.* 1874.

Peyton (John Lewis). Memoir of William M. Peyton, of Roanoke, with some of his speeches, letters, etc. vii, 392 pp. 8°. *London, J. Wilson,* 1873.

Pfizmaier (*Dr.* August). Kritische durchsicht der von Dawidow verfassten wörtersammlung aus der sprache der Aino's. 179 pp. 8°. *Wien, k. k. hof- und staatsdruckerei,* 1851. s
[KAISERLICHE akademie der wissenschaften. *Vienna.* Publications].

Pharmacopœa germanica. The german pharmacopœia. Translated by C. L. Lochman. xii, 382 pp. 8°. *Philadelphia, D. Elder & co.* 1873.

Phebens (Eggerik Egges). Kronijk van 1565–1594, uitgegeven door mr. H. O. Feith. xiv, 178 pp. 8°. *Utrecht, Kemink en zoon,* 1867. s.
[HISTORISCH genootschap. *Utrecht.* Publications. Werken, nieuwe reeks. no. 7].

Phelps (Austin). Sabbath hours. 157 pp. 24°. *Boston, congregational publishing society,* 1875.
——— The still hour. 136 pp. 16°. *Boston, Gould & Lincoln,* 1860.

Phelps (*Mrs.* Elizabeth Stuart). The sunny side. [*anon.*] 142 pp. 4 pl. 18°. *Philadelphia, am. s.-s. union,* [1851]. s.

Phelps (*Miss* Elizabeth Stuart). Poetic studies. 141 pp. sq. 18°. *Boston, J. R. Osgood & co.* 1875.
——— Trotty's wedding tour. 224 pp. 3 pl. 16°. *Boston, J. R. Osgood & co.* 1874.
——— What to wear? 1 p. l. 92 pp. 16°. *Boston, J. R. Osgood & co.* 1873.

Phelps (J. W. *editor*). Secret societies, ancient and modern. 240 pp. 16°. *Chicago, E. A. Cook & co.* 1873.

Phelps (Lavinia Howe). Dramatic stories. 262 pp. 12°. *Chicago, S. C. Griggs & co.* 1874.

Philadelphia (*Pa.*) *Apprentices' library.* Catalogue of books, boys' department, july 1st, 1874. 248 pp. 1 l. 18°. *Philadelphia, Merrihew & son,* 1874. s.

Philadelphia and its environs. [*anon.*] 72 pp. 1 map. 8°. *Philadelphia, J. B. Lippincott & co.* [1872].
——— Same. 2d ed. rev. [*anon.*] Title, 96 pp. incl. 2 pl. 1 pl. 1 map. 8°. *Philadelphia, J. B. Lippincott & co.* [1873].
——— Same. 3d ed. [*anon.*] Title, xvi, 110, 16 pp. 1 pl. 1 map. 8°. *Philadelphia, J. B. Lippincott & co.* [1875].
——— Same. [*anon.*] 2 v. in 1. xvi pp. 1 pl. 110 pp. 1 pl. 1 map; 50 pp. 8°. *Philadelphia, J. B. Lippincott & co.* [1875].

Philadelphia as it is. 114 pp. 1 map. 18°. *Philadelphia, G. S. Appleton,* 1845.

Philadelphia board of trade. Thirty-sixth to forty-first reports. 1869–1874. 6 v. 8°. *Philadelphia, J. B. Chandler,* 1869–74.

Philagatharches (*pseud.*) Hints on toleration: in five essays. 2d ed. xxiii, 367 pp. 8°. *London, Broxbourn, for Cadell & Davies,* 1811.

Philip II. *king of Spain.* Correspondance de Philippe II sur les affaires des Pay-bas; précédée d'une notice historique par Gachard. 2 v. 2 p. l. ccxvi pp. 1 l. 652 pp. port. 1 pl; 2 p. l. c, 748 pp. port. 1 plan. 4°. *Bruxelles, librairie ancienne et moderne, & C. Muquardt,* 1848–51. s.

Philippe (Mathieu Braussi, *called frère*). Meditations on the holy eucharist. From the french. xvi, 508 pp. 12°. *West Chester, N. Y. catholic protectory,* 1873.
——— Meditations on the sacred heart of Jesus. From the french. 2 p. l. 153 pp. 12°. *West Chester, N. Y. catholic protectory,* 1873.
[*With* PHILIPPE (M. B.) Meditations on the holy eucharist, 1873].

Philips *or* **Phillips** (Ambrose, *editor*). Collection of old ballads. 3 v. 16°. *London, J. Roberts,* 1722–25, [*reprint, London,* 1871].

Phillips (J. S.) The explorers', miners', and metallurgists' companion. 2d ed. 671 pp. 8°. [*San Francisco*], *the author,* 1873.

Phillips (*Rev.* Thomas). The Chinese. 1 p. l. vi, 120 pp. 12°. *London, S. Bagster & sons,* [1854].

Phillips (Waldorf H.) The world to blame. 3 p. l. xi–190 pp. 12°. *Philadelphia, Claxton, Remsen & Haffelfinger,* 1874.

Phin (John). Practical hints on the microscope. 131 pp. 16°. *New York, industrial publication co.* 1875.

Phull (Charles Louis de, *baron*). Essai d'une système pour servir de guide dans l'étude des opérations militaires. Publié par le baron

Phull (C. L. de, *baron*)—continued.
F. de Batz. xlviii, 220, xxxiv pp. 1 l. 2 pl. 8°. *Leipzig, F. A. Brockhaus*, 1853.

Piatt (*Mrs.* Sarah Morgan Bryan). Voyage to the Fortunate isles, etc. vi, 179 pp. 16°. *Boston, J. R. Osgood & co.* 1874.

Piattoli (Scipione). Essai sur les lieux et les dangers des sépultures. Traduit de l'italien. Par [Félix] Vicq d'Azyr. clxvii, 142 pp. 16°. *Paris, P. F. Didot*, 1778.

Picart (Bernard). Recueil de lions. Eng. title, 1 p. l. 6 pp. 36 pl. obl. 16°. *Amsterdam, B. Picart*, 1729.

Piccope (*Rev.* George John, *editor*). Lancashire and Cheshire wills and inventories. 3 v. sm. 4°. [*Manchester*], 1857-61.
[CHETHAM society remains, v. 33, 51, 54].

Pichot (Pierre Amédée). Le jardin d'acclimatation illustré. Animaux et plantes. viii, 336 pp. 41 pl. 8°. *Paris, Hachette & cie.* 1873.

Pick (Bernhard). Luther as a hymnist. 178 pp. 16°. *Philadelphia, lutheran bookstore*, 1875.

Pickering (Edward C.) Elements of physical manipulation. xii, 225 pp. 8°. *New York, Hurd & Houghton*, 1873.

Pico (Giovanni, *della Mirandola*). Ioannis Pici Mirandvlae omnia opera: [etc.] 262 l. unnumb. fol. *Venetiis, per Bernardinū Venetū*, 1498.

——— Same. Opera omnia. Item Cabala Ioannis Reuchlini, ad intelligenda loca quædam Pici, magno usui futura lectori. 16 p. l. 900, 897-923 pp. fol. *Basileæ, per H. Petri*, 1557.

Pico (Giovanni Francesco, *della Mirandola*). Dialogo intitulato La strega, overo de gli inganni de demoni. Tradotto in lingva toscana per il signor abate Turino Turini da Pescia. Eng. title, 4 p. l. 17-126 pp. 1 l. 4°. *Pescia, [L. Torrentino]*, 1555.

Picton (J. A.) Memorials of Liverpool. 2d ed. 2 v. vii, 607 pp; 3 p. l. 533 pp. 12°. *London, Longmans*, 1875.

Pictorial miscellany. Selections from St. Nicholas and from Scribner's monthly [etc.] New ed. 1 p. l. [252] pp. front. 8°. *New York, Scribner & co.* [1875].

Pictures in Tyrol and elsewhere. [*anon.*] x, 313 pp. 63 pl. 12°. *London, Longmans*, 1867.

Picturesque America; or, the land we live in. Edited by William Cullen Bryant. 2 v. Eng. title, viii, 568 pp. 23 pl; eng. title, vi,

Picturesque America—continued.
576 pp. 24 pl. 4°. *New York, D. Appleton & co.* [1872-74].

Pierantoni (Augusto). Gli arbitrati internazionali e il trattato di Washington. 127 pp. 1 l. 8°. *Napoli, fratelli de Angelis*, 1872.

Piétrement (C. A.) Les origines du cheval domestique. xv, 487 pp. 8°. *Paris, E. Donnaud*, 1870.

Pigafetta (Antonio). Beschreibung der von Magellan unternommenen ersten reise um die welt. Aus dem französischen. lxxi, 296 pp. 3 maps. 8°. *Gotha, J. Perthes*, 1801.

Piggot (John). Persia—ancient & modern. xvi, 328 pp. 12°. *London, H. S. King & co.* 1874.

Pigot (Hugh). Hadleigh. The town; the church; and the great men who have been born in, or connected with the parish.
[*In* SUFFOLK institute of archæology. Proceedings. v. 3. 8°. *Lowestoft, S. Tymms*, 1863. 1 p. l. x, 290 pp. 10 pl.]

Pike (James S.) The prostrate state: South Carolina under negro government. 279 pp. 16°. *New York, D. Appleton & co.* 1874.

Pike (Luke Owen). History of crime in England. v. 1. From the roman invasion to the accession of Henry VII. xxx, 539 pp. 1 facs. 8°. *London, Smith, Elder & co.* 1873.

Pike (Nicolas). Sub-tropical rambles in the land of the aphanapteryx. Personal experiences in Mauritius. 1 p. l. xviii, 510 pp. 15 pl. 4 maps. 8°. *New York, Harper & brothers*, 1873.

Pike (Robert, *jr.*) *and* **Pike** (William C.) Mnemonics applied to the acquisition of knowledge. Pts. 1 & 2 in 1 v. 35, 39-100 pp. 8°. *Boston, S. N. Dickinson*, 1844.

Pike (*Rev.* Samuel) *and* **Hayward** (*Rev.* Samuel). Religious cases of conscience answered in an evangelical manner. viii, 527 pp. 16°. *Philadelphia, for R. Campbell*, 1800.

Pilkington (Mary). Tales of the hermitage; english and italian. Translated by V. Peretti. 2d ed. [*anon.*] 1 p. l. xii, 128 pp. front. 12°. *London, for B. Dulau & co.* 1809.

Pilon (Martin Regul). The yanko-sequor; disquisitions upon several things in America. In five books. Book 4. [*anon.*] 8°. *New York, M. R. Pilon*, 1874.

CONTENTS.

Book 4. Discourses and sketches upon the ways to arrive at the demonetization of gold and silver in America, and the establishment of private banks, 186 pp. 1 pl. 1874.

Pilon (M. R.)—continued.

——— Same. The yanko-sequor on free trade. In two books. Book 2. 8°. *New York, authors' publishing co.* 1875.

CONTENTS.

Book 2. Disquisitions upon the ways to arrive at the demonetization of gold and silver, and upon the establishment of private banks. 1 p. l. 186 pp. 1 pl. 1875.

Pinamonti (Giovanni Pietro, *s. J.*) Exorcista rite edoctus, seu accurata methodus omne maleficiorum genus probe, ac prudenter curandi. 95 pp. incl. 1 port. 16°. *Venetiis, ac Bassani, apud J. A. Remondinum,* 1740.

——— Le leggi dell'impossibile ovvero le regole dell'astrologia per rintracciare l'avvenire esposte alla luce. 156 pp. 18°. *Firenze, P. M. Miccioni & M. Nestenus,* 1700.

Pinckard (*Mrs.* M. E.) Bread of heaven, and husks of swine. [*anon.*] 304 pp. 12°. *Baltimore, J. Y. Slater,* 1874.

Pindar. Extant odes translated into english, with an introduction by Ernest Myers. 23, 176 pp. 12°. *London, Macmillan & co.* 1874.

Pine (Cuyler). Ecce femina. [*anon.*] 46 pp. 8°. *New York, Schuyler & Gracie,* 1874.

——— Same. 133 pp. 12°. *New York, G. W. Carleton & co.* 1875.

Pineau (— *m. d.*) Mémoire sur les dangers des inhumations précipitées. 136 pp. 1 l. 8°. *Niort, P. Elies,* 1776.

Pinkerton (Allan). Allan Pinkerton's detective stories. 3 v. 12°. *New York & Chicago, W. B. Keen, Cooke & co.* 1874–75.

CONTENTS.

1. The expressman and the detective. 278 pp. 14 pl. 1874.
2. Claude Melnotte as a detective, and other stories. 11, 9–282 pp. 18 pl. 4 facs. 1875.
3. The detective and the somnambulist. The murderer and the fortune teller. 241 pp. 10 pl. 1875.

Pinkerton (John). Modern atlas. 1 p. l. 7 pp. 61 maps. fol. *Philadelphia, T. Dobson & son,* 1818.

Pinner (Moses). Compendium des hierosolymitanischen und babylonischen thalmud. Uebersetzt von M. Pinner. 1ster band. Entstehung, sprache, aechtheit des thalmud, [etc.] xlviii, 132 pp. 4°. *Berlin, verfasser,* 1831.

Pinto (M. *pseud?*) Don Pirlone a Roma. Da m. Pinto [*pseud?*] 306 pl. obl. 4°. [*n. p. about* 1850].

Pirie (*Rev.* Alexander). Dissertation on baptism. 150 pp. 18°. *Whitehall, for A. Young,* 1803.

Pischon (Friedrich August). Denkmäler der deutschen sprache. 6 v. 8°. *Berlin, Duncker & Humblot,* 1838–50.
[Imperfect: wanting v. 6, 2te abth.]

Pitts (*Dr.* J. R. S.) Life and bloody career of the executed criminal, James Copeland, [etc.] 2d ed. 1 p. l. 220 pp. 4 pl. 8°. *Jackson, Miss. pilot publishing co.* 1874.

Plain facts for practical people. [*anon.*] 336 pp. 12°. *Philadelphia, Devlin, Dickey & co.* [1873].

Planché (James Robinson). The conqueror and his companions. 2 v. xxii, 268 pp; vi, 304 pp. 8°. *London, Tinsley brothers,* 1874.

——— Recollections and reflections, a profes- fessional autobiography. 2 v. xv, 316 pp. 3 facs; xii, 308 pp. 4 facs. 8°. *London, Tinsley brothers,* 1872.

——— Regal records: or, a chronicle of the coronations of the queens regnant of England. xiv, 170 pp. front. 16°. *London, Chapman & Hall,* 1838.

Plateau (Félix). Recherches sur les phénomènes de la digestion chez les insectes. 1 p. l. 124 pp. 3 pl. 4°. *Bruxelles, F. Hayez,* 1874. S.

Platina *or* **Piadena** (Bartolommeo de Sacchi). B. Platinæ cremonensis opus, de vitis ac gestis summorum pontificium ad Sixtum IV. pont. max. deductum. 24 p. l. 672 pp. 18°. [*Lugduni Batavorum*], 1664.

Plato. Dialogues, translated into english. By B. Jowett. 4 v. 8°. *Oxford, Clarendon press,* 1871.

Platt (*Rev.* S. H.) Power of grace over acquired habits, special inborn perversities, and the natural appetites. 185 pp. 3 l. 16°. *Brooklyn, S. Harrison & co.* 1874.

——— Princely manhood. A private treatise. 115 pp. 18°. *Bridgeport, Conn. the author,* 1873.

——— Queenly womanhood. A private treatise. 167 pp. 18°. *Brooklyn, S. Harrison & co.* 1875.

Plimsoll (Samuel, *m. p.*) Our seamen. Popular ed. vii, 128 pp. 1 map. 12°. *London, Virtue & co.* 1873.

Ploennies (Luise von). Mariken von Nymwegen. x, 280 pp. 16°. *Berlin, A. Duncker,* 1853.

Plumer (William S.) Hints and helps in pastoral theology. 381 pp. 8°. *New York, Harper & brothers,* 1874.

Plumptre (Anne). Narrative of a three years' residence in France, 1802 to 1805. 3 v. 8°. *London, for J. Mawman,* [*etc.*] 1810.

Pocahontas: a historical drama. [*anon.*] 240 pp. 12°. *New York, G. Dearborn,* 1837.

Poe (Edgar Allan). Works. With a study on his life and writings, from the french of C. Baudelaire. viii, 676 pp. 3 pl. 1 facs. 12°. *London, J. C. Hotten,* [1873].

——— Poems. Complete. With memoir by R. H. Stoddard. 380 pp. port. 1 facs. 3 pl. 12°. *New York, W. J. Widdleton,* 1875.

——— Poems and essays; with the letters, addresses and poems of the ceremonies at the monumental dedication. Memorial ed. clxxvi, 5–270 pp. 3 pl. 2 facs. port. 12°. *New York, W. J. Widdleton,* 1876.

——— Aventures d'Arthur Gordon Pym. Eureka. Traduction de C. Baudelaire. 2 p. l. 518 pp. 16°. *Paris, M. Lévy frères,* 1870.

[BAUDELAIRE (C.) Oeuvres complètes. 16°. *Paris,* 1868–73. v. 7].

——— Histoires extraordinaires. Traduction de C. Baudelaire. 2e éd. 2 p. l. 524 pp. 16°. *Paris, M. Lévy frères,* 1873.

[BAUDELAIRE (C.) Oeuvres complètes. 16°. *Paris,* 1868–73. v. 5].

——— Nouvelles histoires extraordinaires. Traduction de C. Baudelaire. 2 p. l. 544 pp. 16°. *Paris, M. Lévy frères,* 1869.

[BAUDELAIRE (C.) Oeuvres complètes. 16°. *Paris,* 1868–73. v. 6].

Poems for catholics & convents. By the sisters of mercy, st. Catherine's convent, New York city. 1 p. l. xii, 282 pp. 12°. *West Chester, N. Y. catholic protectory,* 1873.

Poetical account of the american campaigns of 1812 and 1813. [etc. *anon.*] 139 pp. 12°. *Halifax, J. Howe, jr.* 1815.

Poey (Felipe). Curso elemental de mineralogia. 183 pp. 1 pl. 8°. *Habana, A. Pego,* 1872. s.

Poitou (Eugène Louis). Spain and its people. From the french. With illustrations by V. Foulquier. xiii, 11–497 pp. incl. 24 pl. & 2 ports. 12°. *London, T. Nelson & sons,* 1873.

Polain (Matthieu Lambert). Esquisses ou récits historiques sur l'ancien pays de Liége. 3e éd. 4 p. l. iij, 375 pp. 8°. *Bruxelles, Hauman & co.* 1842.

Pollard (Josephine). Gipsy in New York. 190 pp. incl. 1 pl. 16°. *New York, Nelson & Phillips,* [1873].

——— Gipsy's adventures. 174 pp. incl 3 pl. 18°. *New York, Nelson & Phillips,* [1875].

Pollard (Josephine)—continued.

——— Gipsy's early days. 182 pp. incl. 1 pl. 16°. *New York, Nelson & Phillips,* [1873].

——— Gipsy's travels. 187 pp. incl. 3 pl. 16°. *New York, Nelson & Phillips,* [1874].

Polwhele (*Rev.* Richard). Cornish-english vocabulary. 1 p. l. 98 pp. 4°. *Truro, J. Tregoning, for Cadell & Davies, London,* 1808.

[POLWHELE (R.) History of Cornwall. v. 6].

——— History of Cornwall. New ed. 7 v. in 2. 4°. v. 1–3, *Falmouth, T. Flindell, for Cadell & Davies, London,* 1803; v. 4–7, *London, for Law & Whittaker,* 1816.

——— History of Devonshire. 3 v. in 1. fol. *Exeter, Trewman & son,* 1793–1806.

Polybius, *megalopolitanus.* Histoire générale de la république romaine.

[*In* BUCHON (J. A. C). Ouvrages historiques de Polybe, etc. 8°. *Paris,* 1838. pp. 1–567].

Pomp (N.) Kurzgefasste prüfungen der lehre des ewigen evangeliums. xvi, 200 pp. 12°. *Philadelphia, H. Miller,* 1774.

Pond (Enoch, *d. d.*) Review of Bushnell's "God in Christ." xi, 118 pp. 12°. *Bangor,* [*Me.*] *E. F. Duren,* 1849.

Pontis (Louis de). Memoirs. Englished by Charles Cotton. 4 p. l. 288 pp. fol. *London, for J. Knapton,* 1694.

Pontoppidan (*Dr.* Erik). Oanedubme dr. Erik Pontoppidan čilgitusast. Samas jorgali professor J. A. Friis.—Udtog af dr. Erich Potoppidans forklaring ved H. U. Sverdrup. 311 pp. 16°. *Kristianiast, A. Grøndahl,* 1873. s.

[*In* parallel pages, quänian and norwegian].

Poole (Margaret E.) Pictures of cottage life in the west of England. ix, 302 pp. 12°. *London, Macmillan & co.* 1870.

Poole (Stanley Lane). Coins of the eastern khaleefehs in the British museum. xx, 263 pp. 8 autotype pl. 8°. *London, trustees,* 1875

[BRITISH museum. Catalogue of oriental coins. v. 1].

Poole (William Frederick). Anti-slavery opinions before 1800. [Also] a fac simile reprint of dr. George Buchanan's oration on the moral and political evil of slavery. 2 parts in 1 v. 82 pp; 20 pp. 8°. *Cincinnati, R. Clarke,* 1873.

Poor (Henry V.) Manual of the railroads of the United States, for 1874–75, 1875–76. 7th–8th series. 2 v. 8°. *New York, H. V. & H. W. Poor,* 1874–75.

Poot (Hubert Korneliszoon). Het groot natuur- en zedekundigh werelttoneel of woor-

Poot (H. K.)—continued. denboek van meer dan 1200 aeloude egiptische, griekscbe en romeinsche zinnebeelden of beeldenspraek. 3 v. fol. *Delft, R. Boitet,* 1743.

Pope (Mary E.) Poems. 150 pp. 1 port. 12°. *Philadelphia, J. B. Lippincott & co.* 1872.

Popular encyclopedia. New ed. 7 v. 8°. *Glasgow,* [*etc.*] *Blackie & son,* [1865–66].
Note.—Known as "Blackie's encyclopedia."

Porchat (Jean Jacques). Trois mois sous la neige. Éd. revue et corrigée. 166 pp. 16°. *Philadelphia, F. Leypoldt,* 1864.

Porta (Giambattista della). Commedie. 4 v. 16°. *Napoli, G. Muzio,* 1726.

Porte-feuille de Buonaparte, pris à Charleroi le 18 juin 1815. 128 pp. 1 facs. 8°. *Paris, Le Normant,* 1815.
[NAPOLEON pamphlets, v. 23].

Porter (*Mrs.* Ann Emerson). Millie Lee. 316 pp. 2 pl. 16°. *Boston, D. Lothrop & co.* [1873].

——— Uncle Jerry's letters to young mothers. 144 pp. 16°. *Boston, J. P. Jewett & co.* 1854.

Porter (Charles T.) Treatise on the Richards steam-engine indicator. Revised, with notes, by F. W. Bacon. 2d ed. 155 pp. incl. 24 diagrams, 1 pl. 16°. *New York, D. Van Nostrand,* 1873.

Porter (David D. *admiral, U. S. n.*) Memoir. xi, 427 pp. 25 pl. port. 8°. *Albany, J. Munsell,* 1875.

Porter (Duvall). Poems. vii, 275 pp. 12°. *Lynchburg, Va. J. P. Bell & co.* 1875.

Porter (George Richardson). Tropical agriculturist. xii, 429 pp. incl. 30 pl. 8°. *London, Smith, Elder & co.* 1833.

Porter (James, *d. d.*) Revised compendium of methodism. 506 pp. port. 12°. *New York, Nelson & Phillips,* [1875].

——— The winning worker. 300 pp. incl. front. 1 l. 16°. *New York, Nelson & Phillips,* 1875.

Porter (Linn Boyd). Caring for no man. 173 pp. 8°. *Boston, W. F. Gill & co.* 1875.

Porter (Rose). The winter fire. 231 pp. 16°. *New York, A. D. F. Randolph & co.* [1874].

——— The years that are told. 6 p. l. 234 pp. 16°. *New York, A. D. F. Randolph & co.* [1875].

Portfolio. Artistic periodical. Edited by Philip Gilbert Hamerton. Monthly. Jan. 1870, to dec. 1875. v. 1–6. fol. *London, Seeley, Jackson & Halliday,* 1870–75.

Portsmouth monumental cook book, compiled by the ladies of the soldiers' aid society of Portsmouth, Ohio. 185 pp. 8°. *Portsmouth, J. W. Newman,* 1874.

Portulano de la America setentrional. Construido en la direccion de trabajos hidrograficos. Divido en quatro partes, 1809. Aumentado y corregido en 1818. [*anon.*] 2 p. l. 121 maps, 3 l. obl. fol. *Madrid,* [1818]?

Post (Loretta J.) Scenes in Europe. 336 pp. 12 pl. 16°. *Cincinnati, Hitchcock & Walden,* 1874.

Postola sögur. Legendariske fortællinger om apostlernes liv. Udgivne af C. R. Unger. 3 p. l. xxx pp. 1 l. 936 pp. port. 8°. *Christiania, B. M. Bentzen,* 1874. s.

Potiquet (Alfred). Institut national de France, 1795–1869. 1 p. l. xx, 474 pp. 8°. *Paris, Didier & cie.* 1871.

Potter (Humphrey Tristram). New dictionary of all the cant and flash languages. 16, 9–62 pp. 8°. [*London*], *W. Mackintosh,* [1795?]

Potts (*Rev.* John Vinton). 1774. Christian co-operation in actual life; or, "united brethren in Christ." A review of their origin and progress. In five parts. 404 pp. 12°. *Dayton, Ohio, united brethren publishing house,* 1874.

Potts (Thomas). Potts's discovery of witches in the county of Lancaster, from the original ed. of 1613. With notes by J. Crassley. 2 p. l. lxxix, 235, 6 pp. sm. 4°. [*Manchester*], 1845.
[CHETHAM society remains, v. 6].

Poullain de Saintfoix (Germain François). Essais historiques sur Paris. 4e éd. 6 v. 16°. *Paris, veuve Duchesne,* 1766.

Poussin (Guillaume Tell). États-Unis d'Amérique. 1815–1873. 242 pp. 1 l. 8°. *Paris, E. Dentu,* 1874.

Povey (Charles). The virgin in Eden. 2d ed. 1 p. l. 118 pp. 12°. *London, J. Roberts,* 1741.

Powell (Frederick). Bacchus dethroned. 268 pp. 12°. *New York, national temperance society,* 1873.

Powell (John J.) The golden state and its resources. 219 pp. 16°. *San Francisco, Bacon & co.* 1874.

Powell (Warington Baden). Canoe travelling. xv, 172 pp. 3 pl. 1 map. 8°. *London, Smith, Elder & co.* 1871.

Powell (Willis J.) *and* **Rarey** (J. S.) Tachyhippodamia; or, the new secret of taming horses. 161 pp. 8 pl. 16°. *Philadelphia, Hubbard bros.* [1874].

Power (John Carroll). Abraham Lincoln. His life, death and great funeral. Monumental ed. 352 pp. port. 1 map, 1 plan. sq. 12°. *Springfield, Ill. E. A. Wilson & co.* 1875.

Powers (Horatio N.) Through the year. viii, 288 pp. 16°. *Boston, Roberts brothers,* 1875.

Poynder (Frederick). Dictionary of the english language. 3d ed. 2 p. l. 447 pp. sq. 18°. *London, soc. for promoting christian knowledge,* [1870].

Practical receipts of experienced housekeepers. Compiled by the ladies of the seventh presbyterian church of Cincinnati. 191 pp. 8 l. 8°. *Cincinnati,* 1874.

Praet (Jan). Speghel der wijsheit of leeringhe der zalichede, uitgegeven van wege der koninklijke akademie van Belgie, door J.-H. Bormans. 2 p. l. xv, 208 pp. 8°. *Brussel, F. Hayez,* 1872. s.

Pranceriana. Select collection of pieces, published since the appointment of the present provost of the university of Dublin. [*anon.*] 253 pp. 2 pl. 16°. *Dublin,* 1775.

Pratt (Daniel J.) Annals of public education in the state of New York.—Founding of King's (afterward Columbia) college, [etc.] 169–234 pp; 205–236 pp. 2 pam. in 1 v. 8°. [*Albany ?* 1875].

Pratt (I. Loring). Bonnie Aerie. By "L. L." [*anon.*] 337 pp. front. 16°. *Boston, D. Lothrop & co.* [1875].

——— Branches of palm. By L. L. [*anon.*] 334 pp. 2 pl. 16°. *Boston, D. Lothrop & co.* 1873.

——— Broken fetters. By L. L. [*anon.*] 357 pp. 2 pl. 16°. *Boston, D. Lothrop & co.* [1874].

Pratt (L. Maria). Sunshine for baby land. [*anon.*] 368 pp. incl. 71 pl. 12°. *Boston, D. Lothrop & co.* [1875].

Pratt (*Mrs.* Mary E.) Rhoda Thornton's girlhood. 273 pp. 11 pl. 16°. *Boston, Lee & Shepard,* 1874.

Pratt (Parley Parker). Autobiography. Edited by his son. 502, x pp. 6 pl. 8°. *New York, for the editor,* 1874.

——— Key to the science of theology. 3d ed. xv, 178 pp. 12°. *Salt Lake city, Deseret news establishment,* 1874.

Pratt (Parley Parker)—continued.

——— Voice of warning and instruction to all people. 9th ed. xi, 171 pp. 12°. *Salt Lake city, Deseret news establishment,* 1874.

Pre-adamite man. [*anon.*] xvi, 333 pp. 7 pl. 12°. *London, Saunders, Otley & co.* 1860.

Preble (George Henry). First cruise of the U. S. frigate Essex. 1 p. l. 108 pp. 8°. *Salem, Essex institute,* 1870. s.

Prentice (George Dennison). The poems of George D. Prentice; edited, with a biographical sketch, by John James Piatt. 216 pp. port. 12°. *Cincinnati, R. Clarke & co.* 1876.

Prentiss (*Mrs.* E.) Religious poems. [*anon.*] viii, 200 pp. 12°. *New York, A. D. F. Randolph & co.* [1873].

——— Urbané and his friends. 287 pp. 12°. *New York, A. D. F. Randolph & co.* [1874].

Presbyterian church in the United States. Book of hymns and tunes. Prepared by authority of the assembly of 1873. Edited by E. Thompson Baird and C. C. Converse. 1 p. l. 409 pp. 8°. *Richmond, presbyterian committee of publication,* [1874].

——— The presbyterian digest: a compend of the acts and deliverances of the general assembly. By William E. Moore, d. d. 1873. 718 pp. 8°. *Philadelphia, presbyterian board of publication,* [1874].

Presbyterian cook book, compiled by the ladies of the first presbyterian church, Dayton, Ohio. 183 pp. incl. 2 pl. 8°. *Dayton, O. Crook & co.* 1873.

Prescott (Albert B.) Outlines of proximate organic analysis. 192 pp. 12°. *New York, D. Van Nostrand,* 1875.

Prescott (C. E.) New York; its past and present. 174 pp. 8°. *New York, mercantile publishing co.* 1874.

Prescott (Mary N.) Matt's follies, and other stories. 164 pp. incl. 1 pl. 12°. *Boston, J. R. Osgood & co.* 1873.

Prescott (William Hickling). History of Philip the second. New ed. Edited by John Foster Kirk. 3 v. 12°. *Philadelphia, J. B. Lippincott & co.* 1874.

——— History of the conquest of Mexico. New ed. Edited by John Foster Kirk. 3 v. 12°. *Philadelphia, J. B. Lippincott & co.* 1874.

——— History of the conquest of Peru. 2 v. 1 p. l. v–xl, 527 pp. 1 port. 1 map; 1 p. l. viii–xix, 547 pp. 1 port. 1 facs. 8°. *Philadelphia, J. B. Lippincott & co.* 1874.

Prescott (William H.)—continued.

——— Same. New ed. Edited by John Foster Kirk. 2 v. xxxvi, 510 pp. 1 pl. 1 map; xx, 530 pp. 1 pl. 1 facs. 12°. *Philadelphia, J. B. Lippincott & co.* 1874.

Preston (Harriet W.) Love in the nineteenth century. 2 p. l. 153 pp. 16°. *Boston, Roberts brothers,* 1873.

Preston (John, *d. d.*) The breast-plate of faith and love. 4th ed. 3 v. in 1. sm. 4°. *London, for N. Bourne,* 1634.

Preston (Margaret J.) Cartoons. 1 p. l. 240 pp. 16°. *Boston, Roberts brothers,* 1875.

Preston (*Very rev.* Thomas S.) Lectures upon the devotion to the most sacred heart of Jesus Christ. 189 pp. 12°. *New York, R. Coddington,* 1874.

Prévost d'Exiles (Antoine François). Pensées, précédées de l'abrégé de sa vie. xlviij, 218 pp. 1 l. 16°. *Amsterdam, Arské & Merckus,* 1764.

Prévost-Paradol (Lucien Anatole). Essai sur l'histoire universelle. 2e éd. 2 v. 3 p. l. iv, 517 pp; 7 p. l. 532 pp. 16°. *Paris, L. Hachette & cie.* 1865.

——— Études sur les moralistes français. 3e éd. 2 p. l. vii, 303 pp. 16°. *Paris, Hachette & cie.* 1873.

——— Quelques pages d'histoire contemporaine. 1–4 séries. 4 v. 16°. *Paris, M. Lévy frères,* 1864–71.

Price (Bartholomew). Treatise on infinitesimal calculus. 2d ed. 4 v. 8°. *Oxford, [Eng.] university press,* 1857–68.
Note.—Volume 4 is 1st ed.

Price (Bonamy). Currency and banking. 4 p. l. 176 pp. 12°. *London, H. S. King & co.* 1876.

Price (Isaiah). History of the ninety-seventh regiment, Pennsylvania volunteer infantry, during the war of the rebellion. viii, 3–608 pp. 1 l. 7 ports. 8°. *Philadelphia, author,* 1875.

Price (John). Historical & topographical account of Leominster [Eng.] 5 p. l. 273 pp. 7 pl. 8°. *Ludlow, H. Procter,* 1795.

Prichard (Sarah J.) Aunt Saidee's cow. 357 pp. incl. 1 pl. 16°. *New York, R. Carter & brothers,* 1873.

Prime (Edward Dorr Griffin, *d. d.*) Forty years in the Turkish empire; or, memoirs of rev. William Goodell, d. d. xii, 489 pp. 8°. *New York, R. Carter & brothers,* 1876.

Prime (Samuel Irenæus.) The Alhambra and the Kremlin. xxiv, 482 pp. incl. 17 pl. 8°. *New York, A. D. F. Randolph & co.* [1873].

——— Life of Samuel F. B. Morse, ll. d. xii pp. 1 l. 776 pp. 4 ports. 5 pl. 1 facs. 8°. *New York, D. Appleton & co.* 1875.

——— Under the trees. 313 pp. 8°. *New York, Harper & brothers,* 1874.

——— Walking with God. 1 p. l. 101 pp. 18°. *New York, A. D. F. Randolph & co.* [1872].

——— *editor.* Songs of the soul. Gathered out of many lands and ages. viii, 661 pp. 1 port. 8°. *New York, R. Carter & brothers,* 1874.

Prime (William C.) I go a-fishing. 365 pp. 8°. *New York, Harper & brothers,* 1873.

Pritchard (H. Baden). Tramps in the Tyrol. xii, 267 pp. incl. front. 12°. *London, Tinsley brothers,* 1874.

Prittwitz (M. von). Die arbeiterfrage und deren lösung. 4 p. l. 132 pp. 8°. *Berlin, L. Simion,* 1873.
[ARBEITERFREUND, 1873, v. 11, supplementheft].

Probasco (Henry). Catalogue of the collection of books, [etc.] belonging to mr. H. Probasco, Cincinnati, Ohio. iv, 407 pp. 8°. [*Cambridge, Mass. Welch, Bigelow & co.*] 1873.

Procter (George H.) Fishermen's memorial and record book, a list of vessels and their crews, lost from Gloucester from 1830 to oct. 1, 1873. iv, 172 pp. 8°. *Gloucester, [Mass.] Procter brothers,* 1873.

Procter brothers, (*compilers*). Fishermen's ballads and songs of the sea. 1 p. l. 204 pp. 16°. *Gloucester, Mass. Procter brothers,* 1874.

Proctor (Richard A.) Borderland of science. viii pp. 1 l. 438 pp. port. *London, Smith, Elder & co.* 1873.

——— Essays on astronomy. xiv pp. 1 l. 401 pp. 10 pl. 8°. *London, Longmans,* 1872.

——— The moon. xvi, 394 pp. 22 pl. 3 photos. 12°. *London, Longmans,* 1873.

——— The universe and the coming transits. xiv, 303 pp. 22 pl. 8°. *London, Longmans,* 1874.

Proffatt (John). Woman before the law. vii, 137 pp. 12°. *New York, G. P. Putnam's sons,* 1874.

Prosateurs français vivans, fragmens extraits des ouvrages de mm. Ampère, Ballanche, Balzac (etc.) 112 pp. 18°. *Paris,* 1833.

Protestant episcopal church in the United States. Debates of the house of deputies in

Protestant episcopal—continued.
general convention, New York, october, 1874. 426 pp. 8°. *Hartford, M. H. Mallory & co.* 1874.

——— Journals of general conventions, 1785–1835. Edited by W. S. Perry. 3 v. 8°. *Claremont, N. H. Claremont manufacturing co.* 1874.

——— Livre des prières publiques: avec le psautier. Nouv. éd. par rev. A. Verren. viii pp. 14 l. 464 pp. 12°. *New York, T. & J. Swords,* 1831.

——— Hymnal. Rev. ed. 502 pp. 16°. *New York, Pott, Young & co.* 1875.

——— Shorter prayer book. 361 pp. 18°. *Hartford, Conn. M. H. Mallory & co.* 1874.

Proud (Joseph). Hymns and spiritual songs, for the use of the lord's new church. 3d ed. xxiv, 347 pp. 16°. *London, E. Hodson,* 1798.

Proudhon (Pierre Joseph). Correspondance, précédeé d'une notice par J.-A. Langlois. 14 v. 8°. *Paris, A. Lacroix & cie.* 1875.

Prudhomme (Louis). Miroir historique, politique et critique de l'ancien et du nouveau Paris, [etc.] 3e éd. v. 1–5. 24°. *Paris,* 1807.
[Imperfect: v. 6 wanting; also, pl. 15, v. 4; pl. 48 and 100, v. 5].

Prutz (Robert Eduard). Aus der heimat. Neue gedichte. viii, 345 pp. 16°. *Leipzig, F. A. Brockhaus,* 1858.

——— Geschichte des deutschen journalismus. v. 1. xiv, 422 pp. 8°. *Hannover, C. F. Kius,* 1845.

Pryme (Abraham de la). Diary of A. de la Pryme, the Yorkshire antiquary. xxxii, 3 l. 348 pp. 2 pl. 1 pedigree. 8°. *Durham,* 1870.
[SURTEES society. Publications, v. 54].

Public characters, or cotemporary biography. [*anon.*] viii, 496 pp. 8°. *Baltimore, Bonsal & Niles,* 1803.

Publishers' trade list annual, jan. 16, 1873, to june 27, 1874. 8°. *New York, office of the publishers' weekly,* 1874.

Pueyrredon (Manuel Alejandro). Memoria sobre la escuela militar. 152 pp. 8°. *Buenos Aires, Bernheim y Boneó,* 1861. S.

Puliga (*Comtesse de —, pseud?*) Madame de Sévigné, her correspondents and contemporaries. 2 v. xvi, 400 pp; xii, 373 pp. port. 1 facs. 1 tab. 8°. *London, Tinsley brothers,* 1873.

Pullen (Henry William). Modern christianity, a civilized heathenism. 14th thousand.

Pullen (H. W.)—continued.
[*anon.*] 159 pp. 12°. *Salisbury,* [*Eng*]. *Brown & co.* 1875.

Pullman (James M.) Pullman's reply to Talmage. 100 pp. 8°. *New York, J. C. Baldwin & co.* 1875.

Putlitz (Gustav Heinrich Gans, *edler herr zu*). Die Alpenbraut. Novelle. 128 pp. 16°. *Berlin, C. Duncker,* 1870.

Putnam (Alfred P.) Singers and songs of the liberal faith. xxiii, 556 pp. 12°. *Boston, Roberts brothers,* 1875.

Putnam (Allen). Bible marvel workers. 238 pp. 12°. *Boston, Colby & Rich,* 1873.

Putnam (H. A.) Through trials to triumph. 277 pp. incl. 3 pl. 16°. *New York, Nelson & Phillips,* [1873].

Putnam (Rufus, *of Chillicothe, O.*) Pioneer record, and reminiscences, of the early settlers, and settlement of Fayette county, Ohio. 1 p. l. 120 pp. 8°. *Cincinnati, Applegate, Pounsford & co.* 1872.

Puton (Alfred). L'aménagement des forêts. 2e éd. xii, 218 pp. 16°. *Paris, J. Rothschild,* 1874.

Puttenham (George). The arte of english poesie. London, R. Field, 1589. xxxviii pp. 5 l. 258 pp. 7 l. 1 pl. sm. 4°. *London,* [*reprinted*] *for R. Triphook,* 1811.
[HASLEWOOD (J. *editor*). Ancient critical essays upon english poets and poësy, v. 1].

Puttrich (*Dr.* Ludwig) *and* **Geyser** (G. W. *jun.*) [Denkmale der baukunst des mittelalters in Sachsen. Mit einer enleitung von C. L. Stieglitz]. i. abth. v. 1, lfrg. 1–3. ii. abth. v. 1, lfrg. 1–8. 6 v. in 1. 4°. *Leipzig, F. A. Brockhaus,* 1835–39.

Puzzlewell (Peter, *pseud.*) Choice collection of riddles, charades, rebusses, &c. Part second. 108 pp. front. 18°. *London, for E. Newbery,* 1796.

Pycroft (Samuel). Reflections upon the nature of contentment. 4 p. l. 112 pp. 8°. *Cambridge,* [*Eng.*] *C. Crownfield,* 1714.

Pyl (Theodor, *editor*). Pommersche genealogien. 2ter band [heft 2]. 2 p. l. 81–396 pp. 2 pl. 3 tab. 8°. *Greifswald, vereinsschrift der rügisch-pommerschen abtheilung der gesellschaft für pommersche geschichte* [*etc.*] 1873. S.

Quadrado y De-Roó (*Don* Francisco de Paula). Elogio histórico del señor don Antonio de Escaño. 2 p. l. xv, 486 pp. 2 l. 8°. *Madrid, Real academia de la historia,* 1852. S.

Quaker art of courtship. [*anon.*] 120 pp. 16°. *Glasgow*, 1770.

Quaritch (Bernard). General catalogue of books. x, 1889 pp. 8°. *London*, [*G. Norman & son*], 1874.

Quatrefages de Bréau (Jean Louis Armand de). Natural history of man. From the french, by Eliza A. Youmans. 152 pp. front. 12°. *New York, D. Appleton & co.* 1875.

Quenstedt (Friedrich August). Epochen der natur. vi, 853 pp. 8°. *Tübingen, H. Laupp*, 1861.

——— Petrefactenkunde Deutschlands. 1ste abth. v. 1–3. 8°. & atlas, fol. *Tübingen, L. F. Fues & Fues's verlag*, 1846–75.

Quérard (Joseph Marie). Les supercheries littéraires dévoilées. 2e éd. par G. Brunet et P. Jannet. 3 v. 8°. *Paris, P. Daffis*, 1869–70.

Question (The) of hell. An essay in new orthodoxy. [*anon.*] 102 pp. 16°. *New Haven, Wilson & co.* 1873.

Quevedo y Villegas (Francisco de). The visions of Quevedo. From the spanish. By W. Elliot. 216 pp. 18°. *Philadelphia, H. H. Porter*, 1832.

Quillinan (Edward). Dunluce castle. Edited by sir Egerton Brydges. 3 p. l. 68 pp. 4°. *Private press of Lee priory*, 1814.

Quinby (Hosea, *d. d.*) The prison chaplaincy. 198 pp. 12°. *Concord, N. H., D. L. Guernsey*, 1873.

Quincy (Josiah). Speeches in the congress of the United States: 1805–1813. Edited by his son. xii, 412 pp. 8°. *Boston, Little, Brown & co.* 1874.

Quincy (Josiah, 3*d*). Memoir of the life of Josiah Quincy, junior: 1744–1775. By his son. 2d ed. xv, 431 pp. 2 facs. 8°. *Boston, J. Wilson & son*, 1874.

Quinlan (James Eldridge). History of Sullivan county, [N. Y.] 700 pp. 8°. *Liberty, N. Y., G. M. Beebe & W. T. Morgans*, 1873.

Quinn (P. T.) Money in the garden. A vegetable manual. 268 pp. 1 pl. 12°. *New York, tribune association*, 1871.

Quintilianus (Marcus Fabius). Quintilianus cum commento [Raph. Regii]. 202 l. unnumb. fol. [*At end*] *Venetiis per Bonetum Locatellum*, MCCCCLXCIII, [1493].

Quinton (M. A.) The nobleman of '89. From the french, by Ernest Legarde. 1 p. l. 816 pp. front. 12°. *Baltimore, Kelly, Piet & co.* 1874.

R. (H. O.) The governing race. [*anon.*] 102 pp. 8°. *Washington, T. McGill*, 1860.

R * * * (J.) Voyage à la Martinique. [*anon.*] viii, 5–196 pp. 8°. *Paris, L. Pelletier*, 1804.

R. (M.) Memoirs of the life of mr. Ambrose Barnes, of Newcastle-upon-Tyne. [*anon.*] xvi, 511 pp. 8°. *Durham*, 1867.
[SURTEES society. Publications, v. 50].

R. (S.) The new scholar. [*anon.*] 108 pp. incl. 1 pl. 12°. *Philadelphia, american s. s. union*, [1850]. s.

R. B. R.'S (The): my little neighbors. A story. [*anon.*] 104 pp. 4 pl. sq. 16°. *Boston, Walker, Wise & co.* 1860.
[ALL the children's library].

Rabaut de Saint Étienne (Jean Paul). Le vieux cevenol, anecdotes de la vie d'Ambroise Borély; par W. Jesterman [*pseud.*] Traduit de l'anglais. 115, 105 pp. 8°. *Londres*, 1784.
[MISCELLANEOUS pamphlets, v. 1008 : 3, 4].

——— *and* **Lacretelle** (Charles Joseph). Précis historique de la révolution française. 3 v. 8°. *Bruxelles, A. Wahlen*, 1817–18.

Rabener (Gottlieb Wilhelm). Satirical letters. From the german. 2 v. xxiii, 317 pp; 3 p. l. 325 pp. 16°. *London, A. Linde*, 1757.

Rademacher (Johann Gottfried). Rechtfertigung der von den gelehrten misskannten, verstandesrechten erfahrungsheillehre der alten scheidekünstigen geheimärzte. 3te ausg 2 v. xxvii, 873 pp; xiv, 809 pp. 8°. *Berlin, G. Reimer*, 1848.

Rae (William Fraser). Wilkes, Sheridan, Fox: the opposition under George the third. viii, 462 pp. 8°. *London, W. Isbister & co.* 1874.

Raffaello Sanzio da Urbino. Collection des cinquante-deux fresques du Vatican, connues sous le nom de loges de Raphaël. 2 p. l. 52 pl. 52 l. obl. fol. *Paris, Castel de Courval*, [*etc.*] 1825.

Raffei (Stefano, *s. J.*) Dissertazioni VII. da servire di supplemento all'opera dei monumenti antichi inediti di Giovanni Winckelmann. 164 pp. 17 pl. fol. *Roma, C. Mordacchini*, 1821.
[WINCKELMANN (J. J.) Monumenti antichi inediti, v. 3].

Raikes (Thomas). Personal reminiscences.
[*In* BRIC-À-BRAC series. Edited by Richard Henry Stoddard. 16°. *New York, Scribner, Armstrong & co.* 1875. v. 7, pp. 165–332, 2 ports.

Railway clearing house. *London.* Regulations. Jan. 1871. [274] pp. 8°. *London, J. Truscott & son*, 1871.

Raine (*Rev.* James, *editor*). Historia Dunelmensis scriptores tres, Gaufridus de Coldingham, Robertus de Graystanes, et Willielmus de Chambre. xlviii, 156, ccccxciii pp. 8°. *London,* 1839.

[SURTEES society. Publications, v. 9].

——— Priory of Hexham. 2 v. cxci, 220, cxci, 1 pp. 5 pl; cvi, 1 l. 203 pp. 3 pl. 8°. *Durham,* 1864–65.

[SURTEES society. Publications, v. 44, 46].

——— Testamenta Eboracensia, or wills registered at York, from MCCC. downwards. 4 v. 8°. *London,* 1836–69.

[SURTEES society. Publications, v. 4, 30, 45, 53].

——— Wills and inventories from the registry of the archdeaconry of Richmond. xxv, 294 pp. 8°. *Durham,* 1853.

[SURTEES society. Publications, v. 26].

——— Wills and inventories illustrative of the history, manners, &c. of the northern counties of England, from the eleventh century downwards. 2 v. xi, 443 pp. 1 facs; viii, 414 pp. 8°. *Durham,* 1835–60.

[SURTEES society. Publications, v. 2, 38].

Raisson (Horace Napoléon). Histoire populaire de la révolution française. 3e éd. 4 v. 16°. *Paris, B. Renault,* 1835.

Ralph and Robbie: a tale. [*anon.*] 135 pp. incl. 4 pl. 18°. *New-York, Carlton & Phillips,* 1856. s.

Ralston (Thomas N. *d. d.*) Ecce unitas: or, a plea for christian unity. By Eureka [*pseud.*] 157 pp. 16°. *Cincinnati, Hitchcock & Walden,* 1875.

Ralston (William Ralston Shedden). Russian folk-tales. 1 p. l. v–xvi, 382 pp. 12°. *London, Smith, Elder & co.* 1873.

Ram (Pierre François Xavier de). De laudibus quibus veteres lovaniensium theologi efferri possunt; oratio. xi, 164 pp. 8°. *Lovanii, Valinthout & Vandenzande,* [1847].

——— *editor.* Documents relatifs aux troubles du pays de Liége, sous les princes-évêques Louis de Bourbon et Jean de Horne. 4 p. l. xxvi, 964 pp. 3 ports. 1 pl. 4°. *Bruxelles, M. Hayez,* 1844.

[BELGIUM. *Académie royale des sciences, des lettres et des beaux-arts.* Collection des chroniques belges inédites].

Ramage (Craufurd Tait). Beautiful thoughts from french and italian authors. 2d ed. 4 p. l. xi–xx, 619 pp. 18°. *Liverpool, E. Howell,* 1875.

——— Beautiful thoughts from latin authors. 2d ed. xix, 745 pp. 16°. *Liverpool, E. Howell,* 1869.

Ramazzini (Bernardino). Treatise of the diseases of tradesmen. Now done into english. 6 p. l. 274 pp. 12°. *London, for A. Bell,* [*etc.*] 1705.

"**Rambler**" (*pseud.*) Guide to Florida. 146 pp. 8 pl. 1 map. 12°. *New York, american news co.* 1875.

Rambles (The) of the emperor Ching Tih in Këang Nan. Translated by Tkin Shen, with a preface by J. Legge, d. d. [*anon.*] 2 v. viii, 320 pp; 2 p. l. 322 pp. 8°. *London, for Longman,* [*etc.*] 1843.

Ramsay (Andrew C.) The old glaciers of Switzerland and north Wales. 3 p. l. 116 pp. 8 pl. 1 map. 16°. *London, Longmans,* 1860.

Ramsay (*Mrs.* C. H.) A summer in Spain. viii, 421 pp. front. 8°. *London, Tinsley brothers,* 1874.

Ramsay (William, *d. d.*) Spiritualism, a satanic delusion. iv, 9–122 pp. 12°. *Peace Dale, R. I., H. L. Hastings,* 1856.

Ramsey (James Beverlin, *d. d.*) The spiritual kingdom. xxxv, 518 pp. 8°. *Richmond, Va. presbyterian committee of publication,* 1873.

Rand (*Rev.* Asa). Familiar sermons. 393 pp. 12°. *Portland,* [*Me.*] *mirror office,* 1825.

Randolph (Anson Davis Fitz, *compiler*). Narrative of messrs. Moody and Sankey's labors in Scotland and Ireland. Also in England. [*anon.*] 122 pp. 8°. *New York, A. D. F. Randolph & co.* 1875.

——— Same. New ed. [*anon.*] 2 pts. in 1 v. 1 p. l. 122 pp; 2 p. l. 125 pp. 8°. *New York, A. D. F. Randolph & co.* 1875.

Rankin (Fannie W.) True to him ever. By F. W. R. [*anon.*] 290 pp. 12°. *New York, G. W. Carleton & co.* 1874.

Rankin (*Rev.* Jeremiah E.) Gems for the bridal ring. 3 p. l. xi–xvi, 142 pp. 18°. *Boston, W. J. Holland & co.* 1867.

Rankin (Melinda). Twenty years among the Mexicans. 199 pp. 12°. *Cincinnati, Chase & Hall,* 1875.

Ratzeburg (Julius Theodor Christian). Die forst-insecten. 3 pts. in 1 v. 4°. *Berlin, Nicolai,* 1839–44.

——— Forstwissenschaftliches schriftsteller-lexikon. xi, 516 pp. 4°. *Berlin, Nicolai,* 1874.

Raumer (Karl von). Palästina. 2te aufl xvi, 488 pp. 3 maps, 1 pedigree. 8°. *Leipzig, F. A. Brockhaus,* 1838.

Rawlinson (*Rev.* George). Historical illustrations of the old testament. x, 237 pp. 16°. *Boston, H. A. Young & co.* 1873.

Rawlinson (*Sir* Henry Creswicke). England and Russia in the east. xvi, 393 pp. 1 col. map. 8°. *London, J. Murray*, 1875.

Rawstorne (Lawrence). Gamonia: the art of preserving game. 208 pp. 15 col. pl. 8°. *London, for the proprietor*, 1837.

Ray (*Rev.* D. B.) *and* **Lucas** (*Rev.* J. R.) Church discussion: baptists and disciples. 505 pp. 12°. *Cincinnati, for the author*, 1873.

Ray society. Publications. 2 v. fol. & 8°. *London, R. Hardwicke*, [*etc.*] 1862–73.

CONTENTS.

CARPENTER (W. B.) PARKER (W. K.) *and* JONES (T. R.) Introduction to the study of the foraminifera. xxii, 319 pp. 21 l. 22 pl. 1862.

LUBBOCK (J.) Monograph of the collembola and thysanura. x, 276 pp. 78 pl. 1873.

Raymond (Rossiter Worthington). Brave hearts. By Robertson Gray [*pseud.*] iv, 284 pp. 6 pl. 12°. *New York, J. B. Ford & co.* 1873.

——— The man in the moon and other people. Eng. title, 2 p. l. 9–347 pp. 10 pl. sq. 12°. *New York, J. B. Ford & co.* 1875.

——— Silver and gold: an account of the mining and metallurgical industry of the United States. 2 p. l. 7–566 pp. 9 pl. 8°. *New York, J. B. Ford & co.* 1873.

Raymond (Samuel, *compiler*). Memorial volume. The record of Andover during the rebellion. viii, 232 pp. 8°. *Andover*, [*Ms.*] *W. F. Draper*, 1875. S.

Raynolds, *or* **Reynolds**, *or* **Rainolds** (William) *and* **Gifford** (William, *archbishop of Rheims*). Calvino-tvrcismvs, id est, calvinisticæ perfidiæ, cvm mahvmetana collatio, et dilvcida vtrivsqve sectae confutatio: quatuor libris explicata. 8 p. l. 1106 pp. 8 l. 16°. *Coloniæ Agrippinæ, apud A. Hierat*, 1603.

Reade (Charles). A simpleton, and the wandering heir. Household ed. 2 p. l. 296 pp. 12°. *Boston, J. R. Osgood & co.* 1873.

——— *and* **Boucicault** (Dion). Foul play. A novel. 136 pp. 6 pl. 8°. *Boston, Ticknor & Fields*, 1868.

Reade (H. L.) Success in business, or money, and how to make it. 2 p. l. ix-605 pp. eng. dedication, 8 pl. 6 incl. in pag. 1 port. 8°. *Hartford, S. S. Scranton & co.* 1875.

Reade (Winwood). African sketch book. 2 v. 1 p. l. v–x, 483 pp. 6 pl. 6 maps; 2 p. l. 529 pp. 4 pl. 6 maps. 12°. *London, Smith, Elder & co.* 1873.

Real characters, and genuine anecdotes. [*anon.*] xi, 107 pp. 18°. *London, for W. Bingley*, 1769.

[DUANE pamphlets, v. 116: 2].

Reavis (L. U.) Change of national empire; or arguments in favor of the removal of the national capital from Washington to the Mississippi valley. 170 pp. 2 maps. 8°. *St. Louis, J. F. Torrey*, 1869.

Rebello da Silva (Luiz Augusto). Corpo diplimatico portuguez; desde o seculo xvi até os nossos dias. Publicado de ordem da academia real das sciencias de Lisboa. v. 1–4. 4°. *Lisboa, typographia da academia real das sciencias*, 1862–70.

Reber (George). The Christ of Paul; or, the enigmas of christianity. 397 pp. 12°. *New York, C. P. Somerby*, 1876.

Rebouças (Antonio Pereira). Recordações da vida parlamentar. 2 v. 2 p. l. 562 pp. 1 port; 2 p. l. 580 pp. 8°. *Rio de Janeiro, typ. universal de Laemmert*, 1870.

Recherches sur le commerce. [*anon.*] 2 v. in 4. 8°. *Amsterdam, M. M. Rey*, 1778–84.

Recueil de chansons, vers, discours, règlemens, qui concernent les loges des fransmaçons & la maçonnerie. [*anon.*] 2 p. l. 124 pp. 12°. *Amsterdam, J. F. Joly*, 1752.

Recueil d'observations curieuses, sur les mœurs, les coutumes, [etc.] de différens peuples de l'Asie, de l'Afrique, & de l'Amérique. [*anon.*] 4 v. 18°. *Paris, David le jeune*, 1749.

Redden (Laura C.) Sounds from secret chambers. 197 pp. 18°. *Boston, J. R. Osgood & co.* 1873.

Redford (A. H. *d. d.*) Western cavaliers: history of the methodist episcopal church in Kentucky from 1832 to 1844. 1 p. l. 5–548 pp. 12°. *Nashville, southern methodist publishing house*, 1876.

Redford (John C.) The student's library. 2 p. l. 146 pp. 12°. *Petersburg*, [*Va.*] 1818.

Redgrave (Samuel). Dictionary of artists of the english school. vii, 473 pp. 8°. *London, Longmans*, 1874.

Reed (Isaac George, *jr.*) From heaven to New York. 1 p. l. 114 pp. 12°. *New York, Murray hill publishing co.* 1876.

[AMERICAN authors' series, no. 1].

Reed (John J.) My sabbath school scrapbook. 407 pp. 12°. *New York, M. L. Byrn*, 1874.

Reed (William W.) Head light, for locomotive engineers and machinists. 189 pp. 16°. *Paterson, N. J. "press" steam print*, 1874.

Reemelin (Charles). Treatise on politics as a science. vii, 186 pp. 8°. *Cincinnati, R. Clarke & co.* 1875.

Rees (James). Life of Edwin Forrest. 2 p. l. 21–524 pp. port. 12°. *Philadelphia, T. B. Peterson & brothers*, [1874].

Reese (John J. *m. d.*) Manual of toxicology. xvi, 13–507 pp. 8°. *Philadelphia, J. B. Lippincott & co.* 1874.

Reeve (Henry). Royal and republican France. A series of essays. 2 v. xvi pp. 421 pp; 3 p. l. 395 pp. 8°. *London, Longmans,* 1872.

Reeve (John). Spiritual hymns upon Solomon's song. 2 p. l. 210 pp. 12°. *London, for the author,* 1693.

Reference catalogue of current literature. 8°. *London, J. Whitaker*, 1874.

——— Same. 8°. *London, J. Whitaker*, 1875.

Reflections on freedom of writing. [*anon.*] 6 l. 168 pp. 8°. [*n. p.*] 1794.
[HAZARD pamphlets, v. 78].

Reformed church in America. Liturgy. 128 pp. 12°. *New York, board of publication r. c. A.* 1873.

Reformed episcopal church. Book of common prayer. xvi, 588 pp. 18°. *Philadelphia, J. A. Moore,* 1874.

——— Hymns. 223 pp. 18°. *Philadelphia, C. W. Quick*, 1874.

——— Same. 223 pp. 18°. *Philadelphia, C. W. Quick*, 1874.
[*With* PROTESTANT episcopal church. Mission service book].

——— Mission service book. 223 pp. 18°. *Philadelphia, C. W. Quick*, 1874.

Regel (Eduard). Aufzaehlung der von Radde in Baikalien, Dahurien und am Amur sowie der vom herrn von Stubendorff auf seiner reise durch Sibirien und der von Rieder, Kussmisscheff und anderen in Kamtschatka gesammelten pflanzen. i. abth. heft 1–2 in 1 v. vii, 447 pp. 9 pl. 8°. *Moscau, buchdruckerei der k. universität*, 1861–62.
[RADDE (G.) Reisen in den süden von Ostsibirien in 1855–59. Botanische abth. v. 1].

Reghellini de Schio (M.) La maçonnerie, considérée comme le résultat des réligions égyptienne, juive et chrétienne; par le f. M. R. de S. [*anon.*] 3 v. 8°. *Paris, J. P. Aillaud*, 1842.

Reginald, *dunelmensis*. Libellus de vita et miraculis s. Godrici, heremitæ de Finchale. xl, 499 pp. 8°. *London,* 1847.
[SURTEES society. Publications, v. 20].

Reginald, *dunelmensis*—continued.

——— Libellus de admirandis beati Cuthberti virtutibus quæ novellis patratæ sunt temporibus. xviii, 336 pp. 8°. *London,* [1835].
[SURTEES society. Publications, v. 1].

Register (The) and magazine of biography. 2 v. 8°. *Westminster, Nichols & sons; London, R. Hardwicke,* 1869.

Regius *or* **König** (Urban). Dialogus von der schönen predigt, Luc. 24. 4 p. l. 297 l. numb. 3 l. 4°. *Wittemberg, Joseph Klug*, 1539.

Regnault-Warin (Jean Baptiste Joseph Innocent Philadelphe). Spinalba. Aus dem französischen von Friedrich von Oertel. 2 v. 1 p. l. 294 pp; 342 pp. 18°. *Leipzig, J. G. Beygang*, 1804.

Reiche (Friedrich, *editor*). Der führer auf dem lebenswege. 3te aufl. xvi, 237 pp. 1 pl. 18°. *Berlin, C. Heymann*, [1843].

Reid (Alexander). Dictionary of the english language. 23d ed. 564 pp. 12°. *Edinburgh, Oliver & Boyd,* 1873.

Reid (H. G.) Past and present or social and religious life in the north. 2 p. l. iii, 304 pp. 4 pl. 12°. *Edinburgh, Edmonston & Douglas,* [1871].

Reid (Numa Fletcher, *d. d.*) Life, sermons and speeches. 536 pp. port. 12°. *New York, E. J. Hale & son,* 1874.

Reid (T. Wemyss). Cabinet portraits, sketches of statesmen. viii, 303 pp. 12°. *London, H. S. King & co.* 1872.

Reinhard (*Dr.* Franz Volkmar). Memoirs and confessions. From the german by O. A. Taylor. 164 pp. port. 12°. *Boston, Peirce & Parker*, 1832.

Reland (Adrien). Hadriani Relandi Palaestina, ex monumentis veteribus illustrata. Eng. title, 7 p. l. 787 [+1] pp. 41 l. 15 pl. 4°. *Norimbergae, apud P. C. Monathum*, 1716.

Relation des troubles de Gand sous Charles-quint. [*anon.*] 4 p. l. lxxviii, 778 pp. 1 l. 1 pl. 4°. *Bruxelles, M. Hayez*, 1846.
[BELGIUM. *Académie royale des sciences, des lettres et des beaux-arts.* Collection des chroniques belges inédites].

Relation fidèle et détaillée de la dernière campagne de Buonaparte. 3e éd. [*anon.*] 2 p. l. 107 pp. 8°. *Paris, J. G. Dentu*, 1815.
[NAPOLEON pamphlets, v. 21].

Rengger (Johann Rudolph). Reise nach Paraguay in den jahren 1818 bis 1826. xxxviii, 496 pp. port. 3 pl. 1 map. 8°. *Aarau, H. R. Sauerlænder*, 1835.

Rétif *or* **Restif de la Bretonne** (Nicolas Edme). Les nuits de Paris, ou le specta-

Rétif de la Bretonne (N. E.)—continued. teur nocturne. [*anon.*] 15 v. [parties]. 16°. *Londres,* 1788–90.

Reuchlin (Hermann). Pascal's leben und der geist seiner schriften. xx, 392 pp. 8°. *Stuttgart, J. G. Cotta,* 1840.

Reumont (Alfred von). The Carafas of Maddaloni: Naples under spanish dominion. From the german. xiv, 465 pp. port. 12°. *London, H. G. Bohn,* 1854.
[BOHN's standard library].

Reusch (Erhard). Capita deorvm et illvstrivm hominvm pacis belliqve artibvs clarissimorvm nec non hieroglyphica, abraxea et amvleta qvædam. 4 p. l. 226 pp. 11 l. 17 pl. fol. *Francofvrti & Lipsiæ,* 1721.

Reusens (Edmund Heinrich Joseph). Syntagma doctrinæ theologicæ Adriani sexti. lvi, 264 pp. 8°. *Lovanii, Valinthout et socii,* 1862. s.
[LOUVAIN. *Universitas catholica.* S. facultas theologica. 1861–62. no. 263].

Reuter (Fritz). Ut mine stromtid. 3 v. 8°. *Wismar,* [*etc.*] *Hinstorff,* 1865.
[OLLE kamellen, iii–v].

Revelations revealed. [*anon.*] 144 pp. 18°. *Philadelphia, W. P. Hazard,* 1862.

Review of doct. Emmons's theory of God's agency on mankind. [*anon.*] viii, 13–388 pp. 8°. *New York, J. Sayre,* 1821.

Reviglio (D. Maurizio). Elementi fisicochemici. 210 pp. 1 l. 8°. *Fossano, G. Berutti,* 1842. s.

Revue bibliographique universelle. Polybiblion. Revue bibliographique universelle. [Monthly. Feb. 1868–dec. 1874]. v. 1–12. 8°. *Paris, aux bureaux de la revue,* 1868–74.

——— Same. Partie littéraire. 2e sér. v. 1. [Jan.-june, 1875]. 8°. *Paris, aux bureaux du polybiblion,* 1875.

Revue de bibliographie analytique. Par mm. [Emmanuel] Miller et [Adolphe] Aubenas. 1840–45. 6 v. 8°. *Paris, M. Aurel, B. Duprat,* 1840–45.

Revue de France. 15 feb.–9 dec. 1871. 1e série. v. 1, 4°. v. 2, 8°. *Paris, Dubuisson & cie.* 1871.

——— Same. Jan. 1872–june, 1875. 2e–5e année. v. 1–14. 8°. *Paris, bureaux de la revue de France,* 1872–75.

——— Supplément. Actes du gouvernement révolutionnaire de Paris. 2 v. in 1. cxx pp; 77 pp. 4°. [*Paris, bureaux de la revue,* 1871].

Revue des deux mondes. Table générale, 1831–1874. 2 p. l. viii, 477 pp. 1 l. 8°.

Revue des deux mondes—continued. *Paris, bureau de la revue des deux mondes,* 1875.

Révy (J. J.) Hydraulics of great rivers. The Paraná, the Uruguay, and the La Plata estuary. xvi, 163 pp. 8 pl. fol. *London, E. & F. N. Spon,* 1874.

Rezzonico (Antonio Giuseppe, *conte* della Torre). Disqvisitiones Plinianae. 2 v. xii, 308 pp. 2 ports; xxii, 432 pp. 1 port. fol. *Parmae, excvdebant Borsii fratres,* 1763.

Rhéal (Sébastien). Les divines féeries de l'orient et du nord. 3e éd. Eng. title, 2 p. l. viii, 280 pp. 31 pl. 8°. *Paris, Fournier,* 1843.

Rheil (Marie). The farm of Muiceron. From the french by mrs. A. B. Storrs. 154 pp. 8°. *New York, catholic publication society,* 1874.
[*With* DUBOIS (C.) Madame Agnes].

Rhodes (Albert). The French at home. 2 p. l. 9–256 pp. front. sq. 18°. *New York, Dodd & Mead,* [1875].

Ribadeneira (Pedro, *s. J.*) Vita Ignatii Loiolæ. 558 pp. 16 l. 18°. *Antverpiae, ex officina C. Plantini,* 1587.

Ribeyre (Félix). Histoire de la guerre du Mexique. viii, 360 pp. port. 1 pl. 8°. *Paris, E. Pick de l'Isère,* 1863.

Ribot (Th.) English psychology. From the french. viii, 328 pp. 12°. *London, H. S. King & co.* 1873.

——— Heredity. From the french. x, 393 pp. 12°. *London, H. S. King & co.* 1875.

Rice (Harvey). Nature and culture. 202 pp. 12°. *Boston, Lee & Shepard,* 1875.

Rice (Roswell). Oration on messiah's king dom, with a variety of poetry. For 1875 1 p. l. 395–520 pp. port. 16°. *Albany, Munsell,* 1874.

Rice (Thomas Jefferson). Departure. viii, 399 pp. 1 l. 12°. *Toledo,* [*O.*] *blade printing & paper co.* 1875.

Rich (*Rev.* A. B.) Gleanings from the fields of science, art and history. 109 pp. 18°. *Boston, Mass. s.-s. society,* [1864].

Richard (Jean, *avocat*). Discours moraux sur les evangiles de tous les dimanches de l'année. v. 1. [*anon.*] 8 p. l. 533 pp. 1 l. 18°. *Paris, J. Couterot,* 1680.

Richards (*Rev.* C. H.) Will Phillips. [*anon.*] 363 pp. 2 pl. 16°. *Boston, D. Lothrop & co.* 1873.

Richards (John). Mechanical humour. vii, 150 pp. 12°. *London, G. Richards,* [1874].

Richards (John)—continued.
——— On the arrangement, care, and operation of wood-working factories and machinery. xi, 189, v pp. 16°. *New York, [printed in London], E. & F. N. Spon*, 1873.

Richards (William, *c. e.*) The gas-consumer's guide. [Am. ed. *anon.*] 148 pp. 12°. *Boston, A. Moore*, 1871.

Richardson (Abby Sage). History of our country from its discovery to the celebration of the centennial anniversary of its declaration of independence: [etc.] 600 pp. incl. 7 pl. 2 pl. 8°. *Boston, H. O. Houghton & co.* 1875.

Richardson (Benjamin Ward, *m. d.*) On alcohol. 9th ed. 3 p. l. 122 pp. 16°. *London, Macmillan & co.* 1875.

Richardson (*Mrs.* Charles *or* Constance). Memoirs of the private life and opinions of Louisa, queen of Prussia. 2d ed. xii, 331 pp. 1 port. 12°. *London, R. Bentley*, 1848.

Richardson (Jabez). Monitor of free-masonry. 192 pp. 16°. *New York, L. Fitzgerald*, [1873].

Richardson (John, *of Hull, Eng.*) Statical estimates of the materials of brewing. xxiv, 244 pp. 4 l. 1 pl. 8°. *London, for G. Robinson*, [*etc.*] 1784.
[MISCELLANEOUS pamphlets, v. 791 : 3].

Richardson (R) Communings in the sanctuary. 179 pp. 16°. *Lexington, Ky. Transylvania printing & publishing co.* 1872.

Richardson (Richard). Memoir of Josiah White. 135 pp. port. 3 pl. 12°. *Philadelphia, J. B. Lippincott & co.* 1873.

Richardson (Samuel, 1689–1761). Clarissa. Condensed by C. H. Jones. 2 p. l. 515 pp. 16°. *New York, H. Holt & co.* 1874.
[LEISURE hour series].

Richardson (Thomas, *m. a.*) *and* **Watts** (Henry, *b. a.*) Complete practical treatise on acids, alkalies, and salts. 2d ed. 3 v. 8°. *London, H. Baillière*, 1865–67.
[LIBRARY of illustrated standard scientific works, v. 14–16].

Richardson (William). Poems. 3 p. l. 111 pp. 16°. *Glasgow, R. & A. Foulis*, 1774.
[*With* BUSHE (Amyas). Socrates, a dramatic poem].

Richardson (William A.) Practical information concerning the public debt of the United States. 2d ed. 186 pp. 2 tab. 8°. *Washington, D.C., W. H. & O. H. Morrison*, 1873.

Riche (*Rev.* Auguste). The family. Translated by mrs. J. Sadlier. 147 pp. 18°. *New York, D. & J. Sadlier*, 1875.

Richmond (*Mrs.* E. J.) The fatal dower. 219 pp. 1 pl. 18°. *New York, national temperance society*, 1874.
——— Hope Raymond. 229 pp. incl. 3 pl. 16°. *New York, Nelson & Phillips*, [1875].
——— The two paths. 238 pp. incl. front. 18°. *New York, Nelson & Phillips*, [1875].
——— Zoa Rodman. 262 pp. 1 pl. 16°. *New York, national temperance society*, 1874.

Richmond (*Rev.* J. F.) Diamonds, unpolished and polished. 1 p. l. 7–249 pp. 4 pl. 16°. *New York, Nelson & Phillips*, 1873.

Rico y Sinobas (Manuel). Memoria sobre las causas meteorológico-físicas que producen las constantes sequías de Murcia y Almeira. 392 pp. 9 pl. 8°. *Madrid, imprenta á cargo de D. S. Compagni*, 1851. s.

Riddell (*Mrs.* J. H. *i. e.* Charlotte Eliza Lawson). Home, sweet home. 3 v. 12°. *London, Tinsley brothers*, 1873.

Riddle (Albert G.) Alice Brand. 384 pp. 12°. *New York, D. Appleton & co.* 1875.
——— The portrait. 378 pp. 16°. *Boston, Nichols & Hall*, 1874.

Ridgaway (Henry B. *d. d.*) Life of the rev. Alfred Cookman. 480 pp. port. 12°. *New York, Harper & brothers*, 1873.

Ridpath (John Clark). History of the United States. 479 pp. incl. front. 6 col. maps, 6 col. charts. 8°. *Cincinnati, Jones brothers & co.* [1875].

Riego (Miguel del, *editor*). Coleccion de obras poeticas españolas. 1 p. l. [275] pp. 7 l. inserted, 5 pl. 4°. *Londres, C. Wood*, 1843.

Riffault (Jean René Denis), **Vergnaud** (Amand Denis), *and* **Toussaint** (G. Alvar). Practical treatise on the manufacture of colors for painting. From the french by A. A. Fesquet. 659 pp. 8°. *Philadelphia, H. C. Baird*, 1874.

Rifle shots at past and passing events. A poem. [*anon.*] 112 pp. 8°. *Philadelphia, T. B. Peterson & brothers*, [1862].

Rigault (Ange Hippolyte). Histoire de la querelle des anciens et des modernes. 3 p. l. iv, 490 pp. 1 l. 8°. *Paris, L. Hachette & cie.* 1856.

Rigby (*Rev.* N. L.) United testimony of two hundred pedobaptist scholars to christian baptism. 115 pp. 18°. *Philadelphia, Grant, Faires & Rodgers*, 1875.

Rigg (James H. *d. d.*) The living Wesley, as he was in his youth and in his prime. 269

Rigg (James H. *d. d.*)—continued. pp. port. 12°. *New York, Nelson & Phillips*, 1874.

——— National education in its social conditions and aspects. x, 517 pp. 12°. *London, Strahan & co.* 1873.

Rigg (Jonathan). Dictionary of the Sunda language of Java. xvi, 537, v pp. 4°. *Batavia, Lange & co.* 1862.

[BATAVIAASCH genootschap van kunsten en wetenschappen. Verhandelingen, v. 29].

Riggs (Elias, *d. d.*) Suggested emendations of the authorized english version of the old testament. 130 pp. 12°. *Andover*, [*Ms.*] *W. F. Draper*, 1873.

Rights of women. [*anon.*] 104 pp. 12°. *London, Trübner & co.* 1875.

Ŕig-veda-sanhitá, the sacred hymns of the brahmans; with the commentary of Sâyaṇacharya. Edited by F. Max Müller. v. 5–6. Published under the patronage of her majesty's secretary of state for India in council. 4°. *London, W. H. Allen & co.* 1872–74. s.

Riley (H. H.) The Puddleford papers. 1 p. l. 5–386 pp. 4 pl. 12°. *Boston, Lee & Shepard*, 1875.

Rinaldo (Ottavio). Memorie istoriche della città di Capua. 2 v. 8 p. l. 472 pp. 2 l. 1 tab; xx, 387 pp. 1 tab. sm. 4°. *Napoli, G. di Simone*, 1753–55.

Ripon (*Collegiate church of ss. Peter and Wilfrid*). Acts of chapter. 1452–1506. 2 p. l. viii, 411 pp. front. 8°. *Durham, for the society*, 1875.

[SURTEES society. Publications, v. 64].

Risdon (Tristram). Chorographical description or survey of the county of Devon. New ed. xvi, xxxvii, 442 pp. 8°. *London, Rees & Curtis*, 1811.

Ritchie (*Mrs.* Anna Cora Mowatt). Italian life and legends. 299 pp. incl. 1 pl. 6 pl. 12°. *New York, Carleton*, 1870.

Ritchie (Leitch). Windsor castle and its environs. 2d ed. Eng. title, viii, 312 pp. 14 pl. 1 plan. 8°. *London, H. G. Bohn*, 1848.

Ritter (Frederic Louis). History of music. 2d series. 320 pp. 16°. *Boston, O. Ditson & co.* 1874.

Rivail (Léon Hippolyte Denisart). Experimental spiritism. Book on mediums. By Allan Kardec [*pseud.*] Translated by Emma A. Wood. 1 p. l. 458 pp. 12°. *Boston, Colby & Rich*, 1874.

Rivers (Pearl, *pseud.*) Lyrics. By Pearl Rivers [*pseud.*] 131 pp. 12°. *Philadelphia, J. B. Lippincott & co.* 1873.

Rivers (William J.) Chapter in the early history of South Carolina. 110 pp. 8°. *Charleston, S. C., Walker, Evans & Cogswell*, 1874.

Rivet (André). Antidotum contra pestem & malorum omnium ἀλέξημα. 4 p. l. 227 pp. 1 l. 64 pp. 1 l. 18°. *Arnhemii, ex officina J. Biesii*, 1638.

[*With* RIVET (A.) Suspiria pœnitentis afflicti].

——— Suspiria pœnitentis afflicti. Ed. 2a. 8 p. l. 298 pp. 1 l. 18°. *Arnhemii, ex officina J. Biesii*, 1638.

Robbins (E. Y.) The soldier's foe; pocket treatise on health and hygiene. 109 pp. 24°. *Cincinnati, Moore, Wilstach, Keys & co.* 1861.

Robbins (*Mrs.* S. S.) Brentford parsonage. [*anon.*] 455 pp. front. 16°. *New York, R. Carter & brothers*, 1876.

——— Doors outward. [*anon.*] 404 pp. 1 pl. 16°. *New York, R. Carter & brothers*, 1875.

——— Mabel Hazard's thoroughfare. [*anon.*] 334 pp. 1 pl. 16°. *New York, R. Carter & brothers*, 1874.

Röbert (Charles E.) Nashville and her trade for 1870. 1 p. l. 480 pp. 8°. *Nashville, Roberts & Purvis*, 1870.

Roberts (Joseph). Hand-book of artillery, for the service of the United States. 10th ed. 336 pp. 8 tab. sq. 18°. *New York, D. Van Nostrand*, 1875.

Roberts (J. P.) Dizionario italiano-inglese e inglese-italiano. 2 v. in 1. 2 p. l. xxxii, (1), 525 pp; 1 p. l. xvi, (1), 455 pp. 12°. *Londra, Trübner e c.* 1873.

Roberts (Louis A.) *and* **Stebbens** (George S. *m. d.*) High art: pictures from the poets from the brush of L. A. Roberts, and sport from the quill of Ikabod Izax [*pseud.*] 61 l. inc. 28 pl. 8°. *Springfield, Mass. D. E. Fisk & co.* [1873].

——— Same. 128 pp. incl. 59 pl. 8°. *Springfield, Mass. D. E. Fisk & co.* [1875].

Roberts (Maggie). Shadows and silver sprays. By Eiggam Strebor [*anagram*]. viii, 123 pp. 5 pl. 12°. *New York, J. F. Trow & son*, 1875.

Roberts (Robert). Twelve lectures on the teaching of the bible in relation to the faiths of christendom. 5th ed. 370 pp. 12°. *Birmingham*, [*Eng.*] *the author*, 1869.

Roberts (Sarah). My childhood. 144 pp. 2 pl. 18°. *New York, general prot. episc. s. s. union*, 1852.

Robertson (James Burton). Lectures on the life, writings, and times, of Edmund Burke. xliii, 407 pp. 12°. *London, J. Philp*, [1868].

Robertson (*Rev.* Norvell). Church-members' hand-book of theology. 1 p. l. 323 pp. 12°. *Memphis, for the author*, 1874.

Robertson (Théodore). Dictionnaire idéologique: recueil des mots, des phrases, des idiotismes et des proverbes de la langue française. 2 p. l. xxviii, 480 pp. 8°. *Paris, A. Derache*, 1859.

Robertson (*Rev.* William). Journal of a clergyman during a visit to the Peninsula, 1841. 2 p. l. ii, v, 401 pp. 6 pl. 8°. *Edinburgh, W. Blackwood & sons*, 1845.

Robertson (William, *d. d.*) History of the reign of Charles the fifth. With an account of the emperor's life after his abdication. By W. H. Prescott. New ed. 3 v. 12°. *Philadelphia, J. B. Lippincott & co.* 1875.

Robin (*L'abbé* Claude). Recherches sur les initiations anciennes et modernes. Par m. l'abbé R.... [*anon.*] 116 pp. 16°. *Dresde, frères Walther*, 1781.

——— Same. Ueber die einweihungen in alten und neuern zeiten. Vom abt R.... [*anon.*] 128 pp. 16°. *Memphis & Braunschweig*, [*Petersburg, Logan*], 5782, [1782].

Robins (E. W.) Cause and effect: as applied to mathematics. vii, 104 pp. incl. 1 pl. 18°. *Vermillion, D. T., W. L. H. Owens*, 1874.

Robinson (Charles). New South Wales. 1 p. l. iii, 110, 4 pp. 12°. *Sydney, T. Richards*, 1873. s.

Robinson (*Rev.* Charles John). The mansions of Herefordshire and their memories. 1 p. l. viii, 318, 2 pp. 1 pl. 4°. *London, Longmans*, 1872.

Robinson (Charles S. *d. d.*) The memorial pulpit.—Church life: sermons. viii, 318 pp. 12°. *New York, A. S. Barnes & co.* 1873.

——— Same. v. 2. Bethel and Penuel: twenty-six sermons. viii, 317 pp. 12°. *New York, A. S. Barnes & co.* [1874].

——— *compiler.* Psalms and hymns, and spiritual songs. Manual of worship for the church of Christ. 515 pp. 8°. *New York, A. S. Barnes & co.* [1875].

——— Same. [New ed.] 3 p. l. 290 pp. sq. 16°. *New York, A. S. Barnes & co.* [1875].

——— Songs for the sanctuary. vi, 86 pp. 4 l. 482 pp. 8°. *New York, A. S. Barnes & co.* 1874.

Robinson (Frederic). Seven gray pilgrims. [*anon.*] 2 p. l. 292 pp. 12°. *Boston, A. Williams & co.* 1874.

Robinson (Frederick W.) Her face was her fortune. 3 v. 12°. *London, Hurst & Blackett*, 1873.

——— Little Kate Kirby. 3 v. 12°. *London, Hurst & Blackett*, 1873.

Robinson (*Rev.* John B.) Infidelity answered by the father-God and his family. 268 pp. 2 pl. 12°. *Boston, J. P. Magee*, 1875.

Robinson (*Dr.* J. H.) Cepherine; or the secret cabal. 114 pp. incl. 9 pl. 8°. *New York, F. A. Brady*, [1862].

Robinson (Thomas, *d. d.*) Suggestive commentary on st. Paul's epistles to the Romans. 2 v. xi, 520 pp; 3 p. l. 379 pp. 12°. *New York, D. Appleton & co.* 1873.

[VAN DOREN (W. H.) A suggestive commentary on the new testament].

Robinson (W.) Mushroom culture. x, 172 pp. front. 12°. *London, F. Warne & co.* 1870.

Roby (Henry John). Grammar of the latin language. Part 2:—book 4. Syntax. Also prepositions &c. cxii, 555 pp. 16°. *London, Macmillan & co.* 1874.

Roca (Ramon de la). Cartas á D. F. M. sobre la variacion de nuestro sistema gubernativo. Escritas en el año de 1813 por Maron Dáurico [*pseud.*] 6 p. l. 133 pp. 18°. *México, oficina de Benavente*, 1815.

Rocafuerte (Vicente). Bosquejo ligerisimo de la revolucion de Mégico. [*anon.*] xi, 300 pp. 3 l. 24°. *Philadelphia, Teracrouef & Naroajeb*, [*i. e. Habana, Rocafuerte & Bejarano*], 1822.

[*With* ROCAFUERTE (V.) Memoria politico-instructiva, enviada desde Filadelfia, 1821].

——— Ideas necesarias á todo pueblo Americano independiente, que quiera ser libre. [*anon.*] 227 pp. 24°. *Puebla, impresas en Filadelfia, P. de la Rosa*, 1823.

[*With* ROCAFUERTE (V.) Memoria politico-instructiva, enviada desde Filadelfia, 1821].

——— Memoria politico-instructiva, enviada desde Filadelfia en agosto de 1821, á los gefes independentes del Anáhuac. [*anon.*] 126 pp. 2 l. 24°. *Filadelfia, J. F. Hurtel*, 1821.

Rochefort (Charles de). Natuurlyke en zedelyke historie van d' eylanden, de voor-eylanden van Amerika. Vertaalt in nederduytsch door H. Dullaart. Eng. title, 19 p. l. 475 [+ 1] pp. 5 l. sm. 4°. *Rotterdam, A. Leers*, 1662.

Rocquancourt (Jean Thomas). Cours élémentaire d'art et d'histoire militaires. 3e éd. 3 v. 8°. *Bruxelles, L. Hauman & ce.* 1836-40.

Rodenbough (Theophilus Francis, *compiler*). From everglade to cañon with the second dragoons, (U. S. cavalry). 1836–1875. 561 pp. 6 col. pl. 2 pl. 2 maps. 8°. *New York, D. Van Nostrand,* 1875.

Rodriguez (José Ignacio). Vida de don José de la Luz y Caballero. xii, 327 pp. port. 12°. *Nueva York, imprenta de "el mundo nueva—la America ilustrada",* 1874.

Rodriguez Velasco (Francisco de Paula). Biografia del doctor d. José A. Rodriguez Aldea. 265 pp. 12°. *Santiago, imprenta del ferrocarril,* 1862.

Roe (—). Military memoir of colonel John Birch; with commentary by the rev. John Webb. Edited by the rev. T. W. Webb. 2 p. l. xv, 240 pp. 4°. [*Westminster, J. B. Nichols & sons*], 1873.

[CAMDEN society. Publications, new series, no. vii].

Roe (*Rev.* Edward Payson). From jest to earnest. 548 pp. 12°. *New York, Dodd & Mead,* [1875].

——— Opening a chestnut burr. 2 p. l. 7–561 pp. 12°. *New York, Dodd & Mead,* [1874].

——— What can she do? xii, 509 pp. 12°. *New York, Dodd & Mead,* [1873].

Roger (P.) La noblesse de France aux croisades. 399 pp. 13 pl. 8°. *Paris, Derache,* 1845.

Rogers (Augustus C. *editor*). Sketches of representative men, north and south. 612 pp. 68 ports. 4°. *New York, Atlantic publishing co.* 1872.

——— United States diplomatic and consular service. Our representatives abroad. xii, 469 pp. 40 ports. 4°. *New York, Atlantic publishing co.* 1874.

Rogers (*Rev.* Charles, *editor*). Three scottish reformers, Alexander Cunningham, Henry Balnaves and John Davidson, of Prestonpans. iv, 168 pp. port. 8°. *London, english reprint society,* 1874.

Rogers (Ebenezer P. *d. d.*) Everything in Christ. 125 pp. 12°. *New York, board of publication of the reformed protestant dutch church,* 1858.

——— The precious things of st. Peter. 237 pp. 18°. *New York, A. D. F. Randolph & co.* [1874].

Rogers (Henry). Life and character of John Howe. New ed. xii, 454 pp. port. 8°. *London, religious tract society,* 1863.

Rogers (*Mrs.* Hester Ann). Short account of the experience of Mrs. H. A. Rogers.

Rogers (*Mrs.* Hester Ann)—continued. 256 pp. 1°. *New York, for the methodist connection in the U. S.* 1811.

Rogers (James Edwin Thorold). Cobden and modern political opinion. Essays. xix, 382 pp. 8°. *London, Macmillan & co.* 1873.

Rogers (*Rev.* John). Διαπολιτεία. A christian concertation with mr. Prim, mr. Baxter, mr. Harrington, for the true cause of the commonvvealth. 6 p. l. 124 pp. 4°. *London, L. Chapman,* 1659.

Roget (Peter Mark). Thesaurus of english words and phrases. Edited by Barnas Sears, d. d. New am. from last Lond. ed. 567 pp. 8°. *Boston, Gould & Lincoln,* 1873.

Rohault de Fleury (Georges) La Toscane au moyen âge, lettres sur l'architecture civile et militaire en 1400. 2 v. viii, 461 pp. 1 plan; 2 p. l. 484 pp. 8°. *Paris, veuve A. Morel & cie.* 1874.

Rohde (Levin Joergen). The universal sea language; a complete code of signals. From the danish, by H. E. Dahlerup. 2d ed. xxviii, 174 pp. 8°. *London, A. W. Webster,* 1835. s.

Rohlfs (Gerhard). Adventures in Morocco. viii, 371 pp. incl. port. 1 map. 8°. *London, S. Low, Marston, Low & Searle,* 1874.

Rohner (Beat). Die wunder der göttlichen liebe. Eng. title, 1 p. l. 526 pp. 2 pl. 24°. *Einsiedeln,* [*etc.*] *gebr. K. & N. Benziger,* 1874.

Rolleston (George, *m. d.*) Forms of animal life. clxviii, 268 pp. 12 pl. 8°. *Oxford, Clarendon press,* 1870.

Rollins (John R.) Records of families of the name of Rawlins or Rollins, in the United States. xix, 348 pp. port. 8°. *Lawrence, Mass. G. S. Merrill & Crocker,* 1874.

Rolt (Richard). New dictionary of trade and commerce. 2 p. l. 450 l. 1 pl. fol. *London, for T. Osborne & J. Shipton,* [*etc.*] 1756.

Roman catholic church. Recueil des allocutions consistoriales encycliques et autres lettres apostoliques des souverains pontifes Clément XII. Benoît XIV. Pie VI. Pie VII. Léon XII. Grégoire XVI. et Pie IX. citées dans l'encyclique et le syllabus du 8 décembre 1864. Suivi du concordat de 1801 et de divers autres documents. [Latin et français]. 4 p. l. 576 pp. 8°. *Paris, A. Le Clere & cie.* 1865.

——— Rituale romanum Pauli V. pont. max. jussu editum et a Benedicto XIV. auctum et

Roman catholic church—continued. castigatum. Ed. Ratisbonensis prima. viii, 312, 154, 16 pp. 8°. *Ratisbonae, F. Pustet*, 1872.

——— Same. 546 pp. 12°. *Baltimori, J. Murphy*, 1873.

Romancero (Le) du Pays Basques. [*anon.*] 137 pp. 16°. *Paris, F. Didot frères, fils & cie.* 1859.

Romans (Les) de la table ronde, mis en nouveau langage et accompagnés de recherches sur l'origine et le caractère de ces grandes compositions par Paulin Paris. v. 1–3. 16°. *Paris, L. Techener*, 1868–72.

CONTENTS.

ARTUS (*Le roi*). Livre iv. v. 2.
JOSEPH d'Arimathie. Livre i. v. 1.
LANCELOT du lac. v. 3.
MERLIN. Livre iii. v. 2.
SAINT-GRAAL (Le). Livre ii. v. 1.

Römer (Christian). Amalie, oder: treu bis in den tod. 156 pp. 18°. *Regensburg*, [*etc.*] *F. Pustet*, 1874.

Roosa (Daniel B. St. John, *m. d.*) Practical treatise on the diseases of the ear. 535 pp. 1 pl. 8°. *New York, W. Wood & co.* 1873.

Roosevelt (Robert B.) Progressive petticoats. 316 pp. 12°. *New York, G. W. Carleton & co.* 1874.

Roper (Stephen). Catechism of high pressure or non-condensing steam engines. 218 pp. incl. 12 pl. 18°. *Philadelphia, Claxton, Remsen & Haffelfinger*, 1874.

——— Hand-book of land and marine engines. 598 pp. incl. 25 pl. & 2 ports. 16°. *Philadelphia, Claxton, Remsen & Haffelfinger*, 1875.

——— Hand-book of the locomotive. 324 pp. incl. 1 port. 18°. *Philadelphia, Claxton, Remsen & Haffelfinger*, 1874.

Rosa (Gabriele). Storia generale delle storie. 2da ed. xvi, 520 pp. 12°. *Milano, U Hoepli*, 1873. s.

Roscher (Wilhelm). Principes d'économie politique. Traduit sur la deuxième éd. par m. Wolowski. 2 v. cxii, 375 pp; 2 p. l. 480 pp. 8°. *Paris, Guillaumin & cie.* 1857.

Roscoe (Henry Enfield). Spectrum analysis. 3d ed. xx, 484 pp. 10 pl. 8°. *London, Macmillan & co.* 1873.

Roscoe (Thomas). The tourist in Italy. 2 v. 4 p. l. 271 pp. 26 pl; 4 p. l. 287 pp. 26 pl. 12°. *London, R. Jennings*, 1831–32.
[LANDSCAPE annuals for 1831 and 1832].

Rose (A. C.) Widow's souvenir. 128 pp. 18°. *New York, Lane & Scott*, 1852.

Rose (Stewart). Ignatius Loyola and the early jesuits. 3 p. l. 518 pp. port. 8°. *London, Longmans*, 1870.

Rose (*Rev.* William). History of Joseph. A poem. 6 p. l. 179 pp. 6 pl. 8°. *London, J. Knapton*, 1712.

Rose (The) culturist. [*anon.*] 125 pp. 18°. *New York, W. H. Starr*, 1846.

Rosell (Cayetano). Historia del combate naval de Lepanto. 1 p. l. 260 pp. 1 map. 1 pl. 8°. *Madrid, Real academia de la historia*, 1853. s.

Rosenthal (L.) Catalog der Hebraica und Judaica aus der L. Rosenthal'schen bibliothek. Bearbeitet von M. Roest. 2 v. viii, 910 pp; 1 p. l. 911–1218 pp. 1 p. l. 502 pp. 1 l. 8°. *Amsterdam*, [*J. Clausen*], 1875. s.

Rosina: a novel. [*anon.*] 5 v. 16°. *London, for W. Lane*, 1793.

Rosini (Giovanni). La monaca di Monza. 12a ed. 2 v. 2 p. l. iv, 298 pp. 1 l; 2 p. l. 306 pp. 1 l. 16°. *Parigi, Baudry*, 1846.

Ross (James, *m. d.*) On protoplasm. 2 p. l. 125 pp. 16°. *London, R. Hardwicke*, 1874.

Rosseeuw-Saint-Hilaire (Eugène François Achille). Études religieuses et littéraires. xii, 335 pp. 12°. *Paris, Dentu*, 1863.

Rossel (Louis Nathaniel). Posthumous papers. From the french. ix, 294 pp. 12°. *London, Chapman & Hall*, 1872.

Rossetti (Maria Francesca). Shadow of Dante: an essay towards studying himself, his world and his pilgrimage. 5 p. l. 296 pp. 4 pl. port. 12°. *London, Rivingtons*, 1871.

Rossi (Domenico de). Romanæ magnitvdinis monvmenta qvæ vrbem illam velvt redivivam exhibent. 138 pl. incl. title. obl. fol. *Romæ*, 1699.

Rossi (*Rev.* Gaudentius). The christian trumpet. Compiled by Pellegrino [*pseud.*] 2d thousand. xvi, 272 pp. 12°. *Boston, P. Donahoe*, 1873.

Rossini (Pietro). Il mercurio errante delle grandezze di Roma. 7ma ed. 2 v. in 1. 4 p. l. 192 pp; 1 p. l. 146 pp. 4 l. 18°. *Roma, a spese di F. Amidei*, 1750.

Rothschild (C.) *and* **Rothschild** (A. de). History and literature of the Israelites. 2 v. 2 p. l. viii, 640 pp. map; viii, 332 pp. 12°. *London, Longmans*, 1870.

Round lake camp-meeting, New York. Fraternal camp-meeting sermons, preached by ministers of the various branches of methodism, july, 1874. 498 pp. front. 12°. *New York, Nelson & Phillips*, 1875.

Rouquette (Adrien). Les savanes. Poésies américaines. Par Adrien * * * [*anon.*] 3 p. l. 306 pp. 16°. *Paris, J. Labitte,* 1841.

Rousseau (Jean Jacques). Complete dictionary of music. From the french. By W. Waring. 2d ed. 1 p. l. 468 pp. 8°. *London, for J. Murray,* 1779.

——— Dissertation on political economy: [also], a treatise on the social compact. 1st am. ed. 72, 214 pp. 1 l. 1 pl. 16°. *Albany, Barber & Southwick,* 1797.

——— Lettres inédites à Marc Michel Rey, publiées par J. Bosscha. xxii, 319 pp. 2 facs. 8°. *Amsterdam, F. Muller,* 1858.

Roussel (Pierre Joseph Alexis). Histoire secrète du tribunal révolutionnaire. Par m. de Proussinale [*pseud.*] 2 v. 2 p. l. iv, 336 pp; 2 p. l. 326 pp. 8°. *Paris, Lerouge,* 1815.

Rousselet (Louis). India and its native princes. Travels in central India and in Bombay and Bengal. Edited by lieut.-col. Buckle. xviii, 579 pp. 113 pl. 5 maps. 4°. *London, Chapman & Hall,* 1876.

Rousselin (Alexandre Charles). Vie de Lazare Hoche. 2e éd. 3 p. l. 1–335, 356–372, 353–493 pp. 2 plans, 1 map. port; 2 p. l. ii, 490 pp. 8°. *Paris, C. F. Buisson, an* VI [1798].

Roustan (Honoré Joseph Fortuné). Les subtilités de la librairie parisienne. La bande noire et la révision. [etc. *anon.*] viii, 288 pp. 8°. *Versailles, Roustan,* 1864–65.

Routledge (Edmund). Modern speaker and reciter. vi, 571 pp. 1 pl. 16°. *London, G. Routledge & sons,* [187–].

Rowe (Horace). The years of youth: poems. 151 pp. sq. 16°. *Philadelphia, J. B. Lippincott & co.* 1873.

Rowlands (Cadwalader). Henry M. Stanley. The story of his life. 1 p. l. v–184 pp. 8 pl. 3 facs. 8°. *London, J. C. Hotten,* [1873].

Rowley (Hugh, *editor*). More puniana. viii, 303 pp. sq. 12°. *London, Chatto & Windus,* 1875.

Roy (Just Jean Étienne). Captain Rougemont. [*anon.*] From the french [of Théophile Ménard, *pseud.*] by mrs. Mary Huntington. 180 pp. incl. front. 8°. *New-York, Benziger brothers,* 1875.

——— Lucille. By Stéphanie Ory [*anagram.*] From the french. 140 pp. 1 pl. 18°. *New York, D. & J. Sadlier & co.* 1873.

——— Priest of Auvrigny. [*anon.*] From the french [of Just Girard, *pseud.*] by mrs. Mary

Roy (Just Jean Étienne)—continued.
C. Monroe. 181 pp. incl. front. 8°. *New-York, Benziger brothers,* 1875.

——— Recluse of Rambouillet. By Stéphanie Ory [*anagram.*] From the french. 138 pp. 1 pl. 18°. *New York, D. & J. Sadlier & co.* 1873.

Roy (Rammohun). Bengalee grammar. 2 p. l. 140 pp. 8°. *Calcutta, unitarian press,* 1826.

Rucker (James M.) The sphere and cylinder. viii, 100 pp. 8°. *Lynchburg,* [*Va.*] *Bryant & Browne,* 1873.

Rudge (*Rev.* Thomas). History of the county of Gloucester; to 1803. 2 v. xviii, 402 pp. xvii–cxx pp. 1 map; 2 p. l. 409 pp. 1 pl. 8°. *Gloucester, for the author, by G. F. Harris,* 1803.

Rudolphy (John). Pharmaceutical directory of all the crude drugs now in general use. 2d ed. 114 pp. 8°. *New-York, W. Radde,* 1872.

Ruehle (Hugo). Pulmonary consumption and acute miliary tuberculosis.

[*In* ZIEMSSEN (H. W. von, *editor*). Cyclopædia of the practice of medicine. 8°. *New York, W. Wood & co.* 1875. v. 5, pp. 471–630].

Rufus (William, *of Charleston, S. C.*) Rufiana. 144 pp. 12°. *New-York, G. & C. Carvill,* 1826.

Ruggles (C. Lorain). Perils of scout-life. 399 pp. 8 pl. 8°. *New York, M. L. Byrn,* 1873.

Ruhkopf (Julie) *and* **Moritz** (August). Nannie's jewel-case. From the german by Trauermantel [*pseud.*] 3 p. l. 223 pp. 3 col. pl. 16°. *Boston, Crosby, Nichols & co.* 1858.

Rümker (*Dr.* Carl). Handbuch der schiffahrts-kunde, mit seemans- tafeln [etc.] 6t aufl. xii, 372, xii, 546 pp. 5 maps & charts, 2 pl. 8°. *Hamburg, Perthes-Besser & Mauke,* 1857. S.

Rump: or an exact collection of the choycest poems and songs relating to the late times. 1639 to 1661. London, for H. Brome, & H. Marsh, 1662. 2 v. Eng. title, 3 p. l. 376 pp. front; 1 p. l. 200 pp. 16°. [*London reprinted,* 1874] ?

Rumsey (Henry W.) Essays and papers on some fallacies of statistics concerning life and death, health and disease. xv, 322 pp. 8°. *London, Smith, Elder & co.* 1875.

Runkel (*Col.* William M.) Wontus, or the corps of observation. 363 pp. 14 pl. 12°. *Philadelphia, J. B. Lippincott & co.* 1874.

Rupp (I. Daniel). Brief biographic memorial of Joh. Jonas Rupp, and genealogical family register of his descendants, from 1756 to 1875. 1 p. l. 292 pp. port. 12°. *West Philadelphia, L. W. Robinson,* [1875].

—— Collection of upwards of thirty thousand names of german, swiss, dutch, french and other immigrants in Pennsylvania from 1727 to 1776. 2d ed. with german translation. x, 495 pp. 8 pl. on 4 l. 12°. *Philadelphia, I. Kohler,* 1876.

Ruprecht (Rudolph). Bibliotheca chemica et pharmaceutica. 1858 bis ende 1870. 1 p. l. 125 pp. 8°. *Göttingen, Vandenhoeck & Ruprecht,* 1872.

Ruskin (John). Art culture: a hand-book of art technicalities and criticisms, selected from the works of J. Ruskin, by rev. W. H Platt. xxvii, 485 pp. 22 pl. 12°. *New York, J. Wiley & son,* 1873.

—— Frondes agrestes. Readings in "Modern painters," chosen by the younger lady of the Thwaite, Coniston. [*anon.*] vii, 184 pp. 16°. *Sunnyside, Orpington, Kent,* [*London printed*], *G. Allen,* 1875.

Rusling (James F.) Across America. 503 pp. 8 pl. 1 map. 8°. *New York, Sheldon & co.* 1874.

Russell (Addison P.) Library notes. 1 p. l. 401 pp. 12°. *New York, Hurd & Houghton,* 1875.

Russell (*Rev.* Frank). What Jesus says. 381, xii pp. 12°. [*Kalamazoo, Mich.*] *Kalamazoo publishing co.* 1875.

Russell (*Count* Henry). Pau and the Pyrenees. viii, 79 pp. 16°. *London, Longmans,* 1871.

Russell (John, *earl*). Essays on the rise and progress of the christian religion. xvi, 348 pp. 8°. *London, Longmans,* 1873.

—— Recollections and suggestions, 1813–1873. x, 475 pp. 8°. *London, Longmans,* 1875.

Russell (William, *ll. d.*) History of America. 2 v. Title, 596 pp. 6 pl. 3 maps; 630 pp. 2 pl. 7 maps. 4°. *London, Walker,* 1800.

Russell (W. Clark). Book of authors. Collection of criticisms, ana, môts, personal descriptions, etc. wholly referring to english men of letters. iv, 516 pp. front. containing 7 ports. 16°. *London, F. Warne & co.* [1871].

Rüstow (W.) The war for the Rhine frontier, 1870. From the german by John Layland Needham. 3 v. 8°. *Edinburgh, W. Blackwood & sons,* 1871–72.

Rutebeuf. Oeuvres complètes. Recueillies par Achille Jubinal. 2 v. xxxii, 480 pp; 2 p. l. 522 pp. 2 l. 8°. *Paris, É. Pannier,* 1839.

Rutherford (John). The troubadours. x, 356 pp. 12°. *London, Smith, Elder & co.* 1873.

Rutherford (*Rev.* Samuel). Joshua redivivus: or, three hundred and fifty-two religious letters. 9th ed. xxxii, 526 pp. 8°. *Glasgow, J. Bryce,* 1765.
[Imperfect: wanting pp. 107–110].

Ruttley (J. H. *m. d.*) Nature's secrets and the secrets of woman revealed. v. 1. 1 p. l. ii, 210 pp. port. 12°. *San Francisco, J. H. Ruttley,* 1875.

Ryan (Richard). Dramatic table talk. 3 v. 16°. *London, J. Knight & H. Lacey,* 1825–30.

S. (R. R.) Daily praise and prayer. [*anon.*] 3 p. l. 370 pp. 12°. *Boston, american unitarian association,* 1876.

S. (W. H.) Gleanings, historical and literary. [*anon.*] xxiv, 400 pp. 12°. *London, Simpkin & Marshall,* 1837.

Sabin (*Rev.* Elijah R.) Journey from Egypt to Jerusalem. 204 pp. 16°. *Boston, E. Olliver,* 1811.

Saboureux de la Bonnetrie (Charles François *or* Charles Louis). Traduction d'anciens ouvrages latins relatifs à l'agriculture et à la médecine vétérinaire. 6 v. 8°. *Paris, P. F. Didot je.* 1771–75.

CONTENTS.

1. CATO (Marcus Porcius). L'économie rurale. v. 1.
2. COLUMELLA (Lucius Junius Moderatus). L'économie rurale. v. 3–4.
3. PALLADIUS (Rutilius Taurus Æmilianus). L'économie rurale. v. 5.
4. VARRO (Marcus Terentius). L'économie rurale. v. 2.
5. VEGETIUS (Flavius Renatus). L'art vétérinaire, ou l'hippiatrique. v. 6.

Sacchi (Archimede). Architettura pratica. Le abitazioni. xix, 743 pp. 6 l. 8°. *Milano, U. Hoepli,* 1874. s.

Sacheverell (William). Account of the Isle of Man, with a voyage to I-Columb-Kill. Edited by the rev. J. G. Cumming. xvi, 204 pp. 8°. *Douglas,* [*Isle of Man*], 1859.
[MANX society. Publications, v. 1].

Sachs (Hans). Ernstliche trauerspiele, liebliche schauspiele, seltsame fastnachtsspiele, [etc.] Herausgegeben von dr. J. G. Büsching. 3 v. 12°. *Nürnberg, J. L. Schrag,* 1816–24.

Sachs (Julius). Text-book of botany morphological and physiological. Translated by Alfred W. Bennett [and] W. T. Thiselton Dyer. xii, 858 pp. 8°. *Oxford,* [*Eng.*] *Clarendon press,* 1875.

Sackville-West (Reginald Windsor, *baron Buckhurst*). Historical notices of the parish of Withyham in Sussex. [*anon.*] viii, 100 pp. 14 pl. 4°. *London, J. R. Smith*, 1857.

Sad (The) mistake. [*anon.*] 179 pp. 18°. *Philadelphia, am. s.-s. union*, [1854].

Sadeler (Rafael), **Sadeler** (Johann) *and* **Collaert** (Adrian). [Les pères du désert. 5 v. in 1. obl. 4°. *Paris, G. Iollain*, 1654–56].

Saguí (Francisco). Los últimos cuatro años de la dominacion española en el Rio de la Plata desde 1806 hasta 1810. xiv, 324 pp. 4 ports. 4 pl. 8°. *Buenos Aires, imprenta americana*, 1874. s.

Saigey (Émile). Unity of natural phenomena. From the french. By T. F. Moses. 2 p. l. 7–255 pp. 12°. *Boston, Estes & Lauriat*, 1873.

[SCIENCE for the people, no. 1].

St. Bridget's manual. [*anon.*] Eng. title, vi, 3–731 pp. port. 6 col. pl. 24°. *New York, T. Kelly*, [1874].

Saint Cecilia. A modern tale. [*anon.*] 3 v. 12°. *London, S. Low, Marston, Low & Searle*, 1872.

St. Clair (Henry). United States criminal calendar. 356 pp. 13 pl. 5 incl. in pag. 12°. *Boston, C. Gaylord*, 1835.

St. Dominique (*Countess* C. * * de, *pseud.*) Animal magnetism (mesmerism) and artificial somnambulism. x, 234 pp. 12°. *London, for the authoress*, 1874.

Saint-Félix (Jules de). Avventure di Cagliostro. 128 pp. 1 l. 1 pl. 16°. *Milano, fratelli Ferrario*, [*about* 1840].

St. George (Richard, *Norroy king of arms*). Visitation of the county palatine of Lancaster, in 1613. Edited by rev. F. R. Raines. 2 p. l. xx, 142 pp. sm. 4°. [*Manchester*], 1871.

[CHETHAM society remains, v. 82].

Saint-Germain (Bertrand de, *m. d.*) Des manifestations de la vie et de l'intelligence à l'aide de l'organisation. vii, 421 pp. 8°. *Paris, L. Leclerc*, 1848.

Saintine (Joseph Xavier Boniface). Myths of the Rhine. From the french by prof. M. Schele de Vere. Illustrated by Gustave Doré. 1 p. l. xii, 423 pp. incl. 14 pl. 8°. *New York, Scribner, Armstrong & co.* 1875.

St. John (*Mrs.* Eugenia). Bella; or, the cradle of liberty. 351 pp. 12°. *Boston, N. D. Berry*, 1874.

St. Louis. *Mercantile library.* Classified catalogue. xiii, 762 pp. 8°. *St. Louis, for the association*, 1874.

Saint-Marc Girardin (Marc Girardin, *called*). La Fontaine et les fabulistes. 2 v. viii, 448 pp; 2 p. l. 484 pp. 8°. *Paris, M. Lévy frères*, 1867.

Saint Marcel (*Chevalier* de, *pseud.*) Commerce de lettres entre mlle. Julie du * * *, et le chevalier de S. Marcel [*pseud.*] 8 p. l. 227 pp. 1 l. 1 pl. 16°. *Amsterdam, J. Dusauzet*, 1723.

Saint-Martin (Louis Claude de). Man: his true nature and ministry. From the french. By E. B. Penny. xiii, 499 pp. 12°. *London, W. Allan & co.* 1864.

St. Onge (L. N.) Alphabet yakama, contenant les prières, les cantiques et le catéchisme dans la même langue. 1 p. l. 104 pp. 1 photog. port. 18°. *Montréal, imprimé à la Providence*, 1872. s.

St. Paul library association. Catalogue, 1873. 134 pp. 8°. *St. Paul, Ramaley, Chaney & co.* 1873.

Saint-Réal (César Vischard de). Conspiracy of the Spaniards against the state of Venice. Out of french. [*anon.*] 111 pp. 16°. *London, J. D. for R. Chiswell*, 1675.

——— Same. [New ed.] xiv, 127 pp. 16°. *London, J. Carpenter & son*, 1823.

Sainte-Beuve (Charles Augustin). Lettres à la princesse. 3e éd. 2 p. l. iii, 367 pp. 16°. *Paris, M. Lévy frères*, 1873.

——— Notice sur m. Littré. 2 p. l. 107 pp. 8°. *Paris, L. Hachette & cie.* 1863.

——— Nouveaux lundis. v. 13. 12°. *Paris, M. Lévy frères*, 1872.

——— Tableau historique et critique de la poésie française et du théâtre français au XVIe siècle. Nouv. éd. 2 p. l. 500 pp. 16°. *Paris, Charpentier & cie.* 1869.

Sainte-Marthe (Gaucher II. *called* Scévole I. de). Scævolæ Sammarthani opera. 3 p. l. 318 pp. 1 port; 4 p. l. 278 pp. 5 l. 12°. *Lvtetiae, apud P. Dvrand*, 1616.

——— Pædotrophia; or, the art of nursing and rearing children. From the latin of Scevole de St. Marthe. With notes. By H. W. Tytler. cxci, 224 pp. 8°. *London, for the author*, 1797.

Sainte-Palaye (Jean Baptiste de la Curne de). Dictionnaire historique de l'ancien langage françois. v. 1. A—Ao. 4°. *Niort, L. Favre*, 1875.

Saissy (Jean Antoine, *m. d.*) Essay on the diseases of the internal ear. From the french, by N. R. Smith. 228 pp. 1 pl. 8°. *Baltimore, Hatch & Dunning*, 1829.

Salem. *North church and society.* First centenary of the north church and society in Salem. July 19, 1872. vi, 222 pp. 7 ports. 8°. *Salem, for the society,* 1873. s.

Sallengre (Albert Henri, *editor*). Pièces échapées du feu. [*anon.*] 8 p. l. 292 pp. 2 l. 16°. *Plaisance,* [*Holland*], 1717.

CONTENTS.

Polichinelle demandant une place dans l'académie. Comédie. [*anon.* Par Nicolas de Malezieu].
Remarques sur l'Angleterre faites en 1713. Par S. G. [*anon.* Par Dubois de Saint-Gelais?]
Histoire de Léonice et de Mendosa, par m. de S. [*anon.*]
Des lettres, des contes et poésies diverses.

Salter (Joseph). The asiatic in England; sketches of sixteen years' work among orientals. 3 p. l. ix, 303 pp. 6 pl. 1 facs. 12°. *London, Seeley, Jackson & Halliday,* 1873.

Saltus (Francis S.) Honey and gall. Poems. 231 pp. 12°. *Philadelphia, J. B. Lippincott & co.* 1873.

Salvolini (Francesco). Campagne de Rhamsès-le-grand (Sésostris), contre les Schèta et leurs alliés. 124 pp. 2 pl. 8°. *Paris, ve. Dondey-Dupré,* 1835.

Salyards (Joseph). Idathea. A poem. 308 pp. 16°. *New Market, Va. Henkel, Calvert & co.* 1875.

Salzmann (Christian Gotthilf). What God does is well done. From the german. By miss E. T. Disosway. 304 pp. 16°. *Cincinnati, Hitchcock & Walden,* 1875.

Sâma-veda. Sâmavedârcikam: die hymnen des Sâma-veda, übersetzt von Theodor Benfey. 2 v. 2 p. l. 256 pp; lxvi, 307 pp. 8°. *Leipzig, F. A. Brockhaus,* 1848.

Sampson (Henry). History of advertising. x, 616 pp. 5 pl. incl. 1 col. 11 facs. 12°. *London, Chatto & Windus,* 1874.

Sanchez (Tomas, *s. J.*) Patris Thomæ Sanchez de sancto matrimonii sacramento disputationum, tomi tres. Posterior & accuratior editio. 3 v. in 1. fol. *Venetiis, apud B. Milochum,* 1672.

Sandeau (Léonard Silvain Jules). Fernand. Vaillance. Richard. 6e éd. rév. 2 p. l. 328 pp. 16°. *Paris, Charpentier,* 1868.

Sanders (Robert). New book of martyrs. By Henry Southwell, ll. d. [*pseud.*] 466 pp. 4 l. 42 pl. fol. *London, J. Cooke,* [*about* 1775].

Sandham (Alfred). Ville-Marie, or, sketches of Montreal. xiii, 393 pp. 18 pl. 1 plan. 8°. *Montreal, G. Bishop & co.* 1870.

Sandys (George). Relation of a iourney begun 1610. Fovre bookes. 2d ed. Eng. title, 1 p. l. 309 pp. incl. 1 pl. 1 map. fol. *London, for W. Barren,* 1621.

Sané (Alexandre Marie). Tableau des peuples des quatre parties du monde. 2 v. 2 p. l. 486 pp; 2 p. l. 506 pp. 8°. *Paris, Carteret,* 1801.

Sanford (*Mrs.* D. P.) Frisk and his flock. 184 pp. 32 pl. sm. 4°. *New York, E. P. Dutton & co.* 1875.

Sanford (*Mrs.* E. B.) The christian mother. 275 pp. 16°. *Hartford, Conn. M. H. Mallory & co.* 1871.

——— Names, and their meanings. 168 pp. 8 pl. 18°. *New York, E. P. Dutton & co.* 1874.

Sanford (*Mrs.* Lucy E.) History of two lives. 132 pp. 1 pl. 18°. *New York, national temperance soc. & publ. house,* 1875.

San Francisco (*City of*). *Mercantile library.* Catalogue. viii, 958 pp. 8°. *San Francisco, Francis & Valentine,* 1874. s.

Sangiovanni (Giosuè) *and* **Guarini** (Giovanni). De' rimedii incompatibili ossia de' farmachi che mescolati fra lora si scompongono. v. 1. [A–Fal.] xii, 216 pp. 16°. *Napoli, dai torchi del tramateur,* 1835. s.

Saratoga illustrated. [*anon.*] 1 p. l. 118 pp. 15 pl. 2 maps, 1 port. 18°. *New York, Taintor brothers & co.* 1875.

Sardo (Joaquin). Relacion de la portentosa imagen de n. sr. Jesucristo crucificado aparecida en una de las cuevas de s. Miguel de Chalma, hoy real convento y santuario de este nombre [etc.] 7 p. l. 386 pp. 1 pl. sm. 4°. [*México*], *Arizpe,* 1810.

Sardou (Victorien). Ragabas. Comédie. 27e éd. 2 p. l. 210 pp. 16°. *Paris, M. Lévy frères,* 1872.

Sargent (Eli Densmore, *m. d.*) The immaterial elements. 100 pp. 12°. *Chicago, author,* 1873.

Sargent (Epes). School manual of english etymology. 264 pp. 16°. *Philadelphia, J. H. Butler & co.* [1873].

[NEW american series].

——— Velasco; a tragedy. 115 pp. 16°. *Boston, Eastburn's press,* 1837.

[MISCELLANEOUS pamphlets, v. 270: 2].

Sargent (Nathan). Public men and events from 1817 to 1853. 2 v. 349 pp; 407 pp. 8°. *Philadelphia, J. B. Lippincott & co.* 1875.

Sarmiento (Domingo Faustino). Argyropolis, ou la capitale des états confédérés du Rio de la Plata. Traduit par J.-M.-B. Le-

Sarmiento (D. F.)—continued.
noir. 2e éd. 3 p. l. viii, 150 pp. 1 map. 8°. *Paris, E. Belin,* 1851.

Sasnett (*Rev.* William J.) Progress: considered with particular reference to the methodist episcopal church, south. 320 pp. 12°. *Nashville, Tenn. southern methodist publishing house,* 1856.

Saunders (Frederick). A festival of song: choice selections from the greatest poets of the english language. 1 p. l. vii–xvi, 376 pp. 6 pl. 1 port. 8°. *St. Louis,* [*etc.*] *F. A. Hutchinson & co.* [1874].

——— Same. xv, 376 pp. 10 ports. 10 facs. 8°. *St. Louis, Scammell & co.* 1876.

Saussure (Henri de). Études sur les insectes orthoptères, et les myriapodes. 5 p. l. 516 pp. 8 pl. 8 l. 4°. *Paris, imprimerie impériale & nationale,* 1870–74. s.

[FRANCE. *Ministère de l'instruction publique.* Mission scientifique au Mexique et dans l'Amérique centrale. 6e partie].

——— Mémoires pour servir à l'histoire naturelle du Mexique, des Antilles et des État-Unis. 4me mémoire. v. 2. 1 ptie. 4°. *Genève et Bâle, H. Georg,* 1871. s.

CONTENTS.

v. 2, pt. 1. Synopsis des mantides américaines. 1 p. l. 186 pp. 2 pl. 1871.

Sautier (Heinrich). Apologie der ersten frage: Warum soll ich ein freymäurer werden? Von Erich Servati [*pseud.*] xvi, 158 pp. 16°. *Basel, J. J. Flick,* 1787.

——— Bruchstücke zur geschichte der deutschen freymäurerey, gesammelt von Erich Servati [*pseud.*] 336, 367–525, xiv pp. 1 pl. 16°. *Basel, J. J. Flick,* 1787.

——— Warum soll ich ein freymäurer werden? von Erich Servati [*pseud.*] xiv, 256 pp. 1 l. 1 tab. 18°. *Basel, J. J. Flick,* 1786.

Sauzade (John S.) Cecil's tryst. [*anon.*] 3 v. 12°. *London, Tinsley brothers,* 1872.

——— Mark Gildersleeve. 379 pp. 12°. *New York, G. W. Carleton & co.* 1873.

Sauzay (A.) Marvels of glass-making in all ages. xx, 272 pp. 12°. *London, S. Low, son, & Marston,* [1869].

Savage (Minot Judson). Christianity the science of manhood. x, 187 pp. 12°. *Boston, Noyes, Holmes & co.* 1873.

Savérien (Alexandre). Histoire des philosophes anciens. 5 v. 16°. *Paris, Bleuet,* 1773.

——— Histoire des philosophes modernes. 2e éd. 7 v. 16°. *Paris, Brunet,* 1761–69.

Savornin (M. — *de*) Sentimens d'un homme de guerre sur le nouveau systême du chevalier de Folard. Par monsieur D * * *. [*anon.*] 7 p. l. 168 pp. 1 pl. 4°. *Paris, Briasson,* 1733.

Saward (Frederick E.) The coal trade. 2 p. l. 104 pp. 8°. *New York,* 1875.

Saxe (John Godfrey). Leisure-day rhymes. 268 pp. 1 l. 16°. *Boston, J. R. Osgood & co.* 1875.

——— Poems. Complete ed. xii, 308 pp. sq. 18°. *Boston, J. R. Osgood & co.* 1873.

Sayce (Archibald Henry). Assyrian grammar. xvi, 188 pp. 12°. *London, Trübner & co.* 1872.

Sayer & Noble. Guide to the N. Y. Midland r. r. 162 pp. 1 map. 18°. *Deckertown, Sayer & Noble,* 1873.

Sayre (Lewis A. *m. d.*) Practical manual of the treatment of club-foot. 2d ed. 117 pp. 12°. *New York, D. Appleton & co.* 1874.

Scadding (Henry, *d. d.*) Toronto of old. xii, 594 pp. 2 ports. 8°. *Toronto, Adam, Stevenson & co.* 1873.

Scaliger (Giulio Cesare). Exotericarvm exercitationvm liber xv. de subtilitate, ad H. Cardanvm. 8 p. l. 1129 [+1] pp. 46 l. 16°. *Francoforti, apud Andreæ Wecheli heredes, C. Marnium, & J. Aubrium,* 1592.

——— Poemata sacra. Quibus adiecimus A. Frvsii epigrammata in haereticos correcta & aucta. 2 v. in 1. 156 pp; 115 [+1] pp. 18°. *Coloniæ, apud B. Gualtheri,* 1600.

Scammon (Charles M.) Marine mammals of the north-western coast of North America, described and illustrated. 320, vi pp. 27 pl. 4°. *San Francisco, J. H. Carmany & co.* 1874.

Scarborough (William). Collection of chinese proverbs translated. viii, xxxvi, 478 pp. 12°. *Shanghai, american presbyterian mission press,* 1875.

Schack (Adolf Friedrich von). Stimmen vom Ganges. Eine sammlung indischer sagen. 2 p. l. 266 pp. 18°. *Berlin, W. Hertz,* 1857.

Scharf (J. Thomas). Chronicles of Baltimore. viii, 356 pp. 8°. *Baltimore, Turnbull brothers,* 1874.

Schattenrisse edler teutscher frauenzimmer. [*anon.*] 2 v. 4 p. l. 402 pp. 11 pl; xii, 340 pp. 7 pl. 16°. *Halle, J. C. Hendel,* 1784–85.

Schauplatz des gegenwærtigen kriegs. Von 1756–1763. 10 theile in 1 v. 9 titles, 160 pl. 6 l. indexes. obl. fol. *Nürnberg, auf kosten der Raspischen buchhandlung,* [17—].

Note.—24 small charts inserted.

Scheel (Heinrich Othon von). Treatise on artillery. From the french. 154 pp. 8°. *Philadelphia*, 1800.

[WOLCOTT pamphlets, v. 37. Wanting title and an atlas].

Schell (I. Herman). Die einheit des seelenlebens aus den principien der Aristotelischen philosophie entwickelt. xiii, 269 pp. 1 l. 8°. *Freiburg im Breisgau, F. J. Scheuble*, 1873. s.

Schellen (H.) Spectrum analysis in its application to terrestrial substances, and the physical constitution of the heavenly bodies. From the 2d german ed. by Jane and Caroline Lassell. Edited by W. Huggins. xxvi, 662 pp. 13 pl. 8°. *London, Longmans*, 1872.

Scherer (Theodor). Life of Guendaline, princess Borghese. From the german, by A. Francis Hewit. 119 pp. 18°. *New York, P. O'Shea*, 1851.

Schieffelin (Samuel B.) Milk for babes, and children's bread. viii, 69, 180 pp. 18°. *New York, board of publication of the reformed church in America*, 1874. s.

Schiller (Johann Christoph Friedrich von). Cabal and love, a tragedy. From the german. 3 p. l. 119 pp. 1 l. 8°. *London, for T. Boosey*, 1795.

[MISCELLANEOUS pamphlets, v. 674 : 2].

——— Essays, æsthetical and philosophical. Newly translated. 2 p. l. 435 pp. 12°. *London, G. Bell & sons*, 1875.

[BOHN'S standard library].

——— Die Piccolomini. Edited by J. M. Hart. lxxi, 178 pp. 1 col. map. 18°. *New York, G. P. Putnam's sons*, 1875.

[GERMAN classics for american students, v. 2].

Schleicher (Auguste). Les langues de l'Europe moderne. Traduit par H. Ewerbeck. viii, 319 pp. 8°. *Paris, Ladrange*, 1852.

Schleiden (*Dr.* Matthias Jakob) *and* **Schmid** (*Dr.* Ernst Erhard). Encyclopädie der gesammten theoretischen naturwissenschaften in ihrer anwendung auf die landwirthschaft. v. 1-2. 8°. *Braunschweig, F. Vieweg & sohn*, 1850. s.

CONTENTS.

v. 1. SCHMID (*Dr.* E. E.) Physik, anorganische chemie und mineralogie. xviii, 520 pp. 1 l.
v. 2. SCHMID (*Dr.* E. E.) Organische chemie, meteorologie, geognosie, bodenkunde und düngerlehre. xii pp. 1 l. 557 pp.

Schleiermacher (Friedrich Ernst Daniel). Sämmtliche werke. 1ste abth. band 1-8, 11-13. 2te abth. band 1-4, 7-10. 3te abth. band 1-9. 28 v. 8°. *Berlin, G. Reimer*, 1835-62.

Schleiermacher (F. E. D.)—continued.

——— Monologen. 3te ausg. 3 p. l. 126 pp. 18°. *Berlin, G. Reimer*, 1822.

Schliemann (*Dr.* Heinrich). Troy and its remains. Translated [from the german]. Edited by P. Smith. lv, 392 pp. 1 map, 2 plans, 52 pl. 8°. *London, J. Murray*, 1875.

Schmarda (Ludwig Karl). Zoologie. 2 v. x, 372 pp; xii, 584 pp. 8°. *Wien, W. Braumüller*, 1871-72.

Schmid (*Dr.* Ernst Erhard). Organische chemie, meteorologie, geognosie, bodenkunde und düngerlehre. Für landwirthe. xii pp. 1 l. 557 pp. 8°. *Braunschweig, F. Vieweg & sohn*, 1850. s.

[SCHLEIDEN (*Dr.* M. J.) *and* SCHMID (*Dr.* E. E.) Encyclopädie der gesammten theoretischen naturwissenschaften, v. 2].

——— Physik, anorganische chemie und mineralogie. Für landwirthe. xviii, 520 pp. 1 l. 8°. *Braunschweig, F. Vieweg & sohn*, 1850. s.

[SCHLEIDEN (*Dr.* M. J.) *and* SCHMID (*Dr.* E. E.) Encyclopädie der gesammten theoretischen naturwissenschaften, v. 1].

Schmid (Heinrich). The doctrinal theology of the evangelical lutheran church, exhibited, and verified from the original sources. From the 5th ed. by Charles A. Hay and rev. Henry E. Jacobs. 1 p. l. 7-696, 3-14 pp. 8°. *Philadelphia, lutheran publication society*, 1876.

Schmidl (*Dr.* A. Adolf). Das Bihar-gebirge. (Mit einer geodätischen abhandlung, von J. Wastler). xvi, 442 pp. 3 col. pl. 3 pl. 1 tab. 1 map. 8°. *Wien, Förster & Bartelmus*, 1863. s.

Schmidt (Julian). Neue bilder aus dem geistigen leben unserer zeit. 2 p. l. 402 pp. 8°. *Leipzig, Duncker & Humblot*, 1873.

Schmidt (Oscar). Doctrine of descent and Darwinism. 2d ed. 1 p. l. vii, 334 pp. 12°. *London, H. S. King & co.* 1875.

[INTERNATIONAL scientific series, v. 12].

Schneck (Benjamin S. *d. d.*) Mercersburg theology inconsistent with protestant and reformed doctrine. xii, 9-188 pp. 12°. *Philadelphia, J. B. Lippincott & co.* 1874.

——— *editor.* Die deutsche kanzel: eine sammlung auserlesener predigten der neuesten zeit. 2te aufl. 572 pp. 8°. *Chambersburg, druckerei der hochdeutsch-reformirten kirche*, 1845.

Schneider (L.) Krieg der triple-allianz (Brasilien, Argentinische conföderation und Uruguay) gegen Paraguay. 3 v. 8°. *Berlin, B. Behr's buchhandlung*, 1872-75.

Schneider (Louis). Die preussischen orden, ehrenzeichen u. auszeichnungen. Geschichtlich, bildlich, statistisch. 6 v. 4°. *Berlin, A. Duncker*, 1857-72. s.

CONTENTS.

Der rothe adler-orden. 3 eng. titles, viii, 139, 106 pp. 22 col. pl. 1857-68.
Das buch vom schwarzen adler-orden. 1 p. l. [205] pp. 8 col. pl. 1870.
Der königliche kronen-orden. 1 p. l. [116] pp. 2 col. pl. 1871.
Das buch vom eisernen kreuze. 1 p. l. [211] pp. 2 pl. (1 col.) 1872.
Das verdienst-kreuz für frauen und jungfrauen. Eng. title, 12, 39 pp. 1 col. pl. 1872.
Die kriegsdenkmünze für den feldzug 1870-71. 1 p. l. 18 pp. 1 l. 1 pl. 1872.

Schoettgen (Christian). [Horae hebraicae et talmudicae]. 2 v. 13 p. l. 1280 pp. 18 l. port; 16 p. l. 996 pp. 30 l. 4°. *Dresdae et Lipsiae, apvd F. Hekel*, 1733-42.

CONTENTS.

v. 1. Horae hebraicae et talmudicae in universum novum testamentum. 1733.
v. 2. Horae hebraicae et talmudicae in theologiam Jvdaeorvm dogmaticam antiqvam et orthodoxam de Messia impensae. 1742.

Schöll (A.) Carl-August-büchlein. iv, 170 pp. 1 l. 16°. *Weimar, H. Böhlau*, 1857.

Schönaich (Christoph Otto, *freiherr* von). Arminius: or, Germania freed. From the 3d ed. of the original, written by baron Cronzeck [*pseud.*] With preface by Gottsched. 2 v. liv, 192 pp; 216 pp. 16°. *London, for T. Becket & P. A. de Hondt*, 1764.

Schopenhauer (Arthur). Schopenhauer-lexikon. Bearbeitet von Julius Frauenstädt. 2 v. in 1. ix, 382 pp; 2 l. 508 pp. 8°. *Leipzig, F. A. Brockhaus*, 1871.

Schreiber (Egid). Herpetologia europaea. xvii, 639 pp. 8°. *Braunschweig, F. Vieweg u. sohn*, 1875. s.

Schroeckh (Johann Matthias). Historia religionis et ecclesiae christianae. Ed. 6a. xviii, 333 pp. 8°. *Berolini, apvd A. Mylivm*, 1818.

Schroeder (Carl). Diseases of the female sexual organs. Translated by Edward Schauffler, m. d. Leonard Wheeler, m. d. William M. Richardson, m. d. viii, 575 pp. 8°. *New York, W. Wood & co.* 1875.

[ZIEMSSEN (*Dr.* Hugo Wilhelm von, *editor*). Cyclopædia of the practice of medicine. 8°. *New York, W. Wood & co.* 1875. v. 10].

Schroeder (Leopold). Ueber die formelle unterscheidung der redetheile im griechischen und lateinischen. x, 562 pp. 3 pl. 8°. *Leipzig, K. F. Köhler*, 1874. s.

Schubert (F. C.) Handbuch der landwirthschaftlichen baukunde. viii, 212 pp. 12°. *Berlin, G. Bosselmann*, 1860. s.

Schubert (Friedrich Wilhelm von). Reise durch Schweden, Norwegen, Lappland, Finnland und Ingermannland in 1817, 1818 und 1820. 3 v. 8°. *Leipzig, J. C. Hinrichsche buchhandlung*, 1823-24.

Schubert (Gotthilf Heinrich von). Reise in das morgenland in 1836 und 1837. Neue aufl. 3 v. 8°. *Erlangen, J. J. Palm & E. Enke*, 1840.

Schück (Johann Joseph). Sammlung auserlesener abhandlungen über den gebrauch des kalten wassers. v. 1. viii, 206 pp. 1 l. 16°. *Wien, J. B. Wallishausser*, 1849. s.

Schuckers (J. W.) Brief account of the finances and paper money of the revolutionary war. 2 p. l. 128 pp. 8°. *Philadelphia, J. Campbell & son*, 1874.

——— Life and public services of Salmon Portland Chase. xv, 669 pp. 4 pl. 2 facs. port. 8°. *New York, D. Appleton & co.* 1874.

Schultes (Henry). Dissertation on the public fisheries of Great Britain. 1 p. l. 101 pp. 8°. *London, for the author*, 1813.

[MISCELLANEOUS pamphlets, v. 837: 5].

Schultz (Johann Carl). Danzig und seine bauwerke. 3 v. obl. folio. *Danzig, autor*, [1855]. s.

Schulze (Ernst). Gothisches glossar. 2 p. l. xxii, 456 pp. 4°. *Magdeburg, E. Baensch*, [1848].

Schulze-Delitzsch (Hermann). Die genossenschaften in einzelnen gewerbszweigen. xii, 408 pp. 12°. *Leipzig, E. Keil*, 1873.

——— Jahresbericht für 1872 über die auf selbsthilfe gegründeten deutschen erwerbs- und wirthschaftsgenossenschaften. 1 p. l. 112 pp. fol. *Leipzig, J. Klinkhardt*, 1873.

Schumann (F.) Formulas and tables for architects and engineers in calculating the strains and capacity of structures in iron and wood. viii, 246 pp. 18°. *Washington, W. Choate & co.* 1873.

Schuster (Ignaz, *d. d.*) Abridged history of the old and new testaments. From the german. 103 pp. incl. front. sq. 18°. *St. Louis, B. Herder*, 1874.

——— Illustrated bible history of the old and new testaments. From the 58th german ed. xiv, 274 pp. incl. front. 16°. *St. Louis, B. Herder*, 1875.

Schwab (Gustav). Schwaben. 2te aufl. 200 pp. 30 pl. 8°. *Leipzig, C. A. Haendel's verlag*, [1847].

[MALERISCHE (Das) und romantische Deutschland, v. 1].

Schwabe (H.) Königliche haupt- und residenzstadt Berlin. Resultate der volkszählung und volksbeschreibung vom 1. dec. 1871. viii pp. 1 l. xii, 178 pp. 1 l. 1*-286* pp. 1 map, 10 pl. 8°. *Berlin, in comm. L. Simion*, 1874.

Schwartz (Marie Sophie). Gerda. From the swedish by S. Borg and M. A. Brown. 344 pp. 12°. *Philadelphia, Porter & Coates*, [1874].

——— Little Karin. From the swedish by S. Borg and M. A. Brown. 293 pp. port. 8°. *Hartford, R. W. Bliss & co.* 1873.

——— Son of the organ-grinder. From the swedish by S. Borg and M. A. Brown. 1 p. l. 353 pp. 1 pl. 12°. *Philadelphia, Porter & Coates*, [1873].

Schweinfurth (*Dr.* Georg). The heart of Africa. Translated by Ellen E. Frewer. 2 v. xvi, 559 pp. 15 pl. 1 map; x, 521 pp. 11 pl. 1 map. 8°. *London, Low, Marston, Low & Searle*, 1873.

Scitivaux (Roger de). Voyage en Orient. 2 p. l. xi, 121 pp. 2 l. 25 pl. fol. *Paris, vve. A. Morel & cie.* 1873.

Scotland (*Free church of*). Memoirs of mrs. W. Veitch, mr. T. Hog of Kiltearn, mr. H. Erskine, and mr. J. Carstairs. Issued by the committee of the general assembly, for the publication of the works of scottish reformers and divines. 1 p. l. v, 152 pp. 12°. *Edinburgh, for the assembly's committee*, 1846.

Scott (Alfred T.) The happy life. 132 pp. 24°. *Philadelphia, tract depository*, 1859.

——— The need of the church. vii, 13-105 pp. 18°. *Philadelphia, Perkinpine & Higgins*, 1860.

Scott (Clement W.) Round about the islands. xii, 355 pp. incl. front. 8°. *London, Tinsley brothers*, 1874.

Scott (*Mrs.* Hugh Roy). Rome as it is. 291 pp. 8 pl. 12°. *Philadelphia, J. B. Lippincott & co.* 1874.

Scott (Jane A.) Letters on christian holiness. xvi, 13-173 pp. 18°. *Philadelphia, tract depository*, 1859.

Scott (John, *d. d.*) Pulpit echoes. 312 pp. 12°. *Cincinnati, C. A. Scott*, 1873.

Scott (*Sir* Walter). Ivanhoe. Traduit par A. Dumas. 2 v. 2 p. l. 305 pp; 2 p. l. 287 pp. 16°. *Paris, M. Lévy frères*, 1862.

[DUMAS (A. D.) Oeuvres complètes. 16°. *Paris*, 1862. v. 147-148].

Scott (William B.) Albert Durer; his life and works. xvi, 324 pp. 3 ports. 3 pl. 8°. *London, Longmans*, 1869.

Scratchley (Arthur). Industrial investment and emigration. 2d ed. xxiv, 309 pp. 8°. *London, J. W. Parker*, 1851.

Scribble (Timothy, *pseud.*) Norfolk poetical miscellany. 2 v. xvi, 416 pp; 2 p. l. 427 pp. 8°. *London, author*, 1744.

Scudder (Horace Elisha). Doings of the Bodley family in town and country, [etc. *anon.*] 250 pp. incl. 19 pl. sm. 4°. *New York, Hurd & Houghton*, 1875.

Scudder (John M. *m. d.*) On the reproductive organs. 393 pp. 6 pl. 8°. *Cincinnati, Wilstach, Baldwin & co.* 1874.

——— Specific diagnosis. iv, 9-387 pp. 12°. *Cincinnati, Wilstach, Baldwin & co.* 1874.

Scudery (Georges de). Curia politiae: or, the apologies of severall princes: justifying to the world their most eminent actions. Now faithfully render'd into english. Eng. title, 8 p. l. 190 pp. 1 l. 7 pl. fol. *London, H. Moseley*, 1654.

Searle (Arthur). Outlines of astronomy. xvi, 415 pp. 13 pl. 12°. *Boston, Ginn brothers*, 1874.

Sebald (Hugo). Zeichnen-schule. 268 pp. 1 l. 8°. *Philadelphia*, [*Collins*], 1874.

Sébillotte (L. A.) Bassins de radoub de Marseille. 2 p. l. 204 pp. 1 pl. 4°. *Marseille, M. Olive*, 1873. S.

[MÉDITERRANÉE (*Compagnie des travaux publics de la*). Publications].

Secret warfare of freemasonry against church and state. From the german. [*anon.*] lxiii, 288 pp. 12°. *London, Burns, Oates & co.* 1875.

Seddall (*Rev.* Henry). Malta: past and present. xii, 355 pp. 1 map. 8°. *London, Chapman & Hall*, 1870.

Seeley (John Robert). Roman imperialism, and other lectures and essays. 335 pp. 16°. *Boston, Roberts brothers*, 1871.

Seelye (*Rev.* Julius H.) Christian missions. 207 pp. 12°. *New York, Dodd & Mead*, [1875].

Segar (*Sir* William). Honor, military, and ciuill, contained in foure bookes. 256 pp. incl. 2 ports. 7 ports. fol. *London, R. Barker*, 1602.

Segneri (Paolo, *s. J.*) Lenten sermons. v. 2. 1 p. l. 314 pp. 16°. *New York, catholic publication society*, 1874.

Segni (Bernardo). Storie fiorentine dall'anno 1527 al 1555. 3 v. 8°. *Milano, società tipografica de' classici italiani*, 1805.

Seguier (Frederick Peter). Critical and commercial dictionary of the works of painters between 1250 and 1850. xvi, 241 pp. 8°. *London, Longmans,* 1870.

Ségur (Louis Gaston, *monseigneur* de). The wonders of Lourdes. From the french by Anna T. Sadlier. 1 p. l. 7–249 pp. 18°. *New York, D. & J. Sadlier & co.* 1874.

Ségur (Philippe Paul, *comte* de). Histoire et mémoires. 7 v. 8°. *Paris, F. Didot frères, fils & cie.* 1873.

——— Mélanges. 2 p. l. 528 pp. 8°. *Paris, F. Didot frères, fils & cie.* 1873.

Seidl (Johann Gabriel). Tyrol und Steyermark. 2te aufl. 392 pp. 60 pl. 8°. *Leipzig, C. A. Haendel,* 1847.

[MALERISCHE (Das) und romantische Deutschland, v. 10].

Seidlitz (Georg). Die Darwin'sche theorie. xxxviii, 230 pp. 1 tab. 8°. *Dorpat, C. Mattiesen,* 1871.

Seiler (Emma). The voice in speaking. From the german by W. H. Furness, d. d. 164 pp. 12°. *Philadelphia, J. B. Lippincott & co.* 1875.

Seisl (Martin, *s. J.*) Die geleise des kirchenjahres und der wege Gottes in der gründung seines reiches auf erden. iv, 356 pp. 8°. *Regensburg,* [*etc.*] *F. Pustet,* 1875.

Seiss (Joseph A.) *and* **Engelmann** (Charles Pilling). Church song. Part first. Musical responses, chants, etc. of the evangelical lutheran church. 2d ed. Part second. Metrical tunes, [etc.] 2 pts. in 1 v. 75 pp; 148 pp. 12°. *Philadelphia, lutheran book store,* 1875.

Select collection of favourite scotish ballads. [*anon.*] 2 v. in 1. 1 p. l. 92 pp. 6 l. 1 pl; 1 p. l. 96 pp. 1 pl. 16°. *Perth, R. Morison, jun. for R. Morison & son,* 1790.

Select sentences: designed as a moral guide-book for young Israelites. [*anon.*] 200 pp. 32°. *Philadelphia,* 5614, [1854]. s.

Sells (*Mrs.* S. E.) Amy's temptation. 300 pp. 6 pl. 16°. *Cincinnati, Hitchcock & Walden,* 1875.

Semple (Barbara). Guildford-street stories. v. 1–3. 18°. *New York, Nelson & Phillips,* [1875].

CONTENTS.

v. 1. Jeanie Nesbit and Jack's theft. 68 pp.
2. Malcolm Dykes, and four other stories. 73 pp.
3. Very disobliging, and eight other stories. 141 pp.

Senft (Ferdinand). Synopsis der mineralogie und geognosie. 1ste abth: mineralogie. xxxvi, 932 pp. 8°. *Hannover, Halm,* 1875. s.

[LEUNIS (J.) *and* SENFT (F.) Synopsis der drei naturreiche. 3ter theil, 1ste abtheilung].

Sennert (Daniel). Epitome natvralis scientiæ. Ed. tertia. 8 p. l. 632 pp. 10 l. 18°. *Oxoniæ, excudebat I. Lichfield impensis H. Cripps,* 1632.

Seraphical (The) young shepherd. Translated by Cornelius Caley jun. [*anon.*] 178 pp. 18°. *Boston, D. Carlisle for J. West,* 1806.

Serasquier (The) Bassa: an historical novel. Out of french. [*anon.*] 4 p. l. 136 pp. 18°. *London, H. Rhodes,* [*about* 1700].

Sewall (*Rev.* Frank). Pillow of stones. Divine allegories in their spiritual meaning. 226 pp. 12°. *Philadelphia, J. B. Lippincott & co.* 1876.

Sewall (*Rev.* Jotham). Memoir of rev. Jotham Sewall, of Chesterville, Maine. By his son. 408 pp. 1 port. 12°. *Boston, Tappan & Whittemore,* 1853.

Seward (William). Biographiana. 1 v. in 2. Eng. title, 1 p. l. viii, iv, 631 pp. 10 pp. music, 4 pl. 8°. *London, J. Johnson,* 1799.

Seward (William Henry). Travels around the world. xii, 730 pp. 8°. *New York, D. Appleton & co.* 1873.

Sewel (Willem), **Holtrop** (Jan), *and* **Berry** (T.) New pocket dictionary of the flemish, english, and french languages. In three parts. 3d ed. 3 v. in 2. 12°. *Duynkerken, Men vind-se te koopen tot Gend, by P. & P. Gimblet,* 1793.

Sewell (Elizabeth Missing). Journal kept during a summer tour. [*anon.*] 3 pts. in 1 v. 12°. *New-York, D. Appleton & co.* 1859–65.

Seymour (*Mrs.* Mary H.) Recompense. 2 p. l. 226 pp. 3 pl. 16°. *New York, T. Whittaker,* 1874.

Sgroppo (—). Royaume des deux Siciles. Costumes. Dessinés sur les lieux. Eng. title, 100 col. pl. 4°. *Paris, P. Marino,* [1826].

Shaffner (Taliaferro P.) Odd fellowship illustrated. 1 p. l. 368 pp. front. 8°. *New York, Russell brothers,* 1874.

Shairp (John Campbell). Culture and religion. (From the Edinburgh ed.) 197 pp. 12°. *New York, Hurd & Houghton,* 1871.

Shakespeare (William). Hamlet. [Traduit par A. Dumas] en société avec M. Paul Meurice.

[*In* DUMAS (A. D.) Théâtre complet. 16°. *Paris, M. Lévy frères,* 1864. v. 7, pp. 285–386].

——— Midsummer-night's dream. With illustrations by A. Fredericks. 101 pp. incl. 2 pl. 4°. *New York, D. Appleton & co.* 1874.

——— New variorum edition of Shakespeare edited by H. H. Furness. v. 2. Macbeth. xix, 491 pp. 8°. *Philadelphia, J. B. Lippincott & co.* 1873.

——— Othello. [Italian and eng.] The italian as performed by signor Salvini. 135 pp. 8°. *New York, G. F. Nesbit & co.* 1873.

Shakespeare's library, 1875. *See* **Hazlitt** (W. C. *editor*).

Shankland (*Mrs.* E. R.) Matron's household manual. 118 pp. 4 l. 18°. *Dubuque,* [*Iowa*], [*Palmer, Winall & co.*] 1875.

Sharon (Thomas). Viola. [*anon.*] 422 pp. 2 pl. 12°. *Chicago, R. R. McCabe & co.* 1874.

Sharp (Granville). Three tracts on the syntax and pronunciation of the hebrew tongue. 2 p. l. [385] pp. 16°. *London, Vernor & Hood,* [1803–]1804.

Sharp (Leander J.) Vindication of the character of the late col. Solomon P. Sharp. . 140 pp. 8°. *Frankfort,* [*Ky.*] *A. Kendall & co.* 1827.

Sharp (Thomas, *d. d.*) Life of John Sharp, d. d. Edited by Thomas Newcome. 2 v. xxxii, 449 pp. 1 port; 1 p. l. 337 pp. 1 port. 8°. *London, C. & J. Rivington,* 1825.

Shaw (E. M.) Fire surveys. vii, 103 pp. 12°. *London, E. Wilson,* 1872.

Shaw (Henry W.) Everybody's friend, or; Josh Billing's [*pseud.*] encyclopedia of wit and humor. 617 pp. 16 pl. port. 8°. *Hartford, american publishing co.* 1874.

Shaw (*Rev.* James). History of the temperance reforms of the nineteenth century. x, 9–505 pp. 21 pl. 14 ports. on 2 pl. 8°. *Cincinnati, for the author,* [1875].

Shaw (*Rev.* Lachlan). History of the province of Moray. New ed. 4 p. l. 498 pp. 15 pl. 4°. *Elgin, J. Grant,* 1827.

Shaw (Richard Norman). Architectural sketches from the continent. Eng. title, 6 p. l. 100 phot.-lith. pl. fol. *London, for the proprietors,* 1872.

Shaw (Thomas Budd). New history of english literature. Prepared on the basis of "Shaw's manual" by Truman J. Backus. 1 p. l. v–xv, 5–404 pp. 1 map, 5 charts. 12°. *New York, Sheldon & co.* 1874.

Sheahan (James W.) Universal historical atlas. 282 pp. incl. 41 col. charts, 24 col. maps. fol. *Chicago, Warren, Cockcroft & co.* 1873.

Shedd (*Mrs.* Julia A.) Famous painters and paintings. vi, 326 pp. 10 pl. 8 ports. 8°. *Boston, J. R. Osgood & co.* 1876.

Shedd (*Rev.* William Greenough Thayer). Discourses and essays. 271 pp. 12°. *Andover, W. F. Draper,* 1856.

Shee (Martin Archer). Rhymes on art. 3d ed. 1 p. l. lxvi, 116 pp. 16°. *London, for J. Murray,* [*etc.*] 1806.

——— Same. 3d ed. 1 p. l. lxv, 116 pp. 16° *London, for W. Miller,* 1809.

Shelley (Percy Bysshe). Poetical works. From the author's original editions. 3 v. 16°. *London, J. C. Hotten, & Chatto & Windus,* [1874–]1875.

CONTENTS.

1st series. "Queen Mab" and the early poems. With memoir by Leigh Hunt.
2d series. Laon and Cythna, the Cenci and later poems. Edited by the author of Tennysoniana.
3d series. Posthumous poems. The masque of anarchy. The wandering jew. The Shelley papers. Notes to queen Mab and Hellas. Edited with notes by R. H. Shepherd.

——— Same. Poetical works. With a memoir by J. R. Lowell. 704 pp. port. 10 pl. sq. 16°. *New York, J. Miller,* 1875.

Shelton (Edward). Dictionary of every-day difficulties in reading, writing and speaking. 2 p. l. 364 pp. 12°. *London, Ward, Lock & Tyler,* [1874].

Shenstone (William). Essays on men and manners. 204 pp. 18°. *Philadelphia, W. W. Morse, for S. F. Bradford, & J. Conrad & co.* 1804.

[SELECT british classics, v. 39].

Shepard (J. S.) Over the dovrefjelds. 2d ed. 3 p. l. 217, viii pp. front. 16°. *London, H. S. King & co.* 1874.

Shepherd (Henry E.) History of the english language. 227 pp. 12°. *New York, E. J. Hale & son,* 1874.

Sheppard (Francis H.) Love afloat. 1 p. l. 483 pp. 12°. *New York, Sheldon & co.* [1875].

Sheppard (John). On dreams, in their mental and moral aspects. xxiv, 179 pp. 18°. *London, Jackson & Walford,* 1847.

Sheridan (Charles Francis). Essay on the true principles of civil liberty. [*anon.*] xxiv, 150 pp. 8°. *London,* 1793.

[MISCELLANEOUS pamphlets, v. 699: 4. Imperfect: wanting title].

Sheridan (Richard Brinsley). Works. Edited by F. Stainforth. viii, 656 pp. 3 ports. 7 pl. 12°. *London, Chatto & Windus,* 1875.

Sherman (*Mrs.* Ellen Ewing, *compiler*). Memorial of Thomas Ewing of Ohio. 291 pp. 3 pl. 8°. *New York, catholic publication society,* 1873.

Sherman (William Tecumseh). Memoirs. By himself. 2 v. 405 pp; 409 pp. 1 map in cover. 12°. *New York, D. Appleton & co.* 1875.

—— Same. 2 v. in 1. 405 pp; 1 p. l. 5–409 pp. 12°. *New York, D. Appleton & co.* 1876.

Sherring (M. A.) History of protestant missions in India, from 1706 to 1871. xi, 482 pp. 1 map. 8°. *London, Trübner & co.* 1875.

Sherwood (Robert). Dictionaire anglois et françois. 105 l. fol. *London,* 1672.

[*With* COTGRAVE (Randle). A french and english dictionary. 1673].

Shibata (M.) *and* **Koyas** (T.) English and japanese dictionary. New ed. 4 p. l. 1548 pp. 8°. *Yokohama, Ni-shu-sha printing office,* [1873].

Shillaber (Benjamin P.) Lines in pleasant places. 305 pp. port. 16°. *Chelsea,* [*Mass.*] 1874.

Shipley (*Rev.* Orby, *editor*). The church and the world: [second series:] essays. By various writers. viii, 567 pp. 8°. *London, Longmans,* [*etc.*] 1867.

Shiras (*Rev.* Alexander). Life and letters of rev. James May, d. d. 185 pp. port. 12°. *Philadelphia, protestant episcopal book society,* [1865].

Sibbald (*Sir* Robert, *m. d.*) History of the sheriffdoms of Fife and Kinross. New ed. xvi, 468 pp. 3 l. 4 pl. 8°. *Cupar-Fife, R. Tullis,* 1803.

Sibley (John Langdon). Biographical sketches of graduates of Harvard university. v. 1. 1642–58. xx, 618 pp. 3 l. 8°. *Cambridge,* [*Mass.*] *C. W. Sever,* 1873.

Sidney (Henry, *earl of Romney.*) Diary of the times of Charles the second. Edited with notes, by R. W. Blencowe. 2 v. cii, 307 pp. 1 port. 1 tab. 1 facs; vii, 390 pp. 1 port. 8°. *London, H. Colburn,* 1843.

Sikes (*Mrs.* Wirt, *formerly* Olive Logan). They met by chance. 1 p. l. 7–320 pp. 12°. *New York, Adams, Victor & co.* [1873].

Siliad (The); or, the siege of the seats. By the authors of "The coming k—." [*anon.*] Ill. title, xv, 236 pp. 16°. *London, Ward, Lock & Tyler,* [1874].

[BEETON (S. O.) Humorous books, no. 28].

Sillar (David). Poems. 247 pp. 8°. *Kilmarnock,* [*Scotland*], *J. Wilson,* 1789.

Sime (James). History of Germany. Edition for american readers. xiv, 282 pp. 16°. *New York, H. Holt & co.* 1874.

[FREEMAN's historical course for schools].

Simms (Joseph, *m. d.*) Nature's revelations of character. xxiv, 600 pp. 1 pl. 8°. [*London*], *for the author,* 1873.

Simon (Johann). Lexicon manuale hebraicum et chaldaicum. 4 p. l. 1082 pp. 24 l. 8°. *Amstelædami, apud J. a Wetstein,* 1757.

Simond (Louis). Voyage en Suisse, fait dans les années 1817, 1818 et 1819. 2 v. 1 p. l. v–viii, 656 pp. 1 pl; 1 p. l. 596 pp. 8°. *Paris, Treuttel & Würtz,* 1822.

Simonds (William). Our little ones in heaven. [*anon.*] 248 pp. 18°. *Boston, Gould & Lincoln,* 1858.

Simons (*Rev.* Ezra D.) Divine pictures of the christian centuries. iv, 328 pp. 16°. *Troy, N. Y., W. H. Young,* 1875.

Simons (John W.) The beauseant; a manual for the use of knights templar. 245 pp. 1 l. 1 pl. 12°. *New York, D. Sickels & co.* 1874.

—— Knights templars' manual, for the use of commanderies of masonic knighthood. 139 pp. incl. 1 pl. 12°. *New York, masonic publishing co.* 1873.

Simpson (Edward, *U. S. n.*) Report on a naval mission to Europe. 2 v. 341 pp. 45 pl; 300 pp. 27 pl. 4°. *Washington, government printing office,* 1873.

[UNITED STATES. *Navy department. (Bureau of ordnance)*].

Simpson (William). Meeting the sun: a journey all round the world. xii, 413 pp. 44 pl. 8°. *London, Longmans,* 1874.

Simrock (Karl). Rheinland. 2te aufl. 376 pp. 60 pl. 8°. *Leipzig, C. A. Haendel,* [1847].

[MALERISCHE (Das) und romantische Deutschland, v. 8].

Sinclair (*Rev.* John). Memoirs of sir John Sinclair, bart. 2 v. 3 p. l. vi, ii, 362 pp; 2 p. l. ii, 427 pp. 12°. *Edinburgh, W. Blackwood & sons,* 1837.

Sizer (Nelson). What to do, and why. 504 pp. 1 port. 8°. *New York, E. C. Fisher, & co.* 1874.

Skinner (*Rev.* John). The scottish endowment question. xv, 309 pp. 8°. *Glasgow, J. Symington & co.* 1838.

Skinner (John, *d. d. editor.*) The pastoral relation—what are its securities? 107 pp. 12°. *Lexington, Va. Winn & Carter,* 1847.

Skinner (John, *d. d. editor*)—continued.
——— Sundry papers in the Lexington church case. 2 p. l. 104 pp. 12°. *Lexington, Va. S. Gillock*, 1848.
[*With* SKINNER (J.) The pastoral relation. 1847].

Skinner (J. Ralston). Key to the hebrew-egyptian mystery in the source of measures originating the british inch [etc.] 1 p. l. xvi, 324 pp. 8°. *Cincinnati, R. Clarke & co.* 1875.

Slafter (*Rev.* Edmund F. *editor.*) Sir William Alexander and american colonization. ix, 283 pp. 1 pl. 1 map. sm. 4°. *Boston, Prince society*, 1873.
[PRINCE society publications, no. 7].

Slaughter (Linda Warfel). The freedmen of the south. 201 pp. 12°. *Cincinnati, Elm street printing co.* 1869.

Sleigh (John). History of the ancient parish of Leek, in Staffordshire. 3 p. l. 312 pp. 17 pl. 2 facs. 8°. *Leek, R. Nall*, 1862.

Slight (James) *and* **Burn** (Robert Scott). Book of farm implements and machines. Edited by Henry Stephens. xxii, 648 pp. 40 pl. 8°. *Edinburgh, W. Blackwood & sons*, 1858.

Sloan (Edward L. *compiler.*) Gazetteer of Utah, and Salt Lake city directory. 1874. [v. 2]. 3 p. l. 17–326 pp. 1 col. map. 8°. *Salt Lake city, "Salt Lake herald" publishing co.* [1874].

Small (George G.) Trip of the Porgie; or, tacking up the Hudson. By Bricktop [*pseud.*] 1 p. l. 124 pp. 8° *New York, Collin & Small*, 1874.

Smalley (Elam, *d. d.*) Worcester pulpit. 562 pp. 12°. *Boston, Phillips, Sampson & co.* 1851.

Smart (Bath C. *m. d.*) *and* **Crofton** (H. T.) Dialect of the english gypsies. 2d ed. xxiii, 302 pp. 1 facs. 8°. *London, Asher & co.* 1875.

Smart (Charles, *m. d.*) Driven from the path. [By Polywarp Oldfellow, m. d. *pseud.*] 467 pp. 12°. *New York, D. Appleton & co.* 1873.

Smead (Wesley). Guide to wealth. 110 pp. 16°. *Cincinnati, E. Mendenhall*, 1856.

Smedley (A. B.) Manual of jurisprudence and co-operation of the patrons of husbandry. xvi, 200 pp. 16°. *Des Moines, [Iowa,] Mills & co.* 1875.

Smee (Alfred). My garden, its plan and culture. 2d ed. 2 p. l. vii–xx, 650 pp. 24 pl. 8°. *London, Bell & Daldy*, 1872.

Smet (Joseph Jean de, *abbé.*) Recueil des chroniques de Flandre. 4 v. 4°. *Bruxelles, M. Hayez*, 1837–65. s.
[BELGIUM. *Académie royale d'histoire, des lettres, et des beaux-arts.* Collection des chroniques belges inédites].

Smet (*Rev.* Peter J. de, *s. J.*) New Indian sketches. 175 pp. 2 pl. 18°. *New York, D. & J. Sadlier & co.* [1865].

Smiddy (*Rev.* Richard). Essay on the Druids, the ancient churches, and the round towers of Ireland. ix, 320 pp. 16°. *Dublin, W. B. Kelly*, 1871.

Smiles (Samuel). Huguenots in France. xiv, 430 pp. 12°. *London, W. Isbister & co.* 1874.

Smillie (James) *and* **Walter** (Cornelia W.) Mount Auburn. Eng. title, 119 pp. 18 pl. 4°. *New York, Martin & Johnson*, [1848].

Smith (Alfred Russell, *bookseller*). Bibliotheca americana. Catalogue of books and pamphlets, illustrating the history & geography of America. vi, 182 pp; 681–733 pp. 8°. *London, A. R. Smith*, 1874.

Smith (Buckingham). Rudo ensayo, tentativa de una prevencional descripcion geographica de la provincia de Sonora. [*anon.*] x, 208 pp. sm. 4°. *San Augustin de la Florida*, [*Albany printed, J. Munsell*], 1863.

Smith (Butler Kennedy). Series of discourses on various subjects. vii, 320 pp. port. 12°. *Indianapolis, printing & publishing house print*, 1874.

Smith (*Mrs.* Caroline L.) Home arts for old and young. 198 pp. 16°. *Boston, Lee & Shepard*, 1873.
——— Home games for old and young. vi, 3–190 pp. 16°. *Boston, Lee & Shepard*, 1873.

Smith (Charles). New treatise on the diseases and lameness of the horse. 214 pp. 16°. *Binghamton, N. Y., Malette & Reid*, 1873.

Smith (Charles A. *d. d.*) Inlets and outlets. Familiar talks about the five senses. 224 pp. incl. 4 pl. 16°. *Philadelphia, presbyterian board of publication*, [1873].

Smith (Charles H.) Bill Arp's [*pseud.*] peace papers. 271 pp. incl. front. 12°. *New York, G. W. Carleton & co.* 1873.

Smith (Dexter, *jr.*) Poems. 128 pp. 16°. *Boston, G. D. Russell & co.* 1868.

Smith (*Rev.* Elias). Sermons containing an illustration of the prophecies to be accomplished. 300 pp. 16°. *Exeter, [N. H.] for the author*, 1808.

Smith (Fannie Morris). Shiftless folks. By Christabel Goldsmith [*pseud.*] 454 pp. 12°. *New York, G. W. Carleton & co.* 1875.

Smith (*Mrs.* Frances Burge). The bishop and Nannette. 329 pp. 5 pl. 12°. *New York, T. Whittaker,* [1874].

——— Jimmy Don. 128 pp. 3 pl. 18°. *Boston, american tract society,* [1869].

Smith (Francis S.) The young magdalen; and other poems. 280 pp. 1 port. 8°. *Philadelphia, T. B. Peterson & brothers,* [1874].

Smith (George). Assyrian discoveries; explorations on the site of Nineveh, during 1873 and 1874. xvi, 461 pp. 1 map, 3 pl. 3 photos. 1 plan. 8°. *London, S. Low, Marston, Low & Searle,* 1875.

Smyth (William Woods). The bible and the doctrine of evolution. viii, 390 pp. 1 l. 12°. *London, H. K. Lewis,* 1873.

Smythe (William H. B.) Commercial index to first hands, in iron, steel, and kindred branches, [for fall and winter, 1873–74. 122 pp. 12°. *New York, W. H. B. Smythe,* 1873].

Sobolewski (Serge). Catalogue de la collection de livres formant la bibliothèque de feu m. Serge Sobolewski dont le vente se fera le 14 juillet 1873 à Leipzig. xviii, 314 pp. 8°. *Leipzig, List & Francke,* 1873.

Sociétés de sécours aux blessés militaires des armées de terre et de mer. Conférences internationales tenues à Paris en 1867. 1e ptie. 2e éd. & 2e ptie. 2 v. in 1. 10, iii–xvi, 372 pp; 1 p. l. viii, 3–286 (+250 quater) pp. 4 pl. 8°. *Paris, commission générale des délégués,* 1867.

Solorzano-Pereyra (Juan de). Decada segvnda de los emblemas de don Ivan de Solorçano Pereyra. Tradvcidos por el dotor Lorenço Matheu y Sanz. Eng. title, 334 pp. 1 l. 18°. *Valencia, B. Noguès,* 1658.

——— Dispvtationem de Indiarvm ivre. 2 v. 14 p. l. 751 pp. 50 l; 26 p. l. 1076 pp. 68 l. fol. *Matriti, F. Martinez,* 1629–39.

Solvyns (François-Balthazar). Les Hindous. 4 v. fol. *Paris, l'auteur,* 1808–12.

Southworth (*Mrs.* Emma Dorothy Eliza Nevitte). Victors triumph. 1 p. l. pp. 19–348. 12°. *Philadelphia, T. B. Peterson & brothers,* [1874].

——— *editor.* Mystery of dark hollow. 1 p. l. 21–366 pp. 12°. *Philadelphia, T. B. Peterson & brothers,* [1875].

Souvestre (Émile). Pleasures of old age. From the french. xii, 344 pp. 1 pl. 16°. *London, G. Routledge & sons,* 1868.

Spalding (J. L.) Life of M. J. Spalding, archbishop of Baltimore. 468 pp. 1 port. 8°. *New York, catholic publication society,* 1873.

Spangler (Helen King). The physician's wife. 305 pp. 12°. *Philadelphia, J. B. Lippincott & co.* 1875.

Spaulding (M. C. *compiler*). Handbook of statistics of the United States. 1 p. l. 216 pp. 12°. *New York, G. P. Putnam's sons,* 1874.
[PUTNAM'S handy book series].

Speechiana. A collection of speeches and recitations. [*anon.*] 1 p. l. 144 pp. 16°. *New York, happy hours co.* [1875].

Speer (William). God's rule for christian giving. 272 pp. 16°. *Philadelphia, presbyterian board of publication,* [1875].

Spencer (Herbert). Study of sociology. xiv, 423 pp. 12°. *New York, D. Appleton & co.* 1874.
[INTERNATIONAL scientific series, v. 5].

Spencer (*Rev.* Jesse A.) Course of english reading. 299 pp. 16°. *New York, J. Miller,* 1873.

Spencer (*Rev.* Oliver M.) Narrative; comprising an account of his captivity among the Mohawk Indians. 2d ed. 281 pp. 18°. *London, J. Mason,* 1842.

Spencer (*Elder* Orson). Letters exhibiting the most prominent doctrines of the church of Christ of latter-day saints. 5th ed. viii, 252 pp. 12°. *Salt Lake city, Deseret news,* 1874.

Spenser (Edmund). Faerie queene. New ed. with notes, by Ralph Church. 4 v. 8°. *London, W. Faden,* 1758–59.

Sperry (*Mrs.* N. S.) Recognition of the creator in daily life. [*anon.*] 284 pp. 16°. *Hartford, Case, Lockwood & Brainard,* 1873.

Spiegel (Friedrich). Die altpersischen keilinschriften. 4 p. l. 223 pp. 8°. *Leipzig, W. Engelmann,* 1862.

Spielhagen (Friedrich). What the swallow sang. From the german by M S. 1 p. l. 306 pp. 16°. *New York, Holt & Williams,* 1873.
[LEISURE hour series].

Spielmann & Brush, *civil engineers.* Insurance maps of Jersey city, N. J. 1873. 6 v. fol. *Hoboken, N. J., Spielmann & Brush,* [1873].

CONTENTS.

v. 1–2. Jersey city portion.
v. 3–4. Hudson city portion.
v. 5–6. Bergen city portion.

Spinster's (A) tour in France, the states of Genoa, &c. during 1827. [*anon.*] iv, 427 pp. 12°. *London, for Longman,* [*etc.*] 1828.

Spitzel *or* **Spizelius** (Gottlieb, *or* Theophilus). Elevatio relationis montezinianæ de repertis in America tribubus israeliticis. 12 p. l. 128 pp. 12°. *Basiliæ, J. König,* 1663.

Spon (E.) *and* **Spon** (F. N.) Spons' dictionary of engineering. Edited by Byrne and Spon. 3 v. viii, 3131 pp. 8°. *London, E. & F. N. Spon,* 1873–74.

Spon (Jacob). Histoire de Genève. 2 v. 2 p. l. xv, 556 pp. 3 pl; 7 p. l. 518 pp. 12 pl. 4°. *Genève, Fabri & Barrillot,* 1730.

Sporschil (Johann). Sachsen. 2te aufl. 168 pp. 30 pl. 8°. *Leipzig, C. A. Haendel's verlag,* [1847].

[MALERISCHE (Das) und romantische Deutschland, v. 5].

Spottswood (Lucy, *pseud?*) Alice Dunbar. 155 pp. port. 2 pl. 18°. *Philadelphia, presbyterian board of publication,* [1875].

Sprague (Charles). Writings, now first collected. 124, 58 pp. 8°. *New York, C. S. Francis,* 1841.

Sprague (Homer B.) Masterpieces in english literature. In four books. v. 1. 437 pp. 6 ports. 8°. *New York, J. W. Schermerhorn & co.* 1874.

Sprague (William B. *d. d.*) Life of Jedidiah Morse, d. d. viii, 333 pp. port. 8°. *New York, A. D. F. Randolph & co.* [1874].

Spratt (Thomas Abel Brimage, *r. n.*) *and* **Forbes** (*Prof.* Edward). Travels in Lycia, Milyas, and the Cibyratis. 2 v. xxiv, 302 pp. 18 pl; viii, 332 pp. 8 pl. 1 map. 8°. *London, J. Van Voorst,* 1847.

Sprigg *or* **Sprigge** (Joshua). Anglia rediviva; England's recovery. New ed. 1 p. l. xvi, iii, 336 pp. 1 tab. 1 map. 8°. *Oxford, university press,* 1854.

Note.—Walker, in his history of independency, p. 32, states that col. Nathaniel Fiennes is the real author of this work.

Spring (Gardiner, *d. d.*) Dissertation on the rule of faith. 104 pp. 8°. *New York, Leavitt, Trow & co.* 1844.

Spring (Samuel, *d. d.*) Friendly dialogue, between Philalethes & Toletus, upon the nature of duty. 160, 32 pp. 18°. *Newbury-port,* [*Ms.*] *J. Mycall,* 1784.

Springer (Rebecca Ruter). Beechwood. 288 pp. 12°. *Philadelphia, J. B. Lippincott & co.* 1873.

Springfield, (*Mass.*) *City library association.* Catalogue. xii, 668 pp. 1 pl. 8°. *Springfield, S. Bowles & co.* 1871.

Sproul (E. R.) Mystery. [Or mental philosophy adapted to the bible]. vi, 3–734 pp. 8°. *San Francisco, for the author,* 1875.

Squier (Miles P. *d. d.*) The problem solved; or, sin not of God. 255 pp. 12°. *New York, M. W. Dodd,* 1855.

Staël-Holstein (Anne Louise Germaine Necker, *baronne* de). Corinne; or, Italy. Translated by Isabel Hill. xxvii, 5–396 pp. 12°. *New York, Mason, Baker & Pratt,* 1873.

Stainton (Henry Tibbats). Tineina of southern Europe. vii, 370 pp. 1 pl. 8°. *London, J. Van Voorst,* 1869,

——— Tineina of Syria and Asia Minor. vi pp. 1 l. 84 pp. 8°. *London, J. Van Voorst,* 1867.

Stanhope (Louisa Sidney). Madelina. 4 v. 16°. *London, for A. K. Newman & co.* 1814.

Stanhope (Philip Dormer, *earl of Chesterfield*). Wit and wisdom of the earl of Chesterfield: selections from his miscellaneous writings. Edited, by W. Ernst-Browning. xii, 400 pp. port. 8°. *London, R. Bentley & son,* 1875.

Stanley (Arthur Penrhyn, *d. d.*) Lectures on the history of the jewish church. 2 v. xl, 460 pp. 2 maps, 1 pl; xxv, 518 pp. 3 maps. 8°. *London, J. Murray,* 1870.

Stanley (*Hon.* Henry, *editor*). The east and the west. Essays by different hands. vii, 271 pp. 12°. *London, Hatchard & co.* 1865.

Stanley (Henry Morton). Coomassie and Magdala. xiv, 510 pp. 13 pl. 3 ports. 2 maps. 8°. *New York, Harper & brothers,* 1874.

——— My Kalulu. xvi, 432 pp. 16 pl. 12°. *New York, Scribner, Armstrong & co.* 1874.

Stansfield (F. W. H.) Life of gen'l U. S Grant. 2 p. l. 17–104 pp. 12°. *New York, T. R. Dawley,* [1864].

Stark (Adam). History and antiquities of Gainsburgh. 2d ed. viii, 630 pp. 5 pl. 8°. *London, Longman,* 1843.

Stary (James P.) Choisy. 131 pp. 8°. *Boston, J. R. Osgood & co.* 1872.

Stebbins (George S. *m. d.*) Victims of ignorance. A treatise on the diseases and deformities of children. 404 pp. 11 pl. 12°. *Springfield, Mass. D. E. Fisk & co.* [1873].

Stebbins (Jane E.) Earthly trials and glory of the immortal life. Eng. title, 2 p. l. 576 pp. 7 pl. 2 l. 8°. *Hartford, L. Stebbins,* 1875.

Stedman (Edmund Clarence). Poetical works. Complete ed. 2 p. l. ix–xii, 342 pp. 1 port. 16°. *Boston, J. R. Osgood & co.* 1873.

——— Victorian poets. xxv, 441 pp. 12°. *Boston, J. R. Osgood & co.* 1876.

Steele (*Mrs.* Anne). Works. Heretofore published under the title of Theodosia. 2 v. 328 pp; 300 pp. 12°. *Boston, Munroe, Francis & Parker,* 1808.

Steele (Daniel, *d. d.*) Love enthroned. 416 pp. 12°. *New York, Nelson & Phillips,* 1875.

Steele (I. Dorman). Brief history of France. [*anon.*] 299, xxx pp. 2 col. maps. 12°. *New York, A. S. Barnes & co.* 1875.
[BARNES's one term history].

Steele (James W.) Sons of the border. 260 pp. 8°. *Topeka, Ks. commonwealth printing co.* 1873.

Steffens (Heinrich). Anthropologie. 2 v. iv, 476 pp. 2 l; 2 p. l. 456 pp. 2 l. 2 tab. 8°. *Breslau, J. Max,* 1822.

Steiger (Ernest). Periodical literature of the United States. 5 p. l. 139 pp; 2 p. l. 14 pp. 8°. *New York, E. Steiger,* 1873.

Steinwehr (A. von). Centennial gazetteer of the United States. 1016 pp. 1 pl. 8°. *Philadelphia, Ziegler & McCurdy,* [1874].

Stenhouse (Thomas B. H.) The Rocky mountain saints. xxiv, 761 pp. 24 pl. port. 8°. *New York, D. Appleton & co.* 1873.

Stenhouse (*Mrs.* Thomas B. H. *i. e.* Fanny). "Tell it all": the story of a life's experience in mormonism. 623 pp. incl. 16 pl. 2 pl. 8°. *Hartford, Conn. A. D. Worthington & co.* 1874.

Stennett (Samuel, *d. d.*) Remarks on the christian minister's reasons for administering baptism by sprinkling. xx, 146 pp. 16°. *London, for G. Keith,* [*etc.*] 1772.

Stephen (James Fitzjames). Liberty, equality, fraternity. 4 p. l. 350 pp. 8°. *London, Smith, Elder & co.* 1873.

Stephen (Leslie). Essays on freethinking and plainspeaking. 5 p. l. 362 pp. 12°. *London, Longmans,* 1873.

Stephens (*Mrs.* Ann Sophia Winterbottom). Bellehood and bondage. 2 p. l. 21–458 pp. 12°. *Philadelphia, T. B. Peterson & brothers,* [1873].

——— Bertha's engagement. 2 p. l. 21–552 pp. 12°. *Philadelphia, T. B. Peterson & brothers,* [1875].

Stephens (*Mrs.* A. S. W.)—continued.

——— Lord Hope's choice. 2 p. l. 21–312 pp. 12°. *Philadelphia, T. B. Peterson & brothers,* [1873].

——— The old countess. 1 p. l. 21–301 pp. 12°. *Philadelphia, T. B. Peterson & brothers,* [1873].

——— Phemie Frost's experiences. 3 p. l. 9–408 pp. 12°. *New York, G. W. Carleton & co.* 1874.

Stephens (J. W.) Every man his own doctor! 192 pp. 32°. *Newark, N. J. author,* 1873.

Stephens (Philetus J.) Record of the surgical clinics of Wm. Tod Helmuth. A synopsis of the clinics of 1873–'74. 207 pp. port. 8°. *New York,* 1875.

Stephenson (Charles). Cuban martyrs and other poems. 204 pp. 12°. *Rock Island, Ill. union printing co.* 1874.

Stetson (Charles B.) Technical education. iv, 284 pp. 16°. *Boston, J. R. Osgood & co.* 1874.

Stevens (*Dr.* Abel). Geschichte der bischöflichen methodistenkirche in den Ver. Staaten von Nordamerika. Frei aus dem englischen übersetzt von H. Liebhart. 2 v. 424 pp. port; 444 pp. port. 12°. *Cincinnati, Hitchcock & Walden,* [1867]–72.

Stevens (Charles Asbury). Camping-out series. v. 6. On the Amazons. 227 pp. 8 pl. 16°. *Boston, J. R. Osgood & co.* 1874.

——— Young moose hunters. By C. A. Stephens [*pseud.*] 288 pp. incl. front. 12°. *Boston, H. L. Shepard & co.* 1874.

Stevens (Henry). Bibliotheca geographica & historica, or, catalogue of a nine days sale of books, maps, (etc.) Part 1. 2 p. l. 361 pp. 1 photo. 8°. *London, H. Stevens,* 1872.

——— Bibliotheca historica. Or a catalogue of 5000 volumes relating chiefly to America. xvi, 234 pp. 8°. *Boston, H. O. Houghton & co.* 1870.

Note.—This collection was sold at Boston, April 13–15, 1870.

Stevens (H. I.) *and* **Stevens** (A.) Scott & Scotland; with illustrations by George Cattermole, &c. Eng. title, viii, 264 pp. 28 pl. port. 8°. *London, H. I. & A. Stevens,* [18—].

Stevenson (*Rev.* Joseph, *editor*). Documents illustrative of the history of Scotland, 1286–1306. 2 v. lv, 432 pp; xxii, 532 pp. 8°.

Stevenson (*Rev.* J. *editor*)—continued. *Edinburgh, h. m. general register house,* 1870. s.

[GREAT BRITAIN. *Treasury. General register house, Edinburgh*].

——— Narratives of the expulsion of the English from Normandy, 1449–1450. Edited from mss. 1 p. l. xiv pp. 1 l. 527 pp. 8°. *London, Longmans,* 1863.

[GREAT BRITAIN. (*Public record office*). Rerum britannicarum medii aevi scriptores, no. 32].

Stevenson (Sarah Hackett). Boys and girls in biology; based upon lectures of prof. T. H. Huxley. Illustrated by miss M. A. I. Macomb. 186 pp. 12°. *New York, D. Appleton & co.* 1875.

Stewart (Agnes M) The Limerick veteran. 2 p. l. 253 pp. 12°. *Baltimore, Kelly, Piet & co.* 1873.

Stewart *or* **Stuart** (*Sir* James, *of Goodtrees*) *and* **Stirling** (*Rev.* James, *of Paisley*). Naphtali; or, a true and short deduction of the wrestlings of the church of Scotland for the kingdom of Christ. [*anon.*] 510 pp. 3 l. 16°. *Edinburgh, D. Paterson,* 1761.

Stieglitz (Christian Ludwig). Von altdeutscher baukunst [und] xxxiv kupfer [dazu]. 2 v. viii, 248 pp; eng. title, 34 pl. 4° & fol. *Leipzig, G. Fleischer,* 1820.

Stigliani (Tommaso). Del mondo nvovo. Venti primi canti. [etc. Ed. 1a]. 700 pp. 3 l. 18°. *Piacenza, A. Bazacchi,* 1617.

Stillingfleet (Edward, *d. d.*) Irenicvm. 2d ed. 14 p. l. 447 pp. sm. 4°. *London, for H. Mortlock,* 1662.

Stillman (George A.) Life—real. A poem. 137 pp. 12°. *New York, J. C. Derby,* 1855.

Stillman (Samuel, *d. d.*) Select sermons on doctrinal and practical subjects. xxiv, 382 pp. 1 l. 8°. *Boston, Manning & Loring,*

Stillman (William J.) Cretan insurrection of 1866–7–8. 196, 199–203 pp. 12°. *New York, H. Holt & co.* 1874.

Stimson (Hiram K.) From the stage coach to the pulpit, an auto-biographical sketch. 427 pp. port. 12°. *Saint Louis, R. A. Campbell,* 1874.

Stockbridge (Virgil D.) Digest of patents relating to breech-loading and magazine small arms, granted in the United States from 1836 to 1873. 1 p. l. 176 pp. incl. 84 photolith. 1 l. 4°. *Washington,* 1874.

Stockmar (E. von, *baron*). Memoirs of baron von Stockmar. By his son. From the german by G. A. M. 2 v. cx, 391 pp; xiii, 555 pp. 12°. *London, Longmans,* 1872.

Stockton (Frank R.) What might have been expected. 292 pp. 12 pl. 16°. *New York, Dodd & Mead,* [1874].

——— *and* **Stockton** (Marian). The home. 5–182 pp. 12°. *New York, G. P. Putnam & sons,* 1873.

[PUTNAM'S handy-book series, no. 10].

Stocqueler (John Henry). Familiar history of the british army, from 1660 to the present time. 4 p. l. xvi, 349 pp. sm. 4°. *London, E. Stanford,* 1871.

——— Personal history of the horse-guards from 1750 to 1872. x, 292 pp. 8°. *London, Hurst & Blackett,* 1873.

Stodart (*Miss* M. A.) Female writers. 4 p. l. 203 pp. 16°. *London, R. B. Seeley & W. Burnside,* 1842.

Stoddard (Charles Warren). South-sea idyls. 354 pp. 18°. *Boston, J. R. Osgood & co.* 1873.

——— Summer cruising in the South seas. 319 pp. 22 pl. 12°. *London, Chatto & Windus,* [1874].

Stoddard (Richard Henry). Poems. viii, 127 pp. 12°. *Boston, Ticknor, Reed & Fields,* 1852.

——— *editor.* Personal recollections of Lamb, Hazlitt, and others. xxii, 322 pp. port. 1 facs. 12°. *New York, Scribner, Armstrong & co.* 1875.

[BRIC-À-BRAC series, v. 9].

Stoddard (S. R.) The Adirondacks: illustrated. vi, 204 pp. 2 pl. 1 map. 12°. *Albany, Weed, Parsons & co.* 1874.

——— Lake George; (illustrated). 1 p. l. 115 pp. 16°. *Albany, Weed, Parsons & co.* 1873.

Stoddard (William Osborn). Verses of many days. 1 p. l. 172 pp. 12°. *New York, J. Miller,* 1875.

Stone (Andrew, *m. d.*) New gospel of health. xviii, 519 pp. 2 pl. port. 8°. *Troy, N. Y. lung and hygienic institute,* 1875.

Stone (Barton Warren). Biography of eld. Barton Warren Stone, written by himself. ix, 404 pp. port. 12°. *Cincinnati, for the author,* 1847.

Stone (David M.) Frank Forrest. 143 pp. incl. 3 pl. 18°. *New York, M. W. Dodd,* 1850.

Stone (John Benjamin). Tour with Cook through Spain. viii, 229 pp. 4 autotype pl.

Stone (John Benjamin)—continued. 12°. *London, S. Low, Marston, Low & Searle,* 1873.

Stone (*Rev.* Richard Cecil). Life incidents of home, school and church. viii, 352 pp. port. 16°. *St. Louis, southwestern publishing co.* 1874.

Stone (William Leete). Reminiscences of Saratoga and Ballston. 2 p. l. 451 pp. 8 pl. 12°. *New York, Virtue & Yorston,* 1875.

Storer (Henry Sargent) *and* **Storer** (James Sargent). Views in Edinburgh and its vicinity. 2 v. Eng. title, 2 p. l. 192 pp. 26 pl. 26 l. 2 plans; eng. title, 1 p. l. 70 pl. 71 l. 8°. *Edinburgh, A. Constable & co.* 1820.

Storer (James Sargent) *and* **Greig** (John). Views in North Britain. Eng. title, 3–61 pp. 19 pl. 8°. *London, Vernor & Hood,* 1805.

Stories for children by eleven sophomores. [*anon.*] 118 pp. sq. 16°. *Boston, Roberts brothers,* 1875.

Stork (Theophilus, *d.d.*) Afternoon. 360 pp. 1 phot. 12°. *Philadelphia, J. B. Lippincott & co.* 1874.

Storm (Theodor). Novellen. 3 p. l. 262 pp. 16°. *Schleswig, schulbuchhandlung (H. Heiberg),* 1868.

——— Sommer-geschichten und lieder. viii, 150 pp. 16°. *Berlin, A. Duncker,* 1851.

Stormonth (*Rev.* James). Etymological and pronouncing dictionary of the english language. 2d ed. viii, 777 pp. 12°. *Edinburgh, W. Blackwood & sons,* 1874.

Storrs (Richard S. *d. d.*) Conditions of success in preaching without notes. 233 pp. 12°. *New York, Dodd & Mead,* 1875.

Story (William Wetmore). Nero, an historical play. viii, 275 pp. sq. 16°. *Edinburgh, W. Blackwood & sons,* 1875.

Stowe (*Mrs.* Harriet Elizabeth Beecher). Palmetto-leaves. 2 p. l. 321 pp. 1 pl. 16°. *Boston, J. R. Osgood & co.* 1873.

——— We and our neighbors. 480 pp. 8 pl. 12°. *New York, J. B. Ford & co.* 1875.

——— Woman in sacred history. 96 l. unp. 16 col. pl. 8°. *New York, J. B. Ford & co.* 1874.

Strachey (William). Proceedings of the english colonie in Virginia since 1606, till this present 1612. By W. S. [*anon.*] 2 p. l. 110 pp. 4°. *Oxford, J. Barnes,* 1612.

[*In* SMITH (*Capt.* John). A map of Virginia. sm. 4°. *Oxford,* 1612].

Strada (Famiano, *s. J.*) De bello belgico, decas prima. 8 p. l. 630 pp. 1 l. 12 ports. 16°. *Venetiis, apud L. Basilium,* 1730. s.

Strahan (Edward). The new Hyperion. With illustrations by Gustave Doré and others. 271 pp. 8°. *Philadelphia, J. B. Lippincott & co.* 1875.

Stratmann (Francis Henry). Dictionary of the old english language. 2d ed. xii, 594 pp. 4°. *Krefeld, author; London, Trübner & co.* 1873.

Strauch (Adolphus). Spring Grove cemetery. [*anon.*] viii, 199 pp. 1 phot. 8°. *Cincinnati, R. Clarke & co.* 1869.

Straus-Dürckheim (Hercule Eugène G.) Théologie de la nature. 3 v. 8°. *Paris, l'auteur,* 1852.

Strauss (David Friedrich). The old faith and the new. Authorized translation from the 6th ed. by Mathilde Blind. Am. ed. 2 v. in 1. xxxiii, 223 pp; 224 pp. 12°. *New York, H. Holt & co.* 1873.

Street (George Edmund). Some account of gothic architecture in Spain. 2 pts. in 1 v. xiv, 527 pp. 51 pl. 25 plans. 8°. *London, J. Murray,* 1865.

Stretch (Richard H.) Illustrations of the zygænidæ & bombycidæ of North America. v. 1. vii, 3–242 pp. 10 col. pl. 8°. [*San Francisco*], 1872–73.

Strickland (Hugh Edwin, *m. a.*) *and* **Melville** (A. G. *m. d.*) The dodo and its kindred. 2 pts. in 1 v. 4 p. l. 1-6 pp. 1 l. 7–141 pp. 12 pl. 3 col. pl. 3 facs. incl. 1 col. 4°. *London, Reeve, Benham & Reeve,* 1848.

Strickland (*Capt.* P.) Voice from the deep. 189 pp. 2 pl. 12°. *Boston, A. Williams & co.* 1873.

Strong (*Rev.* Nathan). Sermons. 2 v. 396 pp; 408 pp. 8°. *Hartford, Hudson & Goodwin, & for O. D. & I. Cooke,* 1798–1800.

Strutt (Joseph). History and description of Colchester. [*anon.*] 2 v. 1 p. l. 276, 22 pp. 1 pl; 2 p. l. 232 pp. 2 l. 5 pl. 12°. *Colchester, W. Keymer,* 1803.

Stuart (Andrew). Letters to lord Mansfield. 196 pp. 8°. *Dublin,* 1775.

[DUANE pamphlets, v. 23: 6. MISCELLANEOUS pamphlets, v. 668: 7].

Stuart (James, *of Armagh*). Poems on various subjects. 22, 192 pp. 16°. *Belfast, J. Smyth,* 1811.

Stuart-Glennie (John Stuart, *m. a.*) In the morningland; or the law of the origin and transformation of christianity. v. 1. xiii, 432 pp. 8°. *London, Longmans,* 1873.

Stubbs (*Rev.* William). Constitutional history of England. v. 1. viii, 638 pp. 12°. *Oxford, Clarendon press*, 1874.

[CLARENDON press series].

——— *editor.* Chronicles and memorials of the reign of Richard I. 2 v. clxxxix pp. 1 l. 468 pp; clxxxvii pp. 2 l. 574 pp. 8°. *London, Longmans*, 1864–65.

CONTENTS.

v. 1. Itinerarium peregrinorum et gesta regis Ricardi, auctore, ut videtur, Ricardo, canonico sanctae trinitatis londoniensis.

v. 2. Epistolae cantuarienses, 1187–1199.

[GREAT BRITAIN. (*Public record office*). Rerum britannicarum medii aevi scriptores, no. 38].

——— ——— Memorials of saint Dunstan. 4, cxxiii, 490 pp. 8°. *London, Longmans*, 1874.

[GREAT BRITAIN. (*Public record office*). Rerum britannicarum medii aevi scriptores, no. 63].

Student's (The) France. [*anon.*] xii, 730 pp. front. 12°. *New York, Harper & brothers*, 1871.

Studer (Jacob H.) Columbus, Ohio: its history, resources, and progress. 584 pp. incl. 12 pl. 9 pl. 1 map. 8°. [*Columbus, O., J. H. Studer*, 1873].

Sturm (Christoph Christian). Beauties of nature delineated. Selected from Sturm's reflections, by rev. Thaddeus M. Harris. 2d ed. 237 pp. 16°. *Charlestown*, [*Ms.*] *L. Etheridge*, 1801.

Sturtevant (E. Lewis, *m. d.*) *and* **Sturtevant** (Joseph N.) The dairy cow. Monograph on the Ayrshire breed of cattle. 252 pp. 5 pl. 12°. *Boston, A. Williams & co.* 1875.

Suares (*Rev.* M. R.) The great mystery: God manifest in the flesh, and other discourses. 192 pp. port. 12°. *Philadelphia, Grant, Faires & Rodgers*, 1875.

Suckling (*Sir* John). Poems, plays and other remains. New ed. 2 v. lxxxiv, 204 pp. 1 l. port; 2 p. l. 286 pp. 1 facs. 12°. *London, F. & W. Kerslake*, 1874.

Suddoth (*Mrs.* H. A. B.) An orphan of the old dominion. By Lumina Silvervale [*pseud.*] 390 pp. 12°. *Philadelphia, J. B. Lippincott & co.* 1873.

Sue (Marie Joseph, *called* Eugène). Marquis of Létorière. (From the french). C. G. C. [Caroline Green Cotting. *anon.*] 193 pp. 18°. *Boston, Nichols & Hall*, 1873.

——— The wandering jew. New translation, by Henry L. Williams. 1 p. l. viii, 368 pp. port. 12°. *London, E. Appleyard*, 1873.

Sullivan (Robert). Dictionary of derivations. 14th ed. 304 pp. 1 pl. 16°. *Dublin, Sullivan bros.* 1872.

Summers (Thomas O.) Pocket anatomy. 224 pp. 18°. *Nashville, A. H. Redford*, 1876.

Sumner (Charles). Works. v. 5–9. 12°. *Boston, Lee & Shepard*, 1873–74.

——— Prophetic voices concerning America. 2 p. l. 176 pp. 1 port. 8°. *Boston, Lee & Shepard*, 1874.

Sumner (William G.) History of american currency. iv, 391 pp. 2 tab. 8°. *New York, H. Holt & co.* 1874.

Supernatural religion. 4th ed. [*anon.*] 2 v. xx, 485 pp; vi, 512 pp. 8°. *London, Longmans*, 1874.

Surr (Thomas Skinner). A winter in London: a novel. 2d ed. 3 v. 16°. *London, for R. Phillips*, 1806.

Surtees society. Publications. v. 1–64. 8°. *London and Durham*, 1835–75.

Sussex archæological society. Sussex archæological collections. 25 v. 8°. *London, J. R. Smith; Lewes, G. P. Bacon*, 1848–73.

Sutherland (Thomas Jefferson). Loose leaves, from the port folio of a late patriot prisoner in Canada. [*anon.*] 216 pp. 18°. *New York, W. H. Colyer*, 1840.

Sutton (Charles). The New York Tombs. Edited by J. B. Mix and S. A. Mackeever. 669 pp. incl. 14 pl. 8°. *New York, United States publishing co.* 1874.

Svedelius (G.) Hand-book for charcoal burners. From the swedish by R. B. Anderson. xv, 217 pp. 12°. *New York, J. Wiley & son*, 1875.

Svetchine (Sophie Soymonof). Lettres inédites. 2 p. l. vii, 495 pp. 2 l. 8°. *Paris, A. Vaton*, 1866.

Swedenborg *or* **Svedberg** (Emmanuel, *baron von*). Angelic wisdom concerning the divine providence. From the latin. From the last London ed. xiii, 308 pp. 8°. *New York, am. Swedenborg printing and publishing society*, 1873.

——— Apocalypse revealed. From the latin. New ed. 2 v. 480 pp; 339, 136 pp. 8°. *New York, am. Swedenborg printing & publishing society*, 1873.

——— Same. From the latin. Rotch ed. 1 p. l. 572 pp; 1 p. l. 573–1202 pp. 12°. *Philadelphia, J. B. Lippincott & co.* 1875.

Sweeny (*Mrs.* M. S.) Rock farm. iv, 168 pp. 18°. *Baltimore, W. J. C. Dulany & co.* 1873.

Sweet (Homer D. L.) New atlas of Onondaga co. N. Y. 110 pp. incl. 35 col. maps on 56 l. 4°. *New York, Walker bros. & co.* 1874.

Sweet (James Bradby). Memoir of Henry Hoare. xxiv, 552 pp. 8°. *London, Rivingtons*, 1869.

Sweet (S. H.) Report on the proposed Chesapeake bay and Potomac river tide-water canal, from Washington to Annapolis. viii, 103 pp. 8°. *Albany, argus co.* 1866. s.

Sweetser (Matthew Foster). Europe for $2 a day. 120 pp. 18°. *Boston, J. R. Osgood & co.* 1875.

——— *editor.* The maritime provinces. A guide to Canada. xi, 336, 24 pp. 4 maps, 4 plans. 16°. *Boston, J. R. Osgood & co.* 1875.

——— The middle states: a handbook for travellers. xvi, 470, 26 pp. 20 maps and plans, 2 maps in pockets. 16°. *Boston, J. R. Osgood & co.* 1874.

——— New England: a handbook for travellers. xvi, 399 pp. 14 maps and plans, 1 map in pocket. 16°. *Boston, J. R. Osgood & co.* 1873.

——— Same. New ed. xvi, 431 pp. 17 maps and plans. 16°. *Boston, J. R. Osgood & co.* 1874.

Sweetser (S.) The ministry we need. 123 pp. 16°. *Boston, american tract society*, [1873].

Sweringen (H. V.) Pharmaceutical lexicon. [viii], 17–576 pp. 8°. *Philadelphia, Lindsay & Blakiston*, 1873.

Swinburne (Algernon Charles). Bothwell: a tragedy. 2d ed. 4 p. l. 532 pp. 12°. *London, Chatto & Windus*, 1874.

——— Essays and studies. xiv, 380 pp. 12°. *London, Chatto & Windus*, 1875.

Swing (*Rev.* David). Sermons. 144 pp. 1 pl. 8°. *Chicago, W. B. Keen, Cooke & co.* 1874.

——— Trial of the rev. David Swing before the presbytery of Chicago. 1 p. l. 286 pp. 8°. *Chicago, Jansen, McClurg & co.* 1874.

——— Truths for to-day. 291 pp. 12°. *Chicago, Jansen, McClurg & co.* 1874.

Swinton (William). Outlines of the world's history. xi, 498 pp. 6 col. maps. 16°. *New York, Ivison, Blakeman, Taylor & co.* 1874.

Sybel (Heinrich C. L. *von*). History of the french revolution. From the german, by Walter C. Perry. 4 v. 8°. *London, J. Murray*, 1867–69.

Note.—v. 3 & 4 from the 3d ed. of the original german.

Syckelmoore (William, *publisher*). Centennial city. Illustrated handbook of Philadelphia. 1 p. l. 146, xxii pp. 1 l. 1 map, 1 pl. 12°. *Philadelphia, W. Syckelmoore*, [1875].

Symeon *of Durham.* Opera et collectanea. v. 1. lxxxi pp. 1 l. 301 pp. 1 l. 8°. *Durham*, 1868.

[SURTEES society. Publications, v. 51].

Symson (*Rev.* Andrew). Large description of Galloway. 9–224, 4 pp. 12°. [*Kirkcudbright, J. Nicholson*, 1841].

[*With* MACKENZIE (*Rev.* William). The history of Galloway, v. 2. Imperfect; title-page, etc. wanting].

Sypher (Josiah R.) Art of teaching school. New ed. 327 pp. 12°. *Philadelphia, J. M. Stoddart & co.* [1872].

Szold (*Rabbi* Benjamin, *compiler*). Israelitish prayer book, for all the public services of the year. Hebrew and english ed. by M. Jastrow. 4 p. l. 590 pp. 5 l. 16°. *Philadelphia, editor*, 1873.

——— Songs and prayers and meditations. From the german by M. Jastrow. iv, 104 pp. 12°. *Philadelphia, translator*, 1873.

[*With* SZOLD (B.) Israelitish prayer book].

Taber (C. A. M.) Rhymes from a sailor's journal. viii, 215 pp. 12°. *Cambridge*, [*Mass.*] *for the author*, 1873.

Tabor (Eliza). Aston-royal. [*anon.*] 3 v. 12°. *London, Hurst & Blackett*, 1872.

——— Diary of a novelist. [*anon.*] 3 p. l. 317 pp. 12°. *London, Hurst & Blackett*, 1871.

——— Hagar. [*anon.*] 3 v. 12°. *London, Hurst & Blackett*, 1870.

——— Jeanie's quiet life. [*anon.*] 3 v. 12°. *London, Hurst & Blackett*, 1868.

Taillandier (René Gaspard Ernest, *called* Saint-René). Drames & romans de la vie littéraire. La comtesse d'Ahlefeldt, Henri et Charlotte Stieglitz, Henri de Kleist. 2e éd. 2 p. l. iv, a–h, 258 pp. 1 l. 16°. *Paris, librairie des bibliophiles*, 1871.

Taine (Hippolyte Adolphe). Essais de critique et d'histoire. 2e éd. 2 p. l. xxvii, 410 pp. 16°. *Paris, L. Hachette & cie.* 1866.

——— Notes sur Paris. 3e éd. xi, 347 pp. 16°. *Paris, L. Hachette & cie.* 1867.

——— Same. Translated by J. A. Stevens. 1 p. l. ix, 372 pp. 12°. *New York, H. Holt & co.* 1875.

——— Nouveaux essais de critique et d'histoire. 2 p. l. 396 pp. 16°. *Paris, L. Hachette & cie.* 1865.

——— On intelligence. From the french by T. D. Haye. xxxix, 514 pp. 8°. *New York, Holt & Williams*, 1872.

——— Philosophy of art. Art in Greece. Translated by John Durand. vi, 168 pp. 16°. *New York, Holt & Williams*, 1871.

Taine (Hippolyte Adolphe)—continued.
——— Same. 2d ed. 190 pp. 16°. *New York, Holt & Williams*, 1873.
——— Philosophy of art. Art in Italy. Translated by John Durand. 156 pp. 16°. *New York, H. Holt & co.* 1875.
——— Tour through the Pyrenees. Translated by J. Safford Fiske; with illustrations by Gustave Doré. xvi, 523 pp. incl. 45 pl. 8°. *New York, H. Holt & co.* 1874.

Takings; or, the life of a collegian. A poem. Illustrated by twenty-six etchings, from designs by R. Dagley. [*anon.*] xlvii, 184 pp. 26 pl. 8°. *London, J. Warren*, 1821.

Tales and sketches. [*anon.*] 2 p. l. 13–248 pp. 12°. *New-York, J. & J. Harper*, 1829.

Tallis (John). Tallis's history and description of the crystal palace, and the exhibition of 1851. Edited by J. G. Strutt. 3 v. containing 141 pl. 4°. *London, J. Tallis & co. and London publishing co.* [1852].

Talmage (*Rev.* Thomas De Witt). Around the tea-table. 504 pp. incl. 12 pl. 12°. *Philadelphia, Cowperthwait & co.* 1874.
——— Old wells dug out: a third series of sermons. 2 p. l. 13–432 pp. 12°. *New York, Harper & brothers*, 1874.
——— One thousand gems. Edited by William H. Larrabee. xvi, 13–360 pp. port. 12°. *New York, N. Tibbals & son*, 1873.
——— Sports that kill. 241 pp. 12°. *New York, Harper & brothers*, 1875.

Talmud. Talmudis babylonici codex succa. Latinitate donavit F. B. Dachs. 8 p. l. 580 pp. 8 l. sm. 4°. *Trajecti ad Rhenum, apud Gysbertum a Paddenburg*, 1726.
——— Same. Talmud babylonicum. I. Tractatus macot cum scholiis hermeneuticis, auctore dr. H. S. Hirschfeld. vi, 174 pp. 8°. *Berolini, M. Simion*, 1842.
——— Same. Talmud de Babylone, traduit en langue française. Par l'abbé L. Chiarini. 2 v. in 1. 1 p. l. 414 pp; 1 p. l. 373 pp. 8°. *Leipzic, J. A. G. Weigel*, 1831.

Tapia Zenteno (Carlos de). Noticia de la lengua huasteca. 5 p. l. 128 pp. 12°. *México, imprenta de la bibliotheca mexicana*, 1767.

Tardieu (Jules). Only a pin! From the french of J. T.; de St.-Germaine by P. S. [*anon.*] 206 pp. 16°. *New York, catholic publication society*, 1873.

Tassy (Louis). Études sur l'aménagement des forêts. 2e éd. 3 p. l. xxxiv, 498 pp. 8°. *Paris, J. Rothschild*, 1872.

Tastu (Sabine-Casimir-Amable Voïart, *dame*). Poésies. 7e éd. 2 p. l. 315 pp. 1 pl. 18°. *Paris, Didier*, 1839. s.

Tatler (The) and the guardian. By Joseph Addison [and others]. Edited by G. W. Greene. 520 pp. port. 12°. *Philadelphia, J. B. Lippincott & co.* 1876.

Tautphœus (Jemima Montgomery, *baronin* von). The initials. 1 p. l. 402 pp. 12°. *Philadelphia, T. B. Peterson & brothers*, [1872].

Taylor (*Rev.* Alfred). Peeps at our sunday-schools. 252 pp. 12°. *New York, Nelson & Phillips*, [1874].
——— *compiler.* The tabernacle chorus. 160 pp. 24°. *New York, Biglow & Main*, 1874.

Taylor (Bayard). Egypt and Iceland in 1874. 282 pp. 18°. *New York, G. P. Putnam's sons*, 1874.
——— Home pastorals, ballads and lyrics. viii, 214 pp. 12°. *Boston, J. R. Osgood & co.* 1875.
——— Lars: a pastoral of Norway. 144 pp. 12°. *Boston, J. R. Osgood & co.* 1873.
——— The prophet: a tragedy. 3 p. l. 9–300 pp. 12°. *Boston, J. R. Osgood & co.* 1874.
——— School history of Germany. 1 p. l. v–x, 608 pp. 1 pl. 12°. *New York, D. Appleton & co.* 1874.
——— *editor.* Illustrated library of travel. 12°. *New York, Scribner, Armstrong & co.* 1874.

CONTENTS.

TAYLOR (Bayard). Central Asia. 365 pp. 20 pl 1 map. 1874.

Taylor (Benjamin Franklin). Old-time pictures and sheaves of rhyme. 2 p. l. 9–194 pp. 12°. *Chicago, S. C. Griggs & co.* 1874.
——— Pictures of life in camp and field. 1 p. l. 270 pp. *Chicago, S. C. Griggs & co.* 1875.
——— The world on wheels. Eng. title, 1 p. l. 9–258 pp. 1 pl. 12°. *Chicago, S. C. Griggs & co.* 1874.

Taylor (F.) Ella V—; or, the july tour. [*anon.*] 2 p. l. 219 pp. 12°. *New York, D. Appleton & co.* 1841.

Taylor (George). Memoir of Robert Surtees. New ed. by James Raine. xxi, 441 pp. 1 pl. 8°. *Durham*, 1852.
[SURTEES society. Publications, v. 24].

Taylor (*Rev.* Isaac). Etruscan researches. xii, 388 pp. front. 8°. *London, Macmillan & co.* 1874.

Taylor (John, *the water poet*). Works, not included in the folio volume of 1630. Second collection. [370] pp. 4°. [*Manchester*], *for the Spenser society*, 1873.
[SPENSER society. Publications, no. 14].

Taylor (John, *d.* 1832). Personal reminiscences.
[*In* BRIC-À-BRAC series. 16°. *New York, Scribner, Armstrong & co.* 1875. v. 8. pp. 183–329, port.]

Taylor (Joseph). Curious antiquities. 108 pp. 18°. *New-York, S. Wood & sons*, 1820.

Taylor (Joseph). Fast life on the modern highway; being a glance into the railroad world. 220 pp. incl. 8 pl. 12°. *New York, Harper & brothers*, 1874.

Taylor (Samuel W.) The storming of Quebec, a poem. 126 pp. 18°. *Philadelphia, J. Gray*, 1829.

Taylor (Theodore). Golden treasury of thought. vii, 466 pp. 12°. *London, Chatto & Windus*, [1873].

Taylor (Thomas, *the Platonist*, 1758–1835). Eleusinian and bacchic mysteries. 3d ed. Edited by Alexander Wilder. xxii, 174 pp. 8°. *New York, J. W. Bouton*, 1875.

Taylor (Tom). Leicester square. viii, 495 pp. 8 pl. 4 ports. 2 facs. 2 photos. 12°. *London, Bickers & son*, 1874.

Taylor (T.) John Richmond. 248 pp. incl. 3 pl. 16°. *New York, Nelson & Phillips*, [1873].

Taylor (William M. *d. d.*) David, king of Israel. 443 pp. 12°. *New York, Harper & brothers*, 1875.

——— The lost found, and the wanderer welcomed. 3 p. l. 170 pp. 12°. *New York, Scribner, Armstrong & co.* 1873.

Temminck (Coenraad Jacob). Coup-d'œil général sur les possessions néerlandaises dans l'Inde archipélagique. 3 v. 8°. *Leide, A. Arnz & co.* 1846–49.

Tempelhoff (Georg Fr.) Extracts from [his] history of the seven years war, [etc.]
[*In* LINDSAY (C.) Extracts from col. Tempelhoffe's history of the seven years war [etc.] 8°. *London, for T. Cadell*, 1793. v. 1, pp. 1–214, & v. 2, pp. 215–264].

Temple (Josiah Howard) *and* **Sheldon** (George). History of the town of Northfield, Mass. for 150 years. viii, 636 pp. 5 pl. 2 ports. 8°. *Albany, J. Munsell*, 1875.

Ten Brink (B.) Levensbeschrijving van Rijklof Michaël van Goens. x pp. 1 l. 340 pp. 1 l. 8°. *Utrecht, C. van der Post, jr.* 1869. s.

Ten Brook (Andrew). American state universities, their origin and progress. vi, v–viii, 410 pp. 8°. *Cincinnati, R. Clarke & co.* 1875.

Tercentenary (The) book. Containing an account of the "tercentenary celebration" as observed by the presbyterians of Philadelphia nov. 20, 1872. With an introduction by rev. Henry McCook. 232 pp. incl. 7 pl. 12°. *Philadelphia, presbyterian board of publication*, [1873].

Terhune (*Mrs.* Mary Virginia Hawes). "Common sense in the household" series. Breakfast, luncheon and tea. By Marion Harland [*pseud.*] 3 p. l. 459 pp. 12°. *New York, Scribner, Armstrong & co.* 1875.

——— From my youth up. By Marion Harland [*pseud.*] 390 pp. 12°. *New York, G. W. Carleton & co.* 1874.

——— Jessamine. By Marion Harland [*pseud.*] 387 pp. 12°. *New York, G. W. Carleton & co.* 1873.

Tétôt (—, *archiviste*). Répertoire des traités de paix d'alliance, de commerce, etc. conclus entre toutes les puissances du globe principalement depuis la paix de Westphalie jusqu'à nos jours. Partie alphabétique. 1493–1867. 4 p. l. 595 pp. 8°. *Paris, Amyot*, [1873].

Teuffel (Wilhelm Sigismund). History of roman literature. Translated by W. Wagner. 2 v. 2 p. l. 549 pp; 2 p. l. 624 pp. 8°. *London, G. Bell & sons*, 1873.

Thackeray (Anne Isabella). Bluebeard's keys and other stories. 3d ed. x, 412 pp. 12°. *London, Smith, Elder & co.* 1875.

——— Old Kensington. 1 p. l. 9–182 pp. 1 pl. 8°. *New York, Harper & brothers*, 1873.

Thaddæus (Joannes). Reconciler of the bible. By J. T. [*anon.*] 4 p. l. 348 pp. sq. 12°. *London, S. Miller*, 1656.

Thalheimer (M. E.) History of England. 287 pp. 2 col. maps. 12°. *Cincinnati, Wilson, Hinkle & co.* [1875].

——— Manual of mediæval and modern history. 480 pp. 12 maps. 8°. *Cincinnati, Wilson, Hinkle & co.* 1874.

Thatcher (Benjamin Bussey). Memoir of rev. S. Osgood Wright. 2d ed. 122 pp. 18°. *Boston, Light & Horton*, 1835.

Thaxter (Celia). Among the Isles of Shoals. 184 pp. 4 pl. 18°. *Boston, J. R. Osgood & co.* 1873.

——— Poems. [Enlarged ed.] 188 pp. 18°. *New York. Hurd & Houghton*, 1874.

Thébaud (*Rev.* Aug. J. *s. J.*) The irish race in the past and the present. xxiv, 532 pp. 8°. *New York, D. Appleton*, 1873.

Théry (Augustin). Tableau des littératures anciennes et modernes. 2 v. xii, 400 pp; 2 p. l. 392 pp. 8°. *Paris, Dezobry, E. Magdeleine & cie.* [1856].

Thiéblin (Nicolas Léon.) Spain and the spaniards. 2 v. 3 p. l. 330 pp. 1 l; 3 p. l 316 pp. 12°. *London, Hurst & Blackett*, 1874.

——— Same. 404 pp. 16°. *Boston, Lee & Shepard*, 1875.

Thielens (Armand). Flore médicale belge. 2 p. l. 335 pp. 12°. *Bruxelles & Leipzig. A. Lacroix, Verboeckhoven & cie.* 1862. s.

Thomas (Artus, *sieur d'Embry*). Description de l'îsle des hermaphrodites. 3 p l. 352 pp. 1 pl. 16°. *Cologne, les héritiers de H. Demen*, 1724.

——— Same. 3 p. l. 352 pp. 1 pl. 16°. *Cologne, les héritiers de H. Demen*, 1726.

Thomas (Francis Sheppard). Notes and materials for the history of public departments [of Great Britain. *anon.*] xi, 216 pp. sm. fol. *London, W. Clowes & sons*, 1846.

Thomas (Frederick William). Howard Pinckney. [*anon.*] 2 v. 227 pp; 216 pp. 12°. *Philadelphia, Lea & Blanchard*, 1840.

Thomas (John, *m. d.*) Chronikon hebraikon; or the chronology of the scriptures. 43 pp 8°. *New York, E. O. Jenkins, for the author*, 1866.

[*With* THOMAS (J. *m. d.*) Elpis israel].

——— Elpis israel; being an exposition of the kingdom of God. 4th ed. vi, 410 pp. 8°. *West Hoboken, N. J. author*, 1867.

Thomas (J. W.) Star-beams. 363 pp. 16°. *Providence, Angell, Burlingame & co.* 1875.

Thomas (*Rev.* Thomas). Memoirs of Owen Glendower. 6 p. l. xxiv, 240 pp. 12°. *Haverford-west, [Wales], for the author*, 1822.

Thomé (Otto Wilhelm). Lehrbuch der zoologie. 2ter abdruck. viii, 416 pp 8°. *Braunschweig, F. Vieweg & sohn*, 1874.

Thomes (William H.) Life in the East Indies. 354 pp. 4 pl. 12°. *Boston, Lee & Shepard*, 1873.

[OCEAN-LIFE series].

——— Running the blockade; or, U. S. secret service adventures. 474 pp. 8 pl. 12°. *Boston, Lee & Shepard*, 1875.

Thompson (Benjamin, *count Rumford*). Complete works. v. 1. [v], 493 pp. 18 pl. 8°. *Boston*, 1870.

Thompson (*Mrs.* Clara M.) Hawthorndean. 426 pp. 12°. *Philadelphia, P. F. Cunningham*, 1873.

Thompson (Edith). History of England. xvi, 252 pp. 16°. *New York, H. Holt & co.* 1873.

[FREEMAN (E. A.) Historical course for schools, v. 2].

Thompson (Edward Healy, *editor*). Library of religious biography, v. 5. Life of the venerable Anna Maria Taigi, the roman matron. [1769–1837]. xxiii, 414 pp. port. 16°. *New York, F. Pustet*, 1874.

Thompson (*Mrs.* Ella W.) Beaten paths. 274 pp. 16°. *Boston, Lee & Shepard*, 1874.

Thompson (*Mrs.* Helen S.) Ponapé; or, light on a dark shore. 1 p. l. 240 pp. 4 pl. 16°. *Philadelphia, american baptist publication society*, [1874].

Thompson (Joseph Parish). Church and state in the United States. 1 p. l. 166 pp. 16°. *Boston, J. R. Osgood & co.* 1873.

——— Jesus of Nazareth: his life for the young. xviii, 438 pp. 52 pl. 8°. *Boston, J. R. Osgood & co.* 1876.

Thompson (J. W.) Sketches of noted Maine horses. xv, 25–331 pp. 2 pl. 12°. *Portland, Hoyt & Fogg*, 1874.

Thompson (Lewis O.) The presidents and their administrations. 320 pp. 1 map. 16°. *Indianapolis, J. W. Robinson*, [1873].

Thompson (Maurice). Hoosier mosaics. 196 pp. 18°. *New York, E. J. Hale & son*, 1875.

Thompson (Noyes L.) History of Plymouth church. 1847 to 1872. 310 pp. 10 pl. 12°. *New York, G. W. Carleton & co.* 1873.

Thompson (Robert Ellis). Social science and national economy. 415 pp. 12°. *Philadelphia, Porter & Coates*, 1875.

Thoms (William J.) Human longevity, its facts and fictions. xii, 320 pp. 12°. *London, J. Murray*, 1873.

Thomson (John Lewis). History of the indian wars and war of the revolution. 402 pp. incl. 14 pl. 8°. *Philadelphia, J. B. Lippincott & co.* 1873.

Thomson (Richard). Lecture on the most characteristic features of illuminated manuscripts from the VIII. to the XIII. century. [Also] lecture on the materials and practice of illuminators; [etc.] 1 p. l. vi, 138 pp. 8°. *London, [not published]*, 1857. s.

Thomson (William). Prospects and observations; on a tour in England and Scotland. By Thomas Newte [*pseud.*] viii, 1–184, 177–440 pp. 23 pl. 1 map. 4°. *London, for G. G. J. & J. Robinson*, 1791.

Thoré (Théophile Étienne Joseph). Histoire des peintres de toutes les écoles. École anglaise, par m. W. Bürger [*pseud.*] 2 p. l. 16, [267] pp. 4 l. fol. *Paris, vve. J. Renouard*, 1863.

[*With* BLANC (C.) *and others.* Histoire des peintres de toutes écoles. École espagnole. fol. *Paris, vve. J. Renouard*, 1869].

Thornbury (Walter) Criss-cross journeys. 2 v. 2 p. l. 329 pp; 1 p. l. 342 pp. 12°. *London, Hurst & Blackett*, 1873.

Thorne (Olive). Little folks in feathers and fur, and others in neither. 357, xi pp. sq. 12°. *Hartford, Dustin, Gilman & co.* 1875.

Thornton (*Mrs.* Alice). Autobiography. xv, 373 pp. 2 tab. 8°. *Durham, for the society*, 1875.

[SURTEES society. Publications, v. 62].

Thornton (John Wingate). Historical relation of New England to the english commonwealth. 105 pp. 8°. [*Boston, A. Mudge & son*], 1875.

Thornton (William Thomas). Indian public works. xi, 278 pp. 1 map. 12°. *London, Macmillan & co.* 1875.

——— Old-fashioned ethics and common-sense metaphysics. xi, 298 pp. 8°. *London, Macmillan & co.* 1873.

Thornwell (James Henley, *d. d.*) Collected writings. v. 3–4. 8°. *Richmond, presbyterian committee of publication*, 1873.

Thorpe (Kamba). Little Joanna. A novel. 2 p. l. 131 pp. 8°. *New York, D. Appleton & co.* 1876.

[APPLETON'S library of american fiction].

Throop (George H.) Lynde Weiss. [New ed.] 188 pp. 6 pl. 12°. *Philadelphia, Claxton, Remsen & Haffelfinger*, 1873.

Throsby (John). History and antiquities of Leicester. 3 p. l. 424 pp. 44 pl. 2 plans, 1 facs. 3 pl. containing 15 ports. 4°. *Leicester, printed by J. Brown, for the author*, 1791.

——— Select views in Leicestershire. 2 v. Eng. title, viii, 354 pp. 57 pl. 1 port. 1 tab. 4 facs. 4°. *London, J. Throsby*, 1789.

——— Supplementary volume to the Leicestershire views. Eng. title, 536 pp. 17 pl. 1 map. 4°. *London, for the author*, 1790.

Tibullus (Albius). Elegies. Translated into english verse, with life of the poet, by James Cranstoun. xxvi, 217 pp. 12°. *Edinburgh, W. Blackwood & sons*, 1872.

Tiffany (John K.) Philatelical library. Catalogue of stamp publications. vi pp. 2 l. 110 pp. 1 l. sm. 4°. *St. Louis, [Cambridge, Ms. printed], privately printed*, 1874.

Tileston (Mary W. *compiler*). Quiet hours. A collection of poems. [*anon.*] ix, 182 pp. 18°. *Boston, Roberts brothers*, 1874.

Tillotson (John). The golden Americas. xi, 376 pp. 12 pl. 12°. *London, Ward, Lock, & Tyler*, [186–].

Tilton (Theodore). Tempest-tossed. 606 pp. 8°. *New York, Sheldon & co.* 1874.

Timbs (John). Doctors and patients. 2 v. viii, 288 pp; vi, 287 pp. 12°. *London, R. Bentley & son*, 1873.

——— Eccentricities of the animal creation. 352 pp. 8 pl. 16°. *London, Seeley, Jackson & Halliday*, 1869.

——— English eccentrics and eccentricities. xvi, 578 pp. col. front. 12°. *London, Chatto & Windus*, 1875.

Timmins (Samuel, *editor.*) Resources, products, and industrial history of Birmingham and the midland hardware district. xiii, 721 pp. 8°. *London, R. Hardwicke*, 1866.

Timrod (Henry). Poems. 205 pp. 16°. *New York, E. J. Hale & son*, 1873.

Todd (John). John Todd, the story of his life told mainly by himself. 529 pp. 4 p. l. port. 12°. *New York, Harper & brothers*, 1876.

Todhunter (Isaac). Conflict of studies and other essays on education. xi, 242 pp. 8°. *London, Macmillan & co.* 1873.

Toland (John). Amyntor: a defence of Milton's life. [*anon.*] 2 p. l. 172 pp. 8°. *London*, 1699.

Tomlinson (Charles). The sonnet; its origin, structure, and place in poetry. With translations from Dante, Petrarch, etc. xix, 227 pp. 12°. *London, J. Murray*, 1874.

Toner (Joseph Meredith, *m. d.*) Contributions to the annals of medical progress and medical education in the United States before and during the war of independence. 118 pp. 8°. *Washington, government printing office*, 1874.

[UNITED STATES. *Interior department.* (*Bureau of education*)].

Tonge (Thomas, *Norroy king of arms*). Heraldic visitation of the northern counties in 1530. Edited by W. H. D. Longstaffe. xi, 103, xc pp. 8°. *Durham*, 1863.

[SURTEES society. Publications, v. 41].

Tonna (Charlotte Elizabeth). Judæa capta: by Charlotte Elizabeth [*pseud.*] 222 pp. 18°. *New York, J. S. Taylor & co.* 1845.

Topin (Marius). The man with the iron mask. Translated by H. Vizetelly. xvi, 368 pp. 1 facs. 12°. *London, Smith, Elder & co.* 1870.

Torrey (Joseph). A theory of fine art. xi, 290 pp. 16°. *New York, Scribner, Armstrong & co.* 1874.

Touchatout, *pseud.* Histoire de France tintamarresque depuis les temps les plus reculés jusqu'à nos jours. 1 p. l. 796 pp. incl. 11

Touchatout, *pseud.*—continued. col. pl. front. 8°. *Paris, aux bureaux du journal l'éclipse*, 1872.

Toussaint (François-Vincent). Histoire des passions. Ouvrage traduit de l'anglois. 1 & 2 partie. [*anon.*] 4 p. l. 356 pp. 2 l. 16°. *La Haye, J. Neaulme*, 1751.

Towle (Nancy). Vicissitudes illustrated. 2d ed. 310 pp. incl. front. 18°. *Portsmouth,* [*N. H.*] *for the authoress*, 1833.

Towler (John, *m. d.*) The silver sunbeam: a text-book on sun drawing and photographic printing. 8th ed. 1 p. l. xvii, 18, 9-574 pp. 6 l. 1 tab. 8°. *New-York, E. & H. T. Anthony & co.* 1873.

——— Same. El rayo solar. xiv, 439 pp. 2 photos. 8°. *Nueva York, D. Appleton & ca.* 1876.

Towneley (The) mysteries. xxi, 352 pp. 1 pl. 8°. *London*, 1836.

[SURTEES society. Publications, v. 3].

Note.—Known also as the Widkirk mysteries.

Townsend (Calvin). Analysis of letter-writing. viii, 181 pp. 8°. *New York, Ivison, Blakeman, Taylor & co.* 1873.

——— Shorter course in civil government. vi, 240 pp. 12°. *New York, Ivison, Blakeman, Taylor & co.* 1875.

Townsend (George Alfred). Washington, outside and inside. 751 pp. 20 pl. 8°. *Hartford, J. Betts & co.* 1873.

Townsend (George H.) William Shakespeare not an impostor. [*anon.*] vi, 122 pp. 16°. *London, G. Routledge & co.* 1857.

Townsend (Luther Tracy, *d. d.*) The arena and the throne. 264 pp. 1 pl. 16°. *Boston, Lee & Shepard*, 1874.

——— Lost forever. 448 pp. 16°. *Boston, Lee & Shepard*, 1875.

Townsend (Virginia Frances). Elizabeth Tudor. [*anon.*] 325 pp. 3 pl. 16°. *New York, Nelson & Phillips*, [1874].

——— One woman's two lovers. 284 pp. 12°. *Philadelphia, J. B. Lippincott & co.* 1875.

——— Six in all. 447 pp. 1 pl. 8°. *Boston, Loring*, [1873].

——— Temptation and triumph, with other stories. 389 pp. 16°. *Cincinnati, Hitchcock & Walden*, [1863].

——— That queer girl. 299 pp. 6 pl. 16°. *Boston, Lee & Shepard*, 1875.

[MAIDENHOOD series].

Trafton (*Miss* Adeline). Katherine Earle. 325 pp. 5 pl. 12°. *Boston, Lee & Shepard*, 1874.

Traits of attractive women, and philosophy of love affairs. [*anon.*] 240 pp. 12°. *Philadelphia, Belmont publishing co.* [1874].

Trall (Russell Thatcher, *m. d.*) Mother's hygienic hand-book. 186 pp. 12°. *New York, S. R. Wells*, 1874.

Trammell (William Dugas). Ça ira. A novel. 358 pp. 12°. *New York, United States publishing co.* 1874.

Trappen (J. E. van der). Herbarium vivum. 2 v. xvi, 747 pp; 1 p. l. xvi, 953 pp. 8°. *Haarlem, V. Loosjes* [*&*] *erven V. Loosjes*, 1839-43. s.

Treat (E. B.) Treat's illustrated New York, Brooklyn and surroundings. Ill. title, 100 pp. 8°. *New York, E. B. Treat*, 1874.

Trelles (Joseph Manuel). Asturias ilustrada. v. 1. 10 p. l. 491 pp. 10 l. fol. *Madrid, J. Sanchez*, 1736. s.

Trench (Richard Chenevix). Plutarch; his life, his lives and his morals. iii, 131 pp. 16°. *London, Macmillan & co.* 1873.

Trent (*Capt.* William). Journal, from Logstown to Pickawillany a. d. 1752. With letters of governor Robert Dinwiddie, [etc.] Edited by Alfred T. Goodman. 117 pp. 8°. *Cincinnati, for W. Dodge*, 1871.

Trevelyan (George Otto). The ladies in parliament and other pieces. 4 p. l. 196 pp. 12°. *Cambridge,* [*Eng.*] *Deighton, Bell & co.* 1869.

Tribune (The) association. Memorial of Horace Greeley. 265 pp. 4 pl. 8°. *New York, the tribune association*, 1873.

Triggs (J. H.) History of Cheyenne and northern Wyoming embracing the gold fields of the Black hills, [etc.] 143 pp. 1 map. 8°. *Omaha, herald printing house*, 1876.

Tripp (F. E.) British mosses. xxii, 235 pp. 39 pl. sm. 4°. *London, Bell & Daldy*, 1868.

Tristram (Henry Baker). The land of Moab. With a chapter on the persian palace of Mashita, by Jas. Fergusson. xvi, 408 pp. 10 pl. 1 col. map, 1 plan. 12°. *London, J. Murray*, 1873.

Triumph (The) of benevolence. [By the author of the Vicar of Wakefield. *anon.* Not by Goldsmith]. 2 v. in 1. 1 p. l. 214 pp. 1 pl; 238 pp. 16°. *Berlin, A. Mylius*, 1786.

Trobriand (Régis de). Quatre ans de campagnes à l'armée du Potomac. 2 v. in 1. 348 pp; 397 pp. 8°. *Paris, librairie internationale*, 1867-68.

Troilo (Franz Ferdinand von). Orientalische reise-beschreibung. Eng. title, 14 p. l. 669

Troilo (F. F. von)—continued. [+1] pp. 4°. *Dresden, M. Bergens sel. nachgelassene wittwe und erben*, 1677.

Trollope (Anthony). The golden lion of Granpere. 2 p. l. 353 pp. 12°. *London, Tinsley brothers*, 1872.

——— Lady Anna. 2 v. in 1. 1 p. l. v–viii, 317 pp; 1 p. l. v–viii, 314 pp. 16°. *London, Chapman & Hall*, 1874.

——— Phineas Redux. 1 p. l. 255 pp. 8°. *New York, Harper & bros.* 1874.

——— Sir Harry Hotspur of Humblethwaite. viii, 324 pp. 12°. *London, Hurst & Blackett*, 1871.

——— The vicar of Bullhampton. 2 pts. in 1 v. 141 pp. 9 pl; 1 p. l. 142–300 pp. 13 pl. 8°. *Philadelphia, J. B. Lippincott & co.* 1870.

——— The way we live now. 408 pp. incl. 2 pl. 8°. *New York, Harper & brothers* 1875.

Trollope (Frances). Life and adventures of Jonathan Jefferson Whitlaw. 3 v. in 1. 8°. *London, R. Bentley*, 1836.

Tröltsch (Anton von). Lehrbuch der ohrenheilkunde. 5te aufl. xiv, 554 pp 8°. *Leipzig, F. C. W. Vogel*, 1873 s.

Tronchin du Breuil (Jean). Relation du voyage de sa majesté britannique en Hollande. Eng. title, 5 p. l. 108 pp. 14 pl. fol. *La Haye, A. Leers*, 1692.

Tronk (Herman B. van). Rechts-handbuch. 264 pp. 12°. *Philadelphia, selbstverlag des verfassers*, 1874.

Troschel (Franz Hermann). Handbuch der zoologie. 7te aufl. viii, 788 pp. 8°. *Berlin, C. G. Lüderitz*, 1871.

Trotter (Lionel James). History of India. lvi, 414 pp. 8 pl. 1 col. map. 12°. *London, society for promoting christian knowledge*, [1874].

Trowbridge (John Townsend). Doing his best. 279 pp. 4 pl. 16°. *Boston, J. R. Osgood & co.* 1873.

——— The emigrant's story, and other poems. 1 p. l. v–vi, 173 pp. 1 pl. 16°. *Boston, J. R. Osgood & co.* 1875.

——— Fast friends. 282 pp. 6 pl. 16°. *Boston, J. R. Osgood & co.* 1875.

——— The old battle-ground. 276 pp. 1 pl. 18°. *New York, Sheldon & co.* 1860.

——— The young surveyor. 290 pp. 7 pl. 16°. *Boston, J. R. Osgood & co.* 1875.

Trowbridge (William P.) Heat as a source of power. ix, 209 pp. 33 pl. 8°. *New York, J. Wiley & son*, 1874.

True (Charles K.) John Winthrop and the great colony. 207 pp. incl. 2 pl. 16°. *New York, Nelson & Phillips*, [1875].

Truman (*Major* Ben. C.) Semi-tropical California. 204 pp. 8°. *San Francisco, A. L. Bancroft & co.* 1874.

Tryon (George Washington, *jr.*) American marine conchology. 208 pp. 44 col. pl. 8°. *Philadelphia, by the author*, [1873–74]. s.

——— Amy Cassonet. Opera. Vocal score. 1 p. l. 12, 5–127 pp. 4°. *Philadelphia, Lee & Walker*, [1875]

Tuke (Daniel Hack, *m. d.*) Illustrations of the influence of the mind upon the body. xvi, 444 pp. 8°. *London, J. & A. Churchill*, 1872.

Tulk (Alfred, *m. r. c. s.*) *and* **Henfrey** (Arthur, *a. l. s.*) Anatomical manipulation. xvi, 413 pp. 16°. *London, J. Van Voorst*, 1844.

Tulloch (John, *d. d.*) Rational theology and christian philosophy in England in the seventeenth century. 2 v. xiv, 463 pp; 3 p. l. 500 pp. 8°. *Edinburgh, W. Blackwood & sons*, 1872.

Tunnels (The) and water system of Chicago. [*anon.*] 112 pp. incl. 19 pl. 8°. *Chicago, J. M. Wing & co.* 1874.

Tupper (Martin Farquhar). Cithara: a selection from [his] lyrics. Eng. title & dedication, xi, 350 pp. 12°. *London, Virtue brothers & co.* 1863.

Turgénieff (Ivan Sergheïevitch). Dimitri Roudine. From the french and german versions. 271 pp. 16°. *New York, Holt & Williams*, 1873.
[LEISURE hour series].

——— Liza. From the russian by W. R. S. Ralston. 318 pp. 16°. *New York, Holt & Williams*, 1873.
[LEISURE hour series].

——— On the eve. From the russian by C. E. Turner. Am. ed. vi, 272 pp. 16°. *New York, Holt & Williams*, 1873.
[LEISURE hour series].

——— Spring floods; from the russian by mrs. Sophie Michell Butts. A Lear of the steppe; from the french by William Hand Browne. 1 p. l. 219 pp. 16°. *New York, H. Holt & co.* 1874.
[LEISURE hour series].

Turner (Bessie A.) A woman in the case. A story. 288 pp. albertype port. 12°. *New York, G. W. Carleton & co.* 1875.

Turner (Dawson). Muscologiæ hibernicæ spicilegium. 2 p. l. xi, 200, xiv pp. 16 pl. 8°. *Yermuthæ, J. Black*, 1804.

Turner (Juliana Frances). The harp of the beech woods. xi, 156 pp. 12°. *Montrose. Penn. A. Waldie*, 1822.

Turner (Thomas Hudson, *editor*). Manners and household expenses of England in the thirteenth and fifteenth centuries. 5 p. l. xcv, 622 pp. 4°. *London, W. Nicol*, 1841.
[ROXBURGHE club. Publications].

Turner (William). Compleat history of the most remarkable providences, which have hapned in this present age. 3 pts. in 1 v. fol. *London, for J. Dunton*, 1697.

Tussaud (*Madame* —, *born* Grosholtz). Memoirs and reminiscences of France. Edited by Francis Hervé. 1 p. l. xvi, 506 pp. 2 ports. 8°. *London, Saunders & Otley*, 1838.

Tuttle (Charles Richard). History of the border wars of two centuries. 608 pp. 8 pl. 8°. *Chicago, C. A. Wall & co.* 1874.

——— An illustrated history of Wisconsin. To 1875. 800 pp. incl. 102 ports. front. 1 col. map. 8°. *Boston, B. B. Russell*, 1875.

Tweedie (Alexander, *m. d. editor*). Dissertations on diseases of the digestive, urinary, and uterine organs. 516 pp. 8°. *Philadelphia, Lea & Blanchard*, 1841.

Tweedie (William K. *d. d.*) Home; or, the parents' assistant and children's friend. 2 p. l. 7–423 pp. 4 pl. 12°. *Norwich, Conn. H. Bill publishing co.* [1873].

Twells (*Mrs.* J. H.) The mills of the gods. 366 pp. 12°. *Philadelphia, J. B. Lippincott & co.* 1875.

Twelve mormon homes visited. [*anon.*] 2 p. l. 158 pp. 8°. *Philadelphia* [*W. Wood, for private circulation*], 1874.

Twining (Elizabeth). Illustrations of the natural orders of plants. Reduced from the folio ed. 2 v. 2 p. l. xii pp. 80 l. numb. & 80 col. pl; 3 p. l. 81–160 l. numb. & 81–160 col. pl. 161–172 pp. 8°. *London, S. Low, son, & Marston*, 1868.

Twisleton (Edward). The tongue not essential to speech. iv, 232 pp. 12°. *London, J. Murray*, 1873.

Tyerman (L.) Life and times of John Wesley. [2d ed.] 3 v. 8°. *London, Hodder & Stoughton*, 1872–75.

Tyndall (John). The advancement of science. Inaugural address at Belfast, aug. 19, 1874, with biographical sketch. Opinions of prof. H. Helmholtz, and articles of prof. Tyndall and sir Henry Thompson on prayer. 105 pp. port. 12°. *New York, A. K. Butts & co.* 1874.

Tyndall (John)—continued.

——— Address delivered before the British association assembled at Belfast. 7th thousand. xxxvi, 83 pp. 8°. *London, Longmans*, 1874.

——— A hö mint a mozgás egyik neme. Fordította Jezsovics Károly. 1 p. l. xxviii, 590 pp. 1 pl. 8°. *Budapest, kiadja a termeszettudomanyi társulat*, 1874. s.
[BUDAPEST. Kiralyi Magyar természettudományi társulat, no. 5].

——— Lectures on light. 194 pp. 12°. *New York, D. Appleton & co.* 1873.

Tyroff (Konrad). Wappenbuch des gesammten adels des königreichs Baiern. 19 v. in 9. 8°. *Nürnberg, wappen-, kunst- und kommissions-bureau* [*&*] *I. A. Tyroff*, 1818–56.

——— Same. General-register. 1ter bis 14ter band. 1 p. l. 50 pp. 8°. [*Nürnberg, I. A. Tyroff*, 1846.
[*In* TYROFF (K.) Wappenbuch des königreichs Baiern, v. 13–14].

——— ——— Same. [1ter–16ter band]. 1 p. l. 54 pp. 8°. [*Nürnberg, I. A. Tyroff*, 1850].
[*With* TYROFF (K.) Wappenbuch des gesammten adels des königreichs Baiern, v. 15–16].
See, also, WAPPENBUCH.

Tyrwhitt (*Rev.* Richard St. John). Christian art and symbolism. xii, 292 pp. 1 l. 3 pl. 12°. *London, Smith, Elder & co.* 1872.

Tyson (James, *m. d.*) Guide to the practical examination of urine. viii, 13–182 pp. 1 pl. 12°. *Philadelphia, Lindsay & Blakiston*, 1875.

Tyson (Robert A.) History of East St. Louis. 152 pp. 1 l. 1 pl. 1 map. 8°. *East St. Louis*, [*Ill.*] *J. Haps & co.* 1875.

Tyson (*Miss* —). The queen of the kitchen. A collection of "old Maryland" family receipts for cooking. 412 pp. 12°. *Philadelphia, T. B. Peterson & brothers*, [1874].

U. (A.) Overland, inland, and upland. [*anon.*] viii, 342 pp. 6 pl. 12°. *London, Seeley, Jackson, & Halliday*, 1873.
Note.—Travels to India by way of Egypt.

Ueber die alten und neuen mysterien. [*anon.*] 5 p. l. viii, 380 pp. 16°. *Berlin, F. Maurer*, 1782.

Ueberweg (Friedrich, *d. d.*) History of philosophy. Translated from the 4th germ. ed. by Geo. S. Morris. v. 2.—History of modern philosophy. viii, 561 pp. 8°. *New York, Scribner, Armstrong & co.* 1874.
[SMITH (H. B.) *and* SCHAFF (P.) Theological and philosophical library. v. 2 of the philosophical division].

Ulman (H. Charles). Trow's legal directory and lawyers' record of the United States. 1875. 8°. *New York, J. F. Trow*, [1875].

Ulrici (Hermann). Strauss as a philosophical thinker. Translated by C. P. Krauth. 1 p. l. 7–167 pp. 16°. *Philadelphia, Smith, English & co.* 1874.

Uncle Charles (*pseud.*) Social visits. Eng. title, 229 pp. 1 pl. 18°. *Charleston,* [*S. C.*] *southern baptist publication society,* 1854. s.

Uncle Paul (*pseud.*) The Nesbits, and other tales. 246 pp. 16°. *New York, catholic publication society,* [1872].

Underwood (Francis H.) Lord of himself. 512 pp. 12°. *Boston, Lee & Shepard,* 1874.

United States. *Congress.* Congressional directory. 43d cong. 2d session. Compiled by B. P. Poore. 1st ed. 8°. *Washington, government printing office,* 1874.

——— ——— Congressional globe: third session forty-second congress. By F. & J. Rives & George A. Bailey. 3 v. 4°. *Washington, office of the congressional globe,* 1873.

——— ——— Congressional record: containing the proceedings and debates of the forty-third congress. Special session of the senate of the United States. March 4 to 26, 1873. v. 1. 4°. *Washington, government printing office,* 1874.

——— ——— Same, forty-third congress, first session. [Dec. 1, 1873–june 23, 1874]. v. 2 and index in 7 v. 4°. *Washington, government printing office,* 1874.

——— ——— Same, forty-third congress, second session. [Dec. 7, 1874–mar. 3, 1875] v. 3 and index in 4 v. 4°. *Washington, government printing office,* 1875.

——— ——— Constitution of the United States: Jefferson's manual, and Barclay's digest. 1st sess. 43d cong. 280, 254 pp. 8°. *Washington, government printing office,* [1873].

——— ——— Same. 2d sess. 43d cong. 280, 264 pp. 8°. *Washington, government printing office,* [1874].

——— ——— Same. 1st sess. 44th cong. 231, 262 pp. 8°. *Washington, government printing office,* [1875].

——— *Department of justice.* Catalogue of law books of the department of justice. 1873. 251 pp. 8°. *Washington, government printing office,* 1873.

——— ——— Register of the department of justice. To sept. 1, 1874. 4th ed. 231 pp. 8°. *Washington, government printing office,* 1874.

——— *Interior department.* Register of officers and agents in the service of the United States, 30th sept. 1873. xv, 1022 pp. 8°. *Washington, government printing office,* 1874.

——— *Navy department.* Polaris investigation. 184 pp. 8°. [*Washington, government printing office,* 1873].

——— *Treasury department.* Catalogue of the library, july 1, 1873. 2 p. l. 131 pp. 8°. *Washington, government printing office,* 1873.

——— ——— General regulations under the customs and navigation laws. vii, 656 pp. 5 pl. 8°. *Washington, government printing office,* 1874.

——— ——— United States treasury register, 1874. ix, 257 pp. 8°. *Washington, government printing office,* 1874.

——— *War department.* Cavalry tactics. 530 pp. 18°. *New York, D. Appleton & co.* 1874.

Unseen (The) universe. [*anon.*] 3d ed. xvii, 197 pp. 12°. *New York, Macmillan & co.* 1875.

Note.—Attributed generally to Balfour Stewart and Peter Guthrie Tait.

Upham (Charles Wentworth). Life of Timothy Pickering. v. 2–4. 8°. *Boston, Little Brown & co.* 1873.

Upham (Francis William). The star of our lord. xlii, 370 pp. 12°. *New York, Nelson & Phillips,* 1873.

——— The wise men. v, 253 pp. incl. 1 map. 12°. *New York, Nelson & Phillips,* 1873.

Upham (Thomas Cogswell, *d. d.*) Absolute religion. 312 pp. 12°. *New York, G. P. Putnam's sons,* 1873.

Upton (*Bvt. maj.-gen.* Emory). Infantry tactics. Rev. ed. 445 pp. 24°. *New York, D. Appleton & co.* 1874.

Ure (Andrew). Ure's dictionary of arts, manufactures, and mines, by Robert Hunt assisted by F. W. Rudler [etc.] 7th ed. 3 v. 8°. *London, Longmans,* 1875.

Urlin (R. Denny). John Wesley's place in church history. xv, 272 pp. front. 16°. *London, Rivingtons,* 1870.

Urmy (*Rev.* W. S.) The king of day. 196 pp. incl. front. 18°. *New York, Nelson & Phillips,* [1875].

——— Lost and found. 176 pp. 4 pl. 16°. *Cincinnati, Hitchcock & Walden,* 1875.

——— Wonders in the air. 123 pp. incl. 7 pl. 16°. *New York, Carlton & Lanahan,* [1870].

——— Wonders of fire and water. 125 pp. incl. 9 pl. 16°. *New York, Carlton & Lanahan,* [1870].

Vacani (Camillo, *barone, di Forteolivo*). Della laguna di Venezia e dei fiumi nelle attigue provincie, memoria. 1 p. l. 477 pp. 1 map. 8°. *Firenze, tipografi e litografia degli ingegneri*, 1867. s.

Vacquer (Theod.) Nouveau recueil de monumens funéraires. 60 l. numb. incl. 59 pl. 18°. *Paris, Caudrilier*, [1862].

Vadé (Jean Joseph) *and* **Lécluse** (N. Fleury, *called*). Oeuvres poissardes. 216 pp. 5 pl. 18°. *Paris, Didot jeune*, 1796.

Vahey (*Rev.* J. W.) Julia; or, sister Agnes. 178 pp. 16°. *Milwaukee, Bray bro's*, 1875.

Vaille (Frederick Ozni) *and* **Clark** (Henry Alden, *compilers*). The Harvard book. By various authors. 2 v. 347 pp. incl. 1 pl. 33 heliot. pl. 1 facs. pl. 2 lithog. pl. on 1 l. 57 ports; 447 pp. 25 heliot. pl. 4°. *Cambridge, [Ms.] Welch, Bigelow & co.* 1875.

Valdez (Francisco Travassos). Africa occidental. v. 1. x, xxiv, 406 pp. 18 pl. 8°. *Lisboa, imprensa nacional*, 1864.

Valentin de Cullion (Ch. Fr.) Examen de l'esclavage. Par V. D. C. [*anon.*] 2 v. xii, 298 pp; 1 p. l. 305 pp. 8°. *Paris, Desenne, an* XI—1802.

Valentin de la madre de Dios (*P. fr.*) Fuero de la conciencia. Parte 2da. Ed. 4ta. 4 p. l. 536 pp. sm. 4°. *Madrid, P. Aznar*, 1771. s.

Valeriano-Bolzani (Giovanni Pietro) *and others.* Ioannis Pierii Valeriani hieroglyphica. Editio nouissima. 4 v. in 1. [1279] pp. 4°. *Francofvrti ad Moenvm, sumptibus A. Hierati, excudebat E. Kempffer*, 1614.

Vallejo (*Father* Joseph Ignatius). Life of st. Joseph. [Also] Lives of saint Joachim and saint Anne, by father S. Binet, s. J. 391 pp. 8 pl. 8°. *New York, E. Dunigan & brother*, 1858–64.

[*With* GENTILUCCI (R.) Life of the most blessed virgin Mary. 1857].

Vallemont (Pierre Lorrain, *known as l'abbé de*). La physique occulte. [*anon.*] 2 v. in 1. Eng. title, 9 p. l. 275 pp. 6 pl; 1 p. l. 246 pp. 15 pl. 18°. *La Haye, A. Moetgens*, 1722

Vallès (M. F.) Études sur les inondations. xvi, xv, 528 pp. 1 pl. 8°. *Paris, V. Dalmont*, 1857.

Valley (The) of Wyoming. [*anon.*] 153 pp. 12°. *New York, R. H. Johnston & co.* 1866.

Vambéry (Ármin). Central Asia. Translated by F. E. Bunnètt. viii, 385 pp. 12°. *London, Smith, Elder & co.* 1874.

Van Buren (William H. *m. d.*) *and* **Keyes** (Edward L. *m. d.*) Practical treatise on the surgical diseases of the genito urinary organs. xv, 672 pp. 8°. *New York, D. Appleton & co.* 1874.

Vance (Susa S.) Lois Carrol. 327 pp. 12°. *Philadelphia, J. B. Lippincott & co.* 1874.

Vance (Zebulon B.) Sketches of North Carolina. ix, 175 pp. 8°. *Norfolk, Va Norfolk landmark*, 1875.

Van Cleve (B. Frank). The english and american mechanic. A collection of over 3000 receipts. 1 p. l. 283 pp. 12°. *Philadelphia, F. Van Cleve*, [1875].

——— "Van Cleve's receipts." 1 p. l. 235, viii pp. 12°. *Philadelphia, inquirer printing office*, 1873.

Vandenbussche (*Mme.* —). Ivan. From the french of Marie Émery [*pseud.*] 1 p. l. 5–176 pp. 1 pl. 18°. *New York, D. & J. Sadlier & co.* 1873.

Vander-Velde (Carel Franz). Christine et sa cour. Traduit par m. Le Mart. v. 1. 2 p. l. xxiv, 208 pp. 18°. *Paris, Bernard & cie.* 1827. s.

Van Fleet (*Rev.* J. A.) Old and new Mackinac. 2d ed. 173 pp. 1 map. 8°. *Cincinnati, western methodist book concern*, 1874.

Van Horne (Thomas B.) History of the army of the Cumberland. With campaign and battle maps by Edward Ruger. 2 v. xiv, 454 pp; v, 478 pp. Atlas; 1 p. l. iv pp. 22 col. maps. 8°. *Cincinnati, R. Clarke & co.* 1875.

Van Lede (Charles). De la colonisation au Brésil. viii, 427 pp. 5 tab. 2 maps. 8°. *Bruxelles, A. Decq*, 1843.

Van-Lennep (Henry John, *d. d.*) Bible lands: their modern customs illustrative of scripture. 832 pp. 2 pl. 2 col. maps. 8°. *New York, Harper & brothers*, 1875.

——— Ten days among greek brigands. 271 pp. 2 pl. 16°. *Boston, congregational pub. soc.* 1874.

Van Praet (Jules). Essays on the political history of the fifteenth, sixteenth, and seventeenth centuries. Edited by sir E. Head. li, 464 pp. 8°. *London, R. Bentley*, 1868.

Van Rhyn (G. A. F.) What and how to read: guide to recent english literature. xxx, 221 pp. 12°. *New York, D. Appleton & co.* 1875.

Varley (Henry). The christian ambassador and other addresses. viii, 240 pp. port 12°. *Boston, Willard tract repository*, [1875]

Varney (George J.) Young people's history of Maine; to 1842. xviii, 13–258 pp. incl. 1 pl. 12°. *Portland, Me., Dresser, McLellan & co.* 1873.

Varnhagen (Francisco Adolpho de). Os Indios Bravos e o sr. Lisboa, Timon 3°. [*anon.*] iv, 124 pp. sm. 4°. *Lima, na impressa liberal*, 1867.

Vasey (George). Monograph of the genus bos. xvi, 192 pp. front. 8°. *London, J. R. Smith*, 1857.

——— Philosophy of laughter and smiling. xix, 17–166 pp. 32 pl. 12°. *London, J. Burns*, 1875.

Vasi (Mariano). Itinéraire instructif de Rome ancienne et moderne. 2 v. xxiv, 261 pp. 32 pl. 2 plans; iv, 267–560 pp. 16 pl. 16°. *Rome, l'auteur*, 1817.

——— Itinéraire instructif de Rome à Naples. 2 p. l. vii–viii, 280 pp. 34 pl. 1 map, 1 plan. 16°. *Rome, l'auteur*, 1817.

Vattier (*Madame* Valentine). The fisherman's daughter. From the french by mrs. Mary C. Monroe. 180 pp. incl. front. 8°. *New-York, Benziger brothers*, 1875.

Vaumorière (Pierre Dortigue de). The grand Scipio. Written in french. Rendered into english by G. H. 2 pts. in 1 v. 3 p. l. 125 pp; 111–250 pp. sm. fol. *London, for H. Mosely, T. Dring, & H. Herringman*, 1660.

Vaux (William Sandys W.) Ancient history from the monuments. Persia to the arab conquest. 192 pp. incl. front. 18°. *London, society for promoting christian knowledge*, [1875].

Vegetius (Flavius Renatus). L'art vétérinaire, ou l'hippiatrique. 8 p. l. 395 pp. 8°. *Paris, P. F. Didot*, 1775.

[*In* SABOREUX DE LA BONNETRIE (C. F. *or* C. L.) Traduction d'anciens ouvrages latins relatifs à l'agriculture et à la médecine vétérinaire. 1771–5. v. 6].

Velasco (José Francisco). Noticias estadisticas del estado de Sonora. 350 pp. 8°. *México, I. Cumplido*, 1850.

Velazquez de la Cadena (Mariano). Dictionary of the spanish and english languages, abridged. viii, 847 pp. 12°. *London, Trübner & co.* 1873.

Venable (W. H. *editor*). The amateur actor. 288 pp. 12°. *Cincinnati, Wilson, Hinkle & co.* [1874].

——— Dramas and dramatic scenes. 336 pp. 12°. *Cincinnati, Wilson, Hinkle & co.* [1874].

——— School stage. 234 pp. 12°. *Cincinnati, Wilson, Hinkle & co.* 1873.

Venner (Tobias). Via recta ad vitam longam. Or a treatise for attaining to a long and healthfull life, [etc.] 2 p. l. 404 pp. 4 l. port. sm. 4°. *London, for A. Roper*, 1660.

Vercruysse (*Rev.* Bruno, *s. J.*) New practical meditations for every day in the year. 2 v. x, 607 pp. 1 plan; x, 621 pp. 1 map. 12°. *New-York, Benziger brothers*, [1875].

Vereker (*Lt. col.* Charles Smyth). Scenes in the sunny south. 2 v. xvi, 307 pp; xi, 296 pp. 12°. *London, Longmans*, 1871.

Verey (Joseph). The open air or sketches out of town. 1 p. l. ii, 283 pp. 12°. *London, Tinsley brothers*, 1869.

Verne (Jules). Adventures in the land of the behemoth. 14th thousand. 190 pp. 20 pl. 12°. *Boston, H. L. Shepard & co.* 1874.

——— The Baltimore gun club. (From the earth to the moon). Translated by Edward Roth. 2 p. l. 442 pp. 12 pl. 1 map. 12°. *Philadelphia, King & Baird*, [1874].

——— Doctor Ox, and other stories. From the french, by George M. Towle. Authorized ed. 1 p. l. v–vi, 292 pp. 18°. *Boston, J. R. Osgood & co.* 1874.

——— From the clouds to the mountains. Translated by A. L. Alger. 1 p. l. 285 pp. 5 pl. 12°. *Boston, W. F. Gill & co.* 1874.

[GILL's select novels].

——— The mysterious island. Wrecked in the air. Authorized ed. [Part 1]. 2 p. l. 110 pp. 1 map. 8°. *New York, Scribner, Armstrong & co.* 1875.

——— Stories of adventure. I. Meridiana. II. A journey to the centre of the earth. 2 v. in 1. 1 p. l. viii, 232 pp. 48 pl; 2 p. l. 305 pp. 20 pl. 12°. *New York, Scribner, Armstrong & co.* 1874.

——— Tour of the world in eighty days. 291 pp. incl 1 pl. 18°. *Boston, J. R. Osgood & co.* 1873.

——— Voyages and adventures of captain Hatteras. From the french. With illustrations by Riou. xiv, 440 pp. 77 pl. 8°. *Boston, J. R. Osgood & co.* 1875.

——— Wreck of the Chancellor. Translated by George M. Towle. 285 pp. 18°. *Boston, J. R. Osgood & co.* 1875.

Note.—Contains also: Martin Paz.

Verneilh (Félix de). L'architecture byzantine en France. Saint-Front de Périgueux et les églises à coupoles de l'Aquitaine. 316 pp. 20 pl. 4°. *Paris, V. Didron*, 1851.

Vertot (René Aubert de Vertot d'Aubeuf, *known as the abbé* de). Révolutions de Por-

Vertot (R. A. de V. d'A.)—continued. tugal. 3e éd. viii, 360 pp. 12 l. 16°. *Paris, F. Barois*, 1728.

Veuillot (Louis). Jésus-Christ. Avec une étude sur l'art chrétien par E. Cartier. 2e éd. viii, 572 pp. 16 col. pl. 7 helio. pl. 8°. *Paris, F. Didot frères, fils & cie.* 1875.

——— Same. Life of our lord Jesus Christ. Translated into english by A. Farley. From the 7th french ed. 509 pp. 12°. *New York, the catholic publication society*, 1875.

Vico (Giovanni Battista). Oeuvres choisies de Vico. Précédées d'une introduction sur sa vie et ses ouvrages par m. Michelet. 2 v. 2 p. l. viii, 1, 418 pp. front; 392 pp. 8°. *Paris, L. Hachette*, 1835.

Vienna. *Welt-ausstellung* 1873 *in Wien.* Amtlicher catalog der im reichsrathe vertretenen koenigreiche und laender Oesterreichs. 2 p. l. 1, 520 pp. 3 pl. 8°. *Wien, verlag der general-direction*, 1873.

——— ——— Officieller general-catalog. 2te aufl. x, 1028 pp. 1 pl. 8°. *Wien, verlag der general-direction*, 1873.

Vilas (Charles Harrison, *compiler*). Genealogy of the descendants of Peter Vilas. 221 pp. 4 ports. 8°. *Madison, Wis. editor*, 1875.

Villarena (Vincenzo Mortillaro, *marchese di*). Reminiscenze de' miei tempi. ix, 318 pp. 1 l. 8°. *Palermo, P. Pensante*, 1865.

Villemain (Abel François). Life of Gregory the seventh. Translated by J. B. Brockley. 2 v. vii, 400 pp; viii, 357 pp. 8°. *London, R. Bentley & son*, 1874.

Villemessant (Hippolyte Cartier, *dit de*). Mémoires d'un journaliste. 4 v. 16°. *Paris, E. Dentu*, 1867–75.

CONTENTS.

[1e série. Souvenirs de jeunesse].
2e série. Les hommes de mon temps.
3e série. À travers le Figaro.
4e série. Derrière le rideau.

Villetard de Prunières (Charles Edmond). History of the international. From the french, by Susan M. Day. ix, 259 pp. 12°. *New Haven, G. H. Richmond & co.* 1874.

Vincent (Francis). History of the state of Delaware. [v. 1]. 1 p. l. 478 pp. 8°. *Philadelphia, J. Campbell*, 1870.

Vincent (Frank, *jr.*) The land of the white elephant: sights and scenes in south-eastern Asia. (1871–2). xix, 316 pp. 34 pl. 3 maps. 8°. *New York, Harper & brothers*, 1874.

——— Through and through the tropics, thirty thousand miles of travel in Oceanica, Australasia, and India. 304 pp. 12°. *New York, Harper & brothers*, 1876.

Vinton (John Adams). The Symmes memorial. xvi, 184 pp. port. 8°. *Boston, for the author*, 1873.

Viollet-Le-Duc (Eugène Emmanuel). Discourses on architecture. Translated, with an introductory essay, by Henry Van Brunt. xxii, 517 pp. 37 pl. 8°. *Boston, J. R. Osgood & co.* 1875.

——— Story of a house. From the french by George M. Towle. vi, 284 pp. 15 pl. 12°. *Boston, J. R. Osgood & co.* 1874.

Virgilius Maro (Publius). The works of Virgil: translated into literal english prose. By C. Alexander. 674 pp. 8°. *Worcester, Mass. for D. West, of Boston*, 1796.

Note.—With the latin text.

——— Bvcolica: Aeneidos I–VI. Poems of Virgil. v. 1. Containing the pastoral poems and six books of the Æneid. x, 184 pp. 1 l. 188 pp. 12°. *Boston, Ginn brothers*, 1874.

——— The XIII. bukes of Eneados translated into scottish metir, bi Gawin Douglas.

[DOUGLAS (G. *bishop of Dunkeld*). Poetical works. 12°. *Edinburgh, W. Paterson*, 1874. v. 2–4].

Visdelou (Claude de) *and* **Galland** (Antoine). Bibliothèque orientale. Pour servir de supplément à celle de m. d'Herbelot. 2 p. l. iv, 284 pp. 3 tab. fol. [*Maestricht, Dufour*], 1780.

——— Same.

[*With* HERBELOT (B. d'). Bibliothèque orientale. fol. 1776].

Vizetelly (Henry). Wines of the world characterized & classified. Ill. title, 7 p. l. 9–202 pp. 12°. *London, Ward, Lock & Tyler*, 1875.

Vocal (The) lyre. [*anon.*] viii, 152 pp. 18°. *New-York, W. Borradaile*, 1825.

Vogel (*Dr.* Hermann). Handbook of photography. From the german. 2d ed. 404 pp. 8°. *Philadelphia, Benerman & Wilson*, 1875.

——— Photographer's pocket reference-book and dictionary. From the german by Edward F. Moelling. Am. ed. 119 pp. 12°. *Philadelphia, Benerman & Wilson*, 1873.

Volcano (The) diggings. [*anon.*] 131 pp. 12°. *New York, J. S. Redfield*, 1851.

Volckmar (*Dr.* Karl). Sammlung deutscher gedichte. 3te aufl. ix, 470 pp. 8°. *Göttingen, Vandenhoeck & Ruprecht*, 1865.

Voltaire (François Marie Arouet de). Les vraies lettres de Voltaire à l'abbé Moussinot, publiées par Courtat. 2 p. l. xliv, 259 pp. 8°. *Paris, A. Lainé*, 1875.

Voorhees (Daniel W.) Speeches. Compiled by his son, C. S. Voorhees. xii, 585 pp. port. 8°. *Cincinnati, R. Clarke & co.* 1875.

Vose (George Leonard). Manual for railroad engineers and engineering students. 2 v. xix, 570 pp; 31 pl. 8°. *Boston, Lee & Shepard,* 1873.

Vosmaer (Arnoult). Description d'un receuil d'animaux rares, des Indes Orientales, et Occidentales. Ci devant appartenantes à son altesse m. le prince d'Orange-Nassau. 33 pts. in 1 v. Ill. title, viii, [374] pp. 35 col. pl. sm. 4°. *Amsterdam, J. B. Elwe,* 1767–1805.

Wadsworth (*Rev.* Benjamin). Guide for the doubting, and cordial for the fainting, saint. 3d impression. 2 p. l. 254 pp. 3 l. 18°. *Boston, re-printed for N. Buttolph,* 1720.

Wagenaar (Jan). Amsterdam, in zyne opkomst, aanwas, geschiedenissen [etc.] 3 v. fol. *Amsterdam, I. Tirion,* 1760–67.

Waggoner (J. Frederick). Tried and true recipes. Home cook book of Chicago. [*anon.*] 288 pp. 8°. *Chicago, J. F. Waggoner,* 1874.

——— Same. Tried, tested, proved. [*anon.*] 9th thousand. 394 pp. 12°. *Chicago, J. F. Waggoner,* 1876.

——— Same. Home cook book of Chicago. [*anon.*] 9th thousand. 394 pp. 12°. *Chicago, J. F. Waggoner,* 1876.

Wagner (Wilhelm Richard). Art life and heories, selected from his writings and translated by Edward L. Burlingame. xiii, 305 pp. 3 pl. 12°. *New York, H. Holt & co.* 1875.
[AMATEUR series.]

Wahl (O. W.) The land of the czar. xvi, 389 pp. 8°. *London, Chapman & Hall,* 1875.

Waisbrooker (Lois). Nothing like it. 336 pp. 12°. *Boston, Colby & Rich,* 1875.

Wakeley (J. B. *d. d.*) American temperance cyclopædia of history, biography, anecdote, and illustration. 1 p. l. xv, 13–243 pp. port. 12°. *New York, national temperance society & publication house,* 1875.

——— The bold frontier preacher. A portraiture of rev. William Cravens. 119 pp. 18°. *Cincinnati, Hitchcock & Walden,* [1869].

Walcott (*Rev.* Mackenzie Edward Charles). Sacred archæology. xvi, 640 pp. 8°. *London, L. Reeve & co.* 1868.

——— Traditions and customs of cathedrals. viii, 159 pp. 12°. *London, Longmans,* 1872.

Waldron (George). Description of the Isle of Man. Edited by William Harrison. xxiii pp. 2 l. 155 pp. 1 pl. 8°. *Douglas,* [*Isle of Man*], 1865.
[MANX society. Publications, v. 11].

Walker (Charles D.) Memorial, Virginia military institute. Biographical sketches of the graduates and élèves of the Virginia military institute who fell during the war between the states. 585 pp. 8°. *Philadelphia, J. B. Lippincott & co.* 1875.

Walker (C. H.) *and* **Jewett** (C. F.) County atlas of Tioga, Penn. 109 pp. incl. 44 colored maps and plans & 2 pl. fol. *New York, F. W. Beers & co.* 1875.

Walker (*Mrs.* Edward Ashley). The pilgrim's progress. By John Bunyan. In words of one syllable. 335 pp. 10 col. pl. 16°. *New York, G. A. Leavitt,* [1869].

Walker (Francis A.) The indian question. 268 pp. 1 map. 12°. *Boston, J. R. Osgood & co.* 1874.

Walker (George). The vagabond. A novel. 1st am. from 4th eng. ed. xii, 228 pp. 16°. *Boston, for West & Greenleaf,* 1800.

Walker (James Barr, *d. d.*) Doctrine of the holy spirit. 4th ed. 255 pp. 12°. *Chicago, S. C. Griggs & co.* 1874.

Walker (Jeanie Mort). Life of capt. Joseph Fry, the cuban martyr. 589 pp. 13 pl. 3 ports. 8°. *Hartford, the J. B. Burr publishing co.* 1874.

Walker (Obadiah). Of education. [*anon.*] 5th impression. 5 p. l. 309 pp. 16°. *Oxford, A. Curteyne,* 1687.

Wallace (John H. *of Muscatine, Iowa*). American trotting register. v. 2. 710 pp. 8°. *New York, Hurd & Houghton,* 1874.

Wallace (Lewis). The fair god. xiv, 586 pp. 12°. *Boston, J. R. Osgood & co.* 1873.

Waller (S. E.) Six weeks in the saddle: a painter's journal in Iceland. 3 p. l. 177 pp. 6 pl. 12°. *London, Macmillan & co.* 1874.

Wallez (—). Précis historique des négociations entre la France et Saint-Domingue. 4 p. l. 488 pp. 8°. *Paris, Ponthieu,* [*etc.*] 1826.

Walling (H. F. *editor*). Atlas of the state of Michigan. 162 pp. incl. 84 maps, 16 l. fol. *Detroit, R. M. & S. T. Tackabury,* [1873].

Walpole (Spencer). Life of the rt. hon. Spencer Perceval. 2 v. xii, 376 pp. port; viii, 332 pp. 8°. *London, Hurst & Blackett,* 1874.

Walras (Léon). Éléments d'économie politique pure. viii, 208 pp. 2 pl. 8°. *Lausanne, L. Corbaz & cie.* 1874.

Walsh (Thomas). Essays on Gladstone and the Vatican, liberalism, free masonry and the secret societies. 2 pts. in 1 v. 77 pp; 82 pp. 8°. *Syracuse, N. Y. Truair, Smith & co.* 1875.

Walsingham (Charlotte). Annette. 1 p. l. ix–374 pp. 12°. *Philadelphia, Claxton, Remsen & Haffelfinger,* 1875.

——— O'er moor and fen. 422 pp. 12°. *Philadelphia, Claxton, Remsen & Haffelfinger,* 1876.

Walton (Izaak) *and* **Cotton** (Charles). Complete angler. With notes by sir Harris Nicolas. ccv, 320 pp. 48 pl. 2 facs. 1 eng. title, 3 ports. 12°. *London, Chatto & Windus,* 1875.

Wansey (Henry) *and* **Hoare** (*Sir* Richard Colt, *bart.*) Hundred of Warminster. x, 133 pp. 3 pl. 1 pedigree. fol. *London, J. B. Nichols & son,* 1831.

[HOARE (*Sir* R. C.) The history of modern Wiltshire. v. 3, part 2].

Wappenbuch der oesterreichischen monarchie. [*anon.*] v. 1–17 in 9 v. 8°. *Nürnberg, I. A. Tyroff,* 1831–50.

Wappenbuch der preussischen monarchie. [*anon.*] 29 v. in 13. 8°. *Nürnberg, I. A. Tyroff,* 1832–67.

Wappenbuch der regierenden monarchen Europas. [*anon.*] Eng. title, 1 p. l. 51 pl. 4°. *Nürnberg, J. A. Tyroff,* 1846.

Wappenbuch der gesammten adels im königreich Würtemberg. [*anon.*] 4 v. in 2. 8°. *Nürnberg, Tyroff'sche kunstverlagshandlung,* 1833–50.

Ward (Andrew Henshaw). Genealogical history of the Rice family. viii, 379 pp. 8°. *Boston, C. B. Richardson,* 1858.

——— The Ward family. 265 pp. 2 ports. 8°. *Boston, S. G. Drake,* 1851.

Ward (Caroline). National proverbs. iv, 176 pp. 18°. *London, J. W. Parker,* 1842.

Ward (*Mrs.* Ellen E.) Angels messages. 408 pp. 12°. *Nashville, Wheeler, Marshall & Bruce,* 1875.

Ward (Henry George). Gedrängtes gemälde des zustandes von Mexiko im jahre 1827. Übertragen von F. A. Rüder. xxvi, 158 pp. 8°. *Leipzig, C. F. H. Hartmann,* 1828.

Ward (Hetta Lord Hayes). Davy's jacket. Miss Elsie's boys and girls. 176 pp. 3 pl. 18°. *Boston, D. Lothrop & co.* [1873].

——— Memoir of mrs. Hetta L. Ward, [by her husband], with selections from her writings. 136 pp. 12°. *Boston, T. R. Marvin,* 1843.

Ward (John). Borough of Stoke-upon-Trent, [Staffordshire], in the commencement of the reign of Victoria. xvi, 600, lxviii, 16 pp. 20 pl. port. 8°. *London, W. Lewis & son,* 1843.

Ward (John, *of New York*). Overland route to California, and other poems. 296 pp. sm. 4°. *New York,* [*K. Tompkins*], 1875.

Warden (*Rev.* John). System of revealed religion. xv, 736, xvii pp. 4°. *London, for E. & C. Dilly,* 1769.

Warden (Robert B.) Account of the life of Salmon Portland Chase. xxiii, 11–838 pp. port. 8°. *Cincinnati, Wilstach, Baldwin & co.* 1874.

Warder (George W.) Poetic fragments. 136 pp. 12°. *St. Louis, southwestern book & publishing co.* 1873.

Wardlaw (*Dr.* L. J.) Oregon as it is. 187 pp. port. 8°. *San Francisco, women's co-operative printing union,* 1875.

Ware (Samuel Hibbert). Lancashire memorials of the rebellion, 1715. 2 v. in 1. 3 p. l. x, 56 pp; xxviii, 292 pp. 1 pl. sm. 4°. [*Edinburgh*], 1845.

[CHETHAM society remains, v. 5].

Ware (William). Julian. 2 v. in 1. vi, 271 pp; 3–270 pp. 12°. *New York, J. Miller,* 1874.

Warfield (*Mrs.* Catherine Ann Ware). A double wedding. 1 p. l. 19–406 pp. 12°. *Philadelphia, T. B. Peterson & brothers,* [1875].

——— Hester Howard's temptation. 1 p. l. 19–569 pp. 12°. *Philadelphia, T. B. Peterson & brothers,* [1875].

——— Miriam Monfort. [*anon.*] 556 pp. 12°. *New York, D. Appleton & co.* 1873.

Waring (George E. *jr.*) A farmer's vacation. 251 pp. sq. 8°. *Boston, J. R. Osgood & co.* 1876.

——— Whip and spur. 245 pp. 18°. *Boston, J. R. Osgood & co.* 1875.

Waring (John Burley). Ceramic art in remote ages. Ill. title, 1 p. l. ii, 127 pp. 55 pl. fol. *London, J. B. Day,* 1874.

——— Record of my artistic life. 1 p. l. 312, 11 pp. 14 pl. 12°. *London, Trübner & co.* 1873.

Warner (Anna B.) The fourth watch. 149 pp. 24°. *New York, A. D. F. Randolph & co.* [1874].

——— Miss Tillers vegetable garden and the money she made by it. 140 pp. 16°. *New York, A. D. F. Randolph & co.* [1873].

Warner (Charles Dudley). Baddeck, and that sort of thing. 191 pp. 18°. *Boston, J. R. Osgood & co.* 1874.

Warner (I. de Ver, *m. d.*) *and* **Warner** (Lucien C. *m. d.*) Popular treatise on man. 1

Warner (I. de V. *and* L. C.)—continued. p. l. 5–13, 23–337 pp. 12°. *New York, Manhattan publishing co.* 1873.

Warner (Lucien C. *m. d.*) Popular treatise on the functions and diseases of woman. 17, 25–345 pp. 12°. *Cortland, N. Y.* [*author*], 1873.

Warner (*Rev.* Richard). Miscellanies. Collecta undique. 2 v. vii, 176 pp; 2 p. l. 218 pp. 12°. *Bath,* [*Eng.*] *R. Cruttwell,* 1819.

Warner (Susan). Bread and oranges. [*anon.*] 434 pp. 3 pl. 16°. *New York, R. Carter & brothers,* 1875.

——— The flag of truce. [*anon.*] 1 p. l. 5–397 pp. 3 pl. 16°. *New York, R. Carter & brothers,* 1875.

——— The little camp on Eagle hill. [*anon.*] 2 p. l. 7–429 pp. 3 pl. 16°. *New York, R. Carter & brothers,* 1874.

——— The rapids of Niagara. [*anon.*] 436 pp. 3 pl. 16°. *New York, R. Carter & brothers,* 1876.

——— Sceptres and crowns. [*anon.*] 427 pp. 3 pl. 16°. *New York, R. Carter & brothers,* 1875.

——— Willow brook. [*anon.*] 348 pp. 3 pl. 16°. *New York, R. Carter & brothers,* 1874.

Warren (Edward, *m. d.*) Life of John Warren, m. d. xv, 568 pp. port. 8°. *Boston, Noyes, Holmes & co.* 1874.

Warren (*Rev.* Henry W.) Sights and insights. 299 pp. incl. 3 pl. 16°. *New York, Nelson & Phillips,* 1874.

Warren (Israel P.) Chauncey Judd. 314 pp. 5 pl. 12°. *New York, Warren & Wyman,* [1875].

——— The three judges. xii, 5–303 pp. 7 pl. 16°. *New York, Warren & Wyman,* [1873].

Warren (John H. *jr.*) Thirty years' battle with crime. 400 pp. 16 pl. 8°. *Poughkeepsie, N. Y., A. J. White,* 1874.

Warren (S. Edward). Stereotomy. Problems in stone cutting. xi, 126 pp. 10 pl. 8°. *New York, J. Wiley & son,* 1875.

Warriner (Edward A.) Victor La Tourette [*anon.*] 406 pp. 16°. *Boston, Roberts brothers,* 1875.

Warring (Charles B.) Mosaic account of creation, the miracle of today. xviii, 9–292 pp. 1 pl. 12°. *New York, J. W. Schermerhorn & co.* 1875.

Washburn (Edward A. *d. d.*) Social law of God. 2d ed. 2 p. l. 212 pp. 12°. *New-York, T. Whittaker,* [1875].

Washburn (Israel, *jr. of Maine*). Notes, historical, descriptive, and personal, of Livermore, in Androscoggin county, Maine. [*anon.*] 169 pp. 3 photos. 8°. *Portland, Bailey & Noyes,* 1874.

Washburn (Katherine Sedgwick). The italian girl. 1 p. l. 7–390 pp. 16°. *Boston, Lee & Shepard,* 1874.

——— Perfect love casteth out fear. 319 pp. 12°. *Boston, Lee & Shepard,* 1875.

Washington (Elizabeth). Dorothy's ladder. [*anon.*] 252 pp. incl. 1 pl. 16°. *Philadelphia, am. s. s. union,* [1873].

——— How Marjorie watched. 161 pp. incl. 3 pl. 16°. *New York, Nelson & Phillips,* 1873.

Waterbury (Jared Bell, *d. d.*) Book for the sabbath. viii, 222 pp. 12°. *Andover,* [*Ms.*] *Gould, Newman & Saxton,* 1840.

Watson (*Miss* E. H.) New and not new. Epipsychidion series. v. 1. [*anon.*] 194 pp. 12°. *Boston, A. Williams & co.* 1874.

Watson (*Rev.* Samuel). The clock struck three. 352 pp. port. 12°. *Chicago, S. S. Jones,* 1874.

——— A Memphian's trip to Europe with Cook's educational party. 352 pp. port. 12°. *Nashville, Tenn., southern methodist pub. house,* 1874.

Watson (Samuel James). Constitutional history of Canada. v. 1. 157 pp. 16°. *Toronto, Adam, Stevenson & co.* 1874.

Watts (Henry) *and others.* Dictionary of chemistry. Second supplement. 3 p. l. 1215 pp. 1 tab. 8°. *London, Longmans,* 1875.

Wayland (Francis, *d. d.*) Elements of moral science; abridged. 223 pp. 18°. *Boston, Gould & Lincoln,* 1873.

——— Elements of political economy. Revised ed. 406 pp. 12°. *Boston, Gould & Lincoln,* 1873.

Waylen (James). Chronicles of the Devises, a history of the castle, parks and borough of that name. 2 p. l. 9–160, 139–362 pp. front. 8°. *London, author,* 1839.

Weatherhead (George Hume, *m. d.*) Treatise on headachs. viii, 109 pp. 16°. *London, S. Highley,* 1835.

Weaver (*Lieut.* William A. *U. s. n.*) Journals of the ocean; and other poems. [*anon.*] 228 pp. 12°. *New-York, G. C. Morgan,* 1826.

Webb (Ann Eliza). Wife no. 19, by Ann Eliza Young. 2 p. l. 9–605 pp. 9 pl. 3 ports. 8°. *Hartford, Dustin, Gilman & co.* 1875.

Webb (Charles Henry). John Paul's book. By John Paul [*pseud.*] Eng. title, 2 p. l. ix-621 pp. port. 30 pl. 8°. *Hartford, columbian book co.* 1874.

Webb (Henry, *editor*). Dogs. New ed. 2 p. l. [334] pp. 6 photos. 12°. *London, Dean & son,* [1873].

—— Same. New ed. 2 p. l. 330 pp. + 64 A-D. 12°. *London, Dean & son,* [1874].

Webb (James M.) Mary's vision. [*anon.*] 180 pp. 16°. *Hartford, the Case, Lockwood & Brainerd co.* 1874.

Webb (*Rev.* John). Some plain and necessary directions to obtain eternal salvation. 2d ed. 4 p. l. 166 pp. 1 l. 18°. *Boston, for S. Eliot,* 1741.

Webber (Charles Wilkins). Old Hicks, the guide. 2 p. l. 356 pp. 12°. *New York, Harper & brothers,* 1848.

—— Wild scenes and wild hunters. Eng. title, 1-4, 9-10, 17-610 pp. front. 12°. *Philadelphia, Claxton, Remsen & Haffelfinger,* 1875.

Webster (Noah, *ll. d.*) Collection of papers on bilious fevers. x, ix, 246 pp. 8°. *New York, Hopkins, Webb & co.* 1796.

—— People's illustrated dictionary of the english language. From the quarto dictionary. By William A. Wheeler. xl, 1000 pp. incl. 30 pp. of pl. port. 8°. *Hartford, S. S. Scranton & co.* 1874.

Webster (Richard). Principles of monetary legislation. viii, 192 pp. 8°. *London, Longmans,* 1874.

Webster (Thomas, *d. d.*) Woman man's equal. ix, 297 pp. 16°. *Cincinnati, Hitchcock & Walden,* 1873.

Webster (William Bullock). Ireland considered as a field for investment or residence. xi, 123 pp. 1 map. 16°. *Dublin, Hodges & Smith,* 1852.

Webster's ready-made love letters. [*anon.*] 192 pp. 16°. *New York, R. M. De Witt,* [1873].

Wedgwood (Julia). John Wesley and the evangelical reaction of the eighteenth century. xi, 412 pp. 12°. *London, Macmillan & co.* 1870.

Wedmore (Frederick). Two girls. 2 v. iv, 274 pp; iv, 266 pp. 12°. *London, H. S. King & co.* 1873.

Weed (Joseph). A view of California as it is. 192 pp. 18°. *San Francisco, Byron & Wright,* 1874.

Weeden (William B.) Morality of prohibitory liquor laws. 223 pp. 16°. *Boston, Roberts brothers,* 1875.

Weidinger (G.) Waarenlexikon der chemischen industrie und der pharmacie. 3 p. l. 811 pp. 8°. *Leipzig, H. Haessel,* 1868-69. s.

Weisbach (Julius). Mechanics of engineering. Theoretical mechanics. From the 4th german ed. by Eckley B. Coxe. 4th am. ed. 1112 pp. 8°. *New York, D. Van Nostrand,* 1875.

Weiss (N.) Personal recollections of the wreck of the Ville-du-Havre and the Loch-Earn. From the French. 1 p. l. 208 pp. 16°. *New York, A. D. F. Randolph & co.* [1875].

Weiss (*Rev.* S. W.) Jacob Weller. 2 p. l. 7-322 pp. 16°. *New York, author,* 1873.

Weitzel (*Mrs.* Sophy Winthrop). Miss Roberts' fortune. By Sophy Winthrop. 428 pp. 16°. *New York, A. D. F. Randolph & co.* [1875].

Welch *or* **Welsche** (*Rev.* John). Thirty five sermons, in 1605. xxviii, 198 pp. sm. 4°. *Edinburgh, for W. Gray,* 1744.

[MISCELLANY sermons, [etc.] sm. 4°. *Edinburgh, for W. Gray,* 1744. pt. 1].

Welcker (*Prof.* W. T.) Military lessons: military schools, colleges, and militia. viii, 175 pp. 12°. *New York, Ivison, Blakeman, Taylor & co.* 1874.

Weld (Charles Richard). Last winter in Rome. 2 p. l. ix-xxviii, 589 pp. 4 pl. 12°. *London, Longmans,* 1865.

Welles (Gideon). Lincoln and Seward. viii, 7-215 pp. 12°. *New York, Sheldon & co.* 1874.

Wellington (Arthur M.) Methods for the computation from diagrams of preliminary and final estimates of railway earthwork. 2 v. Pt. 1.—Text. xvi, 163 pp. 12°. Pt. 2.—Plates. 2 p. l. 12 pl. fol. *New York, D. Appleton & co.* 1874.

Wellons (*Rev.* J. W.) Family prayers. 227 pp. 8°. *Baltimore, Sherwood & co.* 1874.

Wells (C. F.) My uncle Toby: his table-talks and reflections. 328 pp. 16°. *Cincinnati, Hitchcock & Walden,* 1875.

Wells (David Ames). Relation of the government to the telegraph. 1 p. l. 170 pp. 8°. *New York,* 1873.

Wells (J. Soelberg, *m. d.*) Treatise on diseases of the eye. 2d am. from the 3d eng. ed. 836 pp. 10 col. pl. 4 pl. test types. 8°. *Philadelphia, H. C. Lea,* 1873.

Wells (Walter). Water-power of Maine. viii, 526 pp. 20 pl. 1 map. 8°. *Augusta, [Me.] Sprague, Owen & Nash*, 1869.

Welsch (Antony). Orbital system of the universe. 161 pp. 6 pl. 8°. *Clinton, Iowa, Allen & Bowers*, 1875.

Wermylierus (Otho). Spiritual and most preciouse perle. [From the german by Miles Coverdale]. Reprinted. xxviii, 225 pp. 12°. *London, Longman*, 1812.

Werner (Ernst). Bound by his vows; or, at the altar. From the german by J. S. L. 1 p. l. 5–343 pp. 16°. *Philadelphia, J. B. Lippincott & co.* [1874].

——— Broken chains. Translated by Frances A. Shaw. 133 pp. 8°. *Boston, J. R. Osgood & co.* 1875.

——— "Good luck!" Translated by Frances A. Shaw. 153 pp. 8°. *Boston, J. R. Osgood & co.* 1874.
[OSGOOD'S library of novels, no. 39].

Wesley (*Rev.* John). Nobility at the cross. Life of monsieur de Renty. 4, 139 pp. 16°. *Boston, J. Bent & co.* 1873.

Wesley (Samuel). Life of our blessed lord & savior Jesus Christ. With sixty copper-plates, by W. Faithorn. 2d ed. 16 p. l. 356 pp. 4 l. 60 pl. incl. eng. title, 2 maps. sm. fol. *London, for C. Harper*, 1697.

Wesleyan university, *Middletown, Conn.* Alumni record. Compiled by Orange Judd, 1869; revised by C. T. Winchester, [etc.] 1873. xxviii, 308 pp. 8°. *Boston, Rand, Avery, & co.* 1873.

West (Henry Josiah, *compiler.*) The chinese invasion. 154 pp. 2 maps. 8°. *San Francisco, Bacon & co.* 1873.

West (*Mrs.* Jane). Letters to a young lady. 503 pp. 8°. *Troy, [N. Y.] O. Penniman & co.* 1806.

West (Maria A.) Romance of missions: or, life and labor, in the land of Ararat. xiii, 710 pp. 1 map. 12°. *New York, A. D. F. Randolph & co.* [1875].

West (Robert A.) Sketches of wesleyan preachers. 400 pp. port. 16°. *New-York, Lane & Tippett*, 1848.

Westcott (Brooke Foss). General view of the history of the english bible. 2d ed. xvi, 359 pp. 12°. *London, Macmillan & co.* 1872.

Westcott (Margaret). Bessie Wilmerton. 384 pp. 12°. *New York, G. W. Carleton & co.* 1874.

Western Texas the Australia of America. [*anon.*] iv, 235 pp. 12°. *Cincinnati, E. Mendenhall*, 1860.

Westfield jubilee: on the two hundredth anniversary of the incorporation of the town, with the historical address of hon. William G. Bates, [etc.] 226 pp. 8°. *Westfield, Mass. Clark & Story*, 1870.

Westmacott (Charles Molloy). Punster's pocket-book. By Bernard Blackmantle [*pseud.*] x, 198 pp. 12 pl. port. 12°. *London, Sherwood, Gilbert & Piper*, 1826.

Westminster drolleries, both parts, of 1671, 1672; a choice collection of songs and poems, sung at court & theatres. Edited, [etc.] by J. Woodfall Ebsworth. [*anon.*] 2 v. in 1. 12°. *Boston, [Eng.] R. Roberts*, 1875.

Westmoreland (John G. *m. d.*) Treatise on acology and therapeutics. x, 391 pp. 8°. *Atlanta, Ga. plantation publishing co's press*, 1873.

Westmoreland (Maria Jourdan). Clifford Troup. 338 pp. 12°. *New York, G. W. Carleton & co.* 1873.

Weston (Daniel C.) Scenes in a vestry. v, 228 pp. 12°. *Augusta, [Ga.] W. R. Smith & co.* 1841.

West Springfield, *Mass.* Account of the centennial celebration, march 25th, 1874. Compiled by J. N. Bagg. 144 pp. 5 pl. 2 ports. 8°. [*Springfield, Mass. C. W. Bryan & co.*] 1874.

Wetherall (John). Sixteen orations. 225 pp. 16°. *Burlington, N. J., S. C. Ustick*, 1803.

Wey (François Alphonse). Rome. Description et souvenirs. Nouv. éd. xii, 732 pp. incl. 72 pl. 1 map. 4°. *Paris, Hachette & cie.* 1873.

——— Trop heureux. 2 p. l. 265 pp. 16°. *Paris, L. Hachette & cie.* 1863.

Whalley abbey. The coucher book or chartulary of Whalley abbey. Edited by W. A. Hulton. 4 v. sm. 4°. [*London and Manchester*], 1847–49.
[CHETHAM society remains, v. 10, 11, 16, 20].

Wharton (Charles). Hand-book on the treatment of the horse in the stable and on the road. 137 pp. 2 pl. 12°. *Philadelphia, J. B. Lippincott & co.* 1873.

What of the churches and clergy? [*anon.*] 120 pp. 12°. *Springfield, Mass. D. E. Fisk & co.* 1874.

Wheatley (Henry B.) Round about Piccadilly and Pall Mall. xii, 405 pp. 3 pl. 1 plan. 8°. *London, Smith, Elder & co.* 1870.

Whedon (Daniel Denison, *editor*). Commentary on the old testament. v. 3–4. 12°. *New York, Nelson & Phillips,* 1873–75.

CONTENTS.

v. 3. Book of Joshua, by D. Steele, d. d. Book of Judges to II. Samuel, by rev. M. S. Terry. 558 pp. incl. 8 pl. 1 map. 1873.
v. 4. Kings to Esther. By rev. Milton S. Terry. 534 pp. incl. 1 col. map, 2 col. maps. 1875.

Wheeler (Ella). Shells. 5 p. l. 9–206 pp. 12°. *Milwaukee, Hauser & Storey,* 1873.

Wheeler (George Augustus, *m d.*) History of Castine, Penobscot, and Brooksville, Maine; including Pentagöet. 401 pp. 6 pl. 2 maps, 2 ports. 8°. *Bangor, Burr & Robinson,* 1875.

Wheeler (Gervase). Choice of a dwelling. xii, 299 pp. 4 pl. 12°. *London, J. Murray,* 1871.

Wheeler (John). Treatise of commerce. 126 pp. sm. 4°. *London, I. Harison,* 1601.

Wheeler (John Hill, *compiler*). Legislative manual and political register of North Carolina, for 1874. 1st annual ed. 388, 2 pp. 1 pl. 1 map, 4 tab. 8°. *Raleigh,* [*N. C.*] *J. Turner, jr.* 1874.

Wheeler (J. Talboys). History of India, from the earliest ages. v. 2–3. 8°. *London, N. Trübner & co.* 1869–74.

CONTENTS.

v. 2. The râmâyana and the brahmanic period.
v. 3. Hindû. Buddhist. Brahmanical revival.

Wheildon (William W.) Contributions to thought. 3 p. l. 236 pp. 12°. *Concord, Ms. author's private printing office,* 1874.

Wheler (*Sir* George). Account of the churches, or places of assembly of the primitive christians; from the churches of Tyre, Jerusalem, and Constantinople. Described by Eusebius. [etc.] 3 p. l. 130 pp. 5 pl. 18°. *London, for R. Clavell,* 1689.

Whelpley (Samuel). The triangle. By investigator. [*anon.*] 396 pp. 8°. *New-York, O. Halsted,* 1832.

Whipple (Squire). Elementary and practical treatise on bridge building. 2d ed. vi, 352 pp. 1 pl. 8°. *New York, D. Van Nostrand,* 1873.

Whitaker (Joseph). Almanack for 1874–76. 3 v. 16°. *London, J. Whitaker,* 1873–[75].

Whitaker (Mary Ann). Alice's dream. 122 pp. 16°. *Boston, Walker, Wise, & co.* 1860.

Whitcombe (*Mrs.* Henry Pennell). Bygone days in Devonshire and Cornwall. xv, 276 pp. 12°. *London, R. Bentley & son,* 1874.

White (Anna L.) Kate Callender. 208 pp. 12°. *Boston, author,* 1870.

White (*Rev.* Henry). Indian battles: with incidents in the early history of New England. 428 pp. 12°. *New York, D. W. Evans & co.* [1859].

White (*Rev.* Homer). The Norwich cadets. 136 pp. 8°. *St. Albans, Vt. A. Clarke,* 1873.

White (John). Sketches from America. viii, 374 pp. 8°. *London, S. Low, son & Marston,* 1870.

White (*Rev.* J. G.) Startling facts; relative to auricular confession. 224 pp. 8°. *Cincinnati, author,* 1875.

White (John Pagen). Lays and legends of the english lake country. xvi, 334 pp. 16°. *London, J. R. Smith,* 1873.

White (Robert Baker, *d. d.*) Reason and redemption. 351 pp. 8°. *Philadelphia, J. B. Lippincott & co.* 1873.

White (Thomas, *b.* 1582, *d.* 1676). De mvndo dialogi tres. 6 p. l. 446 pp. 9 l. sm. 4°. *Parisiis, apud D. Moreav,* 1642.

Whitehead (William A.) East Jersey under the proprietary governments: until the surrender to the crown in 1703. With appendix. 2d ed. 1 p. l. v–viii pp. 1 l. 486 pp. 3 maps. 8°. *Newark, N. J., M. R. Dennis,* 1875.

Whitehill (James C. *m. d.*) *and others.* Cyclopedia of things worth knowing. 544 pp. 8°. *St. Louis, continental publishing co.* [1873].

Whitehurst (Felix M.) Court and social life in France under Napoleon the third. 2 v. vii, 346 pp; 2 p. l. 348 pp. 8°. *London, Tinsley brothers,* 1873.

Whitman (Walt). Poems. Selected and edited by William Michael Rossetti. xii, 403 pp. port. 16°. *London, J. C. Hotten,* 1868.

Whitney (*Mrs.* Adeline D. Train). The other girls. vii, 463 pp. 8 pl. 12°. *Boston, J. R. Osgood & co.* 1873.

Whitney (William Dwight). The life and growth of language. ix, 326 pp. 12°. *New York, D. Appleton & co.* 1875.
[INTERNATIONAL scientific series, v. 16].

——— Oriental and linguistic studies. Second series. xi, 432 pp. 1 chart. 12°. *New York, Scribner, Armstrong & co.* 1874.

Whitson (*Mrs.* L. D.) Gilbert St. Maurice. viii, 337 pp. photo. port. 16°. *Louisville, for the author*, 1875.

Whittier (John Greenleaf). Hazel-blossoms. 1 p. l. 5–133 pp. front. 16°. *Boston, J. R. Osgood & co.* 1875.

——— Legends of New England. 142 pp. 16°. *Hartford, Hanmer & Phelps*, 1831.
[MISCELLANEOUS pamphlets, v. 47: 2].

——— Literary recreations and miscellanies. 432 pp. 12°. *Boston, Ticknor & Fields*, 1854.

——— *editor*. Child life in prose. 301 pp. 1 pl. 8°. *Boston, J. R. Osgood & co.* 1874.

——— ——— Songs of three centuries. xxviii, 352 pp. 12°. *Boston, J. R. Osgood & co.* 1876.

Wichert (Ernst). The green gate. From the german by mrs. A. L. Wister. 374 pp. 12°. *Philadelphia, J. B. Lippincott & co.* 1875.

Wicquefort (Abraham de). Histoire des Provinces-Unies des Païs-Bas. v. 1–2. lv, 538 pp; xx, 715 pp. 8°. *Amsterdam, F. Muller*, 1861–64.
[HISTORISCH genootschap. *Utrecht.* Publications].

Widdifield (Hannah). New cook book. 2 p. l. 23–410 pp. 12°. *Philadelphia, T. B. Peterson & brothers*, [1873].

Wiener (Charles). Essai sur les institutions de l'empire des incas. 104 pp. 5 pl. 4°. *Paris, Maisonneuve & cie.* 1874. s.

Wiener (Wilhelm, *editor*). Gallerie der sipurim. 224 pp. 8°. *Prag, W. Pascheles*, 1847.

Wikoff (Henry). The four civilizations of the world. ix, 416 pp. 12°. *Philadelphia, J. B. Lippincott & co.* 1874.

Wilbur (Asa). Biblical standpoint. Views of the sonship of Christ. 2d ed. 213 pp. 12°. *Boston, A. Williams & co.* 1875.

Wilder (Burt G.) What young people should know. The reproductive function in man and the lower animals. 212 pp. 12°. *Boston, Estes & Lauriat*, [1875].

Wilder (Daniel W.) Annals of Kansas. 691 pp. 8°. *Topeka, G. W. Martin*, 1875.

Wilkes (John). Letters from the year 1774 to the year 1796, to his daughter: with a collection of his miscellaneous poems. 4 v. 16°. *London, for Longman*, [*etc.*] 1804.

Wilkins (William, 1778–1839). Prolusiones architectonicæ; essays on grecian and roman architecture. Pt. 1. iv, 128 pp. 17 pl. 4°. *London, J. Weale*, 1837.

Wilkinson (William Cleaver). A free lance in the field of life and letters. 4 p. l. 340 pp. 12°. *New York, A. Mason*, 1874.

Willett (William M.) Messiah. iv, iii–442 pp. 3 pl. 12°. *Boston, B. B. Russell*, 1874.

William and Mary college. (*Williamsburg, Va.*) History of the college of William and Mary. [*anon.*] 183 pp. 1 l. 8°. *Richmond, J. W. Randolph & English*, 1874.
Note.—Compiled by the faculty.

Williams (Daniel, *d. d.*) Practical discourses. 2 v. [xxxvi], 440 pp; 2 p. l. 520 pp. 8°. *London, J. Wilson*, 1738.

Williams (Edwin, *compiler*). Book of the constitution. 144 pp. 12°. *New York, P. Hill*, 1833.

Williams (Folkestone, *i. e.* Robert Folkestone). Lives of the english cardinals. 2 v. xii, 484 pp; iv, 543 pp. 8°. *London, W. H. Allen & co.* 1868.

——— Memoirs and correspondence of Francis Atterbury. 2 v. xix, 446 pp; xii, 478 pp. 8°. *London, W. H. Allen & co.* 1869.

Williams (Francis S.) Getting to Paris. A book of practice in french conversation. x, 210, 226 pp. 12°. *Boston, Lee & Shepard*, 1875.

Williams (Frank). New pocket-dictionary of the english and german languages. 19th ed. 5 p. l. 392, 290 pp. 18°. *London, F. Warne & co.* 1872.

Williams (James). Life and adventures of James Williams, a fugitive slave. 108 pp. 8°. *San Francisco, women's union print*, 1873.

Williams (James R.) History of the methodist protestant church. 402 pp. 12°. *Baltimore, book committee of the m. p. church*, 1843.

Williams (John). The hamiltoniad: or, an extinguisher for the royal faction of New-England. By Anthony Pasquin, esq. [*pseud.*] 104 pp. 8°. *Boston, for the author*, [1804].
[BAILEY pamphlets, v. 54: 8. DUANE pamphlets, v. 94: 7].

Williams (Joseph, *of Kidderminster*). Extracts from the diary, meditations, and letters, of Joseph Williams. New ed. 314 pp. 12°. *Edinburgh, for Ogle & Aikman*, 1801.

Williams (Joseph S.) Old times in west Tennessee [*anon.*] 2 p. l. 295 pp. 12°. *Memphis, Tenn. W. G. Cheeney*, 1873.

Williams (Katherine). How Tiptoe grew. 254 pp. 5 pl. 16°. *New York, american tract society*, [1875].

Williams (Monier). Indian wisdom or examples of the doctrines of the Hindūs. 2d ed. xlviii, 542 pp. 8°. *London, W. H. Allen & co.* 1875.

Williams (Roger). Letters of Roger Williams. 1632–1682. Edited by John Russell Bartlett. xviii pp. 1 l. 420 pp. 4°. *Providence, R. I.* [*Providence press co.*] 1874.
[NARRAGANSETT club. Publications, v. 6.]

Williams (*Rev.* Samuel Porter). Sermons on various subjects. xx, 306 pp. port. 8°. *Salem,* [*Mass.*] *Essex register office,* 1827.

Williams (Samuel Wells). Syllabic dictionary of the chinese language. lxxiv, 1252 pp. 4°. *Shanghai, american presbyterian mission press,* 1874.

Williams (*Rev.* Solomon). Christ, the king and witness of truth. 2 p. l. 151 pp. 8°. *Boston, Rogers & Fowle, for D. Henchman,* 1744.

Williamson (*Rev.* Alexander). Journeys in north China. 2 v. xx, 444 pp. 6 pl. 1 map; viii, 442 pp. 3 pl. 1 map. 12°. *London, Smith, Elder & co.* 1870.

Williamson (Edward H.) Clayton's rangers. [*anon.*] 294 pp. 5 pl. 12°. *Philadelphia, J. B. Lippincott & co.* 1876.

Williamson (I. D.) Argument for the truth of christianity. 252 pp. 16°. *New York, P. Price & co.* 1836.

Williamson (M. J.) Modern diabolism; commonly called modern spiritualism. 401 pp. 12°. *New York, J. Miller,* 1873.

Willis (Julia A. *pseud.*) What a boy! 362 pp. 1 pl. 12°. *Philadelphia, J. B. Lippincott & co.* 1875.

Willis (Nathaniel Parker). Tortesa the usurer. A play. 149 pp. 12°. *New York, S. Colman,* 1839.
[COLMAN's dramatic library].

Williston (*Rev.* Timothy). Talks to my bible class. 242 pp. 16°. *New York, for the author,* 1875.

Willits (A. A.) Miracles of Jesus. 528 pp. 8°. *Philadelphia, Cowperthwait & co.* [1875].

Willshire (William Hughes, *m. d.*) Introduction to the study & collection of ancient prints. xii, 469 pp. 1 pl. 8°. *London, Ellis & White,* 1874.

Willson (Marcius). Drawing guide. 205 pp. 8 pl. 12°. *New York, Harper & brothers,* 1873.

Wilmer (Margaret E.) The dumb traitor. 332 pp. incl. 1 pl. 16°. *New York, national temperance society,* 1874.

Wilmer (Margaret E.)—continued.
——— The glass cable. 288 pp. 1 pl. 16°. *New York, national temperance society,* 1873.

Wilmot (John). Life of the rev. John Hough, d. d. xvi, 387 pp. 6 pl. 2 facs. 4°. *London, for the author,* 1812.

Wilmshurst (Zavarr). The winter of the heart, and other poems. 100 pp. 12°. *New York, Dodd & Mead,* 1874.

Wilson (Andrew). Elements of zoölogy. xxi, 634 pp. 16°. *Edinburgh, A. & C. Black,* 1873.

Wilson (Augusta Evans). Infelice. 572 pp. 12°. *New York, G. W. Carleton & co.* 1876.

Wilson (*Capt.* A. E. *r. e.*) *and others.* The recovery of Jerusalem. 2 v. in 1. 1 p. l. v–xxvii, 334 pp. 12 pl. & plans, 1 incl. in pag; 1 p. l. 335–554 pp. 10 pl. plans, &c. 2 incl. in pag. 8°. *London, R. Bentley,* 1871.

Wilson (Daniel, *ll. d.*) Caliban: the missing link. 1 p. l. xvi, 274 pp. 8°. *London, Macmillan & co.* 1873.

Wilson (Edward L.) Wilson's lantern journeys. 217 pp. 12°. *Philadelphia, Benerman & Wilson,* 1874.

Wilson (Henry, *vice-president of the United States*). History of the rise and fall of the slave power in America. v. 2. xxii, 720 pp. 8°. *Boston, J. R. Osgood & co.* 1874.

Wilson (*Mrs.* H. E.) Our nig. [*anon.*] 140 pp. 12°. *Boston, G. C. Rand & Avery,* 1859.

Wilson (Jacob). Truths of religion and the bible! 131 pp. 8°. *New York,* 1874.

Wilson (James Grant). Sketches of illustrious soldiers. 486 pp. 4 ports. 12°. *New York, G. P. Putnam's sons,* 1874.

Wilson (John Stainback, *m. d.*) Woman's home book of health. New stereo. ed. 445 pp. port. 12°. *Atlanta, southern publishing co.* 1874.

Wilson (Lea). Bibles, testaments, psalms and other books of the holy scriptures in english, in the collection of Lea Wilson. viii pp. incl. 1 pl. 354 + 129*–136* pp. 8°. *London,* [*Chiswick printed, C. Whittingham*], 1845.

Wilson (Theodore D.) Outline of ship building. xvii, 399 pp. 45 pl. & tab. 8°. *New York, J. Wiley & son,* 1873.

Wilson (Thomas). Complete system of english country dancing. 1 p. l. v–xxvii, 340 pp. 1 tab. 2 diagrams, 4 l. of music. 12°. *London, for Sherwood, Neeley & Jones,* [1815]?

Wilson (*Rev.* Thomas). Miscellanies. With memoirs of his life, by the rev. F. R. Raines. 2 p. l. lxxxix, 230 pp. 2 pl. sm. 4°. [*Manchester*], 1857.
[CHETHAM society remains, v. 45].

Wilson (William). Poems. Edited by Benson J. Lossing. 2d ed. xxi, 210 pp. 2 l. port. 16°. *Poughkeepsie,* [*N. Y.*] *A. Wilson,* 1875.

Wilson (William D.) First principles of political economy. 356 pp. 12°. *Ithaca,* [*N. Y.*] *Fitch & Apgar,* 1875.

Winchell (Alexander). The doctrine of evolution. 148 pp. 12°. *New York, Harper & brothers,* 1874.

Winchester (*Rev.* Samuel Gover). The theatre. 239 pp. 12°. *Philadelphia, W. S. Martien,* 1840.

Wines (Mary J.) The infant harper, and other poems. viii, 339 pp. 16°. *New York, for the author,* 1874.

Winfield (Charles H.) History of the county of Hudson, N. J. vii, 568 pp. 12 pl. 8°. *New York, Kennard & Hay,* 1874.

Wingate (Charles F. *editor*). Views and interviews on journalism. 372 pp. 12°. *New York, F. B. Patterson,* 1875.

Winslow (*Rev.* Hubbard). Christianity applied to our civil and social relations. 184 pp. 12°. *Boston, W. Peirce,* 1835.

Winslow (*Miss* M. E.) Barford mills. 254 pp. front. 16°. *New York, national temperance society,* 1875.

Winter (William). Poems. 143 pp. 12°. *Boston, G. W. Briggs & co.* 1855.

Wirth (Max.) Lois du travail au XIXe siècle. Traduit par la baronne de Crombrugghe. viii, 514 pp. 1 l. 8°. *Bruxelles, C. Muquardt,* 1874.

Wisconsin (*State of*). *Historical society.* Catalogue of the library. Prepared by D. S. Durrie, and I. Durrie. 2 v. 639 pp; 719 pp. 8°. *Madison, by order of the state,* 1873.

——— ——— Same. First supplement. 383 pp. 8°. *Madison, Wis. E. B. Bolens,* 1875.

Wise (Daniel, *d. d.*) Bridal greetings. 160 pp. 1 pl. 18°. *New-York, Lane & Scott,* 1850.

——— Little Peachblossom. By Francis Forrester, esq. [*pseud.*] 230 pp. incl. 9 pl. 16°. *New York, Nelson & Phillips,* [1873].

——— Our king and saviour. 367 pp. incl. 1 map & 22 pl. 12°. *New York, Nelson & Phillips,* [1875].

Wise (Daniel, *d. d.*)—continued.

——— The squire of Walton hall; or, sketches from the life of Charles Waterton. 232 pp. incl. 6 pl. 16°. *New York, Nelson & Phillips,* [1874].

——— Story of a wonderful life; or, incidents in the life of John Wesley. 1 p. l. 318 pp. 6 pl. 16°. *Cincinnati, Hitchcock & Walden,* 1874.

——— Summer days on the Hudson. 288 pp. incl. front. 12°. *New York, Nelson & Phillips,* 1875.

——— Uncrowned kings: sketches of some men who rose from obscurity to renown. 301 pp. 5 pl. port. 16°. *Cincinnati, Hitchcock & Walden,* 1875.

Wise (*Dr.* Isaac M.) The martyrdom of Jesus of Nazareth. 134 pp. 8°. *Cincinnati, office of the american israelite,* [1874].

Withrow (*Rev.* W. H.) The catacombs of Rome, and their testimony relative to primitive christianity. 560 pp. 12°. *New York, Nelson & Phillips,* 1874.

Witt (*Mme.* Cornelis de, *born* Guizot). Marie Derville. From the french, by Mary G. Wells. 239 pp. 12°. *Philadelphia, J. B. Lippincott & co.* 1873.

Wittitterly (John Altrayd). Three months at Pau, in 1859. 4 p. l. 267 pp. 12°. *London, Bell & Daldy,* 1860.

Wixson (Franklin, *m. d.*) Black hills gold mines. 100 pp. 1 l. 2 maps, 1 pl. 12°. *Yankton,* [*Dakota*], *Taylor bros.* 1875.

Wodrow (*Rev.* Robert). Collections as to the life of mr. Robert Bruce, minister at Edinburgh.
[*In* BRUCE (R.) Sermons. 8°. *Edinburgh, for the Wodrow society,* 1843. pp. 1–157].

Wohlfarth (*Dr.* Joh. Fr. Theo.) Abracadabra. 2te ausg. 1 p. l. viii, 348 pp. 16°. *Weimar, B. F. Voigt,* 1843.

Wolfe (Napoleon B. *m. d.*) Startling facts in modern spiritualism. xxvii, 543 pp. 4 ports. 12°. *Cincinnati,* [*author*], 1874.

Wollaston (T. Vernon). Coleoptera Atlantidum. xlvii, 526, 140 pp. 1 map. 8°. *London, J. Van Voorst,* 1865.

——— Coleoptera Hesperidum. xxxix, 285 pp. 1 map. 8°. *London, J. Van Voorst,* 1867.

——— On the variation of species. viii, 206 pp. 12°. *London, J. Van Voorst,* 1856.

Wollenweber (L. A.) Gemälde aus dem pennsylvanischen volksleben. Cyklus 1. 143 pp. 18°. *Philadelphia, Schäfer & Koradi,* 1874.

Woltmann (*Dr.* Alfred). Holbein and his times. Translated by F. E. Bunnètt. xvi, 468 pp. 24 pl. 8°. *London, R. Bentley & son,* 1872.

Wood (De Volson). Treatise on the resistance of materials. 2d ed. x, 313 pp. 1 pl. 8°. *New York, J. Wiley & son,* 1875.

——— Treatise on the theory of the construction of bridges and roofs. x, 249 pp. 1 pl. 8°. *New York, J. Wiley & son,* 1873.

Wood (*Mrs.* Henry). The master of Greylands. 1 p. l. 19–280 pp. 8°. *Philadelphia, T. B. Peterson & brothers,* [1873].

Wood (Horatio C. *jr. m. d.*) Contribution to the history of the freshwater algæ of North America. viii, 262 pp. 21 pl. 19 col. 4°. [*Washington, Smithsonian institution,* 1873]. [SMITHSONIAN contributions to knowledge, v. 19].

——— Treatise on therapeutics. 578 pp. 8°. *Philadelphia, J. B. Lippincott & co.* 1874.

——— Same. 2d ed. 674 pp. 8°. *Philadelphia, J. B. Lippincott & co.* 1876.

Wood (*Rev.* John George). Bible animals. [Also] articles on evolution, by rev. James McCosh, and travel in bible lands, by rev. Daniel March. xxix, 719 pp. 24 pl. 8°. *Philadelphia, Bradley, Garretson & co.* 1875.

——— Man and beast, here and hereafter. 2 v. ix, 336 pp; 2 p. l. 346 pp. 12°. *London, Daldy, Isbister & co.* 1874.

Wood's illustrated hand-book to New York and environs. 215 pp. sq. 16°. *New York, G. W. Carleton & co.* 1873.

Woodbury (Augustus). The second Rhode Island regiment, from the beginning to the end of the war for the union. 633 pp. port. 1 map. 8°. *Providence, Valpey, Angell & co.* 1875.

Woodman (*Rev.* J. M.) God in nature and revelation. 542 pp. 1 l. 21 pl. 8°. *New York,* [*Chico, Cal. printed*], *J. G. Hodge & co.* 1875.

Woodman (M. S.) Choice receipts. By M. S. W. [*anon.*] viii, 7–200 pp. sq. 16°. *Boston, J. R. Osgood & co.* 1875.

Woodruff (George H.) Forty years ago! Contribution to the history of Joliet and Will county, [Ill.] iv, 108 pp. 8°. *Joliet,* [*Ill.*] *J. Goodspeed,* 1874.

Woodruff (Hiram). The trotting horse of America: how to train and drive him. Edited by Charles J. Foster. 18th ed. 487 pp. 1 l. port. 6 pl. 12°. *Philadelphia, Porter & Coates,* 1874.

Woodruff (Julia Louisa Matilda). Holden with the cords. By W. M. L. Jay [*pseud.*] 517 pp. 12°. *New York, E. P. Dutton & co.* 1874.

Woods (C. L.) Kaw-wau-nita, and other poems. 101 pp. 16°. *Stockton,* [*Cal*] *D. H. Berdine,* 1873.

Woods (*Rev.* Edgar). Golden apples. 269 pp. 2 pl. 16°. *New York, R. Carter & brothers,* 1875.

Woods (Harriet F.) Historical sketches of Brookline, Mass. 430 pp. 1 l. 12°. *Boston, for the author,* 1874.

Woods (J. T. *m. d.*) Services of the ninety-sixth Ohio volunteers. 1 p. l. 247 pp. 3 ports. 3 plans. 12°. *Toledo, O. blade printing & paper co.* 1874.

Woodward (Bernard Bolingbroke), **Wilks** (*Rev.* Theodore Chambers), *and* **Lockhart** (Charles). General history of Hampshire including the isle of Wight. 3 v. 4°. *London, Virtue & co.* [1870].

Woodward (E. M. *adjt. 2d Pa. reserves*). Our campaigns. 362 pp. 12°. *Philadelphia, J. E. Potter,* 1865.

Woodward (George E.) *and* **Thompson** (Edward G.) Woodward's national architect. Eng. title, x, 15, 48 pp. 100 pl. 19 pp. 4°. *New York, G. E. Woodward,* [1873].

Woolley (John). Introduction to logic. vii, 162 pp. 1 l. 16°. *Oxford, J. H. Parker,* 1840.

Woolrych (Humphry William). Lives of eminent serjeants-at-law of the english bar. 2 v. xxviii, 451 pp; 2 p. l. 453–900 pp. 8°. *London, W. H. Allen & co.* 1869.

Woolsey (Sarah Chauncey). Mischief's thanksgiving. By Susan Coolidge [*pseud.*] 244 pp. 1 pl. 16°. *Boston, Roberts brothers,* 1874.

——— Nine little goslings. By Susan Coolidge [*pseud.*] 3 p. l. 289 pp. front. 16°. *Boston, Roberts brothers,* 1875.

——— What Katy did at school. By Susan Coolidge [*pseud.*] 2 p. l. 278 pp. 4 pl. 16°. *Boston, Roberts brothers,* 1874.

Woolsey (Theodore Dwight). Helpful thoughts for young men. 41 l. unp. 12°. *Boston, D. Lothrop & co.* 1874.

——— Introduction to the study of international law. 4th ed. 487 + 370*–371* pp. 12°. *New York, Scribner, Armstrong & co.* 1874.

Woolson (Abba Goold). Woman in american society. 271 pp. 16°. *Boston, Roberts brothers,* 1873.

Woolson (Abba Goold)—continued.

——— *editor.* Dress-reform: a series of lectures, on dress as it affects the health of women. 263, 2 pp. 3 pl. 16°. *Boston, Roberts brothers,* 1874.

Woolson (Constance Fenimore). Castle Nowhere. 386 pp. 12°. *Boston, J. R. Osgood & co.* 1875.

Worcester (John). Correspondences of the bible. The animals. iv, 276 pp. 16°. *Boston, Lockwood, Brooks & co.* 1875.

Worcester (*City of, Mass.*) *Free public library.* Supplement to the catalogue of the circulating department. 251 pp. 12°. *Worcester, C. Hamilton,* 1874.

Wordsworth (Christopher, *d. d. bishop of Lincoln*). Athens and Attica. i–viii, xi–xii, 285 pp. 3 pl. 2 maps, 1 facs. 8°. *London, J. Murray,* 1836.

Wordsworth (Dorothy) Recollections of a tour in Scotland, 1803. xliv, 316 pp. 1 l. 12°. *Edinburgh, Edmonston & Douglas,* 1874.

Wordsworth (William). Prose works. Edited by A. B. Grosart. 3 v. 8°. *London, E. Moxon, son & co.* 1876.

Worm (Olaüs). Danicorum monumentorum libri sex. Eng. title, 11 p. l. 526 pp. 8 l. 1 pl. 4°. *Hafniæ, apud I. Moltkenium,* 1643.

——— Fasti danici. Eng. title, 5 p. l. 191 pp. 4 l. 4°. *Hafniæ, apud I. Moltkenium,* 1643.

[*With* WORM (O.) Danicorum monumentorum libri sex, 1643].

Worth (*Mrs.* L. L.) Smith's saloon. 299 pp. 3 pl. 16°. *New York, Warren & Wyman,* [1875].

Worthington (John, *d. d.*) Diary and correspondence. Edited by James Crossley. 2 v. 2 p. l. viii, 398 pp; 2 p. l. 248 pp. sm. 4°. [*Manchester*], 1847–55.

[CHETHAM society remains, v. 13, 36].

Wright (A. O.) Analysis and exposition of the constitution of Wisconsin. 175 pp. 12°. *Madison, Wis. Atwood & Culver,* 1873.

Wright (Caleb E.) Marcus Blair. 165 pp. 7 pl. 16°. *Philadelphia, J. B. Lippincott & co.* 1873.

Wright (D. Thew). Mrs. Armington's ward. 332 pp. 16°. *Boston, Lee & Shepard,* 1874.

Wright (Elizur). Politics and mysteries of life insurance. vii, 238 pp. 2 pl. 12°. *Boston, Lee & Shepard,* 1873.

Wright (George). The bible plain; or superstition, bigotry, [etc.] falling from priestcraft. 255 pp. 24°. *Wilmington, Ill.* 1855. S.

Wright (*Rev.* George Newnham). Shores and islands of the Mediterranean. Drawn from nature, by sir Grenville Temple, W. L. Leitch, major Irton, & lieut. Allen, r. e. With an analysis of the Mediterranean and descriptions of the plates. Eng. title, 156 pp. 63 pl. 1 map. 4°. *London, Fisher, son, & co.* [1840].

Wright (Julia McNair). The early church in Britain. 2 pts. in 1 v. 198 pp; 143 pp. 12°. *Cincinnati, western tract society,* 1875.

——— How could he escape? 1 p. l. 324 pp. 16°. *New York, national temperance society,* 1870.

——— Life cruise of captain Bess Adams. 1 p. l. 413 pp. 2 pl. 16°. *New York, national temperance society,* 1874.

——— Nothing to drink. 399 pp. front. 16°. *New York, national temperance society,* 1873.

Wright (J. R.) Principia or basis of social science. xxix, 19–524 pp. 8°. *Philadelphia, J. B. Lippincott & co.* 1875.

Wright (Richard). The anti-satisfactionist; or, the salvation of sinners. 6 p. l. 17–412 pp. 8°. *Wisbech,* [*Eng.*] *F. B. Wright,* 1805.

Wright (Samuel, *d. d.*) Treatise on that being born again, without which no man can be saved. [Also] communicant's spiritual companion. By rev. Thomas Haweis. 276 pp. 16°. *New York, W. Barlas,* 1813.

Wright (Thomas, "*the journeyman engineer*"). Our new masters. x, 392 pp. 12°. *London, Strahan & co.* 1873.

Wright (Thomas, *f. s. a. editor*). Feudal manuals of english history. xxiv, 184 pp. sm. 4°. *London,* [*for*] *J. Mayer,* 1872.

Wright (William B.) The brook and other poems. 167 pp. 12°. *New York, Scribner, Armstrong & co.* 1873.

Wrigley (Edmund). How to manage building associations. 211 pp. 12°. *Philadelphia, J. K. Simon,* 1873.

——— The working man's way to wealth. 5th ed. vi, 108 pp. 16°. *Philadelphia, J. K. Simon,* 1872.

Wrigley (Henry E.) Special report on the petroleum of Pennsylvania. viii, 122 pp. 1 pl. 4 profiles, 2 maps. 8°. *Harrisburg,* 1875.

[PENNSYLVANIA (*State of*). *2d geological survey:* 1874–5].

Wriothesley (Charles). Chronicle of England during the reign of the Tudors, from a. d. 1485 to 1559. Edited by W. D. Hamilton. v. 1. 2 p. l. xlviii, 226 pp. sm. 4°. *London, for the Camden society,* 1875.

[CAMDEN society. Publications. New series, v. 11].

Wrottesley (*Lieut.-col.* George). Life and correspondence of sir John [F.] Burgoyne. 2 v. 3 p. l. 506 pp. port; 2 p. l. 508 pp. 1 facs. 8°. *London, R. Bentley & son,* 1873.

Wyatt (*Sir* Matthew Digby). Fine art; a sketch of its history, [etc.] viii, 376 pp. 8°. *London, Macmillan & co.* 1870.

Wyeth (John A. *m. d.*) Hand-book of medical and surgical reference. 279 pp. 24°. *New-York, W. Wood & co.* 1873.

Wyeth (Joseph). Anguis flagellatus: or, a switch for the snake. Being an answer to the snake in the grass. 9 p. l. 548 pp. 12°. *London, T. Sowle,* 1699.

Wyeth (*Mrs.* Mary E. C.) Bob Tinker and his friends. 160 pp. 2 pl. 18°. *New York, american tract society,* [1874]

Wyeth (Samuel Douglas). The rotunda and dome of the U. S. capitol. vii, 115–231 pp. incl. 13 pl. 3 photos. 8°. *Washington, Gibson brothers,* 1869.

Wyld (Robert S.) Physics and philosophy of the senses. xvi, 562 pp. 8°. *London, H. S. King & co.* 1875.

Wynkoop (M. B.) Song leaves from the book of life and nature. [*anon.*] 113 pp. 16°. *New York, J. S. Redfield,* 1852.

Wynter (Andrew, *m. d.*) Borderlands of insanity and other papers. 1 p. l. vii, 314 pp. 12°. *London, R. Hardwicke,* 1875.

——— Our social bees; and other papers. 10th ed. viii, 532 pp. 12°. *London, R. Hardwicke,* 1869.

——— Peeps into the human hive. 2 v. 4 p. l. 302 pp; 3 p. l. 303 pp. 12°. *London, Chapman & Hall,* 1874.

——— Subtle brains and lissom fingers. 3d ed. viii, 446 pp. 12°. *London, R. Hardwicke,* 1869.

Xántus (János). Utazás Kalifornia déli részeiben. 5 p. l. 191 pp. 8 col. pl. 1 map. 8°. *Pesten, Lauffer & Stolp,* 1860.

Ximinez (Matteo). Compendio della vita del beato Sebastiano d'Apparizio. xvi, 228 pp. + 223–224 bis. 1 l. sm. 4°. *Roma, stamperia Salomoni,* 1789.

Y—k—f (S. F.) Essai d'une solution en économie politique. [*anon.*] 2 p. l. 355, xiv pp. 8°. *Moscou, W. Gautier,* 1853.

Yaggy (L. W.) Our home counselor, a practical cyclopedia for daily use. 320, 127 pp. 8°. *Chicago, western publishing house,* 1873.

Yale college (*New Haven, Conn.*) Catalogue of the Linonian and Brothers' library. 344 pp. 8°. *New Haven, Tuttle, Morehouse & Taylor,* 1873.

Yates (Edmund Hodgson). A dangerous game. 1 p. l. 200 pp. 8°. *Boston, W. F. Gill & co.* 1875.
[GILL's select novels].

Yeager (George). The garden of Eden. 128 pp. 18°. *Philadelphia, J. B. Lippincott & co.* 1873.

Yeats (John, *ll. d.*) Technical, industrial, and trade education. The growth and vicissitudes of commerce. From b. c. 1500 to a. d. 1789. xxix, [441] pp. 2 maps. 12°. *London, Virtue & co.* 1872.

Yelverton (Thérèse, *viscountess Avonmore*). Teresina peregrina: fifty thousand miles of travel round the world. 2 v. iv, 352 pp. 1 photo; iv, 355 pp. 1 photo. 12°. *London, R. Bentley & sons,* 1874.

Yepes (Joaquin Lopez). Catecismo y declaracion de la doctrina cristiana en lengua otomí, con un vocabulario del misma idioma. 254 pp. 1 l. sq. 12°. *Mégico, A. Valdés,* 1826.

Yonge (Charles Duke). History of France under the Bourbons. 1589–1830. v. 1–4. 8°. *London, Tinsley brothers,* 1866–67.

——— History of the british navy, to the present time. 2d ed. 3 v. 8°. *London, R. Bentley,* 1866.

York (*England*) *Archbishopric of.* The register, or rolls of Walter Gray, lord archbishop of York. lviii, 329 pp. 1 pl. 8°. *Durham,* 1872.
[SURTEES society. Publications, v. 56].

——— *Castle of.* Depositions from the castle of York, relating to offences committed in the northern counties in the seventeenth century. xxxvi, 346 pp. 8°. *Durham,* 1861.
[SURTEES society. Publications, v. 40].

——— *Guild of corpus Christi.* Register. xvi, 362 pp. 1 l. 1 pl. 8°. *Durham,* 1872.
[SURTEES society. Publications, v. 57].

——— *Minster.* The fabric rolls of York minster. xxx, 379 pp. 1 pl. 8°. *Durham,* 1859.
[SURTEES society. Publications, v. 35].

——— ——— Manuale et processionale ad usum insignis ecclesiæ eboracencis. xxviii, 207, 228* pp. 8°. *Durham, for the society,* 1875.
[SURTEES society. Publications, v. 63].

——— ——— Missale ad usum insignis ecclesiæ eboracensis. v. 2. xxiv, 360 pp. 8°. *Durham,* [*Leeds printed*], *for the society,* 1874.
[SURTEES society. Publications, v. 60].

Young (Andrew W.) History of the town of Warsaw, New York. 400 pp. 6 pl. 40 ports. 8°. *Buffalo, Sage, sons & co.* 1869.

Young (Arthur). Arithmétique politique. Traduit par m. Fréville. 2 v. 4 p. l. 464 pp; 3 p. l. 519 pp. 8°. *La Haye, P. F. Gosse,* 1775.

Young (*Dr.* R. F.) Magic wand and medical guide. 1 p. l. 316 pp. 12 pl. 18°. *New York, R. F. Young & co.* 1875.

Zahn (Wilhelm). Ornamente aller klassischen kunst-epochen. 3te aufl. 22 p. l. 100 col. pl. obl. fol. in portfolio. *Berlin, D. Reimer,* 1870.

Zani (Pietro). Enciclopedia metodica critico-ragionata delle belle arti. Parte prima. 19 v. 8°. *Parma, dalla tipografia ducale,* 1819–24.

——— Same. Parte seconda. v. 1–9. 8°. *Parma, dalla tipografia ducale,* 1817–22. [Imperfect; v. 10 wanting].

——— Materiali per servire alla storia dell'origine e de' progressi dell'incisione in rame e in legno. vi, 248 pp. 1 l. intercalated. 1 pl. 8°. *Parma, dalla stamperia Carmignani,* 1802.

Zarate (Augustin de). Conqueste van Indien. [*anon.* Overgezet van Romoldus de Bacquere Regius. 3d ed?] *b. l.* 154 l. 10 unp. l. sm. 4°. *Amstelredam, J. P. Wachter,* 1623.

——— Same. Histoire de la découverte et de la conquête du Pérou, traduite de l'espagnole, par S. D. C. [*i. e.* de Broe, seigneur de Citry de la Guette]. 2 v. xxxj, 317 pp; 2 p. l. 443 pp. 8°. *Paris, aux frais du gouvernement,* 1830.

Zeiller (Martin). M. Z. Topographia Germaniæ—inferioris vel circuli—Burgundici das ist beschreibung der fürnembsten örter in

Zeiller (Martin)—continued.

den niderländischen XVII provincien. [*anon.*] Eng. title, 283 [+1] pp. 10 l. 12 maps, 122 pl. & plans. fol. *Franckfurt am Maÿn, C. Merian,* [1659].

Zell (T. Ellwood, *publisher*). Zell's United States business directory for 1875. Compiled under the supervision of L. Colange. 8°. *Philadelphia, T. E. Zell,* [1875].

Ziemssen (Hugo Wilhelm von, *editor*). Cyclopædia of the practice of medicine. Translated by R. H. Fitz, [etc.] Albert H. Buck, N. Y. editor of am. ed. v. 1–3, 5, 10. 8°. *New York, W. Wood & co.* 1874–75.

Ziethe (*Rev.* W.) Anna Lavater. From the german, by Catherine E. Hurst. 226 pp. 16°. *Cincinnati, Hitchcock & Walden,* 1870.

Zimmermann (*Dr.* Wilhelm). Geschichte der Hohenstaufen für das deutsche volk. 2te aufl. 2 v. in 1. 366 pp. 2 pl; viii, 3–362 pp. 3 pl. 12°. *Stuttgart, Rieger,* 1858.

Zimmern (Helen). Stories in precious stones. 2d ed. xii, 192 pp. incl. 3 pl. front. 12°. *London, H. S. King & co.* 1873.

Zincke (F. Barham). A month in Switzerland. xvi, 272 pp. 12°. *London, Smith, Elder & co.* 1873.

——— Swiss allmends, being a second month in Switzerland. ix, 367 pp. 12°. *London, Smith, Elder & co.* 1874.

Zollikofer (*Rev.* Georg Joachim). Sermons on the dignity of man. From the german by the rev. Wm. Tooke. 1st am. ed. v. 1. xxii, 424 pp. 8°. *Worcester,* [*Ms.*] *for I. Thomas, jun.* 1807.

Zschokke (Heinrich). The rose of Disentis. From the german by James J. D. Trenor. 1 p. l. 284 pp. 12°. *New York, Sheldon & co.* 1873.

LAW-BOOKS.

LAW-BOOKS.

Abbott (Austin). Reports of practice cases in the courts of the state of New York, [1870–1874]. New series. v. 13–15. 8°. *New York, Diossy & co.* 1873–74.

——— Reports of the decisions of the court of appeals of the state of New York, not heretofore reported under official sanction, [1850–1869]. v. 1–4. A–W. 8°. *New York, Diossy & co.* 1873–74.

Abbott (Benjamin Vaughan). Digest of the reports of the United States courts, from may, 1872, to nov. 1874. v. 6. 8°. *New York, Diossy & co.* 1874.

——— United States digest of decisions of the various courts within the United States. From the earliest period [1658] to the year 1870. First series. v. 1–9. 8°. *Boston, Little, Brown, & co.* 1874–75.

——— Same. Annual digests for 1872–1874. New series. v. 3–5. 8°. *Boston, Little, Brown, & co.* 1873–75.

——— *and* **Abbott** (Austin). Digest of the New York statutes and reports from the earliest period. 2d ed. 1873. 6 v. 8°. *New York, Baker, Voorhis & co.* 1873–74.

Abbott (Charles, *baron Tenterden*). Treatise of the law relative to merchant ships and seamen. 11th ed. by W. Shee. liii, 638, cccclxxiii pp. 8°. *London, Shaw & sons,* 1867.

Acollas (Émile). Le droit de l'enfant. L'enfant né hors mariage. 2e éd. x, 160 pp. 1 l. 12°. *Paris, G. Baillière,* 1870.

——— Manuel de droit civil à l'usage des étudiants. v. 3. 8°. *Paris, G. Baillière,* 1871.

Adams (Charles G.) Wrongs and their remedies. 4th ed. by F. S. P. Wolferstan. xcii, 1179 pp. 8°. *London, Stevens & sons,* 1873.

Adams (Frank Mantell). Treatise on the law of trade marks. viii, 176 pp. 8°. *London, G. Bell & sons,* 1874.

Adams (John, *jr. barrister*). Doctrine of equity. 6th am. ed. With notes by G. Sharswood, jr. lxxxv, 831 pp. 8°. *Philadelphia, T. & J. W. Johnson & co.* 1873.

Adams (John B.) *and* **Durham** (Warren J.) Real estate statutes of Illinois. [1809–1874]. 2 v. xxxi, 1060 pp; 1 p. l. 1061–1991 pp. 8°. *Chicago, Callaghan & co.* 1874.

Addison (Charles G.) Treatise on the law of contracts. 3d am. ed. by J. A. Morgan. v. 1. xxxv, 771 pp. 8°. *New York, J. Cockcroft & co.* 1875.

Admiralty jurisdiction, its faults and its defaults. 2d ed. [*anon.*] x, 159 pp. 1 l. 8°. *London, Longmans,* 1861.

Aird (David Mitchell). Blackstone economized. 2d ed. xxv, 29–356, 12 pp. 1 chart. 8°. *London, Longmans,* 1873.

Alabama (*State of*). Acts of the 5th biennial session, 1855; 2d called session, 1861, and 1st regular annual session, 1861; called session, 1863, and 3d regular annual session, 1863; session 1869–70; session 1870–71; session 1871–72; session 1872–73; session 1873. 8 v. 8°. *Montgomery, state printers,* [*etc.*] 1856–74.

——— *Supreme court.* Condensed reports of decisions, 1820–1839, by W. R. Smith. 5 v. 8°. *Tuskaloosa, Ala. W. R. Smith,* [*etc.*] 1870.

——— ——— Digest of decisions, 1820–1869, by R. C. Brickell. v. 2. 8°. *Montgomery, Ala. J. White,* 1874.

——— ——— Reports of cases, v. 44–48, new series, 1870–1872, by T. G. Jones. 8°. *Montgomery, Ala. Barrett & Brown,* 1871–74.

——— ——— Same. v. 49, new series, 1873, by J. W. Shepherd. 8°. *Montgomery, Ala.* [*etc.*] *J. White,* 1875.

Albany law journal. Jan. 1873 to jan. 1875. v. 7–10. 4°. *Albany, Weed, Parsons & co.* 1873–74.

Algeria. Dictionnaire de législation algérienne, 1830–1872, par P. de Ménerville. 3 v. in 2. 8°. *Alger, Bastide,* [*etc.*] 1867–72.

Allard (Albéric). Histoire de la justice criminelle au seizième siècle. viii, 525 pp. 8°. *Gand, H. Hoste,* 1868.

Allen (Charles). Telegraph cases decided in the courts of America, Great Britain, and

Allen (Charles)—continued. Ireland. xvi, 740 pp. 8°. *New York, Hurd & Houghton*, 1873.

Alvarez Posadilla (Juan). Comentarios á las leyes de Toro. 4a ed. 4 p. l. 444 pp. 1 chart. sm. 4°. *Madrid, imprenta que fue de Fuentenebro*, 1833.

——— Práctica criminal por principios. 3a ed. 3 v. sm. 4°. *Madrid, la imprenta que fue de Garcia*, 1815.

Ameline (Edmond). Des nullités du mariage. 2 p. l. 447 pp. 1 l. 8°. *Paris, S. Raçon*, 1866.

American law journal, 1842–1852. *See* **Pennsylvania** law journal reports.

American law record. [July], 1874–[june], 1875. v. 3. 8°. *Cincinnati, Bloch & co.* 1875.

American law register. From jan. 1873 to dec. 1874. New series, v. 12–13, (old series, v. 21–22). 8°. *Philadelphia, D. B. Canfield & co.* 1873–74.

American law review. [Oct.] 1872–[july], 1875. v. 7–9. 8°. *Boston, Little, Brown, & co.* 1873–75.

American law times. 1868–1869. v. 1–2. 4°. *Washington, american law times association*, 1868–69.

——— Same. 1871–1872. v. 4–5. 8°. [*Washington, J. C. & R. Cox*, 1871–72].

——— Same. [1874]. New series. v. 1. 8°. *New York, Hurd & Houghton*, 1874.

American law times reports. [1871–1872]. v. 4–5. 8°. *Washington, R. Cox*, 1872–[73].

——— Same. [1873]. v. 6. 8°. *New York, Hurd & Houghton*, 1874.

——— Same. New series. [1874]. v. 1. 8°. *New York, Hurd & Houghton*, 1875.

American railway reports. [1872–1873]. By J. H. Truman. v. 1. 8°. *New York, J. Cockcroft*, 1873.

——— Same. [1869–1874]. By J. A. Mallory. v. 2–4. 8°. *New York, J. Cockcroft*, [*etc.*] 1874–75.

American reports, v. 7–15, 1868–1874, by Isaac Grant Thompson. 8°. *Albany, J. D. Parsons, jr.* 1873–75.

Ames (James Barr). Selection of cases on pleading at common law, [1474–1873]. viii, 299 pp. 8°. *Cambridge, [Ms.] J. Wilson & son*, 1875.

Ames (Samuel). Law of private corporations aggregate. *See* **Angell** (Joseph K.) *and* **Ames.**

Amory (Robert, *m. d.*) Chapters on poisons. [*In* WHARTON (Francis, *ll. d.*) *and* STILLÉ (Moreton, *m. d.*) Medical jurisprudence. 3d ed. 8°. *Philadelphia, Kay & brother*, 1873. v. 2, pt. 1, pp. 274–368].

Amos (Sheldon). An english code; its difficulties and the modes of overcoming them. 1 p. l. xv, 237 pp. 8°. *London, Strahan & co.* 1873.

——— Science of law. xx, 417 pp. 1 chart. 12°. *New York, D. Appleton & co.* 1874.

Andrews (Horace). Manual of the laws and courts of the United States, and of the several states and territories, with a directory of lawyers. 3 p. l. 444 pp. 8°. *New York, Andrews, Gibson & Bateman*, 1873.

Angell (Joseph K.) *and* **Ames** (Samuel). Treatise on the law of private corporations aggregate. 10th ed. by J. Lathrop. lxiv, 866 pp. 8°. *Boston, Little, Brown & co.* 1875.

Annales du barreau français, depuis Le Maistre, [né 1608], jusqu'à nos jours. Barreau ancien, v. 2–6, in 7 v. 8°. *Paris, B. Warée*, 1822–29.

Note.—v. 1 not yet published.

——— Same. Barreau moderne. 12 v. in 13. 8°. *Paris, B. Warée*, [*etc.*] 1822–47.

Annuaire de législation étrangère. 1e–2e années. 2 v. 8°. *Paris, Cotillon & fils*, 1872–73.

Archbold (John Frederick). Justice of the peace, and parish officer; with the practice of country attorneys in criminal cases. 6th ed. 4 v. 12°. *London, Shaw & sons*, 1855–73.

——— Same. Supplement to the sixth edition. By J. Paterson. xvi, 280 pp. 7 l. 12°. *London, Shaw & sons*, 1863.

[Lettered v. 5].

——— The poor law. 12th ed. by W. C. Glen. 12°. *London, Shaw & sons*, 1873.

[ARCHBOLD'S justice of the peace, v. 3].

Aristarchi *bey* (Gregorius). Législation ottomane, [1839–1870]. 2 v. xxx, 5–427 pp; 1 p. l. 464 pp. 8°. *Constantinople, frères Nicolaïdes*, [*etc.*] 1873–74.

Arizona (*Territory of*). Acts, resolutions and memorials adopted by the sixth and seventh legislative assemblies, 1871–1873. 2 v. 8°. *Tucson*, [*office of*] *the Arizona citizen*, 1871–73.

Arkansas (*State of*). Acts passed at the session of 1873. 8°. *Little Rock, printing co.* 1873.

——— *Supreme court.* Reports of cases, v. 25–27, 1867–1872, by Norval W. Cox. 8°. *Little Rock, state printers*, [*etc.*] 1870–73.

Arnoux (William Henry). The Rollwagen will case, [1873–1874]. Argument of counsel for proponents. 2 p. l. 209 pp. 8°. *New York, Lange, Little & co.* 1874.

Aucoc (Léon). Conférences sur l'administration et le droit administratif faites à l'école impériale des ponts et chaussées. 2 v. xxiii, 681 pp. 1 l; 2 p. l. 540 pp. 8°. *Paris, Dunod*, 1869–70.

Augusta (*City of, Georgia*). Laws incorporating Augusta, and ordinances in force, july, 1814. 8°. *Augusta, Hobby & Bunce*, 1814.

Austria. Das allgemeine bürgerliche gesetzbuch für das kaiserthum Oesterreich, [1725–1873]. Fünfter abdruck. viii, 476 pp. 16°. *Wien, G. J. Manz*, 1873.

——— Die civil- und militär-jurisdictionsnorm. [1774–1873]. 5te auf. xvi, 651 pp. 16°. *Wien, G. J. Manz*, 1873.

——— Katechismus der österreichischen staatsverfassung. 102 pp. 16°. *Wien, G. J. Manz*, 1874.

——— Reichsgesetzblatt. Jahrgang 1870–1872. 3 v. 4°. *Wien, k. k. hof- und staatsdruckerei*, 1870–72. s.

——— Staatsgrundgesetze der österreichischen monarchie. [1222–1861]. Unveränderter neudruck. lxxx, 561 pp. 16°. *Wien, G. J. Manz*, 1871.

——— Same. Supplementheft. März, 1861–december, 1867. x, 250 pp. 16°. *Wien, G. J. Manz*, 1868.

Ayckbourn (Hubert). Forms of proceedings in the high court of chancery. 9th ed. xxiv, 176, 200 pp. 12°. *London, Wildy & sons*, 1873.

Bailliot (Célestin). Guide des opérations de transferts. 2e éd. 4 p. l. 364 pp. 8°. *Paris, A. Chaix et cie.* 1874.

Baker (George Sherston). Handy book on the law of railway companies. 1 p. l. v, 93 pp. 12°. *London, Reeves & Turner*, 1873.

Ball (George W. I.) General railroad laws of the state of Pennsylvania. 1820–1874. 271 pp. 8°. *Philadelphia, Allen, Lane & Scott*, 1875.

Barbour (Oliver Lorenzo). Reports of cases in the supreme court of the state of New York, [1863–1873]. v. 63–65. 8°. *Albany, W. C. Little & co.* 1873.

——— Same. [1847]. v. 1. [2d ed.] 8°. *New York, Banks & brothers*, 1875.

——— Treatise on the practice of the court of chancery. 2d ed. 3 v. 8°. *Albany, Banks & brothers*, 1874–75.

Barlow (William). Index to equity cases in Ireland, 1838–1867. *See* **Gamble** (Richard Wilson) *and* **Barlow.**

Barnard (George G.) Proceedings in the impeachment of George G. Barnard. [Albany, 1872]. 1 v. in 3. 8°. *Oswego, [N. Y.] E. J. Oliphant*, 1875.

Barroll (Francis) *and others.* Cases [at law and opinions, english, 1692–1778]. 178 pp. 4 l. ms. sm. 4°.

Bateman (Joseph). Treatise on the law of auctions. 5th ed. by R. Rouse. xxxvi, 502 pp. 12°. *London, W. Maxwell & son*, 1874.

Battle (William H.) Revisal of the public statutes of North Carolina, 1872–1873. 8°. *Raleigh, Edwards, Broughton & co.* 1873.

Baxter (Wynne E.) Law and practice of the supreme court of judicature. xvi, 428 pp. 12°. *London, Butterworths, [etc.]* 1874.

Baylies (Edwin). Questions and answers for law students. vi, 512 pp. 8°. *Albany, W. Gould & son*, 1873.

Baylis (T. Henry). Rights, duties and relations of domestic servants. 4th ed. by E. P. Monckton. xiv, 80 pp. 1 l. 16°. *London, Butterworths*, 1873.

Bazaine (François Achille). Procès du maréchal Bazaine, [Versailles, 1873]. 400 pp. 1 map; 401–632, 179 pp.

[FOUQUIER (A.) Causes célèbres. 4°. *Paris, H. Lebrun*, 1874, v. 8–9].

Beaulieu (Arthur Léon Michel). De la complicité en droit romain et en droit français. 276 pp. 8°. *Paris, C. Pichon-Lamy*, 1868.

Becker (Henri). De la justice et des avocats en Bavière et en Allemagne. 2 p. l. 38 pp. 8°. *Paris, Cotillon*, 1861.

Beitel (Calvin G.) Digest of titles of corporations chartered by the legislature of Pennsylvania, 1700–1873. 2d ed. viii, 744 pp. 8°. *Philadelphia, J. Campbell & son*, 1874.

Belgium. Code pénal, par J. S. G. Nypels. 8°. *Bruxelles, Bruylant-Christophie et cie.* 1867.

Belime (William). Philosophie du droit. 3e éd. 2 v. viii, 536 pp; 712 pp. 8°. *Paris, A. Durand & Pedone-Lauriel*, 1869.

Belknap (David P.) Probate law and practice of California. 3d ed. xix, 388, ccliv pp. 8°. *San Francisco, A. L. Bancroft & co.* 1873.

Bell (Charles U.) General statutes of Massa chusetts. Reduced to questions and answers. 2 p. l. 183 pp. 12°. *Boston, G. B. Reed*, 1874.

Bench and bar. New series. April, 1871–jan. 1874. v. 1–3. 8°. [*Chicago & New York, Callaghan & Cockcroft, etc.* 1871–74].

Bench and bar review. Jan.–april, 1874. v. 1. 8°. *Baltimore, A. Schaumburg,* [*etc.*] 1874.

Benedict (Robert D.) Reports of cases in the district courts of the United States, second circuit. [1871–1873]. v. 5–6. 8°. *New York, Baker, Voorhis & co.* 1874–75.

Benjamin (Judah Peter). Treatise on the law of sale of personal property. 2d ed. xxix, 790 pp. 8°. *London, H. Sweet,* 1873.

——— Same. 1st am. ed. by J. C. Perkins. liv, 847 pp. 8°. *New York, Hurd & Houghton,* 1875.

Bennett (Edmund Hastings). Fire insurance cases. v. 2–3, from 1840 to 1854. 8°. *New York, Hurd & Houghton,* 1873–74.

Bentley (Alexander J.) Opinions of the attorneys general of the United States, v. 13–14, 1869–1875. 8°. *Washington, government printing office,* 1873–75.

Berry (Charles M.) *and others.* History of the conspiracy case of Pennsylvania *vs.* Chas. M. Berry. [1874]. 43 pp. 16°. *Titusville, Pa. morning herald,* 1874.

Best (William Mawdesley). Law of evidence. 1st am. ed. by J. A. Morgan. v. 1. xix, 526 pp. 8°. *New York, J. Cockcroft & co.* 1875.

Bicknell (George A. *jr.*) Commentary on the bankrupt law of 1841. 2d ed. 100 pp. 8°. *New York, Gould, Banks, & co.* 1842.

Bigelow (Melville M.) Index of the cases overruled, reversed, denied, doubted, modified, limited, explained, and distinguished, by the courts of America, England, and Ireland; from the earliest period to the present time. 566 pp. 8°. *Boston, Little, Brown, & co.* 1873.

——— Leading cases on the law of torts, [1722–1871]. xlii, 754 pp. 8°. *Boston, Little, Brown, & co.* 1875.

——— Reports of life and accident insurance cases to jan. 1875. [From 1800]. v. 3–4. 8°. *New York, Hurd & Houghton,* 1874–75.

Billings (Sidney). The laws relating to pews in churches. 2 p. l. xlviii, 252 pp. 12°. *London, W. Benning & co.* 1845.

Bioren (John). Laws of Pennsylvania, 1700–1802. *See* **Carey** (Mathew) *and* **Bioren.**

Bishop (Joel Prentiss). Commentaries on the law of marriage and divorce. 5th ed. 2 v. lxxv, 701 pp; viii, 747 pp. 8°. *Boston, Little, Brown, & co.* 1873.

——— Commentaries on the law of married women. v. 2. xx, 757 pp. 8°. *Boston, Little, Brown, & co.* 1875.

——— Commentaries on the law of statutory crimes. xvi, 814 pp. 8°. *Boston, Little, Brown, & co.* 1873.

Bispham (George Tucker). Principles of equity. lx, 540 pp. 8°. *Philadelphia, Kay & brother,* 1874.

Bissell (Arthur H.) Statutes at large of the state of Minnesota in force, march 7, 1873. 2 v. xiv, 718 pp; x, 719–1375 pp. 8°. *Chicago, Callaghan & co.* 1873.

Bissell (Josiah H.) Cases in the circuit and district courts of the United States, for the seventh circuit, 1851–1873. v. 1–4. 8°. *Chicago, Callaghan & co.* 1873–75.

Black (James B.) Reports of cases in the supreme court of Indiana, 1870–1874. v. 6–19. [v. 35–48, Indiana reports]. 8°. *Indianapolis, journal co.* 1873–75.

Blackstone (*Sir* William). Analysis of the laws of England. 5th ed. lxxxii, 189 pp. 7 l. 8°. *Oxford, Clarendon press,* 1762.

——— Commentaries reduced to questions and answers. *See* **Devereux** (John C.)

Blackwell (Robert S.) Treatise on the power to sell land for the non-payment of taxes. 4th ed. xliii, 761 pp. 8°. *Boston, Little, Brown, & co.* 1875.

Blake (Henry Nichols). Reports of cases in the supreme court of Montana territory, 1868–1873. v. 1. [v. 1, Montana reports]. 8°. *Virginia City, G. F. Cope,* 1873.

Blatchford (Samuel). Reports of cases in the circuit court of the United States for the second circuit, [1870–1875]. v. 10–12. 8°. *New York, Baker, Voorhis & co.* 1873–75.

Blatchley (J. S.) Digest of fire insurance decisions. *See* **Littleton** (H. A.) *and* **Blatchley.**

Blickensderfer (U.) Abridgment of elementary law. *See* **Dunlap** (M. E.) *and* **Blickensderfer.**

Bliss (George). Law of life insurance. 2d ed. xxiv, 793 pp. 8°. *New York, Baker, Voorhis & co.* 1874.

Bohun (William). The practising attorney. 3d ed. 2 v. 6 p. l. 464 pp; 528 pp. 8°. [*London*], *E. & R. Nutt,* [*etc.*] *for A. Bettesworth,* [*etc.*] 1732.

Bolivia. Código de procederes Santa-Cruz, 1833. 2 p. l. 212, viii pp. 8°. *Chuquisaca, Aillon y Castillo,* [1833].

Bonaparte (*Prince* Pierre). Prince Pierre Bonaparte. [Trial at Tours, 1870, for the murder of Victor Noir].

[*In* MORSE (John T. *jr.*) Famous trials. 8°. *Boston, Little, Brown, & co.* 1874. pp. 256–273].

Bond (H. H.) Mechanics' liens under the law of Massachusetts. 32 pp. 12°. *Springfield, Mass. C. W. Bryan & co.* 1874.

Bonnifield (M. S.) *and* **Healy** (Thaddeus W.) Compiled laws of Nevada, 1861–1873. 2 v. 8°. *Carson City, state printer,* 1873.

Booraem (H. Toler). Reports of cases in the supreme court of California, 1856–1857. v. 1–3. 2d ed. by R. Desty. [v. 6–8, California reports]. 8°. *San Francisco, S. Whitney,* [*etc.*] 1875.

Boorn (Jesse) *and* **Boorn** (Stephen). Trial of Jesse and Stephen Boorn, [at Bennington, 1819], for the murder of Russell Colvin. By L. Sargeant. 48 pp. 8°. *Manchester, Vt. journal job office,* 1873.

Booth (David B.) *and others.* Revision of 1875, of the general statutes of Connecticut. 8°. *Hartford, Case, Lockwood & Brainard,* 1874.

Booth (Walter S.) Justice's manual for Minnesota. 2d ed. 55 pp. 16°. *Rochester, Leonard & Booth,* 1872.

——— Same. 4th ed. 128 pp. 12°. *Rochester, Leonard & Booth,* 1875.

——— Township manual for Minnesota. 31, 60 pp. 16°. *Rochester, Leonard & Booth,* 1873.

——— Same. 2d ed. 128 pp. 12°. *Rochester, Leonard & Booth,* 1874.

Boulet (J. E. B.) Institutes de Gaius. *See* **Caius** (Titius).

Bourgeois (Jules). Des modes de transmission des créances. 180 pp. 8°. *Paris, Pichon-Lamy & Dewez,* 1869.

Bourgeois (Paul). De la compensation. 186 pp. 8°. *Paris, C. Pichon-Lamy,* 1868.

Bourjon (François). Le droit commun de la France, et la coutume de Paris. Nouvelle éd. 2 v. 12 p. l. 1136 pp; 2 p. l. xxvii, 864 pp. fol. *Paris, Grangé,* [*etc.*] 1770.

Brandt (Frederick). Games, gaming and gamesters' law. 2d ed. xx, 266 pp. 1 l. 8°. *London, H. Sweet,* 1873.

Bravard-Veyrières (Pierre Claude Jean Baptiste). Manuel de droit commercial. 4e éd. vii, 830 pp. 8°. *Paris, G. Thorel,* 1851.

Brewster (Frederick Carroll). Reports of cases in the supreme court of Pennsylvania and in other courts, [1863–1873]. v. 4. 8°. *Philadelphia, Kay & brother,* 1873.

Brickell (R. C.) Digest of the decisions of the supreme court of Alabama, [1820–1869]. v. 2. Fe.–Wi. xxiii, 549 pp. 4°. *Montgomery, Ala. J. White,* 1874.

Brightly (Frederick Charles). Annual digest of the laws of Pennsylvania for the year 1873. 8°. *Philadelphia, Kay & brother,* 1873.

——— Same. For the years 1873 and 1874. 8°. *Philadelphia. Kay & brother,* 1874.

——— Digest of Pennsylvania laws, 1700–1872. *See* **Purdon** (John).

——— Digest of the decisions of the federal courts. v. 2. 2d ed. [1868–1873]. 461 pp. 8°. *Philadelphia, Kay & brother,* 1873.

——— Supplement to Purdon's digest. 1846–1848. 100 pp. 8°. *Philadelphia, J. Kay, jun. & brother,* 1848. S.

Broom (Herbert) *and* **Hadley** (Edward A.) Commentaries on the laws of England. [1st am. ed.] by W. Wait. 2 v. xxxi, 918 pp. 2 charts; xxii, 821 pp. 8°. *Albany, J. D. Parsons, jr.* 1875.

Brown (Archibald). New law dictionary. lxviii, 392 pp. 8°. *London, Stevens & Haynes,* 1874.

——— Same. With additions, by A. P. Sprague. vi, 418 pp. 8°. *Albany, J. D. Parsons, jr.* 1875.

Brown (Guy A.) General statutes of Nebraska, in force sep. 1, 1873. 8°. *Lincoln, state printers,* 1873.

Brown (William). Compendium of practice in the court of exchequer. 8 p. l. 548 pp. 5 l. 12°. *London, assigns of R. & E. Atkins, for H. Mortlocke,* 1688.

Browne (Albert G. *jr.*) Cases in the supreme court of Massachusetts, 1871–1872, v. 11–13, [v. 107–109, Massachusetts reports]. 8°. *Boston, H. O. Houghton & co.* 1873–74.

——— *and* **Gray** (John C. *jr.*) Cases in the supreme court of Massachusetts, 1872–1873, v. 1–2, [v. 110–111, Massachusetts reports]. 8°. *Boston, H. O. Houghton & co.* 1874–75.

Browne (J. H. Balfour). Treatise on the law of carriers of goods and passengers. xxxii, 656 pp. 8°. *London, Stevens & sons,* 1873.

Browne (William Hardcastle). Pennsylvania legal time table. 123 pp. 8°. *Philadelphia, Kay & brother,* 1875.

Browne (William Henry). Treatise on the law of trade-marks. xxiii, 677 pp. 8°. *Boston, Little, Brown, & co.* 1873.

Bruce (William Downing). Guide to the land registry act. 2d ed. 4 p. l. 124, xix pp. 8°. *London, V. & R. Stevens, sons, & Haynes,* [*etc.*] 1863.

Buckley (H. Burton). Law and practice under the companies acts. xliv, 516 pp. 8°. *London, Stevens & Haynes,* 1873.

Bump (Orlando Franklin). Law and practice in bankruptcy. To may 1, 1873. 6th ed. xxv, 782 pp. 8°. *New York, Baker, Voorhis & co.* 1873.

——— Same, to sep. 1, 1874. 7th ed. xxx, 855 pp. 8°. *New York, Baker, Voorhis & co.* 1874.

——— Same, to august 1, 1875. 8th ed. xxxix, 983 pp. 8°. *New York, Baker, Voorhis & co.* 1875.

——— United States bankrupt law. 70 pp. 8°. *New York, Baker, Voorhis & co.* 1874.

Burch (John C.) Civil, penal and political codes and code of procedure of California, 1873, annotated. *See* **Haymond** (Creed) *and* **Burch.**

——— Civil, penal and political codes of California, 1873. *See* **Haymond** (Creed), **Burch** (John C.) *and* **McKune** (John H.)

Burke (Peter). Loi internationale entre l'Angleterre et la France, sur la propriété des ouvrages littéraires. xii, 158 pp. 16°. *Londres, S. Low & fils,* 1852.
[In french and english on opposite pages].

Burton (John Hill). Law of bankruptcy in Scotland. 1 p. l. xxx, 352 pp. 8°. *Edinburgh, W. Tait,* 1845.

——— Manual of the law of Scotland. 2d ed. xiv, 506 pp. 12°. *Edinburgh, Oliver & Boyd,* 1847.

Busbee (Quentin). Busbee's North Carolina justice, and form book. vii, 486 pp. 8°. *Raleigh, J. H. Enniss,* 1874.

Bush (William P. D.) Reports of cases decided in the court of appeals of Kentucky, 1872–1874. v. 9–10. 8°. *Louisville, Ky. J. P. Morton & co.* 1875.

Byles (*Sir* John Barnard). Treatise of the law of bills of exchange, promissory notes, bank-notes and checks. 6th am. ed. with notes by G. Sharswood. lxiii, 783 pp. 8°. *Philadelphia, T. & J. W. Johnson & co.* 1874.

Byrne (James P.) The new law of divorce and matrimonial causes applicable to Ireland. xii, 118 pp. 1 l. 16°. *Dublin, E. J. Milliken,* 1859.

Cabinet lawyer. *See* **Wade** (John).

Caius (Titius). Gaii institvtionvm commentarios, edidit J. B. E. Boulet. viii, 432 pp. 8°. *Parisiis, F. N. Mansut,* 1827.
Note.—In latin and french on opposite pages.

California (*State of*). Acts amendatory of the codes, passed 1873–1874. ix, 501 pp. 8°. *Sacramento, state printer,* 1874.

——— Civil code of California. [To take effect jan. 1, 1873]. Published under authority of law, by C. Haymond, J. C. Burch, J. H. McKune, commissioners. xcvi, 767 pp. 8°. *Sacramento, state printer,* 1872.

——— Civil, penal and political codes and code of procedure, 1873, annotated by C. Haymond and J. C. Burch. 7 v. 8°. *Sacramento, H. S. Crocker & co.* 1872.

——— Code of civil procedure. 3d ed. 1872–1874, by W. Olney. 16°. *San Francisco, S. Whitney & co.* 1874.

——— Penal code of California. [To take effect jan. 1, 1873]. Published under authority of law, by C. Haymond, J. C. Burch, J. H. McKune, commissioners. lix, 448 pp. 8°. *Sacramento, state printer,* 1872.

——— Political code of California. [To take effect jan. 1, 1873]. Published under authority of law, by C. Haymond, J. C. Burch, J. H. McKune, commissioners. 2 v. lxx, 556 pp; xxxiii, 527 pp. 8°. *Sacramento, state printer,* 1872.

——— Statutes of California, 20th session, 1873-1874. 8°. *Sacramento, state printer,* 1874.

——— *Supreme court.* Citations of cases, 1850–1872, by R. Desty. 8°. *San Francisco, S. Whitney & co.* 1874.

——— ——— Digest of reports, 1868–1873, by R. Desty. 8°. *San Francisco, A. L. Bancroft & co.* [*etc.*] 1875.

——— ——— Reports of cases, v. 2, 1852, by H. P. Hepburn. 2d ed. by R. Desty. 8°. *San Francisco, S. Whitney,* [*etc.*] 1875.

——— ——— Same. v. 6–8, 1856–1857, by H. T. Booraem. 2d ed. by R. Desty. 8°. *San Francisco, S. Whitney,* [*etc.*] 1875.

——— ——— Same. v. 9, 1858, by H. Lee. 2d ed. by R. Desty. 8°. *San Francisco, S. Whitney,* [*etc.*] 1875.

——— ——— Same. v. 14, 1859–1860, by J. B. Harmon. 2d ed. by R. Desty. 8°. *San Francisco, S. Whitney,* [*etc.*] 1873.

——— ——— Same. v. 41–49, 1871–1875, by C. A. Tuttle. 8°. *Sacramento & San Francisco, state printer,* [*etc.*] 1873–75.

Callis (Robert). Reading upon the statute of sewers. 2d ed. 2 p. l. 291 pp. 36 l. sm. 4°. *London, M. Flesher, for T. Basset*, 1685.

Campbell (Robert). Law of negligence. xi, 112 pp. 8°. *London, Stevens & Haynes*, 1871.

Canada (*Dominion of*). Acts of the parliament of the dominion, 36th–38th years of Victoria, 1873–1875. 4 v. 8°. *Ottawa, B. Chamberlin*, 1873–75.

Caparros (Juan Julian). Disciplina eclesiástica. 2a ed. 2 v. viii, 364 pp; viii, 316, 31 pp. sm. 4°. *Madrid, N. Llorenci*, 1847.

Carette (A. A.) *and others*. Recueil des lois et des arrêts de France, fondé par Sirey et continué par Devilleneuve, 1873–1874. 2 v. 4°. *Paris, bureaux de l'administration du recueil*, [1874–75].

Carey (Mathew) *and* **Bioren** (John). Laws of Pennsylvania, 1700–1802. 6 v. 8°. *Philadelphia, J. Bioren*, [*etc.*] 1803.

Caroline Amelia Elizabeth (*Queen, of England*). Trial of queen Caroline, [in the house of lords, 1820]. 3 v. 8°. *New York, J. Cockcroft & co.* 1874.
[CAUSES célèbres, v. 1–3].

Castro (Thomas). The Tichborne trial [1873–1874]. xvi, 302 pp. 8°. *London, Ward, Lock & Tyler*, 1874.

Caudaveine (— de) *and* **Théry** (—). Traité de l'expropriation. 2 p. l. vii, 492 pp. 8°. *Paris, A. Guyot & Scribe*, 1839.

Cauvet (Jules). Le droit pontifical chez les anciens Romains. 92 pp. 8°. *Caen, F. Le Blanc-Hardel*, 1869.

Central law journal. 1874. v. 1. 4°. *St. Louis, Soule, Thomas & Wentworth*, [1874].

Chamberlin (Franklin). American commercial law. [2d ed.] 1024 pp. 8°. *Hartford, O. D. Case & co.* 1875.

Chardon (—). Traité des trois puissances, maritale, paternelle et tutélaire. 3 v. 8°. *Auxerre, G. Maillefer*, 1841–42.

Chevalet (É). Dictionnaire de législation et d'administration militaires. *See* **Saussine** (V.) *and* **Chevalet.**

Chicago legal news. Oct. 1871–sep. 1875. v. 4–7. fol. *Chicago, legal news co.* 1872–75.

Chitty (Joseph, *jr.*) Treatise on the law of contracts. 11th am. ed. by J. C. Perkins. 2 v. cxci, 788 pp; 1 p. l. 789–1745 pp. 8°. *New York, Hurd & Houghton*, 1874.

Cincinnati superior court reporter, by C. P. Taft and others, 1870–1873. v. 1–2. 8°. *Cincinnati, R. Clarke & co.* 1872–73.

Clark (Charles) *and* **Finnelly** (William). Reports of cases in the house of lords, 1831–1846. Edited by J. C. Perkins. 12 v. 8°. *Boston, Little, Brown, & co.* 1873–74.

Clarke (Charles L.) Reports of chancery cases, eighth circuit of the state of New York. [1839–1841]. 3d ed. 8°. *New York, Banks & brothers*, 1873.

Clément (H.) Études sur le droit rural, civil, commercial, administratif et pénal. 527 pp. 8°. *Cambrai, Simon*, 1872.

Código eclesiástico primitivo. 2a ed. lxxiv, 49, cxlv pp. 12°. *Madrid, M. De Burgos*, 1822.

Colas de la Noue (Éd.) Du prêt à intérêt en Grèce, à Rome, en Judée, dans le droit canonique, le droit barbare et dans le droit français. 2 p. l. 274 pp. 8°. *Paris, A. Durand & Pedone-Lauriel*, 1867.

Cole (Chester C.) Reports of cases in the supreme court of Iowa, [1855]. v. 1. 8°. *Des Moines, Mills & co.* 1874.

Colebrooke (Henry Thomas). Two treatises on the hindu law of inheritance. Translated [from the sanscrit]. 1 p. l. xv, 351 pp. 4°. *Calcutta, A. H. Hubbard*, 1810.

Coler (William N.) Treatise on the law of municipal bonds. 2 v. 5–468 pp; 13–498 pp. 1 l. 8°. *New York, the author*, 1873.

Colombia (*United States of*). Código judicial, 1872. 161, xxvii pp. 8°. *Bogotá, M. Rivas*, 1872.

Compleat chancery-practiser. *See* **Jacob** (Giles).

Connecticut (*State of*). Public acts, passed 1874. 8°. *Hartford, Wiley, Waterman & Eaton*, 1874.

——— Revision of 1875. The general statutes. [1639–1874]. 1 p. l. lix, 749 pp. 8°. *Hartford, Case, Lockwood & Brainard*, 1874.

——— Special acts and resolutions passed 1874. 8°. *Hartford, Wiley, Waterman & Eaton*, 1874.

——— *Supreme court.* Reports of cases, v. 1–2. 1814–1818, by T. Day. 2d ed. 8°. *New York, Banks & brothers*, 1875.

——— ——— Same. v. 22–24, 1852–1856, by W. N. Matson. 2d ed. 8°. *New York, Banks & brothers*, 1873.

——— ——— Same. v. 25–28, 1856–1859, by J. Hooker. 2d ed. 8°. *New York, Banks & brothers*, 1873–74.

——— ——— Same. v. 38–41, 1871–1874, by J. Hooker. 8°. *Hartford, Case, Lockwood & Brainard*, 1873–75.

Conover (O. M.) Reports of cases in the supreme court of Wisconsin. 1862-1866. v. 1-5. Republished by W. F. Vilas & E. E. Bryant. [v. 16-20, Wisconsin reports]. 8°. *Chicago, Callaghan & co.* 1874.

——— Same. [1866-1869]. v. 6-8. 2d ed. [v. 21-23, Wisconsin reports]. 8°. *Chicago, Callaghan & co.* 1872-74.

——— Same. 1871-1875. v. 13-21. [v. 28-36, Wisconsin reports]. 8°. *Chicago, Callaghan & co.* 1873-75.

Cook (Robley D.) New York supreme court reports, 1873-1874. *See* **Thompson** (Isaac Grant) *and* **Cook.**

Cooley (Thomas M. *ll. d.*) Treatise on constitutional limitations. 3d ed. lxiii, 827 pp. 8°. *Boston, Little, Brown, & co.* 1874.

Copp (Henry N.) Decisions of the commissioner of the general land office and the secretary of the interior, under the United States mining statutes of 1866, 1870, and 1872. 1 p. l. iv, 3-351 pp. 8°. *San Francisco, A. L. Bancroft & co.* 1874.

——— Public land laws, passed by congress, 1869-1875, with decisions [etc.] xv, 953 pp. 8°. *Washington, the compiler,* 1875.

Corbin (David T.) Revised statutes of South Carolina of 1872. 8°. *Columbia, state printers,* 1873.

Cormenin (Louis Marie de La Haye de). Droit administratif. 5e éd. 2 v. 2 p. l. xliv, 568 pp; 2 p. l. 492, 106 pp. 8°. *Paris, G. Thorel,* [*etc.*] 1840.

Coryton (John). Stageright. viii, 100, lii pp. 8°. *London, D. Nutt,* 1873.

Cowen (Esek). Reports of cases in the supreme court: and in the court of impeachments and errors of the state of New York, [1823-1826]. v. 1-2 and 5. 8°. *New York, Banks & brothers,* 1873.

Cowen (Sidney J.) Treatise on warrants and attachments. [For the state of New York]. 3 p. l. 733 pp. 8°. *Albany, Banks & brothers,* 1874.

Cox (Edward William). Reports of cases relating to joint stock companies. [1870-1872]. v. 5. 8°. *London, H. Cox,* 1873.

Cox (Homersham). Law and science of ancient lights. 2d ed. x, 136 pp. 8°. *London, H. Sweet,* 1871.

Cox (Norval W.) Reports of cases in the supreme court of Arkansas, 1867-1872. v. 1-3, [v. 25-27, Arkansas reports]. 8°. *Little Rock, state printers,* [*etc.*] 1870-73.

Cracroft (Bernard). Trustees' guide. 10th ed. 158 pp. sm. 4°. *London, E. Stanford,* [1873].

Crocker (Uriel H.) *and* **Crocker** (George C.) Notes on the general statutes of Massachusetts. 2d ed. 1874. xiii, 704 pp. 8°. *Boston, H. O. Houghton & co.* 1875.

Crompton (George). Practice common placed. 3d ed. 2 v. 3 p. l. cxv, 379 pp. 3 l; 1 p. l. 480 pp. 4 l. 8°. *London, for T. Whieldon,* 1786.

Crounse (Lorenzo). Reports of cases in the supreme court of Nebraska, 1873-1874. v. 1. [v. 3, Nebraska reports]. 8°. *Lincoln, state journal co.* 1874.

Crump (F. O.) The english law of sale and pledge by factors and agents. 51 pp. 8°. *London, Stevens & sons,* 1868.

Curtis (George Ticknor). Treatise on the law of patents. 4th ed. xxxviii, 749 pp. 8°. *Boston, Little, Brown, & co.* 1873.

Dakota (*Territory of*). Laws and resolutions 2d session, 1862-1863; 9th session, 1870-1871; 10th session, 1872-1873. 3 v. 8°. *Yankton, public printers,* 1862-73.

Daly (Charles P. *judge*). Reports of cases in the court of common pleas for the city and county of New York, [1871-1873]. v. 4. 8°. *New York, Baker, Voorhis & co.* 1874.

Daniel (John M.) Law directory of the United States. 1874. 181, xxxiv pp. 8°. *Louisville, J. P. Morton & co.* 1874.

Dassler (C. F. W.) Digest of the Kansas reports, [1858-1874]. viii, 17-247 pp. 1 l. xxxi pp. 8°. *St. Louis, W. J. Gilbert,* 1874.

Daveis (Edward H.) Reports of cases in the district court of the United States for Maine, 1839-1849. v. 2 [of Ware's decisions]. 2d ed. 8°. *Portland, Loring, Short & Harmon,* 1873.

Davidson (Charles). Precedents and forms in conveyancing. v. 1, 4th ed; v. 2, pt. 2, and v. 3, pts. 1-2, 3d ed; v. 4 and v. 5, pts. 1-2, 2d ed. 8°. *London, Maxwell & son,* 1864-74.

Davis (James Edward). Jurisdiction & practice of the county courts in equity. xlviii, 460 pp. 8°. *London, Butterworths,* 1872.

Day (Thomas). Reports of cases in the supreme court of Connecticut, [1814-1818]. v. 1-2. 2d ed. [v. 1-2, Connecticut reports]. 8°. *New York, Banks & brothers,* 1875.

Deady (Matthew P.) *and others.* General laws of Oregon, 1843-1872. 8°. [*Salem*], *state printer,* 1874.

Deane (Henry Charles). Epitome of the law of corporeal hereditaments and conveyancing. xxiv, 494 pp. 8°. *Boston, Little, Brown, & co.* 1875.

Debacq (Gabriel). De l'action du ministère public en matière civile. 2 p. l. ii, 407 pp. 8°. *Paris, Cotillon,* 1867.

De Colyar (Henry Anselm). Treatise on the law of guarantees and of principal & surety. xxvi, 374 pp. 8°. *London, Butterworths,* 1874.

——— Same. With notes, by J. A. Morgan. li, 534 pp. 8°. *New York, Baker, Voorhis & co.* 1875.

De Gex (John Peter), **Fisher** (F.) *and* **Jones** (H. Cadman). Reports of cases in chancery. Edited by J. C. Perkins, 1859–1862. 4 v. 8°. *Boston, Little, Brown, & co.* 1873.

——— *and* **Jones** (H. Cadman). Reports of cases in chancery. Edited by J. C. Perkins, 1858–1859. v. 2–4. 8°. *Boston, Little, Brown, & co.* 1873.

——— ——— *and* **Smith** (Richard Horton). Reports of cases in chancery, 1863–1865. v. 4. 8°. *London, Stevens & sons,* 1873.

——— ——— ——— Same. Edited by J. C. Perkins, 1862–1865. 4 v. 8°. *Boston, Little, Brown, & co.* 1873–74.

Dejean (Oscar). Traité des expertises. 2 p. l. iv, 600 pp. 8°. *Paris, A. Marescq aîné,* 1875.

Delaware (*State of*). Laws, passed jan. 1873. v. 14, pt. 2. 8°. *Dover, delawarean office,* 1873.

——— Same, passed jan. 1875. v. 15, pt. 1. 8°. *Wilmington, James & Webb,* 1875.

——— Revised statutes of 1852, amended, to 1874. [979] pp. 8°. *Wilmington, James & Webb,* 1874.

——— *Superior court, court of errors and appeals, and criminal courts.* Reports of cases, 1855–1874, by J. W. Houston. v. 2–4. 8°. *Wilmington, James & Webb,* 1871–75.

Demolombe (Jean Charles Florent). Traité des contrats. v. 5. 8°. *Paris, Durande & Pedone Lauriel,* [*etc.* 1873].

Denio (Hiram). Reports of cases in the supreme court and court of errors of the state of New York, [1845–1848]. v. 1–4. 8°. *New York, Banks & brothers,* 1873–75.

Denmark. Constitution de Danemark, 1849; révisée 1866. 2 p. l. 68 pp. 8°. *Copenhague, F. S. Muhle,* 1869.

Desmaze (Charles). Les pénalités anciennes. Supplices, prisons et grâce en France. 2 p. l. 460 pp. 4 pl. 8°. *Paris, H. Plon,* 1866.

Desty (Robert). California citations, [1850–1872]. 2 p. l. 688 pp. 8°. *San Francisco, S. Whitney & co.* 1874.

——— Digest of California reports, [1868–1873]. 3 p. l. 453 pp. 8°. *San Francisco, A. L. Bancroft & co.* [*etc.*] 1875.

——— Manual of practice in the courts of the United States. [459] pp. 16°. *San Francisco, S. Whitney & co.* 1875.

Devereux (John C.) Blackstone's commentaries reduced to questions and answers. New ed. xxiii, 392 pp. 8°. *New York, Baker, Voorhis & co.* 1875.

Devilleneuve (Jean Esprit Marie Pierre Lamoine) *and others.* Recueil des lois et des arrêts de France, fondé par J. B. Sirey. 1872. 4°. *Paris, bureaux de l'administration du recueil,* [1873].

De Witt (E. L.) Reports of cases in the supreme court of Ohio, [1873–1874]. v. 1. v. 24, [Ohio state reports]. 8°. *Cincinnati, R. Clarke & co.* 1875.

Dicey (Albert V.) Treatise on parties to an action. xxiii, 545 pp. 8°. *London, W. Maxwell & son,* 1870.

Dickson (Frederick S.) Analysis of Kent's commentaries. 428 pp. 4°. *Philadelphia, R. Welsh,* 1875.

Dillon (John F.) Cases in the United States circuit courts, eighth circuit, [1871–1873]. v. 2. 8°. *Davenport, Iowa, Day, Egbert & Fidlar,* 1873.

——— Treatise on the law of municipal corporations. 2d ed. 2 v. xii, 526 pp; 2 p. l. 527–988 pp. 8°. *New York, J. Cockcroft & co.* 1873.

District of Columbia. Revision of the laws in relation to the district of Columbia, reported by Thomas J. Durant, [1874]. 2 p. l. 224 pp. 8°. *Washington, government printing office,* 1874.

——— Statutes in force in the district of Columbia. Report of [George P. Fisher and others], 1872. 639 pp. 8°. [*Washington, government printing office,* 1872].

Note.—This report was never adopted.

——— *Supreme court.* Reports of cases, 1873–1874, by A. Mac Arthur. 8°. *Washington, government printing office,* 1875.

——— (*Territory of*). Laws of the district of Columbia. 1871–1872. Acts of the legislative assembly. 8°. *Washington, chronicle publishing co.* 1872.

——— Same. 1871–1873. 2 v. in 1. 8°. *Washington, chronicle publishing co.* 1872–73.

Donaldson (E. N.) Minnesota justices' practice. 596 pp. 8°. *St. Paul, Rameley, Chaney & co.* 1873.

Drake (Charles Daniel). Treatise on the law of attachment. 4th ed. lx, 699 pp. 8°. *Boston, Little, Brown, & co.* 1873.

Drew (James B. C.) Reports of cases in the supreme court of Florida, 1869–71. v. 1. [v. 13, Florida reports]. 8°. *Tallahassee, Fla. state printer,* 1871.

Droz (Jennie). Life and trial, [1872]. 1 p. l. 45 pp. 8°. [*Cleveland, O.* 1874].

Duane (William). View of the relation of landlord and tenant in Pennsylvania. 136 pp. 12°. *Philadelphia, J. Kay, jun. & brother,* 1844.

Du Boys (Albert). Histoire du droit criminel de l'Espagne. xvi, 732 pp. 8°. *Paris, Durand & Pédone Lauriel,* 1870.

Dunlap (M. E.) *and* **Blickensderfer** (U.) Abridgment of elementary law. 308 pp. 1 l. 32°. *Erie, Penn. Dunlap & Blickensderfer,* 1874.

Durham (Warren J.) Real estate statutes of Illinois to 1874. *See* **Adams** (John B.) *and* **Durham.**

Duty (The) of executors and administrators. *See* **Grimké** (J. F.)

Duvergier (Alphonse Marie Guillaume). Médecine légale. 3e éd. 3 v. 8°. *Paris, G. Baillière,* 1852.

Duvergier (J. B.) *and* **Duvergier** (J.) Collection des lois de France, 1872–1873. v. 72–73. 8°. *Paris, directeur de l'administration,* 1872–73.

Edmonds (John W.) Statutes at large of the state of New York, as they existed 1st of jan. 1867. 2d ed. 5 v. 8°. *Albany, Weed, Parsons & co.* 1869.

——— Same. v. 6, general statutes, 1863, 1864, 1865 & 1866. 2d ed. 8°. *Albany, Weed, Parsons & co.* 1869.

——— Same. v. 7, general statutes, 1867, 1868, 1869 & 1870. 2d ed. 8°. *Albany, Weed, Parsons & co.* 1870.

——— Same. v. 9, general statutes, 1871, 1872, 1873 & 1874. By J. W. Edmonds and W. H. Field. 8°. *Albany, Weed, Parsons & co.* 1875.

Eggleston (William). Treatise on the law of boards of commissioners, in Indiana. xiii, 361 pp. 8°. *Indianapolis, journal co.* 1873.

Election commissioners. In the supreme court of Pennsylvania, 1873. *See* **Wells** (Francis) *and others vs.* **Election** (The) commissioners.

Election commissioners—continued.

Emery (George F.) Reports of cases in the district court of the United States for Maine and Massachusetts, [1853–1866]. v. 3, [of Ware's decisions]. 8°. *Portland, Loring, Short & Harmon,* 1874.

English reports, 1872–1874. *See* **Moak** (Nathaniel C.)

Erskine (John, *of Carnock.*) An institute of the law of Scotland. New ed. by J. B. Nicolson. 2 v. civ, 656 pp; 4 p. l. 657–1361 pp. 4°. *Edinburgh, Bell & Bradfute,* 1871.

Favre (Antoine). De Montisferrati dvcatv contra dvcem Mantvæ, pro dvce Sabavdiæ consultatio, [1615]. [614] pp. 15 l. 1 chart. 4°. *Lvgdvni, apvd I. Rovssin,* 1617.

Fay (Joseph D.) Digest of the laws of the state of New York, in force jan. 1, 1874. v. 1–2. 8°. *New York, J. Cockcroft & co.* 1874–75.

——— Guide to changes in the New York statute law since 1858. 1 p. l. 62 pp. 8°. *New York, Baker, Voorhis & co.* 1873.

Field (George W.) Treatise on the county and township officers of Iowa, [to 1874]. xvii, 462 pp. 3 maps. 8°. *Des Moines, Mills & co.* 1875.

Finlason (W. F.) History of law of tenures of land in England and Ireland. vii, 154 pp. 8°. *London, Stevens & Haynes,* 1870.

Finnelly (William). House of lords cases, 1831–1846. *See* **Clark** (C.) *and* **Finnelly.**

Fisher (F.) Chancery reports, 1859–1862. *See* **De Gex** (J. P.) **Fisher** (F.) *and* **Jones** (H. Cadman).

Fisher (George P.) *and others.* Report of a commission to revise the statutes in force in the district of Columbia, 1872. 8°. [*Washington, government printing office,* 1872].

Fisher (Robert Alexander). Digest of the reported decisions of all the courts, including the irish. [Annual]. Hilary term, 1871–hilary term, 1874. 3 v. 8°. *London, H. Sweet,* 1872–74.

Fisher (Samuel Sparks). Reports of cases under letters patent for inventions, in the courts of the United States, [1869–1873]. v. 5–6, [of Fisher's patent cases]. 8°. *Cincinnati, R. Clarke & co.* 1874.

Fisher (William Hubbell). Reports of cases relating to letters patent for inventions, in the supreme and circuit courts of the United

Fisher (William Hubbell)—continued. States, [1821-1850]. v. 1. 8°. *Cincinnati, R. Clarke & co.* 1873.

Fitzherbert (*Sir* Anthony). [Le graunde abridgement]. 3 v. in 2. fol. [*n. p.*] 1516.

Flanders (Henry). Treatise on the law of fire insurance. 2d ed. xxx, 17-668 pp. 8°. *Philadelphia, Claxton, Remsen, & Haffelfinger*, 1874.

Florida (*Provinces of*). Ordinances, by major-general Andrew Jackson, [1821]. 15 l. 8°. *St. Augustine, R. W. Edes*, 1821.

Florida (*Territory of*). Acts [and resolutions], passed at the 13th session, jan. 1835; 17th session, jan. 1839. 2 v. 8°. *Tallahassee, W. Wilson, [etc.]* 1835-39.

——— Laws of the United States relative to the territory, passed prior to 1838. 80 pp. 8°. *Tallahassee, S. S. Sibley*, 1837.

Florida (*State of*). Acts and resolutions, 3d session, [held jan. 1870]; extra session, may, 1870; 4th session, [held jan. 1871]. 3 v. 8°. *Tallahassee, state printer*, 1870-71.

——— *Supreme court.* Reports of cases, v. 13, 1869-1871, by J. B. C. Drew. 8°. *Tallahassee, state printer*, 1871.

Folkhard (Henry C.) Pawnbrokers', factors', and merchants' guide to the law of loans and pledges. xii, 322 pp. 16°. *London, Lockwood & co.* 1873.

Forsyth (William). History of trial by jury. New ed. by J. A. Morgan. x, 388 pp. 8°. *New York, J. Cockcroft & co.* 1875.

Fortescue (*Sir* John). De laudibus legum Angliae. 2 p. l. lxiv, 302 pp. 8°. *Cincinnati, R. Clarke & co.* 1874.

Forum law review. *See* **Bench** and bar review.

Forum. [July-oct. 1874]. v. 2. 8°. *Baltimore & New York, H. Taylor & co. [etc.]* 1874.

Fouquier (A.) Causes célèbres de tous les peuples. Le maréchal Bazaine. [1873]. v. 8-9. 4°. *Paris, H. Lebrun*, 1874.

France. Bulletin des arrêts de la cour de cassation rendus en matière civile. 1872-1874. v. 74-76. 8°. *Paris, imprimerie nationale*, 1873-75.

——— Same. Rendus en matière criminelle, 1872-1874. v. 77-79. 8°. *Paris, imprimerie nationale*, 1873-75.

——— Bulletin des lois. 12e série. 1872-1874. Partie principale. v. 4-9, nos. 77 à 240. 8°. *Paris, imprimerie nationale*, 1872-75.

France—continued.

——— The same. Partie supplémentaire. v. 4-9, in 16 v. nos. 69 à 736. 8°. *Paris, imprimerie nationale*, 1872-75.

——— Les codes de la législation forestière. [1669-1864]. 4e éd. par m. C. Jacquot. 2 p. l. 284 pp. 16°. *Paris, bureau de la revue des eaux et forêts*, 1866.

——— Collection des lois: par J. B. et J. Duvergier. Année 1872-1873. v. 72-73. 8°. *Paris, directeur de l'administration*, 1872-73.

——— Droit musulman. Par A. Querry. 2 v. viii, 768 pp; 2 p. l. 699 pp. 8°. *Paris, imprimerie nationale*, 1871-72.

——— Précis de jurisprudence musulmane, par sidi Khalil. 3e éd. 2 p. l. ii, 234 pp. 8°. *Paris, imprimerie nationale*, 1872.

——— Recueil des lois et des arrêts. Par L. M. Devilleneuve [et autres]. Année 1872. 4°. *Paris, bureaux de l'administration du recueil*, [1873].

——— Same. Par A. A. Carette [et autres]. Années 1873-1874. 2 v. 4°. *Paris, bureaux de l'administration du recueil*, [1874-75].

Franklyn (Henry Bowles). Outlines of military law and the laws of evidence. viii, 152 pp. 32°. *London, Trübner & co. [etc.]* 1874.

Freeman (A. C.) Cotenancy and partition. liv, 59-713 pp. 8°. *San Francisco, S. Whitney & co.* 1874.

——— Treatise on the law of judgments. xxxv, 541 pp. 8°. *San Francisco, A. L. Bancroft & co.* 1873.

——— Same. 2d ed. xliii, 13-648 pp. 8°. *San Francisco, A. L. Bancroft & co.* 1874.

Freeman (Norman L.) Reports of cases in the supreme court of Illinois, 1869-1873 & 1875. v. 26-37 & 46. [v. 56-67 & 76, Illinois reports]. 8°. *Springfield, for the reporter*, 1873-75.

Frith (William). Remarks on the recent state trials. xii, 383 pp. 8°. *London, Bensley & sons, for Clarke & son, [etc.]* 1818.

Gamble (Richard Wilson) *and* **Barlow** (William). Index to cases in equity in Ireland, 1838 to 1867. 2 v. 2 p. l. 4, lii, 664 pp; 2 p. l. 665-1410 pp. 1 l. 4°. *Dublin, Hodges, Smith & Foster*, 1868.

Garbajal (Francisco Leon). Discurso sobre la legislacion de los antiguos Mexicanos. 128 pp. 8°. *México, J. Abadiano*, 1864.

Gardner (Alan Legge). Reports of the proceedings of the house of lords on the claims to the barony of Gardner, [1824-1825]. By

Gardner (Alan Legge)—continued. D. Le Marchant. lxiv, 505 pp. 8°. *London, H. Butterworth*, 1828.

Gatteschi (Domenico). Une nouvelle organisation judiciaire en Égypte. 24 pp. 8°. *Paris, A. Durand & Pedone-Lauriel*, 1867.

Gayarre (Charles). Reports of cases in the supreme court of Louisiana, 1873–1874. v. 1–2. [v. 25–26, Louisiana annual reports]. 8°. *New Orleans, the republican office*, 1873–74.

Georgia (*State of*). Acts [and resolutions], annual session, 1866; called session, july, 1868. 2 v. 8°. *Macon, J. W. Burke & co.* 1867–68.

——— Code of Georgia. [3d ed. 1873]. xviii, 1050 pp. 8°. *Macon, J. W. Burke & co.* 1873.

——— *Supreme court.* Reports of cases, v. 45, 1872, by N. J. Hammond and H. Jackson. 8°. *Macon, J. W. Burke & co.* 1873.

——— ——— Same, v. 46–51, 1872–1874, by H. Jackson. 8°. *Macon, J. W. Burke & co.* 1873–75.

Gerard (James W. *jr.*) Titles to real estate in the state of New York. 2d ed. xvi, 791 pp. 8°. *New York, Baker, Voorhis & co.* 1873.

German empire. Military penal code for the German empire, 1872. 54 pp. 8°. *Washington, D. C.* 1873.

Géry (*Dr.* —, *père*). Caractères qui établissent la viabilité chez les nouveau-nés. 1 p. l. 60 pp. 8°. *Paris, A. Delahaye*, 1869.

Geyer (Henry S.) Digest of the laws of Missouri territory, [1812–1817]. xii, 486, xxvi pp. 15 l. 8°. *St. Louis, J. Charless*, 1818.

Gilbert (Frank). Railway law in Illinois. xvi, 5–337 pp. 8°. *Chicago, Callaghan & co.* 1873.

Gilbert (*Sir* Jeffrey). History and practice of the high court of chancery. 1st am. ed. by S. Tyler. viii, 380 pp. 8°. *Washington, W. H. & O. H. Morrison*, 1874.

Giron (Alfred). Essai sur le droit communal de la Belgique. 350 pp. 8°. *Bruxelles, Bruylant-Christophie & cie.* 1868.

Glenn (Robert George). Manual of the laws affecting medical men. xxxii, 460 pp. 8°. *London, J. & A. Churchill*, [*etc.*] 1871.

Goguet (Antoine). Del origen de las leyes. 5 v. sm. 4°. *Madrid, la imprenta real*, 1791–94.

Gomez de la Serna (Pedro). Motivos de las variaciones en los procedimientos. xv, 266 pp. 8°. *Madrid, revista de legislacion*, 1857.

Gomez de la Serna (P.)—continued.

——— *and* **Reus y Garcia** (José). Código de comercio. 5a ed. 736 pp. 8°. *Madrid, revista de legislacion*, 1869.

Gonzales de Vallejo (Pedro). Discurso canónico-legal. 1 p. l. 274 pp. 1 l. 8°. *Madrid, J. M. Repullés*, 1839.

Gonzalez Huebra (Pablo). Curso de derecho mercantil. 3a ed. 2 v. vii, 536 pp; 264 pp. 8°. *Madrid, Sanchez*, 1867.

Goudsmit (J. E.) The pandects; a treatise on the roman law. Translated from the dutch, by R. De T. Gould. xxii, 368 pp. 8°. *London, Longmans*, 1873.

Gould (W. Reid). Lawyers' diary for the year 1875. [354] pp. 16°. *New York, W. R. Gould*, [1875].

Granger (Moses M.) Reports of cases in the supreme court of Ohio, [1871–1873]. v. 1–2. [v. 22–23, Ohio state reports]. 8°. *Cincinnati, R. Clarke & co.* 1873–74.

Grant (Harding). Questions and answers on the practice of the court of chancery. vi, 192 pp. 12°. *London, A. Maxwell*, 1839.

Grant (James). Treatise on the law relating to bankers and banking companies. 3d ed. by R. A. Fisher. xxviii, 800 pp. 8°. *London, Butterworths*, 1873.

Grattan (Peachy R.) Reports of cases in the supreme court of Virginia, 1872–1874. v. 22–24. 8°. *Richmond, superintendent of public printing*, 1873–75.

Graves (*Rev.* J. R.) Trial, [1858, for slander and libel]. 127 pp. 8°. [*n. p.* 1858].

Gray (John C. *jr.*) Massachusetts reports, v. 110–111, 1872–1873. *See* **Browne** (Albert G. *jr.*) *and* **Gray**.

Great Britain. Annual digest of decisions, by R. A. Fisher, 1871–1873. 3 v. 8°. *London, H. Sweet*, 1872–74.

——— Chancery commission. Report, 1826. 171 pp. 8°. *London, S. Sweet*, [*etc.*] 1826.

——— *Court of common pleas.* Reports of cases, 1864; common bench reports, new series, v. 16, by J. Scott. 8°. *Philadelphia, T. & J. W. Johnson & co.* 1870.

——— *High court of chancery.* Reports of cases, 1858–1859, by J. P. De Gex and H. C. Jones. Edited by J. C. Perkins. v. 2–4. 8°. *Boston, Little, Brown, & co.* 1873.

——— ——— Same, 1859–1862, by J. P. De Gex, F. Fisher and H. C. Jones. Edited by

Great Britain—continued.
J. C. Perkins. 4 v. 8°. *Boston, Little, Brown, & co.* 1873.

—— —— Same, 1863-1865, by J. P. De Gex, H. C. Jones and R. H. Smith. v. 4. 8°. *London, Stevens & sons,* 1873.

—— —— Same, 1862-1865. Edited by J. C. Perkins. 4 v. 8°. *Boston, Little, Brown, & co.* 1873-74.

—— *House of lords.* Reports of cases, 1831-1846, by C. Clark and W. Finnelly. Edited by J. C. Perkins. 12 v. 8°. *Boston, Little, Brown, & co.* 1873-74.

—— *Poor laws commissioners.* Report, [1834]. viii, 363, 128 pp. 8°. *London, B. Fellowes,* 1834.

—— *Privy council.* Reports of cases, 1861-1862, by E. F. Moore. v. 15. 8°. *London, Stevens & sons,* [1862].

—— —— Same, 1867-1869 & 1871-1873, by E. F. Moore. New series, v. 5 & 8-9. 8°. *London, Stevens & sons,* [1869-73].

—— *Privy council in indian appeals.* Reports of cases, 1869-1872, by E. F. Moore. v. 13-14. 8°. *London, Stevens & sons,* [1871-73].

—— Statutes at large, 32 & 33 Victoria, 1868-1869, by G. K. Rickards. v. 29. 4°. *London, G. E. Eyre & W. Spottiswode,* 1869.

Green (Charles Ewing). Reports of cases in the court of chancery of New Jersey. [1866-1867, 1869-1870 & 1872-1874]. v. 3, 5 & 8-9. [v. 18, 20 & 23-24, New Jersey equity reports]. 8°. *Trenton, Hough & Gillespy,* [*etc.*] 1868-74.

Green (N. St. John). Criminal law reports. [1853-1874]. v. 1-2. 8°. *New York, Hurd & Houghton,* 1874-75.

Green (*Capt.* Thomas) *et al.* Tryal, [1705], for piracy, robbery, & murder. 3 p. l. 65 pp. fol. *Edinburgh, heirs of A. Anderson,* 1705.

Grimké (John Faucheraud). Duty of executors and administrators. [*anon.*] xvii, 343 pp. 1 l. 1 chart. 8°. *New York, T. & J. Swords,* 1797.

—— Public laws of South Carolina, [1694-] 1790. lxxvii, 504, 43 pp. 29 l. 4°. *Philadelphia, R. Aitken & son,* 1790.

Grivel (Félicien). Des constructions élevées sur le terrain d'autrui. iv, 272 pp. 8°. *Paris, E. Donnaud,* 1871.

Gross (William L.) Digest of Illinois statutes. v. 3. Acts of 1873. 4°. *Springfield, W. L. Gross,* 1873.

Gross (William L.)—continued.

—— Same. v. 3. 2d ed. Acts of 1873-1874. 4°. *Springfield, W. L. Gross,* 1874.

Guernsey (Rocellus S.) Mechanics' lien laws for New York city. viii, 228 pp. 8°. *New York,* 1873.

Guthrie (William). Law of trade unions in England and Scotland, 1871. xi, 96 pp. 8°. *Edinburgh, Edmonston & Douglas,* 1873.

Gutierrez Fernandez (Benito). Códigos ó estudios sobre el derecho civil español. 3a ed. v. 1-3. 8°. *Madrid, Sanchez,* 1871.

—— Same. Tratado de las obligaciones. 2a ed. v. 4-5. 8°. *Madrid, Sanchez,* 1871.

Guyard (Albert). Des preuves de la filiation légitime. 2 p. l. 365 pp. 1 l. 8°. *Paris, E. Thorin,* 1870.

Hadley (Edward A.) Commentaries on the laws of England. *See* **Broom** (Herbert) *and* **Hadley.**

Hadley (James, *ll. d.*) Introduction to roman law. vii, 332 pp. 12°. *New York, D. Appleton & co.* 1873.

Hagans (John Marshall). Reports of cases in the supreme court of appeals of West Virginia, 1871-1872. v. 5. [v. 5, West Virginia reports]. 8°. *Wheeling, L. Baker & co.* 1873.

Haines (Elijah M.) Compilation of the laws of Illinois relating to township organization. [4th ed.] 392 pp. 8°. *Chicago, E. B. Myers & co.* 1873.

—— Same. [5th ed.] 1874. 5-386 pp. 8°. *Chicago, E. B. Myers & co.* 1874.

—— Same. [6th ed.] 1875. 5-396 pp. 8°. *Chicago, E. B. Myers & co.* 1875.

—— Laws of Wisconsin concerning the organization of towns, [1858]. 159 pp. 8°. *Chicago, W. B. Keen,* 1858.

—— Treatise on justices of the peace in Illinois. 6th ed. 850 pp. 8°. *Chicago, E. B. Myers,* 1873.

Hale (Robert Safford). Mixed commission of american and british claims. Arguments for the United States. [1871-1873]. 2 v. [1384] pp. [1428] pp. 8°. [*Washington & Newport, Judd & Detweiler, etc.* 1871-73].

Halsted (William, *jr.*) Reports of cases in the supreme court of New Jersey, [1796-1831]. 2d ed. 7 v. 8°. [*Trenton, Murphy & Bechtel,* 1875].

Hammick (James T.) Marriage law of England. [464] pp. 12°. *London, Shaw & sons,* 1873.

Hammond (Nathan J.) *and* **Jackson** (Henry). Reports of cases in the supreme court

Hammond *and* **Jackson**—continued. of Georgia, 1872. v. 1. [v. 45, Georgia reports]. 8°. *Macon, J. W. Burke & co.* 1873.

Hargrove (Tazewell L.) Cases in the supreme court of North Carolina, 1873–1875. v 1, 3, & 5-6. [v. 68, 70 & 72–73, North Carolina reports]. 8°. *Raleigh, state printers,* [*etc.*] 1873–75.

Harmon (John B.) Reports of cases in the supreme court of California, 1859-1860. v. 2. 2d ed. By R. Desty. [v. 14, California reports]. 8°. *San Francisco, S. Whitney,* [*etc.*] 1873.

Harrington (Richard) *et al.* Arguments for the prosecution of the trial for conspiracy, 1874. 1 p. l. 67, 214 pp. 8°. *Washington, government printing office,* 1874.

Harris (G. E.) *and* **Simrall** (G. H.) Reports of cases in the supreme court of Mississippi, 1873–1874. v. 1–2. [v. 49–50, Mississippi reports]. 8°. *Jackson & Chicago, pilot publishing co.* [*etc.*] 1874–75.

Harris (George W.) Pennsylvania state reports. Cases in the supreme court, 1849–1850. v. 1. 3d ed. [v. 13, Pennsylvania state]. 8°. *Philadelphia, Kay & brother,* 1873.

Harris (Thomas, *jun*) Modern entries. 2 v. viii, 703 pp; 1 p. l. 800 pp. 83 l. 8°. *Annapolis, F. Green,* 1801.

Hatch (Wolcott). Instructions to executors and administrators in the state of New York. 2d ed. 1 p. l. 30 pp. 8°. *Belmont, N. Y. Allegany co. reporter printing house,* 1873.

Hautesere a Salvaizon (Flavien François de). Notæ & animaduersiones ad indiculos ecclesiasticorvm canonvm Fvlgentii Ferrandi, & Cresconii afri. 8 p. l. 192 pp. 7 l. sm. 4°. *Avgvstoriti Pictonvm, sumptibus Ivliani Thorellii,* 1630.

Hawke (Michael). Grounds of the lawes of England. By M. H. of the middle temple. [*anon.*] 14 p. l. 474 pp. 16 l. 16°. *London, for H. Twyford,* [*etc.*] 1657.

Hawkins (J.) Reports of cases in the supreme court of Louisiana, 1870–1872. v. 4–6. [v. 22–24, Louisiana annual]. 8°. *New Orleans, office of the republican,* 1870–72.

Haymond (Creed) *and* **Burch** (John C.) Civil code of California, annotated. [1873]. 2 v. lxxxvi, 630 pp; xlix, 799 pp. 8°. *Sacramento, H. S. Crocker & co.* 1872.

——— ——— Code of civil procedure of California, annotated. [1873]. 2 v. lxvi, 794 pp; xxxviii, 640 pp. 8°. *Sacramento, H. S. Crocker & co.* 1872.

——— ——— Penal code of California, annotated. [1873]. lxiv, 628 pp. 8°. *Sacramento, H. S. Crocker & co.* 1872.

——— ——— Political code of California, annotated. [1873]. 2 v. lxxiv, 679 pp; xxxiii, 671 pp. 8°. *Sacramento, H. S. Crocker & co.* 1872.

——— ——— *and* **McKune** (John H.) Civil, penal and political codes of California, 1873. 4 v. 8°. *Sacramento, state printer,* 1872.

Haynes (Freeman Oliver) Outlines of equity. 3d ed. xx, 468, xciv pp. 12°. *London, W. Maxwell & son,* 1873.

Hazlitt (William). Law and practice in bankruptcy. *See* **Roche** (Henry Philip) *and* **Hazlitt.**

Healy (Thaddeus W.) Compiled laws of Nevada, 1861–1873. *See* **Bonnifield** (M. S.) *and* **Healy.**

Hecker (George W.) Law reports of cases on warranty on the sale of personal property, [1603–1869]. 464 pp. 8°. *Meadville, Penn.* [*Ashby & Vincent*], 1874.

Heiskell (Joseph B.) Reports of cases in the supreme court of Tennessee, 1871–1872. v. 3–7. 8°. *Nashville, printers to the state,* [*etc.*] 1872–74.

Helm (Alfred) *and* **Hittell** (Theodore H.) Reports of cases in the supreme court of Nevada, 1871–1874. v. 3–5. [v. 7–9, Nevada reports]. 8°. *San Francisco, Bacon & co.* [*etc.*] 1872–74.

Hepburn (H. P.) Reports of cases in the supreme court of California, 1852. v. 1. 2d ed. By R. Desty. [v. 2, California reports]. 8°. *San Francisco, S. Whitney,* [*etc.*] 1875.

Herman (Henry M.) Treatise on the law of executions. 2 p. l. cxxi, 768 pp. 8°. *New York, J. Cockcroft & co.* 1875.

Herrera (Cayetano de). Deberes de las correjidores etc. *See* **Ortiz de Zúñiga** (Manuel L.) *and* **Herrera.**

Heyl (Lewis). United States duties on imports. 1874. viii, 238, 97, 110 pp. 1 l. 8°. *Washington, W. H. & O. H. Morrison,* 1874.

High (James L.) Treatise on extraordinary legal remedies. xxxii, 672 pp. 8°. *Chicago, Callaghan & co.* 1874.

——— Treatise on the law of injunctions. xxxv, 642 pp. 8°. *Chicago, Callaghan & co.* 1873.

Hill (Edward Judson). Chancery jurisdiction and practice of Illinois. lx, 758 pp. 8°. *Chicago, E. B. Myers & co.* 1873.

——— Highway system of Illinois. xiii, 220 pp. 12°. *Chicago, E B. Myers*, 1873.

——— The municipal officer of Illinois. viii, 836 pp. 12°. *Chicago, E. B. Myers*, 1873.

——— Probate jurisdiction and practice in the county courts of Illinois. xii, 404 pp. 8°. *Chicago, E. B. Myers*, 1873.

——— Same. 2d ed. xxi, 407 pp. 8°. *Chicago, E. B. Myers*, 1875.

Hill (Nicholas, *jun.*) Reports of cases in the supreme court and court for the correction of errors of the state of New York, [1841–1845]. v. 1–3 & 7. 8°. *New York, Banks & brothers*, 1873–75.

Hill (Samuel). Clarke's new law list. [1813]. 300 pp. 12°. *London, W. Clarke & sons*, 1813.

Hilliard (Francis). Law of injunctions. 3d ed. li, 787 pp. 8°. *Philadelphia, Kay & brother*, 1874.

——— Law of remedies for torts. 2d ed. lx, 771 pp. 8°. *Boston, Little, Brown, & co.* 1873.

——— Law of torts or private wrongs. 4th ed. 2 v. lxviii, 735 pp; lix, 729 pp. 8°. *Boston, Little, Brown, & co.* 1874.

Hindes (Samuel) *and* **Wood** (Nicholas L.) Record of investigation in the case, upon charges [of] official misconduct, [1866]. lxx, 201 pp. 8°. *Baltimore, W. K. Boyle*, 1866.

Hittell (Theodore H.) Nevada reports, 1871–1874. *See* **Helm** (Alfred) *and* **Hittell.**

Hoffman (Murray). Law and practice as to referees. xxxvi, 438 pp. 8°. *New York, Diossy & co.* 1875.

——— Reports of cases in the court of chancery of the state of New York, [1839–1840]. v. 1. 3d ed. By T. W. Waterman. 8°. *New York, Banks & brothers*, 1874.

Holdsworth (William Andrews). Law of master and servant. viii, 184 pp. 16°. *London, G. Routledge & sons*, 1873.

Hooker (John). Connecticut reports: cases in the supreme court, [1856–1859]. v. 1–4. 2d ed. [v. 25–28, Connecticut reports]. 8°. *New York, Banks & brothers*, 1873–74.

——— Same, [1871–1874]. v. 14–17. [v. 38–41, Connecticut reports]. 8°. *Hartford, Case, Lockwood & Brainard*, 1873–75.

Hopkins (Archibald). Court of claims reports, 1872–1873. *See* **Nott** (Charles C.) *and* **Hopkins.**

Hopkins (Manley). Manual of marine insurance. 1 p. l. xii, 544 pp. 8°. *London, Smith, Elder, & co.* [*etc.*] 1867.

Horrigan (L. B.) *and* **Thompson** (Seymour D.) Select american cases on the law of self defence. [1790–1873]. xiv, 991 pp. 8°. *St. Louis, Soule, Thomas & Wentworth*, 1874.

Houston (John W.) Reports of cases in the courts of Delaware, [1855–1874]. v. 2–4. 8°. *Wilmington, Del. James & Webb*, 1871–75.

Howard (Nathan, *jr.*) Practice reports in the supreme court and court of appeals of the state of New York, [1863–1875]. v. 45–49. 8°. *Albany, W. Gould & son*, 1873–75.

Hubbell (J. H.) Legal directory for the year ending may 1, 1874. 8°. *New York, J. H. Hubbell*, [1873].

——— Same, for the year ending july 1, 1875. 8°. *New York, J. H. Hubbell & co.* [1874].

——— Same, for the year commencing july 1, 1875. 8°. *New York, J. H. Hubbell & co.* [1875].

Humphreys (James). Observations on the english laws of real property. 2d ed. xviii, 400 pp. 1 chart. 8°. *London, J. Murray*, 1827.

Hun (Marcus T.) Reports of cases in the supreme court of the state of New York, 1874–1875. v. 1–4. v. 8–11 [of the official series commenced by Lansing]. 8°. *New York, Banks & brothers*, [1874–75].

Hunter (Benjamin) *and* **Myer** (William G.) Index to the Missouri reports, [1821–1872]. 270 pp. interleaved. 32°. *St. Louis, the authors*, 1873.

——— ——— Index to the Ohio reports, [1816–1872]. 420 pp. interleaved. 32°. *St. Louis, W. J. Gilbert*, 1874.

——— ——— Index to the Tennessee reports, [1791–1872]. 388 pp. 16°. *St. Louis, W. J. Gilbert*, 1875.

Huntington (Samuel H.) Court of claims reports, 1871. *See* **Nott** (Charles C.) *and* **Huntington.**

Hurd (Harvey B.) Revised statutes of Illinois, 1874. 8°. *Springfield, Illinois journal co.* 1874.

Huston (*Rev.* Lorenzo Dow). Trial for seduction, [1872]. 64 pp. 8°. *Baltimore, [Fisher & Denison]*, 1872.

Hyde (Fanny). Trial, [1872], for murder. 5–161 pp. 2 ports. 8°. *New York, J. R. McDivitt*, 1872.

Illinois (*State of*). Incorporation laws of Illinois, 1838. 249, viii pp. 1 l. 8°. *Vandalia, public printer*, 1839.

——— Laws, 10th assembly, 1836-1837; laws, 18th assembly, second session, 1854; public laws, 22d assembly, 1861; private laws, 22d assembly, 1861; public laws, 24th assembly, 1865; public laws, 27th assembly, sessions jan. 4, may 24, oct. 13, nov. 15, 1871; laws, 28th assembly, first session, 1873; laws, 28th assembly, jan. 8, 1873-march 31, 1874; laws, 29th assembly, 1875. 9 v. 8°. *Vandalia & Springfield, public printer*, [*etc.*] 1837-75.

——— Real estate statutes, 1809-1874, by J. B. Adams and W. J. Durham. 2 v. 8°. *Chicago, Callaghan & co.* 1874.

——— Revised statutes, 1874. By H. B. Hurd. viii, 1235 pp. 8°. *Springfield, Illinois journal co.* 1874.

——— Statutes, as revised, 1871-1872, construed by W. H. Underwood. 2 v. 8°. *St. Louis, W. J. Gilbert*, 1873-75.

——— Statutes in force. By W. L. Gross. v. 3. Acts of 1873. xviii, 6-63, 165 pp. 4°. *Springfield, W. L. Gross*, 1873.

——— Same. v. 3. 2d ed. Acts of 1873-4. vii, 504 pp. 4°. *Springfield, W. L. Gross*, 1874.

——— *Supreme court.* Index of reports, 1819-1871, by G. R. Wendling. 8°. *Chicago, E. B. Myers*, 1874.

——— ——— Reports of cases, v. 56-67 & 76, 1869-1873 & 1875, by N. L. Freeman. 8°. *Springfield, the reporter*, 1873-75.

Indermaur (John). Epitome of leading common law cases. v, 50 pp. 8°. *London, Stevens & Haynes*, 1873.

——— Epitome of leading conveyancing and equity cases. viii, 72 pp. 8°. *London, Stevens & Haynes*, 1873.

India. Code of civil procedure, 1871, by A. J. Lewis. 8°. *London, W. H. Allen & co.* 1871.

Indiana (*State of*). Laws, special session, nov. 1872; 48th session, 1873. 2 v. in 1. 8°. *Indianapolis, state printer*, [*etc.*] 1872-73.

——— *Supreme court.* Reports of cases, v. 35-48, 1870-1874, by J. B. Black. 8°. *Indianapolis, journal co.* 1873-75.

Iowa (*State of*). Code. [1873]. xii, 1039 pp. 8°. *Des Moines, state printers*, 1873.

——— Private acts, 14th assembly, 1872; public acts, 14th assembly, 1872; acts, adjourned session, jan. 1873; public laws, 15th assembly, 1874; private acts, 15th assembly, 1874. 5 v. in 3. 8°. *Des Moines, state printer*, 1872-74.

——— *Supreme court.* Abridgment of decisions, 1839-1872, by J. D. Templin. v. 1. 8°. *Des Moines, state printing co.* 1874.

——— ——— Digest of decisions, 1839-1872, by T. F. Withrow and E. H. Stiles. 2 v. 8°. *Chicago, E. B. Myers*, 1874-75.

——— ——— Reports of cases, v. 1, 1855. 2d ed. by C. C. Cole. 8°. *Des Moines, Mills & co.* 1874.

——— ——— Same, v. 33-37, 1871-1873, by E. H. Stiles. 8°. *Ottumwa, the reporter*, 1873-75.

——— ——— Same, v. 38-39, 1873-1874, by J. S. Runnells. 8°. *Des Moines, Mills & co.* 1875.

Ireland (William M.) *and* **McGrew** (J. M.) Postal laws of the United States, 1873. 8°. *Washington, government printing office*, 1873.

Ireland. Index to cases in equity, 1838-1867, by R. W. Gamble and W. Barlow. 2 v. 8°. *Dublin, Hodges, Smith & Foster*, 1868.

Irish reports. Common law series. 1872-1874. v. 6-7. 8°. *Dublin, E. Ponsonby*, 1873-74.

——— Same. Equity series. 1872-1874. v. 6-7. 8°. *Dublin, E. Ponsonby*, 1873-74.

——— Same. By G. A. C. May. Common law series, 1867. v. 1. 8°. *New York, the transcript association*, 1868.

——— Same. Equity series, 1867. v. 1. 8°. *New York, the transcript association*, 1868.

Irwin (David) *and others.* Code of Georgia. 3d ed. 1873. 8°. *Macon, J. W. Burke & co.* 1873.

Italy. Codice civile del regno, [1866]. viii, 527 pp 8°. *Torino, stamperia reale*, [1865].

——— Codice di procedura civile del regno, [1866]. 2 p. l. 309 pp. 1 l. 8°. *Torino, stamperia reale*, [1865].

——— Legge per l'unificazione, 1865. 204 pp. 8°. [*Torino, stamperia reale*, 1865].

Jackson (Henry). Georgia reports, 1872. *See* **Hammond** (Nathan J.) *and* **Jackson.**

——— Reports of cases in the supreme court of Georgia, 1872-1874. v. 1-6. [v. 46-51, Georgia reports]. 8°. *Macon, J. W. Burke & co.* 1873-75.

Jacob (Giles). Compleat chancery-practiser. [*anon.*] v. 1. viii, 474 pp. 8°. [*London*], *E. & R. Nutt*, [*etc.*] 1730.

Jenkyns (Henry). Law of trade marks. *See* **Ludlow** (Henry) *and* **Jenkyns.**

Johnson (William). Reports of cases in the court of chancery of New York, 1816–1822. v. 2–6. 2d ed. 8°. *New York, Banks & brothers*, 1873.

Jones (David). Value of annuities. 2 v. 1 p. l. xxx, 558 pp; 1 p. l. vi, 559–1196, 64 pp. 8°. *London, R. Baldwin*, 1844.

Jones (Hamilton C.) Reports of cases in equity in the supreme court of North Carolina, 1859–1863. v. 5–6. 8°. *Salisbury, N. C., J. J. Bruner*, [1860–]63.

Jones (H. Cadman). Chancery reports, 1858–1859. *See* **De Gex** (J. P.) *and* **Jones.**

——— Same, 1859–1862. *See* **De Gex** (J. P.) **Fisher** (F.) *and* **Jones**.

——— Same, 1862–1865. *See* **De Gex** (J. P.) **Jones** (H. C.) *and* **Smith** (R. H.)

Jones (Samuel) *and* **Spencer** (James C.) Reports of cases in the superior court of the city of New York, [1871–1875]. v. 1–7. v. 33–39, New York superior court reports. 8°. *New York, Diossy & co.* [*etc.*] 1873–75.

Jones (Thomas G.) Reports of cases in the supreme court of Alabama, 1870–1872. v. 2–6. [v. 44–48, Alabama reports, new series]. 8°. *Montgomery, Ala. Barrett & Brown* 1871–74.

Jordan (Francis). Election laws of Pennsylvania. 3d ed. 1874. 8°. *Harrisburg, B. Singerly*, 1874.

Journal du palais. 1872–1874. v. 83–85. 8°. *Paris, bureaux de l'administration*, [1873–75].

Juan y Colom (Joseph). Instruccion de escribanos en órden á lo judicial. 11a ed. v. 1. 10a ed. v. 2. 6 p. l. 348 pp; 4 p. l. 248 pp. sm. 4°. *Madrid, viuda è hijo de Marin*, [*etc.*] 1787–95.

Justinianus (Flavius Anicius). The institutes. Edited by T. E. Holland. xxxvi, 240 pp. 16°. *Oxford, the Clarendon press*, 1873.

Kansas (*State of*). Laws, 13th session, 1873; 14th session, 1874; 15th session, 1875, and special session of 1874. 3 v. 8°. *Topeka, Kansas, public printer*, 1873–75.

——— *Supreme court.* Digest of reports, 1858–1874, by C. F. W. Dassler. 8°. *St. Louis, W. J. Gilbert*, 1874.

——— ——— Reports of cases, v. 8–13, 1871–1874, by W. C. Webb. 8°. *Topeka, Kansas, public printer*, [*etc.*] 1873–75.

Karo (Joseph). Code rabbinique. Eben Haezer, traduit par extraits, par E. Sautayra, et m. Charleville. 2 v. in 1. 183 pp; 360 pp. 8°. *Paris, Challamel*, [*etc.*] 1868.

Keller (Friedrich Ludwig, von Steinbock). De la procédure civil chez les Romains. Traduit par C. Capmas. xl, 477 pp. 1 l. 8°. *Paris, E. Thorin*, 1870.

Kelly (James Henry). The draftsman. xi, 178 pp. 12°. *London, Butterworths*, 1873.

Kent (James). Commentaries on american law. 12th ed. By O. W. Holmes, jr. 4 v. 8°. *Boston, Little, Brown, & co.* 1873.

Kentucky (*State of*). Acts, adjourned session, jan. 3, 1867. 2 v. in 1. 8°. *Frankfort, public printer*, 1867.

——— *Court of appeals.* Reports of cases, 1872–1874, by W. P. D. Bush. v. 9–10. 8°. *Louisville, Ky. J. P. Morton & co.* 1875.

Kerr (William Williamson). Treatise on the law of discovery. xix, 312 pp. 8°. *London, W. Maxwell & son*, 1870.

Khalil (*Sidi*). Précis de jurisprudence musulmane. 3e éd. 8°. *Paris, imprimerie nationale*, 1872.

Kissane, Chapin *brothers, and others.* The Martha Washington case. [Trial for conspiracy, 1853]. 12 pp. 8°. [*n. p.* 1853]?

Kneeland (Stillman F.) Commercial law register. 558 pp. 8°. *Albany, Parker & Herrick*, 1873.

Ku Klux trials. The great Ku Klux trials. 1871. 224 pp. 1 l. 8°. *Columbia*, [*S. C.*] *Columbia union*, 1872.

Kulp (George B.) Digest of laws of Pennsylvania, for the county of Luzerne, 1700–1874. 110 pp. 1 l. 8°. *Wilkes-Barre*, 1874.

Labroüe de Vareilles-Sommières (*Vicomte* Gabriel de). L'hypothèque judiciaire. xvi, 270 pp. 8°. *Paris, Cotillon & fils*, 1871.

Lacey (John F.) Digest of railway decisions. 962 pp. 8°. *Chicago, Callaghan & co.* 1875.

Lackics (Jorge Sigismundo). Derecho público eclesiástico. 4 p. l. 416 pp. 16°. *Valencia, Mallen y Sobrinos*, 1842.

Lafontaine (Paul Albert). Des donations déguisées. 21 pp. 8°. [*Paris*, 1857]?

Lagrange (Eugène). Manuel de droit romain. 11e éd. par J. Lagrange. 606 pp 16°. *Paris, J. B. Mulot*, 1866.

Lagrèze (Gustave Bascle de). Histoire du droit dans les Pyrénées. 2 p. l. xxxii, 526 pp. 8°. *Paris, imprimerie impériale*, 1867.

Lalor (T. M.) Law of real property of the state of New York. xvi, 9–337 pp. 8°. *New York, J. J. Diossy & co.* 1855.

Landis (Jesse). Supplement to Linn's index of reference to cases in the courts of Pennsylvania. [1850-1871]. 550 pp. 8°. *Lancaster, inquirer printing and publishing co.* 1873.

Langdell (Christopher C.) Cases in equity pleading with reference to discovery, [1661-1869]. Pt. 1. iv, 400 pp. 8°. *Cambridge, [J. Wilson & son]*, 1875.

Langston (William S.) *and others.* The Langston tragedy! Murder of mrs. Nancy Langston, and miss Mary Ann Easter. With the trials. 1873. 58 pp. 8°. *Mattoon, Ill. T. E. Woods*, 1873.

Lansing (Abraham). Reports of cases in the supreme court of the state of New York, [1871-1873]. v. 6-7. 8°. *New York, Banks & brothers*, 1873.

Lathrop (John). Cases in the supreme court of Massachusetts, 1874-1875. v. 1-3. [v. 115-117, Massachusetts reports]. 8°. *Boston, H. O. Houghton & co.* 1875.

Latreille (Jacques). Histoire des institutions judiciaires des Romains. v. 1. 2 p. l. 321 pp. 8°. *Paris, A. Marescq aîné*, 1870.

Law journal reports, 1872-1874. New series. v. 41-43 in 9 v. 4°. *London, E. B. Ince*, 1872-74.

Law list. [1873-1875]. 3 v. 16°. *London, Stevens & sons*, [1873-75].

Law magazine and review, [1873-1874]. New series. v. 2-3. 8°. *London, J. F. Monk, [etc.]* 1873-74.

Law reports. Chancery appeal cases. 1871-1874. v. 7-9. 8°. *London, W. Clowes & sons*, 1872-74.

——— Same. 1865-1867. v. 1-2. 8°. *New York, the transcript association*, 1867-68.

——— Court of common pleas. 1871-1874. v. 7-9. 8°. *London, W. Clowes & sons*, 1872-74.

——— Same. 1865-1867. v. 1-2. 8°. *New York, the transcript association*, 1867-1868.

——— Court of exchequer. 1871-1874. v. 7-9. 8°. *London, W. Clowes & sons*, 1872-74.

——— Same. 1865-1867. v. 1-2. 8°. *New York, the transcript association*, 1867-68.

——— Court of queen's bench. 1871-1874. v. 7-9. 8°. *London, W. Clowes & sons*, 1872-74.

——— Same. 1865-1867. v. 1-2. 8°. *New York, the transcript association*, 1867-68.

——— Courts of probate and divorce. 1869-1872. v. 2. 8°. *London, W. Clowes & sons*, 1872.

Law reports—continued.

——— Crown cases reserved. 1865-1872. v. 1. 8°. *London, W. Clowes & sons*, 1872.

——— Digest of cases. By M. Ware. 1868-1871. v. 2. 8°. *London, W. Clowes & sons*, 1872.

——— English and irish appeal cases. 1871-1873. v. 5-6. 8°. *London, W. Clowes & sons*, 1872-74.

——— Same. 1866-1867. v. 1-2. 8°. *New York, the transcript association*, 1867-68.

——— Equity cases. 1871-1874. v. 13-18. 8°. *London, W. Clowes & sons*, 1872-74.

——— Same. 1865-1867. v. 1-4. 8°. *New York, the transcript association*, 1867-68.

——— High court of admiralty, and ecclesiastical courts. 1869-1872. v. 3. 8°. *London, W. Clowes & sons*, 1872.

——— Same. 1865-1867. v. 1. 8°. *New York, the transcript association*, 1868.

——— Privy council appeals. 1871-1874. v. 4-5. 8°. *London, W. Clowes & sons*, 1873-74.

——— Same. 1865-1867. v. 1. 8°. *New York, the transcript association*, 1868.

——— Public general statutes, 1872-1874. v. 7-9. 8°. *London, W. Clowes & sons*, 1872-74.

Law times. Nov. 1872-oct. 1874. v. 54-57. fol *London, office of the law times*, 1873-74.

Law times reports. Sep. 1872-feb. 1875. v. 27-31. 4°. *London, H. Cox*, [1873-75].

Law times bankruptcy reports. [By C. Rice]. 1868-1869. v. 1-2 in 1. 8°. *Washington, american law times association*, 1868-69.

Law times departments reports. [By C. Rice]. 1868-1869. v. 1-2 in 1. 8°. *Washington, american law times association*, 1868-69.

Law times United States courts reports. [By C. Rice]. 1868-1869. v. 1-2 in 1. 8°. *Washington, american law times association*, 1868-69.

Lawrence (William Beach). Administration of equity jurisprudence. v, 176, 47 pp. 8°. *Boston, A. Mudge & son*, 1874.

Laws of the several states in regard to insurance companies from other states. 1 p. l. 142 pp. 8°. *New York, the insurance monitor*, 1874.

Lee (Harvey). Reports of cases in the supreme court of California, [1858]. v. 1. 2d ed. By R. Desty. [v. 9, California reports]. 8°. *San Francisco, S. Whitney, [etc.]* 1875.

Legal intelligencer, 1865–1868 & 1870–1871. *See* **Philadelphia** reports.

Legal profession. By Doctor-in-jure-civili. [*anon.*] viii, 351 pp. 8°. *London, W. Ridgway*, 1873.

Legrand Du Saulle (Henri). La folie devant les tribunaux. 624 pp. 8°. *Paris, F. Savy*, [*etc.*] 1864.

Levita (Carl). Précis de l'histoire du droit pénal allemand. Traduit par L. Bonneville de Marsangy. 34 pp. 8°. *Paris, Cotillon*, 1862.

Levita (Julius). De la réforme hypothécaire en France et en Prusse. 131 pp. 1 l. 8°. *Paris, Videcoq fils aîné*, 1852.

Lewis (Angelo John). Code of civil procedure [of India]. vii, 254, lxxx pp. 1 l. 8°. *London, W. H. Allen & co.* 1871.

Liquor laws of the [several] United States. [96] pp. 12°. *New York, national temperance society and publication house*, 1873.

Littleton (H. A.) *and* **Blatchley** (J. S.) Digest of fire insurance decisions. 3d ed. by C. Bates. [799] pp. 8°. *New York, Baker, Voorhis & co.* 1873.

Livingston (Edward). Complete works. [With] introduction, by S. P. Chase. 2 v. ix, 589 pp; vi, 657 pp. 8°. *New York, the national prison association of the United States of America*, 1873.

——— Rapport sur le projet d'un code pénal, [1822, etc.] xxii, 224 pp. 8°. *Paris, A. A. Renouard*, 1825.

Livingston (John). Law register, for 1853. 8°. *New York, office of the law magazine*, 1853. s.

——— Same, for the two years beginning may, 1856, and ending may, 1858. 8°. *New York*, [*J. Livingston*], 1856.

——— Same, [1859]. 8°. *New York*, [*J. Livingston*], 1859.

Lloyd (Edward). Law of trade marks. 2d ed. xii, 83 pp. 12°. *London*, [*Yates & Alexander*], 1865.

Louisiana (*State of*). Acts, third session, first legislature, 1870, and extra session, march, 1870; first session, 1873; [and] second session, [1874], third legislature. 3 v. 8°. *New Orleans, state printer*, [*etc.*] 1870–74.

——— Civil code, 1874, by A. Voorhies. 8°. *New Orleans, B. Bloomfield & co.* 1875.

——— Code of practice, [1870]. 200 pp. 8°. *New Orleans, office of the republican*, 1870.

Louisiana (*State of*)—continued.

——— Digest of statutes, [1870]. J. Ray, compiler. 2 v. xiii, 779 pp; v, 746 pp. 8°. *New Orleans, republican office*, 1870.

——— Projet d'un code pénal, 1822. Par É. Livingston. 8°. *Paris, A. A. Renouard*, 1825.

——— Revised civil code, [1870]. xii, 503 pp. 8°. *New Orleans, office of the republican*, 1870.

——— *Supreme court.* Reports of cases, 1870–1872, v. 22–24, Louisiana annual, by J. Hawkins. 8°. *New Orleans, office of the republican*, 1870–72.

——— ——— Same, 1873–1874, v. 25–26, Louisiana annual, by C. Gayarre. 8°. *New Orleans, the republican office*, 1873–74.

Love (Henry K.) Abstract of judgments in the circuit and district courts of the United States for Iowa, 1845 to 1874. 2 p. l. 398 pp. 9 l. fol. *Dubuque, Palmer, Winall & co.* 1874.

Lowenstein (Emil). Trial for murder, Albany, 1874. 1 p. l. 352 pp. 1 pl. 8°. *Albany, W. Gould & son*, 1874.

Lowndes (Richard). Law of general average. 2d ed. xliv, 466 pp. 8°. *London, Stevens & sons*, 1874.

Ludlow (Henry) *and* **Jenkyns** (Henry). Treatise on the law of trade-marks. xv, 152 pp. 8°. *London, W. Maxwell & son*, 1873.

Lumbreras (Joaquin). Lecciones de disciplina eclesiástica. *See* **Riegger** (Paul Joseph).

Lyon (George Edward). Hand-book of the law of bills of sale. xi, 157 pp. 12°. *London, G. Smith & co.* [*etc.*] 1873.

McAdam (David). Law days. 45 pp. 8°. *New York, Diossy & co.* 1874.

Mac Arthur (Arthur). Reports of cases in the supreme court of the district of Columbia, 1873–1874. xiii, 721 pp. 8°. *Washington, government printing office*, 1875.

McClellan (Robert H.) Executor's guide. 2d ed. viii, 404 pp. 8°. *Albany, W. Gould & son*, 1873.

——— Practice in probate courts [of the state of New York]. xxiii, 601 pp. 8°. *Albany, W. Gould & son*, 1875.

McClelland (M. A. *m. d.*) Civil malpractice. 74 pp. 8°. *Chicago, W. B. Keen, Cooke & co.* 1873.

McGarrahan (William). The McGarrahan memorial. [270] pp. 1 map. 8°. *San Francisco, Smyth & Shoaff*, 1870.

McGary (William L.) Treatise on pleading in civil actions. 297 pp. 8°. *St. Louis, W. J. Gilbert*, 1875.

McGrew (J. M.) Postal laws of the United States, 1873. *See* **Ireland** (William M.) *and* **McGrew.**

McKune (John H.) Civil, penal and political codes of California, 1873. *See* **Haymond** (Creed), **Burch** (John C.) *and* **McKune.**

McLaren (John). Law of Scotland in relation to wills and succession. 2 v. lxi, 728 pp; viii, 781 pp. 8°. *Edinburgh, Bell & Bradfute*, 1868.

McMaster (R. Bach). Act for the organization of business corporations of New York, 1875. 1 p. l. vi, 3–33, xviii pp. 12°. *New York, Baker, Voorhis & co.* 1875.

McMullen (Joseph F.) New Wisconsin form book. 4th ed. 405 pp. 8°. *Milwaukee, Strickland & co.* 1873.

McVey (A. H.) Digest of the reported decisions of the courts of Ohio. [1816–1874]. 2 v. 9 p. l. 561 pp; 1 p. l. 579 pp. 8°. *Cleveland, Ingham, Clarke & co.* 1875.

Maine (*Sir* Henry Sumner). Ancient law. 5th ed. 1 p. l. ix, 415 pp. 8°. *London, J. Murray*, 1874.

Maine (*State of*). Acts, 49th legislature, 1870; 53d legislature, 1874; 54th legislature, 1875. 3 v. 8°. *Augusta, printers to the state*, 1870–75.

——— Documents printed by order of the legislature, 1873. [694] pp. 8°. *Augusta, printers to the state*, 1873.

——— Railroad laws, 1831–1875, by E. F. Webb. 8°. *Portland, Dresser, McLellan & co.* 1875.

——— *Supreme court.* Reports of cases, v. 60, 1872, by W. W. Virgin. 8°. *Portland, Loring, Short & Harmon*, 1873.

——— ——— Same, v. 61–63, 1867–1874, by E. B. Smith. 8°. *Portland. Loring, Short & Harmon*, [*etc.*] 1874–75.

Mallory (John A.) Railway reports, 1869–1874. *See* **American** railway reports.

Manin (Daniele). De la jurisprudence vénète. Préface et traduction par E. Millaud. 3 p. l. lxxv, 121 pp. 1 l. 8°. *Paris, Guillaumin & cie.* 1867.

Manresa y Navarro (José Maria), **Miquel** (Ignacio) *and* **Reus y Garcia** (José). Ley de enjuiciamiento civil, comentada. 6 v. 8°. *Madrid, revista de legislacion y jurisprudencia*, 1856–69.

Manual of practice. [*anon.*] 153 l. unp. 16°. [*St. Paul*], *tribune printing co.* [1872].

Martindale (James B.) United States law directory for 1874. 860 pp. 8°. *Indianapolis, J. B Martindale & co.* 1874.

Martinez Marina (Francisco). Juicio crítico de la novísima recopilacion. viii, 335 pp. sm. 4°. *Madrid, F. Villalpando*, 1820.

Martinez Salazar (Antonio). Práctica de substanciar pleytos. 4a ed. 2 p. l. 324 pp. 8°. [*Madrid*], *Hurtado*, 1789.

Maryland (*State of*). Laws passed, 1874. 8°. *Annapolis, S. S. Mills & L. F. Colton*, 1874.

——— *Court of appeals.* Reports of cases, v. 36–41, 1872–74, by J. S. Stockett. 8°. *Baltimore, J. Murphy & co.* [*etc.*] 1873–75.

Massachusetts (*State of*). Acts passed, 1873–1875. 3 v. 8°. *Boston, state printers*, 1873–75.

——— General laws and resolves, 1873 [and] 1875. 2 v. 8°. *Boston, state printers*, [1873–75].

——— General statutes, 1860. 2d ed. Edited by W. A. Richardson and G. P. Sanger. xvii, 1126 pp. 8°. *Boston, the commonwealth*, 1873.

——— Same. Supplement. 1867–1870. 4 v. in 1. 8°. *Boston, the commonwealth*, [1867–70].

——— Same. Supplement. 1860–1872. 2d ed. 1116 pp. 8°. *Boston, the commonwealth*, 1873.

——— General statutes to 1874, in questions and answers, by C. U. Bell. 12°. *Boston, G. B. Reed*, 1874.

——— Notes on the general statutes, by U. H. Crocker and G. C. Crocker. 2d ed. to 1874, inclusive. 8°. *Boston, H. O. Houghton & co.* 1875.

——— *Supreme court.* Reports of cases, v. 107–109, 1866–1873, by A. G. Browne, jr. 8°. *Boston, H. O. Houghton & co.* 1873–74.

——— ——— Same, v. 110–111, 1872–1873, by A. G. Browne, jr. and J. C. Gray, jr. 8°. *Boston, H. O. Houghton & co.* 1874–75.

——— ——— Same, v. 115–117, 1874–1875, by J. Lathrop. 8°. *Boston, H. O. Houghton & co.* 1875.

Mathews (Henry M.) Reports of cases in the supreme court of appeals of West Virginia, 1873. v. 1. [v. 6, West Virginia reports]. 8°. *Charleston, J. W. Gentry*, 1875.

Matson (William N) Reports of cases in the supreme court of Connecticut, [1852–1856].

Matson (William N.)—continued. v. 1-3. 2d ed. [v. 22-24, Connecticut reports] 8°. *New York, Banks & brothers,* 1873.

Matthews (William B.) Forms. xviii, 395 pp. 8°. *Richmond, Va. J. W. Randolph & English,* 1873.

May (Henry W.) Treatise on the statutes of Elizabeth against fraudulent conveyances. xlix, 564 pp. 8°. *London, Stevens & Haynes,* 1871.

May (John Wilder) Law of insurance. xxviii, 777 pp. 8°. *Boston, Little, Brown, & co.* 1873.

Medico-legal society of New York. Papers. First series. Revised ed. 1 p. l. xv, 552 pp. 2 pl. 8°. *New York, McDivitt, Campbell & co.* 1874.

Melendez Valdés (Juan). Discursos forenses. 1 p. l. vi, 310 pp. 1 l. 16°. *Madrid, imprenta nacional,* 1821.

Ménerville (Charles Louis Pinson de). Dictionnaire de la législation algérienne. 1830-1860. 2e éd. v. 1. 8°. *Alger, Bastide,* [*etc.*] 1867.

——— Same. 1860-1872. v. 2-3 in 1. 8°. *Alger, A. Jourdan,* [*etc.*] 1872.

Mexico. Código civil, [1866]. Libro 2do. 46 pp. 18°. *México, M. Villanueva,* 1866.

Michigan (*State of*). Acts, passed 1873. 3 v. 8°. *Lansing, state printers,* 1873.

——— *Supreme court.* Reports of cases, v. 24-29, 1871-1874, by H. Post. 8°. *Lansing, state printers,* 1873-75.

Milan. Atti del municipio, 1871. fol. *Milano, L. di G. Pirola,* [1872].

Miller (Samuel F. *associate justice of the supreme court of the United States*). Reports of decisions in the supreme court of the United States. [Condensed, 1855-1859]. v. 1-3. 8°. *Washington, W. H. & O. H. Morrison,* 1874-75.

Minnesota (*State of*). General laws, 14th session, 1872; 15th session, 1873; 16th session, 1874. 3 v. 8°. *Saint Paul, Ramaley, Chaney & co.* [*etc.*] 1872-74.

——— Revised statutes, 1873, by A. H. Bissell. 2 v. 8°. *Chicago, Callaghan & co.* 1873.

——— *Supreme court.* Reports of cases, v. 17-18 & 20, 1871-1874, by W. A. Spencer. 8°. *St. Paul, W. S. Combs,* 1873-75.

Minor (John B.) Institutes of common and statute law. v. 1-2. 8°. *Richmond, Whit-*

Miquel (Ignacio). Ley de enjuiciamiento civil. *See* **Manresa y Navarro** (José Maria), **Miquel** (Ignacio), *and* **Reus y Garcia** (José).

Mississippi (*State of*) Laws, regular session, 1861-1862; regular session, 1872; regular session, 1873; called session, 1873; regular session, 1874; called session, 1874; regular session, 1875; called session, 1875. 8 v. 8°. *Jackson, state printers,* 1862-75.

——— *Supreme court.* Reports of cases, v. 47-48, 1872-1873, by J. S. Morris. 8°. *Chicago, Callaghan & co.* 1873.

——— ——— Same, v. 49-50, 1873-1874, by G. E. Harris and G. H. Simrall. 8°. *Jackson & Chicago, pilot co.* [*etc.*] 1874-75.

Missouri (*State of*). Digest of laws, 1812-1817, by H. S. Geyer. 8°. *St. Louis, J. Charless,* 1818.

——— Laws, 27th assembly, 1873. 8°. *Jefferson city, state printer,* 1873.

——— *Supreme court.* Digest of reports, 1821-1872, by E. W. Pattison. 2 v. 4°. *St. Louis, W. J. Gilbert,* 1873.

——— ——— Index to reports, 1821-1872, by B. Hunter and W. G. Myer. 32°. *St. Louis, the authors,* 1873.

——— ——— Reports of cases, v. 49-59, 1871-1875, by T. A. Post. 8°. *St. Louis, democrat co.* [*etc.*] 1873-75.

Moak (Nathaniel C.) Reports of cases decided by the english courts, [1872-1874]. v. 3-10. 8°. *Albany, W. Gould & sons,* [*etc.*] 1873-75.

Modderman (W.) De wettelijke bewijsleer in strafzaken. 4 p. l. 300 pp. 8°. *Utrecht, C. van der Post, jr.* 1867. s.

Montana (*Territory of*). Acts, 1st assembly, 1864; 4th assembly, 1867; 5th assembly 1868-1869; 6th assembly, 1869-1870; ex. session, 1873; 8th session, 1874. 6 v. 8°. *Virginia city & Helena, D. W. Tilton & co.* [*etc.*] 1866-74.

——— *Supreme court.* Reports of cases, v. 1, 1868-1873, by H. N. Blake. 8°. *Virginia city, G. F. Cope,* 1873.

Montesquieu (Charles de Secondat, *baron de la Brede et de*). Esprit des lois. 2 p. l. 600 pp. 1 port. 12°. *Paris, F. Didot frères, fils & cie.* 1872.

Monthly western jurist. May, 1874, to april 1875. v. 1. 8°. *Bloomington, Ill. Tipton & Hill,* 1875.

Montluc (Léon Adrien de). Des assurances sur la vie. 327 pp. 5 l. 8°. *Paris, A. Lévy,* 1870.

Moon (Clinton A.) Digest of fees of town and county officers in New York. 84 pp. 12°. *Albany, J. Munsell,* 1873.

Moore (Edmund Fitz). Reports of cases determined by the judicial committee and the lords of privy council, 1861–2. v. 15. 8°. *London, Stevens & sons,* [1862].

——— Same, 1867–9 & 1871–1873. New series. v. 5 & 8–9. 8°. *London, Stevens & sons,* [1869–73].

——— Reports of cases determined by the judicial committee and the lords of privy council on appeal from the East Indies, 1869–1872. v. 13–14. 8°. *London, Stevens & sons,* [1871–73].

Moore (Henry). Instructions for preparing abstracts of titles. 2d ed. viii, 181 pp. 12°. *London, Butterworths,* 1852.

——— Same. 3d ed. x, 302 pp. 12°. *London, Wildy & sons,* 1873.

Moore (Ira M.) Civil jurisdiction of justices of the peace and constables in Illinois. 1020 pp. 8°. *Chicago, Callaghan & co.* 1875.

Morgan (Charles F.) Code of civil procedure of Ohio, 1874. 603 pp. 8°. *Albany, W. Gould & son,* 1874.

Morgan (James Appleton). Law of literature. 2 v. xviii, 513 pp; xvii, 817 pp. 8°. *New York, J. Cockcroft & co.* 1875.

Morilla (José Maria). Tratado de derecho administrativo español. vii, 384 pp. 1 l. 8°. *Habana, V. de Torres,* 1847.

Morin (Achille). Les lois relatives à la guerre. 2 v. xx, 576 pp; viii, 598 pp. 8°. *Paris, Cosse, Marchal & Billard,* 1872.

Morris (Joshua S.) Mississippi reports: cases in the supreme court, [1872–1873]. v. 5–6. [v. 47–48, Mississippi reports]. 8°. *Chicago, Callaghan & co.* 1873.

Morse (John T. *jr.*) Famous trials. vi, 5–342 pp. 5 pl. 8°. *Boston, Little, Brown, & co.* 1874.

Moses (Raphael J. *jr.*) *and* **Shinn** (William A.) National bankruptcy register digest, 1867 to 1875. iv, 7–758 pp. 8°. *New York, McDivitt, Campbell & co.* 1875.

Munford (George W.) Code of Virginia. 3d ed. 1874. 8°. *Richmond, J. E. Goode,* 1873.

Murillo Velarde (Pedro). Cursus juris canonici, hispani, et indici. Ed. tertia. 2 v. 20 p. l. 736 pp. 5 charts; 8 p. l. 465 pp. 9 l. fol. *Matriti, in typographia Ulloae a Ramone Ruiz,* 1791.

Murray (Francis P.) Table of cases affirmed, reversed, cited and overruled in the courts of the United States, [1781–1873]. viii, 393 pp. 8°. *Albany, Weed, Parsons & co.* 1873.

Muteau (Charles). Du secret professionnel. xvi, 565 pp. 8°. *Paris, Marescq aîné,* 1870.

Myer (William G.) Index to Missouri reports, 1821–1872. *See* **Hunter** (Benjamin) *and* **Myer.**

——— Index to Ohio reports, 1816–1872. *See* **Hunter** (Benjamin) *and* **Myer.**

——— Index to the Tennessee reports, 1791–1872. *See* **Hunter** (Benjamin) *and* **Myer.**

Nash (Simeon). Pleading and practice under the codes of Ohio, New York, Kansas and Nebraska. 4th ed. 2 v. x, 789 pp; 1 p. l. 791–1441 pp. 8°. *Cincinnati, R. Clarke & co.* 1874.

National bankruptcy register. [1870–1872]. v. 6. 8°. *New York, the United States law association,* 1872.

National bankruptcy register reports, [1867–1872]. v. 1–6. 8°. *New York, J. R. McDivitt & co.* [*etc.*] 1873–74.

——— Same. [A continuation of The national bankruptcy register. 1872–1875]. v. 7–12. 8°. *New York, J. R. McDivitt,* [*etc.*] 1873–75.

Nebraska (*State of*). General statutes in force sep. 1, 1873. By G. A. Brown. xvi, 1304 pp. 8°. *Lincoln, state printers,* 1873.

——— *Supreme court.* Reports of cases, v. 1–2, by J. M. Woolworth. 8°. *Chicago, Callaghan & Cockcroft,* [*etc.*] 1871–73.

——— ——— Same, v. 3, 1873–1874, by L. Crounse. 8°. *Lincoln, state journal co.* 1874.

Nevada (*State of*). Compiled laws, 1861 to 1873, inclusive. By M. S. Bonnifield and T. W. Healy. 2 v. cxlii, 591 pp; lxi, 683 pp. 8°. *Carson city, state printer,* 1873.

——— Statutes, 6th session, 1873; 7th session, 1875. 2 v. 8°. *Carson city, state printer,* 1873–75.

——— *Supreme court.* Reports of cases, v. 7–9, 1871–1874, by A. Helm and T. H. Hittell. 8°. *San Francisco, Bacon & co.* [*etc.*] 1872–74.

New Hampshire (*State of*). Laws, session, 1873; session, 1874; session, 1875. 3 v. 8°. *Concord, state printer,* 1873–75.

——— *Supreme court.* Reports of cases, v. 51–54, 1866–1874, by J. M. Shirley. 8°. *Concord, B. W. Sanborn & co.* [*etc.*] 1873–75.

New Jersey (*State of*). Acts, 59th assembly, 1st–2d sittings, 1834–[1835]; 97th legislature, [1873]; 98th legislature, [1874]. 4 v. 8°. *Trenton, Morristown & Paterson, J. Justice,* [*etc.*] 1835–74.

——— *Court of chancery.* Reports of cases, v. 18, 20 & 23–24, 1866–1867, 1869–1870 & 1872–1874, by C. E. Green. 8°. *Trenton, Hough & Gillespy,* [*etc.*] 1868–74.

——— *Supreme court.* Reports of cases, 1796–1831, by W. Halsted, jr. 2d ed. 7 v. 8°. [*Trenton, Murphy & Bechtel,* 1875].

——— *Supreme court and court of errors and appeals.* Reports of cases, v. 33 & 35, 1867–1869 & 1870–1872, by P. D. Vroom. 8°. *Trenton, W. T. Nicholson,* [*etc.*] 1870–73.

——— ——— Same, v. 36, 1872–1873, by G. D. W. Vroom. 8°. *Trenton, W. S. & E. W. Sharp,* 1874.

New Mexico (*Territory of*). Acts, 21st session, 1873–1874. 8°. *Santa Fé, N. M. public printers,* 1874.

——— Same. Actos, sesion vigésima primera. 8°. *Santa Fé, N. M. public printers,* 1874.

New York (*City of*). *Superior court.* Reports of cases, v. 33–39, 1871–1875, by S. Jones and J. C. Spencer. 8°. *New York, Diossy & co.* [*etc.*] 1873–75.

New York (*City and county of*). *Court of common pleas.* Reports of cases, 1871–1873, by C. P. Daly. v. 4. 8°. *New York, Baker, Voorhis & co.* 1874.

New York (*County of*). *Surrogate's court.* Reports of cases, 1864–1869, by G. J. Tucker. v. 1. 8°. *New York, Banks & brothers,* 1870.

New York (*State of*). Act for the organization of business corporations, 1875, by R. B. McMaster. 12°. *New York, Baker, Voorhis & co.* 1875.

——— Changes in the statute law, 1858–1873, by J. D. Fay. 8°. *New York, Baker, Voorhis & co.* 1873.

——— *Commission of appeals.* Reports of cases, v. 51, 54 & 57, 1872–1874, by H. E. Sickels. 8°. *New York & Albany, Banks & brothers,* [*etc.*] 1873–75.

——— *Court of appeals.* Reports of cases, v. 49–50, 52–53, 55–56 & 58–59, 1871–1874, by H. E. Sickels. 8°. *New York & Albany, Banks & brothers,* [*etc.*] 1873–75.

——— ——— Reports of cases, not heretofore officially reported, 1850–1869, by A. Abbott. v. 1–4. 8°. *New York, Diossy & co.* 1873–74

New York (*State of*)—continued.

——— *Court of chancery.* Reports of cases, 1816–1822, by W. Johnson. v. 2–6. 2d ed. 8°. *New York, Banks & brothers,* 1873.

——— ——— Same, 1839–1840, by M. Hoffman. v. 1. 3d ed. 8°. *New York, Banks & brothers,* 1874.

——— ——— Same, 1839–1841, by C. L. Clarke. 3d ed. 8°. *New York, Banks & brothers,* 1873.

——— ——— Same, 1843–1844, by L. H. Sandford. v. 1. 8°. *New York, Banks & brothers,* 1873.

——— ——— Same, 1836–1839 & 1842–1844, by A. C. Paige. v. 6–7, 2d ed. & v. 10. 8°. *New York, Banks & brothers,* 1863–73.

——— Digest of fees of town and county officers, 1873, by C. A. Moon. 12°. *Albany, J. Munsell,* 1873.

——— Digest of laws in force jan. 1, 1874, by J. D. Fay. v. 1–2. 8°. *New York, J. Cockcroft & co.* 1874–75.

——— Digest of reports, 1869–1872, by W. Wait. 8°. *Albany, W. Gould & son,* 1873.

——— Digest of reports to 1873, by B. V. Abbott and A. Abbott. 2d ed. 6 v. 8°. *New York, Baker, Voorhis & co.* 1873–75.

——— Excise laws, 1873, by W. W. Saxton. 12°. *Albany, Parker & Herrick,* 1873.

——— General statutes for 1874, 97th session. 8°. *Albany, Weed, Parsons & co.* 1874.

——— Laws, 96th–98th sessions, 1873–1875. 3 v. 8°. *Albany, Weed, Parsons & co.* [*etc.*] 1873–75.

——— Reports of practice cases, 1863–1875, by N. Howard, jr. v. 45–49. 8°. *Albany, W. Gould & son,* 1873–75.

——— Same, 1870–1874, by A. Abbott. v. 13–15, new series. 8°. *New York, Diossy & co.* 1873–74.

——— Rules of the courts of record, [1875]. 1 p. l. 120 pp. 8°. *Albany, Banks & brothers,* 1874.

——— Same. viii, 5-84 pp. 8°. *New York, McDivitt, Campbell & co.* 1875.

——— Statutes at large, by J. W. Edmonds. 2d ed. to 1870, inclusive. 7 v. 8°. *Albany, Weed, Parsons & co.* 1869–70.

——— Same, v. 9, 1871–1874. 8°. *Albany, Weed, Parsons & co.* 1875.

——— *Supreme court.* Reports of cases, 1847, by O. L. Barbour. 2d ed. v. 1. 8°. *New York, Banks & brothers,* 1875.

New York (*State of*)—continued.
——— ——— Same, 1863-1873, by O. L. Barbour. v. 63-65. 8°. *Albany, W. C. Little & co.* 1873.
——— ——— Same, 1873-1874, by I. G. Thompson and R. D. Cook. v. 1-4. 8°. *Albany, J D. Parsons, jr.* 1874.
——— ——— Same, v. 6-7, 1871-1873, by A. Lansing. 8°. *New York, Banks & brothers,* 1873.
——— ——— Same, v. 8-11, 1874-1875, by M. T. Hun. 8°. *New York, Banks & brothers,* [1874-75].
——— *Supreme court and court of errors.* Reports of cases, 1823-1826, by E. Cowen. v. 1-2 & 5. 8°. *New York, Banks & brothers,* 1873.
——— ——— Same, 1828-1840, by J. L. Wendell. 2d ed. v. 1-20. 8°. *New York, Banks & brothers,* 1873.
——— ——— Same, 1841-1845, by N. Hill, jun. v. 1-3 & 7. 8°. *New York, Banks & brothers,* 1873-75.
——— ——— Same, 1845-1848, by H. Denio. v. 1-4. 8°. *New York, Banks & brothers,* 1873-75.

Noel (John V. Vavasour, *m. d.*) Divorce case, [1872-1873]. 143, 13 pp. 8°. *Camden, N. J., F. B. Stiles & E. Morgan,* 1873.

North (Levi). Treatise on the practice in probate courts of Illinois. xvii, 418 pp. 8°. *Chicago, Callaghan & co.* 1873.

North Carolina (*State of*). Public laws, passed 1869-1870. 8°. *Raleigh, state printer,* 1870.
——— Revisal of the public statutes, 1872-3. By W. H. Battle. xi, 987 pp. 8°. *Raleigh, Edwards, Broughton & co.* 1873.
——— *Supreme court.* Reports of cases in equity, 1859-1863, by H. C. Jones. v. 5-6. 8°. *Salisbury, N. C., J. J. Bruner,* [1860-]63.
——— ——— Reports of cases, v. 68, 70 & 72-73, 1873-1875, by T. L. Hargrove. 8°. *Raleigh, state printers,* [*etc.*] 1873-75.

North Hempstead (*Town of*) *vs.* **Hempstead** (*Town of*). Trial, [1828.] 400, 152 pp. 1 l. 8°. *New York, W. Grattan,* 1825.

Notaries' hand-book. By a member of the New York bar. [*anon.*] 2d ed. 38 pp. 8°. *New York, Baker, Voorhis & co.* 1874.

Nott (Charles C.) *and* **Huntington** (Samuel H.) Cases in the court of claims, 1871. v. 7. 8°. *Washington, government printing office,* 1873.

Nott (Charles C.)—continued.
——— *and* **Hopkins** (Archibald). Cases in the court of claims, 1872-1873. v. 8-9 [of the court of claims reports, new series]. 8°. *Washington, government printing office,* 1874.

Nypels (Jan Servais Willem). Pasinomie, 1867. Supplément. Code pénal belge. xiv, 5-195 pp. 8°. *Bruxelles, Bruylant-Christophe & cie.* 1867.

Ohio (*State of*). Code of civil procedure, 1874, by G. E. Seney. 8°. *Cincinnati, R. Clarke & co.* 1874.
——— Same, 1874, by C. F. Morgan. 8°. *Albany, W. Gould & son,* 1874.
——— Laws, 60th assembly, 1872; 60th assembly, adjourned session, 1873; 61st assembly, 1874; 61st assembly, 2d session, 1874-[1875]. v. 69-72. 8°. *Columbus, state printers,* 1872-75.
——— Railroad laws to 1874, by J. A. Wilcox. 8°. *Cincinnati, R. Clarke & co.* 1874.
——— *Supreme court.* Digest of all reported decisions, 1816-1874, by A. H. McVey. 2 v. 8°. *Cleveland, Ingham, Clarke & co.* 1875.
——— ——— Index to reports, 1816-1872, by B. Hunter and W. G. Myer. 32°. *St. Louis, W. J. Gilbert,* 1874.
——— ——— Reports of cases, 1871-1873, v. 22-23, Ohio state, by M. M. Granger. 8°. *Cincinnati, R. Clarke & co.* 1873-74.
——— ——— Same, 1873-1874, v. 24, Ohio state, by E. L. De Witt. 8°. *Cincinnati, R. Clarke & co.* 1875.

Oliver (Benjamin L.) Forms of practice. 4th ed. xxxvi, 864 pp. 8°. *Portland, Me. Dresser, McLellan & co.* 1874.

Olney (Warren). Code of civil procedure of California, 1872; amended, 1874. 3d ed. 2 p. l. 859 pp. 16°. *San Francisco, S. Whitney & co.* 1874.

Ontario (*Province of*). *Court of queen's bench.* Reports of cases, 1870-1872, v. 30-32, by C. Robinson. 8°. *Toronto, H. Rowsell,* [*etc.*] 1871-73.
——— ——— Same, 1872-1873, v. 33, by H. C. W. Wethey. 8°. *Toronto, Rowsell & Hutchison,* 1874.
——— Statutes, 2d [and] 4th sessions, 1873-1874. 2 v. 8°. *Toronto, J. Notman,* 1873-74.

Oregon (*State of*). Acts, eighth session, 1874. 8°. *Salem, state printer,* 1874.
——— Organic and general laws. 1843-1872. iv, 922 pp. 1 l. 8°. [*Salem*], *state printer,* 1874.

Ortiz de Zúñiga (Manuel L.) *and* **Herrera** (Cayetano de). Deberes y atribuciones de los correjidores, justicias y ayuntamientos de España. 5 v. sm. 4°. *Madrid, T. Jordan,* 1832–33.

Overton (Daniel Y.) Annotated code of civil practice for Wisconsin and Iowa, [1875]. lxxiv, 767 pp. 8°. *Chicago, Callaghan & co.* 1875.

Pacheco (Joaquin Francisco). El código penal [de España, 1850]. 4a ed. 3 v. 8°. *Madrid, M. Tello,* 1870.

——— Same. Apéndice, por José Gonzales y Serrano. 8°. *Madrid, M. Tello,* 1870.

Paige (Alonzo C.) Reports of cases in the court of chancery of the state of New York, [1836-1839]. v. 6-7. 2d ed. 8°. *New York, Banks & brothers,* 1873.

——— Same. [1842-1844]. v. 10. 8°. *New York, Banks & brothers,* 1863.

Parkersburg (*City of*). Corporation laws, [1820-1873]. By G. Loomis. xv, 9-250 pp 8°. *Parkersburg, Gibbens brothers,* 1874.

Parsons (Theophilus, *ll. d.*) Law of contracts. 6th ed. 3 v. 8°. *Boston, Little, Brown, & co.* 1873.

——— Laws of business. Revised ed. xxii, 694 pp. 2 l. 8°. *Hartford, S. S. Scranton & co.* 1875.

——— Political, personal, and property rights of a citizen of the U. S. xvi, 744 pp. 8°. *Hartford, S. S. Scranton & co.* 1874.

——— Treatise on the law of promissory notes and bills of exchange. 2d ed. 2 v. cxxv, 664 pp; x, 834 pp. 8°. *Philadelphia, J. B. Lippincott & co.* 1875.

Paschal (George Washington). Digest of decisions of the supreme courts of Texas, [1873]. v. 2-3. 8°. *Washington, W. H. & O. H. Morrison,* [*etc.*] 1874–75.

——— Digest of the laws of Texas, 1754-1872. 3d ed. 2 v. 8°. *Washington, W. H. & O. H. Morrison,* 1873.

——— Same, 4th ed. to 1874. 2 v. 8°. *Washington, W. H. & O. H. Morrison,* 1874.

Paterson (James). Supplement to Archbold's justice of the peace. 6th ed. *See* **Archbold** (John Frederick).

Pattison (Everett W.) Digest of the Missouri reports, 1821-1872. 2 v. 8-402 pp. interleaved; 10-166, lxxi, 273-381 pp. interleaved. 4°. *St. Louis, W. J. Gilbert,* 1873.

Peace (Maskell W.) Coal mines regulation act, 1872. 3d ed. 227 pp. 8°. *London, W. M. Hutchings,* [1873].

Peck (Hiram D.) Township officers' guide of Ohio. viii, 388 pp. 12°. *Cincinnati, R. Clarke & co.* 1874.

Pennsylvania (*Province of*). Charters and acts of assembly, [1682-1759]. 2 v. & appendix in 1. 1 p. l. 164 pp; 1 p. l. iii, 116 pp; 1 p. l. 18, 32 pp. fol. *Philadelphia, P. Miller & co.* 1762.

Pennsylvania (*State of*). Abridgment of the laws, 1700-1811, by J. Purdon. 8°. *Philadelphia, Ferrand, Hopkins, Zantzinger & co.* 1811.

——— Annual digest of laws for 1873, by F. C. Brightly. 8°. *Philadelphia, Kay & brother,* 1873.

——— Same, for 1873 & 1874. 8°. *Philadelphia, Kay & brother,* 1874.

——— Digest of titles to corporations, 1700-1873, by C. G. Beitel. 2d ed. 8°. *Philadelphia, J. Campbell & son,* 1874.

——— Election laws, to 1874. By F. Jordan. 3d ed. vi, 293 pp. 8°. *Harrisburg, B. Singerly,* 1874.

——— Laws, 1700-1802, by M. Carey and J. Bioren. 6 v. 8°. *Philadelphia, J. Bioren,* [*etc.*] 1803.

——— Laws. 13th assembly, 2d sitting, 1789. fol. [*Philadelphia, T. Bradford,* 1789].

——— Same. Acts, session, 1804-[05]; session, 1872; session, 1873; session, 1874; session, 1875. 5 v. 8°. *Octoraro & Harrisburg, F. Bailey,* [*etc.*] 1805-75.

——— Purdon's digest of laws, 10th ed. by Brightly, 1700-1872. 2 v. 8°. *Philadelphia, Kay & brother,* 1873.

——— Railroad laws, 1820-1874, by G. W. I. Ball. 8°. *Philadelphia, Allen, Lane & Scott,* 1875.

——— Supplement to Purdon's digest of laws, by F. C. Brightly, 1846-1848. 8°. *Philadelphia, J. Kay, jun. & brother,* 1848.

——— *Supreme court.* Index of parallel reference, 1850-1871, by J. Landis. 8°. *Lancaster, inquirer printing & publishing co.* 1873.

——— ——— Index to reports, 1754-1872, by R. E. Wright. 8°. *Philadelphia, R. Welsh,* 1874.

——— ——— Reports of cases, 1823-1828, by T. Sergeant and W. Rawle, jr. v. 10-17. 3d ed. 8°. *Philadelphia, Kay & brother,* 1873-75.

——— ——— Same, 1849-1850, v. 13, Penn. state, by G. W. Harris. 3d ed. 8°. *Philadelphia, Kay & brother,* 1873.

Pennsylvania (*State of*)—continued.
——— ——— Same, 1871-1874, v. 69-76, Penn. state, by P. F. Smith. 8°. *Philadelphia, Kay & brother*, 1873-75.
——— *Supreme court and other courts.* Reports of cases, 1863-1873, by F. C. Brewster. v. 4. 8°. *Philadelphia, Kay & brother*, 1873.

Pennsylvania law journal, 1842-1852. *See* **Pennsylvania** law journal reports.

Pennsylvania law journal reports. v. 4-5. 8°. *Philadelphia, J. Campbell & son*, 1872-73.

Perkins *junior, m. a.* [*pseud.*] Essays for englishwomen and law students. 4 p. l. 294 pp. 1 chart. 12°. *London, Longmans*, 1873.

Perry (Jairus Ware). Treatise on the law of trusts. 2d ed. 2 v. cxxxi, 577 pp; xiv, 678 pp. 8°. *Boston, Little, Brown, & co.* 1874.

Petersdorff (Charles), Supplement to the last edition of the abridgment of the common law, 1863 to 1870. 2 p. l. 456 pp. 8°. *London, Butterworths*, [*etc.*] 1870.

Petit (G. Albert). Étude sur les injures et la diffamation en droit romain. 158 pp. 8°. *Paris, A. Marescq aîné*, 1868.

Philadelphia reports, 1865-1868 [and] 1870-1871. By H. E. Wallace. v. 6 & 8. 8°. *Philadelphia, J. B. Hunter*, [*etc.*] 1870-73.

Phillimore (*Sir* Robert Joseph). Ecclesiastical law of the church of England. 2 v. lxxx, 1074 pp; 1 p. l. 1075-2385 pp. 8°. *London, H. Sweet*, [*etc.*] 1873.

Phillips (Philip). Statutory jurisdiction and practice of the supreme court of the United States. 2d ed. 512 pp. 8°. *Washington, W. H. & O. H. Morrison*, 1872.
——— Same. Revised ed. oct. 1875. 548 pp. 8°. *Washington, W. H. & O. H. Morrison*, 1876.

Phillips (Samuel Louis). Treatise on the law of mechanics' liens. xxiv, 728 pp. 8°. *Boston, Little, Brown, & co.* 1874.

Phillips (Samuel March). Famous cases of circumstantial evidence. xxxix, 153 pp. 8°. *New York, J. Cockcroft & co.* 1873.

Pinney (S. U.) Reports of cases in the supreme court of the territory of Wisconsin, [1847], and of the state of Wisconsin, [1849-1850]. v. 2. 8°. *Chicago, Callaghan & co.* 1874.

Pittsburgh legal journal. Aug. 1871-aug. 1874. New series, v. 2-4; old series, v. 19-21. fol. *Pittsburgh, J. W. & J. S. Murray*, 1872-74.

Pittsburgh reports. [1865-1873]. v. 3. 8°. *Philadelphia, J. Campbell & son*, 1873.

Pomeroy (John Norton) Introduction to the constitutional law of the United States. 3d ed. 1 p. l. xxv, 580 pp. 8°. *New York, Hurd & Houghton*, 1875.

Porter (A. N.) Iowa probate manual. xi, 232 pp. 8°. *Des Moines, Mills & co.* 1873.

Post (Hoyt). Michigan reports of cases in the supreme court, 1871-1874. v. 2-7. v. 24-29 of the series. 8°. *Lansing, state printers*, 1873-75.

Post (Truman A.) Reports of cases in the supreme court of Missouri, [1871-1875]. v. 8-18. [v. 49-59. Missouri reports]. 8°. *St. Louis, democrat co.* [*etc.*] 1873-75.

Potts (Thomas). Law dictionary. 1 p. l. iv, 620 pp. 16°. *London, for T. Ostell*, 1803.

Pratt (John Tidd). Law relating to friendly societies. xiv, 146 pp. 12°. *London, Longman*, [*etc.*] 1834. s.

Price (Eli K.) Act [of Pennsylvania, passed 1853], for the sale of real estate. xv, 194 pp. 8°. *Philadelphia, Kay & brother*, 1874.

Prideaux (Frederick). Precedents in conveyancing. 7th ed. 2 v. xlv, 793 pp; xlvi, 734 pp. 8°. *London, Stevens & sons*, 1873.

Prontuario jurídico. Enero, 1834-julio, 1842. 3 v. 16°. *Madrid, Rios*, [1839-]42.

Providence (*City of*). Statutes of Rhode Island, and ordinances of the city, [to 1875]. 459 pp. 8°. *Cambridge, riverside press*, 1875.

Purdon (John). Abridgment of the laws of Pennsylvania. xxxi, 637 pp. 8°. *Philadelphia, Ferrand, Hopkins, Zantzinger & co.* 1811. s.
——— Digest of the laws of Pennsylvania, 1700 to 1872. 10th ed. By F. C. Brightly. 2 v. cxxi, 874 pp; ix, 875-1772 pp. 8°. *Philadelphia, Kay & brother*, 1873.

Purkis (Henry Wakeham). Students' guide to criminal law and magisterial practice. 2d ed. viii, 167 pp. 8°. *London, W. Amer*, 1873.

Puterbaugh (Sabin D.) Chancery pleading and practice of Illinois. 718 pp. 8°. *Chicago, L. Puterbaugh*, 1874.
——— Common law pleading and practice of Illinois. 3d ed. 867 pp. 8°. *Peoria, Brown & Cramer*, 1873.

Quarles (James M.) Criminal code [of Tennessee, 1858 to 1874]. xix, 890 pp. 8°. *Nashville, Tavel, Eastman & Howell*, 1874.

Quebec (*Province of*). Statutes passed 37th-38th years of Victoria, 1873-1875. 2 v. 8°. *Quebec, C. F. Langlois*, 1874-75.

Querry (A.) Droit musulman. 2 v. 8°. *Paris, imprimerie nationale*, 1871-72.

Ram (James). Treatise on facts. 486 pp. 8°. *New York, Baker, Voorhis & co.* 1873.

Rattigan (W. H.) De jure personarum; treatise on the roman law of persons. 1 p. l. xiii, 346 pp. 8°. *London, Wildy & sons*, 1873.

——— Hindu law of adoption. xv, 95 pp. 8°. *London, Wildy & sons*, 1873.

Ravelet (Armand). Code manuel de la presse. 2e éd. 2 p. l. viii, 225 pp. 16°. *Paris, F. Didot frères, fils & cie.* 1872.

Rawle (William, *jr.*) Pennsylvania reports, 1823-1828. *See* **Sergeant** (Thomas) *and* **Rawle.**

Rawle (William Henry). Treatise on the law of covenants for title. 4th ed. xlvi, 754 pp. 8°. *Boston, Little, Brown, & co.* 1873.

Ray (John). Digest of the statutes of Louisiana, 1870. 2 v. 8°. *New Orleans, republican office*, 1870.

Recueil de jurisprudence commerciale du Havre, 1872-1874. v. 18-20. 8°. *Havre, A. Brindeau & compe.* 1872-74.

Redfield (Amasa A.) Law and practice of surrogates' courts [of the state of New York]. xxxix, 669 pp. 8°. *New York, Baker, Voorhis & co.* 1875.

——— Law of negligence. *See* **Shearman** (Thomas G.) *and* **Redfield.**

Redfield (Isaac F.) Law of railways. 5th ed. 2 v. c, 727 pp; lxxv, 755 pp. 8°. *Boston, Little, Brown, & co.* 1873.

——— Leading american cases upon the law of wills. lxiv, 778 pp. 8°. *Boston, Little, Brown, & co.* 1874.

Redman (Joseph Haworth). Treatise on the law of arbitrations and awards. xxiii, 328 pp. 8°. *London, Butterworths*, 1872.

Reed (John C.) Handbook of Georgia criminal law, 1872. 390 pp. 8°. *Macon, J. W. Burke & co.* 1873.

Reed (John C. *counsellor*). Suggestions for the management of law-suits. xxiv, 392 pp. 8°. *New York, J. Cockcroft & co.* 1875.

Rendu (Ambroise). Du jeu, du pari en droit romain et en droit français. 2 p. l. v, 486 pp. 8°. *Paris, Pichon-Lamy & Dewez*, 1870.

Répertoire de législation et de jurisprudence forestières, par m. Charles Deville. 1862-1869. v. 1-4. 8°. *Paris, bureau de la revue des eaux et forêts*, 1863-69.

——— Same, par m. Jules Bezou. 1870-1873. v. 5. 8°. *Paris, bureau de la revue des eaux et forêts*, 1873.

Reus y Garcia (José). Código de comercio de España, 1868. *See* **Gomez de la Serna** (Pedro) *and* **Reus y Garcia.**

——— Ley de enjuiciamiento civil. *See* **Manresa y Navarro** (José Maria), **Miquel** (Ignacio) *and* **Reus y Garcia.**

Revue critique de législation et de jurisprudence. 21e-22e année. Nouvelle série. v. 1-2. 8°. *Paris, Cotillon & fils*, [*etc.*] 1871-73.

Revue de législation ancienne et moderne. Année 1873. v. 3. 8°. *Paris, E. Thorin*, 1873.

Rhode Island (*State of*). General statutes, [1872]. xiii, 770 pp. 8°. *Cambridge, Riverside press*, 1872.

——— Public laws, sessions, jan. 1873-jan. 1875. 2 v. 8°. *Providence, printers to the state*, 1874-[75].

——— *Supreme court.* Reports of cases, v. 9-10, 1868-1874, by J. F. Tobey. 8°. *Providence & New York, Hammond, Angell & co.* [*etc.*] 1873-75.

Richardson (J. S. G.) Reports of cases in the supreme court of South Carolina, 1871-1873. v. 3-4. [New series]. 8°. *Columbia, S. C. state printers*, 1873-75.

Richardson (William Adams) *and* **Sanger** (George P.) General statutes of Massachusetts, 1860. 2d ed. 8°. *Boston, the commonwealth*, 1873.

——— ——— Same. Supplement, 1867-1870. 4 v. in 1. 8°. *Boston, the commonwealth*, [1867-70].

——— ——— Same. Supplement, 1860-1872. 2d ed. 8°. *Boston, the commonwealth*, 1873.

Rickards (George Kettilby). Statutes of Great Britain and Ireland. 32 & 33 Vict. 1868-9. v. 29. 4°. *London, G. E. Eyre & W. Spottiswoode*, 1869.

Riegger (*Ritter* Paul Joseph). Lecciones de disciplina eclesiástica, por Joaquin Lumbreras. v. 1. 8°. *Madrid, M. Calero*, 1838.

——— Same. Instituciones de jurisprudencia eclesiástica. v. 2-6. 8°. *Madrid, M. Calero*, [*etc.*] 1838-41.

Roberts (Clay). Magistrates' guide, and criminal code of Tennessee, [1874]. xxxiii,

Roberts (Clay)—continued. 17-440 pp. 8°. *Nashville, Wheeler, Marshall & Bruce,* [1875].

Robertson (David). Treatise on the law of personal succession. xiv, 503 pp. 8°. *Edinburgh, T. Clark,* 1836.

Robiano (Ceslaus Maria de). De jure ecclesiæ. viii, 260 pp. 8°. *Lovanii, Valinthout et socii,* [1864]. s.

Robinson (Christopher). Reports of cases in the court of queen's bench, [Ontario, 1870-1872]. v. 17-19. v. 30-32 of the series. 8°. *Toronto, H. Rowsell,* [*etc.*] 1871-73.

Robinson (Conway). Principles and practice of courts of justice. v. 7. 8°. *Richmond,* [*Va.*] *Woodhouse & Parham,* [*etc.*] 1874.

Roche (Henry Philip) *and* **Hazlitt** (William). Law and practice in bankruptcy. 2d ed. xxxix, 840 pp. 8°. *London, Stevens & Haynes,* 1873.

Roe (Edward T.) Preliminary proceedings in the courts of the United States. 105, iii pp. 8°. *Springfield,* [*Ill.*] *D. & J. B. Brown,* 1874.

Rollwagen (Frederick). N. Y. surrogate's court. [1873-1874]. Synopsis of testimony. 1 p. l. 200 pp. 8°. *New York, Lange, Little & co.* 1874.

——— Same. [1873-1874]. Papers, testimony, and trial. 3 v. 8°. *New York, D. Taylor,* 1874.

Roper (R. S. Donnison). Treatise on the revocation and republication of wills. 239 pp. 8°. *Philadelphia, for P. Byrne,* 1803.

Rorer (David). Treatise on the law of judicial sales. xxxi, 411 pp. 8°. *Chicago, Callaghan & co.* 1873.

Roscoe (Henry). Digest of the law of evidence in criminal cases. 7th am. ed. by G. Sharswood. li, [932]pp. 8°. *Philadelphia, T. & J. W. Johnson & co.* 1874.

Rowell (John W.) Reports of cases in the supreme court of Vermont, [1872-1874]. v. 1-2. [v. 45-46, Vermont reports]. 8°. *Montpelier, J. & J. M. Poland,* 1873-74.

Royall (William L.) Digest of the decisions of the supreme court of Virginia, [1844-1872]. vi, 472 pp. 8°. *New York, Diossy & co.* 1873.

Ruloff (Edward H.) Trial and execution, [Binghamton, N. Y. 1871]. 1 p. l. 19-80 pp. 4 pl. in text. 8°. *Philadelphia, Barclay & co.* [1871].

Runnells (John S.) Reports of cases in the supreme court of Iowa, [1873-1874]. v. 1-2.

Runnells (John S.)—continued. Being v. 38-39 of the series. 8°. *Des Moines, Mills & co.* 1875.

Russell (John A.) Treatise on mercantile agency. 2d ed. xvii, 300 pp. 8°. *London, H. Sweet,* [*etc.*] 1873.

Sandford (Lewis H.) Reports of cases in the court of chancery of the state of New York, [1843-1844]. v. 1. 8°. *New York, Banks & brothers,* 1873.

Sanger (George P.) General statutes of Massachusetts and supplements, 1860-1872. *See* **Richardson** (William A.) *and* **Sanger**.

——— United States statutes at large, 1871-1873. v. 17. 8°. *Boston, Little, Brown, & co.* 1873.

Sanz (Miguel Cayetano). Modo y forma de instruir las causas criminales. xx, 135 pp. sm. 4°. *Madrid, la hija de F. M. Dávila,* 1828.

Saunders (Thomas William). Law of orders of affiliation, and proceedings in bastardy. 6th ed. xiv, 206 pp. 12°. *London, H. Cox,* 1873.

Saussine (V.) *and* **Chevalet** (É.) Dictionnaire de législation et d' administration militaires. v. 1-2. A-L. 8°. *Paris, Berger-Levrault & cie.* 1873.

Sautayra (A.) Manuel pour les aspirans au grade de licencié en droit. v. 1-2 & 4-5. 16°. *Paris, Mansut fils,* 1836-39.

Sawyer (Lorenzo S. B.) Reports of cases in the circuit and district courts of the United States for the 9th circuit, [1870-1874]. v. 1-2. 8°. *San Francisco, A. L. Bancroft & co.* 1873-75.

Saxton (William W.) Excise law of state of New York, 1873. 92 pp. 12°. *Albany, Parker & Herrick,* 1873.

Sayles (John). Notes to the Texas reports, [1846-1869]. 196 pp. 8°. *St. Louis, W. J. Gilbert,* [1873].

——— Treatise on the practice of courts of Texas. 2d ed. 1 p. l. 837 pp. 8°. *Houston, Texas, E. H. Cushing,* 1875.

Schoeppe (Paul). Murder trial, 1869. 61 pp. 8°. *Carlisle,* [*Pa.*] *herald office,* [1869].

Schott (*Dr.* Hermann). Der obligatorische vertrag unter abwesenden. ii, 256 pp. 8°. *Heidelberg, J. C. B. Mohr,* 1873. s.

Schouler (James). Treatise on the law of personal property. lii, 766 pp. 8°. *Boston, Little, Brown, & co.* 1873.

Schouler (James)—continued.

——— Treatise on the law of the domestic relations. 2d ed. lxxii, 719 pp. 8°. *Boston, Little, Brown, & co.* 1874.

Scott (Robert N.) Digest of the military laws of the United States. 510 pp. 8°. *Philadelphia, J. B. Lippincott & co.* 1873.

Scottish jurist, [oct. 1870–nov. 1873]. v. 43–45 & pts. 1–5, v. 46, in 3 v. 4°. *Edinburgh, T. & A. Constable,* 1871–73.

Sedgwick (Theodore). Treatise on the interpretation of statutory and constitutional law. 2d ed. by J. N. Pomeroy. xlviii, 692 pp. 8°. *New York, Baker, Voorhis & co.* 1874.

——— Treatise on the measure of damages. 6th ed. by H. D. Sedgwick. lxxix, 827 pp. 8°. *New York, Baker, Voorhis & co.* 1874.

Seney (George E.) Code of civil procedure of Ohio, [1874]. 2d ed. viii, 872 pp. 8°. *Cincinnati, R. Clarke & co.* 1874.

Sergeant (Thomas). Land laws of Pennsylvania. 203 pp. 8°. *Philadelphia, J. Kay, jun. & brother,* 1838.

——— *and* **Rawle** (William, *jr.*) Reports of cases in the supreme court of Pennsylvania, [1823–1828]. v. 10–17. 3d ed. 8°. *Philadelphia, Kay & brother,* 1873–75.

Sessions (H. C.) Manual for county clerks, sheriffs and constables, [for Michigan]. 181 pp. 16°. *Detroit, Richmond & Backus,* 1873.

Shearman (Thomas G.) *and* **Redfield** (Amasa A.) Treatise on the law of negligence. 3d ed. lxi, 759 pp. 8°. *New York, Baker, Voorhis & co.* 1874.

Sheffield (William P.) *and others.* General statutes of Rhode Island, 1872. 8°. *Cambridge, Riverside press,* 1872.

Shelford (Leonard). Law of railways. 4th ed. by W. C. Glen. 2 v. lxxxviii, 724 pp; xxxii, 909 pp. 8°. *London, Butterworths,* 1869.

Shepherd (J. W.) Reports of cases in the supreme court of Alabama, 1873. v. 1. [v. 49, Alabama reports, new series]. 8°. *Montgomery, Ala.* [*etc.*] *J. White,* 1875.

Shinn (William A.) National bankruptcy register digest, 1867–1874. *See* **Moses** (Raphael J. *jr.*) *and* **Shinn.**

Shirley (John M.) Reports of cases in the supreme court of New Hampshire, [1866–1874]. v. 3–6. [v. 51–54, New Hampshire reports]. 8°. *Concord, B. W. Sanborn & co.* [*etc.*] 1873–75.

Sickels (Hiram E.) Reports of cases in the commission of appeals of the state of New York, 1872–1874. v. 6, 9 & 12 [of Sickels's reports. v. 51, 54 & 57, New York reports]. 8°. *New York & Albany, Banks & brothers,* [*etc.*] 1873–75.

——— Reports of cases in the court of appeals of the state of New York, 1871–1874. v. 4–5, 7–8, 10–11, & 13–14 [of Sickels's reports. v. 49–50, 52–53, 55–56, & 58–59, New York reports]. 8°. *New York & Albany, Banks & brothers,* [*etc.*] 1873–75.

Simmons (James). Digest of Wisconsin reports, 1868 to 1874. v. 2. xlii, 648 pp. 8°. *Albany, W. Gould & son,* 1874.

Simmons (*Capt.* Thomas Frederick). Constitution and practice of courts martial. By F. T. Simmons. 6th ed. xvi, 544 pp. 8°. *London, J. Murray,* 1873.

Simonds (William Edgar). Law of design patents to 1874. ix, 216 pp. 8°. *New York, Baker, Voorhis & co.* 1874.

——— Manual of patent law. 256 pp. 12°. *Hartford, author,* 1874.

Simrall (G. H.) Mississippi reports, v. 49–50, 1873–1874. *See* **Harris** (G. E.) *and* **Simrall.**

Skidmore (Walter A.) Revised statutes of the United States, [1873], relating to mineral lands and mining. 114 pp. 8°. *San Francisco, S. Whitney & co.* 1875.

Smith (Abram D.) Reports of cases in the supreme court of Wisconsin, 1853–1860. v. 1–2, 4 & 7–11. Republished by W. F. Vilas and E. E. Bryant. In 7 v. [v. 1–2, 4 & 7–11, Wisconsin reports]. 8°. *Chicago, Callaghan & co.* 1873–75.

——— Same. [1854–1856]. v. 3 & 5. Republished by L. S. Dixon. [v. 3 & 5, Wisconsin reports]. 8°. *Chicago, Callaghan & co.* 1874–75.

Smith (Edwin B.) Reports of cases in the supreme court of Maine, [1867–1874]. v. 1–3. v. 61–63, Maine reports. 8°. *Portland, Loring, Short & Harmon,* [*etc.*] 1874–75.

Smith (Josiah W.) Manual of equity jurisprudence. 11th ed. 1 p. l. xxxviii, 540 pp. 12°. *London, Stevens & sons,* 1873.

Smith (Persifer Frazer). Pennsylvania state reports. Cases in the supreme court, 1871–1874. v. 19–26. [v. 69–76, Pennsylvania state reports]. 8°. *Philadelphia, Kay & brother,* 1873–75.

Smith (Richard Horton). Chancery reports, 1862–1875. *See* **De Gex** (J. P.) **Jones** (H. Cadman), *and* **Smith.**

Smith (William R.) Reports of decisions in the supreme court of Alabama, [1820–1839. Condensed]. v. 1–5. 8°. *Tuskaloosa, Ala W. R. Smith,* [*etc.*] 1870.

Sontag (*Dr.* Karl Richard). Die redactionsversehen des gesetzgebers insbesondere auf strafrechtlichem gebiet. 2 p. l. 66 pp. 8°. *Freiburg in Br., F. Wagner,* 1874. s.

Sourdat (Auguste). Traité de la responsabilité. 2e éd. 2 v. xv, 715 pp; 2 p. l. 640 pp. 8°. *Paris, Cosse, Marchal & Billard,* 1872.

South Carolina (*Province of*). Acts passed 1733–1736. 60 pp. fol. *Charles-Town, L. Timothy,* 1736.

[*With* TROTT (N.) Laws of South-Carolina, v. 2].

——— Same, 1736–1739. 162 pp. ms. fol.

[*With* TROTT (N.) Laws of South-Carolina, v. 2].

——— Same, 1740–1742. 3–139 pp. fol. [*Charles-Town, L. Timothy,* 1742].

——— Laws, and charters, 1663–1734, by N. Trott. 2 v. fol. *Charles-Town, L. Timothy,* 1736.

outh Carolina (*State of*). Acts, passed sept. and oct. 1776; [march], 1784; march, 1785; march, 1786; march, 1787; feb. 1788; feb. 1790; feb. 1791; dec. 1791; dec. 1792; dec. 1793; april, 1794; nov. and dec. 1795; dec. 1796; dec. 1797; dec. 1798; dec. 1799. 17 v. in 3. fol. *Charlestown, P. Timothy,* [*etc.* 1776–]1800.

——— Same, passed dec. 1823. 8°. *Columbia, D. & J. M. Faust,* 1824.

——— Same, passed session 1871–1872; session 1872–1873; special session 1873 and session of 1873–74; session of 1874–75. 4 v. 8°. *Columbia, state printers,* 1872–75.

[Forming pp. 1–1026 of v. 15, Statutes at large].

——— Constitution, and acts, 1868, with military orders. [241] pp. 8°. *Columbia, printer to the state,* 1868.

——— Evidence taken by the committee of investigation, 1868–69. 1 p. l. 718 pp. 8°. *Columbia, printer to the state,* 1870.

——— Public laws, 1694–1790, by J. F. Grimké. 4°. *Philadelphia, R. Aitken & son,* 1790.

——— Resolutions passed nov. and dec. 1791; jan. and feb. 1791; nov. and dec. 1792; dec. 1793; april and may, 1794; dec. 1795; dec. 1796; nov. and dec. 1797; dec. 1798; dec. 1799. 10 v. in 1. fol. [*Charleston, T. B. Bowen,etc.* 1792–1800].

South Carolina (*State of*)—continued.

——— Revised statutes. [By D. T. Corbin, 1872]. [1137] pp. 8°. *Columbia, state printers,* 1873.

——— *Supreme court.* Reports of cases, v. 3–4, new series, 1871–1873, by J. S. G. Richardson. 8°. *Columbia, S. C. state printers,* 1873–75.

Southern law review. Jan 1873–oct. 1874. v. 2–3. 8°. *Nashville, Roberts & Purvis,* 1873–74.

Spain. Código de comercio, 1868, por Pedro Gomez de la Serna y José Reus y Garcia. 5ta ed. 8°. *Madrid, J. Morales,* 1869.

——— El código penal, 1850, por Joaquin Francisco Pacheco. 4a ed. 8°. *Madrid, M. Tello,* 1870.

——— Same. Apéndice, por Jo é Gonzalez y Serrano. 8°. *Madrid, M. Tello,* 1870.

——— Coleccion legislativa de España. 1872. v. 108–109. 8°. *Madrid, ministerio de gracia y justicia,* 1872.

——— Prontuario jurídico, 1834–1842. 3 v. 16°. *Madrid, Rios,* [1839–]44.

Spalding (Hugh Mortimer). Practice and forms in justices' courts for Indiana. 797 pp. 8°. *Cincinnati, Wilstach, Baldwin & co.* 1875.

——— Practice and forms in justices' courts for Kansas. 832 pp. 8°. *Topeka, G. W. Crane,* 1875.

——— Practice and forms in justices' courts for Ohio. 828 pp. 8°. *Cincinnati, Wilstach, Baldwin & co.* 1875.

——— Township officers' guide for Kansas. Stereotyped ed. 78 pp. 8°. *Topeka, Kansas, G. W. Crane,* [1873].

——— Same. 2d ed. 1 p. l. 5–83 pp. 8°. *Topeka, Kans. G. W. Crane,* [1874].

Speciale Costarelli (Martino). Legislazioni comparate al codice penale italiano. 2a ed. 1 p. l. xxiv, 324 pp. obl. fol. *Catania, M. Barbagallo,* 1868.

Spencer (James C.) New York superior court reports, 1871–1875. *See* **Jones** (Samuel) *and* **Spencer.**

Spencer (William A.) Reports of cases in the supreme court of Minnesota, [1871–1874], v. 8–9 & 11. [v. 17–18 & 20, Minnesota reports]. 8°. *St. Paul, W. S. Combs,* 1873–75.

Spooner (Philip L.) Reports of cases in the supreme court of Wisconsin, 1860–1862, v. 1–4. Republished by W. F. Vilas and E.

Spooner (Philip L.)—continued. E. Bryant. [v. 12-15, Wisconsin reports]. 8°. *Chicago, Callaghan & co.* 1873.

Spring (Arthur). Life and trials, [Philadelphia, 1853]. 5-109 pp. 8°. *Philadelphia, T. B. Peterson & brothers,* [1853].

Stanton (Richard H.) Manual for executors in Kentucky. 2d ed. 1 p. l xii, 227 pp. 12°. *Cincinnati, R. Clarke & co.* 1875.

——— Treatise on the law relating to justices of the peace, in Kentucky. 3d ed. xxix, 854 pp. 8°. *Cincinnati, R. Clarke & co.* 1875.

Sterling (James Hutchison). Lectures on the philosophy of law. 1 p. l. v, 139 pp. 8°. *London, Longmans,* 1873.

Stevenson (John). Tryal, 1759, for murder. 64 pp. 8°. *Middlewich, J. Schofield,* [1759]?

Stiles (Edward H.) Digest of decisions of the supreme court of Iowa, 1839-1872. *See* **Withrow** (Thomas F.) *and* **Stiles.**

——— Reports of cases in the supreme court of Iowa, [1871-1873]. v. 12-16. Being v. 33-37 of the series. 8°. *Ottumwa, the reporter,* 1873-75.

Stillé (Moreton, *m. d.*) Medical jurisprudence. *See* **Wharton** (Francis, *ll. d.*) *and* **Stillé.**

Stockett (J. Shaaff). Reports of cases in the court of appeals of Maryland, 1872-1874. v. 10-15. [v. 36-41, Maryland reports]. 8°. *Baltimore, J. Murphy & co.* [*etc.*] 1873-75.

Storer (Bellamy, *jr.*) Cincinnati superior court reporter, 1870-1871. *See* **Taft** (Charles P.) *and* **Storer.**

Story (Joseph, *ll. d.*) Commentaries on equity jurisprudence. 11th ed. by F. V. Balch. 2 v. 2 p. l. cvii, 877 pp; 1 p. l. v, 971 pp. 8°. *Boston, Little, Brown, & co.* 1873.

——— Commentaries on the constitution of the United States. 4th ed. by T. M. Cooley. 2 v. xxxii, 752 pp; 737 pp. 8°. *Boston, Little, Brown, & co.* 1873.

——— Commentaries on the law of agency. 8th ed. by N. St. J. Green. xl, 706 pp. 8°. *Boston, Little, Brown, & co.* 1874.

——— Pleadings in civil actions. 2d ed. by B. L. Oliver, jun. 709 pp. 8°. *Boston, Carter & Hendee,* 1829.

Story (William W.) Treatise on the law of contracts. 5th ed. by M. M. Bigelow. 2 v. xxii, 813 pp; 2 p. l. 859 pp. 8°. *Boston, Little, Brown, & co.* 1874.

Sugden (Edward Burtenshaw, *baron St. Leonards*). Treatise of the law of vendors and purchasers. 10th ed. 3 v. 8°. *London, S. Sweet,* 1839.

——— Same. 8th am. ed. By J. C. Perkins. 2 v. clxxv, 606 pp; 755 pp. 8°. *Philadelphia, Kay & brother,* 1873.

Swan (Joseph R.) Treatise on the law relating to justices of the peace and constables in Ohio. 10th ed. xxviii, 1002 pp. 8°. *Cincinnati, R. Clarke & co.* 1875.

Swan (Robert). Trial, Washington county, [Md.] 1853. 139 pp. 8°. *Hagerstown, Heard & Williams,* 1853.

Sweden. Loi pénale, 1864. 124 pp. 8°. *Stockholm, P. A. Norstedt & fils,* 1866.

Switzerland. Amtliche sammlung der bundesgeseze und verordnungen der schweizerischen eidgenossenschaft, [1872-1874]. v. 11. 8°. *Bern, Stämpflische buchdrukerei,* 1874.

Taft (Charles P.) *and* **Storer** (Bellamy, *jr.*) Cincinnati superior court reporter, 1870-1871. v. 1. 8°. *Cincinnati, R. Clarke & co.* 1872.

——— *and* **Taft** (Peter R.) Cincinnati superior court reporter, 1872-1873. v. 2. 8°. *Cincinnati, R. Clarke & co.* 1873.

Tamlyn (John). Treatise on the law of evidence. 2d ed. [xxviii], 386 pp. 12°. *London, W. Benning & co.* 1846.

Tardieu (Ambroise). Étude médico-légale sur l'infanticide. viii, 342 pp. 3 col. pl. 8°. *Paris, J. B. Baillière & fils,* 1868.

Tartara (Jules). Nouveau code des bris et naufrages. 3 p. l. xxii, 443 pp. 2 l. 16°. *Paris, E. Lacroix,* 1874.

Tartarin (Éd.) Traité de l'occupation. 234 pp. 8°. *Paris, Marescq aîné,* 1873.

Taylor (Alfred Swayne). Manual of medical jurisprudence. 7th am. ed. by J. J. Reese. 879 pp. 8°. *Philadelphia, H. C. Lea,* 1873.

Taylor (John N.) Treatise on the american law of landlord and tenant. 6th ed. lxiii, 769 pp. 8°. *Boston, Little, Brown, & co.* 1873.

Taylor (John Pitt). Treatise on the law of evidence. 6th ed. 2 v. cxx, 847 pp; 1 p. l. 849-1797 pp. 8°. *London, W. Maxwell & son,* 1872.

Templin (J. D.) Abridgment of decisions by the supreme court of Iowa, [1839-1872]. v. 1. viii, 739 pp. 8°. *Des Moines, state printing co.* 1874.

Tennessee (*State of*). Acts, 2d session, 36th assembly, 1869–70; called session, 37th assembly, 1872; 38th assembly, 1873; 39th assembly, 1875. 4 v. 8°. *Nashville, printers to the state*, 1870–75.

——— Criminal code and decisions, 1858–1874, by J. M. Quarles. 8°. *Nashville, Tavel, Eastman & Howell*, 1874.

——— *Supreme court.* Index to reports, 1791–1872, by B. Hunter and W. G. Myer. 16°. *St. Louis, W. J. Gilbert*, 1875.

——— ——— Reports of cases, 1871–1872, by J. B. Heiskell. v. 3–7. 8°. *Nashville, printers to the state*, [*etc.*] 1872–74.

Terrell (Alexander W.) *and* **Walker** (Alexander S.) Cases in the supreme court of Texas, 1872–1874. v. 1–3. [v. 38–40, Texas reports]. 8°. *Austin, Cardwell & Walker*, [*etc.*] 1874–75.

Texas (*State of*). Digest of laws. By G. W. Paschal. 3d ed. [1754–1872]. 2 v. xliii, 1085 pp; lvi, 1087–1667 pp. 8°. *Washington, W. H. & O. H. Morrison*, 1873.

——— Same. 4th ed. to 1874. 2 v. xlv, 1085 pp; [924] pp. 8°. *Washington, W. H. & O. H. Morrison*, 1874.

——— General laws, passed 13th legislature, 1873. 8°. *Austin, state printer*, 1873.

——— *Supreme court.* Digest of decisions to 1873, by G. W. Paschal. v. 2–3. 8°. *Washington, W. H. & O. H. Morrison*, [*etc*] 1874–75.

——— ——— Notes to cases, 1846–1869, by J. Sayles. 8°. *St. Louis, W. J. Gilbert*, [1873].

——— ——— Reports of cases, v. 34–37, 1862–1873, by E. M. Wheelock. 8°. *Austin & Houston, journal office*, [*etc.*] 1872–74.

——— ——— Same, v. 38–40, 1872–1874, by A. W. Terrell and A. S. Walker. 8°. *Austin, Cardwell & Walker*, [*etc.*] 1874–75.

Thayer (Israel, *jr.*) **Thayer** (Isaac), *and* **Thayer** (Nelson). Trial for murder. [1825]. 2d ed. 1 p. l. 32 pp. 8°. *New York, J. M'Cleland*, [1825].

Thery (—). Traité de l'expropriation. *See* **Caudaveine** (— de) *and* **Thery**.

Thompson (Isaac Grant). American reports, [1868–1874]. v. 7–15. 8°. *Albany, J. D. Parsons, jr.* 1873–75.

——— Digest of The american reports, v. 1–12, 1870–1875. xv, 3–410 pp. 8°. *Albany, J. D. Parsons, jr.* 1875.

——— *and* **Cook** (Robley D.) Cases in the supreme court of New York, 1873 to 1874. v. 1–4. 8°. *Albany, J. D. Parsons, jr.* 1874.

Thompson (Seymour D.) Bankrupt act of 1867, with amendments. 74 pp. 8°. *Saint Louis, Soule, Thomas & Wentworth*, 1874.

——— Same. 2d ed. 61 pp. 8°. *Saint Louis, Soule, Thomas & Wentworth*, 1874.

——— Select american cases on the law of self defence, 1790–1873. *See* **Horrigan** (L. B.) *and* **Thompson.**

Thoms (George Hunter). Treatise on judicial factors. xxiv, 396, cxxxi pp. 8°. *Edinburgh, Bell & Bradfute*, 1859.

Tichborne (*Sir* Roger Charles). Trial for forgery and perjury, 1873–1874. *See* **Castro** (Thomas).

Tichborne trial: comprising autograph letters in fac-simile. [*anon.*] 1 p. l. 16 pp. 8°. *London, S. Tinsley*, 1874.

Tiffany (Alexander R.) Treatise on justices of the peace in Michigan. 5th ed. By A. Howell. vii, 892 pp. 8°. *Adrian, C. Humphrey*, 1873.

——— Same. 6th ed. vii, 933 pp. 8°. *Adrian, C. Humphrey*, 1875.

Tobey (John F.) Reports of cases in the supreme court of Rhode Island, [1868–1874]. v. 1–2. [v. 9–10, Rhode Island reports]. 8°. *Providence & New York, Hammond, Angell & co.* [*etc.*] 1873–75.

Tolhausen (Alexander). Synopsis of the patent laws of various countries. 2 p. l. 31 pp. 12°. *London, Taylor & Francis*, 1857. s.

Tomlins (*Sir* Thomas Edlyne). Digested index to the term reports, 1785–1800. 2d ed. xl, 394 pp. 8°. *London*, 1800.

Tracy (William). Handbook of law for business men. 3d ed. [716] pp. 8°. *New York, D. Appleton & co.* 1874.

Trémoulet (*M.*) Le régime hypothécaire et le sens commun. 2 p. l. vii, 226 pp. 1 l. 2 charts folded. 8°. *Paris, Cotillon*, 1860.

Troplong (Raymond Théodore). De la prescription. 3e éd. 2 v. 2 p. l. xv, 604 pp. 1 l; 2 p. l. 670 pp. 1 l. 8°. *Paris, C. Hingray*, 1838.

——— Des priviléges et hypothèques. 3e éd. v. 2–4. 8°. *Paris, C. Hingray*, 1838.

——— Priviléges et hypothèques. 2 p. l. 464, clix pp. 8°. *Paris, C. Hingray*, 1856.

Trott (Nicholas). Laws of the province of South-Carolina, [1692–1734], and charters, [1663 & 1665]. 2 v. 3 p. l. lxii, 473 pp; 477–624, 59 pp. 14 l. 20 pp. fol. *Charles-Town, L. Timothy*, 1736.

Truman (J. Henry). Railway reports, 1872-1873. *See* **American** railway reports.

Tucker (Gideon J.) Reports of cases in the surrogate's court of the county of New York, [1864-1869]. v. 1. ix, 517 pp. 8°. *New York, Banks & brothers*, 1870.

Tudor (Owen Davies). Leading cases on mercantile and maritime law. Ed. by G. Sharswood. 2 v. xxxvii, 674 pp; iv, 675-1330 pp. 8°. *Philadelphia, T. & J. W. Johnson & co.* 1873.

Tulloch (*Capt.* Alexander Bruce). Elementary lectures on military law. 2d ed. 100 pp. 8°. *London, W. Mitchell & co.* 1873.

Turkey. Législation ottomane, ou recueil des lois, 1839-1870, par Aristarchi bey. 2 v. 8°. *Constantinople, frères Nicolaïdes*, [*etc.*] 1873-74.

Tuttle (Charles A.) Reports of cases in the supreme court of California, 1871-1875. v. 19-27. [v. 41-49, California reports]. 8°. *Sacramento & San Francisco, state printer*, [*etc.*] 1873-75.

Tyler (Ransom H.) Treatise on the law of boundaries and fences. 596 pp. 8°. *Albany, W. Gould & son*, 1874.

——— Treatise on the law of usury. 833 pp. 8°. *Albany, W. Gould & son*, 1873.

Ulman (H. Charles). Trow's legal directory of the United States, 1875. 677 pp. 8°. *New York, J. F. Trow*, [*etc.* 1875].

Underhill (Arthur). Law of torts. xxiv, 212 pp. 12°. *London, Butterworths*, 1873.

Underwood (William H.) Statutes of Illinois, [as revised, 1871-1872], construed. v. 1. 5-392 pp. interleaved. 8°. *St. Louis, W. J. Gilbert*, 1873.

——— Same. v. 1-2 in 1. 5-392 pp; 9-503 pp. 8°. *St. Louis, W. J. Gilbert*, 1873-75.

United States. Bankrupt law to june 22, 1874, by O. F. Bump. 8°. *New York, Baker, Voorhis & co.* 1874.

——— Bankrupt laws, 1867-1874, by S. D. Thompson. 8°. *Saint Louis, Soule, Thomas & Wentworth*, 1874.

——— Same. 2d ed. 8°. *Saint Louis, Soule, Thomas & Wentworth*, 1874.

——— *Circuit courts. 2d circuit.* Reports of cases, 1870-1875, by S. Blatchford. v. 10-12. 8°. *New York, Baker, Voorhis & co.* 1873-75.

——— ——— *5th circuit.* Reports of cases, 1869-1874, by W. B. Woods. v. 1. 8°. *Chicago, Callaghan & co.* 1875.

United States—continued.

——— ——— *8th circuit.* Reports of cases, 1871-1873, by J. F. Dillon. v. 2. 8°. *Davenport, Iowa, Day, Egbert & Fidlar*, 1873.

——— *Circuit and district courts. 7th circuit.* Reports of cases, 1851-1873, by J. H. Bissell. v. 1-4. 8°. *Chicago, Callaghan & co.* 1873-75.

——— ——— *9th circuit.* Reports of cases, 1870-1874, by L. S. B. Sawyer. v. 1-2. 8°. *San Francisco, A. L. Bancroft & co.* 1873-75.

——— ——— *District of Iowa.* Abstract of judgments and decrees, 1845-1874, by H. K. Love. 8°. *Dubuque, Palmer, Winall & co.* 1874.

——— *Court of claims.* Reports of cases, 1871. v. 7, [new series], by C. C. Nott and S. H. Huntington. 8°. *Washington, government printing office*, 1873.

——— ——— Same, 1872-1873, v. 8-9, [new series], by C. C. Nott and A. Hopkins. 8°. *Washington, government printing office*, 1874.

——— ——— Rules, 1874. 46 pp. 8°. *Washington, government printing office*, 1874.

——— *Department of the interior.* (*General land office*). Decisions of the commissioner, and of the secretary, under the mining statutes of 1866, 1870, and 1872, by H. N. Copp. 8°. *San Francisco, A. L. Bancroft & co.* 1874.

——— ——— ——— Public land laws, and decisions, 1869-1875, by H. N. Copp. 8°. *Washington, the compiler*, 1875.

——— *Department of justice.* Catalogue of law books of the department, 1873. 251 pp. 8°. *Washington, government printing office*, 1873.

——— ——— Register of the department. 4th ed. 1874. 231 pp. 8°. *Washington, government printing office*, 1874.

——— ——— (*Attorney general*). Official opinions of the attorneys general. Edited by A. J. Bentley. [1869-1875]. v. 13-14. 8°. *Washington, government printing office*, 1873-75.

——— Digest of reports and statutes, 1872-1874, by B. Vaughan Abbott. v. 6. 8°. *New York, Diossy & co.* 1874.

——— Digest of the military laws, by R. N. Scott. 8°. *Philadelphia, J. B. Lippincott & co.* 1873.

——— *District courts. 2d circuit.* Reports of cases, 1871-1873, by R. D. Benedict. v. 5-6. 8°. *New York, Baker, Voorhis & co.* 1874-75.

——— *District court of Maine.* Reports of cases, 1839-1849, by E. H. Daveis. v. 2, [or

United States—continued.
Ware's decisions]. 2d ed. 8°. *Portland, Loring, Short & Harmon*, 1873.

——— *District court of Maine and Massachusetts.* Reports of cases, 1853-1866, by G. F. Emery. v. 3, [of Ware's decisions]. 8°. *Portland, Loring, Short & Harmon*, 1874.

——— *Federal courts.* Digest of decisions, 1868-1873, by F. C. Brightly. v. 2. 2d ed. 8°. *Philadelphia, Kay & brother*, 1873.

——— ——— Reports of patent cases, 1869-1873, by S. S. Fisher. v. 5-6, [of Fisher's patent cases]. 8°. *Cincinnati, R. Clarke & co.* 1874.

——— *Mixed commission of american and british claims.* Arguments for the United States, 1871-1873, by R. S. Hale. 2 v. 8°. [*Washington & Newport, Judd & Detweiler, etc.* 1871-73].

——— Mining laws to 1875, by W. A. Skidmore. 8°. *San Francisco, S. Whitney & co.* 1875.

——— *Post office department.* Postal laws, by W. M. Ireland and J. M McGrew. 434 pp. 8°. *Washington, government printing office*, 1873.

——— Revision of the United States statutes, [1789-1873], as drafted by the commissioners. 2 v. 2 p. l. cxxx, 1232 pp; 2 p. l. cxxix, 1233-2668 pp. 4°. *Washington, government printing office*, 1872.

——— Same. Revised statutes of the United States, 1873. 2 p. l. ix, 1437 pp. 8°. *Washington, government printing office*, 1875.

——— Same. Relating to the district of Columbia and post roads, with the public treaties. [1468] pp. 8°. *Washington, government printing office*, 1875.

——— Statutes at large, from march, 1871, to march, 1873. By G. P. Sanger. v. 17. 8°. *Boston, Little, Brown, & co.* 1873.

——— Same, from dec. 1873, to march, 1875. v. 18. 8°. *Washington, government printing office*, 1875.

——— *Supreme court.* Condensed reports of cases, 1855-1859, by S. F. Miller. v. 1-3. 8°. *Washington, W. H. & O. H. Morrison*, 1874-75.

——— ——— Patent cases, 1861-1874, by C. S. Whitman. 8°. *Washington, W. H. & O. H. Morrison*, 1875.

——— ——— Reports of cases, 1871-1874, by J. W. Wallace. v. 14-21. 8°. *Washington, W. H. & O. H. Morrison*, 1873-75.

——— ——— Rules, [1874]. 70 pp. 8°. *Washington, government printing office*, 1874.

United States—continued.
——— *Supreme and circuit courts.* Reports of patent cases, 1821-1850, by W. H. Fisher. v. 1. 8°. *Cincinnati, R. Clarke & co.* 1873.

——— *Supreme, circuit and district courts.* Table of cases affirmed, reversed, cited, etc. 1781-1873, by F. P. Murray. 8°. *Albany, Weed, Parsons & co.* 1873.

——— *Treasury department.* Duties on imports, 1874, by L. Heyl. 8°. *Washington, W. H. & O. H. Morrison*, 1874.

——— ——— (*Internal revenue office*). Internal revenue laws, 1873. xix, 203 pp. 8° *Washington, government printing office*, 1873.

United States digest, first series, 1658-1869. 2d ed. by B. V. Abbott. v. 1-9. 8°. *Boston, Little, Brown, & co.* 1874-75.

——— Same, 1872-1874, by B. V. Abbott. New series. v. 3-5. 8°. *Boston, Little, Brown, & co.* 1873-75.

United States jurist, 1873. v. 3. 8°. *Washington, W. H. & O. H. Morrison*, 1873.

Vanier (J. R.) Questions sur les servitudes. 2 p. l. 227 pp. 8°. [*Poitiers, A. Dupré*], 1871.

Van Santvoord (George). Treatise on pleading in civil actions under the New York code of procedure. New [3d] ed. by N. C. Moak. xli, 1019 pp. 8°. *Albany, J. D. Parsons, jr.* 1873.

Vermont (*State of*). Acts and resolves, 2d biennial session, 1872; 3d biennial session, 1874; special session, jan. 1875. 3 v. in 2. 8°. [*Montpelier, J. & J. M. Poland*, [*etc.*] 1873-[75].

——— *Supreme court.* Reports of cases, v. 45-46, 1872-1874, by J. W. Rowell. 8°. *Montpelier, J. & J. M. Poland*, 1873-74.

Vesine Larue (Edgar de). Essai sur l'avortement. 84 pp. 8°. *Paris, A. Delahaye*, 1866.

Villequez (François Ferdinand). Du droit de destruction des animaux malfaisants. xxviii, 488 pp. 12°. *Paris, L. Hachette & cie.* 1867.

Virgin (William Wirt). Maine civil officer. By B. D. Verrill. 3d ed. xxxiv, 624 pp. 12°. *Portland, Loring, Short & Harmon*, 1874.

——— Reports of cases in the supreme court of Maine, [1872]. v. 9. [v. 60, Maine reports]. 8°. *Portland, Loring, Short & Harmon*, 1873.

Virginia (*Colony of*). Acts, [nov. 1769; july, 1771; feb. 1772]. 3 v. fol. *Williamsburg, printer to the colony*, 1770-72.

Virginia (*State of*). Acts passed oct. 1793. fol. *Richmond, printer for the public*, 1794.

——— Same, session of 1872–73. 8°. *Richmond, sup. of public printing*, 1873.

——— *Supreme court.* Digest of decisions, 1844–1872, by W. L. Royall. 8°. *New York, Diossy & co.* 1873.

——— ——— Reports of cases, 1872–1874, by P. R. Grattan, v. 22–24. 8°. *Richmond, superintendent of public printing*, 1873–75.

——— Third edition of the code, to jan. 1, 1874. By G. W. Munford. xix, 1547 pp. 8°. *Richmond, J. E. Goode*, 1873.

Vives y Cebriá (Pedro Nolasco). Traduccion al castellano de los usages y demás derechos de Cataluña. 2a ed. 5 v. 8°. *Barcelona, libreria del plus ultra*, 1861–67.

Voorhies (Albert). Revised civil code of Louisiana, 1874. 702 pp. 8°. *New Orleans, B. Bloomfield & co.* 1875.

Vroom (Garret D. W.) Reports of cases [in] the supreme court, and at law in the court of errors, of New Jersey, [1872–1873]. v. 1. [v. 36, New Jersey law reports] 8°. *Trenton, W. S. & E. W. Sharp*, 1874.

Vroom (Peter D.) Reports of cases in the supreme court and the court of errors of New Jersey, [1867–1869 & 1870–1872]. v. 4 & 6. [v. 33 & 35, New Jersey law reports]. 8°. *Trenton, W. T. Nicholson*, [*etc.*] 1870–73.

Wade (John). Cabinet lawyer. 24th ed. [*anon.*] xxxi, 870 pp. 16°. *London, Longmans*, 1874.

Wade (William P.) Treatise on the law of taxation, of Missouri. 303 pp. 8°. *Kansas city, Mo. Ramsey, Millett & Hudson*, 1874.

Wait (William). Digest of New York reports, 1869 to 1872. 3 p. l. 873 pp. 8°. *Albany, W. Gould & son*, 1873.

——— Practice in all the courts of record in the state of New York. v. 2–6. 8°. *Albany, W. Gould & sons*, [*etc.*] 1873–75.

Walker (Alexander S.) Texas reports, v. 38–40, 1872–1874. *See* **Terrell** (Alexander W.) *and* **Walker.**

Walker (Timothy, *ll. d.*) Introduction to american law. 6th ed. by J. B. Walker. xxiv, 795 pp. 8°. *Boston, Little, Brown, & co.* 1874.

Wallace (Henry E.) Philadelphia reports, v. 6 & 8, 1865–1868 & 1870–1871. 8°. *Philadelphia, J. B. Hunter*, [*etc.*] 1870–73.

Wallace (John William). Cases in the supreme court of the United States, dec. term, 1871–oct. term, 1874. v. 14–21. 8°. *Washington, W. H. & O. H. Morrison*, 1873–75.

Ware (Ashur). Decisions in the U. S. district court of Maine, 1839–1849. *See* **Daveis** (Edward H.)

——— Same. In the U. S. district court of Maine and Massachusetts. 1853–1866. *See* **Emery** (George F.)

Warren (Samuel). Introduction to law studies. Edited by W. M. Scott. viii, 509 pp. 8°. *Albany, W. C. Little & co.* 1872.

Washburn (Emory). Treatise on the american law of easements and servitudes. 3d ed. xxxix, 776 pp. 8°. *Boston, Little, Brown, & co.* 1873.

Waterman (Thomas W.) Treatise on the law of trespass. 2 v. xxxvi, 699 pp; xxxv, 713 pp. 8°. *New York, Baker, Voorhis & co.* 1875.

Watson (James H.) Lawyers' pocket diary, for 1874. 65 pp. 1881. 16°. *Albany, J. H. Watson*, 1874.

Webb (Edmund F.) Railroad laws of Maine, [1831–1875]. 5–720 pp. 8°. *Portland, Dresser, McLellan & co.* 1875.

Webb (W. C.) Reports of cases in the supreme court of Kansas, 1871–1874. v. 3–8. [v. 8–13, Kansas reports]. 8°. *Topeka, Kansas, public printer*, [*etc.*] 1873–75.

Weekly (The) notes: 1873–1874. 2 v. 4°. *London, W. Clowes & son*, [1873–74].

Wells (Francis) *and others vs.* **Election** (The) commissioners. Power of the constitutional convention of Pennsylvania. [1873]. 206 pp. 8°. *Philadelphia, King & Baird*, 1873.

Wells (John G.) Every man his own lawyer. Centennial ed. 5–612 pp. port. 12°. *New York, R. Macoy*, 1875.

Wendell (John L.) Reports of cases in the supreme court, and in the court of impeachments and errors of the state of New York, [1828–1840]. v. 1–20. 2d ed. 8°. *New York, Banks & brothers*, 1873.

Wendling (George R.) Alphabetical index showing the cases in the Illinois reports, [1819–1871]. 5–268 pp. 8°. *Chicago, E. B. Myers*, 1874.

Western jurist. 1873–1874. v. 7–8. 8°. *Des Moines, Mills & co.* 1873–74.

West Virginia (*State of*). Acts, 11th session, 1872–3. 8°. *Charleston, public printer*, 1873.

——— *Supreme court.* Reports of cases, v. 5, 1871–1872, by J. M. Hagans. 8°. *Wheeling, L. Baker & co.* 1873.

——— ——— Same, v. 6, 1873, by H. M. Mathews. 8°. *Charleston, J. W. Gentry*, 1875.

Wethey (H. C. W.) Reports of cases in the court of queen's bench. [Ontario, 1872-1873]. v. 1. [v. 33 of the series]. 8°. *Toronto, Rowsell & Hutchison,* 1874.

Wharton (Francis, *ll. d.*) Treatise on mental unsoundness. 11 p. l. 878 pp. 8°. *Philadelphia, Kay & brother,* 1873.

[WHARTON (F.) and STILLÉ (M.) Medical jurisprudence, 3d ed. v. 1].

——— Treatise on the criminal law of the United States. 7th ed. 3 v. 8°. *Philadelphia, Kay & brother,* 1874.

——— Treatise on the law of negligence. xliii, 889 pp. 8°. *Philadelphia, Kay & brother,* 1874.

——— *and* **Stillé** (Moreton, *m. d.*) Medical jurisprudence. 3d ed. 2 v. in 3. 8°. *Philadelphia, Kay & brother,* 1873.

Wheelock (E. M.) Reports of cases in the supreme court of Texas, 1870-1873. v. 3-6. [v. 34-37, Texas reports]. 8°. *Austin & Houston, journal office,* [*etc.*] 1872-74.

Whitman (Charles Sidney). Patent cases in the supreme court of the United States, [1861-1874]. vii, 791 pp. 8°. *Washington, W. H. & O. H. Morrison,* 1875.

Whitney (James A.) Law concerning patents and trade-marks. 47 pp. 12°. *New York, J. Ross & co.* 1873.

Wilcox (James A.) Railroad laws of the state of Ohio, 1874. vi, 380 pp. 8°. *Cincinnati, R. Clarke & co.* 1874.

Willard (John). Treatise on equity jurisprudence. [3d ed.] by P. Potter. xliv, 1077 pp. 8°. *New York, Banks & brothers,* 1875.

Williams (Thomas Walter). Precedents in conveyancing. v. 1 & 3. 8°. *London, for G. Kearsley,* 1788.

Winniwarter (Joseph Maximilian de). Loi de change autrichienne. viii, 76 pp. 8°. *Vienne, R. Lechner,* 1866.

Wisconsin (*State of*). Code of civil practice, 1875, by D. Y. Overton. 8°. *Chicago, Callaghan & co.* 1875.

——— General laws passed, 1869; private laws, 1869; general laws, 1872; laws, 1873; laws, 1874; laws, 1875. 6 v. 8°. *Madison, state printers,* [*etc.*] 1869-75.

——— *Supreme court.* Digest of reports, 1868-1874, by J. Simmons. v. 2. 8°. *Albany, W. Gould & son,* 1874.

——— ——— Reports of cases, v. 1-5 & 7-11, 1853-1860, by A. D. Smith. 2d ed. 8°. *Chicago, Callaghan & co.* 1873-75.

Wisconsin (*State of*)—continued.

——— ——— Same, v. 12-15, 1860-1862, by P. L. Spooner. 2d ed. 8°. *Chicago, Callaghan & co.* 1873.

——— ——— Same, v. 16-23, 1862-1869, by O. M. Conover. 2d ed. 8°. *Chicago, Callaghan & co.* 1872-74.

——— ——— Same, v. 28-36, 1871-1875, by O. M. Conover. 8°. *Chicago, Callaghan & co.* 1873-75.

——— Synoptical index of laws, [1836] to 1873. 381 pp. 8°. *Madison, Atwood & Culver,* 1873.

Wisconsin (*Territory of*). Acts, 1st-2d sessions, 1836-1837, and special session, june, 1838. [Reprint]. 584 pp. 8°. *Madison, state printers,* 1867.

Wisconsin (*Territory and State of*). *Supreme court.* Reports of cases, 1847-1850, by S. U. Pinney. v. 2. 8°. *Chicago, Callaghan & co.* 1874.

Withrow (Thomas F.) *and* **Stiles** (Edward H.) Digest of decisions of the supreme court of Iowa, 1839 to [1872]. 2 v. lxii, 541 pp; cxxv, 543-1133 pp. 8°. *Chicago, E. B. Myers,* 1874-75.

Wood (H. G) Treatise on the law of nuisances. iv, xxvi, 937 pp. 8°. *Albany, J. D. Parsons, jr.* 1875.

Wood (Nicholas L.) Investigation, upon charges of official misconduct, Baltimore, 1866. *See* **Hindes** (Samuel) *and* **Wood.**

Woods (William B.) Cases in the circuit courts of the United States for the fifth judicial circuit, [1869-1874]. v. 1. 8°. *Chicago, Callaghan & co.* 1875.

Woolworth (James M.) Reports of cases in the supreme court of Nebraska, v. 1-2. [v. 1-2, Nebraska reports]. 8°. *Chicago, Callaghan & Cockcroft,* [*etc.*] 1871-73.

Wright (Robert E.) Index to the Pennsylvania supreme court reports. [1754-1872]. v, 844 pp. 8°. *Philadelphia, R. Welsh,* 1874.

Wright (Robert Samuel). Law of criminal conspiracies. 108 pp. 8°. *London, Butterworths,* 1873.

Wyss (P. Friedrich von). Haftung für fremde culpa nach römischem recht. 3 p. l. 147 pp. 1 l. 8°. *Zürich, F. Schulthess,* 1867. s.

Zachariae (Karl Salomon). Le droit civil français, traduit de l'allemand. 5e éd. Par G. Massé, Ch. Vergé. v. 3-5. 8°. *Paris, A. Durand,* 1857-60.

Zinn (Peter). Leading cases on trusts. viii, 641 pp. 8°. *Cincinnati, R. Clarke & co.* 1873.

INDEX TO SUBJECTS AND TITLES.

INDEX TO SUBJECTS AND TITLES.

Fiction.

Dumas (A. D.) Œuvres complètes.

v. 3-4. Ange Pitou. Nouv. éd. 2 v. 1873.
v. 5-6. Ascanio. Nouv. éd. 2 v. 1872.
v. 7. Une aventure d'amour. Nouv. éd. 1873.
v. 8-9. Aventures de John Davys. Nouv. éd. 2 v. 1872.
v. 10-11. Les baleiniers. Voyage aux terres antipodiques. Journal du docteur Maynard. 2 v. 1861.
v. 12-14. Le bâtard de Mauléon. Nouv. éd. 3 v. 1871.
v. 15. Black. Nouv. éd. 1865.
v. 16-18. Les blancs et les bleus. 3 v. 1868-72.
v. 19. La bouillie de la comtesse Berthe. Nouv. éd. 1871.
v. 20. La boule de neige. Nouv. éd. 1866.
v. 21-22. Bric-à-brac. 2 v. 1861.
v. 23-25. Un cadet de famille. Traduit par Victor Perceval. 3 v. 1860.
v. 26. Le capitaine Pamphile. Nouv. éd. 1873.
v. 27. Le capitaine Paul. Nouv. éd. 1869.
v. 28. Le capitaine Rhino. Nouv. éd. 1873.
v. 29. Le capitaine Richard. Nouv. éd. 1866.
v. 30. Catherine Blum. Nouv. éd. 1867.
v. 31-32. Causeries. 1e-2e série. 2 v. 1860.
v. 33. Cécile. Nouv. éd. 1871.
v. 34-35. Charles le téméraire. Nouv. éd. 2 v. 1871.
v. 36. Le chasseur de sauvagine. Nouv. éd. 1872.
v. 37-38. Le château d'Eppstein. 2 v. 1860.
v. 39-40. Le chevalier d'Harmental. Nouv. éd. 2 v. 1873.
v. 41-42. Le chevalier de Maison-rouge. Nouv. éd. 2 v. 1872.
v. 43-45. Le collier de la reine. Nouv. éd. 3 v. 1873.
v. 46. La colombe. Maître Adam le Calabrais. Nouv. éd. 1871.
v. 47-49. Les compagnons de Jéhu. Nouv. éd. 3 v. 1868.
v. 50-55. Le comte de Monte-Cristo. Nouv. éd. 6 v. 1871.
v. 56-61. La comtesse de Charny. Nouv. éd. 6 v. 1873.
v. 62-63. La comtesse de Salisbury. Nouv. éd. 2 v. 1861.
v. 64-65. Les confessions de la marquise.—Suite et fin des Mémoires d'une aveugle. Nouv. éd. 2 v. 1869.
v. 66-67. Conscience l'innocent. 2 v. 1861.
v. 68-69. Création et rédemption. Le docteur mystérieux. 2 v. 1872.
v. 70-71. Création et rédemption. La fille du marquis. 2 v. 1872.
v. 72-74. La dame de Monsoreau. Nouv. éd. 3 v. 1872.
v. 75-76 La dame de volupté. Mémoires de mlle. de Luynes. Nouv. éd. 2 v. 1865-72.
v. 77-79. Les deux Diane. (Par Paul Meurice). Nouv. éd. 3 v. 1867.
v. 80-81. Les deux reines.—Suite et fin des Mémoires de mlle. de Luynes. Nouv. éd. 2 v. 1870.

Fiction.

Dumas (A. D.) Œuvres complètes.

v. 82-83. Dieu dispose. Nouv. éd. 2 v. 1866.
v. 84-85. Les drames galants.—La marquise d'Escoman. 2 v. 1860.
v. 86-88. Le drame de quatre-vingt-treize. 3 v. 1866-67.
v. 89. Les drames de la mer. Nouv. éd. 1864.
v. 90. La femme au collier de velours. Nouv. éd. 1873.
v. 91. Fernande. Nouv. éd. 1873.
v. 92. Une fille du régent. Nouv. éd. 1873.
v. 93. Filles, lorettes et courtisanes. Les serpents. Nouv. éd. 1874.
v. 94. Le fils du forçat.—M. Coumbes. Nouv. éd. 1873.
v. 95. Les frères corses. (Othon l'archer). Nouv. éd. 1867.
v. 96. Gabriel Lambert. (La pêche aux filets. Invraisemblance. Une âme à naître). Nouv. éd. 1868.
v. 97. Les Garibaldiens. Révolution de Sicile et de Naples. Nouv. éd. 1868.
v. 98. Gaule et France. Nouv. éd. 1862.
v. 99. Georges. Nouv. éd. 1873.
v. 100. Un Gil-Blas en Californie. 1861.
v. 101-102. Les grands hommes en robe de chambre. César. 2 v. 1866.
v. 103-104. Les grands hommes en robe de chambre. Henri IV. Louis XIII et Richelieu. 2 v. 1866.
v. 105-106. La guerre des femmes. Nouv. éd. 2 v. 1868.
v. 107. Histoire d'un casse-noisette. Nouv. éd. 1871.
v. 108. Les hommes de fer. 1867.
v. 109. L'horoscope. 1860.
v. 110-111. L'île de feu. 2 v. 1870.
v. 112. Impressions de voyage. Une année à Florence. Nouv. éd. 1867.
v. 113-115. Impressions de voyage. L'Arabie heureuse. 3 v. 1860.
v. 116. Impressions de voyage. Le capitaine Aréna. Nouv. éd. 1870.
v. 117-119. Impressions de voyage. Le Caucase. 3 v. 1865.
v. 120-121. Impressions de voyage. Le corricolo. Nouv. éd. 2 v. 1872.
v. 122-123. Impressions de voyage. Excursions sur les bords du Rhin. Nouv. éd. 2 v. 1869.
v. 124-125. Impressions de voyage. Midi de la France. Nouv. éd. 2 v. 1865.
v. 126-127. Impressions de voyage. De Paris à Cadix. Nouv. éd 2 v. 1870.
v. 128. Impressions de voyage. Quinze jours au Sinai. Par A. Dumas et A. Dauzats. Nouv. éd. 1868.
v. 129-132. Impressions de voyage. En Russie. 4 v. 1865-66.
v. 133-134. Impressions de voyage. Le speronare. Nouv. éd. 2 v. 1873.
v. 135-137. Impressions de voyage. Suisse. Nouv. éd. 3 v. 1868-69.

Fiction.

Dupuy (E. A.) The hidden sin. 12°. Philadelphia, 1874.
—— How he did it. 12°. Philadelphia, 1871.
—— The mysterious guest. 12°. Philadelphia, 1873.
Dutcher (J. C.) The old home by the river. 16°. New York, 1874.
Dyer (S.) Home and abroad. 16°. Philadelphia, 1872.
Eckel (L. S. J.) Maria Monk's daughter. 12°. New York, 1874.
Edelfrida. 4 v. 16°. London, 1792.
Edwardes (A.) Archie Lovell. 8°. New York, 1867.
—— Estelle. 12°. New York, 1874.
—— Ordeal for wives. 12°. New York, 1873.
—— Ought we to visit her? 8°. New York, 1871.
—— Vagabond heroine. 12°. London, 1873.
Edwards (A. B.) In the days of my youth. 8°. Philadelphia, 1874.
Eggleston (E.) Circuit rider. 12°. New York, 1874.
—— End of the world. 12°. New York, 1872.
—— Schoolmaster's stories. 12°. Boston, 1874.
Eggleston (G. C.) A man of honor. 12°. New York, 1873.
Eiloart (C. J.) Out of her sphere. 3 v. 12°. London, 1872.
Elder (A.) Tales and legends of the Isle of Wight. 2d ed. 16°. London, 1843.
Eldridge (A. *pseud.*) Norman Brill's life-work. 16°. New York, 1875.
Elliot (S. H.) Look at home. New ed. 12°. New York, 1860.
Emma; or the unfortunate attachment. New ed. 2 v. 16°. London, 1787.
Episodes in an obscure life. 2 v. 12°. London, 1871.
Equal to either fortune. 3 v. 12°. London, 1869.
Erckmann (É.) and Chatrian (A.) Histoire d'un sous-maître. 8e éd. 16°. Paris, 1873.
—— —— La maison forestière. 5e éd. 12°. Paris, 1866.
—— —— Same. Forest house and Catherine's lovers. 16°. London, 1871.
Erizzo (S.) Le sei giornate. 8°. Milano, 1805.
Fabre (F.) Abbé Tigrane. 12°. New York, 1875.
Faithfull (E.) Reed shaken with the wind. 12°. New York, 1873.
Falkner (W. C.) Spanish heroine. 12°. Cincinnati, 1851.
Farjeon (B. L.) Joshua Marvel. 3 v. 12°. London, 1871.
—— London's heart. 3 v. 12°. London, 1873.
Farman (E.) Anna Maylie. 16°. Boston, 1873.
—— Girl's money. 16°. Boston, 1874.
—— Grandma Crosby's household. 16°. Boston, 1873.
—— Little woman. 16°. Boston, 1873.
—— White hand. 16°. Boston, 1875.
Fawcett (E.) Purple and fine linen. 12°. New York, 1873.
Feuillet (O.) Led astray. The sphinx. "Bellah." 12°. New York, 1875.

Fiction.

Féval (P. H. C.) Capitaine Simon. La fille de l'émigré. 12°. Paris, 1858.
[*With* About (E. F. V.) Trente et quarante. 12°. Paris, 1859].
Field (M.) Bertha Percy. 12°. New York, 1860.
Finley (M.) Elsie's womanhood. 16°. New York, 1875.
Fish (H. C.) Harry's conflicts. 16°. Philadelphia, 1872.
—— Harry's conversion. 16°. Philadelphia, 1872.
Fisher (F. C.) Daughter of Bohemia. 8°. New York, 1874.
—— Hearts and hands. 8°. New York, 1875.
—— Nina's atonement. 8°. New York, 1873.
—— Question of honor. 12°. New York, 1875.
Fitzgerald (P.) Two fair daughters. 3 v. 12°. London, 1871.
Five hundred dollar prize series. *See separate works.*
Flagg (W.) Good investment. 8°. New York, 1872.
Fleming (M. A.) Guy Earlscourt's wife. 12°. New York, 1873.
—— Mad marriage. 12°. New York, 1875.
—— Terrible secret. 12°. New York, 1874.
—— Wonderful woman. 12°. New York, 1873.
Floy Lindsley and her friends. 16°. New York, 1875.
Floyd (C.) Mice at play. 16°. Boston, 1876.
Floyd (M. F.) The Nereid. 8°. Macon, Ga. 1871.
Foote (E. B.) Sammy Tubbs and "Spousie". 5 v. sq. 18°. New York, 1874.
Forrest (N.) Honest and earnest. 16°. New York, 1872.
Foscolo (U.) Jacques Ortis. Traduit par A. Dumas. 16°. Paris, 1867.
[Dumas (A. D.) Œuvres complètes, v. 149].
Foster (J. H.) Mr. Mackenzie's answer. 16°. New York, 1875.
—— Those boys. 16°. Boston, 1875.
Francis (L.) Kate Parker. 16°. Boston, 1874.
Franco (G. G.) Tigranes. 12°. Philadelphia, 1874.
Fuller (E. W.) Sea-gift. 12°. New York, 1873.
Fulton (J. D.) Show your colors. 16°. New York, 1875.
Gaboriau (E.) Clique of gold. 8°. Boston, 1874.
—— La dégringolade. 5e éd. 2 v. 16°. Paris, 1874.
—— Other people's money. 8°. Boston, 1875.
—— Widow Lerouge. 8°. Boston, 1873.
—— Within an inch of his life. 8°. Boston, 1874.
Galt (J.) Last of the lairds. 12°. New York, 1827.
Gardner (C. E.) Rich Medway's two loves. 12°. New York, 1875.
—— Tested. 12°. New York, 1874.
Gardner (H. C.) Discontent, and other stories. 16°. New York, 1874.
Gasparin (V. B. A. de). Vesper. 12°. New York, 1863.

Fiction.

Fiction.

Law.

ANNUITIES, Value of. D. Jones. 2 v. 8°. Lond. 1844.

ARBITRATIONS and awards, Law of. J. H. Redman. 8°. Lond. 1872.

ARGUMENTS. Discursos forenses. J. Melendez Valdés. 16°. Madrid, 1821.

ARIZONA. Session laws, 6th and 7th leg. ass. 1871–73. 2 v. 8°. Tucson, 1871–73.

ARKANSAS.

Reports, v. 25–27, 1867–72. N. W. Cox. 8°. Little Rock, 1870–73.

Session laws. Acts, 1873. 8°. Little Rock, 1873.

ASSIGNMENTS. Des modes de transmission des créances. J. Bourgeois. 8°. Paris, 1869.

ATTACHMENT.

Law of attachment. C. D. Drake. 4th ed. 8°. Bost. 1873.

Treatise on warrants and attachment for New York. S. J. Cowen. 8°. Albany, 1874.

ATTORNEY, The practising. W. Bohun. 3d ed. 2 v. 8°. Lond. 1732.

AUCTIONS, Law of. J. Bateman. 5th ed. 12°. Lond. 1874.

AUGUSTA, Ga. Laws and ordinances, 1814. 8°. Augusta, 1814.

AUSTRIA.

Allgemeine (Das) bürgerliche gesetzbuch, 1725–1873. 5ter abdruck. 16°. Wien, 1873.

Civil- und militär-jurisdictionsnorm (Die), 1774–1873. 5te auf. 16°. Wien, 1873.

Katechismus der österreichischen staats-verfassung. 16°. Wien, 1874.

Loi de change autrichienne. J. M. de Winniwarter. 8°. Vienne, 1866.

Reichsgesetzblatt. Jahrg. 1870–72. 3 v. 4°. Wien, 1870–72.

Staatsgrundgesetze, 1222–1861. Unveränderter neudruck. 16°. Wien, 1871.

——— Same. Supplementheft. 1861–67. 16°. Wien, 1868.

AVERAGE, Law of general. R. Lowndes. 2d ed. 8°. Lond. 1874.

BAIL. Haftung für fremde culpa nach römischem recht. P. F. von Wyss. 8°. Zürich, 1867.

BANKING. Law relating to bankers and banking companies. J. Grant. 3d ed. 8°. Lond. 1873.

BANKRUPTCY.

Act of 1867, with amendments. S. D. Thompson. 8°. Saint Louis, 1874.

——— Same. 2d ed. 8°. Saint Louis, 1874.

Commentary on bankruptcy law, 1841. G. A. Bicknell, jr. 2d ed. 8°. N. Y. 1842.

Law and practice in bankruptcy, to 1873. O. F. Bump. 6th ed. 8°. N. Y. 1873.

——— Same, to 1874. 7th ed. 8°. N. Y. 1874.

——— Same, to 1875. 8th ed. 8°. N. Y. 1875.

Law and practice in bankruptcy. H. P. Roche and W. Hazlitt. 2d ed. 8°. Lond. 1873.

Law of bankruptcy in Scotland. J. H. Burton. 8°. Edinb. 1845.

United States law of bankruptcy. O. F. Bump. 8°. N. Y. 1874.

BASTARDY, Law of orders of affiliation and proceedings in. T. W. Saunders. 6th ed. 8°. Lond. 1873.

Law.

BAVARIA. De la justice, etc. en Bavière et en Allemagne. H. Becker. 8°. Paris, 1861.

BELGIUM.

Code pénal. J. S. G. Nypels. 8°. Bruxelles, 1867.

Essai sur le droit communal de la Belgique. A. Giron. 8°. Bruxelles, 1868.

BILLS of exchange and promissory notes.

Law of. Sir J. B. Byles. 8°. Philad. 1874.

Treatise on. T. Parsons. 2d ed. 2 v. 8°. Philad. 1875.

BILLS of sale, Law of. G. E. Lyon. 12°. Lond. 1873.

BLACKSTONE.

Commentaries economized. D. M. Aird. 2d ed. 8°. Lond. 1873.

Commentaries reduced to questions and answers. J. C. Devereux. New ed. 8°. N. Y. 1875.

BONDS, Law of municipal. W. N. Coler. 2 v. 8°. N. Y. 1873.

BOUNDARIES and fences, Law of. R. H. Tyler. 8°. Albany, 1874.

BUSINESS.

Every man his own lawyer. J. G. Wells. Centennial ed. 12°. N. Y. 1875.

Handbook of law for business men. W. Tracy. 3d ed. 8°. N. Y. 1874.

Laws of business. T. Parsons. Rev. ed. 8°. Hartford, 1875.

Rechts-handbuch. H. B. van Tronk. 12°. Philad. 1874.

CABINET lawyer. J. Wade. 24th ed. 16°. Lond. 1874.

CALIFORNIA.

Acts amendatory of the codes, 1873–74. 8°. Sacramento, 1874.

Citations of cases, 1850–72. R. Desty. 8°. S. F. 1874.

Civil code, 1873. C. Haymond, J. C. Burch, J. H. McKune. 8°. Sacramento, 1872.

Civil, penal and political codes and code of procedure, 1873. C. Haymond and J. C. Burch. 7 v. 8°. Sacramento, 1872.

Code of civil procedure. W. Olney. 3d ed. 1872–74. 16°. S. F. 1874.

Digest, 1868–73. R. Desty. 8°. S. F. 1875.

Penal code, 1873. C. Haymond, J. C. Burch, J. H. McKune. 2 v. 8°. Sacramento, 1872.

Political code, 1873. C. Haymond, J. C. Burch, J. H. McKune. 2 v. 8°. Sacramento, 187?.

Probate law and practice of California. D. P. Belknap. 3d ed. 8°. S. F. 1873.

Reports, v. 2, 1852. H. P. Hepburn. 2d ed. 8°. S. F. 1875.

——— Same, v. 6–8, 1856–57. H. T. Booraem. 2d ed. 8°. S. F. 1875.

——— Same, v. 9, 1858. H. Lee. 2d ed. 8°. S. F. 1875.

——— Same, v. 14, 1859–60. J. B. Harmon. 2d ed. 8°. S. F. 1873.

——— Same, v. 41–49, 1871–75. C. A. Tuttle. 8°. Sacramento & S. F. 1873–75.

CANADA. Session laws. Acts, 36th–38th Victoria, 1873–75. 4 v. 8°. Ottawa, 1873–75.

CARRIERS, Law of. J. H. B. Browne. 8°. Lond. 1873.

Theology.

Theology.

www.ingramcontent.com/pod-product-compliance
Lightning Source LLC
LaVergne TN
LVHW020122110826
845151LV00001B/244
* 9 7 8 1 4 2 5 5 4 2 2 9 0 *